PHILIP'S

G000296828

STREET ATLAS
Northamptonshire

Corby, Daventry, Kettering, Northampton, Wellingborough

OXFORDSHIRE
COUNTY COUNCIL
www.oxfordshire.gov.uk

Working for you

Not For Loan

Contents

Mobile safety cameras

Key to map symbols

Key to map pages

Route planning

Major administrative and Postcode boundaries

Street maps at 3½ inches to 1 mile

Index of towns, villages, streets, hospitals, industrial estates, railway stations, schools, shopping centres, universities and places of interest

Digital Data

The exceptionally high-quality mapping found in this atlas is available as digital data in TIFF format, which is easily convertible to other bitmapped (raster) image formats.

The index is also available in digital form as a standard database table. It contains all the details found in the printed index together with the National Grid reference for the map square in which each entry is named.

For further information and to discuss your requirements, please contact philips@mapsinternational.co.uk

Mobile speed cameras

The vast majority of speed cameras used on Britain's roads are operated by safety camera partnerships. These comprise local authorities, the police, Her Majesty's Court Service (HMCS) and the Highways Agency.

This table lists the sites where each safety camera partnership may enforce speed limits through the use of mobile cameras or detectors. These are usually set up on the roadside or a bridge spanning the road and operated by a police or civilian enforcement officer. The speed limit at each site (if available) is shown in red type, followed by the approximate location in black type.

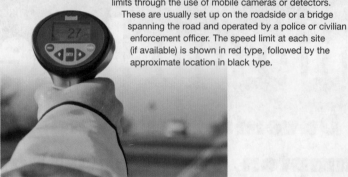

In addition to the routes below, mobile speed enforcement can also take place in local areas of concern requested by residents or as determined by the Police.

A5
60 DIRFT to County Boundary
60 Norton/Whilton Crossroads
30/40 Towcester Racecourse to A43

A6
60 Burton Latimer Bypass

A14
70 Kelmarsh
70 Kelmarsh Junctions 7-10

A43
60 Laxton Turn to A47 Duddington
60 Mawsley to A14 Junc 8 (inc Mawsley Spur)
70 Towcester to M1 Junc 15a

A45
60 M1 Junc 16 to Weedon
60 Stanwick to Raunds

A361
60 Byfield to Chipping Warden

A422
60 Brackley West to A43

A428
60 East Haddon
30/60 Great Houghton to Yardley Hastings

A508
30 Northampton, Plough Gyratory
30 Northampton, St Georges Avenue to Holly Lodge Rd
30 Northampton, St Peters Way to St Georges Avenue
30/60 Stoke Bruerne to A5
70 Wootton Flyover to M1 Junc 15

A509
60 Wellingborough to Isham

A605
40/60 Thrapston to Warmington

A4256
30 Daventry, Eastern Way

A4500
40/60 Great Billing to Earls Barton
30 Northampton, Abington Park to York Rd
30 Northampton, Park Avenue to Booth Lane South
30 Northampton, Weedon Rd to Duston Rd

A5076
40 Mere Way
40 Northampton, Great Billing Way South

A5193
30/40 Wellingborough, London Rd

A6003
50/60 Kettering to Corby

A6014
40/60 Corby, Oakley Rd

B569
50 Irchester to Rushden

B576
60 Desborough to Rothwell

B4038
30/60 Kilsby, Rugby Rd

B4525
40/60 Welsh Lane

B5385
60 Watford to West Haddon

UNCLASSIFIED
30 Brackmills Industrial Estate
30 Northampton, Grange Rd

Key to map symbols

III

22a	Motorway with junction number
	Primary route – dual/single carriageway
	A road – dual/single carriageway
	B road – dual/single carriageway
	Minor road – dual/single carriageway
	Other minor road – dual/single carriageway
	Road under construction
	Tunnel, covered road
30 30	Speed cameras - single, multiple
	Rural track, private road or narrow road in urban area
	Gate or obstruction to traffic (restrictions may not apply at all times or to all vehicles)
	Path, bridleway, byway open to all traffic, road used as a public path
	Pedestrianised area
DY7	Postcode boundaries
	County and unitary authority boundaries
	Railway, tunnel, railway under construction
	Tramway, tramway under construction
	Miniature railway
Walsall	Railway station
	Private railway station
South Shields	Metro station
	Tram stop, tram stop under construction
	Bus, coach station

◆	Ambulance station
◆	Coastguard station
◆	Fire station
◆	Police station
✚	Accident and Emergency entrance to hospital
H	Hospital
+	Place of worship
i	Information Centre (open all year)
🛒	Shopping Centre
P	Parking
P&R	Park and Ride
PO	Post Office
Å	Camping site
🚐	Caravan site
⚑	Golf course
✕	Picnic site
Prim Sch	Important buildings, schools, colleges, universities and hospitals
	Built up area
	Woods
River Medway	Water name
	River, weir, stream
	Canal, lock, tunnel
	Water
	Tidal water
Church	Non-Roman antiquity
ROMAN FORT	Roman antiquity
87 58	Adjoining page indicators

Acad	Academy	Inst	Institute	Recn Gd	Recreation Ground	
Allot Gdns	Allotments	Ct	Law Court			
Cemy	Cemetery	L Ctr	Leisure Centre	Resr	Reservoir	
C Ctr	Civic Centre	LC	Level Crossing	Ret Pk	Retail Park	
CH	Club House	Liby	Library	Sch	School	
Coll	College	Mkt	Market	Sh Ctr	Shopping Centre	
Crem	Crematorium	Meml	Memorial	TH	Town Hall/House	
Ent	Enterprise	Mon	Monument	Trad Est	Trading Estate	
Ex H	Exhibition Hall	Mus	Museum	Univ	University	
Ind Est	Industrial Estate	Obsy	Observatory	W Twr	Water Tower	
IRB Sta	Inshore Rescue Boat Station	Pal	Royal Palace	Wks	Works	
		PH	Public House	YH	Youth Hostel	

■ The small numbers around the edges of the maps identify the 1 kilometre National Grid lines

■ The dark grey border on the inside edge of some pages indicates that the mapping does not continue onto the adjacent page

The scale of the maps on the pages numbered in blue is 5.52 cm to 1 km • 3½ inches to 1 mile • 1: 18103

0		¼		½		¾		1 mile
0	250 m	500 m	750 m	1 kilometre				

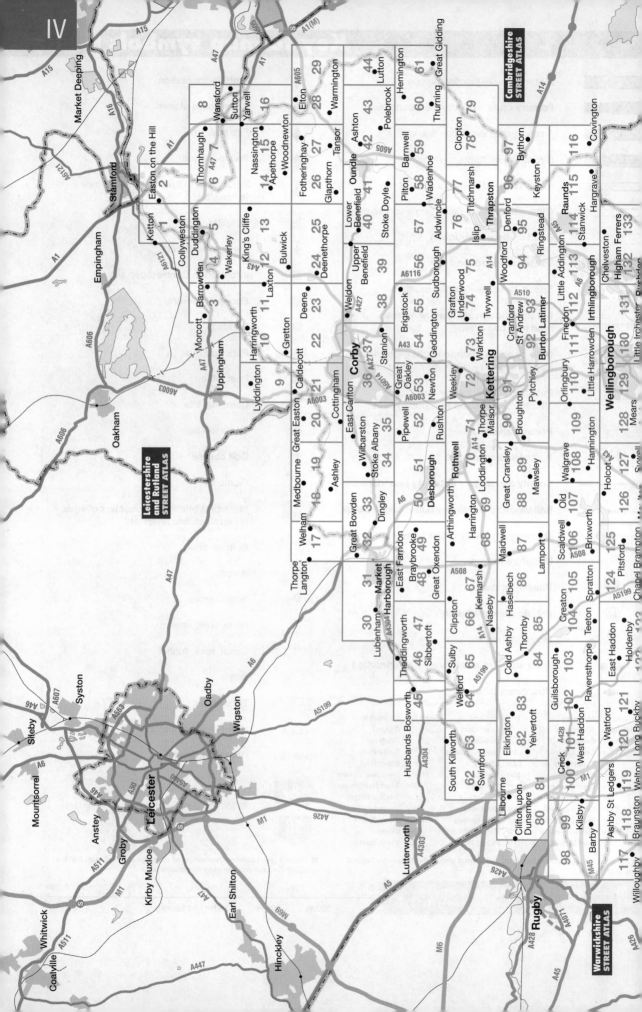

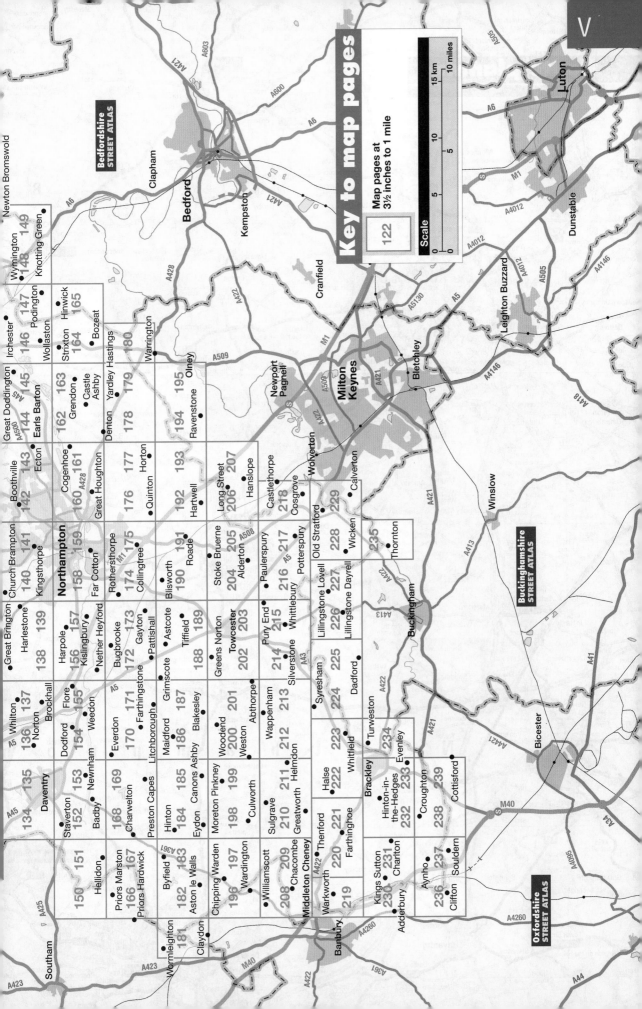

Key to map pages

Map pages at 3½ inches to 1 mile

122

Scale

0 5 10 15 km
0 5 10 miles

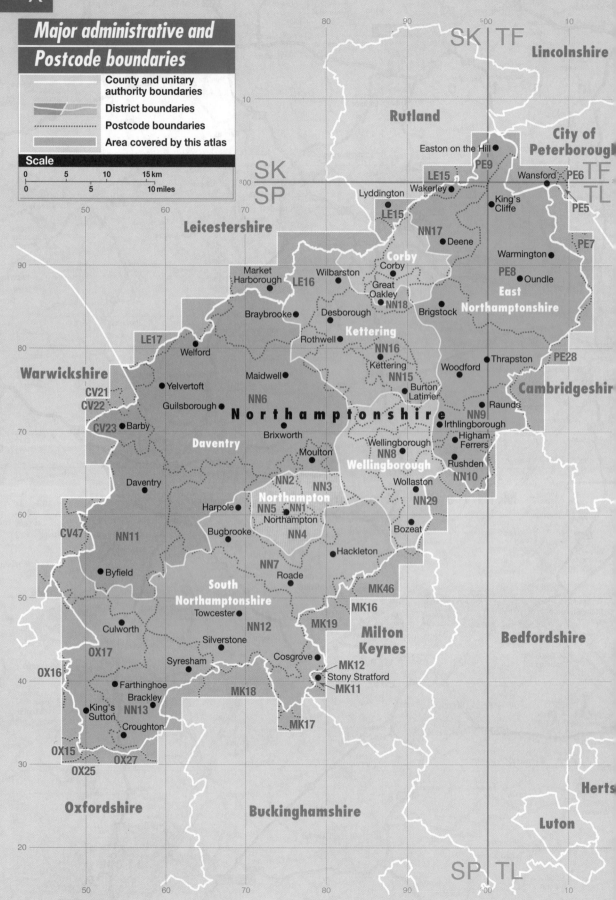

Major administrative and Postcode boundaries

- County and unitary authority boundaries
- District boundaries
- Postcode boundaries
- Area covered by this atlas

Scale

0 5 10 15 km
0 5 10 miles

SK | TF

Lincolnshire

Rutland

City of Peterborough

Easton on the Hill
PE9
LE15
Wansford PE6
TF | TL
Lyddington Wakerley
King's Cliffe PE5
LE15
NN17
SK / SP
Deene
Warmington PE7
Leicestershire
Corby
Corby
PE8 Oundle
East Northamptonshire
Wilbarston
Market Harborough LE16
Great Oakley
NN18
Brigstock
Braybrooke
Desborough Kettering
Rothwell
NN16
Woodford Thrapston PE28
LE17
Kettering NN15
Welford
Burton Latimer
Warwickshire
Maidwell
Raunds
Cambridgeshire
CV21
Yelvertoft
Burton Latimer
NN9
CV22
Guilsborough NN6
Irthlingborough
CV23 Barby
Brixworth
Wellingborough Higham Ferrers
Daventry
Moulton NN8
Rushden
Wellingborough NN10
Northamptonshire
Wollaston
Daventry
NN2
NN29
Harpole NN5 NN1
Bozeat
CV47
NN11
Northampton
Bugbrooke NN4
Byfield
Hackleton
NN7
MK46
Roade
South Northamptonshire
MK16
Towcester MK19
Culworth NN12
Milton Keynes
Silverstone
OX17
Cosgrove MK12
Bedfordshire
OX16
Syresham
Stony Stratford
Farthinghoe MK18 MK11
Brackley
King's Sutton NN13
MK17
Croughton
OX15
OX27
OX25
Herts
Oxfordshire
Buckinghamshire
Luton
SP | TL

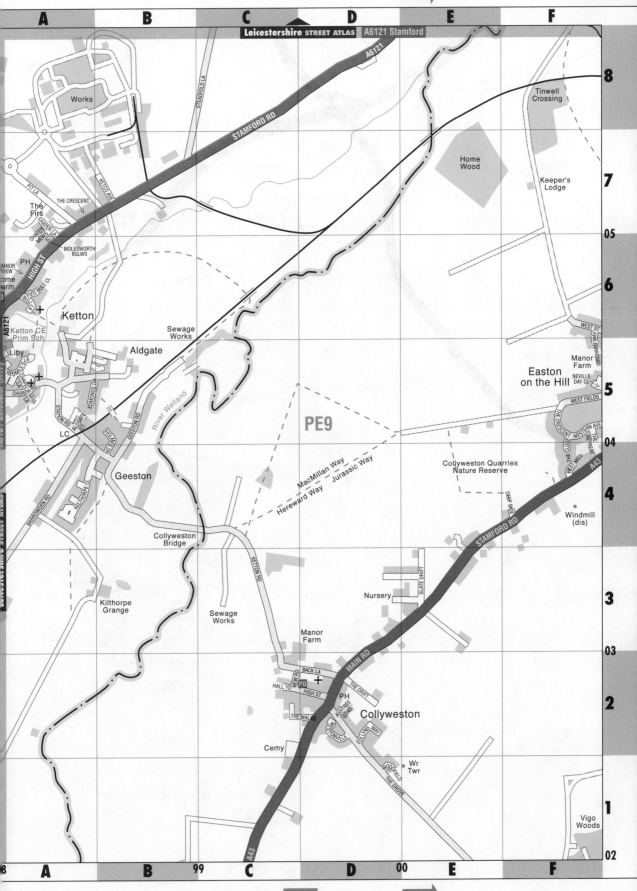

Leicestershire STREET ATLAS A6121 Stamford

A B C D E F

A6121

STAMFORD RD

8

Works

Tinwell
Crossing

Home
Wood

7

Keeper's
Lodge

THE CRESCENT
KETTON AVE

STEADFOLD LA

05

The
Firs

PH

MOLESWORTH
BGLWS

MANOR
VIEW

BULL CL
PIED BULL CL

HIGH ST

HOME
FARM

6

WEST ST

Ketton

Sewage
Works

Manor
Farm

Easton
on the Hill

NEVILLE
DAY CL

Ketton CE
Prim Sch

Aldgate

GRAYDON RD

Liby

REDMILES LA

CHAPEL RD
CHURCH RD

CHURCH LA
EDMUNDS DR

HOT HSE DR
GEESTON RD

River Welland

WEST FIELDS

PE9

THE CRESCENT
WEST MILL
THE CLOSE
THE RETREAT
WESTERN AVE

5

STATION RD
ALDGATE

04

LC

A43

MacMillan Way

Collyweston Quarries
Nature Reserve

Geeston

KELTHORPE CL

Hereward Way Jurassic Way

BARROWDEN RD

DEEP SIDE

Collyweston
Bridge

STAMFORD RD

4

KETTON RD

Windmill
(dis)

Kilthorpe
Grange

Sewage
Works

SLATE DRIFT

Nursery

3

03

Manor
Farm

MAIN RD

BACK LA

NEW RD

PO

THE DRIFT

2

Collyweston

HALL YD

HIGH ST

PH

ASHTREE GDNS

THE WALKS

STONYDALE

COLLYNS WAY

Cemy

WR
Twr

BROADFIELD

THE DROVE

Vigo
Woods

1

A43

02

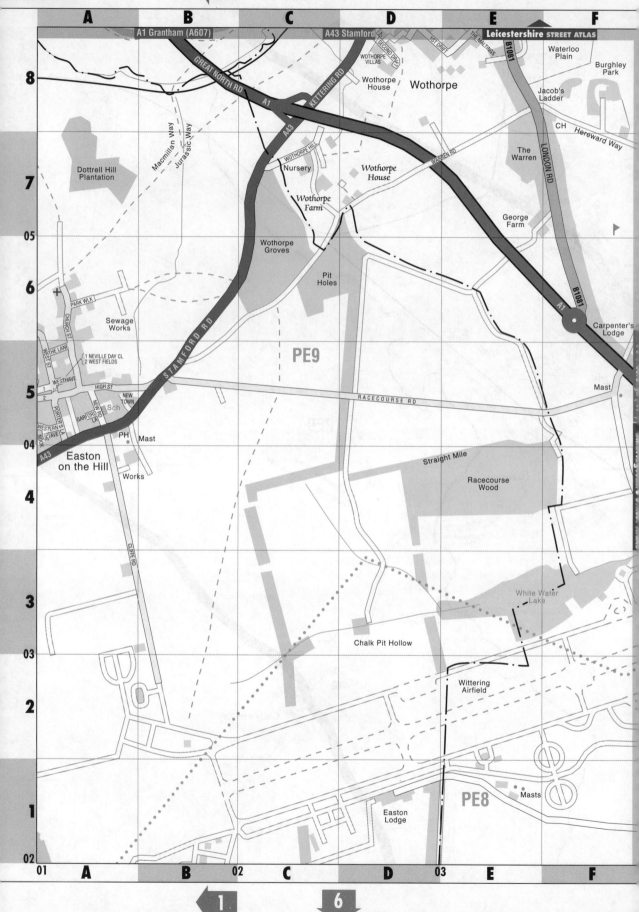

A1 Grantham (A607)
A43 Stamford

GREAT NORTH RD
A1
A43
KETTERING RD
SECOND DRIFT
1ST DRIFT
THE HALTINGS
B1081

WOTHORPE
VILLAS
Wothorpe
House
Wothorpe

Waterloo
Plain

Burghley
Park

Jacob's
Ladder

Macmillan Way
Jurassic Way

Dottrell Hill
Plantation

Nursery

WOTHORPE HILL

Wothorpe
Farm

Wothorpe
House

WARREN RD

CH Hereward Way

The
Warren

LONDON RD

Wothorpe
Groves

George
Farm

Park Wlk

Pit
Holes

Church St

Sewage
Works

B1081
A1

Carpenter's
Lodge

The Lane

West St

1 Neville Day Cl
2 West Fields

PE9

STAMFORD RD

Westhave

High St

New
Town

RACECOURSE RD

Mast

Western La
The Nook
Porters La
Garford La
New Rd La
Sch

PH   Mast

A43

Easton
on the Hill

CLIFFE RD

Works

Straight Mile

Racecourse
Wood

White Water
Lake

Chalk Pit Hollow

Wittering
Airfield

Easton
Lodge

PE8

Masts

A   B   C   D   E   F

8

05

7

6

05

04

5

4

3

03

2

02

1

02

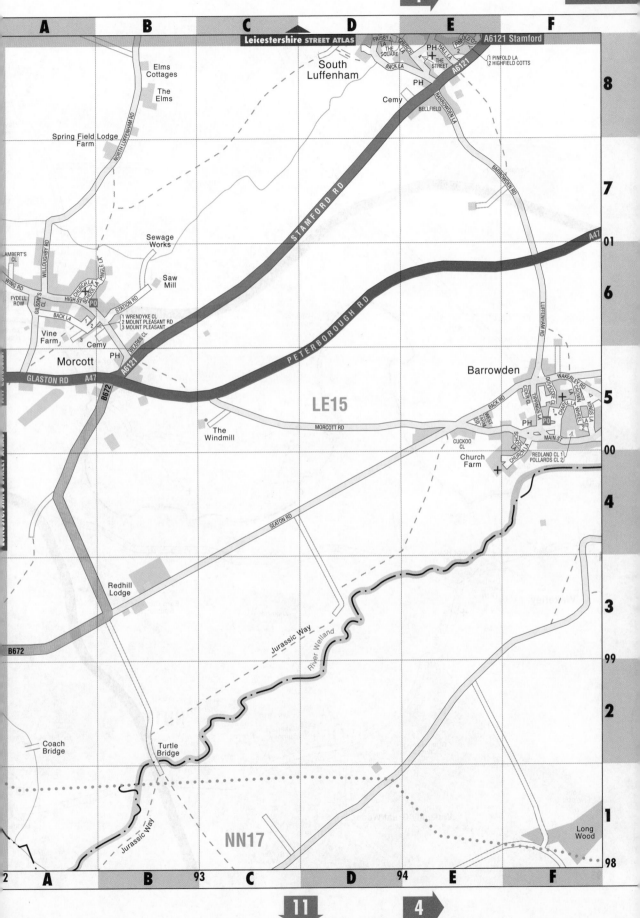

Leicestershire STREET ATLAS

South Luffenham

A6121 Stamford

1 PINFOLD LA
2 HIGHFIELD COTTS

FRISBY LA
THE SQUARE
CHURCH
BACK LA
PH
PH
THE STREET
PINFOLD
A6121

PH
Cemy
Bellfield
BARROWDEN LA

Elms Cottages

The Elms

Spring Field Lodge Farm

NORTH LUFFENHAM RD

STAMFORD RD

BARROWDEN RD

A47
01

Sewage Works

Saw Mill

LUFFENHAM RD

WILLOUGHBY RD

PINGLE LA

CHURCH LA

SCHOOL LA

PO
HIGH ST

STATION RD

PETERBOROUGH RD

LAMBERT'S CL
WING RD
FYDELL ROW
GILSON'S CL
BACK LA
1 WRENDYKE CL
2 MOUNT PLEASANT RD
3 MOUNT PLEASANT

Vine Farm
Cemy
PH
VICARS CL

Morcott

A6121

Barrowden

WAKERLEY RD
CROWN
DOVECOTE CL
CHAPEL LA
KINGS LA
WHEEL LA
TIPPINGS LA
CLIFFE CL
BACK RD
WEST FARM
PH
PO
MAIN ST

GLASTON RD
A47

B672

LE15

MORCOTT RD

The Windmill

CUCKOO CL

Church Farm

SCHOOL LA
CHURCH LA

REDLAND CL 1
POLLARDS CL 2

00

SEATON RD

04

Redhill Lodge

03

Jurassic Way

River Welland

B672

99

02

Coach Bridge

Turtle Bridge

Jurassic Way

NN17

Long Wood

01

98

8
7
6
5
4
3
2
1

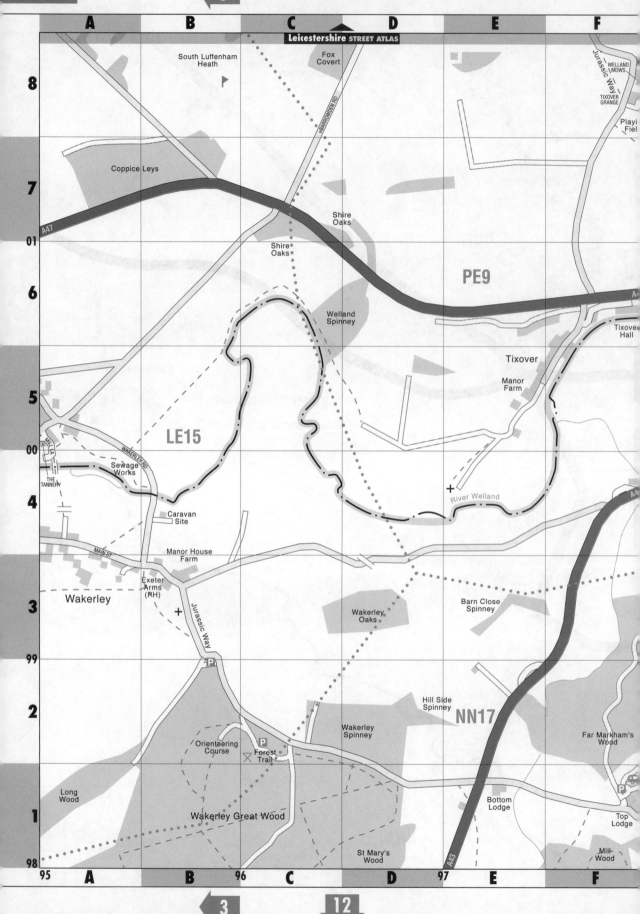
A | B | C | D | E | F

8

South Luffenham
Heath

Fox
Covert

Jurassic Way

WELLAND
MDWS

TIXOVER
GRANGE

Playi
Fiel

Coppice Leys

7

01

A47

Shire
Oaks

PE9

Shire
Oaks

6

BARROWDEN RD

Welland
Spinney

Tixove
Hall

Tixover

5

Manor
Farm

LE15

WAKERLEY RD

00

A47

A1

Sewage
Works

THE
TANNERY

River Welland

4

Caravan
Site

MAIN ST

Manor House
Farm

Exeter
Arms
(RH)

Wakerley

Barn Close
Spinney

3

Jurassic Way

Wakerley
Oaks

99

P

Hill Side
Spinney

2

NN17

Wakerley
Spinney

Orienteering
Course

P

Forest
Trail

Far Markham's
Wood

Long
Wood

P

Bottom
Lodge

1

Wakerley Great Wood

Top
Lodge

St Mary's
Wood

A43

Mill
Wood

98

95 | A | B | 96 | C | D | 97 | E | F

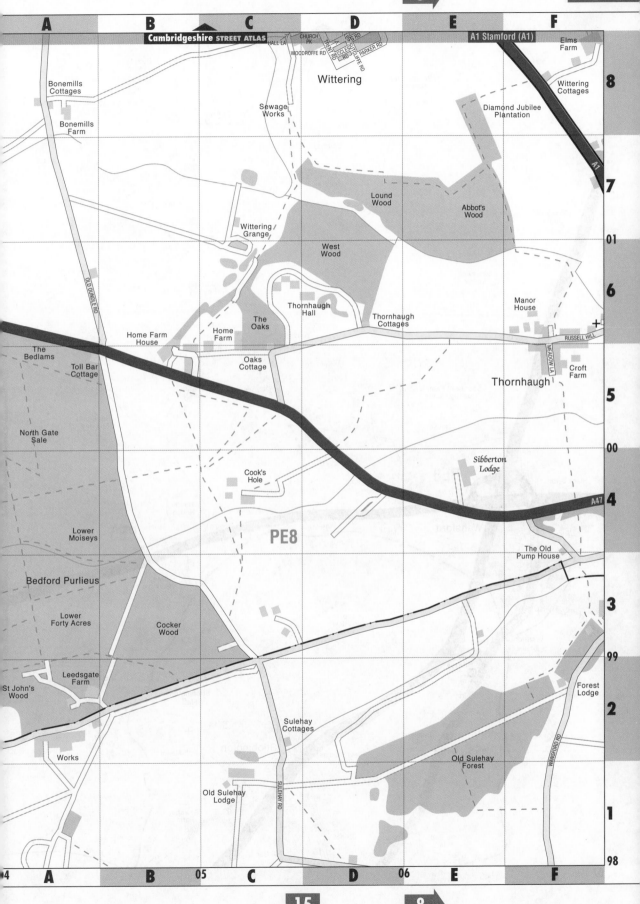

Cambridgeshire STREET ATLAS

Wittering

Bonemills
Cottages

Bonemills
Farm

Sewage
Works

A1 Stamford (A1)

Elms
Farm

Wittering
Cottages

Diamond Jubilee
Plantation

Lound
Wood

Abbot's
Wood

West
Wood

Wittering
Grange

Manor
House

RUSSELL HILL

Thornhaugh
Hall

The Oaks

Thornhaugh
Cottages

Croft
Farm

MEADOW LA

Home Farm
House

Home
Farm

Thornhaugh

The
Bedlams

Toll Bar
Cottage

Oaks
Cottage

North Gate
Sale

Sibberton
Lodge

Cook's
Hole

A47

Lower
Moiseys

The Old
Pump House

PE8

Bedford Purlieus

Lower
Forty Acres

Cocker
Wood

Forest
Lodge

St John's
Wood

Leedsgate
Farm

Sulehay
Cottages

Old Sulehay
Forest

WANSFORD RD

Works

Old Sulehay
Lodge

SULEHAY RD

HALL LA

CHURCH
PK

WOODROFFE RD

TROUT RD

KING RD

ECCLES RD

SUTCLIFFE RD

PARKER RD

A1

7

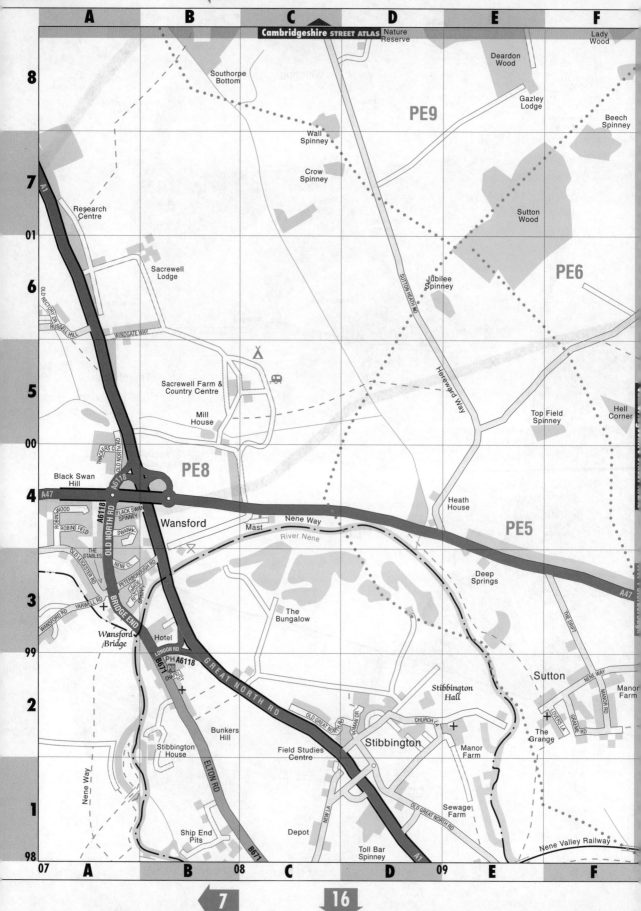

A   B   C   D   E   F

Nature
Reserve

Lady
Wood

Deardon
Wood

8

Southorpe
Bottom

Gazley
Lodge

PE9

Beech
Spinney

Wall
Spinney

7

Crow
Spinney

Research
Centre

Sutton
Wood

01

PE6

Sacrewell
Lodge

6

Jubilee
Spinney

RUSSELL HILL

OLD RECTORY DR

WINDGATE WAY

Hereward Way

Hell
Corner

5

Sacrewell Farm &
Country Centre

Top Field
Spinney

Mill
House

00

PE8

TRACK   CRS CL

OLD NORTH RD

A6118

Black Swan
Hill

Heath
House

4   A47

ROBINS   WOOD

A6118   OLD NORTH RD

Black Swan
Spinney

SWAN

Wansford

Mast

Nene Way

PE5

Robins Field

THE
STABLES

OLD LEICESTER RD

NENE CL

PETERBOROUGH RD

River Nene

Deep
Springs

A47

3   WANSFORD RD   YARWELL RD

BRIDGE END

SILK   ST

The
Bungalow

THE DRIFT

Wansford
Bridge

Hotel

99   B671

LONDON RD

A6118

PH
PO
CHAPEL ST

GREAT NORTH RD

Sutton

Nene Way

Manor
Farm

2

Stibbington
Hall

LOVERS LA   GRAZING RD   MANOR RD

CHURCH LA

The
Grange

Bunkers
Hill

OLD GREAT NORTH RD

JOHNATHON DR

Stibbington

Manor
Farm

Stibbington
House

Field Studies
Centre

1   Nene Way

ELTON RD

NEW LA

Sewage
Farm

Nene Valley Railway

Ship End
Pits

Depot

OLD GREAT NORTH RD

B671

Toll Bar
Spinney

A1

98   07   A   08   B   C   09   D   E   F

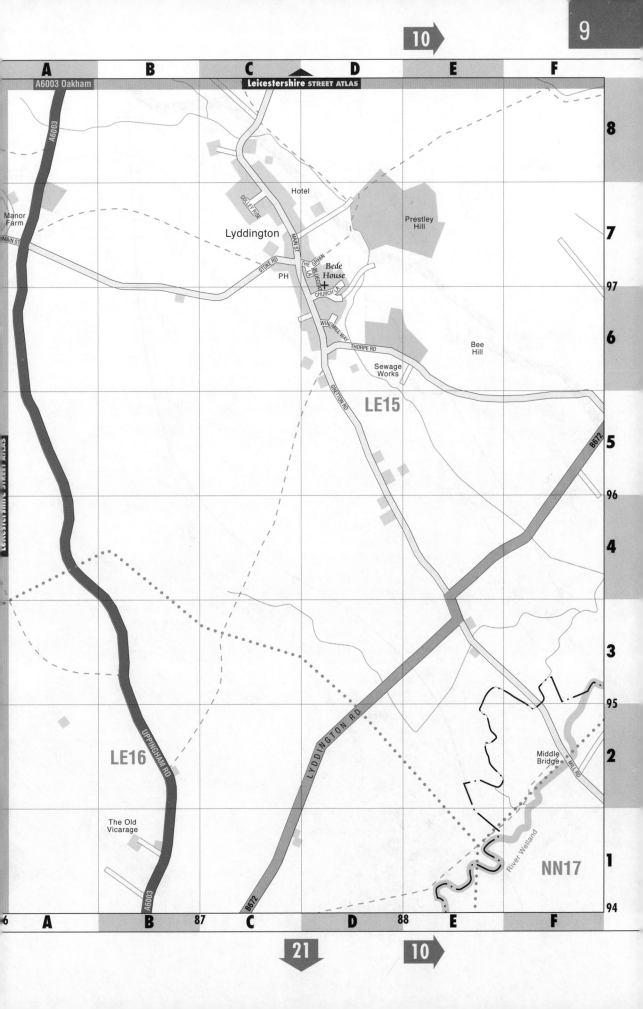

A   B   C   D   E   F

A6003 Oakham

Leicestershire STREET ATLAS

8

Manor
Farm

MAIN ST

COLLEY RISE

Hotel

Prestley
Hill

7

Lyddington

MAIN ST

97

STOKE RD

THE GREEN

BLUECOAT LA

PH

Bede
House

CHURCH LA

6

WINDMILL WAY

THORPE RD

Bee
Hill

Sewage
Works

GRETTON RD

LE15

B672

5

96

4

3

95

LYDDINGTON RD

Middle
Bridge

MILL RD

2

LE16

UPPINGHAM RD

The Old
Vicarage

A6003

B672

River Welland

NN17

1

94

6   A   B   87   C   D   88   E   F

8
7
97
6
5
96
4
3
95
2
1
94

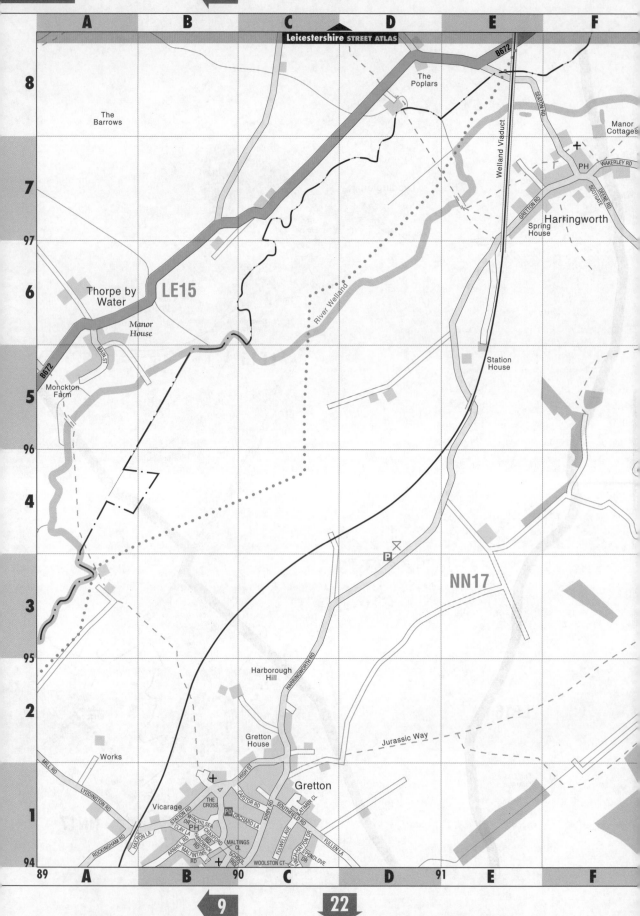

A B C D E F

Leicestershire STREET ATLAS

The Poplars

B672

Manor Cottages

Welland Viaduct

PH WAKERLEY RD

Harringworth

SCOTGATE

DEENE RD

SEATON RD

GRETTON RD

Spring House

The Barrows

8

7

97

Thorpe by Water

LE15

6

River Welland

Manor House

Station House

B672

Monckton Farm

5

96

4

P

NN17

3

95

Harborough Hill

HARRINGWORTH RD

2

Gretton House

Jurassic Way

Works

Gretton

MILL RD

LYDDINGTON RD

ROCKINGHAM RD

HALTON LA

ARNHILL RD

STATION RD

WINCHILSEA DR

CLAY LA

MALTINTINS RD

HARDWICK RD

SCHOOL RD

CRAXFORD RD

PH

Vicarage

THE CROSS

CASTOR RD

HIGH ST

KIRBY RD

ORCHARD LA

MALTINGS CL

WOOLSTON CT

FILWELL AVE

SOUTHFIELD RD

FINCH-HATTON DR

LATIMER CL

SPENDLOVE DR

FULLEN LA

1

94

89 A B 90 C D 91 E F

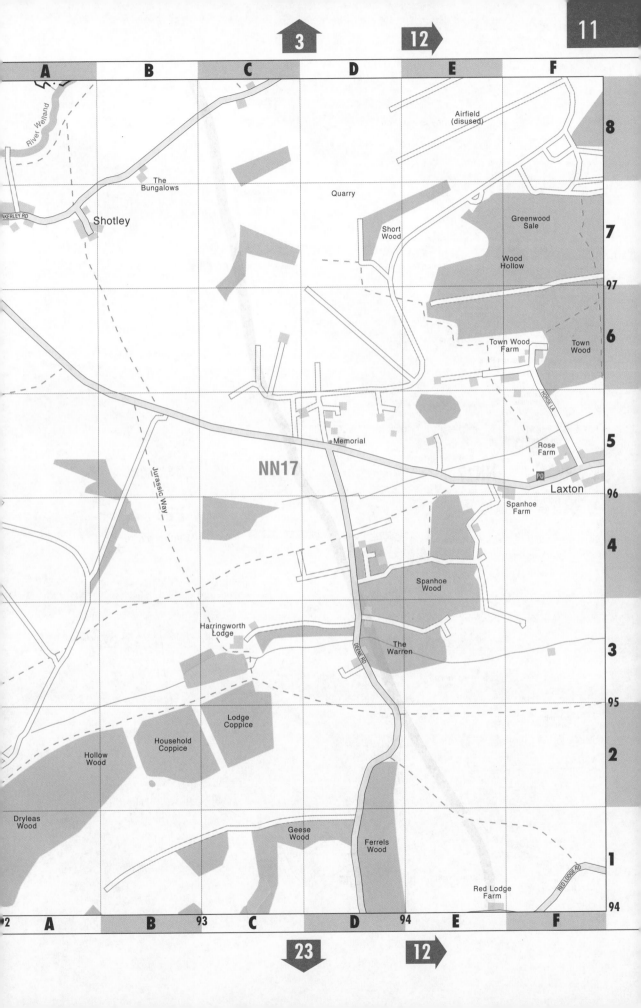

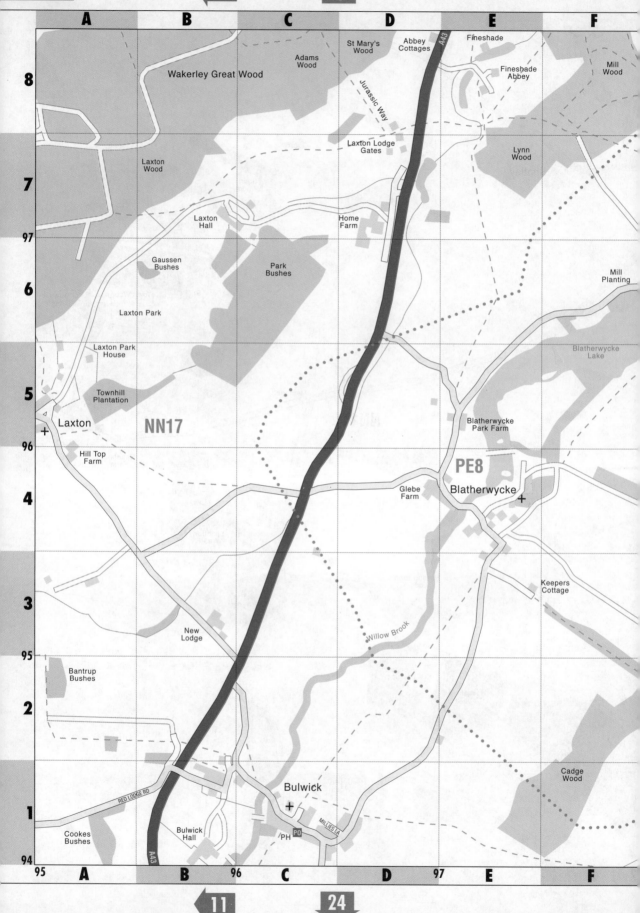

Wakerley Great Wood

Adams Wood

St Mary's Wood

Abbey Cottages

Fineshade

Fineshade Abbey

Mill Wood

Jurassic Way

Laxton Wood

Laxton Lodge Gates

Lynn Wood

Laxton Hall

Home Farm

Gaussen Bushes

Park Bushes

Mill Planting

Laxton Park

Blatherwycke Lake

Laxton Park House

Townhill Plantation

Blatherwycke Park Farm

Laxton

NN17

PE8

Hill Top Farm

Glebe Farm

Blatherwycke

Keepers Cottage

New Lodge

Willow Brook

Bantrup Bushes

Cadge Wood

RED LODGE RD

Bulwick

MILLIES LA

Cookes Bushes

Bulwick Hall

PH   PO

A43

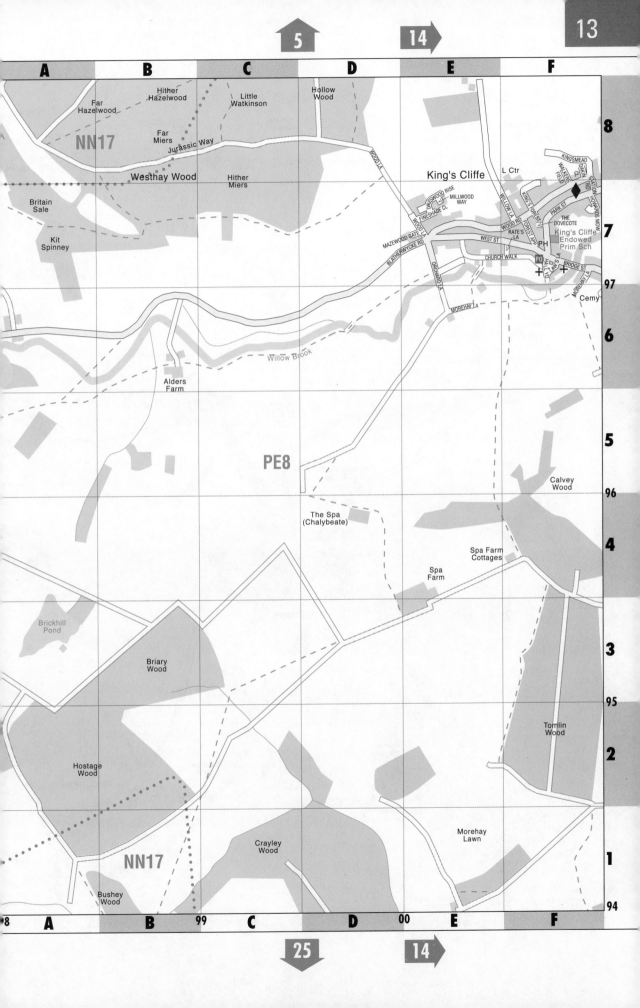

5   14

8

Far
Hazelwood

Hither
Hazelwood

Little
Watkinson

Hollow
Wood

NN17

Far
Miers

Jurassic Way

Westhay Wood

Hither
Miers

WOOD LA

King's Cliffe

L Ctr

KINGSMEAD

WALKERS
FIELD

SEATON HOWARDS MDW

DAKIN
CL

7

Britain
Sale

GLASWOOD RISE

MILLWOOD
WAY

WILLOW LA

KING'S FOREST VW

PARK ST

THE
DOVECOTE

King's Cliffe
Endowed
Prim Sch

Kit
Spinney

FINESHADE CL

WOOD

MAZEWOOD GATE

BLATHERWYCKE RD

ORCHARD LA

WOOD RD

RATE'S
LA

WEST ST

CHURCH WALK

PH

PO

BRIDGE ST

MOREHAY LA

Cemy

97

MOREHAY LA

6

Willow Brook

Alders
Farm

5

PE8

Calvey
Wood

96

The Spa
(Chalybeate)

Spa Farm
Cottages

4

Spa
Farm

Brickhill
Pond

Briary
Wood

3

95

Tomlin
Wood

2

Hostage
Wood

Morehay
Lawn

1

NN17

Crayley
Wood

Bushey
Wood

94

25   14

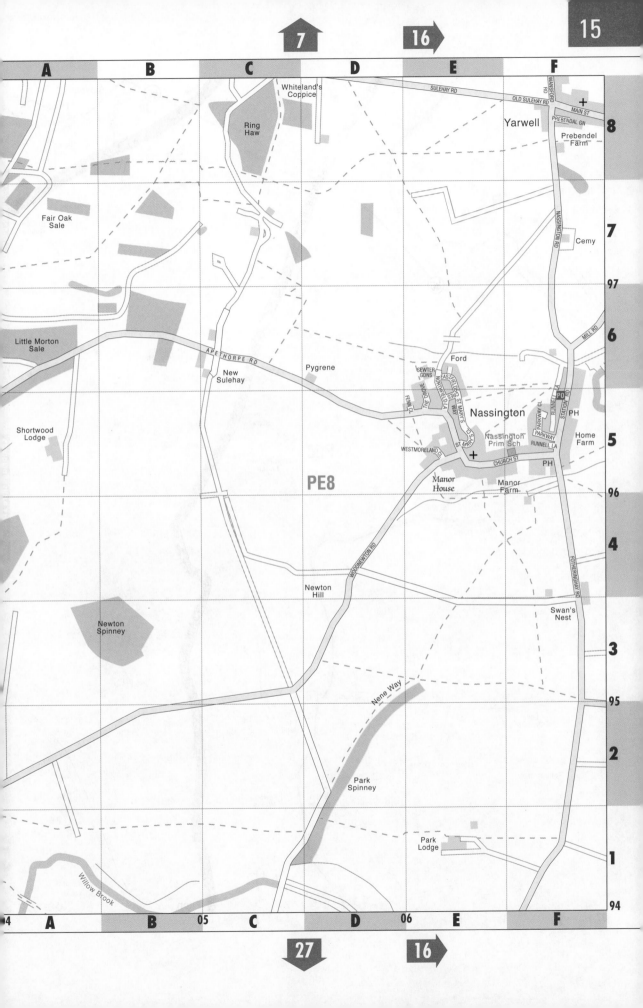

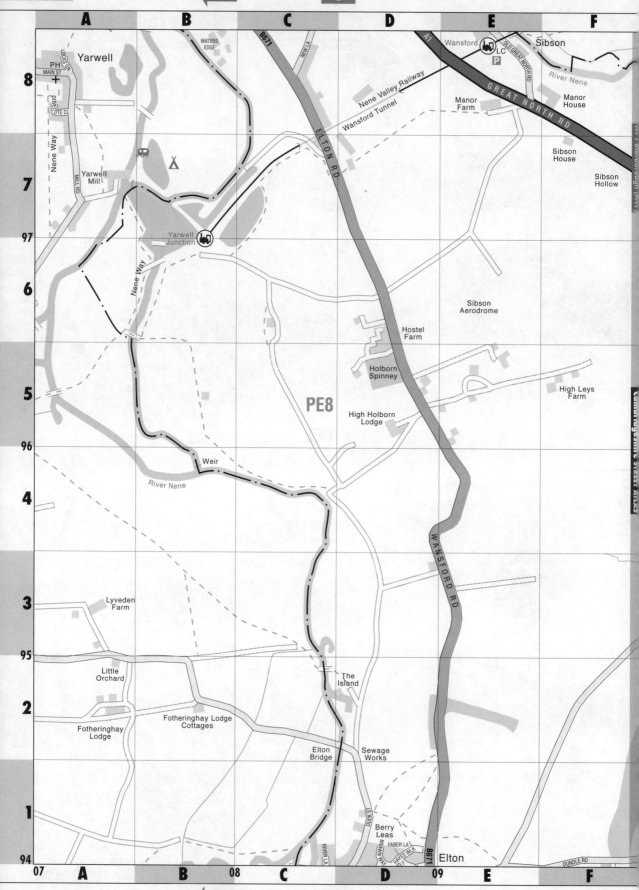

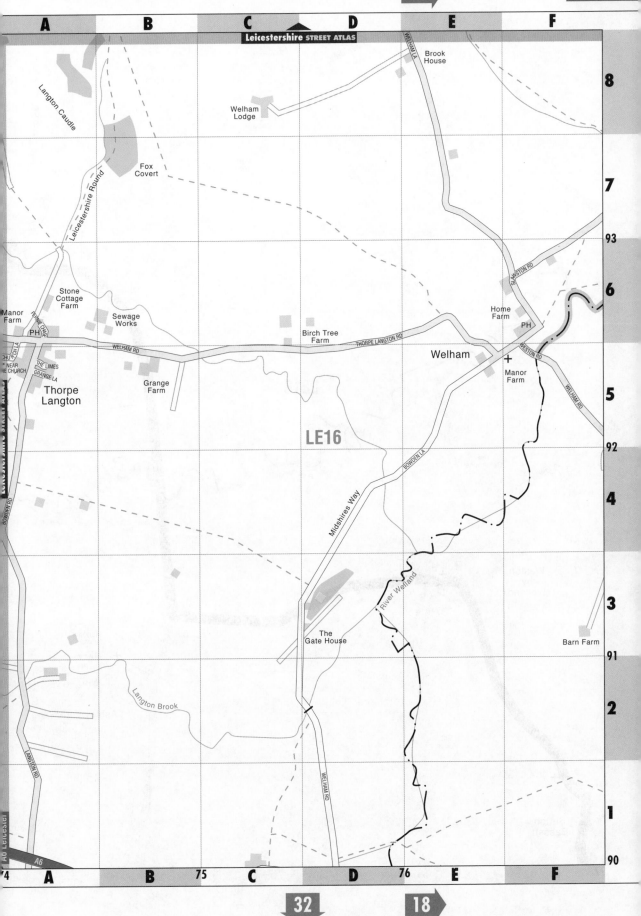

A B C D E F

Leicestershire STREET ATLAS

8

7

93

6

92

5

4

3

91

2

1

90

Langton Caudle

Leicestershire Round

Fox Covert

Welham Lodge

Brook House

WELHAM LA

SLAWSTON RD

Stone Cottage Farm

Manor Farm

PH

FERNIE CHASE

Sewage Works

Birch Tree Farm

THORPE LANGTON RD

Home Farm

PH

WESTON RD

Welham

Manor Farm

WELHAM RD

CHURCH RD

NEAR THE CHURCH

THE LIMES

GRANGE LA

Thorpe Langton

Grange Farm

WELHAM RD

LE16

Midshires Way

BOWDEN LA

River Welland

WELHAM RD

The Gate House

Barn Farm

Langton Brook

LANGTON RD

BOWDEN RD

A6 Leicester

A6

A B 75 C D 76 E F

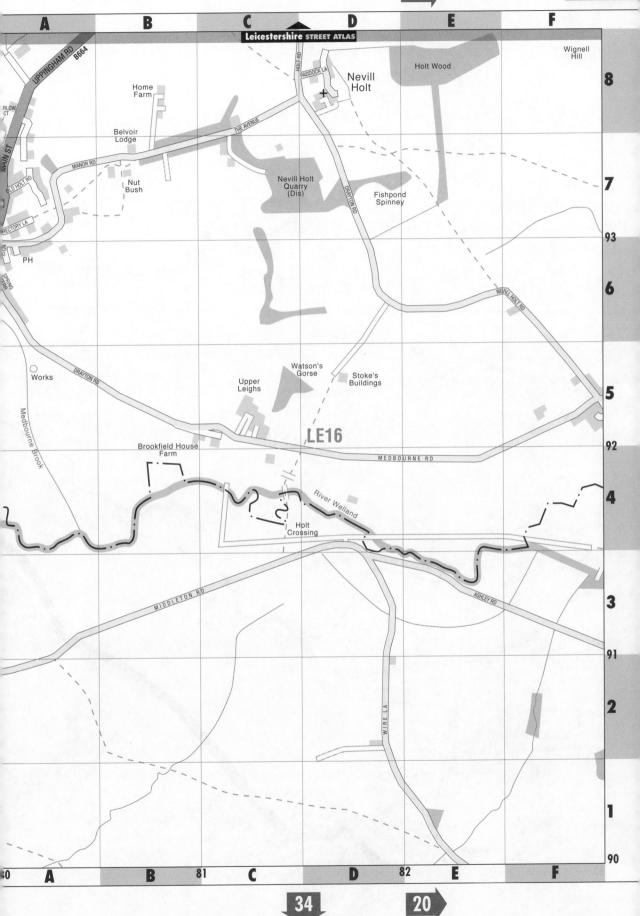

Leicestershire STREET ATLAS

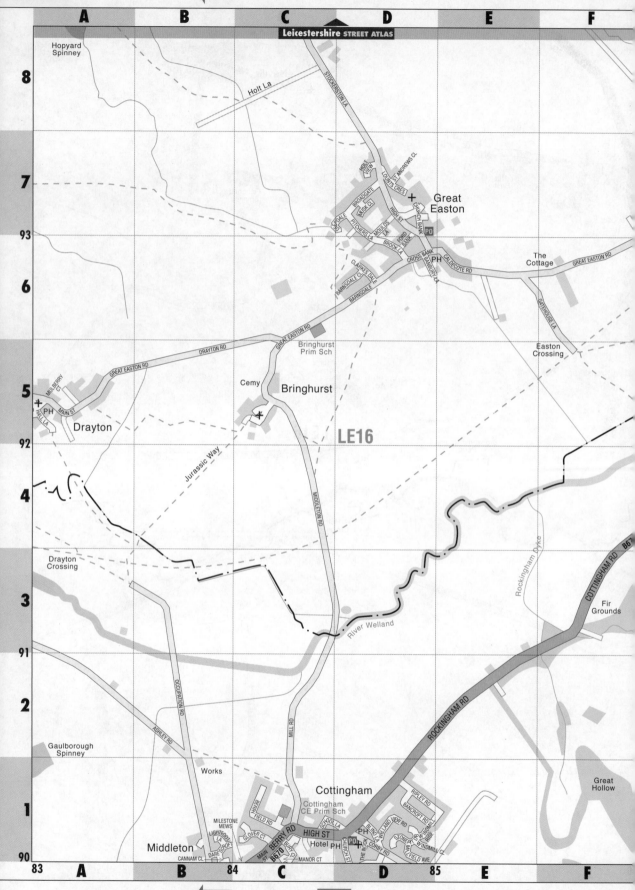

Leicestershire STREET ATLAS

A **B** **C** **D** **E** **F**

8

Hopyard
Spinney

Holt La

STOCKERSTON LA

7

MOLL VIEW

ST ANDREWS CL

LOWINS CRES

Great
Easton

BROADGATE

VESA CL

HIGH ST

CHURCH BANK

93

DEEPDALE

PITCHERS LA

MOULDS LA

BROOK LA

FORD BANK

PO

CHURCH BANK

The
Cottage

GREAT EASTON RD

6

BARNSDALE CL

CLARK'S DALE

CROSS BANK

BARBURY LA

PH

CALDECOTE RD

GATEHOUSE LA

BARNSDALE

BARNSDALE RD

GREAT EASTON RD

DRAYTON RD

GREAT EASTON RD

Bringhurst
Prim Sch

Easton
Crossing

5

MULBERRY CT

MAIN ST

Cemy

Bringhurst

GREAT EASTON RD

PH

HILL LA

Drayton

92

Jurassic Way

LE16

MIDDLETON RD

4

Rockingham Dyke

B6

Drayton
Crossing

COTTINGHAM RD

Fir
Grounds

3

River Welland

91

OCCUPATION RD

ROCKINGHAM RD

2

ASHLEY RD

MILL RD

Gaulborough
Spinney

Works

Great
Hollow

RIPLEY RD

1

Cottingham

BANCROFT RD

Cottingham
CE Prim Sch

MILESTONE
MEWS

BERRY FIELD RD

SCHOOL LA

PH

WELLAND VIEW RD

LIGHTFOOT LA

GLOVER CT

BERRY RD

HIGH ST

CHURCH ST

PO

THE NOOK

DERBY RD

STONEY

WINDMILL LA

RISE

WINDMILL

FIELD AVE

Middleton

CANNAM CL

MAIN ST

B670

Hotel
PH

MANOR CT

90

83 **A** 84 **B** **C** 84 **D** 85 **E** **F**

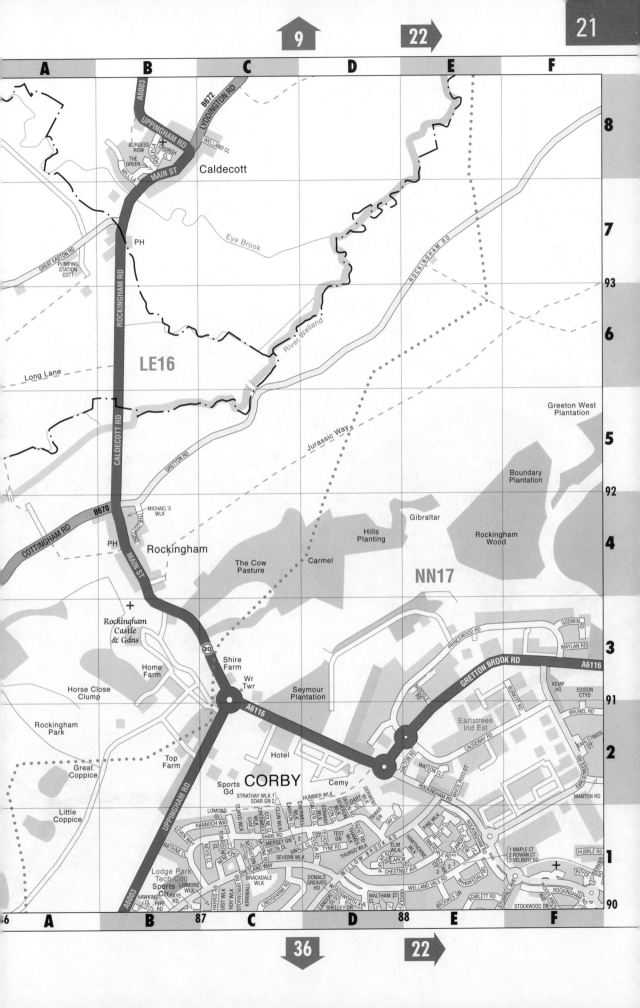

A B C D E F

8

NORTHERN CL

Wr Twr
Gretton Prim Sch

WELLAND CL

STAFORD RD
KIRBY RD
FINCH HATTON DR

Jurassic Way

South Lodge

FULLEN LA

Kirby Hall Farm

7

93

CORBY RD

6

Greeton East Plantation

5

NN17

Keepers Lodge Farm

Kirby Lodge

92

Corby Tunnel

Brookfield Plantation

Forest Nursery

Rockingham Motor Speedway

KIRBY LA

4

GRETTON BROOK RD

P

GRETTON RD

Weldon Lodge

Factory

P

P

3

Greeton Brook Plantation

A6116

MITCHELL RD

Willowbrook East Ind Est

91

FLEMING RD
BRUNEL RD

PHOENIX PARKWAY
HERITAGE WAY

SHELTON CT
SHELTON RD

PRIORS CT 1
ADELAIDE HO 2
MELBOURNE HO 3
PERTH HO 4
DARWIN HO 5
CANBERRA HO 6
ARNSLEY RD 7

2

ALEXANDER CT
BRUNEL CT

Earlstrees Ind Est

MANTON RD

PYWELL CT
PYWELL RD

SONDES RD

BIRCHINGTON RD

Weldon North Ind Est

Corby Gate Bsns P

CORBY

STEEL RD

BARON CT
SALLOW RD

A6116

HUBBLE RD
STANIER RD
CRICK CL
PARSONS GR
LISTER CL
JAMES WAY
STEPHENSON WAY
NEWTON GR
PEG GREEN CL

STOCKBRIDGE RD
MACADAM RD

MARCONI CTYD
RUTHERFORD CT

GENNER RD

GAYDON HO

ARROWRIGHT RD
DARWIN RD

BARD RD
PRIESTLEY CT
CURVER WAY

BOYLE RD

DARWIN RD

CAVENDISH CTYD

Enterprise Ind Pk

HUNTERS RD
BRAKEY RD

Venture

PROBS

1

90

89 A B 90 C D 91 E F

A B C D E F

8
7
93
6
5
92
4
3
91
2
1
90

RED LODGE RD

Mavis
Wood

Bamford
Spinney

Sweethill
Spinney

Deene

Deene
Hall

Gretton Brook

Kirby
Spinney

Parker's
Spinney

Manor
Farm

Kirby Hall

Home
Farm

KIRBY LA

Deene Park

The
Rookery

NN17

Fir
Plantation

Dibbin's
Wood

Hollow
Wood

Bangrave
Wood

Weldon
Little
Wood

CH

A43

Priors
Hall
Quarry

Priors
Hall
Plantation

Lodge
Farm

Shire
Cottage

BIRCHINGTON
RD

GRETTON RD

TANNASTO
LAMMAS RD
CT RD
PRIORS HAW RD

PRIORS CT

STAMFORD RD

Weldon
Park

ARNSLEY RD

A43

92 A B 93 C D 94 E F 90

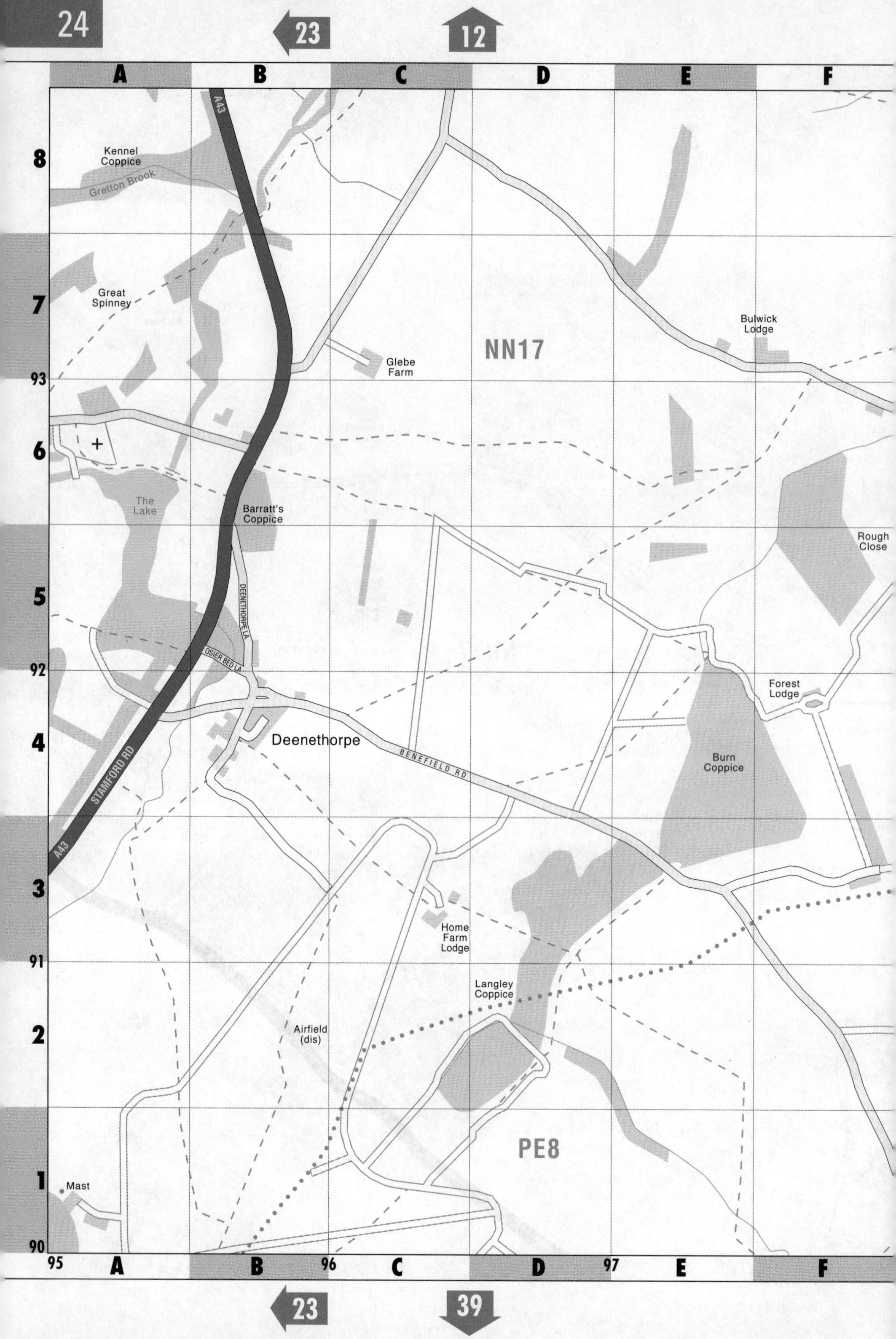

A B C D E F

8

Kennel
Coppice

Gretton Brook

7

Great
Spinney

NN17

Bulwick
Lodge

93

Glebe
Farm

A43

6

+

The
Lake

Barratt's
Coppice

DEENETHORPE LA

Rough
Close

5

OSIER BED LA

92

Forest
Lodge

4

Deenethorpe

BENEFIELD RD

Burn
Coppice

STAMFORD RD

3

A43

Home
Farm
Lodge

91

Langley
Coppice

2

Airfield
(dis)

PE8

1

Mast

90

95 A 96 C D 97 E F
B

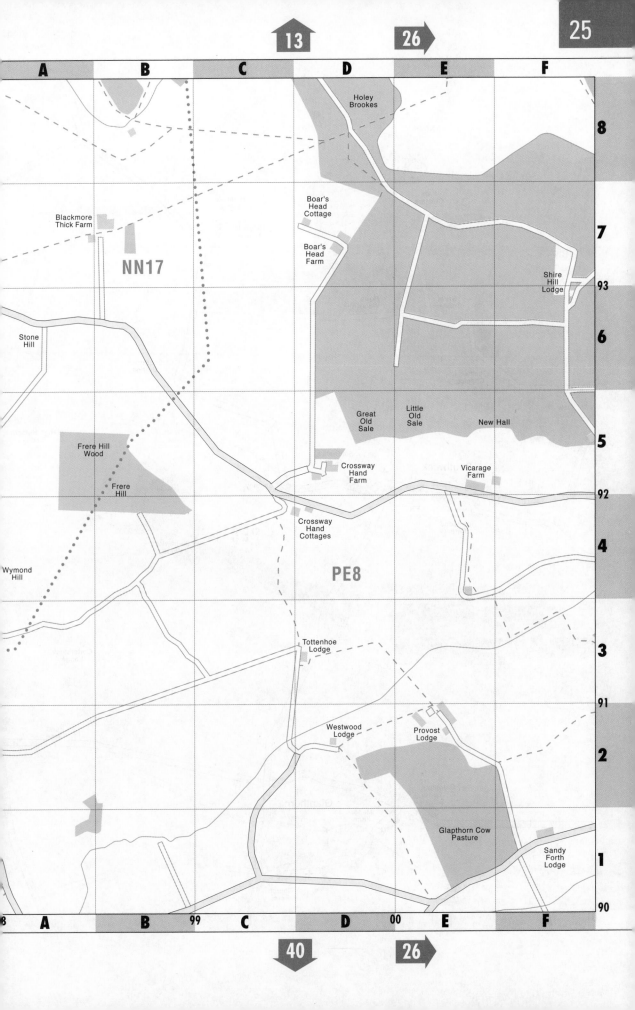

A   B   C   D   E   F

8

Holey
Brookes

Boar's
Head
Cottage

7

Blackmore
Thick Farm

NN17

Boar's
Head
Farm

Shire
Hill
Lodge

93

Stone
Hill

6

Great
Old
Sale

Little
Old
Sale

New Hall

5

Frere Hill
Wood

Crossway
Hand
Farm

Vicarage
Farm

92

Frere
Hill

Crossway
Hand
Cottages

4

Wymond
Hill

PE8

Tottenhoe
Lodge

3

91

Westwood
Lodge

Provost
Lodge

2

Glapthorn Cow
Pasture

Sandy
Forth
Lodge

1

90

← 25
↑ 14

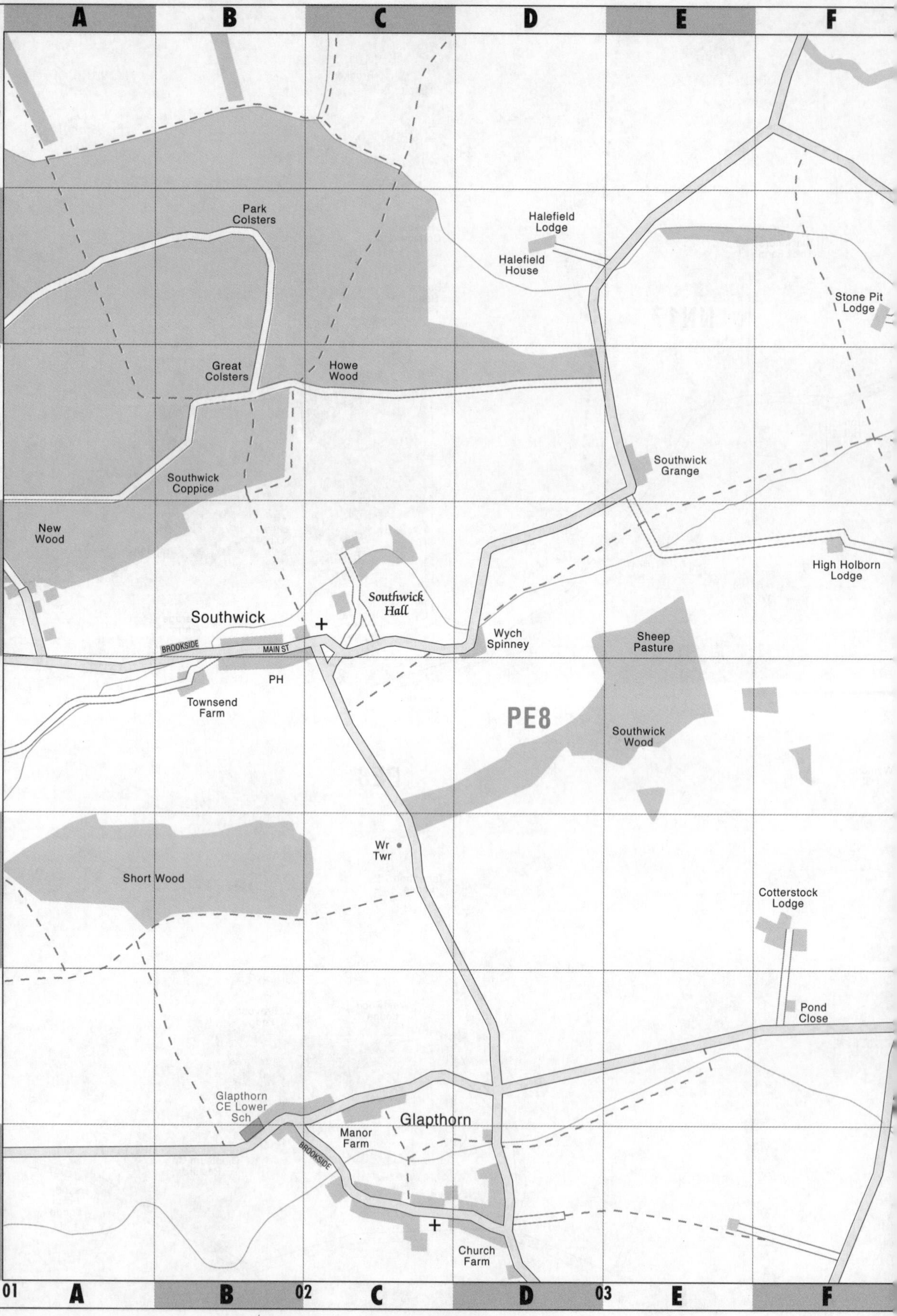

A B C D E F

8

Park
Colsters

Halefield
Lodge

7

Halefield
House

Stone Pit
Lodge

93

Great
Colsters

Howe
Wood

6

Southwick
Grange

Southwick
Coppice

New
Wood

High Holborn
Lodge

5

Southwick

*Southwick
Hall*

Sheep
Pasture

+

92

BROOKSIDE MAIN ST

Wych
Spinney

PH

PE8

Townsend
Farm

Southwick
Wood

4

Short Wood

Wr •
Twr

3

Cotterstock
Lodge

91

Pond
Close

2

Glapthorn
CE Lower
Sch

Glapthorn

Manor
Farm

BROOKSIDE

1

+

Church
Farm

90

← 25
↕ 41

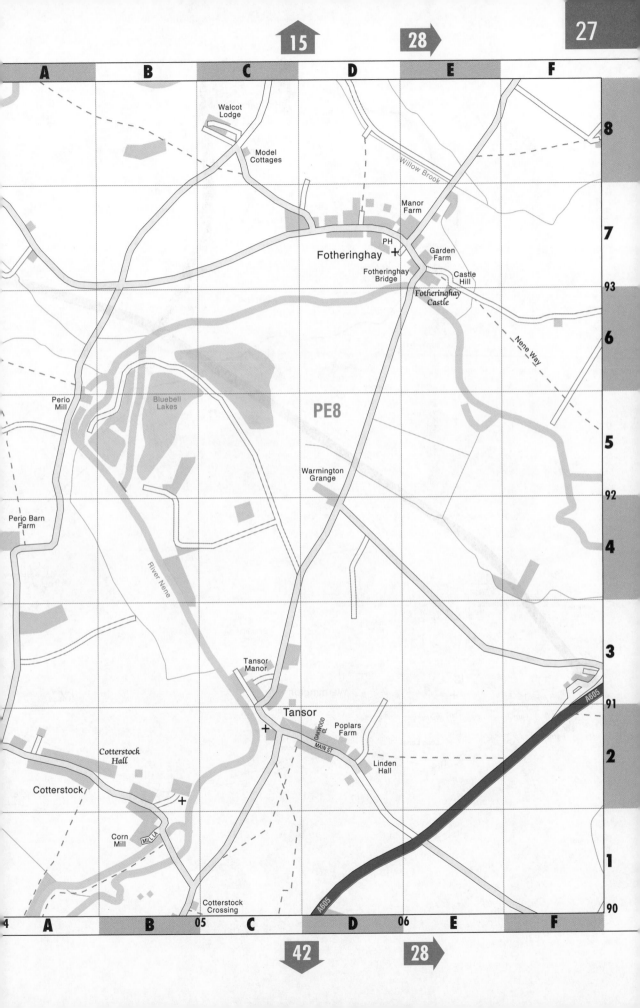

PE8

A605 Peterborough (A1139)

Cambridgeshire STREET ATLAS

Lodge Farm

CH

Elton Furze

Furze Farm

Rectory Farm

Elton Lodge Farm

A605

60

Greenhill Lodge

GREENHILL RD

GREENHILL RD

Bate's Lodge

93

Lawrence's Lodge

PE7

Stockhill Lodge

Bonser's Lodge

92

Tookey Farm

BULLOCK RD

Billing Brook

Morborne Hill

Mast

Mast

Radio Station

Field End Close

PE8

91

Papley Gorse

Long Spinney

Horse Close Hovel

America Farm

Morborne Hill Top

90

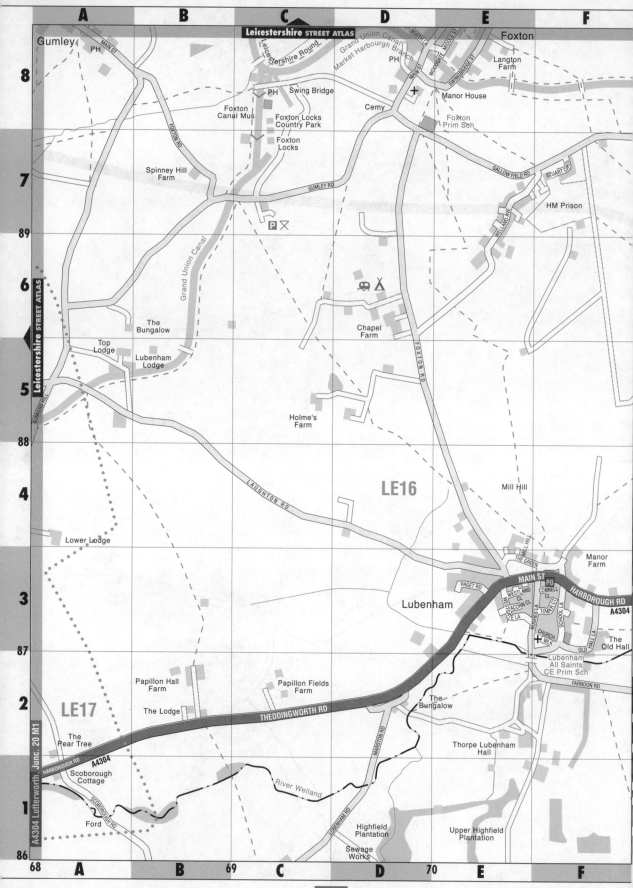

Gumley

Foxton

PH

Main St

Foxton Rd

Leicestershire Round

Grand Union Canal/ Market Harbourgh Branch

North La

Swingbridge St

Woodgate

Middle St

Main St

PH

Langton Farm

Swing Bridge

PH

Foxton Canal Mus

Foxton Locks Country Park

Foxton Locks

Cemy

Manor House

Foxton Prim Sch

Gallow Field Rd

Stuart Crt

Spinney Hill Farm

Gumley Rd

Grand Union Canal

HM Prison

Welland Ave

P

The Bungalow

Chapel Farm

Foxton Rd

Top Lodge

Lubenham Lodge

Bunkers Hill

Holme's Farm

LE16

Laughton Rd

Mill Hill

Lower Lodge

Manor Farm

Mill Hill

The Green

Paget Rd

MAIN ST

PO

Lubenham

Westland Cl

Acorn Cl

Rushes La

Connell Cl

Town Crt

School La

HARBOROUGH RD

A4304

Old Hall La

The Old Hall

Church Wlk

Lubenham All Saints CE Prim Sch

Papillon Hall Farm

Papillon Fields Farm

Farndon Rd

LE17

The Lodge

THEDDINGWORTH RD

The Bungalow

Marston Rd

The Pear Tree

Thorpe Lubenham Hall

A4304 Lutterworth, Junc. 20 M1

Harborough Rd

A4304

Scoborough Cottage

River Welland

Scoborough Rd

Ford

Lubenham Rd

Highfield Plantation

Upper Highfield Plantation

Sewage Works

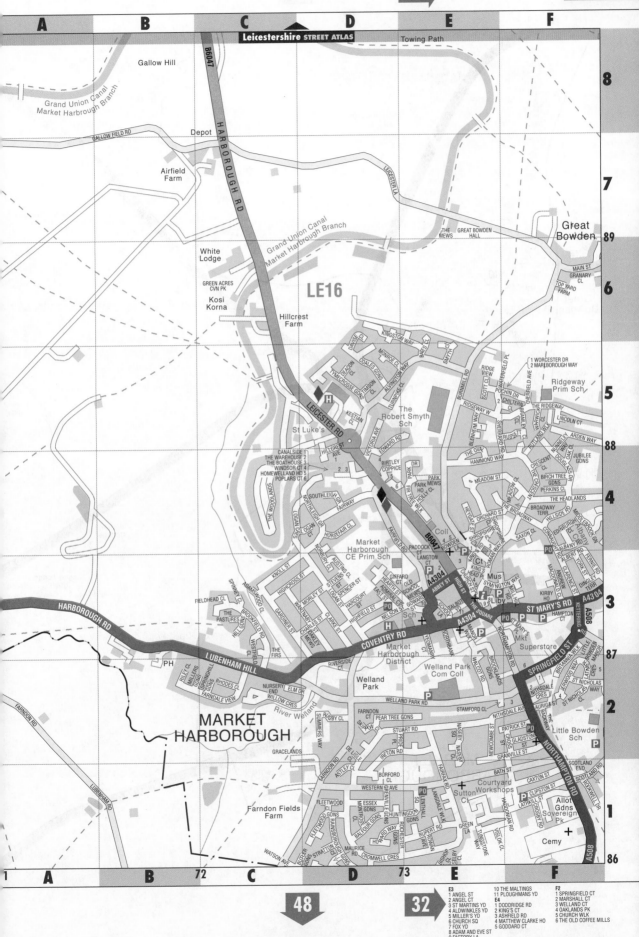

Leicestershire STREET ATLAS

A B C D E F

8
Tin House Farm
Midshires Way
B66
Nurseries
WELHAM LA
WELHAM RD
River Welland

7
Kennels
SUTTON RD
Dingley Grange Cottages
Dingle Grang

89
UPPER GREEN PL
THE PINES
CHATER CL
MANOR RD
MAIN ST
SUTTON RD
Sewage Wks
Dingley La
Lower Lodge

6
Great Bowden
PH
PO
GUN
SBROOK CL
THE GREEN
Great Bowden CE Prim Sch
Cemy
Knight's End
KNIGHT'S END RD
DINGLEY RD

5
Bowden Ridge
THE RIDGEWAY
COUNTRYMAN MEWS
MADELINE CL
BERRY CL
STATION RD
HORSE SHOE LA
BANKFIELD DR
A4304
A427
B664
LE16
HARBOROUGH RD

88
ARDEN WAY
ARDEN CL
THE HEADLANDS
GREAT BOWDEN RD
THE POINT
Euro Bsns Pk

4
ST MARY'S RD
APPLEBROOK GN
Riverside Ind Est
WELLAND CT
RIVERSIDE
Welland Bsns Pk
VALLEY WAY
ROCKINGHAM RD
Meadowdale Prim Sch
MEADOWDALE
FERNFIELD CL
RYLANDS CL
Lodge Farm
Warren Cottage
Sandpits Wood
MAIN RD A42

3
A4304
HARROD DR
Market Harborough
Rockingham Ind Est
CLARK AVE
ANTONY DR
BORRA LA
WILSON CL
DEENE CL
RIPLEY
CL
HOLLYWORTH
DR
DENBY
CL
HAGLEY
CL
THE FURLONGS
STOCKWELL
WOODBRECK DR
ASHLEY WAY
LONGWHILEY
LONGBRIDGE
PICKS
CL
STINFORD LEYS
FOTHERGILL CL
Dingley Lodge Hotel
Dingley Warren
Woodlands

1 WOBURN CL
2 GOODWOOD CL
3 STANWAY CL
4 BURGHLEY CL
5 ROSEMOOR CL
6 BAMBURGH CL
7 BALMORAL CL
8 FLAXLAND CL

87
ROLLESTON
ST MARY'S RD
BELLFIELDS LA
RECTOR
CHURCH WLK
THORNBOROUGH WAY
STABLEGATE
MIDDLEDALE RD
OVERDALE CL
GLEBE RD
PETWORTH DR
SANDRINGHAM WAY
LONGLEAT CL
WOODGATE CL
AUDLEY CL
GILBERT CL
THE LONGLANDS
ASKELAND CL
ROUNDHILL CL

2
BELLFIELDS ST
Little Bowden LC
SCOTLAND RD
LAUNDE PK
QUEEN ST
DUNSLADE CL
DUNSLADE GR
SHREWSBURY AVE
KETTERING RD
FERN LEYS CL
THE HEIGHTS
ROUNDHILL CL
Clack Ridge
Clack Hill
HARBOROUGH RD

1
DUNMORE RD
Windy Ridge
MARKET HARBOROUGH
BRATBROOKE RD
River Jordan

86
74 A B 75 C D 76 E F

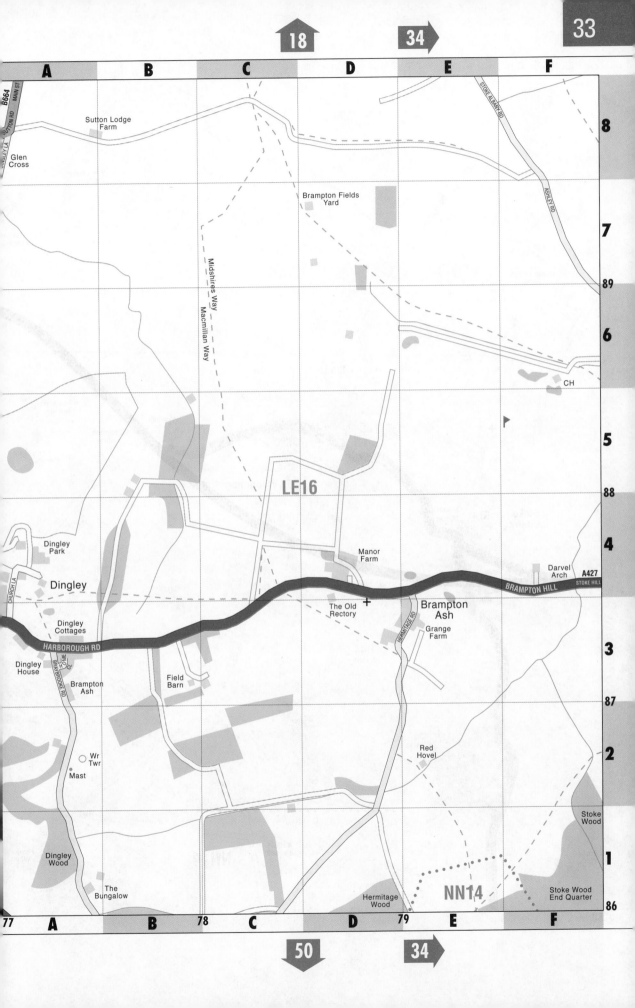

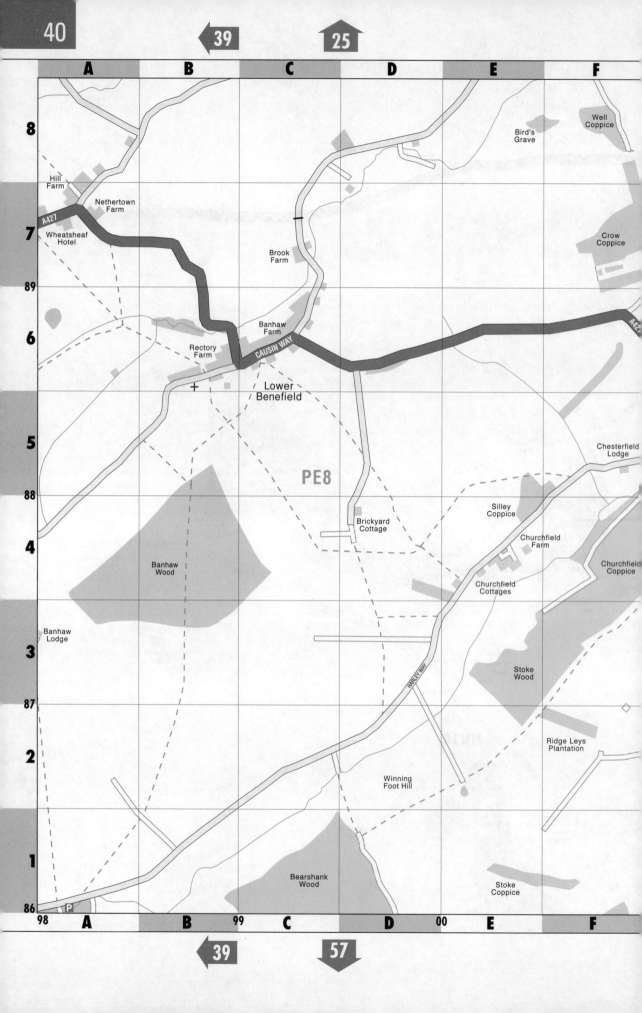

A B C D E F

8
Sewage
Works

Oundle &
Kings
Cliffe Mid
Sch

7
Biggin
Hall

ST PETERS RD
CULM CL
WENTWORTH DR
ROCKINGHAM HILLS
WATSON CL
RAY CL
COTTERSTOCK RD
BELLAMY RD
ST WILFRIDS RD
MONSON WAY
LACOMBES CL
SIDDONS CL
CLOLEY HILL CT
LIME AVE
NENE WAY

Park
Wood
CREED RD
HILLFIELD RD
PH
GLAPTHORN RD
SPRINGFIELD RD
LATHAM ST
ROCK RD
89

SEYMOUR PL 1
WALCOT CL 2
NEWBOLD CL 3
NENE VIEW
GORDON RD
NEW RD

Playing
Fields
OUNDLE
6

Biggin
Grange
PAVILION DR

Heron
Rogers
Wood
STRONGLANDS
CT
FLETTON
Liby

HERONS WOOD CL
WYATT RD
MILDMAY CL
WHITWELL CL
ST ANN'S CT
MILTON RD
Oundle
CE
Prim Sch

HARLEY WAY
Biggin
Fish
Pond
BENEFIELD RD
CH
WAKERLEY
CL
CLIFTON DR
PEXLEY CT
A427
SPURLINGS
INKERMAN WAY
TURNERS YD
5
WEST ST
88

PE8
WARREN
BRIDGS
Cemy
Stoke Hill
Oundle Mus
South
Bridge
BREWERY
DANFORDS
SOUTH RD
BRIDGE RD
MILL RD
SHIP LA
2
1 SETCHELLS YD
2 DANFORD CL

Oundle
Wood

WOOD LA
STOKE DOYLE RD
Barnwell
Country Park
Visitor
Ctr
BARNWELL RD
Marina
4

Feoffee
Lodge

Oundle
Lodge
River Nene
Nene Way
3

Barnwell Mill
Bridge
87

PH
Barnwell
Mill
Farm
2

Stoke
Doyle
OLD
FARM
HATCHDOYLE LA
PH
CHURCH LA
1

The
Old
Rectory
86

A B C D E F

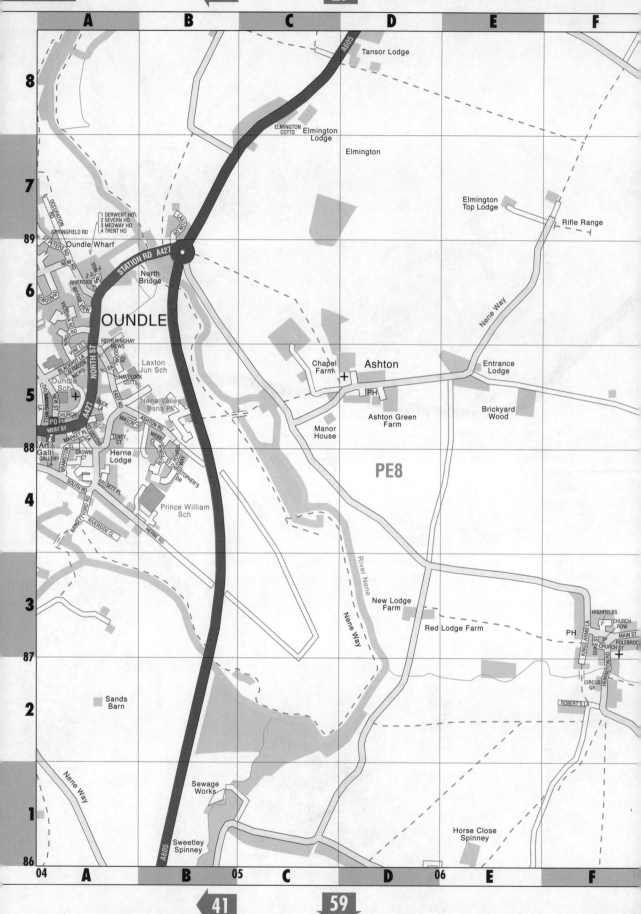

41
27

A · B · C · D · E · F

8

Tansor Lodge

A605

ELMINGTON COTTS · Elmington Lodge

Elmington

7

Elmington Top Lodge

Rifle Range

89

OCCUPATION RD
SPRINGFIELD RD
Oundle Wharf
1 DERWENT HO
2 SEVERN HO
3 MEDWAY HO
4 TRENT HO
ST PETERS RD
NEW RD
RIVERSIDE
STATION RD A427
North Bridge
LAXTON RD

Nene Way

6

OUNDLE
BRIDGE VIEW
VICTORIA RD
KINGS RD
VINE CL
GORDON RD
FOTHERINGHAY MEWS
EASTWOOD RD
Laxton Jun Sch
HAVELOCK COTTS
NORTH ST

Chapel Farm

Ashton

Entrance Lodge

5

Oundle Sch
CHURCH LA
POST ST
DRUMMING WELL LA
NEW ST
EAST RD
MASON'S CL
Nene Valley Bsns Pk
Ashton Rd
A427
WEST ST
i
Art Gall
GALLERY LA

Manor House

Ashton Green Farm

PH

Brickyard Wood

88

BRAMSTON CT
CROWN CT
MARKET PL
TANEY CT
WEBB CL
Herne Lodge
CHRISTOPHER'S DR
KNOWEL WAY

PE8

4

SOUTH RD
BASSETTFORD RD
BASSETT PL
RIVERSIDE CL
Prince William Sch
HERNE RD

3

River Nene

Nene Way

New Lodge Farm

Red Lodge Farm

PH

HIGHFIELDS
KINGS ARMS LA
CHURCH ROW
DYKE ST
MAIN ST
POLEBROC
CHURCH ST
HEMINGTON RD

87

CIRCUS GR

2

Sands Barn

L ROBERT'S LA

1

Nene Way

Sewage Works

Horse Close Spinney

86

A605
Sweetley Spinney

04 · A · B · 05 · C · D · 06 · E · F

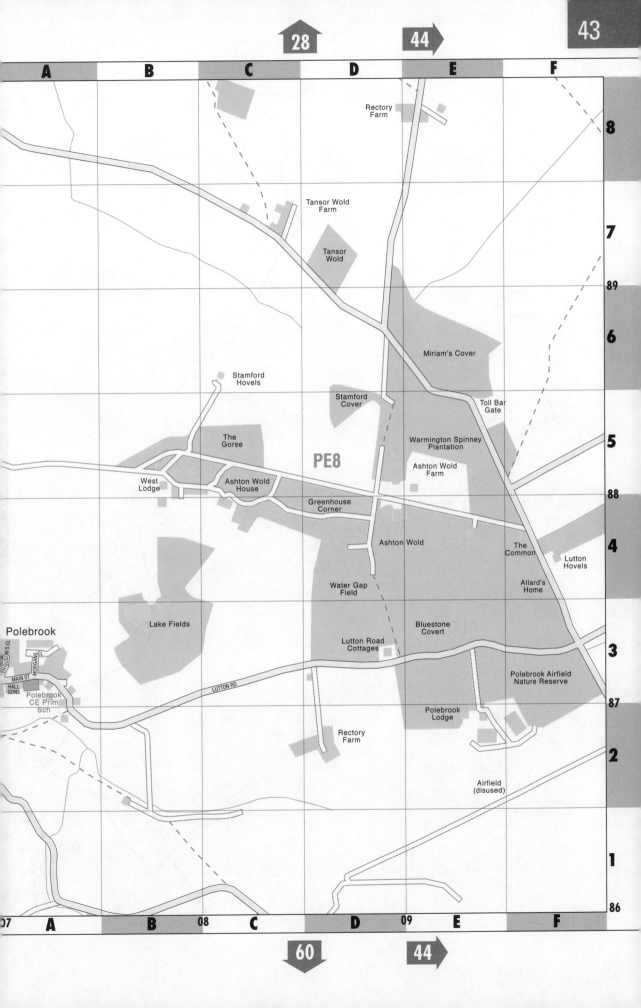

A B C D E F

8

7

89

6

Rectory Farm

Tansor Wold Farm

Tansor Wold

Miriam's Cover

5

88

Stamford Hovels

Stamford Cover

Toll Bar Gate

The Gorse

Warmington Spinney Plantation

PE8

Ashton Wold Farm

West Lodge

Ashton Wold House

Greenhouse Corner

Ashton Wold

The Common

4

Lutton Hovels

Water Gap Field

Allard's Home

Lake Fields

Bluestone Covert

Polebrook

Lutton Road Cottages

Polebrook Airfield Nature Reserve

3

87

FERGUSON'S CL

MORGANS CL

MAIN ST

HALL GDNS

Polebrook CE Prim Sch

LUTTON RD

Polebrook Lodge

Rectory Farm

2

Airfield (disused)

1

86

A B C D E F

43
29

A B C D E F

8

New Farm

Cold
Harbour

Ongutein Manor
Farm

PE7

Lodge
Farm

7

89

Papley
Cottages

Papley

Field
Farm

6

Papley
Coppice

WASHINGLEY LA

Papley
Farm

Ringmoor
Spinney

BULLOCK RD

5

Grange
Farm

Lutton Farm

88

Woodbine
Farm

Chapel
End

Milton Terr

Lutton

4

Manor
Farm

The Old
Rectory

Lutton Lodge
Farm

PE8

3

87

2

High Holborn
Farm

Long
Plantation

PE28 →

1

Top
Lodge

86

10 A B 11 C D 12 E F

43
61

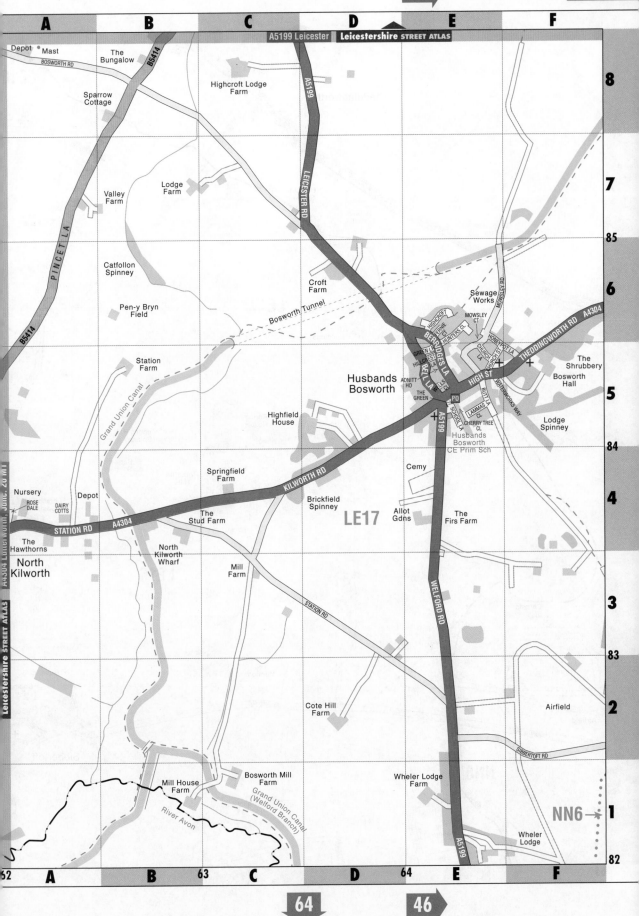

A5199 Leicester **Leicestershire STREET ATLAS**

Leicestershire STREET ATLAS

A4304 Lutterworth, June. 20 M 1

8

7

85

6

Depot   • Mast

BOSWORTH RD

The Bungalow

B5414

Sparrow Cottage

Highcroft Lodge Farm

A5199

Valley Farm

Lodge Farm

PINCET LA

Catfollon Spinney

Pen-y Bryn Field

LEICESTER RD

Croft Farm

Bosworth Tunnel

Sewage Works

HIGHCROFT CT
FERNIE CT
HUNTERS CL
MOWSLEY CT

BERRIDGES LA

GREEN LA
HILLCREST
BUTLER LA

MOWSLEY RD

HONEYPOT LA
CHURCH LA
CHURCH ST

THEDDINGWORTH RD A4304

The Shrubbery

Bosworth Hall

B5414

Station Farm

Grand Union Canal

Highfield House

Husbands Bosworth

ADNITT HO
THE GREEN
WELLS ST

HIGH ST

PO
BUTT LA

WATERWORKS WAY

Lodge Spinney

5

84

Nursery
ROSE DALE

DAIRY COTTS

Depot

Springfield Farm

KILWORTH RD

Brickfield Spinney

Cemy

LAMMAS CL
CHERRY TREE CL

A5199

SCHOOL LA

Husbands Bosworth CE Prim Sch

4

The Hawthorns

STATION RD   A4304

The Stud Farm

North Kilworth Wharf

Mill Farm

Allot Gdns

LE17

The Firs Farm

North Kilworth

STATION RD

3

83

Cote Hill Farm

WELFORD RD

Airfield

SIBBERTOFT RD

2

Mill House Farm

Bosworth Mill Farm

Grand Union Canal (Welford Branch)

River Avon

Wheler Lodge Farm

A5199

Wheler Lodge

NN6 →

1

82

Leicestershire STREET ATLAS A4304 Market Harborough

A B C D E F

The Crown (PH)

A4304

Monksley Rd · Station Rd · Cemy · The Bungalows · Works · LE16

Main St · Hothorpe Rd · Harborough Rd

8

Theddingworth

Bank Cotts · Pebble Cotts

Theddingworth Rd

Bosworth Rd

7

Dene Lodge · Damside Spinney · Old Folly · Quiet Fields

Pebble Hall · Home Farm

Woodside Farm

85

Hothorpe Hall

Theddingworth Rd

6

A4304 · LE17

Broxhill Buildings

River Welland

5

Spring Hollow · Nichol's Hill Spinney

Gravel Pit Spinney

84

Long Spinney · Barn-hill Spinney

Hothorpe Hills · Coombe-hill Spinney

4

LE16

3

Carland Spinney

83

The Roserie

The Wrongs · Coombes Farm

2

Welford Rd · Westhorpe · Beeches Cl · Welland Rise · PH · Berkeley's

Airfield · Sibbertoft Rd

Sibbertoft

Naseby Rd · Church St

NN6

Jurassic Way

1

Depot · Sulby Lodge

Sulby Rd · Sulby Hall Old Dr

The Kennels

82

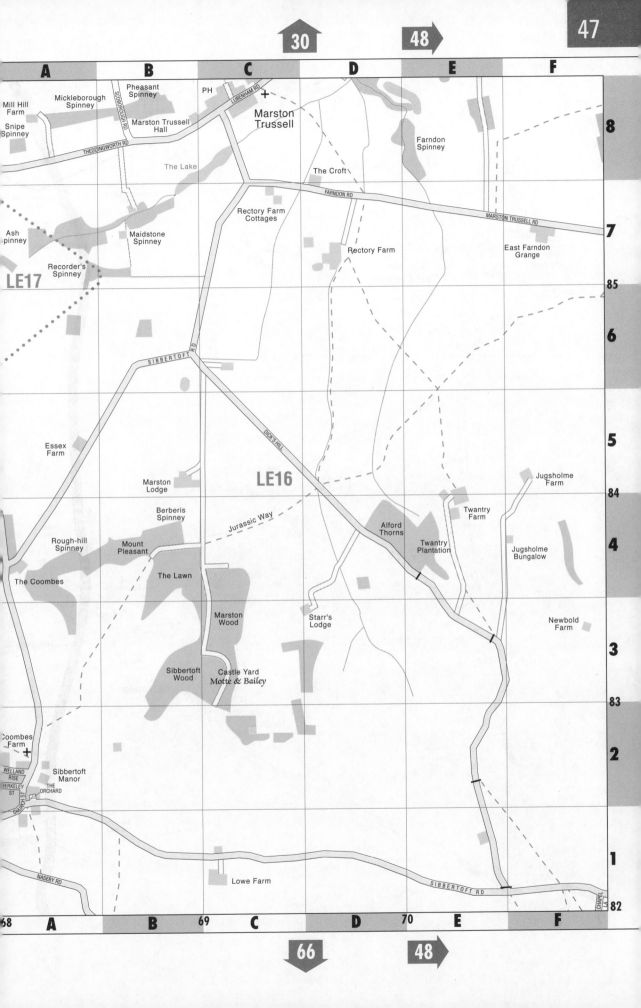

A B C D E F

8

Brierley Farm

Leisure Ctr

WATSON AVE
HARRISON CL
MAURICE RD
BARNARD GDNS
GERRARD GDNS
RAINSBOROUGH GDNS
LINDSEY GDNS
ASKEW CL
FN FIELDS
RITCHIE PK
ARGYLE PK
BISHOP CL
DIGBY CL
DALLISON CL
VAUGHAN CL

LUBENHAM RD
HARBOROUGH RD
THE LEACLAND

New House Farm

Farndon Fields Prim Sch

NORTHAMPTON RD · A508

TORCH WAY

Oxendon Lodge Farm

Oxendon Lodge Cottages

JUSTIN PARK CVN SITE

7

MARSTON LA

The Dales

East Farndon Hall

COUNCIL HO S
HOME FARM CL
BACK LA
MAIN ST

East Farndon

CH

85

Jurassic Way

6

+ RECTORY CT

Farn Wood

OXENDON RD

Jurassic Way

Allot Gdns

5

CLIPSTON RD

FARNDON RD

The Lodge

Little Oxendon

LE16

84

HARBOROUGH RD

+ Waterloo House

4

The Spinney

MEWS COTTS
OXENDON HALL

West End

MAIN ST

PH

BRAYBROOKE RD

3

CLIPSTON LA

Oxendon House

Great Oxendon

Midshires Way

83

HARBOROUGH RD

2

CLIPSTON RD

Sewage Works

Station Cottage

NORTHAMPTON RD
A508

OXENDON R

1

SIBBERTOFT RD

OXENDON RD

82

71 A B 72 C D 73 E F

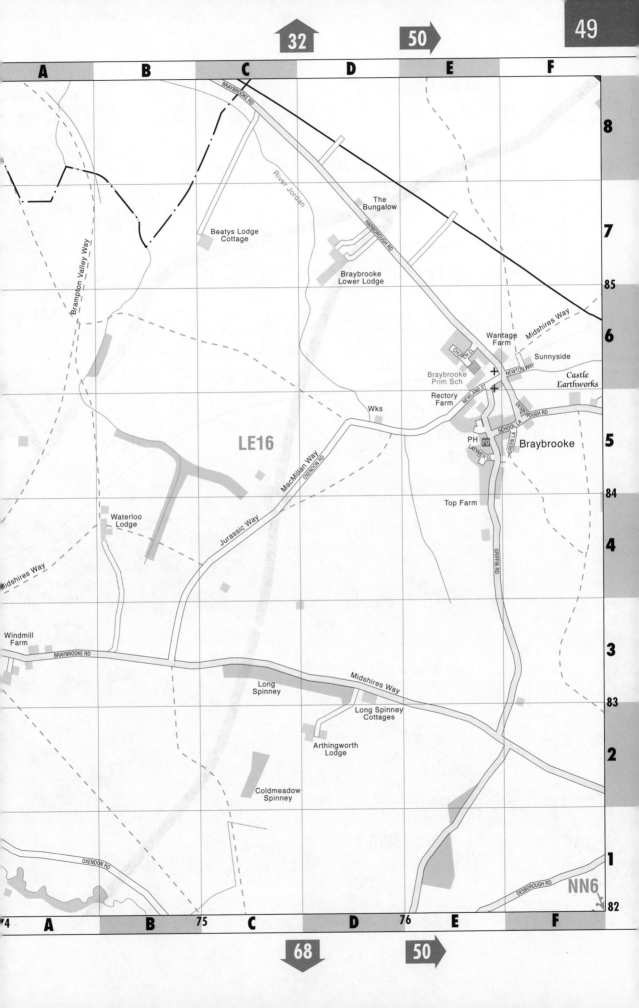

A B C D E F

8

7

85

6

River Jordan

The Bungalow

Beatys Lodge
Cottage

HARBOROUGH RD

Braybrooke
Lower Lodge

Wantage
Farm

Midshires Way

Sunnyside

CHURCH CL

NEWTON WAY

Castle
Earthworks

Braybrooke
Prim Sch

Rectory
Farm

NEWLAND ST

DESBOROUGH RD

Braybrooke 5

Wks

MacMillan Way

OXENDON RD

SCHOOL LA

GREEN LA

PH PO

LATYMER CL

LE16

84

Top Farm

Brampton Valley Way

Waterloo
Lodge

Jurassic Way

GRIFFIN RD

4

Midshires Way

Windmill
Farm

BRAYBROOKE RD

3

Long
Spinney

Midshires Way

83

Long Spinney
Cottages

2

Arthingworth
Lodge

Coldmeadow
Spinney

1

OXENDON RD

NN6

DESBOROUGH RD

82

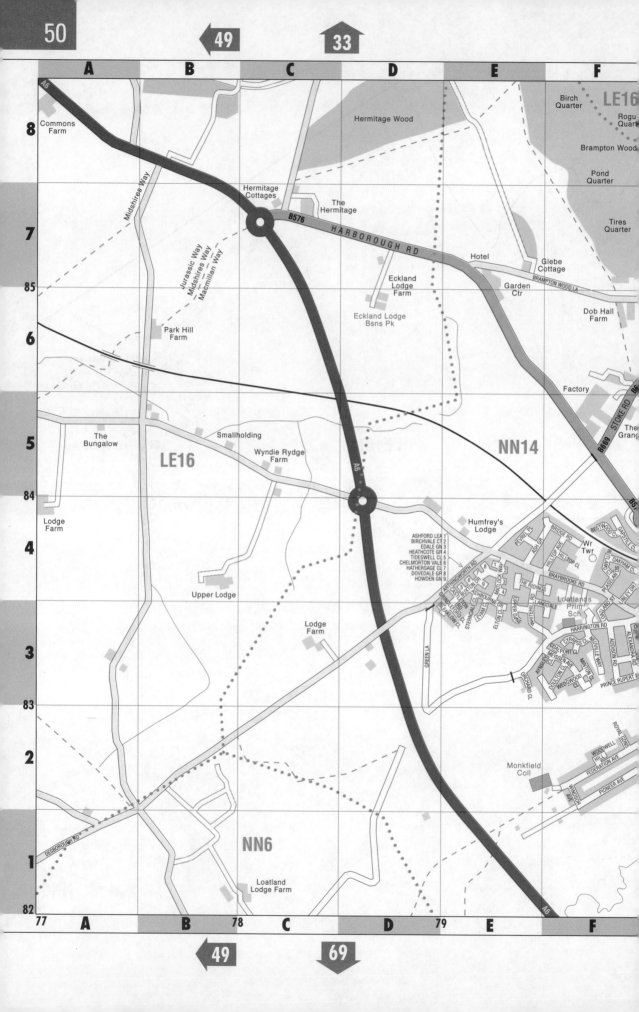

Rawshaw Wood

Hedgerow Spinney

The Old Red House

Harper's Brook

Home Farm

OAKLEY RD

Lower Lodge Farm

NN18

Pipewell Hall

Pipewell

Pipewell Lodge

Shangri-La

White Lodge Farm

UPPINGHAM RD

A6003

RYDER CT.

SAXON WA W

Oakr Ha Ind Est

SAXON WAY W

HEAD

Hilton's End Spinney

Alder Wood

Storefield Wood

Town's Close Lodge

Forty Acre Spinney

New Wood

NN14

Storefield Lodge

OAKLEY RD

Lady Mary's Spinney

Rectory Farm

Rushton Triangular Lodge

The Privet   The Wilderness

Manor Farm

MIDLAND COTTS

Rushton Prim Sch

BESWICK CL

White Gates Farm

DESBOROUGH RD

MATTHEWS CL

STATION RD

PH

CHAPEL LA

HIGH ST

MANOR RD

Rushton

RNIB Rushton Hall Sch

Whitegate Farm

Glendon Sidings

Birch Spinney

Hovel Spinney

Sewage Works

River Ise

Crownest Spinney

Hogs Hole Spinney

Glendon Iron Ore Works

Kettering North Junction

A B C D E F

8

Little
Oakley

Moat
Farm

The
Manor
Farm

Rising
Bridge

A43

FEATHERBED LA

Start
Wood

NN18

7

Cobley Lodge
Farm

Birch Tree
Lawn

Great Hames
Sale

85

Woodlands

6

Great
Brand

Geddington Chase

Pedlar's
Wells

Newton
Spinney

Crab Tree
Hills

Langley Quarter

STAMFORD RD

Little
Brand

Pale
Hill

5

Chase
Lodge

Clay Dick

84

Lardours
Wood

Cotton
Hills

4

Red
House

Bright
Trees

NN14

Bright Trees Rd

FERN VALE CL

CHASE VIEW RD

CHASE HILL

WOOD ST

THE WOODLANDS

3

Geddington

1 LEE'S WAY
2 WORMLEIGHTON WAY
3 BAKEHOUSE HILL
4 CHURCH HILL
5 CASTLE GDNS

NEWTON RD

30

QUEEN ELEANOR RD

WEST ST

MALTING LA

Round
Coppice

Pitmans
Sale

Sedge
Hills

83

Queen
Eleanor's
Cross

PH

PRIORY CT

HALL'S CL

MAGDALENE CL

CHASE FARM

Geddington CE
Prim Sch

DALLINGTON CL

SKEFFINGTON CL

NEW RD

CHAPEL LA

QUEEN ST

PO

Ford

GRAFTON RD

Sawmill

Kennel
Quarter

Boughton
Wood

2

GRANGE RD

MILLBY LA

30

Thomas Rippin
Cl

Bancroft
Wood

Boughton
Wood
Lodge

Thorny
Coppice

1

KETTERING RD

STAMFORD RD

A43

Sewage
Works

New Ground
Spinney

82

89 A B 90 C D 91 E F

A B C D E F

8

7

85

6

5

84

4

83

3

2

1

82

Harpers Brook

BELLS CL
SWAN AVE
STANION RD
NEWTOWN
OLD DRY LA
A6116 RD
BENEFIELD RD

FERMYN CL
WOODYARD CL
CHURCH CL
BACK LA
FARM CL
HIGH ST
PH
1 WOODLANDS MEWS
2 WOODLANDS CL
3 HALL HILL
KENNEL HILL
STABLE HILL
MONTERLY GATE
LYVEDEN RD
SANDLANDS AVE
MAURICE'S AVE
SUDBOROUGH RD

DUSTHILL RD

Playing Field

PO
Sch
Brigstock
The Manor House
BRIDGE ST
LATHAM ST
MILL
PARK WALK
HARPER'S CT
SANDLANDS CL

Chase Farm

Park Farm

Sewage Works

NN14

Bullymore's Lodge

Old Lodge Farm

GRAFTON RD

Park Cottages

Hillside Farm

Breakhill Cottage

Long Sale

Fox Earth

Roadside Quarter

Barn Quarter

Old Head Wood

Stevenson's Quarter

Schich's Corner

Great Bull Sedge

Snapes Wood

92 A B 93 C D 94 E F

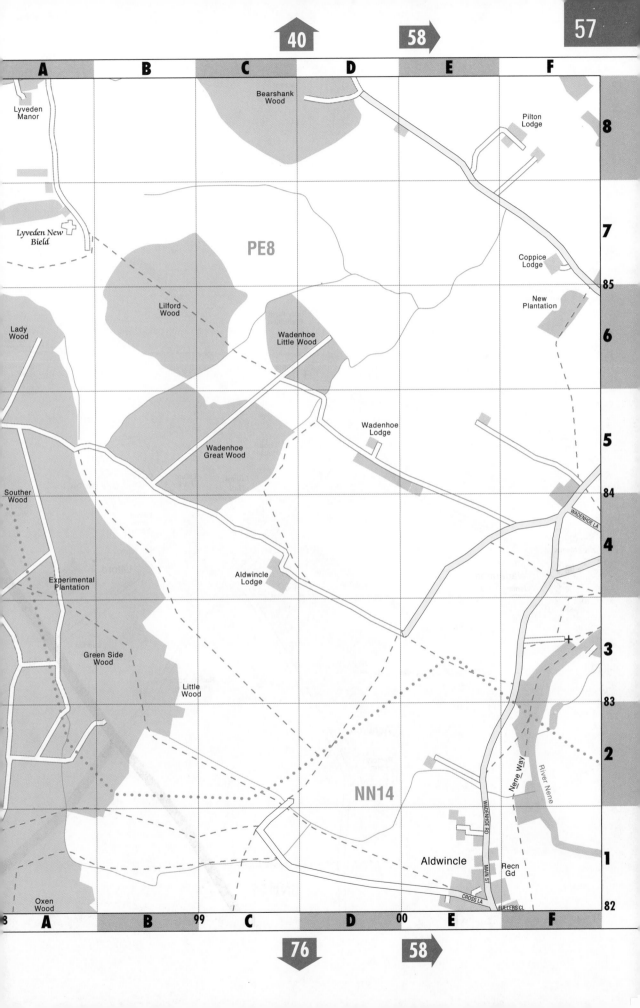

A B C D E F

Lyveden
Manor

Bearshank
Wood

Pilton
Lodge

8

Lyveden New
Bield

PE8

7

Coppice
Lodge

85

Lilford
Wood

New
Plantation

Lady
Wood

Wadenhoe
Little Wood

6

Wadenhoe
Lodge

5

Souther
Wood

Wadenhoe
Great Wood

84

WADENHOE LA

4

Experimental
Plantation

Aldwincle
Lodge

+

3

Green Side
Wood

83

Little
Wood

2

Nene Way

River Nene

NN14

WADENHOE RD

Aldwincle

Recn
Gd

1

MAIN ST

CROSS LA

Oxen
Wood

FULLERS CL

82

A 99 B C D 00 E F

A B C D E F

8

Manor House

Great Ground Spinney

7

PE8

85

Pilton Lodge Farm

6

Petty Fields Plantation

Pilton Grange

Manor House

Pilton

River Nene

5

Boat Houses

Lilford Park

Wr Twr

84

Lilford Hall

Lilford Woods

Lilford Bridge

Lilford Home Farm

4

WADENHOE
THE GREEN
Meml
GLEBE CT
PILTON RD

Lilford

PO

Wadenhoe

MAIN ST

Wadenhoe House

The Linches

OAKLEE CL
CHURCH ST
MILL LA

Sudden's Plantation

PH

3

Ratling Irons Plantation

P

Nene Way

83

Achurch

2

Rectory Farm

B662

River Nene

1

A605

NN14

82

01 A 02 B C 02 D 03 E F

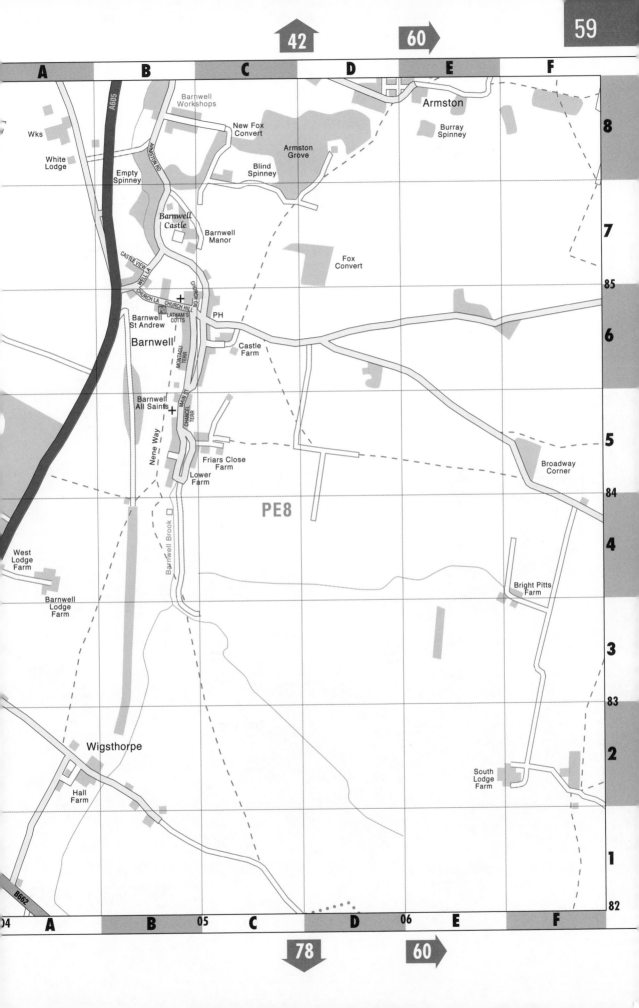

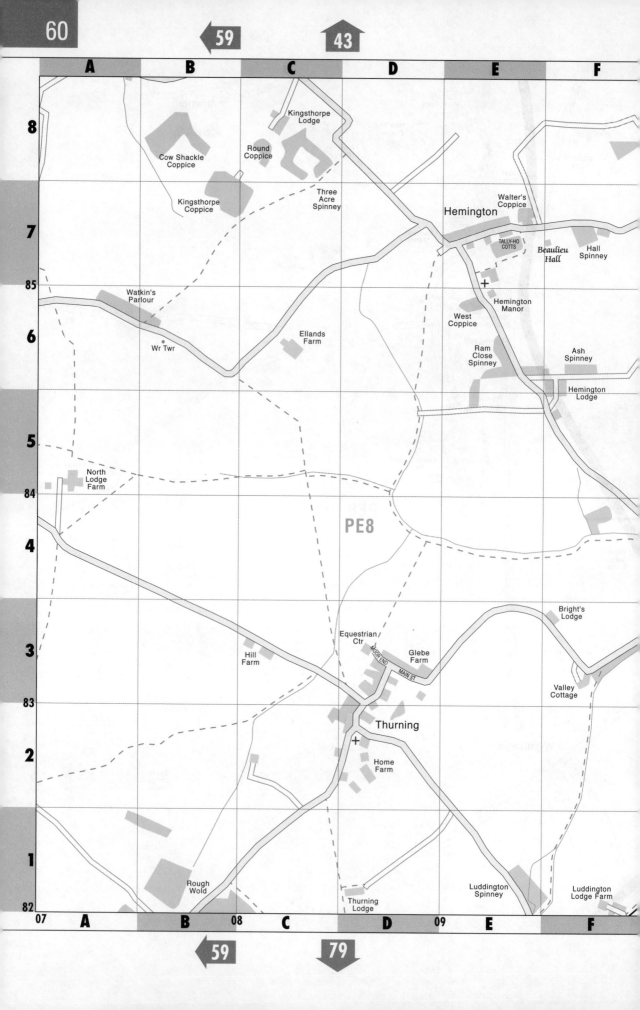

A B C D E F

8

Kingsthorpe
Lodge

Cow Shackle
Coppice

Round
Coppice

Walter's
Coppice

Hemington

Three
Acre
Spinney

Kingsthorpe
Coppice

7

TALLY-HO
COTTS

Hall
Spinney

Beaulieu
Hall

85

Watkin's
Parlour

West
Coppice

Hemington
Manor

6

Wr Twr

Ellands
Farm

Ram
Close
Spinney

Ash
Spinney

Hemington
Lodge

5

North
Lodge
Farm

84

PE8

4

3

Hill
Farm

Equestrian
Ctr

MOOR END

MAIN ST

Glebe
Farm

Bright's
Lodge

83

Thurning

Valley
Cottage

2

Home
Farm

1

Rough
Wold

Thurning
Lodge

Luddington
Spinney

Luddington
Lodge Farm

82

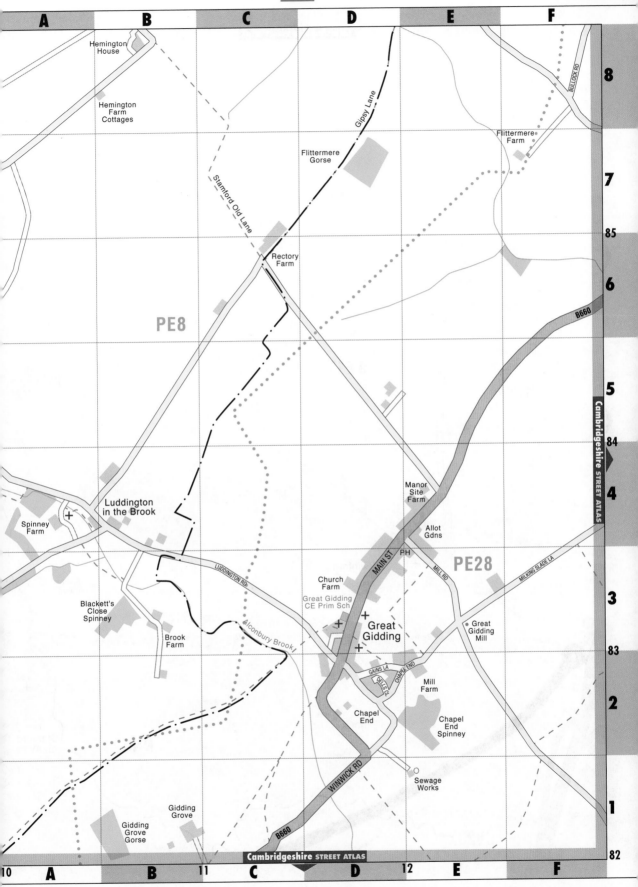

A   B   C   D   E   F

Hemington
House

Hemington
Farm
Cottages

Gipsy Lane

Flittermere
Gorse

Flittermere
Farm

Stamford Old Lane

BULLOCK RD

B660

PE8

Rectory
Farm

Spinney
Farm

Luddington
in the Brook

Manor
Site
Farm

Allot
Gdns

MAIN ST

PH

MILL RD

PE28

MILKING SLADE LA

Blackett's
Close
Spinney

Brook
Farm

LUDDINGTON RD

Church
Farm

Great Gidding
CE Prim Sch

Great
Gidding

Great
Gidding
Mill

Alconbury Brook

Mill
Farm

GAINS LA
WELLS ST
CHAPEL END

Chapel
End

Chapel
End
Spinney

WINWICK RD

Sewage
Works

Gidding
Grove

Gidding
Grove
Gorse

B660

Cambridgeshire STREET ATLAS

8
85
7
6
5
84
4
3
83
2
83
1
82

10   A   B   11   C   D   12   E   F

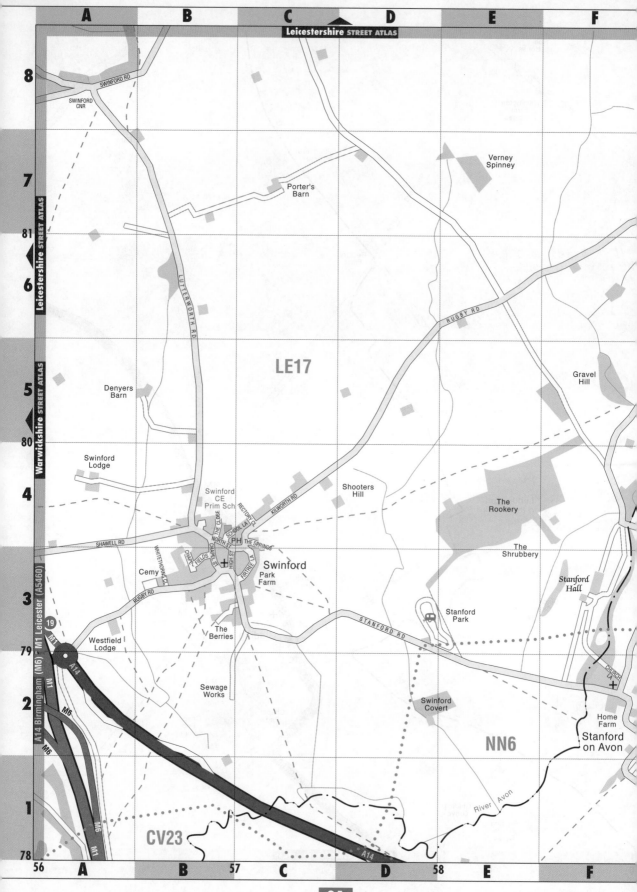

LE17

NN6

CV23

Verney
Spinney

Porter's
Barn

Gravel
Hill

RUGBY RD

SWINFORD RD

SWINFORD
CNR

LUTTERWORTH RD

Denyers
Barn

Swinford
Lodge

Swinford
CE
Prim Sch

KILWORTH RD

Shooters
Hill

The
Rookery

The
Shrubbery

Stanford
Hall

SHAWELL RD

RECTORY CL

SCHOOL LA

THE CLOSE

NORTH ST

HIGH ST

FIRTREE LA

THE SPRINGS

PH

CHAP

FIELDS

CHAPEL ST

WHITETHORNS CL

Cemy

RUGBY RD

Swinford
Park Farm

Swinford

Stanford
Park

Stanford
Hall

STANFORD RD

CHURCH LA

The
Berries

Westfield
Lodge

19

M1

A14

A14 Birmingham (M6)

M1 Leicester (A5460)

M6

M6

M1

Sewage
Works

Swinford
Covert

Stanford
on Avon

Home
Farm

River Avon

A14

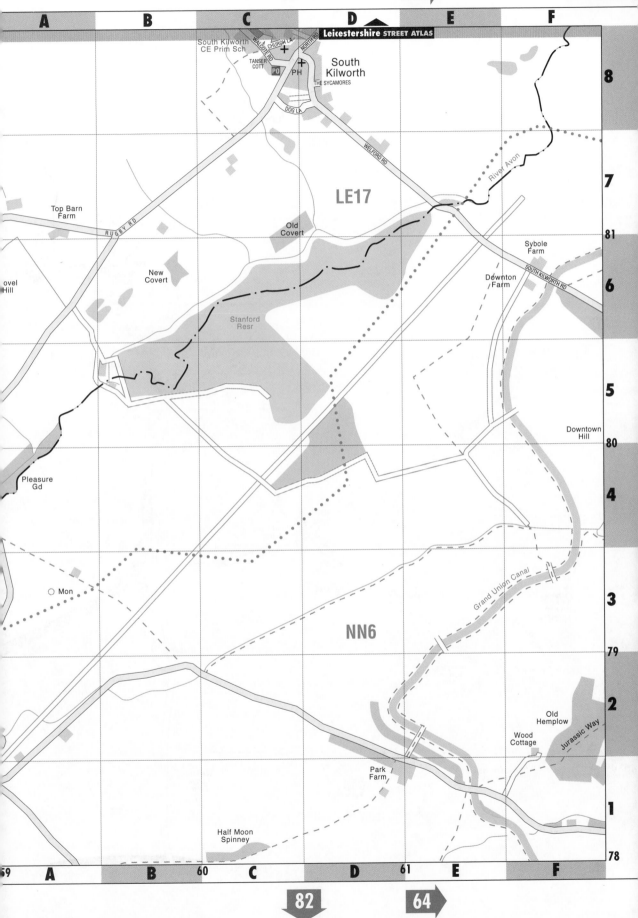

South Kilworth
CE Prim Sch

TANSER
COTT

PO

PH

South
Kilworth

THE SYCAMORES

DOG LA

WALCOTE RD

CHURCH LA

NORTH RD

WELFORD RD

LE17

River Avon

Top Barn
Farm

RUGBY RD

Old
Covert

Sybole
Farm

SOUTH KILWORTH RD

ovel
Hill

New
Covert

Downton
Farm

Stanford
Resr

Downtown
Hill

Pleasure
Gd

Mon

Grand Union Canal

NN6

Old
Hemplow

Wood
Cottage

Jurassic Way

Park
Farm

Half Moon
Spinney

A B C D E F

8

Grand Union Canal

Glebe Farm

Grand Union Canal (Welford Branch)

LE17

River Avon

7

Sybolds Spinney

Lodge Farm

81

Marina

Hill House

Welford Resr

Grange Lodge

6

Hotel

Sewage Works

Welford Grange Farm

NASEBY RD

Allot Gdns

1 CHAMBERS ROW
2 DOVEHOUSE CL
3 THE SQUARE

Sulby Lodge Farm

WESTFIELD CREST

WEST ST

SALFORD RD

ORCHARD TERR

ATOM FIELDS

Welford Sibbertott & Sulby Endowed Sch

HIGH ST

PH

PO

Welford

Hallfield Cottage

5

SOUTH KILWORTH RD

WAKEFIELD DR

CHURCH LA

WEST END

CHRISTOPHER CT

THE LEYS

WOODFORD GLEBE

NEWLANDS RD

80

Jurassic Way

Court Lane Farm

COURT LA

NORTHAMPTON RD

3

Fish Pond Covert

NN6

The Glebe

79

Hemplow Hills

HEMPLOW DR

West Hill Farm

Hemploe Lodge Farm

A5199

2

Dark Spinney

Prince of Wales Spinney

Watts Lodge Farm

Welford Lodge Farm

1

78

A14

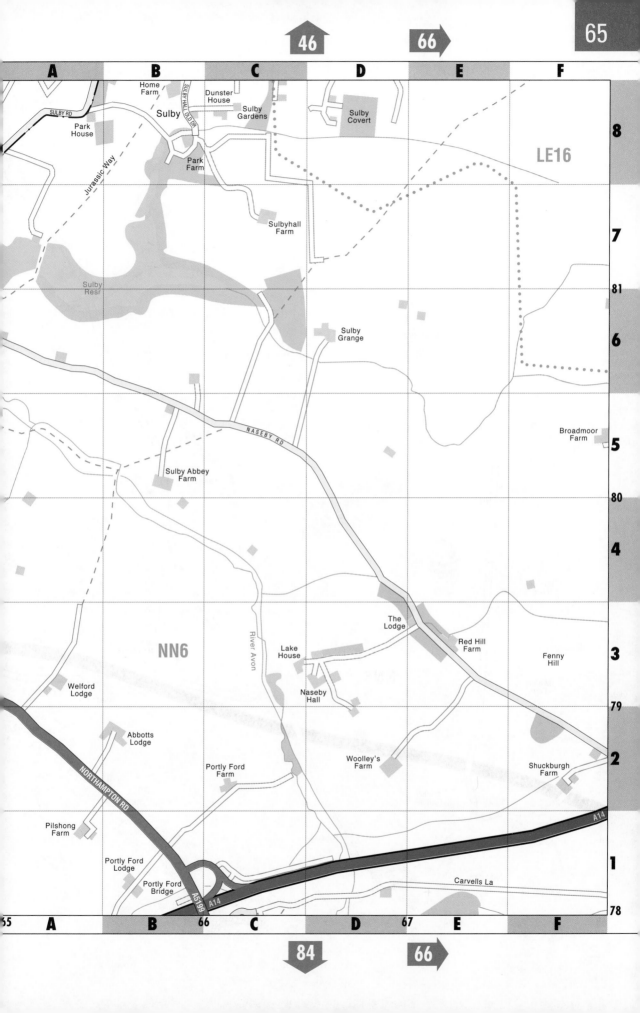

A B C D E F

8

The Old Manse

Clipston

NOBOLD
CT

The Chestnuts

The Paddocks

7

Longhold
Lodge

LE16

81

Prince Rupert's
Farm

6

Dust
Hill

Long Hold
Spinney

Dust Hill
Farm

5

Mon

The Plantation

80

P

Naseby
Covert

4

Paisnell
Spinney

Naseby
Field

Mill
Hill

3

New-House
Farm

NN6

A14

Mill Hill
Farm

Mast

79

2

A14

Clothill
Spinney

1

Obelisk

Naseby

PH

Carvells La

NEWLANDS

Naseby CE
Prim Sch

HIGH ST

78

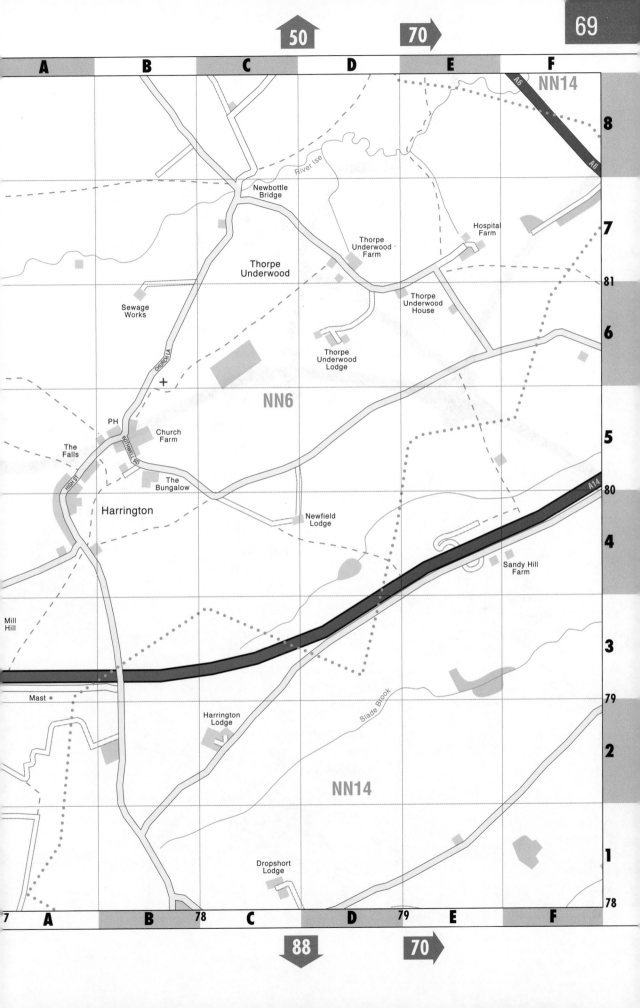

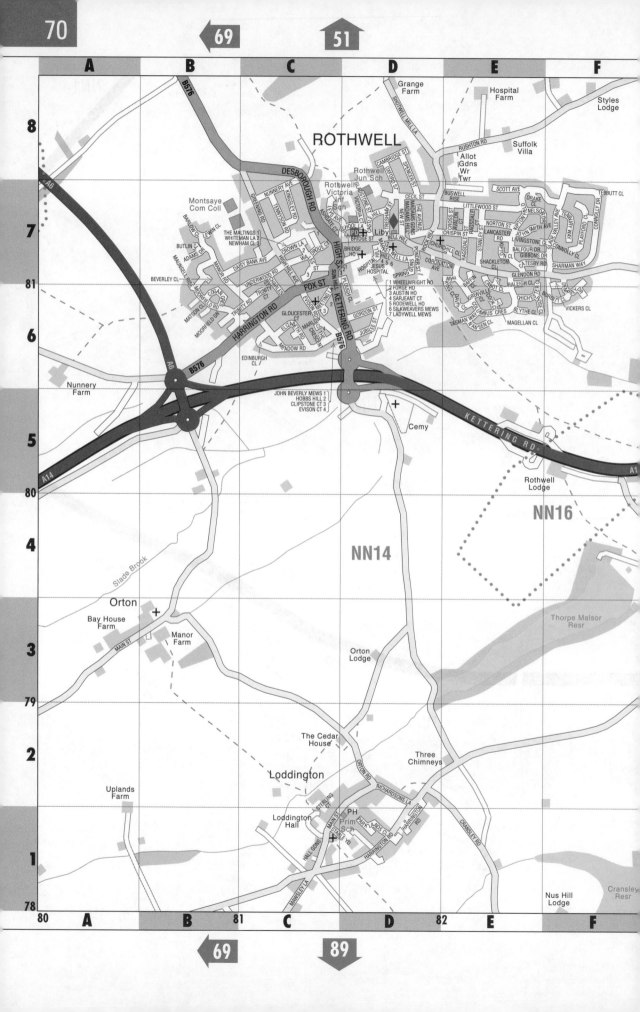

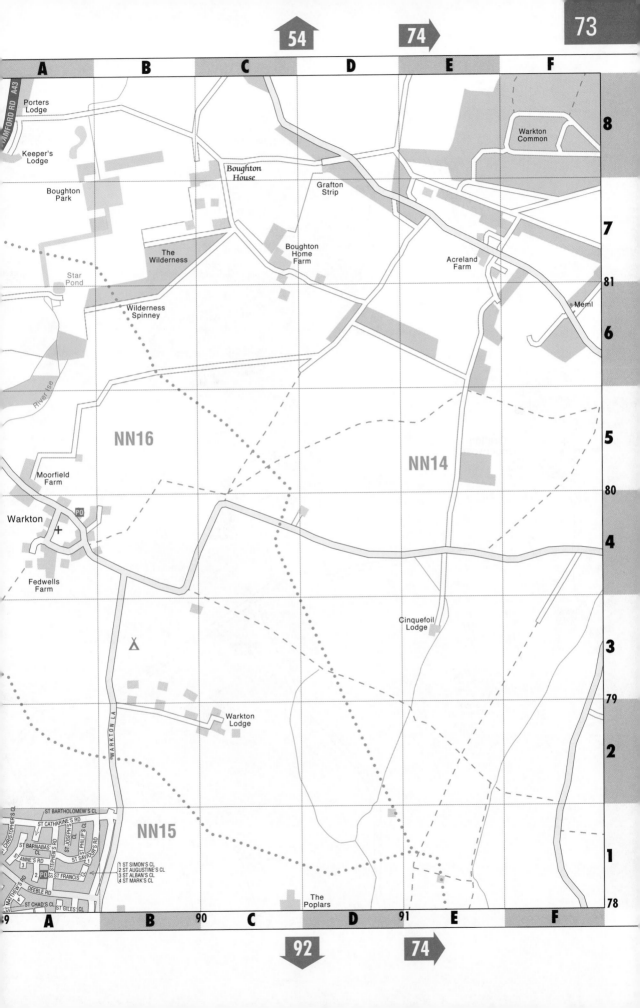

A B C D E F

STAMFORD RD A43

Porters
Lodge

Keeper's
Lodge

Boughton
Park

Boughton
House

Grafton
Strip

Warkton
Common

8

The
Wilderness

Boughton
Home
Farm

Acreland
Farm

7

Star
Pond

81

Wilderness
Spinney

Meml

6

River Ise

NN16

NN14

5

Moorfield
Farm

80

PO

Warkton

4

Fedwells
Farm

Cinquefoil
Lodge

3

79

Warkton
Lodge

WARKTON LA

2

ST BARTHOLOMEW'S CL
ST CATHARINE'S RD
ST CHRISTOPHER'S CL
ST STEPHEN'S RD
ST PHILIP'S RD
ST JOSEPH'S CL
ST SAVIOUR'S RD
ST BARNABAS CL
ST ANNE'S RD
ST FRANCIS CL
ST MATTHEW'S RD
PO
DEEBLE RD
ST CHAD'S CL
ST GILES CL

NN15

1 ST SIMON'S CL
2 ST AUGUSTINE'S CL
3 ST ALBAN'S CL
4 ST MARK'S CL

1

The
Poplars

78

9 A B 90 C D 91 E F

A B C D E F

8

Round
Green

Long
Lown
Wood

7

Grafton Park
Wood

Eker
Cpps

81

6

Freer
Wood

Little
Green
Wood

Park
Lodge

Keeper's
Cottage

Sale
Hill
Wood

Grafton
Park
Farm

PO

5

Grafton
Underwood

NN14

Whitehouse
Farm

The
Manor
House

80

Kirtley
Barn

Kirtley
Coppice

4

Sewage
Works

3

Cranford
Wood

79

Glebe
Farm

Bushy
Covert

SLIPTON LA

2

GORDON
TERR

HIGH ST

THE
HOMESTEAD

1

78

92 A B 93 C D 94 E F

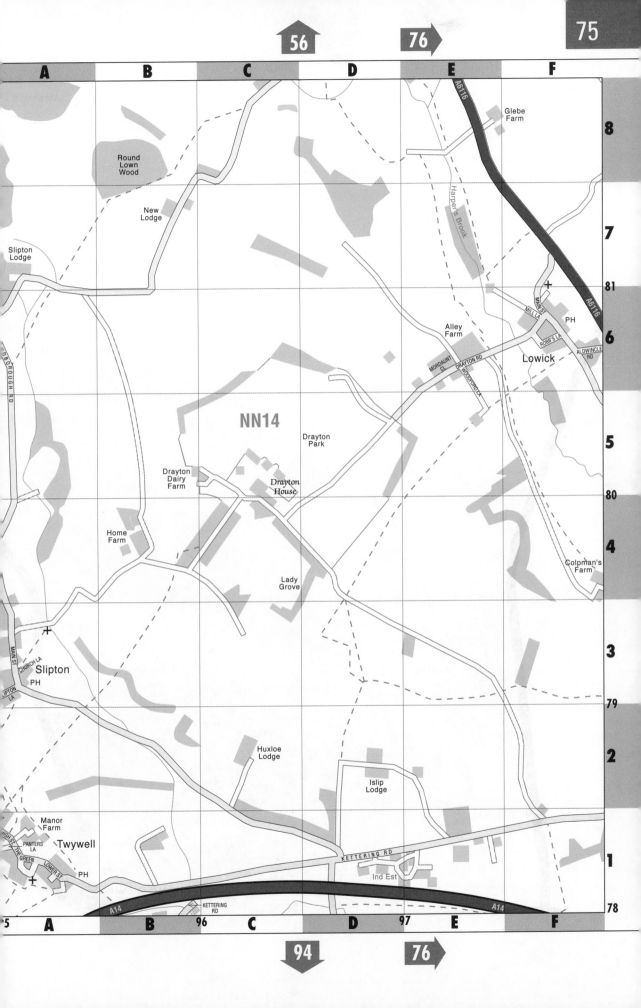

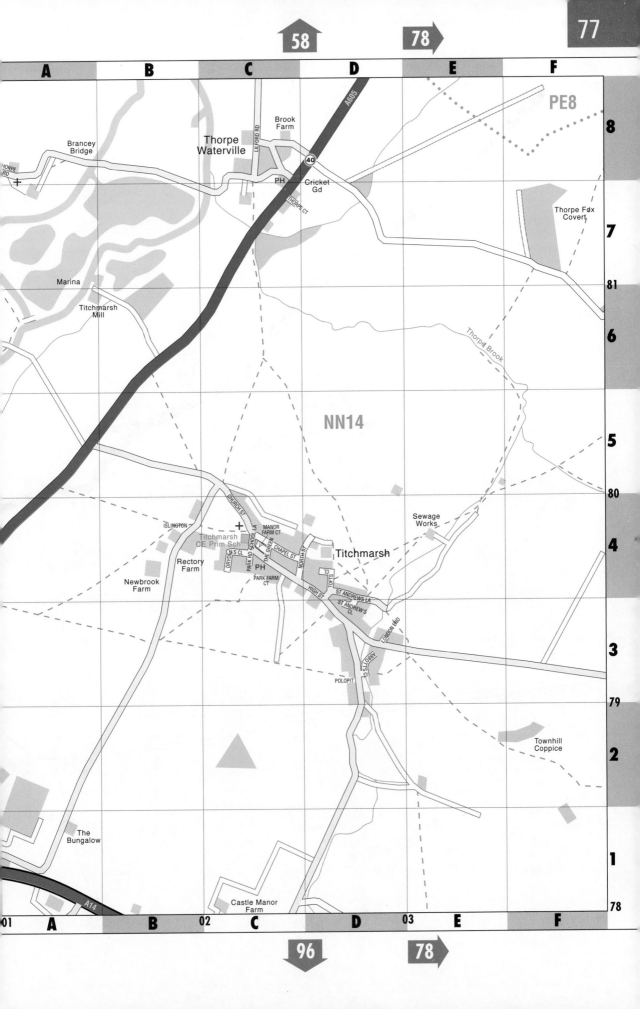

A   B   C   D   E   F

PE8

B662

PE8

8

Towcester Hill
Spinney

Bull Nose
Coppice

Alvaston

Long Thong
Coppice

7

Long Thong
Farm

81

Blackthorn
Coppice

6

Ash Pole
Coppice

BERRY GREEN PK

Home
Farm

PO

Clopton

5

NN14

Skulking Dudley
Copse

Clopton
Hall

B662

80

+

4

Ringdales
Wood

Bidwell
Farm

Crows
Nest
Farm

3

79

Foxholes
Farm

2

Fayway

WARREN LA

Chequer
Hill
Coppice

1

Warren
Lodge
Farm

78

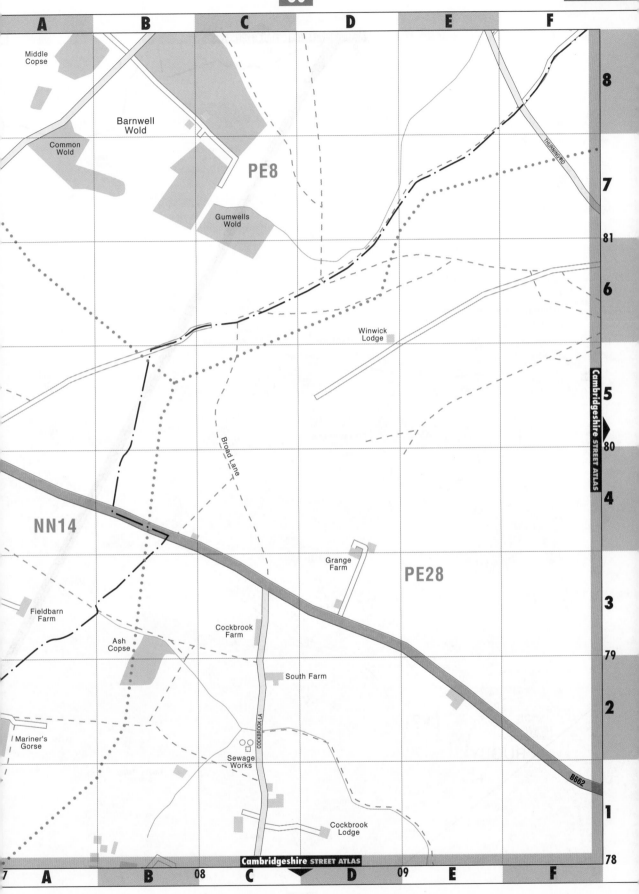

A B C D E F

Middle
Copse

Barnwell
Wold

Common
Wold

PE8

Gumwells
Wold

8

7

81

6

Winwick
Lodge

5

80

Broad Lane

4

NN14

Grange
Farm

PE28

Fieldbarn
Farm

3

79

Ash
Copse

Cockbrook
Farm

South Farm

2

Mariner's
Gorse

COCKBROOK LA

Sewage
Works

B662

1

Cockbrook
Lodge

78

7 A B 08 C D 09 E F

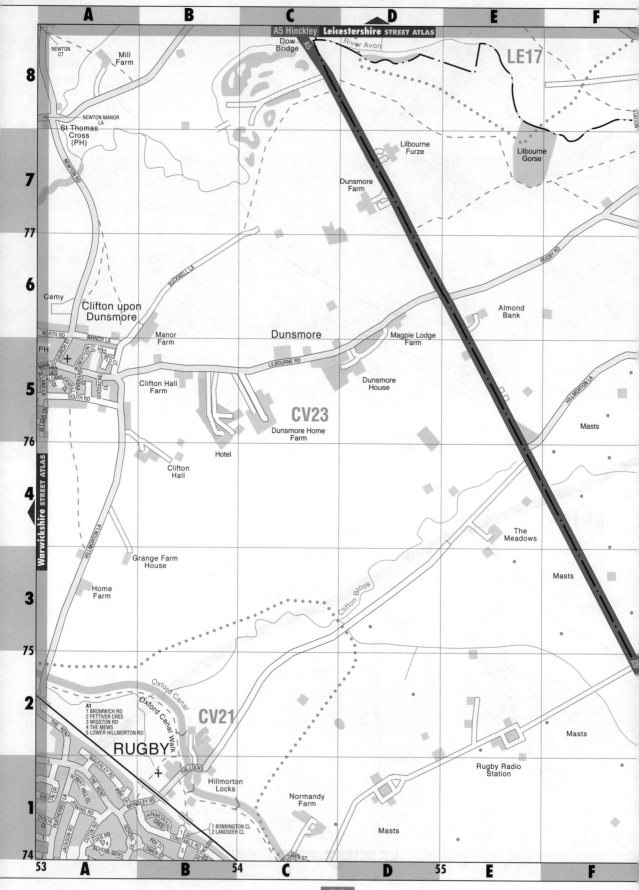

LE17

CV23

CV21

A1
1 BROMWICH RD
2 PETTIVER CRES
3 WIGSTON RD
4 THE MEWS
5 LOWER HILLMORTON RD

RUGBY

1 BONNINGTON CL
2 LANDSEER CL

Warwickshire STREET ATLAS

Key labels (map):

NEWTON CT

Mill Farm

NEWTON MANOR LA

St Thomas Cross (PH)

Dow Bridge

River Avon

Lilbourne Furze

Lilbourne Gorse

Dunsmore Farm

NEWTON RD

BUCKWELL LA

RUGBY RD

Cemy

Clifton upon Dunsmore

Dunsmore

Almond Bank

NORTH RD

MANOR LA

Manor Farm

Magpie Lodge Farm

HILLMORTON LA

PH

CHURCH ST

PO

ROBERTSON CL

HADFIELD CL

LILBOURNE RD

Dunsmore House

MAIN ST

Masts

YT SM

EVERARD CL

ALLANS CL

HEWEL CL

Clifton Hall Farm

GOODACRE CL

SOUTH RD

Dunsmore Home Farm

ALLANS DR

Hotel

Clifton Hall

HILLMORTON LA

The Meadows

Grange Farm House

Masts

Home Farm

Clifton Brook

Oxford Canal

THE KENT

Oxford Canal Walk

Masts

WAVERLEY RD

ROBT HILL CL

PINE GR

BRINDLEY RD

THE LOCKS

Rugby Radio Station

GIBBS CL

GIBSON CL

THE KENT

JENKINS RD

EVER RD

GAINSBOROUGH CRES

Hillmorton Locks

DYSON CL

JACKSON RD

FEATHERBED LA

COTTON RD

SCHOOL ST

FOX CL

SCHOOL GDNS

CONSTABLE RD

REYNOLDS CL

LOWER ST

Normandy Farm

Masts

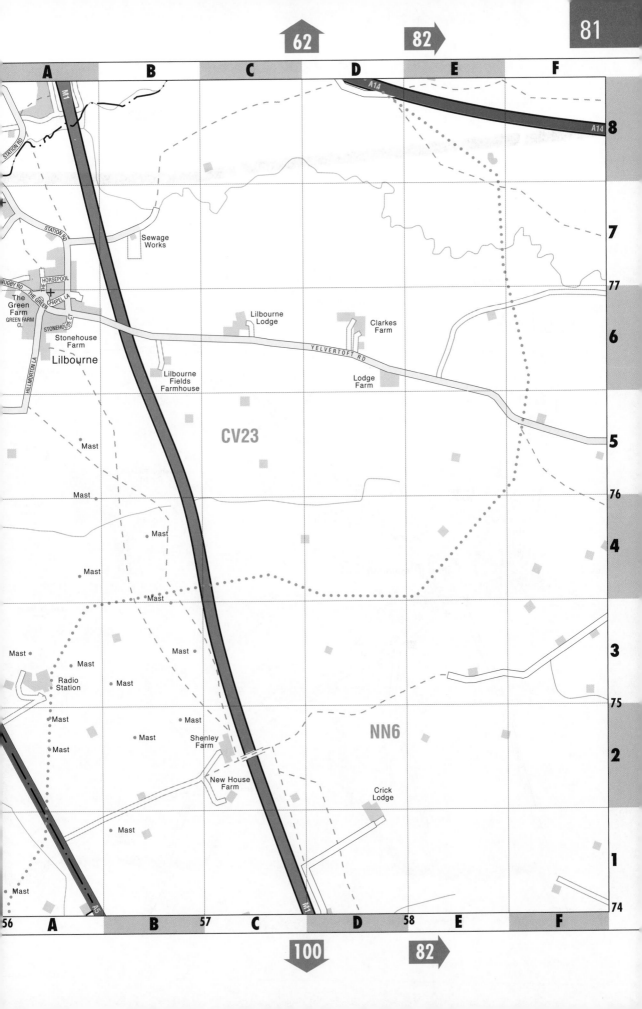

A   B   C   D   E   F

8

A14

A14

7

77

Sewage
Works

The
Green
Farm

Lilbourne
Lodge

Clarkes
Farm

6

YELVERTOFT RD

Stonehouse
Farm

Lilbourne

Lilbourne
Fields
Farmhouse

Lodge
Farm

CV23

Mast

5

76

Mast

Mast

4

Mast

Mast

Mast

3

Mast

Radio
Station

Mast

75

Mast

Mast

NN6

Mast

Mast

Mast

Shenley
Farm

2

Mast

New House
Farm

Crick
Lodge

1

Mast

74

81
63

A   B   C   D   E   F

8   A14

Stanford Mear

Pages Lodge Farm

Jurassic Way

A14

Manor Farm

7

Manor Farm

Blackdown Farm

77

Rectory Farm

Clay Coton

Willow Farm Cottages

6

Buffs Farm

Elkington Farm Cottage

THE PADDOCKS

5   YELVERTOFT RD

Yelvertoft Fieldside Covert

Mountain Barn

Sewage Works

76

BROOKSIDE CL 1
ORCHARD CL 2
BROOKSIDE MEWS 3

NN6

Grand Union Canal

Hall

TARRYS END

4   Yelvertoft Prim Sch

SCHOOL LA

2 3

ASHWELLS LA

BRIDGEND CL

LYNGTON RD

Yelvertoft

Glebe Farm

HILLMORTON LA

SCHOOL CL

KINGS LA

SWINNERTONS LA   ELKINS CL

MERRYCOT LA

KIRKHAMS CL

Winwick Manor Farm

HIGH ST   STYLES PL

WARDS LA

PH

3   PO

Cemy

Grand Union Canal

75

CRICK RD

2

Flint Hill Farm

New House Farm

1

Winwick Grange

74

59   A   B   60   C   D   61   E   F

81
101

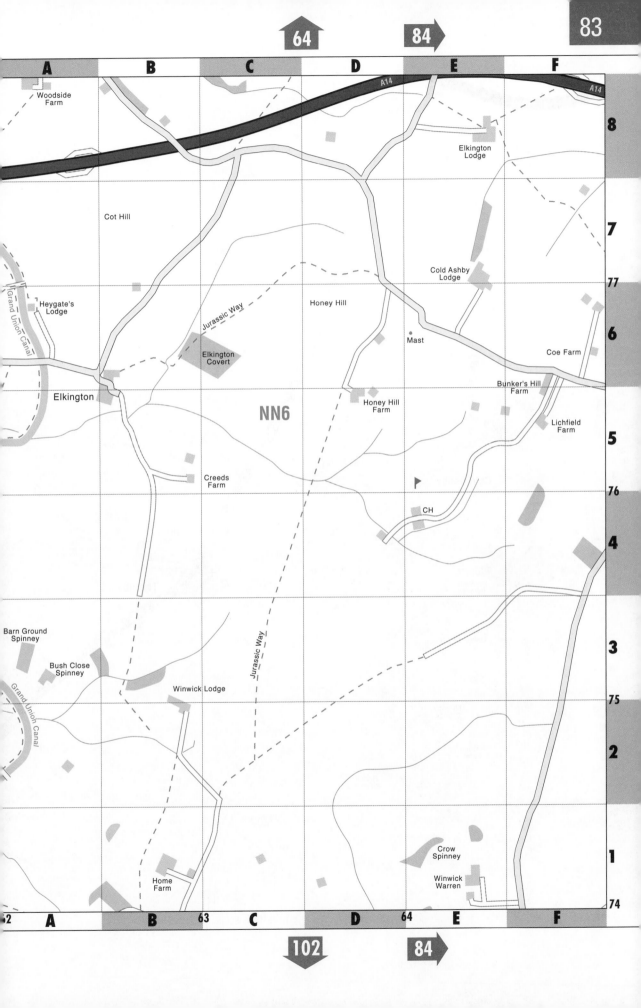

A B C D E F

A14

A5199

A14

A5199

Naseby Resr

Fulbrook Farm

Reservoir Farm

STANFORD RD RD

BRIDLE LA

STANFORD CL

WEST HADDON LA

MAIN ST

CROSSTREE LA

PH

CHURCH LA

PARK SPINNEY CL

THORNBY RD

Cold Ashby

NN6

Lodge Farm

Park Spinney

Thornby Hall

COLD ASHBY RD

WELFORD RD

ST HELENS CL

PH

NASEBY RD

Thornby House Farm

CHURCH LA

STONE HOUSE MEWS

Thornby

Doebank Spinney

Lovells Lodge

Firetail Covert

Firetail

Thornby Grange

Grange Farm

Rabbit Spinney

Nortoft Lodge

Ashbylane Farm

West Lodge

A B C D E F

8

7

77

6

5

76

4

3

75

2

1

74

Reservoir
Farm
SCHOOL LA
KNIGHTS HILL
PH
CHURCH ST
GYNWELL
PO
HIGH ST
BAKEHOUSE RISE
Cromwell
Farm
FAIRFAX RISE
SKIPPONS
CT
NUTCOTE
Naseby
CATTON CL
Brankley
Farm
Hospital
Farm
NASEBY RD

THORNBY RD
Naseby
Battle & Farm
Mus

Oak
Farm

The Grange
Farm

Purser's
Hills

NN6

New
Covert

Vale
Farm

Old
Covert

Stubb
Purlieu

Calender
Farm

Cott Hill
Spinney

Cottesbrooke
Park

Hanwell
Spinney

A5199

Foalfoot
Spinney

A   B   C   D   E   F

Mast

8

Bassetts Lodge
Farm

MAIDWELL RD

Haselbech
Grange

Haselbech

Manor
Farm

Scotland Wood
Farm

NASEBY RD

7

Haselbech
Hall

+

The
Rectory

Dale
Wood

77

Maidwell
Dale

6

Black
Hall

Dale
Farm

Haselbech
Hill

Maidwell
Lodge

5

Shutterdown
Spinney

76

NN6

4

Blueberry
Lodge

Mitley
Spinney

Houseground
Spinney

3

Macmillan Way

75

Moss Hall
Spinney

Gamboro
Plantation

2

Rickleboro Hill
Spinney

Park
Spinney

Blueberry
Grange

1

74

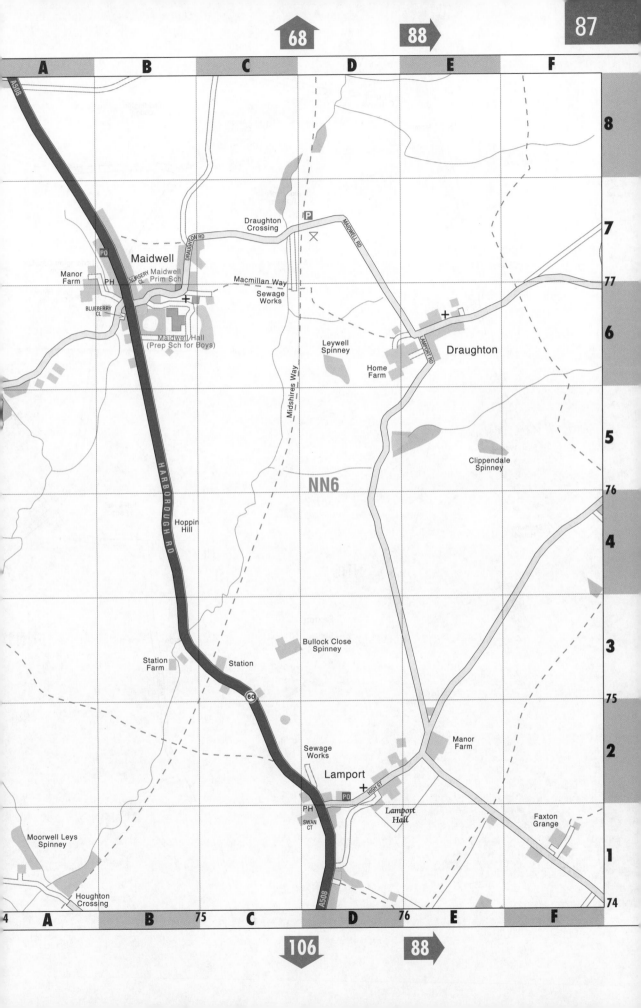

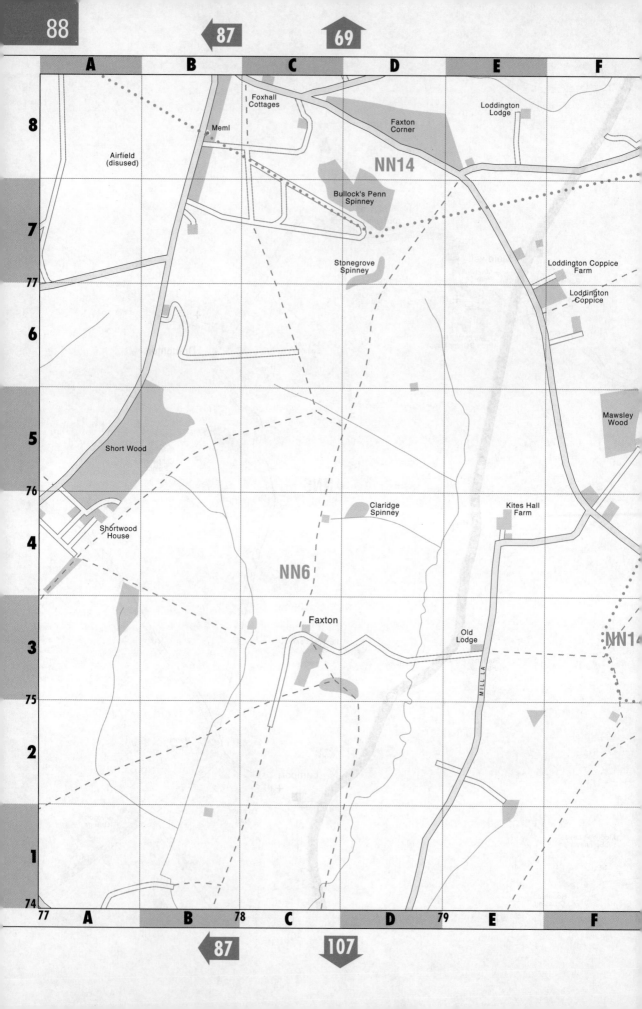

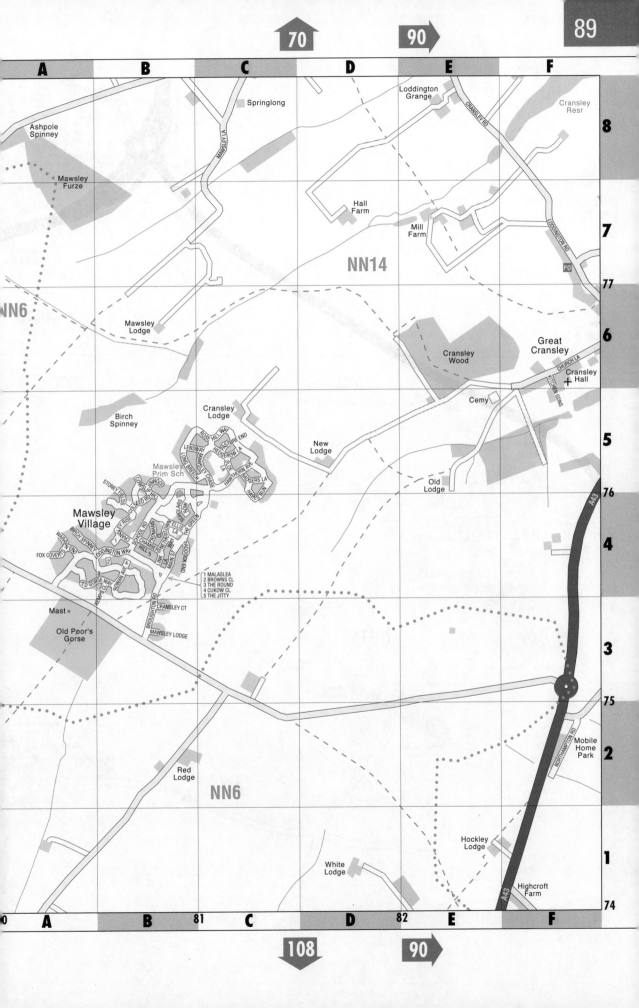

A B C D E F

8

White Hill
Lodge

Allotment
Spinney

7

The Gorse

Works

77

NN15

6

PH
CHURCH LA
BROUGHTON HILL
HOLLY LA

Sewage
Works

Broughton
Grange

5

A43

Little
Cransley

Allot
Gdns

GRANGE RD
THE BANKS
CRANE CL
THURSTONE
PYTCHLEY RD
KETTERING RD

1 GOODHEW CL
2 HEMERY WAY
3 BRAITHWAITE CL

NORTHAMPTON RD
A6013
A14
A43
Prim Sch
REDGRAVE CL
MERRIVALE CL

76

Broughton
Prim Sch

COX'S LA
WEST ST
SILVER ST
CHAPEL
VIEW
IVYDENE TERR
CRANSLEY HILL
HIGH ST
ST ANDREWS
MANOR FARM CL
BROOKVIEW CL
GATE LA

Manor
Farm

Allot
Gdns

Cemy

Recn
Gd

Rathmine
Farm

ASHBROOK CL
PO
ST ANDREWS WAY 1
CHURCH VIEW 2
DAWKINS CT 3
BAKEHOUSE MEWS 4
1
3
4
2
ST ANDREW'S CT
CHURCH ST

4

Broughton

Pytchley
Lodge

BURTON CL
OAK CL
GLEBE AVE
HUTCHINSON AVE
NORTHAMPTON RD
MEADHAM CL
DONALDSON AV
BAKER ST
THODAY CL
RIGGAL CL
PODMORE WAY
CARTER AVE
WELLINGBOROUGH RD
LIME CL
GLEBE AVE
KERFE CL
LENTON CL

NN14

3

Headlands
Farm

New
Covert

Underwood's Hill
Spinney

75

Manor Farm
House

2

Pytchley New
Covert

Stud
Farm

BROUGHTON RD

Pytchley

BLACKSMITHS LA
MANOR CL
TOP END
HIGH ST
BUTCHER'S LA
ORCHARD
WEST
SNOPS

Pytchley
Endowed CE
Prim Sch

OLLINGBURY RD

1

Spencer
Lodge

74

91
73

A B C D E F

8

7

77

6

5

76

4

3

75

2

1

74

KETTERING

Barton Seagrave

Warkton Spinney

ST MATTHEW'S RD
ST JAMES' CL
ST LUKE'S RD
ST JOHN'S RD
BERWICK WAY
LONSETT CL
NORRIS CL
TYNAN
HANOVER CT
MOORE
HOCKNEY AVE
CONSTABLE DR
HARTLEY DR
HOGARTH DR
NASH CT
LAWRENCE DR
ALLCOTT
REYNOLDS CL
TURNER DR
BLAKE
SUBS LA
KEATING CL
GAINSBOROUGH AVE
POPLAR'S FARM RD
RIDGWAY RD
WESTLEIGH RD
WARKTON LA

A6003

1 BUCKINGHAM CT
2 WATERHOUSE GDNS
3 BEARDSLEY GDNS

Shaft Field Spinney

The Osier Bed

The Grange

Stubbs Spinney

TOP DYSONS

NN14

Latimer Com Arts Coll
WREN CL
The Lodge
BELVOIR DR
LINNET DR
RAVEN DR
ROBIN
LINNET DR
BEAUFORT DR
FERNIE CL
WOODLAND AVE
COTTESMORE AVE
FITZWILLIAM DR
Sch
BARTON RD
SWALLOW CL
BARTON RD
CRAMPTON
ACORN CL
LAXTON CT
LAVENDON CT
CRAMPTON
KATE'S CL
SALEM CL

Hayfield Lodge

CRANFORD RD

A14

1 RUFFORD CL
2 GROSVENOR CL
3 TAVISTOCK RD
4 BELGRAVE CL
5 SALCEY CL
6 EPPING CL
7 ROSSENDALE DR
8 QUANTOCK CL
9 BOWLAND DR

Blackbridge Farm

CRANFORD RD

WINDMILL COTTS

A6003

GROSVENOR WAY
GROSVENOR RD
GARNWOOD DR
RADNOR WAY
ASHDOWN CL
FINCHSHADE CL
ROXTON CT
KINGTON RISE
NENE CL
KIELDER CT
QUENDER CL

A6

Mast

NN15

ALTENDIEZ WAY

Double Dug Spinney

Burton Latimer Hall

Rectory Plantation

ELM RD
WOODLAND DR
THE CRESCENT
POPLAR RD
ACORN PK
HURST CL
COPPICE CL
COPSE CL
FOREST CL
CRANFORD RD
SPINNEY RD
LANSOM CL
GEORGE ST
BIRD ST
WOODCOCK ST

HEATH WAY
GLADE CL

Football Gd

KETTERING RD
NORTH AVE
WEST AVE
EAST AVE
SOUTH AVE
STATION RD
VICTORIA
WILLIAM
PIONEER AVE
POWELL LA
POWELL LA

CHURCH VIEW
CHURCH ST
PRESTON CL
SPRING GDNS
ST CRISPIN CL
BAKEHOUSE LA
DENTON CT
MEETING LA
YEOMAN CL
BARYE CL
WHEATFIELD DR
STURGESS CT

Cemy

WOLD RD

Recn Ctr
Meadowside Jun & Inf Schs
REGENT CL
BRIDLE RD
MALLARD
EIDER CL
BUNTING
KINGFISHER
SANDPIPER
REGENT RD
SHAKESPEARE DR
NENE RD
CONWAY
MORRISON
LANGLEY CL
PARK RD
SEVERN CL
SHANNON WAY
THAMES CL
CHURCHILL WAY
WELLAND

P
PO
Sch
DUKE ST
DUKES CT
LATIMER CL

1 BURTON HO
2 CROXEN CL

1 HERON CL
2 SWAN CL
3 BRENT CL

ALEXANDRA ST
COLES CL
SPENCER ST
NEWMAN
Liby
PIGOTT'S LA
ROSEBERY
CORNFIELD
ROWLANDS
HARVEST CL

TRENT CRES
TWEED CL
FINEDON ST
TRENT CRES

QUEENSWAY
WHITNEY RD
EASY RD
MILLER RD
VILLA GDNS
ROSEBERY
ENSLEIGH CL
CORNFIELD
BROOKS CL
HIGHAM RD

BURTON LATIMER

Hog's Hole
DIANA WAY
ALICE DR
HAW
GRACE CT 1
HAWTHORN RD 2
HILLCREST AVE 3

1 BARLOW CT 1
2 MACKINTOSH CT
3 MEADS CT
4 MORBY CT

White Lodge Farm

A6

89 A 90 B C 90 C D 91 E F

91
111

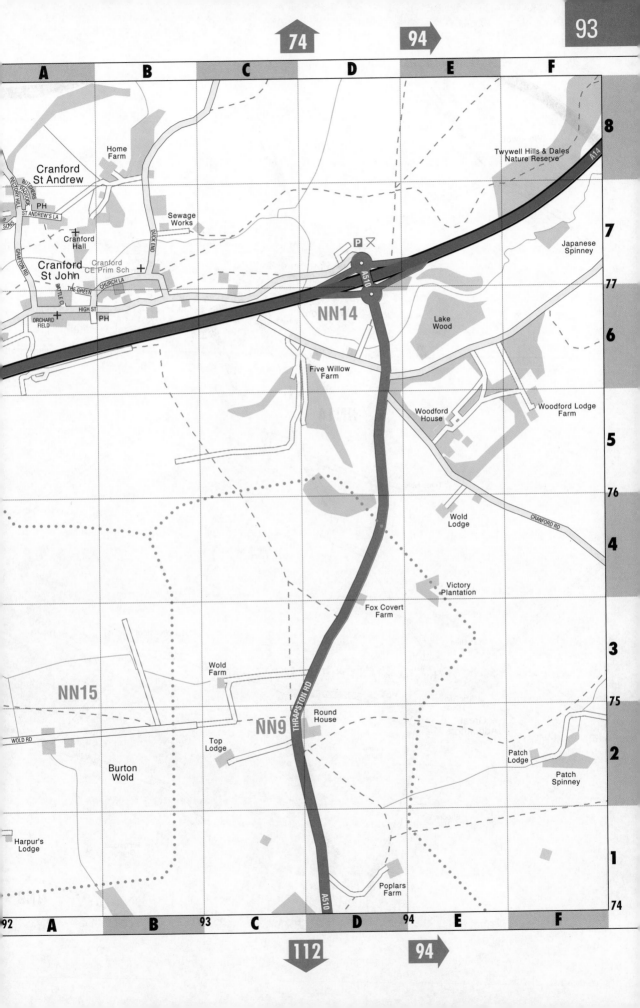

74
94
112
94

Twywell Hills & Dales
Nature Reserve

Japanese
Spinney

Home
Farm

Cranford
St Andrew

BUTCHERS

PADDOCK

PH

ST ANDREW'S LA

Sewage
Works

DUCK END

Cranford
Hall

Cranford
CE Prim Sch

Cranford
St John

CHURCH LA

THE GREEN

BATTLE CL

HIGH ST

PH

ORCHARD
FIELD

GRAFTON RD

RECTORY HILL

P ✕

A510

NN14

Lake
Wood

Five Willow
Farm

Woodford
House

Woodford Lodge
Farm

Wold
Lodge

CRANFORD RD

Victory
Plantation

Fox Covert
Farm

NN15

Wold
Farm

NN9

Round
House

THRAPSTON RD

WOLD RD

Top
Lodge

Burton
Wold

Patch
Lodge

Patch
Spinney

Harpur's
Lodge

Poplars
Farm

A510

A14

← 95
77

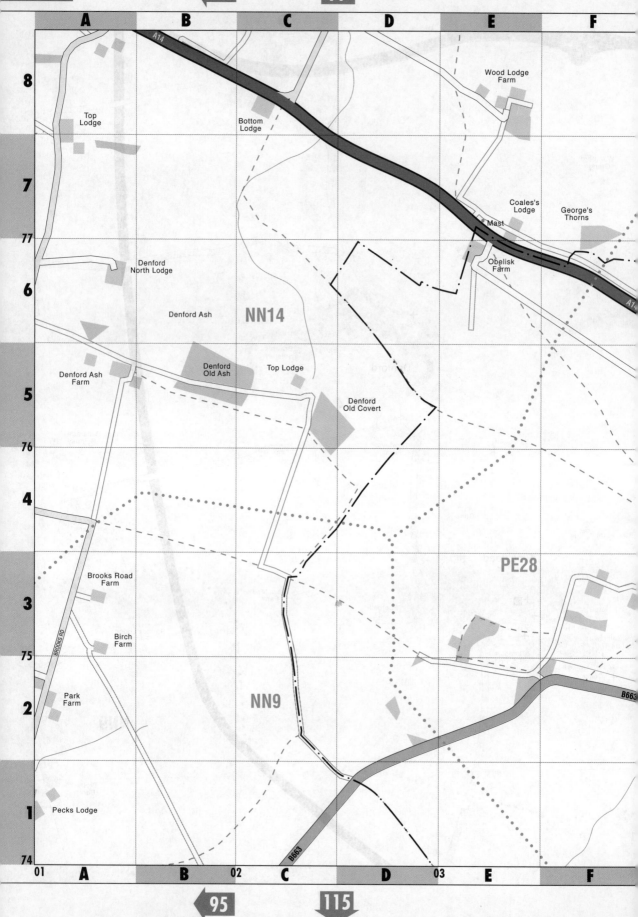

A B C D E F

8

Top
Lodge

Wood Lodge
Farm

Bottom
Lodge

7

Coales's
Lodge

George's
Thorns

77

Mast

Denford
North Lodge

Obelisk
Farm

6

Denford Ash

NN14

Denford Ash
Farm

Denford
Old Ash

Top Lodge

5

Denford
Old Covert

76

4

PE28

BROOKS RD

Brooks Road
Farm

3

Birch
Farm

75

NN9

B663

Park
Farm

2

Pecks Lodge

1

B663

74

01 A B 02 C D 03 E F

A14

NN14

PE28

Firing
Range

Slipe
Cotts

Smith's
Farm

Scott's
Farm

CHURCH
LA

Bythorn

Keyston

Bythorn
House

PH

Manor
Farm

HILLSIDE
COTTS

The Acres

LOOP RD

CHURCH VIEW

THE
PARK

PH

LINDEN GR

Clack La

Crow's Nest Hill

CHAINBRIDGE LA

CHAINBRIDGE LA

TOLL BAR LA

B663

TOLL BAR LA

WARREN LA

SCHOOL LA

MAIN ST

WARREN LA

A14 Huntingdon

Cambridgeshire STREET ATLAS

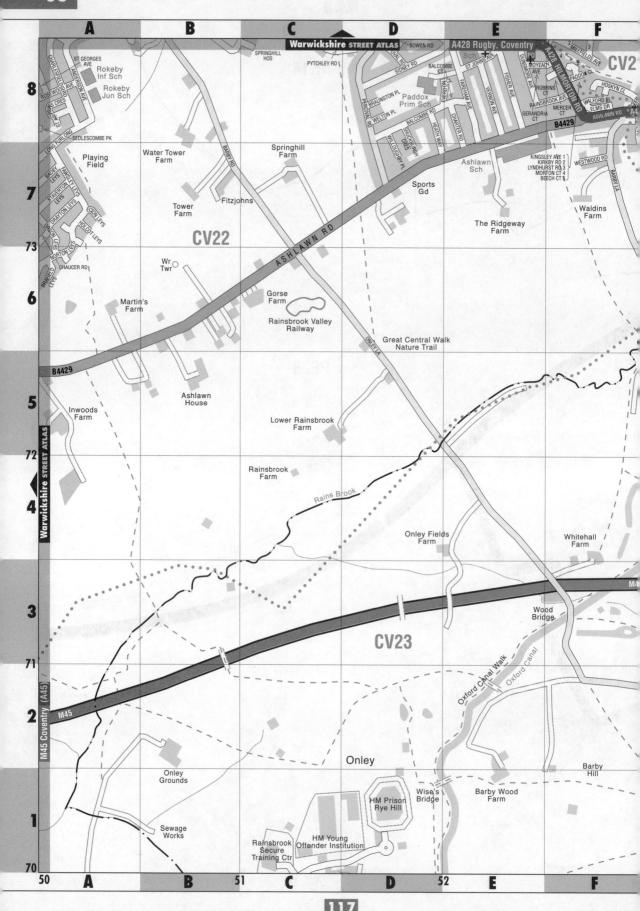

A B C D E F

8

St Georges Ave
Rokeby Inf Sch
Rokeby Jun Sch

SPRINGHILL HOS

BOWEN RD

PYTCHLEY RD

A428 Rugby, Coventry
Sch

MILLFIELDS AVE

CV2

CHARLESFIELD RD
ANDERSON AVE
ROSEWOOD AVE

SEDLESCOMBE PK

OVAL RD
SIDNEY RD
PERCIVAL RD

BRAUNSTON PL
Paddox Prim Sch
WELTON PL
BALCOMBE RD

BALCOMBE CT
ST JOHNS AVE
FAREHAM AVE
VERNON AVE

ROBBINS CT
MOYEACH AVE
DUNSMORE AVE
A428 HILMORTON RD

RAINSBROOK AVE
MERCER CT
GERANDRIA CT
GERARDIA

PADDOX CL
WALFORD PL
HOSKYN CL
ELMS DR
ASHLAWN RD
B4429

A4

Water Tower
Farm

Playing
Field

LONG FURLONG
BABY
FANSLEY LEYS
STAVERTON LEYS
EGON LEYS
DRAYTON LEYS
HOLCOT LEYS
NORTON LEYS
BRAEFIELD LEYS
CHAUCER RD

BARBY RD

Springhill
Farm

Tower
Farm

Fitzjohns

CV22

FISHER AVE
CHARTER RD
HEATH WAY
STUCKBURGH CRES
WILLOUGHBY PL

Ashlawn
Sch

Sports
Gd

KINGSLEY AVE 1
KIRKBY RD 2
LYNDHURST RD 3
MORTON CT 4
BEECH CT 5

WESTWOOD RD

BARBY LA

7

ASHLAWN RD

The Ridgeway
Farm

Waldins
Farm

73

Wr
Twr

Martin's
Farm

Gorse
Farm

Rainsbrook Valley
Railway

ONLEY LA

Great Central Walk
Nature Trail

6

B4429

Ashlawn
House

Inwoods
Farm

Lower Rainsbrook
Farm

5

Warwickshire STREET ATLAS

72

Rainsbrook
Farm

Rains Brook

Onley Fields
Farm

Whitehall
Farm

M4

4

3

Wood
Bridge

M45 Coventry (A45)

71

Oxford Canal Walk
Oxford Canal

CV23

Onley

Barby
Hill

2

M45

Onley
Grounds

Wise's
Bridge

Barby Wood
Farm

HM Prison
Rye Hill

1

Sewage
Works

Rainsbrook
Secure
Training Ctr

HM Young
Offender Institution

70

50 A B 51 C D 52 E F

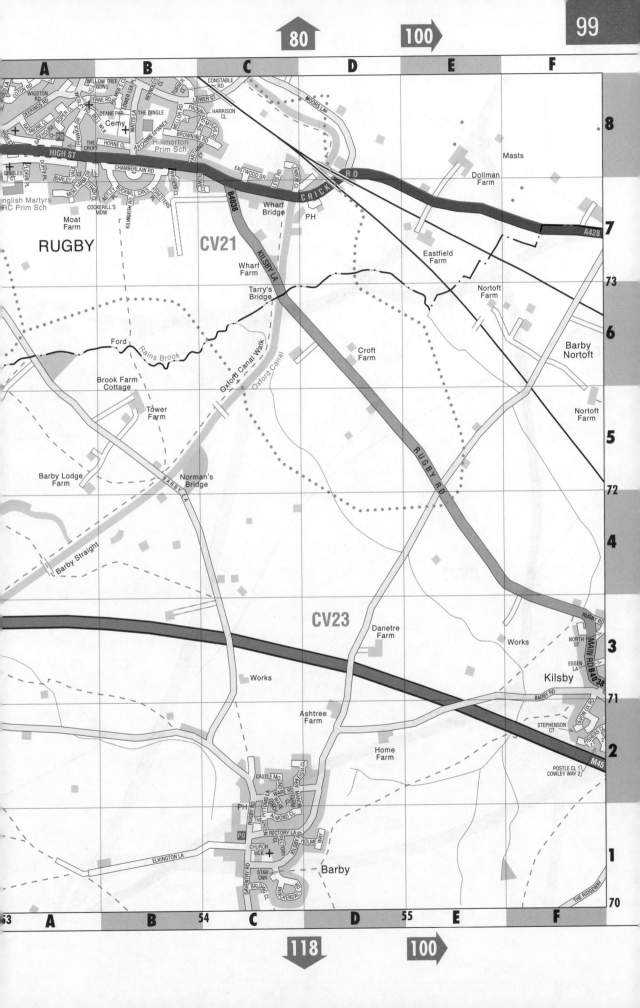

NN6

Winwick

Warren
Covert

White House
Farm

Mill House

Springfield
Farm

Pasture
Farm

Glebe
Farm

Jurassic Way

Wayside
Farm

Manor
Farm

Bungalow
Farm

Marrowell
Farm

West Haddon
Grange

A428   CRICK RD

WEST END
KELMERFORT RD
SYLES CL
WORCESTER
CL
PARTWELL CL
MORRISON PARK RD
CHURCH
CL
ELIZABETH RD
LATTIMORE CL
ELEANOR
CT
GUILSBOROUGH RD
THE
OLD BRICKYARD

ALMSHOUSES
VICTORIA CL
PITCHER CL
WESTFIELD
CT
MUNCASTER
CL
ATTERBURY CL
FIELD CL
DAIRY CL

West Haddon
Endowed CE
Prim Sch

THE GREEN

CROWN LA
HIGH ST
SPENCER
CT
MUDVIS

PO
NORTHAMPTON RD
OLD FORGE DR

STAFFORDS LA RD
HARDAYS LA
HILLSIDE
PH

FITZROY
CT

West Haddon

The Hall

WATFORD RD
FOXHILL RD

Torkington
Lodge

Lodge
Farm

Washbrook
Spinney

Hungerwell
Barn

Home Farm

Grove Farm

Foxhill

Park House

A428

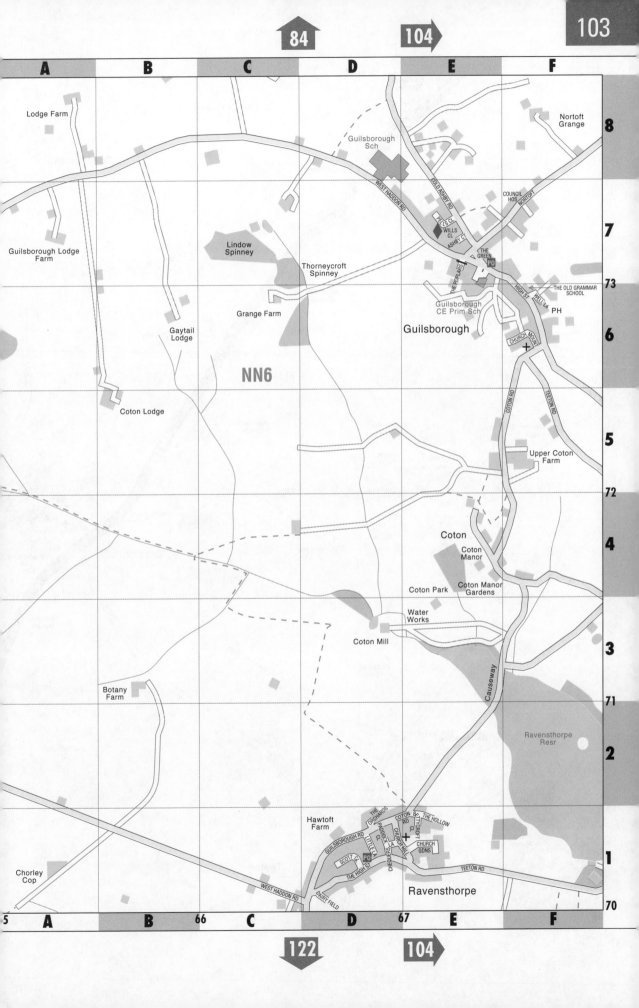

A B C D E F

8
7
73
6
5
72
4
3
71
2
1
70

68 A B 69 C D 70 E F

Blackpits Spinney
A5199
Square Hedge Spinney
Lodges Spinney
Cottesbrooke
Oak Spinney
Cottage Farm
The Green Lane
Hollowell Resr
Hollowell Grange
Great Creaton Lodge
NN6
Neaturn Lodge
Hollowell Lodge
WELFORD RD
HOME FARM CL
Hollowell
Home Farm
HOME FARM YD
LANGHAM CT
GUILSBOROUGH HILL
BRIXWORTH RD
ORCHARD CL
THE GREEN
Creaton Rd
Hollowell Rd
LITCHFIELD LA
HIGH ST
HORSESHOE CL
THE
BG COURT HOUSE
SPRING CL
PO
CHURCH HILL
HIGHFIELD PK
VIOLET LA
Great Creaton Prim Sch
Creaton
PH
Sewage Works
Blackberry Hill Farm
JUDGES CT
TEETON LA
Highgate House
A5199
Pastures Farm
Macmillan Way
Ravensthorpe Lodge
Landymoors Farm
Ravensthorpe Resr
Water Works
Hall
Teeton Lodge
FIVEWAYS
Teeton

8

Midshires Way

Manor Farm

Lamport Grange

Scaldwell Spinney

Scaldwell Lodge

Clint Hill

MANOR WLK

PO

MANOR RD

THE CROFT

TOWNSEND

A508

Hanging Houghton

7

Clint Hill Fox Covert

73

6

HARBOROUGH RD

Lodge Farm

Scaldwell

COUNCIL HOUSES

POPLARS CT

WEST END

The Grange

PETERS LA

BACK LA

BACK LA

HIGH ST

SCHOOL END

OLD RD

HOLCOT

5

NN6

72

4

Pytchley Hunt Kennels

STATION RD

SCALDWELL RD

Rectory Farm

3

Home Farm

THE PADDOCKS

STAVELEY WAY

Ind Est

MORGAN DR

AMOR AVE

SILVER ST

HALL FARM CL

HIGH ST

HARBOROUGH RD

FERRO FIELDS

IRONSTONE WAY

QUARRY RD

CHURCH ST

CROSS HILL

BRIXWORTH HALL PK

71

PH

Isham Charity Farm

Laundon's Lodge

HOLCOT RD

2

Brixworth

FROG HALL

LATCHFIELD

GRANGE CT

NEW LANDS

KENNEL TERR

THE MEWS

RAVENSMEAD

CL

EAGLEHURST

TANTREE WAY

WATERPIKE

BURROWS VALE

HORSESHOE CL

THE RHOMBS

GRASS SLADE

1 DEMSWELL
2 BREACH CL
3 DAMHERST PIECE

NEW ST

PYTCHLEY CL

PYTCHLEY WAY

HUNT CL

HUNTERS' WAY

STANNARD WAY

THE SLIP

BRACKEN BOROUGH

THE KNOLL

THE ASHWAY

WOODSFIELD

SAXON HO

Liby

LONE PINE CT

SOUTH VIEW

1

Park Farm

SPRATTON RD

PARRFIELD RD

ST DAVIDS RD S

CANDLANDS

RYE HOLME

OATHILL CL

BRAMPTON WAY

NORTHAMPTON WAY

Brixworth CE Prim Sch

LESSON RD

EASTFIELD RD

IRON PITS

THE ASHWAY

1 WHADDON FIELD
2 JUNIPER THORN
3 WATERLEE FURLONG
4 GRANDBOROUGH CL

Grange Farm

FROXHILL WLK

ST DAVIDS CL

BROAD ST

OLDE FORDE CL

PORTWEY CL

RYNGWELL CL

THE PICKERING

KNIGHTONS CL

A508

Pitsford Water

WINDMILL GRANGE

DAIRY CL

FROXHILL CRES

SHELLEYCOTES RD

P

HILLTOP CL

70

88
108

A B C D E F

8

7

73

6

5

72

4

3

71

2

1

70

Oak
Spinney

OLD RD

SCALDWELL RD
or LAMPORT RD

MILL LA

BROUGHTON RD

CHAPEL LA
CHARLES CL
CLEAVERS LA
TOWNSON CL
BARNES CL
HARRINGTON RD
FAXTON
END

Wold Farm
Ind Pk

Old

Grange
Farm

PH

BRIDLE RD

WALGRAVE RD

CHERRY HILL

OLD RD
TOWNSEND RD
SPRINGFIELD
HILL
CL
ORCHARD
CL

Ford

Mill
Farm

HOLCOT RD

Cemy

NN6

Rectory
Farm

Works

ST END

HOLCOT LA

Brixworth
Fox Covert

Pitsford Water

Grange Farm
Cottages

HOLCOT RD

New Grange
Farm

P

Causeway
BRIXWORTH RD

WALGRAVE RD

The
Lodge

'7 A B 78 C D 79 E F

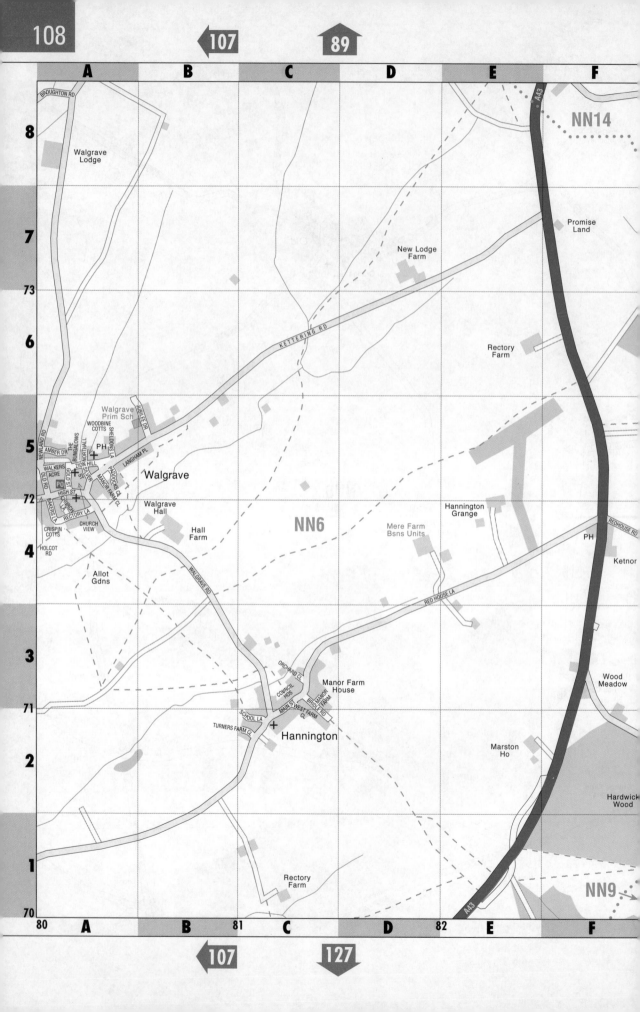

A B C D E F

8

Broughton Rd

Walgrave
Lodge

NN14

7

73

6

Kettering Rd

New Lodge
Farm

Promise
Land

Rectory
Farm

A43

5

Walgrave
Prim Sch

Woodbine
Cotts

Jubilee Dr

Sheldons La

Northall

Zion Hill

Amber Dr

The
Bungalows

PH

Langham Pl

Walgrave

New Land Old Rd

Walkers
Acre

Old Rd

Gold St

Silver St

PO

High St

Paddocks Cl

Manor Farm Cl

Church

Bakers La

Rectory La

Church View

Crispin
Cotts

Walgrave
Hall

NN6

Hannington
Grange

Mere Farm
Bsns Units

Ketnor

PH

Redhouse Rd

72

Holcot
Rd

Hall
Farm

Walgrave Rd

4

Allot
Gdns

Red House La

Wood
Meadow

3

Orchard Cl

Council
Hos

Main St

Manor Farm
House

Bridle Rd

West Farm
Cl

Manor
Farm

71

School La

Turners Farm Cl

Hannington

Marston
Ho

2

Hardwick
Wood

A43

1

Rectory
Farm

NN9

70

A43

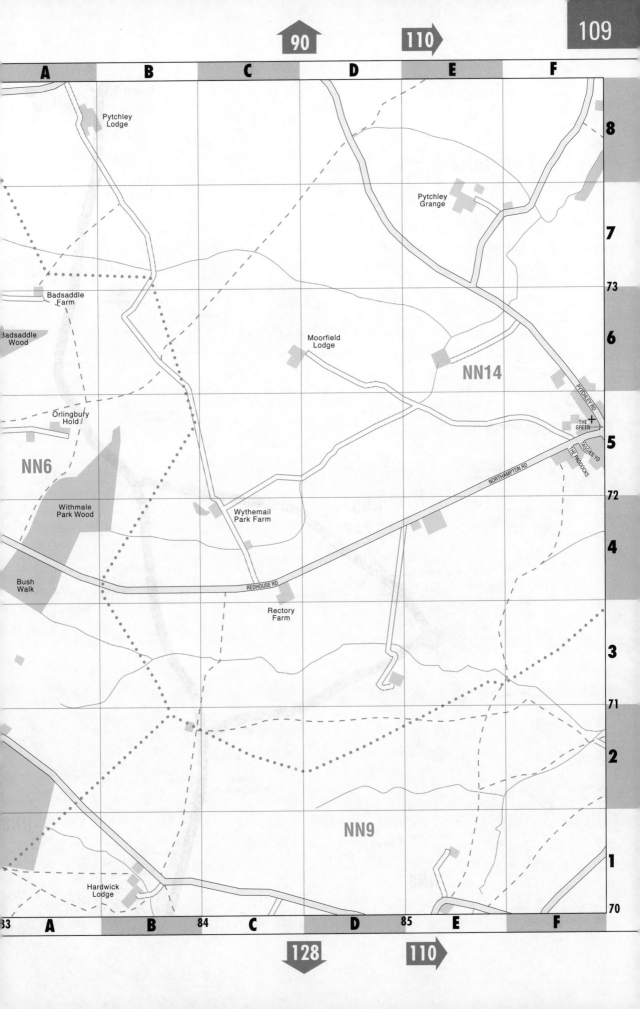

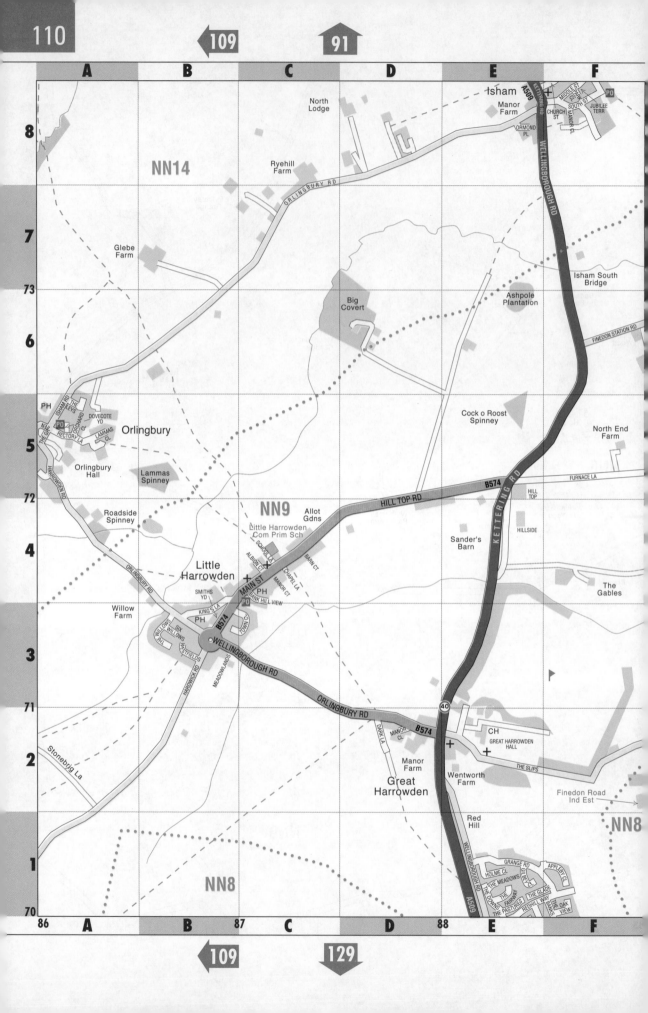

A B C D E F

NN14

HILLCREST AVE

NN15

THE RUSHES
RIVERVIEW

Quarry
(dis)

Buccleuch
Farm

8

FINEDON RD

Barnfield Lodge
Farm

Quarry
(dis)

A6

Black
Lodge

7

Isebrook
Bridge

73

BURTON RD

Quarry
(dis)

6

FINEDON STATION RD

STATION RD

Sewage
Works

A6

1 ST MARY'S AVE
2 BERRY GREEN CT
3 ST MARY'S CT
4 APPLETREE CT
5 WATERLOW BRIDGE
6 THE WELLS

Furnace
Lane
Ind Est

Westfield
Lodge

Cemy

TINGDENE RD
ORCHARD RD
ALBERT RD
VICTORIA RD
TANN RD
ROSE
HILL

5

River Ise

Debdale
Grove

TH
Liby

ORCHARD
TERR
HIGH ST
WELL ST
WALKER'S RD

A510

72

FURNACE
COTTS

FURNACE LA

Finedon
Hall

HOLLY WLK
MACKWORTH DR
DOLBEN CL
CHURCH
HILL
STOCKS
AVENUE RD
AVENUE
CHURCH ST
REGENT ST
BELL HILL
IVY LA

L Ctr
PO

SUMMERLEE RD
MILNER RD
CROMER RD
EVENFIELD RD

4

NN9

Finedon

WELLINGBOROUGH RD

HALL OR
VENMAUR RD

1 SUMMERLEE MEWS
2 PARKERS TERR
3 IRONSTONE CT
4 MACKWORTH GN

GROVE WAY

Allot
Gdns

Eleanor's
Wood

Harrowden Rd

RYEBURY HILL

3

71

Great
Harrowden
Lodge

THE SLIPS

Hillside
Farm

2

WELLINGBOROUGH RD

Quarry
(dis)

BRADFIELD RD
MAUK RD
YELDON CT
SANDERS RD
BRADFIELD CL
STEWARTS RD
BRIDLE CL
STANTON CL
SANDERS CL
BENTLEY RD
PATERSON RD

Sports
Gd

Ryebury
Farm

Finedon Road
Ind Est

Works

NN8

Works

A510
SIDEGATE LA

Carrol Spring
Farm

1

A510

70

39 A B 90 C D 91 E F

A   B   C   D   E   F

8

NN14

Finedon Poplars

Poplar's Bungalow

7

Poplar Lodge

Finedon Lodge

THRAPSTON RD

A510

73

6

Burrows Barn

Mast

Allot Gdns

Bank Farm

Finedon

NN9

Knightlands

HYDE DR

ROCK LEIGH CL

MILLER'S CL

ALMSTON RD

EASTLANDS RD

WENTWORTH RD

HIGHFIELD RD

ROCK RD

EASTFIELD

REGENCY CT

ALLEN RD

ALLEN CT

HAYDEN AVE

FREEMAN WAY

OXFORD ST

WAY

5

A510

HIGH ST

OBELISK RD

ROSE HILL

MULSO RD

HAWTHORNE RD

WILLIAM

UNION ST

NBLE CRES

COWPER RD

OVEL CT

72

Finedon Mulso CE Jun Sch

Wr Twr

IRTHLINGBOROUGH RD

4

Townside Farm

Garrow Close Spinney

Poplar Barn Farm

FINEDON RD

TURNBROOK CL

By Pass Farm

B5348

SCOTS CL

Huxlow Science Coll

FINEDON RD

WICKLEY CL

MEREFIELDS GDNS

MOUNTFIELD

LONG ACRES DR

MIDDLE GRASS

DRAYTON RD

KNIGHTLANDS RD

PORTLAND RD

DRAY

A6

B571

B5348

SCHARPWELL

3

GATES CL

SPRING TERR

RICHFIELD CT

PIPERS CL

FERNHAM CT

ADDINGTON RD

STATION RD

71

Nevilles Lodge

IRTHLINGBOROUGH

Irthlingborough Jun & Inf Schs

NURSERY GDNS

EXCELSIOR CT

SCARBOROUGH ST

MARKET CROSS

PO

Liby

LIME ST

PETER'S WAY

NENE CT

LILLEY TERR

B571

THE FLATLETS

MALTHOUSE CL

2

MANTON RD

COLLEGE ST

WARREN RD

CHURCH ST

OAK TERR

Cricket Gd

HARGRAVE CT

MUSSON CL

RECTORY GDNS

BRIARS RD

HIGH ST

THE CLOSE

MEADOW WAY

Nene Way

QUEEN'S CL

JUBILEE

Liby

MEADOWVALE

NN8

WINDMILL RD

LEES ST

GEORGE ST

VICTORIA ST

STRAW

CHERRY ST

CHERRY RD

CROUCH RD

MEADOWVALE

F2

1 BROOK TERR

2 ARCHFIELD TERR

3 EASTFIELD RD

4 SPRING ST

5 CHURCH WLK

6 OAK TERR

7 THE LOUISA LILLEY HOMES

8 SPINNEY TERR

9 MEADOW WLK

10 GORSEHOLM CT

11 THE LIMES

12 LOVEL CT

13 NEENE CT

1

Factory

B571 WELLINGBOROUGH RD

SHERIFF HO

NICHOLAS LA

COWPER CL 1

MARRIOTT CL 2

PRESLAND WAY

B5348

BBW VALE RD

ALLEN RD

70

92   A   B   93   C   D   94   E   F

94
114

A B C D E F

8

Sewage Works

AMEN PL
WATERVILLE WAY
WEEKLY CL
AMEN CNR
HIGH ST
BACK LA
BAKEHOUSE HILL

Top Lodge

Burrows Farm

THE GREEN
BURROWS FARM LA
PH
CHURCH WLK
S END
ROSE COTTS
CHAPEL HILL
EVERGREEN DR
DOVECOTE DR
IRTHLINGBOROUGH RD

Little Addington

Addington Park Ind Est

HILL FARM EST

NN14

Mallows Cotton

Hog Dyke

7

73

A45

MEADOW LA

6

Freestones Lodge

PH

WELFORD CL 1
FESTIVAL CL 2

RUGBY DR
CHURCHILL AVE
GARDENFIELDS CL
KETTERING RD
LANGLEY CRES
WELFORD AVE

NN9

Nene Way

River Nene

5

NOBLE AVE
ALEXANDER RD
ADDINGTON RD
THE SKIRTS
WINDMILL AVE
PALMER AVE
CLERK CL

PO

72

Needham Rd

4

NEEDHAM RD
ALFRED ST
LAURENCE WAY
RECTORY CT
DOLBEN AVE
MANSFIELD ST
SCHOOL ST
JOHN EAGLE CL
GREEN LA
SPENCER PAR
VILLA RD
SAMUELS CL
HILLSTONE CT
HILL
HIGH GRANGE RD
DOVEHOUSE CL
HIGHAM RD
HOUSE GDNS

Stanwick

Crow Hill

Ford

WEST ST

The Hall

3

71

/Diamonds Bsns Ctr

MARSH LA

Hall Farm

B571

B5348
STATION RD

ASTLEY WAY
DIAMOND WAY

Nene Park (Rushden & Diamonds FC)

Factory

STATION RD

Netherfield

Dieren

2

LIME ST

STATION RD

The Quarries

Caravan Site

Redlands Farm

1

Nene Way

Chowns Mill Bsns Pk

A6
A45

NN10

STANWICK RD

70

← 113
95

A B C D E F

8

New Barn Farm

Blotts Barn Bsns Ctr

BRICK KILN RD

Northdale Farm

1 CHESTNUT CT
2 PENNY LA
3 BRIDGE ST
4 TITHE BARN CL
5 DOVECOTE CL

Brooks Farm

Scalley Farm

ST CRISPIN WAY

Kepwick

WELLS CL

7

WARTH PARK WAY

CATLOW CL

NICHOLS WAY

WHITTAM CL

ORWELL CL

NENE CL

DEAN

ENTERPRISE RD

WESTER CL

Ind Est

MIDLAND RD

WEBB RD

ELLISON

POPHAM

MALLOWS DR

MCINNES WAY

NOTTON ROW

NORTH ST

B663

BLOMSTEAD RISE

WHEELWRIGHT

HERITAGE WAY

MATRON CT

Cemy

YORK WAY

FAIROAKS DR

LUNDIE CL

DE FERNEUS DR

HARRIS

CHURCH ST

RICHARDSON WAY

B663

RAMSAY CL

WHITEFIELD

GARDNER WAY

OAKLEIGH

BUGBY WAY

EAST

LANGHAM

HIGH ST

MANOR HOUSE

STREY PL

BUTTS RD

DERLING DR

Scalley Farm

73

WELBOURNE CL

POPLARS

LEE WAY

WINDMILL VIEW

LANGHAM

MANOR ST

PETERS

ROMAN

HOLMFIELD DR

KINGSMITH WAY

MEADOW LA

Windmill Prim Sch

MILL

MILLER

WINDMILL AVE

Liby

ST PETERS

PORTS

SPENCER ST

MANOR FARM RD

VICENTO'S

BROAD CL

SAXON WAY

MOUNT

6

Mast

London Rd

THE ELMES

CART HILL ST

MARSHALL'S DR

MARSHALLS CT

P

SQUARE

WESLEY CT

CHURCH ST

CHERRADENE

P

COLEMAN

LAWSON ST

GLADSTONE ST

SACKVILLE

Schs

Manor Farm

RAUNDS

BELMONT GDNS

ASHFIELD

GRIMSON

LO AVE

ROSE

EVELYN WLK 1
CHRISTINE CT 2
SHELMERDINE RISE

RED ROW

ASHFIELD AVE

CLARE ST

HARCOURT ST

BROOK ST

PRIMROSE

HILL

PARK AVE

DRYDEN ST

MACKENZIE RD

SMITHFIELD PL

P

PRIMROSE

HILL

LIONS

GROVE ST

5

Sewage Works

Hog Dyke

SHFIELD CT

TITTY HO

SFIELD CT

CHAMBERLAIN WAY

RUSHMERE

WEBBRIDGE WAY

STREATHER

SMITH CT

THE FORRESTERS

WARWICK CL

HOLMES AVE

NEW TOWN RD

SHORTWOODS CL

SANDS WAY

CHERRY WLK

ORCHARD RD

WELLINGTON RD

GLOVERS LA

Thorpe House Farm

KESTON WAY

ANDRE

MILES CL

HARVEY

WHITNEY CL

72

COURTMAN RD

CASTERTON CL

COLLINGHAM CL

FRANCIS TERR

LAWRENCE CL

STANWICK RD

THE PADDOCK

CL

MANNINGHAM

QUICTENHALL RD

WESTFIELD DR

WESTFIELD AVE

ANTONA DR

ANTONA CL

ANTONA GDNS

MAPLETOFT

NN9

POTTER CT

CUMBERLAND AVE

RAUNDS RD

P

Darsdale Farm

SHELTON RD

Stanwick

PH

Stanwick Prim Sch

MANOR GDNS

NEWBRIDGE LA

PO

CHURCH ST

COURTWOOD

CHAPEL LA

THE HOLLOW

BROOKSIDE

THE AVENUE

GRANGE RD

EAST ST

3

MARKS CL

THE WOODLANDS

Cemy

CHELVESTON RD

71

2

Pastures Lodge Farm

B663

Kiriandra House

New Covert

1

Pasture Barn

Stanwick Pastures

70

98 A B 99 C D 00 E F

← 113
133

PRETORIA COTTS

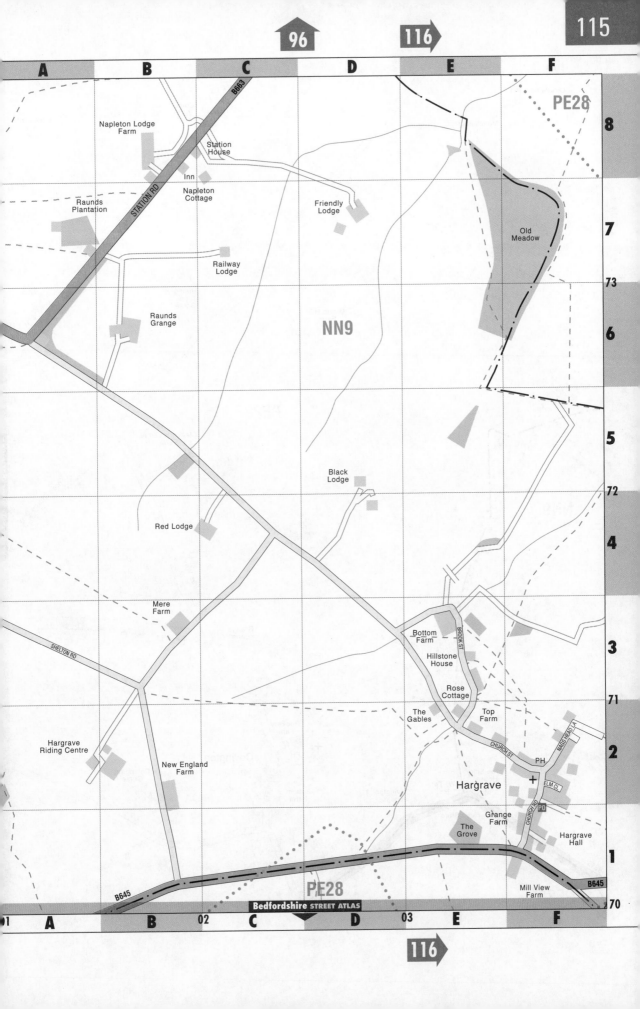

PE28

8

Napleton Lodge
Farm

Station
House

Inn

Napleton
Cottage

Raunds
Plantation

Friendly
Lodge

STATION RD

B663

Old
Meadow

7

73

Railway
Lodge

Raunds
Grange

NN9

6

5

Black
Lodge

72

Red Lodge

4

Mere
Farm

Bottom
Farm

BROOK ST

3

Hillstone
House

SHELTON RD

Rose
Cottage

71

The
Gables

Top
Farm

Hargrave
Riding Centre

CHURCH ST

NAGS HEAD LA

PH

2

New England
Farm

Hargrave

ELM CL

CHURCH RD

PO

Grange
Farm

Hargrave
Hall

The
Grove

1

PE28

Mill View
Farm

B645

B645

70

115
97

A   B   C   D   E   F

8

Crow's Nest Hill

Manchester
Lodge

Clack La

Clack
Barn

CHAINBRIDGE
LA

Molesworth
Lodge
Farm

MICKLE HILL

7

Mickle
Hill

73

Hunt's
Close
Gorse

6

Mickle Hill
Farm

PE28

5

Cleaver's Lodge
Farm

Three Shires Way

72

NN9

Three Shires Way

4

Grange
Farm

3

71

Rookery
Farm

CROSS ST

Covington

2

CHURCH LA

PH

THE PENTELOWES

Covington
Gorse

Three Shire
House

Wr Twr

Covington
Lodge

KEYSTON RD

Bottom
Farm

1

Three Shire
Stone

B645

PE28

B645

70

04   A   B   05   C   D   06   E   F

115

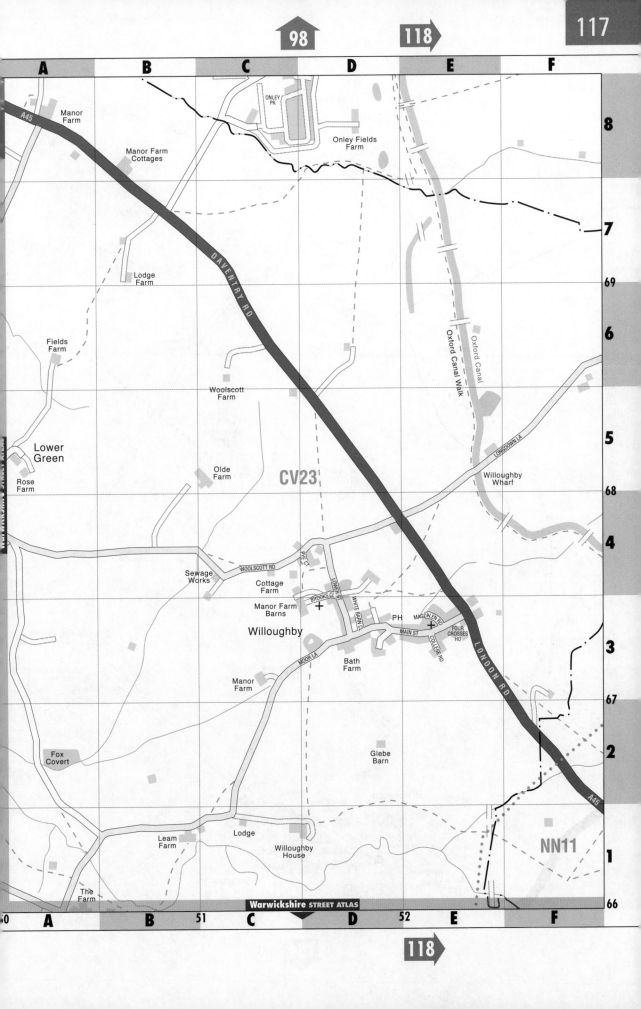

A   B   C   D   E   F

8
7
69
6
5
68
4
3
67
2
1
66

A45
Manor Farm
Manor Farm Cottages
ONLEY PK
Onley Fields Farm
DAVENTRY RD
Lodge Farm
Fields Farm
Oxford Canal Walk
Oxford Canal
Woolscott Farm
LONGDOWN LA
Willoughby Wharf
Lower Green
Rose Farm
Olde Farm
CV23
WOOLSCOTT RD
PYE CT
Sewage Works
Cottage Farm
LOWER ST
BROOKS CL
WHITE BARN CL
Manor Farm Barns
Willoughby
PH
MAGDALEN RD
Four Crosses Ho
MAIN ST
COLLEGE RD
LONDON RD
MOOR LA
Bath Farm
Manor Farm
Glebe Barn
NN11
Fox Covert
Leam Farm
Lodge
Willoughby House
A45
The Farm

A **B** **C** **D** **E** **F**

8

Barby

Barby Hill

Arnills Gate

MITCHISON RD

Barby CE Prim Sch

Briccle Wood

Hillfields

Mast

Ashby Home Wood

Barby Mill

Wr Twr

DAVENTRY RD

THE RIDGEWAY

CV23

7

LONGDOWN LA

Chapel Farm

Longdown

Willow Edge

69

Willoughby Lodge

Tiltup's Wood

High Park

6

Willoughby Fields

Tiltup's Holt Farm

Cleves Hill

Cleves Farm

5

Braunston Fields

Fawcliff Village

Braunston Cleves

Ashby Grange

68

4

Braunston Lodge Farm

Fir Tree Farm

3

Bragborough Lodge

Oxford Canal Walk

Oxford Canal

Jurassic Way

Lodge Farm Spinney

NN11

67

2

BARBY LA

Braunston

Braunston CE Prim Sch

WALNUT CL

SANDERS CL

COUNTRYSIDE

FIELD VIEW

GREENWAY

HAZEL CROFT

TOMPSON CL

DANE CT

ASHBY RD

NORTH CL

SPINNEY HILL

MAPLE CL

GOULD CL

MILL CL

CHURCH RD

PO

THE GREEN

SCHOOL CL

SOUTH CL

WELTON RD

1

A45

LONDON RD

HIGH ST

NIBBITS LA

CROSS LA

ARCHER AVE

MAKEPEACE HO

EAST CL

Ventor Lodge

Little Braunston

Windmill

Home Farm

66

A45

DARK LA

53 **A** **54** **B** **C** **55** **D** **E** **F**

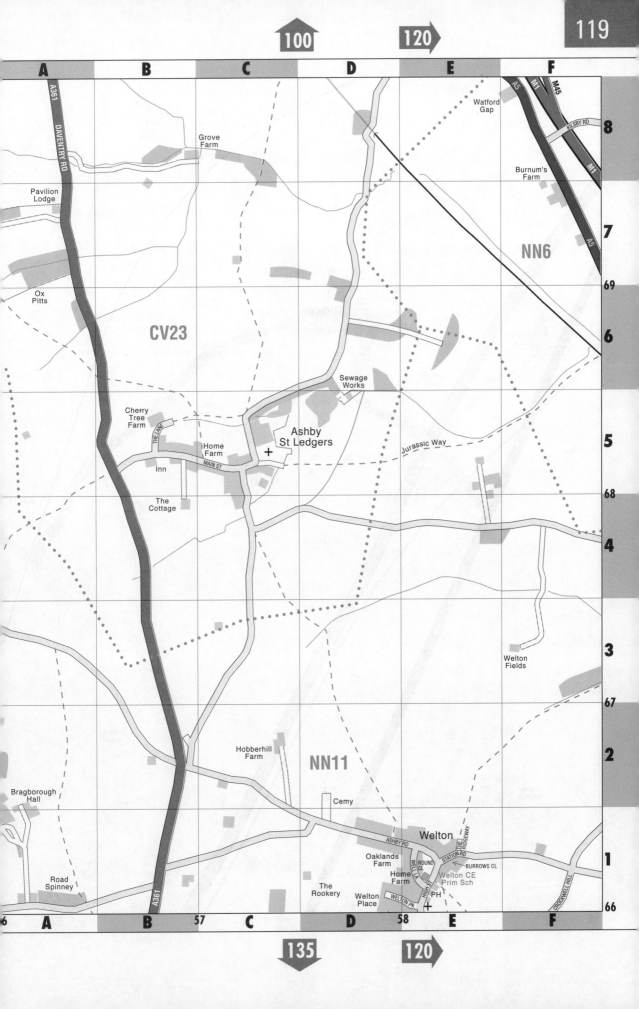

A   B   C   D   E   F

8

Long Spinney

Barleypiece Spinney

Watford Lodge Farm

M1

KILSBY RD

Jurassic Way

WEST HADDON RD

7

Cemy

A5

69

Bluebell Spinney

WOODLANDS CT

CHURCH ST

+

Park House

Jurassic Way

Watford Locks

PARK LA

PARK CL

HENLEY CT

EDEN CT

PO

MAIN ST

Watford

6

Grand Union Canal

Sewage Works

STATION RD

Watford Lodge

LONG BUCKBY RD

5

Foxholes

Watford Gap Service Area

Mast

NN6

B5385

FOG COTTS

68

Brockhill Lodge

Murcott

B53...

4

Welton Lodge Farm

Langborough Barn

3

Mill House

67

NN11

Sewage Works

2

Welton Grange

Ryehill Lodge

White Barn Farm

1

Welton Hythe

A5

M1

Greenhill Farm

66

59   A   B   60   C   D   61   E   F

A B C D E F

8
7
69
6
5
68
4
3
67
2
1
66

NN6

Foxhill Farm

Buckby Lodge

Leighton Lodge

Hinde Mills Barn

Grange Farm

Paynes Lodge

Vanderplank's Covert

Gale House

Gale Lodge

Covert Barn

A428

A428

B5385

Lodge La

Mast

Highfields

Uplands Farm

Lodge Farm

Mast

COTTON END

Old Coopers

Murcott CL

Long Buckby Pocket Park

Long Buckby

Church Farm

The Banks
The Chase
Lawrence Ct
Armley Cl
Downs Pno
The Leys
Miles
Holyoake Terr
The
Applegarth
Berryfield
Orchard Rise
Spennnose Cl
Lime Ave

EAST ST

Grove Farm Cl

Rye Close

MURCOTT

WEST ST

Church St
Sanders Terr
Pytchley Dr
Rebdt Cl
Leys Cl
St Simin
Lexs Cl
Hammas Leys
Clifton Cl
Kingstone Cl
Phillips
Way
Ashmore

Jubilee Cl
Parkfield Rd
Syers Green Cl
Syers Green La
Holmfield Terr
Harbids La
KING ST
Market Pl
The Mews
PO
High St
The Poplars
Spicer Cl
Windsor Rd
Salem Cl
Luck Rd
Greenhill
Ryehill Cl
Greenhill Ct
South Cl
Cook's Wey
Harry Cl
Watts Wk
Maynos Rd
High Stack La

The Mounts
Sharpes La
Liby
Inf Sch
HIGH ST
Whitscroft
Skin Yard
Hall Dr
Grass Croft
Station Cl
William Rd
South Cl
Brington Rd
Cook's La

Oak Lodge Farm

Lodge La

Long Buckby Jun Sch

Rockhill Rd
Cook's Terr
Station Rd
Watson Rd

1 Charles Cl
2 Chestnut Cl

Gravel Pit Lodge

Hoborough Hill

P

Long Buckby

Floyers Farm

Panther's Lodge

Patford Bridge

Brook's Barn

Perkin's Lodge

NN7

A   B   C   D   E   F

Sewage Works

8

Steepleton Lodge

7

Oak Spinney

Washbrook Bridge

69

NN6

Buckby Folly Covert

Vicarage Farm

6

Covert Farm

Ryehills Farm

Millhouse

Sewage Works

A428

PH

East Haddon

B5385

Home Farm

Hall

Buckby Folly

BARN ACRE

TILBURY RISE

ORCHARD CL

NORTHFIELD GN

PANENTHORPE RD

PH

5

TILBURY RD

PRIESTWELL CT

HALL GDNS

LODGE FLATS

HOLDENBY RD

MAIN ST

Grovelands Farm

HADDON CT

ST ANDREWS RD

Fry's Farm

Brickhill Spinney

VICARAGE LA

East Haddon CE Prim Sch

Cemy

68

Haddonstone Show Garden

CLIFDEN TERR

CHURCH LA

4

Tire Hill Farm

Home Farm

Tire Hill Spinney

Rowell Leyes

3

67

East Haddon Grange

2

Garretts Barn

Willow Cottage

A428

The Gables

East Haddon Hill

Works

1

NN7

NN7

Althorp Meer

Langland's Plantation

66

65 A   B 66 C   D 67 E   F

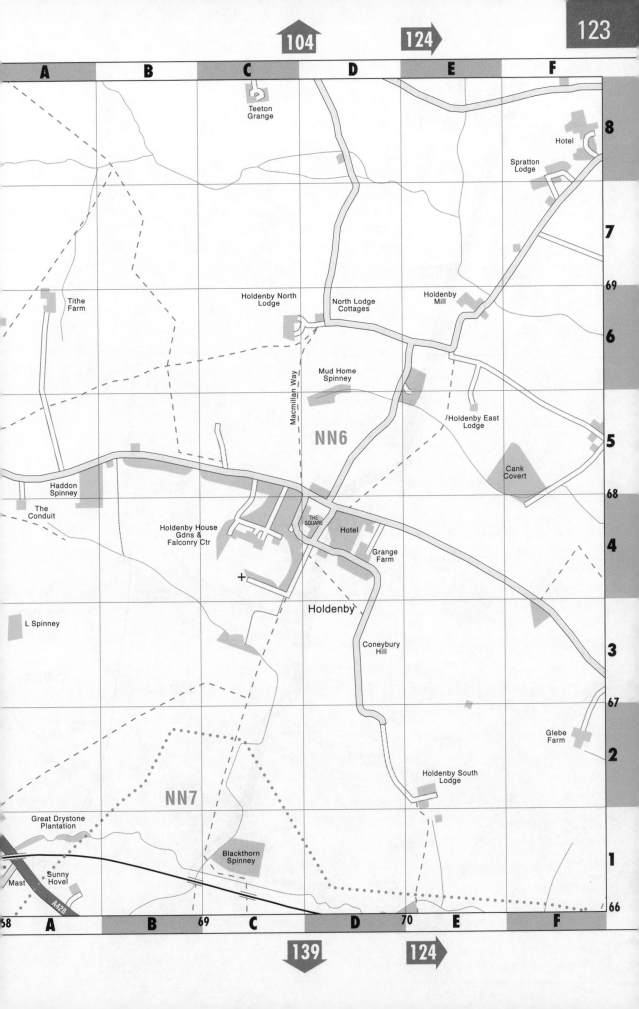

A   B   C   D   E   F

8

Teeton
Grange

Hotel

Spratton
Lodge

7

69

Holdenby North
Lodge

North Lodge
Cottages

Holdenby
Mill

6

Tithe
Farm

Mud Home
Spinney

Macmillan Way

Holdenby East
Lodge

NN6

5

Haddon
Spinney

Cank
Covert

68

The
Conduit

Holdenby House
Gdns &
Falconry Ctr

THE
SQUARE

Hotel

Grange
Farm

4

L Spinney

Holdenby

Coneybury
Hill

3

67

Glebe
Farm

2

Holdenby South
Lodge

NN7

Great Drystone
Plantation

Blackthorn
Spinney

1

Mast

Sunny
Hovel

A428

66

58   A   B   69   C   D   70   E   F

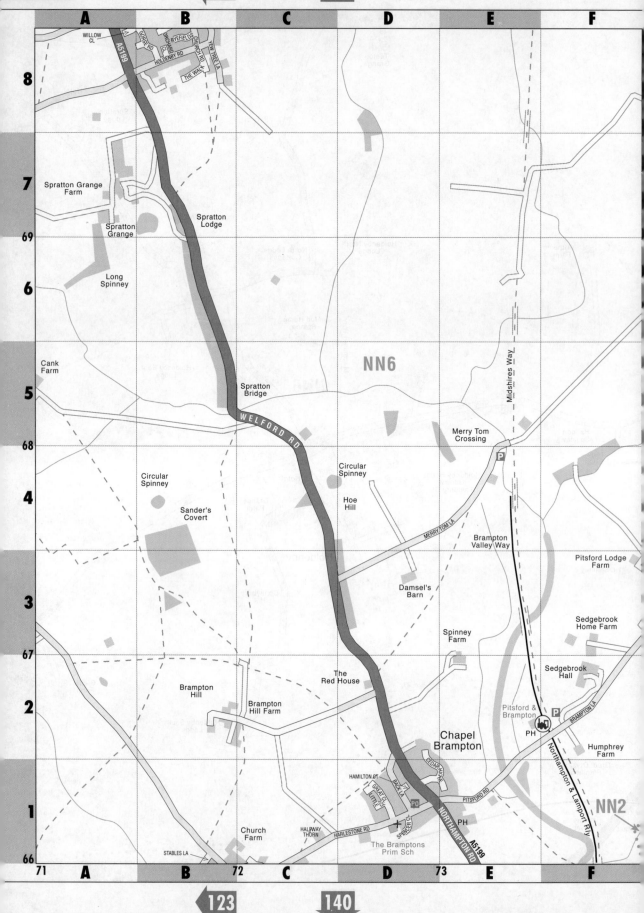

A   B   C   D   E   F

8
7
69
6
5
68
4
3
67
2
1
66

71   A   B   72   C   D   73   E   F

WILLOW CL
GORSE RD
ORCHARD RYEFIELDS
HOLDENBY RD
CHURCH RD
YEW TREE LA
THE WALK
A5199

Spratton Grange Farm
Spratton Grange
Spratton Lodge
Long Spinney
Cank Farm
Spratton Bridge
WELFORD RD
Circular Spinney
Circular Spinney
Hoe Hill
Sander's Covert
Merry Tom Crossing
Midshires Way
NN6
Merry Tom La
Damsel's Barn
Brampton Valley Way
Pitsford Lodge Farm
Sedgebrook Home Farm
Spinney Farm
Brampton Hill
Brampton Hill Farm
The Red House
Sedgebrook Hall
Pitsford & Brampton
Chapel Brampton
PH
Bramnton La
Humphrey Farm
NN2
Northampton & Lamport Rlv
Hamilton CT
GREAT CL
LITTLE CL
BACK LA
CEDAR RD
SPENCER CL
PO
PH
Pitsford Rd
NORTHAMPTON RD
A5199
Church Farm
STABLES LA
HALFWAY THORN
HARLESTONE RD
The Bramptons Prim Sch

A   B   C   D   E   F

8

7

69

6

5

68

4

3

67

2

1

66

South
Lodge

HILLTOP
CL

STONEHILL WAY
SAXON HILL'S
FAR BROOK
PORKY LEY'S
KNIGHTONS WAY
SALT PIKES
HIGH SLADE

THE ASHWAY 1
WHEATENS CL 2

NORTHAMPTON RD

A508

Pitsford
Hill

Hill
Farm

Mon

NN6

Brixworth
Country Park

Visitor
Ctr   P

Northampton
Sailing Club

Pitsford Water

Moulton Grange
Cottages

Moulton
Grange

P   GRANGE LA

RESERVOIR
HOS

Springhill
Farm

THE DOVECOTE
CHURCH LA
GLEBE LA
ORCHARD
COTTS

Pitsford
Pitsford Prim Sch

MANOR RD
BROADLANDS
THE CHASE

The Dairy
Farm

Longman's
Hill

THE SQUARE
HIGH ST
PO
PH

DRUMMOND CL

STABLE CT

Northamptonshire
Gram Sch

HOME FARM LA

Home
Farm

Mast

Sedgebrook
Grange

BRAMPTON LA

Hillcrest

Pitsford
Ctr

PITSFORD RD

67

NN3

Duke's
Clump

Fox Covert
Hall

Grotto
Spinney

NN2

Bunkers
Hill Farm

MOULTON RD

Sedgebrook Lodge
Farm

Butcher's
Spinney

BUTCHER'S LA

SPECTACLE LA

Ford

Moulton
Mill

Brickhill
Spinney

Boughton Park

PH

BUTCHER'S LA
SPRING
CL

A508

125
107

	A	B	C	D	E	F

8

Lower Brixworth Lodge

BRIXWORTH RD

RECTORY LA

WALGRAVE RD

PO

PH

PUDDLES LA

MAIN ST

FARM CL

WINSLAND CT

GLEBE CL

Manor Farm

BACK LA

BRITTENS VIEW

SUNNY BANK

Holcot

The Hawthorns

Equestrian Ctr

SYWELL RD

Pitsford Water

NN6

7

Northfields

MOULTON RD

Moulton Grange Farm

HOSPITAL BUNGALOW

TITHE CL

69

Hillcrest

Moulton Lodge Farm

6

North Farm

Tithe Farm

5

South Lodge

HOLCOT RD

Overstone Old Rectory

68

Slade Farm

Grange Cottages

4

Moulton Lodge

BOUGHTON FAIR LA

Overstone Grange

NN3

3

Hog Hole Spinney

Marsh Spinney

KETTERING RD

A43

67

PITSFORD RD

2

Holcot Centre

Cemy

BROWNS CL

THE GROVE

Grove Farm

Sandy Hill Farm

PARK VIEW

Moulton

CHURCH VIEW

GROVE FARM LA

NN6

THE HOLLIES

THE COLLEGE GROUNDS

Moulton Coll

Moulton Prim Sch

CHURCH MEWS

SCHOOL LA

TARRANT CT

SANDY HILL LA

Sewage Works

STEWART CL

THE LAURELS

CHURCH HILL

PYTCHLEY VIEW

TARRANT WAY

SIDDONS WAY

Overstone Farm

ARNSBY CRES

WEST ST

HOMESTEAD CL

OVERSTONE RD

FADY CT

Sandy Hill Farm

1

JEFFS CL

PYNON CL

POUND CT

THE PADDOCKS

SCHOOL LA

HIGH ST

CROSS ST

HIGH ST

PH

PO

OAKLEY LA

PRINCE OF WALES ROW

THE CRESCENT

ASHLEY LA

OVERSTONE CL

WANTAGE CL

PARK VIEW CL

OVERSTONE LA

SYWELL RD

POUND LA

CAREY CL

Liby

CAREY CT

Moulton Sch & Coll

LUNCHFIELD GDNS

LUNCHFIELD

ASHBY LA

NORTHAMPTON LA

BARLOW LA

A43

THE AVENUE

BILLING LA

66

77	A	B	78	C	D	79	E	F

C1
1 LEONARD LA
2 BLUEBELL PK CVN PK
3 THE NURSERIES
4 ASHBY GDNS
5 CHAPPELL HO
6 WELLS CT
7 LUNCHFIELD WLK
8 STOCKS HILL

108 128

A B C D E F

Hardwick Short Wood

8

NN9

Sywell Wood

7

Rifle Range

69

New College Farm

SYWELL RD

White House

6

Teacaddy Farm

Sywell Grange

NN6

New Inn Spinney

Sywell Lodge Farm

Northampton (Sywell) Airport

5

Rectory Farm

KETTERING RD

68

Ind Est

Sywell Airport Bsns Pk

Hotel

4

Overstone Grange

NN3

WELLINGBOROUGH RD

Park Pond

Sywell

Rectory Farm

WEBBS LA

WESTLEA RD

STONELEA RD

HOLDGT LA

PH

Sywell Hall

3

Cowpasture Spinney

PIE CHR

OVERSTONE HTS

CHURCH LA

The Rectory

Sywell House

HORSE SHOE COTTS

67

OVERSTONE RD

Sywell CE Prim Sch

Bonfire Bank

Long Spinney

BREAMBRIDGE CL

PARK CL

WOODFORD CHASE

New Plantation

Lavender Hill Farm

PO

Ass Bank

ECTON LA

2

Ferny Bank

Cottage Farm

Overstone Prim Sch

SYWELL RD

OVERSTONE CRES

WOODLAND AVE

Highlands

Large Quarter

New Hayes Wood

1

Overstone

Parson's Wood

Young Spinney

ASHDALE CL

WOODSIDE

SE CRES

New Hayes Wood

Hayes Wood

Gashouse Spinney

PARKLANDS

HIGH WOODS

66

30 A B 81 C D 82 E F

143 128

A B C D E F

8

NN9

7

69

6

Sywell
Wood

Hardwick
Grange

Hardwick

Hardwick
House

Manor
House

Merrydal
Farm

HARDWICK RD

Appleby
Gate

SYWELL RD

Appleby
Lodge

Cheesecake
Spinney

MOONSHINE GAP

Highfield
Lodge

Wilby
Hall

Corries
Spinney

Wood Lodge
Farm

5

68

4

NN6

NN8

The
Rookery

HIGHFIELD RD

Wr Twr

The
Grange

Poultry
Farm

3

67

Manor
Farm

GLEBE RD

Mears Ashby
Prim Sch

Mears
Ashby

2

NORTH ST

TINKERS
CRES

EARLS BARTON RD

MANOR RD

CHURCH ST

NURSERY CT

BAKEHOUSE
LA

VICARAGE LA

DALE FARM
COTTS

WELLINGBOROUGH RD

LADY'S LA

DALE CL

THE BARNS

DUCHESS END

WILBY RD

Dale Farm
Cotts

Sywell
Bottom

Recn
Gd

PADDOCK

Hill
Farm

PH

Mast

MEARS ASHBY RD

Glebe
Barn

SYWELL RD

1

66

83 A B 84 C D 85 E F

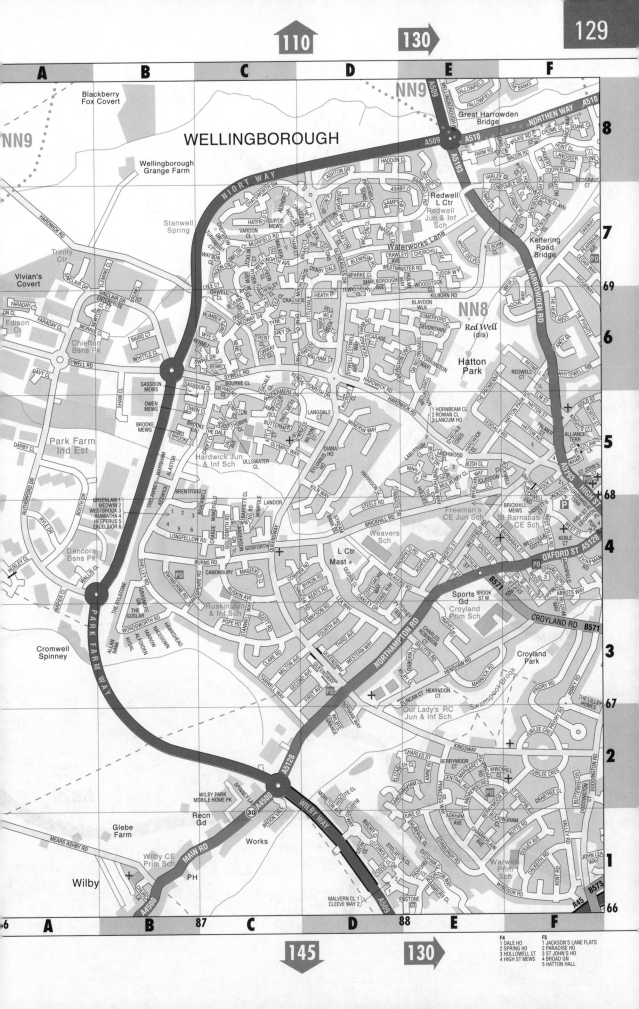

A4
1 CHURCH WAY
2 ANGEL LA
3 MARKET SQ
4 PEBBLE LA
5 CHEESE LA
6 SWANS LA
7 CORN LA
8 SPRING LA

9 The Swansgate Ctr

A5
1 CHARNWOOD
2 ALLIANCE CT
3 BAKER ST
4 PERKINS CT
5 BELL CT
6 LITTLE PARK ST
7 UPPER HAVELOCK ST
8 PARK CRES
9 SALEM LA

10 BENGEWORTH CT
11 HERRIOTTS CT
B5
1 LODGE CT
2 MANOR CT
3 HOWARD CT
4 LAUREL CT
5 STANLEY MEWS

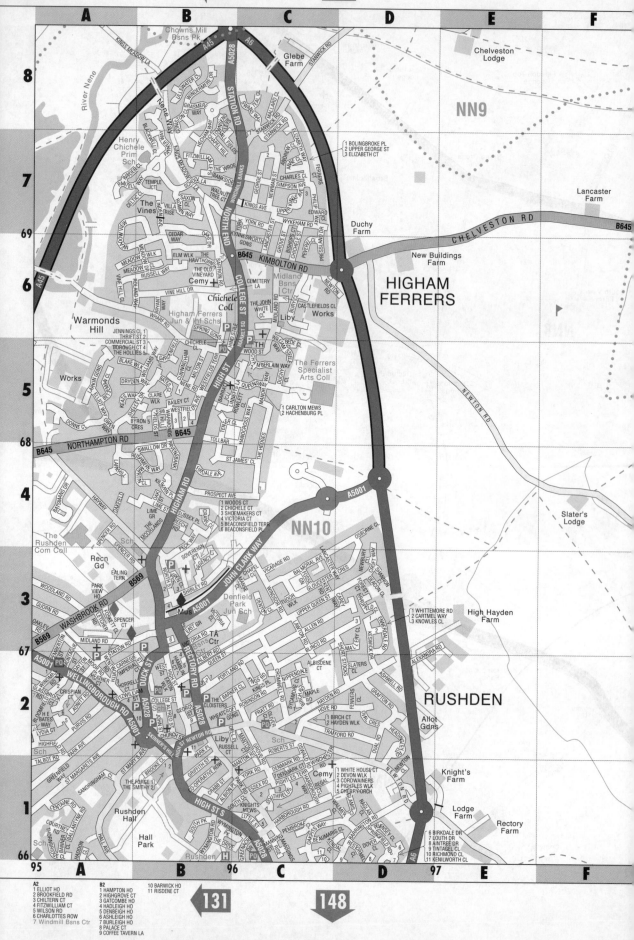

A2
1 ELLIOT HO
2 BROOKFIELD RD
3 CHILTERN CT
4 FITZWILLIAM CT
5 WILSON RD
6 CHARLOTTES ROW
7 Windmill Bsns Ctr

B2
1 HAMPTON HO
2 HIGHGROVE CT
3 GATCOMBE HO
4 HADLEIGH HO
5 DENBEIGH HO
6 ASHLEIGH HO
7 BURLEIGH HO
8 PALACE CT
9 COFFEE TAVERN LA

10 BARWICK HO
11 RISDENE CT

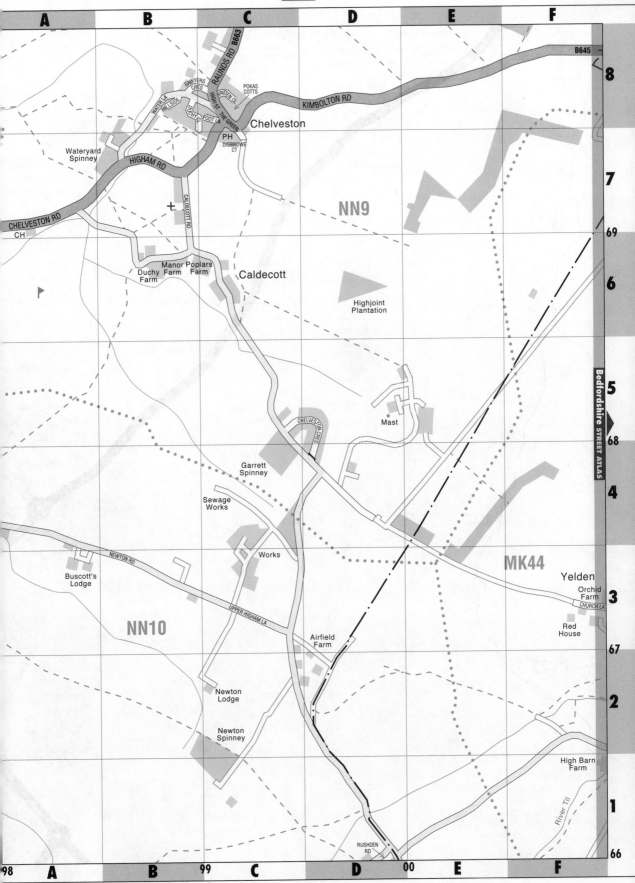

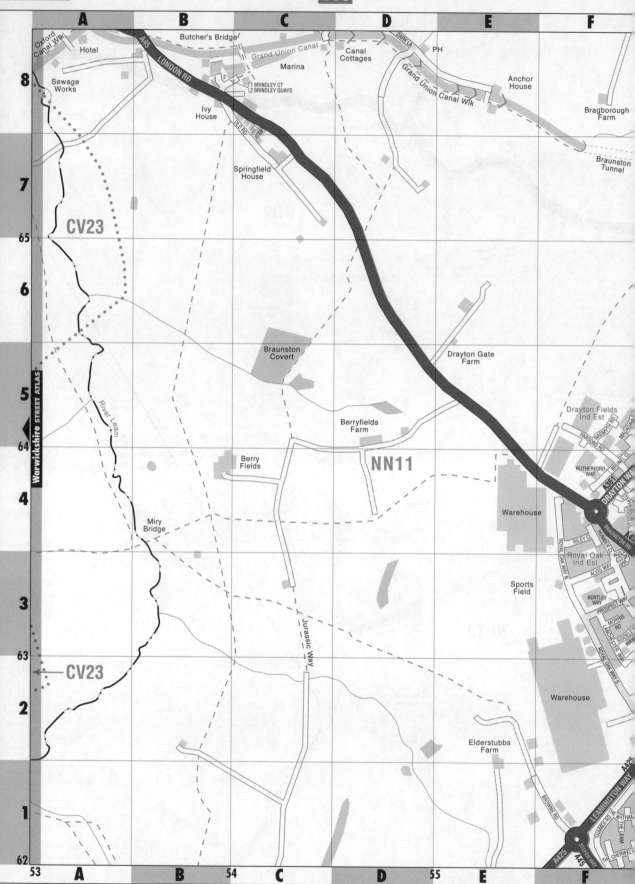

A   B   C   D   E   F

8   Crockwell Farm   Cornerhill Spinney   Buckby Top Lock   Rye Hill Farm   NN6   Surney Cottage

Norton Junction   NEWBRIDGE

Swing Bridge   PH   THE COUNCIL HOS   Surney Farm

Grand Union Canal

7   Grand Union Canal Wlk   Thrupp Grounds   B4036   Long Buckby Wharf

Thrupp Lodge

65   Thrupp Covert   Norton Lodge Farm   WHILTON LODGE   Whilton Locks

6

B4036   SPOTTED COW LA

5   NN11   Marina

64   Sewage Works   DAUNTRY RD   Beehive Lodge

EAGLESFIELD HOME FARM CT BAKERS   Norton Hall Farm   Pant Y Owen Farm

4   MANOR GDNS

PH   Norton   Watling Lodge

Allot Gdns   WEEDON LA   THE BROADWAY

3   Noborough Lodge

63

2   The Woodyard   Heart of The Shires Sh Village

Underhill Spinney   NN7

Noborough Farm

Mast   Noborough Spinney   Ivy House Farm

1   Borough Hill Plantation

62

59   A   60   B   C   61   D   E   F

138 →

A   B   C   D   E   F

Surney Bridges

The Bungalow

Perkin's Lodge

NN6

8

Sewage Works

NN7

7

65

NN11

THE GREEN

WALK CLOSE LA

SOUTH VIEW

THE GARDENS

MANOR LA

Whilton

Roughmoor Grounds

6

Whilton Mill

LONGTON RISE

Hill Top

Home Farm

Gipsy Spinney

5

Windmill Barn

64

4

Greenclose Spinney

Violet Spinney

Ashpole Spinney

Gazewell Farm

Muscott

Muscott House

Gazewell Spinney

Acre Spinney

3

63

Whiltonbrook Spinney

NN7

Diamond Bridge

Brockhall

THE MEWS

Brockhall Manor

2

Grand Union Canal

The Hall

Grand Union Canal Wlk

Flore Fields Farm

Burton Wood

Butlin's Farm

Flore Fields House

1

The Dial House

A5

M1

Flore Fields Spinney

62

138 →

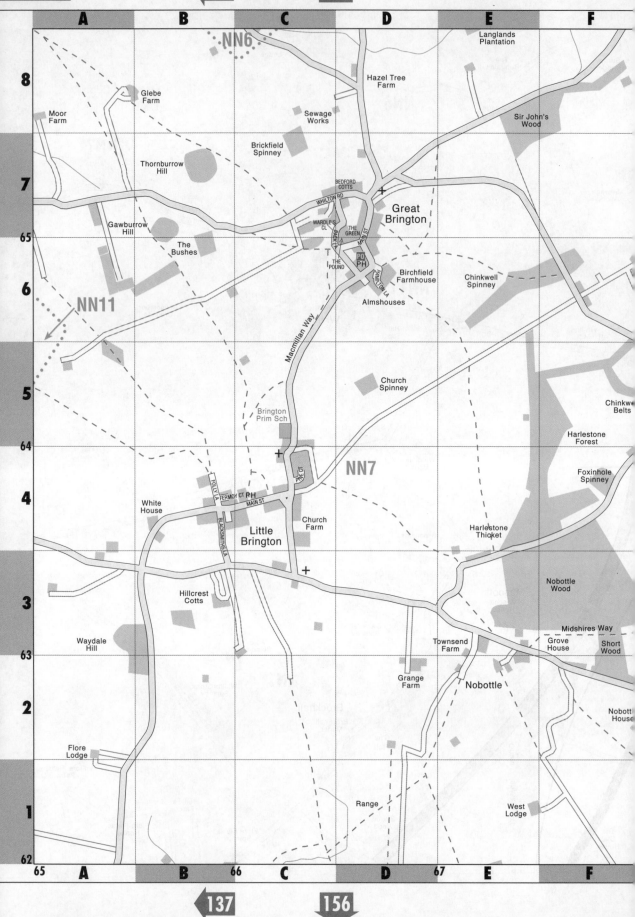

A   B   C   D   E   F

NN6

Langlands
Plantation

8

Moor
Farm

Glebe
Farm

Hazel Tree
Farm

Sir John's
Wood

Sewage
Works

Brickfield
Spinney

Thornburrow
Hill

7

BEDFORD
COTTS

Great
Brington

WHILTON RD

Gawburrow
Hill

WARDLE'S
CL

65

The
Bushes

THE
GREEN

PARK LA

MAIN ST

PO
PH

T

THE
POUND

Birchfield
Farmhouse

Chinkwell
Spinney

6

NN11

HAMILTON LA

Almshouses

Church
Spinney

Chinkwe
Belts

5

Bringhton
Prim Sch

Macmillan Way

Harlestone
Forest

64

Foxinhole
Spinney

NN7

PYKE CT

4

White
House

FOLLY LA

FERMOY CT

PH

MAIN ST

Church
Farm

Harlestone
Thicket

BLACKSMITHS LA

Little
Brington

Nobottle
Wood

3

Hillcrest
Cotts

Midshires Way

Waydale
Hill

63

Townsend
Farm

Grove
House

Short
Wood

Grange
Farm

Nobottle

Nobott
House

2

Flore
Lodge

1

Range

West
Lodge

62

A B C D E F

NN6

8

7

65

6

5

64

4

NN5

3

NN7

63

2

1

62

A428

Millholme
Plantation

Lucas's Field
Plantation

Pedigree
Buildings Farm

East
Lodge

Delf
Spinney

Glebe
Farm

Althorp

Old Lodge
Plantation

Glebe
Cotts

GLEBE LA

Dog
Pond

Althorp
Park

Three Corner
Plantation

New Park
Plantation

Oaktree
Stew

Obelisk

PARK FARM
BARNS

CHURCH LA

HARLESTONE RD

Mill

Great
Stew

Harlestone
Prim Sch

CH

30

PH

Lower
Harlestone

Chinkwell
Clumps

The Paddocks

PO

A428

Harlestone

Midshires Way

Yew Tree
Farm

THE
GREEN

Sand
Pit

Upper
Harlestone

SWEDISH
HOS

Yewtree
Spinney

Standingwell
Spinney

Round Oak
Plantation

Broadgow
Spinney

PORT RD

Fleetland
Farm

Sowditch
Thicket

Nobottle Belt

Oldfield
Thicket

Heath
Farm

BERGERAC CL

ANJOU CT

SANDY LA

TOURAINE CL

ALSACE CL

MACON CL

BEAUVAIS
CT

RICHELLE WAY

VELOCETTE
WAY

Wr Twr

Lodge
Barn

MARSEILLES CL 1
HIRONDELLE CL 2

PROVENCE CT

BEAUN
CL

NORTHAMPTON

The
Lodge

BLOSSAC
CT

ST EMILION CL

WESSEX FARM RD

ANGER CL

AQUITAINE CL

POITIERS
CT

BORDEAUX
CL

TRIUMPH GDNS

BORDEAUX
CT

BROUGH
CL

SPEEDEX

58 69 70

A B C D E F

8

Church Brampton

Manor Farm House
Brampton Brook Plantation
STABLES LA
CHURCH LA
TEN COTTS
WALKERS LA
HARLESTONE RD
GOLF LA

Brampton Grange

Boughton Mill

NORTHAMPTON RD
A5199

7

RAILWAY COTTS
Sandy La
CH
CH

NN6

PH
BRAMPTON LA
P

65

Sewage Works

Fox Covert

Meadow View

6

NN7

Midshires Way

NN2

THE AVENUE
FAIRMEAD RISE
HARROW CL
GASSDALL
WESERDALE
CEDRUS CT
SHERWOOD

WELFORD RD
A5199

5

Saw Mill

COVERDALE
FLINGDALE
DELTA CL

HARVEST WAY 1
MARTINDALE 2
ARNDALE 3
WESTERDALE 4
GLAISDALE CL 5
CROXDALE CL 6

CATTON CRES
KERSTONE CL

64

A428

Harlestone Heath

Dallington Heath

Grange Farm

4

Round Oak Plantation

NN5

3

Dallington Brook
Heath Spinney

King's Heath

SWALE DR
RIBBLE CL
WHARFE GN
HUMBER CL
TRENT CL

63

SANDY LA
ALPINE WAY
SHALE END
KNIGHTON CL
QUARRY RD
PO

HARLESTONE RD

LODGE WAY
BARN WAY
CORNHILL CL
RYEHILL

MEDWAY CL
WELLAND
NENE GN
NENE DR
EAST OVAL
PARK CRES E

2

PORT RD
PHYTONE CL
PINE COPSE CL
LORE CL
CORBIERES CL
AVIGNON CL
CHARDONNAY
DORCHESTER CF
DUSTON WILDES
LARCH LA

New Duston

THE io Centre
Lodge Farm Ind Est

SHEEP CL
GRAFTON WAY
BELVOIR CL
HILL CL
PYTCHLEY WAY
WOODLAND RD
COTTESMORE CL

Britannia Trad Ctr
MONTAGUE CRES
GODWIN
MITCHELL
PERCIVAL
SIWARD VIEW

TEVIOT CL
CONWAY WAY
TAMAR CL
COLNE WAY

CHURCH WLK
PARK CRES
NORTH OVAL
WITHAM
PARK SQ
Sch
PO

1

ST JULIEN
MICHELLE
REIMS CT
LIMOGES CT
HOLMWOOD
WYCHWOOD
ELMWOOD
BROXHOLM
DEANCROFT DR
BRETTON CL
WOODLEY CHASE
MAIN RD
PARK LA
BEAUFORT DR
GIPSY VIEW
WOODHILL CT

40

LENNOX WLK
Hopping Hill

TRESHAM CL
CHADWICK
GODING
MORDAUNT LA
KNIGHTSMOOR CL

1 ROKEBY WLK
2 STONELEIGH CHASE
3 WENLOCK WAY
Allot Gdns

WOODSIDE WLK
BROOKSIDE MDNS
PAGET HO
WOODSIDE WAY

HEATHVILLE
WAVENEY AV
MILL LA

62

VELOCETTE WAY
WRENBURY RD
PRESTBURY RD
MATCHLESS CL
ARIEL CL
RAWLEY CRES
HANDLEY AV
RYELAND WAY
RYELAND RD
GRANGE AVE
ASHCROFT CL
ELDEAN RD
NORTHFIELD RD
WHITEFIELD RD
EASTFIELD RD
LIMEHURST RD
EASTFIELD CL
DARWIN
FREEGHAM CL
MARKHAM CT
NEWTON CL
LIBERTY DR
CIRCUS END
FARNWORTH RD
OAKLEIGH DR
GOXTON CL
UPTON CL
KNIGHTSCLIFFE WAY
EDGEHILL WAY
HOPPING HILL GDNS

A428
Cemy
St Mary's RC Prim Sch

DERWENT CL
SOUTH OVAL
PARK DR

A B C D E F

F1
1 THE CROFT
1 THE BARTONS CL
2 ST MARGARET'S GDNS
3 KG House Bsns Ctr

A   B   C   D   E   F

8

Boughton Grange
Grange Farm

Boughton Hall
Butcher's La

Boughton Prim Sch

MOULTON LA

Church (remains of)
Holly Lodge

Boughton

Boughton Green

St John's Spring

7

NN6
Rectory Farm

BRAMPTON LA

Obelisk

Westleigh Pk 1
Rowley Way 2
Jackson Cl 3
Jacorrin Cl 4
Briscoe Cl 5

RED HOUSE RD   A5076

65

White Hills

LYNTON AVE

Northampton Science Pk

6

Whitehills Prim Sch

Mast

All Saints CE Mid Sch

Northants Ent Pk

KYOTO CL

Spring Park

HOLLY LODGE DR

A5076

Cemy

Sch

Northants Ent Pk

Nene Univ Coll Northampton

5

DELTA WAY

Sunnyside

1 SPENS RD
2 RHYMER HO
3 BERWICK HO
4 SILVERSTONE CL
5 BRADDEN CL
6 COURTENHALL CL

Kingsthorpe Com Coll

NN3

1 HAYCROFT WLK
2 LARWOOD C
3 SHEPHERD CL
4 COLERAINE CL

Hill Top

Allot Gdns

64

WELFORD RD

HARBOROUGH RD

1 CHEVIOT HO
2 YARROW HO
3 HAMILTON HO
4 USHER HO
5 MIDDLETON CL
6 RADSTONE WAY
7 CHARLTON CL
8 SYRESHAM WAY
9 KINGSTHORPE HO 10

GROSVENOR HO

Sch

Northampton Sch for Girls

4

NN2

PRINCESS ANNE BLDG 1
MESCALERO 2
NEWLAND SQ 3

1 BROCKHALL CL
BROCKHALL CL

1 CHURCHFIELD CL
2 BADBY CL
3 HELLIDON CL

Kingsthorpe

NBC DEPOT

3

Kingsthorpe Village Prim Sch

MANOR CT 1
OLD YEW CT 2
HIGH GN 3
TYBECK CT 4
GARFIELD HO 5

The Green

Allot Gdns

63

NN5

FREMEAUX TERR

ST DAVID'S RD

Schs

Crocket Cl

Kingsthorpe Bsns Ctr

Allot Gdns

Northgate Sch

NORTHAMPTON   CH

Allot Gdns

Kingsley Park

A5123

NN1

2

Kingsheath Workshops

Kingsfield Bsns Pk

Queens Park Ind Est

Queen's Park

Fairfields Sch

Unity Coll

Kingsthorpe Hollow

WEBBS FACTORY
Univ Coll Northampton

A5085

A5123 KETTERING RD

Phippsville

1

62

74   A   B   75   C   D   E   76   F

C3
1 CRANFORD HO
2 KINGSTHORPE SH CTR
3 ETON CT
4 STABLE CT
5 ALEXANDRA TERR
6 CRANFORD TERR
↓ 159

↓ 142

E1
1 BETHANY HOMESTEAD
2 DARDIS CL
3 KINGSLEY GDNS
4 METHODIST HOMESTEAD

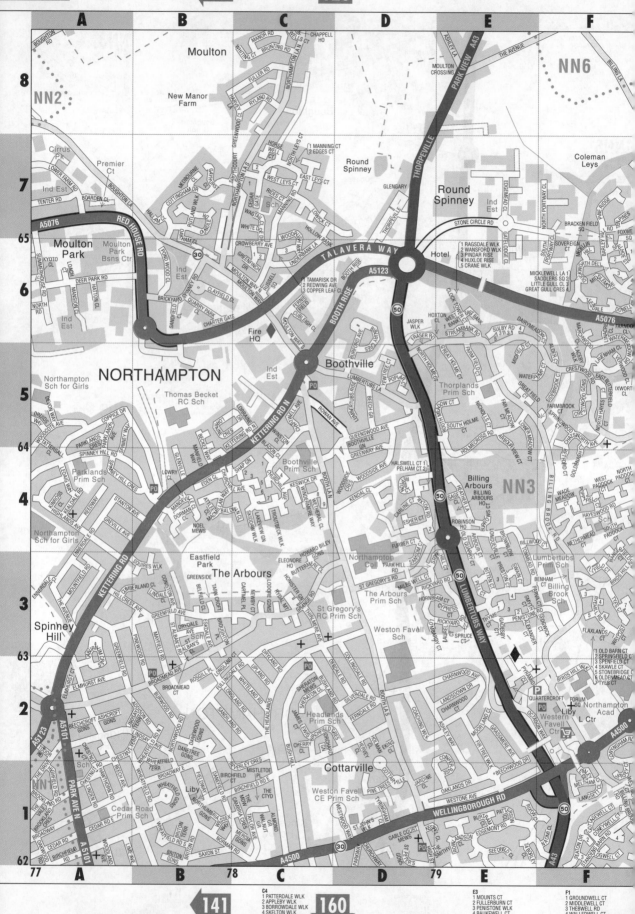

C4
1 PATTERDALE WLK
2 APPLEBY WLK
3 BORROWDALE WLK
4 SKELTON WLK
5 CALDBECK WLK
6 DALSTON WLK
7 KIRKSTONE WLK
8 LANERCOST WLK
9 AMBLESIDE CL

E3
1 MOUNTS CT
2 FULLERBURN CT
3 PENISTONE WLK
4 BAUKEWELL CT

F1
1 GROUNDWELL CT
2 MIDDLEWELL CT
3 THEBWELL RD
4 WALLEDWELL CT
5 RUNNEYMEDE GDNS

A B C D E F

8

Trafalgar Covert

Ward's Barn

Field Barn

NN8

Sywell Resr

Brookhill House

Sywell Country Park

Hockerhill Farm

Brookhill Farm

A45

7

P

Sandp Barn

P

Visitors Ctr

65

Sandwell Spinney

WASHBROOK LA

MEARS ASHBY RD

Main Road Farm

Cemy

6

Ecton East Lodge

Copplemore Barn

White House Ind Est

MAIN RD

Allot Gdns

BARTON AVE

WELLINGBOROUGH RD

TITLEY BAWK AVE

The Grange

EARLS BARTON TURN

B573

Ash Spinney

New Lodge

Elizabeth Way

MALLARD MEWS

THE PYGHTLE

BROOKSIDE

Ind Est

Grange Farm

5

Earls Barton Bridge

GRANGE

HORNBY RD

King St

Victoria St

New Barton

Ecton Lodge

NORTHAMPTON RD

TOWNLEY WAY

STREETON WAY

WHITE WAY

MANOR LA

Elizabeth CL

VICTORIA CL

PRINCE

NORTH RD

Queen St

STEVENS CT

64

A4500

BERRY CL

WEST WAY

KNIGHTS CT

HIGH ST

MANOR HOUSE CL

Nightingale Walk

Dutch Walk

HARDWICK LA

TERBUTT CL

THE DELL

CHURCHILL RD

MILLS CL

SPENCER CL

ST CRISPIN RD

NN6

AUSTINS YD

THE SQUARE

Earls Barton Jun & Inf Schs

FAIRHURST WAY

CLARKE CT

4

The Clump

WEST ST

B573

HARCOURT SQ

Liby

PO

DODDINGTON RD

B57

The Wilderness

ROSGATE WAY

PARK AVE

PARK ST

SAXON RISE

BLACKWEL CL

BROAD ST

DOWTHORPE END

CORDON CRES

BURM

KEAT

SUNNY SIDE

LONDON END

Mus

BARKER WAY

MOUNT PLEASANT

SCHEFIELD

SHURVILLE CL

MILBURY

OXFORD CL

CLAP

South Lodge

WIV SON WAY

DOWTHORPE HILL

3

Ryehill Spinney

Earls Barton

Robersacks Spinney

STATION RD

COMPTON WAY

ALLEBONE RD

Blackthorn Spinney

63

THORPE RD

Crow Spinney

Nene Way

A45

2

A45

B573

Sewage Works

Comander's Spinney

GRENDON RD

NN3

STATION RD

Sports Ground

1

Wind Spinney

NN7

River Nene

River Nene

62

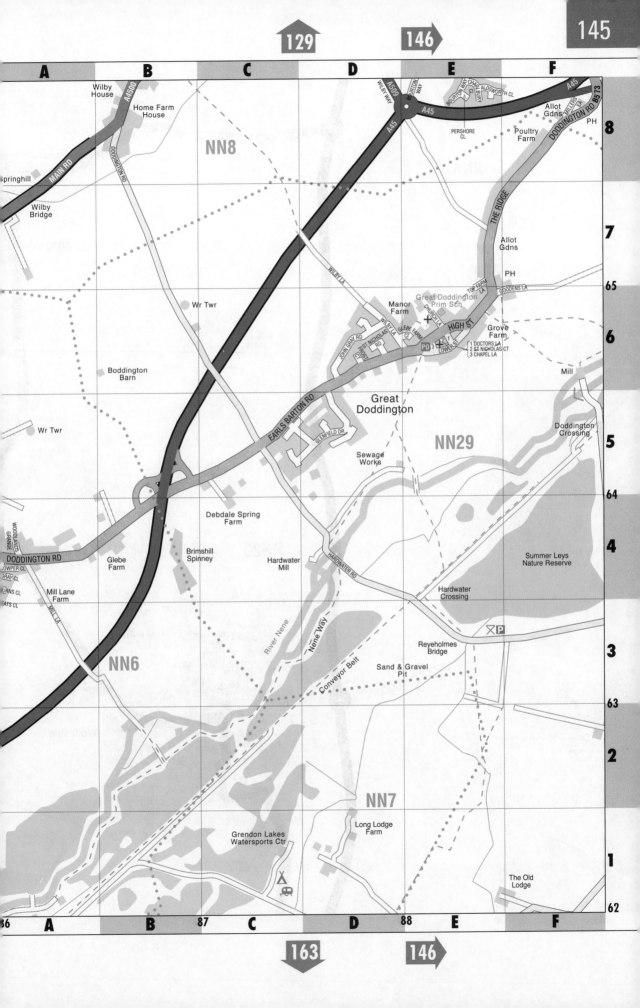

A   B   C   D   E   F

8

7

65

6

5

64

4

3

63

2

1

62

MILLERS PK
HM
Prison

NN8

Nene Way
River Nene

A509 LONDON RD

Mus
B570

Irchester Country Pk
P
GIPSY LA
BRADSHAW WAY
GIPSY LANE TURN
B570
B569

PROSPECT AVE 1
WOODLANDS RD 2

WOLLASTON RD

B569 L

Wollaston
Lodge

Vicarage
Farm

Nene
Lodge

NN29

Fox
Covert

Long
Plantation

IRCHESTER RD

Cringle Farm
Cotts

Cringle
House

FELLOWS
CL

York RD
LITTLE LA
RED HILL GRES
PRIORY RD
PROSPECT
CL
DUCK END
ABBEY RISE
MONKS RD
CHURCH LA
Prospect
Farm
1 BRAMLEY CT
2 ABBEY CT
3 THE MALTINGS

Hall

Wr Twr
Tower
Farm
TOWER CT

FRANCIS DICKINS CL

LANCASTER CL
NENE CL
UNITY CL
ROSES CL
MANCHESTER RD
2
3
ORCHARD CL
COBB'S LA
Cemy

BELL END

Wollaston
Com Prim Sch
SHELTON CT 1
ST MICHAEL'S LA 2
COUNSIL ST 3
HOWARD'S CT 4
NEWTON RD 5
Mus
HIGH ST
COLLEGE ST
SOUTH ST
BACKWAY
EASTFIELD RD
HOLYOAKE RD
THE GAP
THE HEATHERS
Wollaston
Sch
HODGKINS PATH

QUEENS RD
Liby
QUEENS RD
WINDMILL CL

Wollaston

LONDON RD
ROTTEN ROW
THRIFT ST
PO
9
HOWARD RD
STOKE CL
ST MARYS RD
PARK ST
GREEN ST
POPLAR PL

PEARSON
MEWS
HINWICK RD
PH
ST ALBANS
PL
WILLIAMS WAY
RAYMOND CL
Ind
Est
Works
HINWICK RD

Lovett's
Farm

THE
GROVE
FEAST
FIELD CL
BRIARWOOD
WAY
Works

HAZELDEN
CL
LONDO CL
THE PYGHTLES

LONDON RD
B569
A509

Allot
Gdns

SHEPHERDS HILL

A B C D E F

8

1 CHAPEL HILL
2 SHARWOOD TERR
3 ALEXANDER CT
4 ROSE CT
5 NEW STREET CT
6 WANTAGE PL
7 CRADDOCK CT

Irchester Com Prim Sch
School Hill
High St
Townwell La
Liby
Factory
School La
Bakers Cres
Alfred St
New St
Wantage Rd
Garden Fields Ct
B569
STATION RD
NORMAN WAY
Recn Gd
PO
East St
The Orchard
London End
Parsons Rd
Denton Cl
Manor Cl
Saxon Rise
Austin Cl
Arkwright Rd
EVELYN WAY
WOLLASTON RD
GRAY ST
Redwood Cl
Poplar Cl
Berrill St
Oak Cres
Ash Cl
Edward Cl
Chapmans Cl
Grange Way
Grange Cl
Swan Way
Warren Cl
James St
Prospect Ave
Clear Cl
Pine Cl
Woodlands Rd
COULON CL

Knuston High Farm

FRANCISCAN CL 1
BENEDICT CL 2
BOUGHTON DR 3

BLACKFRIARS
TRINTON
GRANGEWAY
BALHAM CL
FARNHAM CL
FARNHAM DR
ASFORD WY
STILMOND GDNS
PO
Schs

Irchester

FARNDISH RD

7

65

Irchester Grange

NN10

6

Mast

5

64

NN29

White's Barn

4

Farndish

Grange Farm

Manor Farm

Rectory Farm

IRCHESTER RD

ICHESTER RD

HINWICK RD

Wellwound Plantation

WYMINGTON RD

3

63

Wr Twr

Manor Farm

2

Long Plantation

Hall Farm House

HORNBEAM CL

OLD ST

HIGH ST

VICARAGE LA

PO

Podington

Glebe Farm

Hinwick Hall Coll of F Ed

STABLE MEWS

CORNER CL

Christopher Reeves Lower Sch

Knapwell Farm

1

Hall Lane Spinney

St Giles House

HINWICK RD

Nursery

62

92
A
B
93
C
D
94
E
F

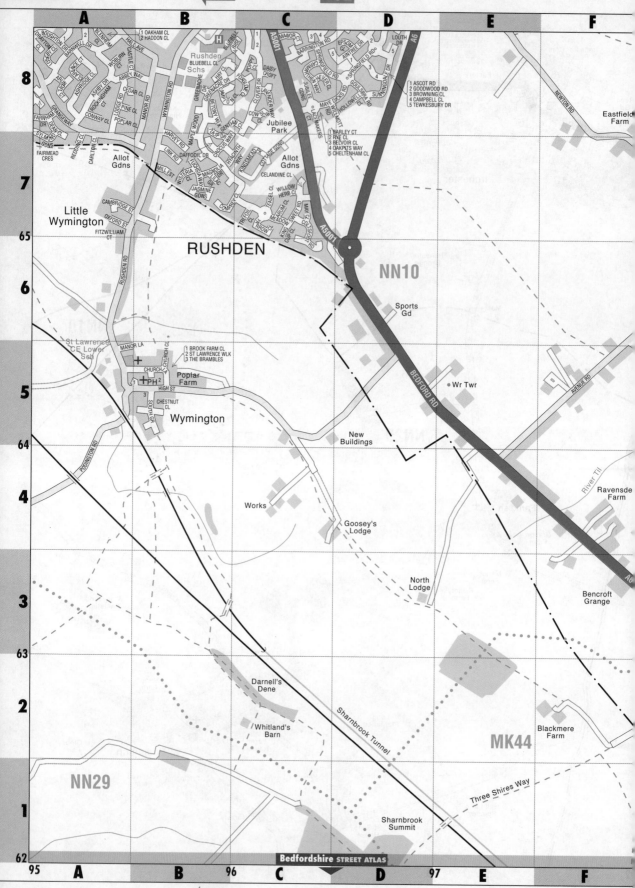

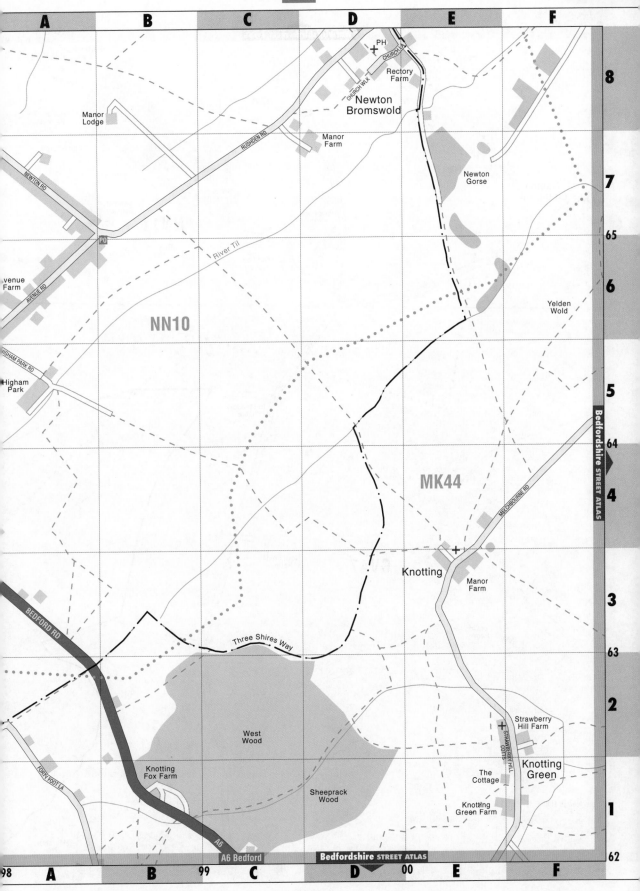

A B C D E F

8

Manor
Lodge

PH

Rectory
Farm

CHURCH WLK

CHURCH LA

Newton
Bromswold

RUSHDEN RD

Manor
Farm

Newton
Gorse

7

NEWTON RD

65

PO

6

venue
Farm

River Til

AVENUE RD

NN10

Yelden
Wold

HIGHAM PARK RD

Higham
Park

5

64

MK44

MELCHBOURNE RD

4

Knotting

Manor
Farm

BEDFORD RD

3

Three Shires Way

63

2

West
Wood

Strawberry
Hill Farm

STRAWBERRY HILL COTTS

Knotting
Green

FORTY FOOT LA

Knotting
Fox Farm

The
Cottage

Sheeprack
Wood

Knotting
Green Farm

1

A6

A6 Bedford

Bedfordshire STREET ATLAS

62

98 A B 99 C D 00 E F

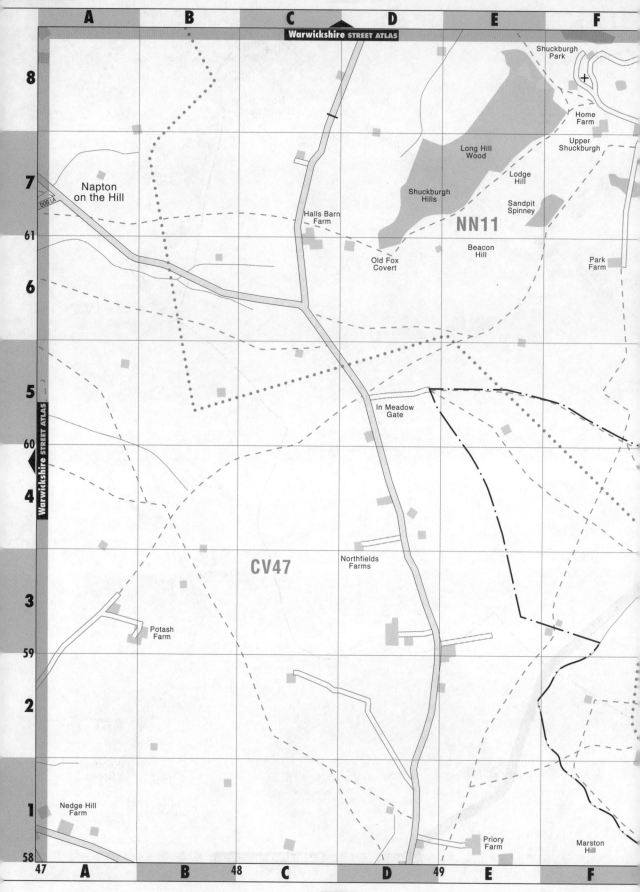

Shuckburgh
Park

Home
Farm

Long Hill
Wood

Upper
Shuckburgh

Napton
on the Hill

DOG LA

Lodge
Hill

Shuckburgh
Hills

Sandpit
Spinney

NN11

61

Halls Barn
Farm

Beacon
Hill

Park
Farm

Old Fox
Covert

6

5

In Meadow
Gate

60

4

CV47

Northfields
Farms

3

Potash
Farm

59

2

1

Nedge Hill
Farm

Priory
Farm

Marston
Hill

58

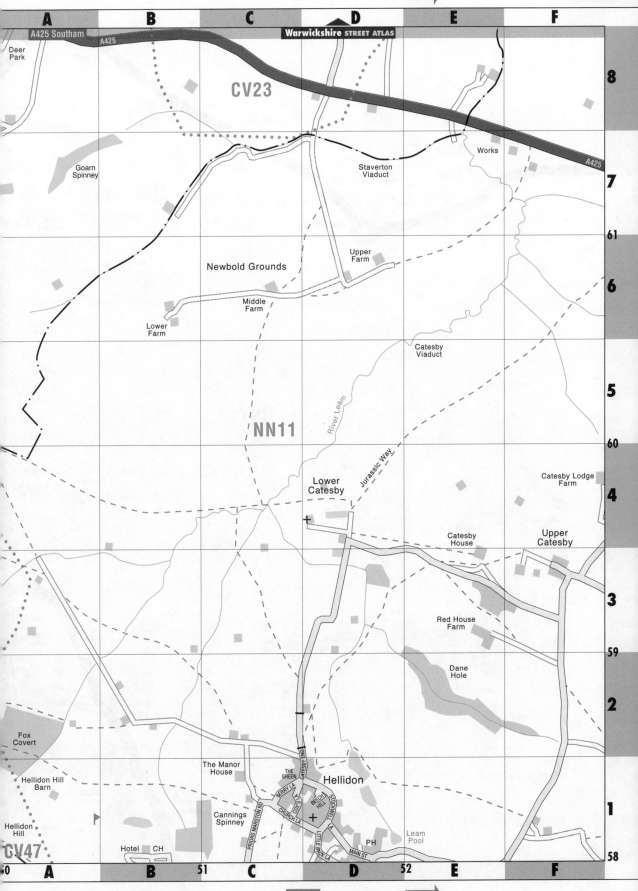

A **B** **C** **D** **E** **F**

8

Drayton
Lodge

WELLAND CL 1
THAMES RD 2
STAVERTON RD

Hall
Farm

Sewage
Works

CH

Woodhollow
Cottages

Stepnell
Spinney

Hotel

Manor
House

Staverton CE
Prim Sch

HOME CL

BRAUNSTON LA

CROFT LA

GLEBE LA

MANOR RD

DADHAM LA

WELL LA

THE WOODLANDS

Compton
Cottage

Oak
Spinne

7

A425

THE
GREEN
THE ORCHARD

PH

1 WINDMILL LA
2 WINDMILL GDNS
3 CHURCH FIELDS

DAVENTRY RD

PO
1
2
CHURCH
DAVENTRY RD
3

Staverton
Clump

Staverton
Wood

Big Hill

Pond
Spinney

Staverton Hill
Farm

Mast

Staverton
Acres

Staverton

61

Bates
Farm

Broiler Breeder
Farm

Jurassic Way

Vine Tree
Farm

Sports
Gd

Badby Lodge
Farm

6

Staverton
Fields

Markleys

NN11

Badby
Fields

5

60

Bridge Hill
Farm

4

Studborough
Hill

Studborough
Clump

Longridge
Farm

Staverton
Lodge

Barehill
Farm

ORCHARD
CL

PH

Badby
Sch

PINGELD RD

POND LA

SCHOOL LA

3

59

Arbury
Hill

STONE WAY

MAIN ST

VICARAGE
HILL

BUNKERS HILL

CHURCH HILL

2

Highfield
Farm

Haycock Hill
Farm

Konigssee
Farm

The
Beeches

Badby
Plantation

A361

Badby
Down

1

58

53 **A** 54 **B** **C** 54 **D** 55 **E** **F**

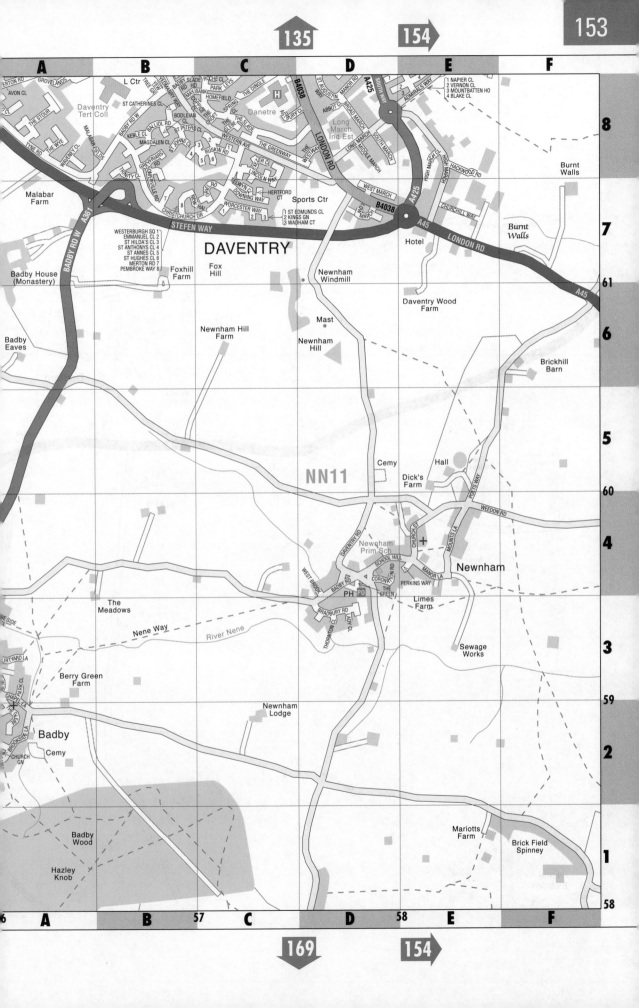

153
136

A B C D E F

8

Borough Hill Farm

Dodford Holt

Dodford Lodge

Hill Farm

7

Newnham Grange Farm

Wagoners Cottage

Newnham Grange

61

Lower Farm

A45

6

Willow End

Brookfield Farm

Dodford

THE GREEN

Manor House

HILLTOP

5

Grange Farm

A45

Newnham Grounds

The Cottages

Four Views

60

NN11

NN7

4

Newnham Lodge

Dodford Mill Farm

ORDNANCE RD

3

River Nene

59

Dairy Farm

QUEEN ST

2

Nene Way

1

Everdon Hall

Little Everdon

Home Farm

FARTHINGSTONE RD

58

59 A B 60 C D 61 E F

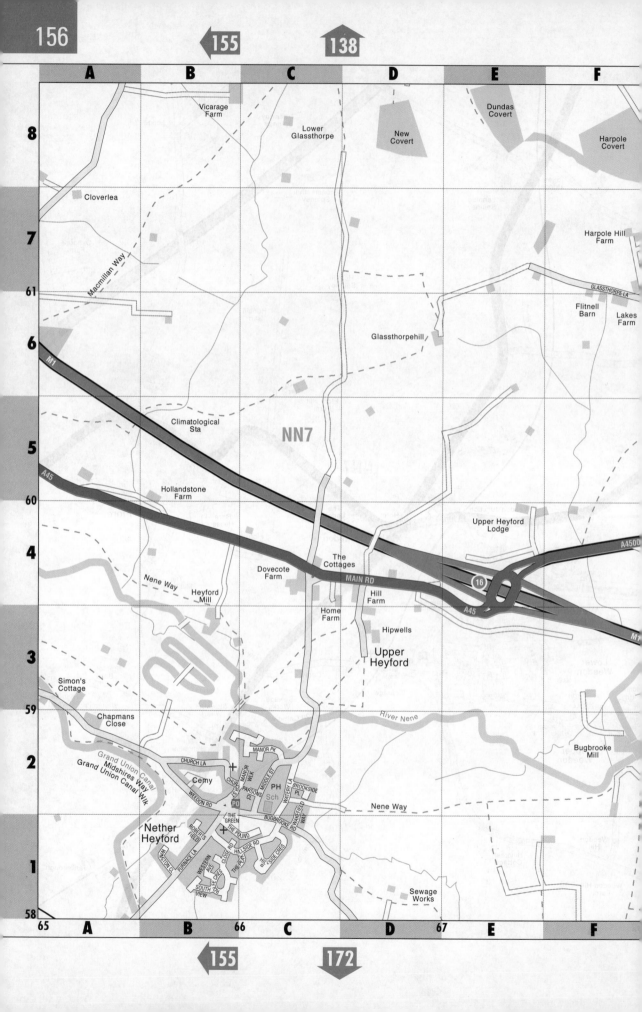

A B C D E F

Brices
Spinney

Wood
Farm

Harpole
Grange

VIENNE CL
WEGGS FARM RD
MARTEL CL
PLIDGE MEWS
WRIGHT RD

EXCELSIOR GDNS 1
DOUGLAS RD 2
GRIFFITHS CL 3

BERRYWOOD RD

VINCENT CL
ENFIELD
LUKE'S
ST

8

HEFFORD RD
DENT
LOWAN RD
LD DR
HOLYOAK RD

MANOR
CRES

61

NORTH MEADOW

7

MOUNT PLEASANT WAY
UPPER HIGH ST
LARKHALL WAY
GARNERS WAY
CORY GDNS

Norwood
Farm

SANDY LA

NN5

CHESTER AVE
SCHOOL LA
THE MOTTS
GLASSTHORPE LA
MANOR CL
ORCHARD WAY
CARR'S WAY
SHEPHERDS WLK
Harpole
Prim Sch

LARKHALL LA

6

HALL CL
DUCK LA
HIGH ST
PO
PARK LA
Hall

Harpole

The
Lake

NORTHAMPTON RD

PH

Hotel
WEEDON RD
SOUTH VIEW
A4500

5

NN7

60

Sewage
Works

River Nene

RIVERSIDE CT

Old
Rectory

Kislingbury

4

PH

PH
HODGES LA
BEECH LA

PH Sch
SCHOOL LA
HA'
CL

WEIR

Harpole Mill
(dis)

PO
STARMERS LA
THE ORCHARD
CHURCH LA
LICHFIELD CL

Weir

Nene Way

TWIN VIEW
NENE WAY
MILL RD
MILL LA
THE GREEN

CAMP LA

3

Weir

DUKES GREEN RD
BUGBROOKE RD
ASHBY CT
TWIGDEN RD

ROTHERSTHORPE RD

59

MILLER'S CL

Mill
Cottages

Works

2

Island
Barn

JOHNS RD

1

M1

58

68 A B 69 C D 70 E F

A B C D E F

8

7

61

6

5

60

4

NN7

3

59

2

1

58

71 A 72 B C 72 D 73 E F

The Duston Sch

Berry Wood

Cemy

Duston

1 BEECHWOOD RD
2 POND FARM CL
3 STARMER'S YD
4 SQUIRREL LA
5 GOUGHS COTTS

1 EDINBURGH HO
2 LIMEHURST SQ
3 WINDSOR HO
4 GIFFORD CT
5 STEPHEN BENNETT CL
6 ROSETTE CL

Liby

INGLEBOROUGH WAY

Chiltern Prim Sch

Dallington

HARLESTONE RD

WARWICK HO
HARLESTONE CT

Lyncrest Prim Sch

St Luke's CE Prim Sch

Millway Prim Sch

Hospital Farm

Princess Marina

Upton Lodge

Ind Est

Superstore

The Bsns Ctr

WEEDON RD

WEEDON RD

Upton

NN5

Quinton House Sch

Park House

Hotel

Sixfields L Complex

Northampton Town FC

Sixfields Stad

EDGAR MOBBS WAY

CLICKERS PL

CLICKERS DR

BLACK CAT DR

Upton Hall Farm

Bottom Spinney

Upton Mill

Nene Way

RAINSBOROUGH CRES

NEWSTONE CRES

Duston Mill (dis)

Works

1 TOWER HILL CL
2 TALLYFIELD END
3 CHEVIOT CT
4 LANGLEY CL
5 LIMLOW CL

UPTON WAY

Briar Hill

NN4

Camp Hill

Hunsbury Hill Spinney

DANES CAMP WAY

A5076

River Nene

BLY LA

1 MILLSTONE CL
2 COBBLESTONE CT
3 BRINDLESTONE CL
4 DAPPLESTONE CL
5 QUARTERSTONE

Pineham Barn

Mus

Hunsbury Hill

Hupsbury Park Prim Sch

Hunsbury Hill Country Park

1 WHITESANDS WAY
6 CAULDECOTT CL
7 LYNMORE CL
8 KEYSTONE

SWAN VALLEY WAY

M1

A5123

A4500

A5076

TOWCESTER RD

YEOMAN MDW

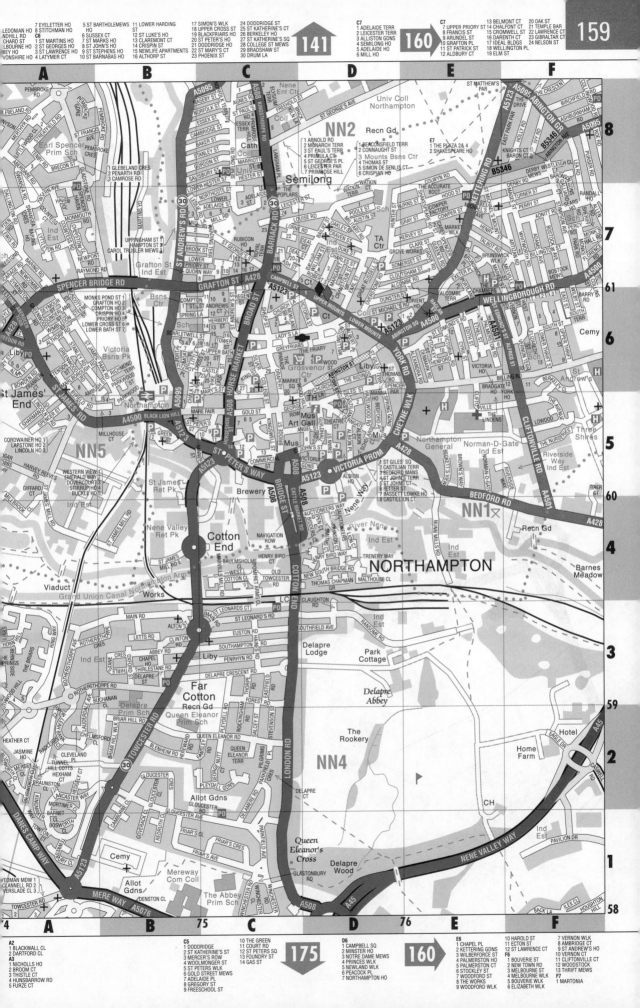

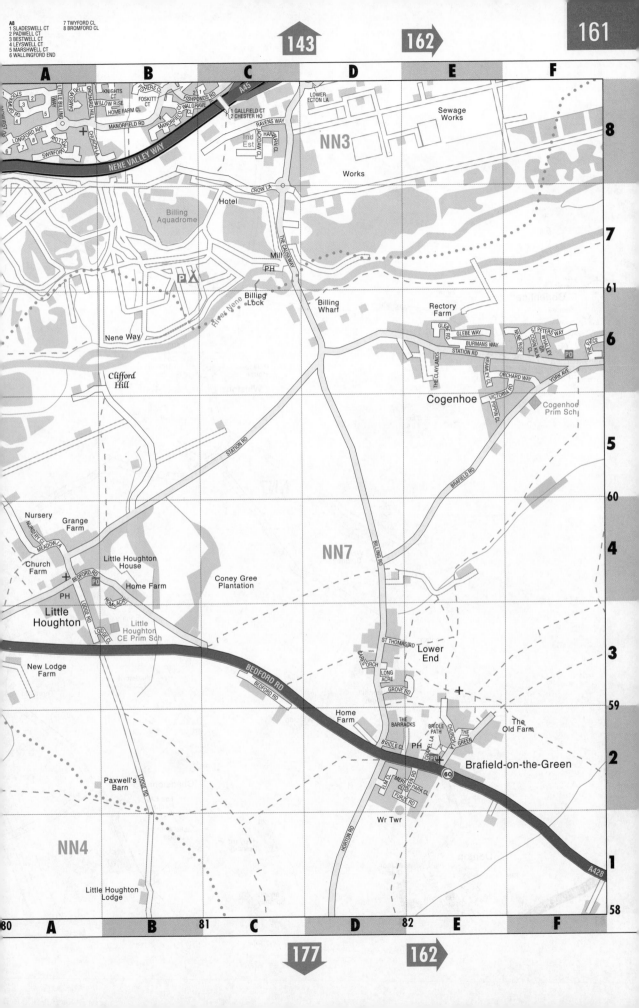

AB
1 SLADESWELL CT
2 PADWELL CT
3 BESTWELL CT
4 LEYSWELL CT
5 MARSHWELL CT
6 WALLINGFORD END
7 TWYFORD CL
8 BROMFORD CL

A B C D E F

143   162

8

NN3

Sewage
Works

Works

Hotel

7

Billing
Aquadrome

CROW LA

THE CAUSEWAY

61

Mill

PH

Billing
Lock

Billing
Wharf

Rectory
Farm

GLEBE RD
GLEBE WAY
BURMANS WAY

ST PETERS WAY
WHITLEY
COTTON MILL CL
NENE RISE

THE PIECE

PO

6

Nene Way

RAVENS WAY

LOWER
ECTON LA

Ind
Est

1 GALLFIELD CT
2 CHESTER HO

HARBOUR CL

JACKDAW LA

A45

NENE VALLEY WAY

River Nene

P

Clifford
Hill

THE CLAYLANDS
BRAMLEY CL

VICTORIA ST
PIPPIN CL

ORCHARD WAY
YORK AVE

Cogenhoe
Prim Sch

Cogenhoe

STATION RD

5

STATION RD

BRAFIELD RD

60

Nursery

Grange
Farm

NN7

BILLING RD

4

Church
Farm

Little Houghton
House

Home Farm

Coney Gree
Plantation

MEADOW LA
NURSERY CL

BEDFORD RD
PO
HOME ACRE

Little
Houghton

Little
Houghton
CE Prim Sch

LODGE RD
LODGE CL

PH

St Thomas RD
CARE's ORCH

Lower
End

LONG
ACRE

GROVE RD

3

New Lodge
Farm

BEDFORD RD
BEDFORD RD

Home
Farm

The
Barracks

BRIDLE
PATH

The Old
Farm

59

BRIDLE CL
PH

CHAPEL LA

THE
GREEN

CHURCH RD

Brafield-on-the-Green

60

2

Paxwell's
Barn

LODGE RD

ELM CL

MERE
CL
GREEN RD

FURZE RD

CHURCH RD
PARK CL

PO

HORTON RD

Wr Twr

NN4

A428

1

Little Houghton
Lodge

58

80   A   B   81   C   D   82   E   F

177   162

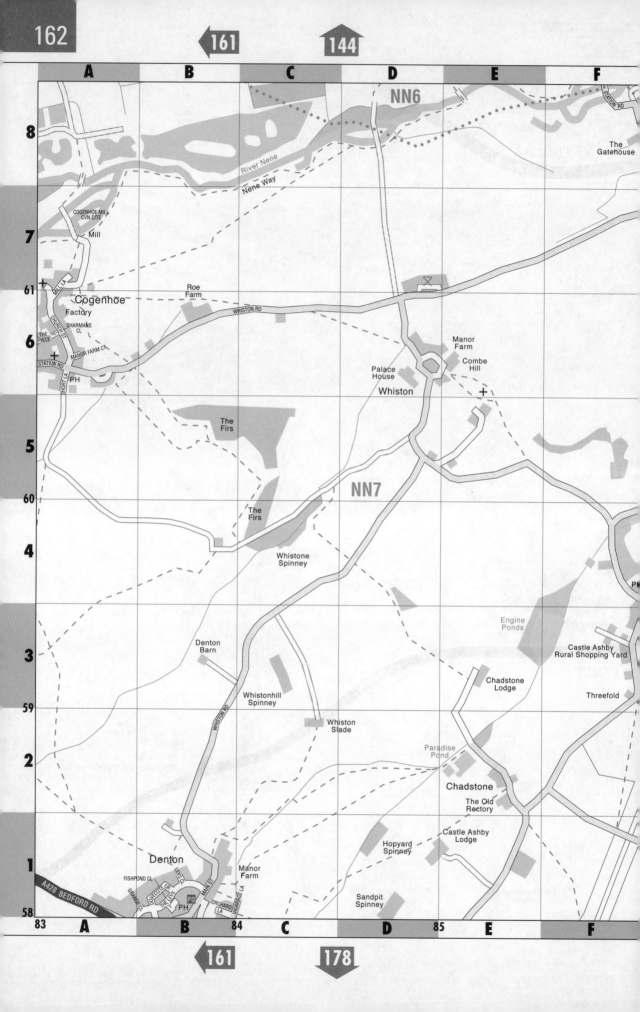

A B C D E F

8

NN6

The Gatehouse

STATION RD

River Nene

Nene Way

Cogenhoe Mill
CVN CITE

Mill

7

61

Roe Farm

Cogenhoe

Factory

WHISTON RD

SHARMANS CL

THE PIECE

CHURCH ST

MANOR FARM CT

6

STATION RD

SHORT LA

PH

Manor Farm

Combe Hill

Palace House

Whiston

The Firs

5

60

NN7

The Firs

4

Whistone Spinney

Engine Ponds

Castle Ashby Rural Shopping Yard

Denton Barn

3

Chadstone Lodge

Threefold

Whistonhill Spinney

WHISTON RD

59

Whiston Slade

Paradise Pond

2

Chadstone

The Old Rectory

Castle Ashby Lodge

Denton

Manor Farm

Hopyard Spinney

1

FISHPOND CL

LEYS CL

MAIN ST

VICARAGE LA

ORCHARD LA

THE LEYS

FOXCOTE CL

GRANGE CL

PO

PH

A428 BEDFORD RD

Sandpit Spinney

58

83 A 84 B C D 85 E F

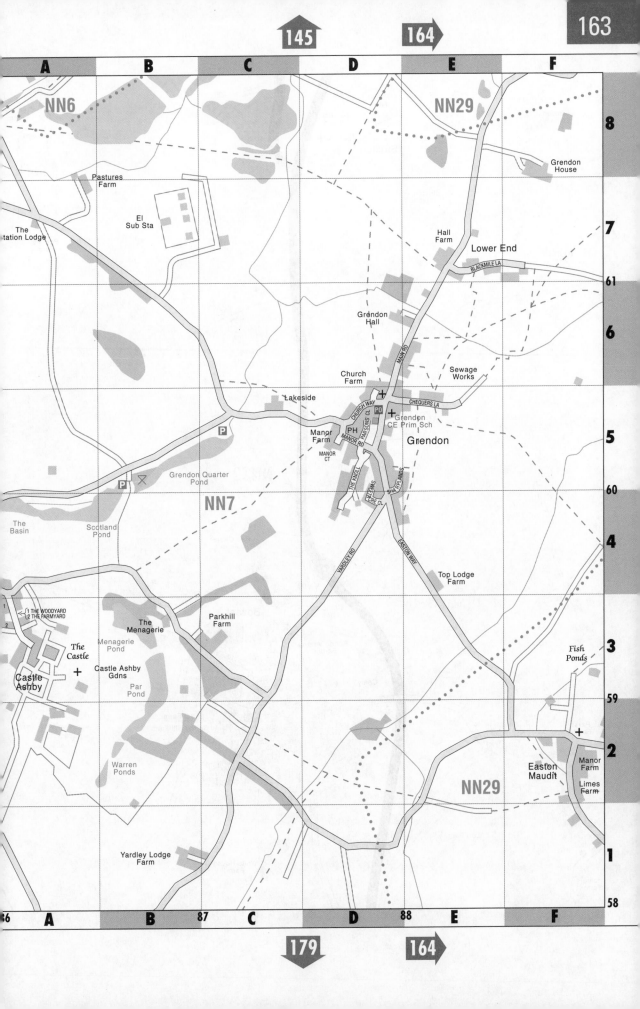

A B C D E F

NN6

NN29

8

Pastures
Farm

Grendon
House

El
Sub Sta

The
Station Lodge

Hall
Farm

7

Lower End

BLACKMILE LA

61

Grendon
Hall

6

Sewage
Works

Church
Farm

Lakeside

CHEQUERS LA

P

PO

Grendon
CE Prim Sch

5

Manor
Farm

PH

MANOR RD

PARSONS CL

CHURCH WAY

Grendon

MANOR
CT

Grendon Quarter
Pond

THE KNOLL

SHARTLANDS

60

P

NN7

PRE CL

NEEMS

The
Basin

Scotland
Pond

EASTON WAY

4

YARDLEY RD

1 THE WOODYARD
2 THE FARMYARD

Top Lodge
Farm

1

Fish
Ponds

3

2

The Menagerie

Parkhill
Farm

Menagerie
Pond

The
Castle

Castle Ashby
Gdns

59

Castle
Ashby

Par
Pond

Manor
Farm

2

Warren
Ponds

Easton
Maudit

Limes
Farm

NN29

1

Yardley Lodge
Farm

58

86 A B 87 C D 88 E F

163
146

A **B** **C** **D** **E** **F**

8

Hillmount
Spinney

Manor
Farm

Church
Farm

Strixton Manor
Bsns Ctr

Strixton

Lodge
Farm

SHEPHERDS HILL

A509

B569

B569

Strixton
Plantation

7

NN7

Poplars
Farm

61

6

Greenfield
Lodge

WOLLASTON RD

5

NN29

60

4

Red Gables
Farm

FULLWELL RD

HOPE ST

Church
Farm

COUNCIL ST

BULL CL

ALLENS HILL

PEAR TREE CL

Glebe
Farm

Three Fields
Farm

Bozeat

1 CHURCH FARM CL
2 PUDDING BAG LA
3 THE ORCHARD
4 BURTON TERR

Spring Vale
Farm

MALLOWS CL

CHURCH WLK

HARROLD RD

3

Slype
Farm

HENSMANS LA

MILE ST

LONDON RD

Bozeat Com
Prim Sch

DYCHURCH LA

Cemy

BURLEIGH
TERR

HIGH ST

MANOR CL

59

EASTON LA

PH

Park
Farm

STONEY
PIECE
CL

SELBY
GDNS

WYMAN RD

ST HEWLETT'S CL

WRIGHTS CL

GOFFS
YD

East Farm

DAG LA

BROADSIDE

Spring Hill Farm

2

ABBEY CL

MILL RD

DUERY ST

CLAYLAND
CL

ROBERTS ST

ST MARY'S RD

HILLSIDE CL

FIR TREE GR

LITTLE CL

5 WARNERS HILL
6 CAMDEN SQ
7 WHEELRIGHTS YD
8 SPENCER GDNS
9 COBBLER'S PL

Low Farm

1

White House
Farm

A509

Home
Farm

58

89 **A** **B** 90 **C** **D** 91 **E** **F**

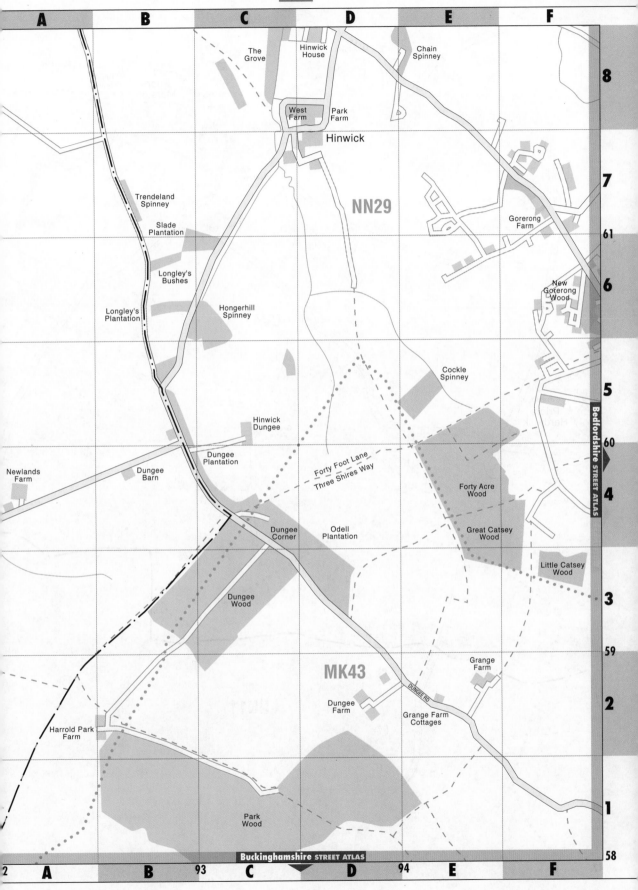

The Grove
Hinwick House
Chain Spinney
West Farm
Park Farm
Hinwick

NN29

Trendeland Spinney
Slade Plantation
Gorerong Farm

Longley's Bushes
New Gorerong Wood

Longley's Plantation
Hongerhill Spinney

Cockle Spinney

Hinwick Dungee
Dungee Plantation

Newlands Farm
Dungee Barn
Forty Foot Lane
Three Shires Way
Forty Acre Wood

60

Dungee Corner
Odell Plantation
Great Catsey Wood

Little Catsey Wood

Dungee Wood

59

MK43
Grange Farm

Dungee Farm
Grange Farm Cottages

DUNGEE RD

Harrold Park Farm

Park Wood

58

93
94

The Meadows

TURVINS MDW

PO

Priors Marston

Hill Farm

Marston Hill

The Priors Sch

ST LEONARDS CL 1
WESTFIELD BARNS 2

PH

Westover Farm

Chestnuts Farm

Manor Farm

Sewage Works

CV47

St MARY'S CL

Church End

THE CLOISTERS

Priors Hardwick

PH

AGRICULTURAL HOS

Grange Farm

London End

WELSH RD

The Old Vicarage

Rump Hall

Fields Farm

NN11

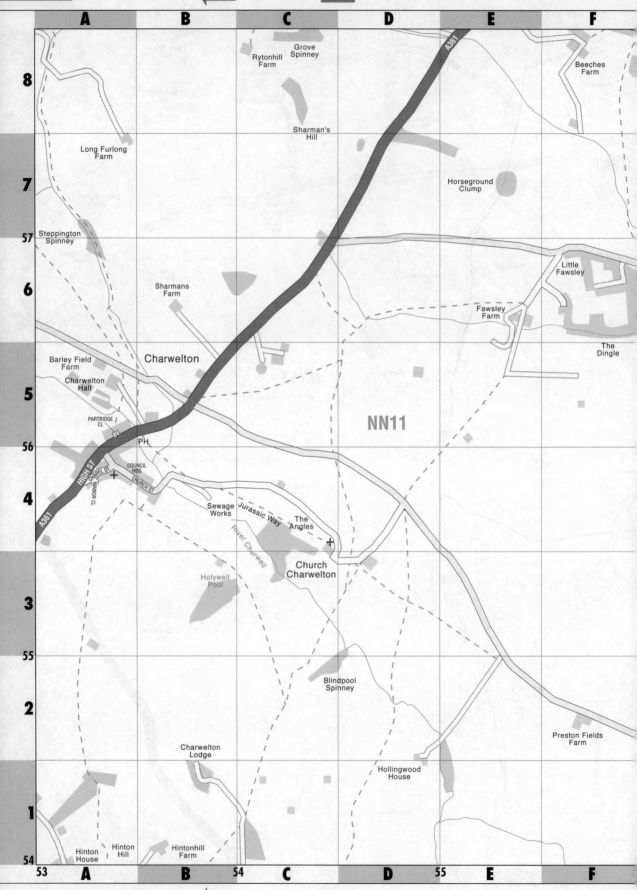

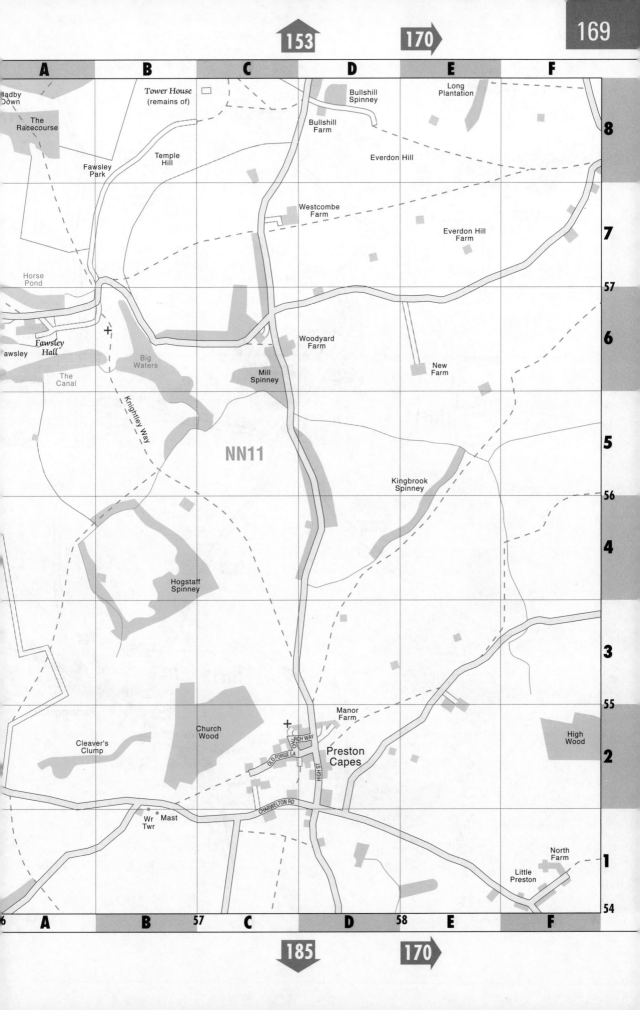

A   B   C   D   E   F

8

Nene Way

Everdon

Weedon Villa

Sewage Works

Weedon Lodge Cottage

LONG ROW CL.

FAWSLEY RD   THE GREEN

SCHOOL LA

HIGH ST   WELL LA

PH

College Farm

BETHEL LA

STUBBS RD

The Manor House

Weedon Lodge

NN7

Fern Hollow

FARTHINGSTONE RD

7

Wood Farm

Joban

57

6

Everdon Wood

Everdon Stubbs Woodland Trust Wood

Castle Dykes

Snorscomb Mill

Everdon Stubbs Nature Trail

Castle Dyke Farm

Meg Spinney

NN11

Wr Twr

Farthingstone Heath

Snorscomb

5

56

Snorscomb Farm

Cockcrow Spinney

4

Fernhill Lodge

Hen Wood

3

Mantles Heath

Hotel   CH

Knightley Way

NN12

Park Farm

COUNCIL HOS 1
MANOR GDNS 2
CATTLE E 3

Manor Farm

EVERDON RD

LITCHBOROUGH RD

WEEDON RD

PH

MAIN ST

Earls Farm

55

Church Farm

Farthingstone

High Wood

2

Macmillan Way

Little Court

Littlecourt Yard

MAIDFORD RD

Little Court Farm

Knightley Wood

Cemy

Glebe Farm

1

54

59   A   B   **60**   C   D   **61**   E   F

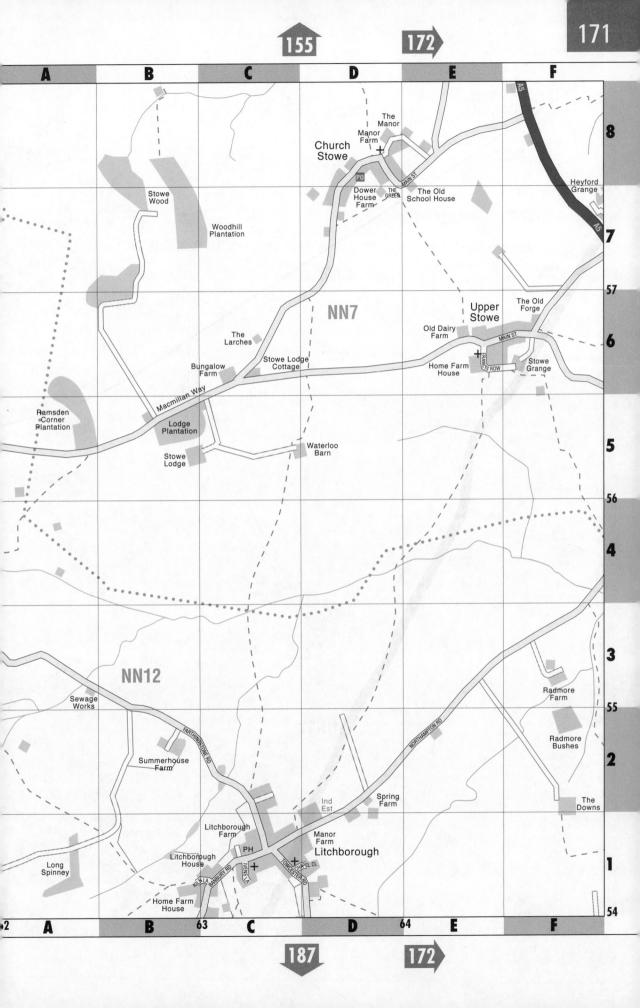

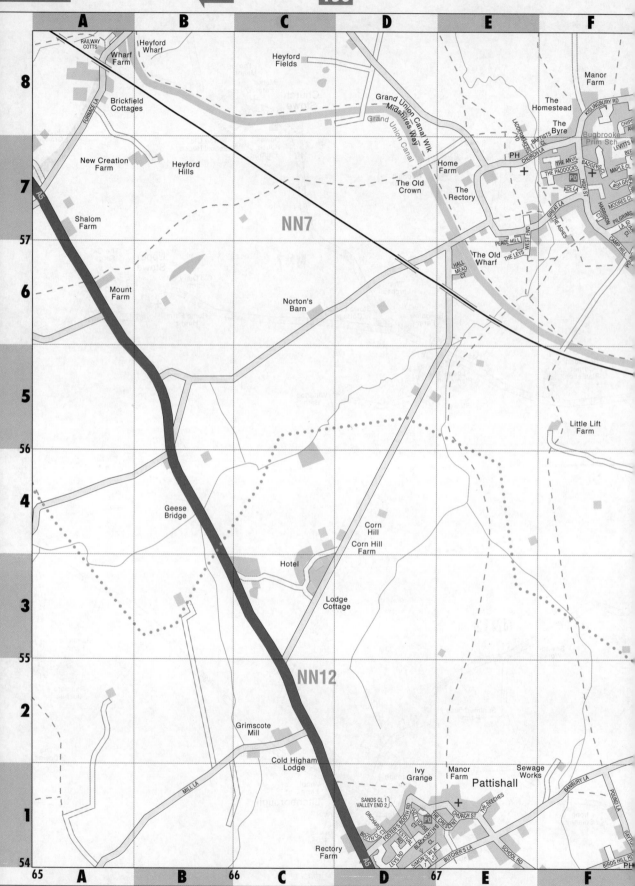

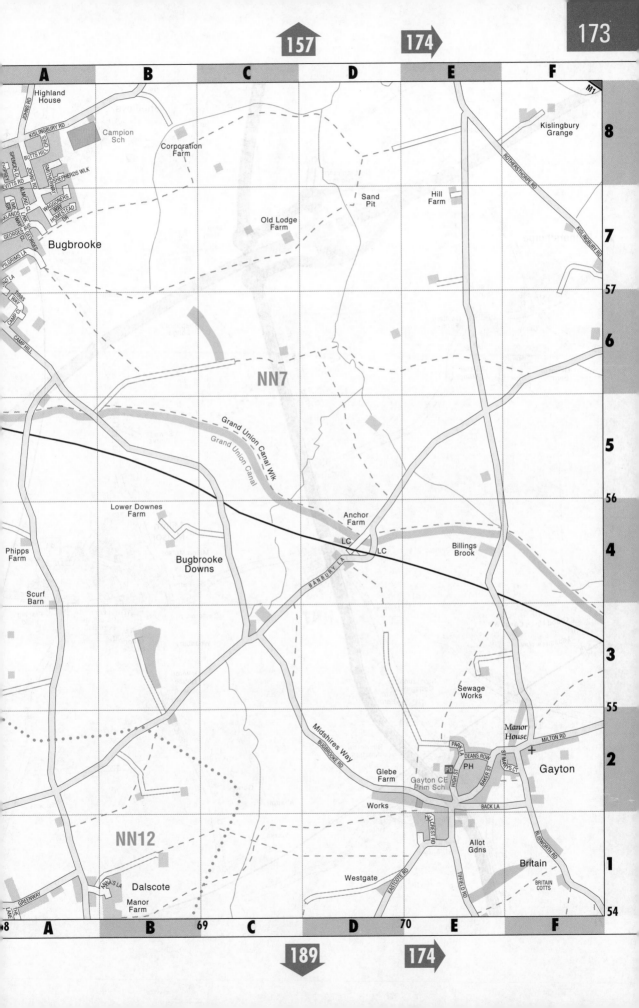

175
160

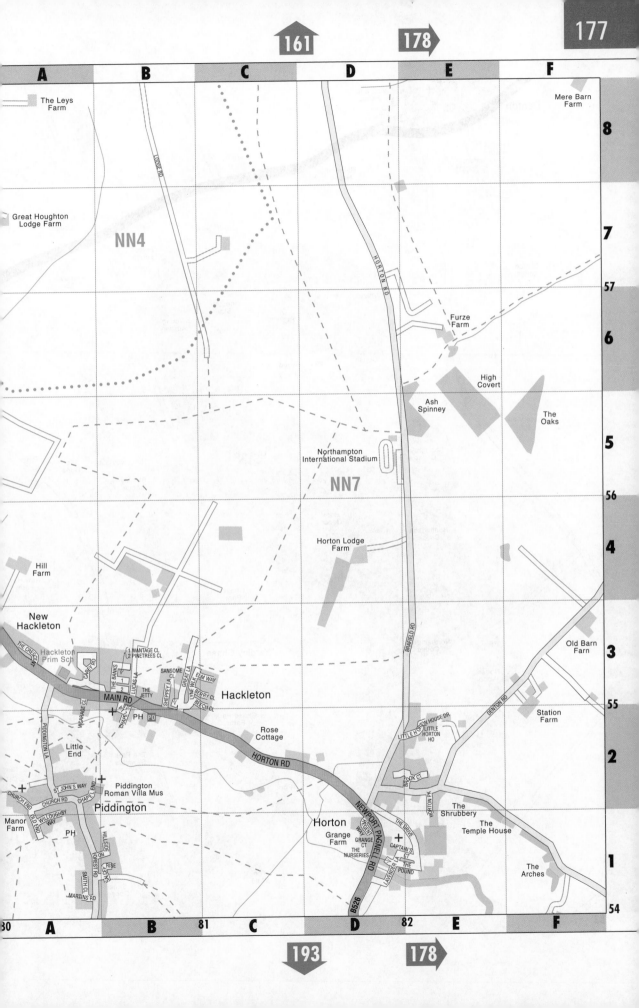

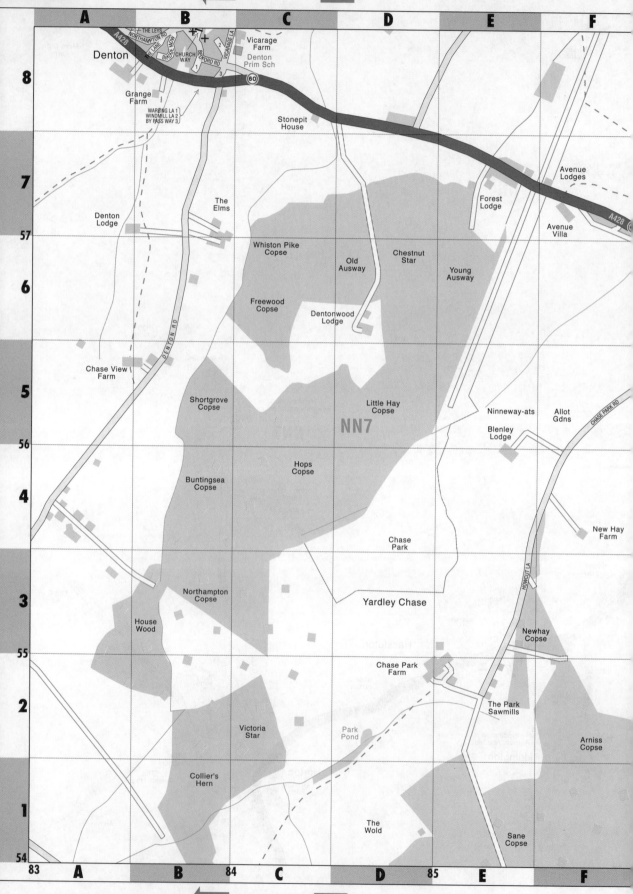

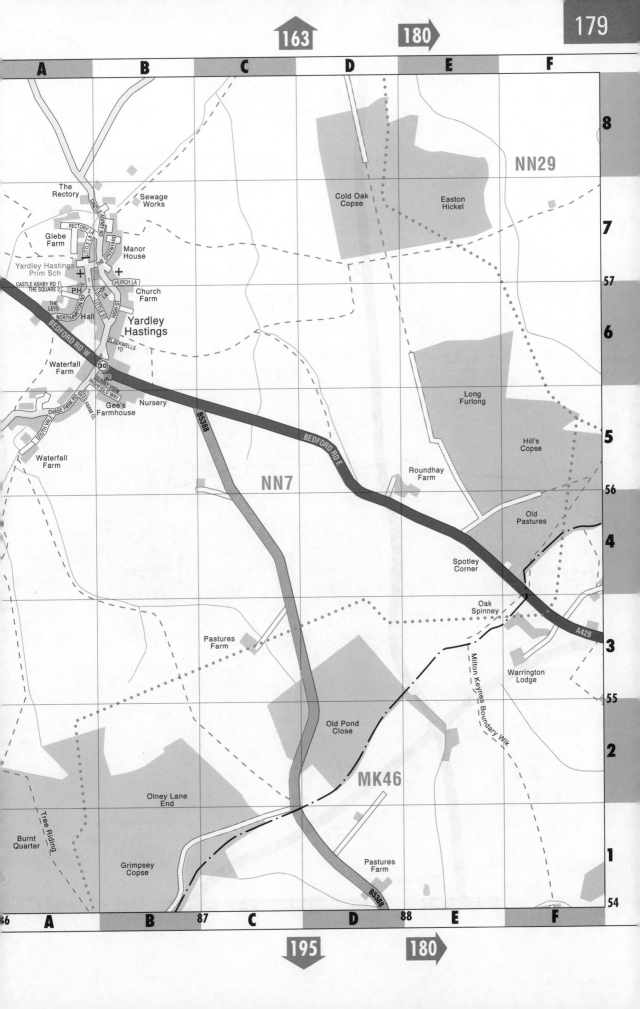

A B C D E F

8

NN29

The Rectory

Sewage Works

Cold Oak Copse

Easton Hickel

7

57

Glebe Farm

RECTORY LA

CASTLE ASHBY RD

THE GREENYARD

LITTLE LA

Manor House

Yardley Hastings Prim Sch

CASTLE ASHBY RD 1

THE SQUARE 2

CHURCH LA

57

PH

SHOP LA

Church Farm

THE LEYS

NORTHAMPTON RD

LITTLE ST

HIGH ST

Hall

Yardley Hastings

6

BLACKWELLS YD

Waterfall Farm

30

PO

BEDFORD RD W

SUNNY VIEW

HIGHFIELD WAY

Nursery

Long Furlong

Hill's Copse

5

CHASE PARK RD

GEES FARM CL

SOUTH VALE RD

Gee's Farmhouse

B5388

BEDFORD RD E

Roundhay Farm

Old Pastures

56

Waterfall Farm

NN7

56

Spotley Corner

4

Pastures Farm

Oak Spinney

A428

3

Warrington Lodge

Milton Keynes Boundary Wlk

55

Old Pond Close

MK46

2

Olney Lane End

Tree Riding

Burnt Quarter

Grimpsey Copse

Pastures Farm

B5388

1

54

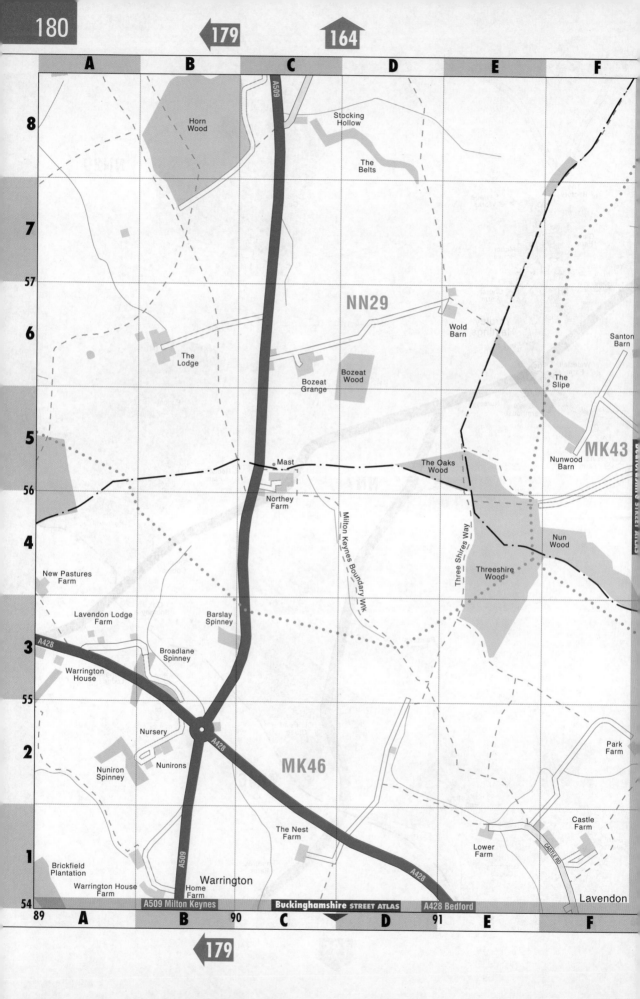

A B C D E F

8

7

57

6

NN29

5

56

Horn
Wood

Stocking
Hollow

The
Belts

A509

Wold
Barn

Santon
Barn

The
Slip

The Lodge

Bozeat
Wood

Bozeat
Grange

Nunwood
Barn

MK43

Mast

The Oaks
Wood

Northey
Farm

Nun
Wood

4

New Pastures
Farm

Milton Keynes Boundary Wlk

Three Shires Way

Threeshire
Wood

Lavendon Lodge
Farm

Barslay
Spinney

3

A428

Broadlane
Spinney

Warrington
House

55

Park
Farm

2

Nursery

Nunirons

MK46

A428

Nuniron
Spinney

Lower
Farm

Castle
Farm

CASTLE RD

1

The Nest
Farm

Brickfield
Plantation

Warrington House
Farm

Warrington

Home
Farm

A509

A428

A428 Bedford

Lavendon

54

89   A   B   90   C   D   91   E   F

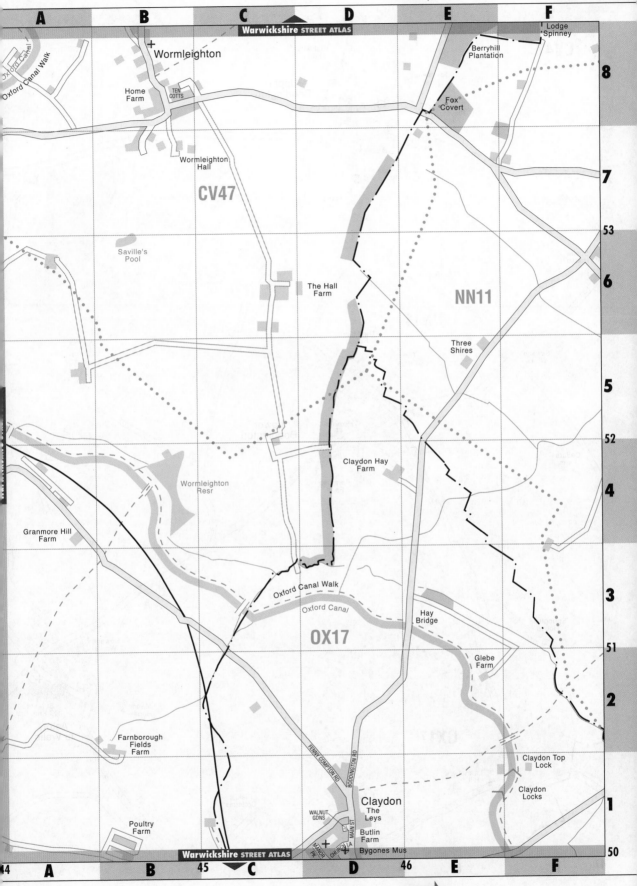

Warwickshire STREET ATLAS

A B C D E F

8

Lodge
Spinney

Berryhill
Plantation

Wormleighton

Home
Farm

TEN
COTTS

Oxford Canal Walk

Fox
Covert

Wormleighton
Hall

CV47

7

53

Saville's
Pool

The Hall
Farm

NN11

6

Three
Shires

5

52

Claydon Hay
Farm

4

Wormleighton
Resr

Granmore Hill
Farm

Oxford Canal Walk

Oxford Canal

OX17

Hay
Bridge

3

51

Glebe
Farm

2

Farnborough
Fields
Farm

FENNY COMPTON RD

BODDINGTON RD

Claydon Top
Lock

Claydon
Locks

Poultry
Farm

Claydon
The
Leys

WALNUT
GDNS

MANOR
PK

CHURCH LA

MAIN ST

Butlin
Farm

Bygones Mus

1

50

44 A B 45 C D 46 E F

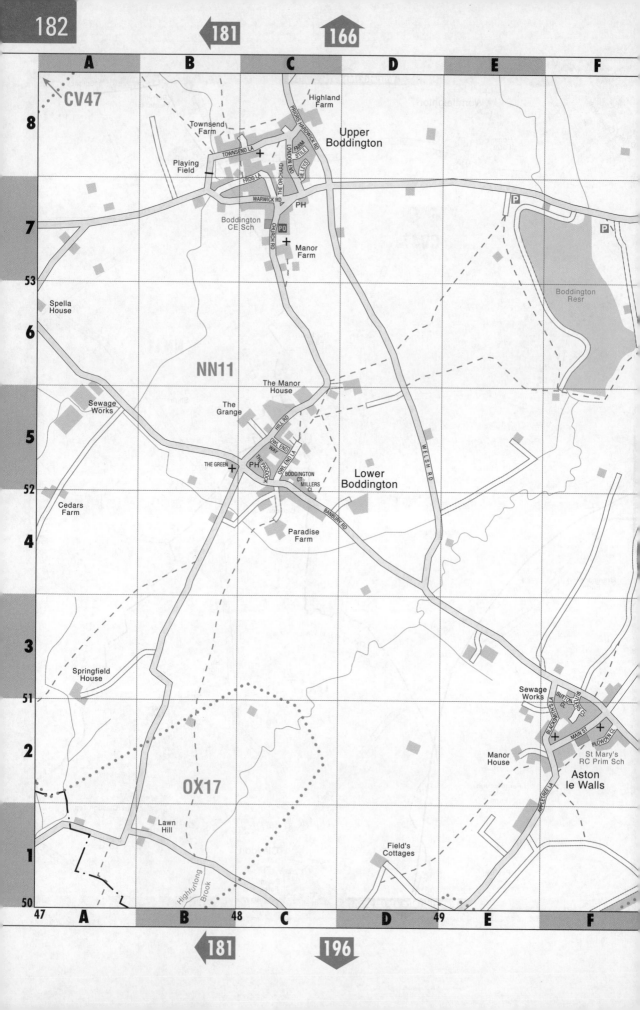

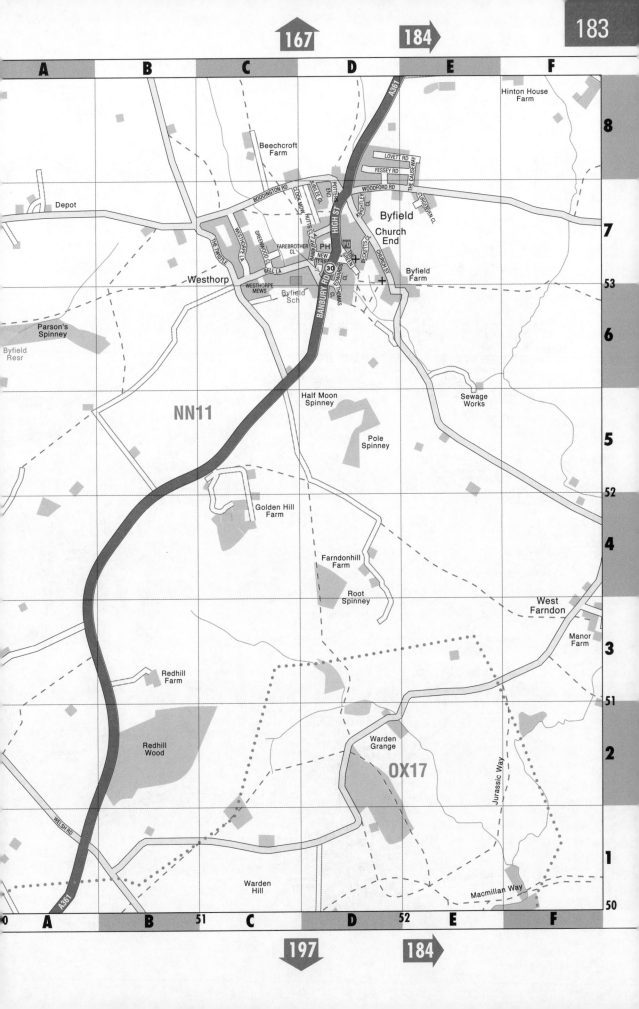

A   B   C   D   E   F

8

7

53

6

5

52

4

3

51

2

1

50

The Beaver
Ctr

BLUEBELL
CL

Mast

FAY CL
DRYDEN CL

BYFIELD RD

Woodford
Halse

Liby

SCHOOL ST

SCRIVENS HILL

Foxhill
Farm

Hinton

CHESTNUT
CL

HAWTHORNE
CL

KINGFISHER
CL

Woodford Halse
CE Sch

MOUNT
PLEASANT

PH

COBLEY CL

Woodford Hill
Farm

Woodfor
Hill

Pool Farm
Ct

BROMLEY
FARM
CT

POOL CL

Gravel
Farm

1 EBONY CT
2 STATION CT
3 KINGS CORNER CL

River Cherwell

Jurassic Way

Sewage
Works

NN11

Gravelfield
Barn

Dairy
Farm

Cherry
Tree

Eydonhill

Moors
Farm

Tile
Barn

Cedars
Farm

Crockwell
Farm

Ashby's
Farm

WOODFORD RD

PRESTON RD

HILL VIEW

MORETON RD

Eydon

PO

BLACKSMITHS
LA
PH

DOCTORS LA

Macmillan Way

Cemy

SCHOOL LA

Sewage
Works

53   A   B   54   C   D   55   E   F

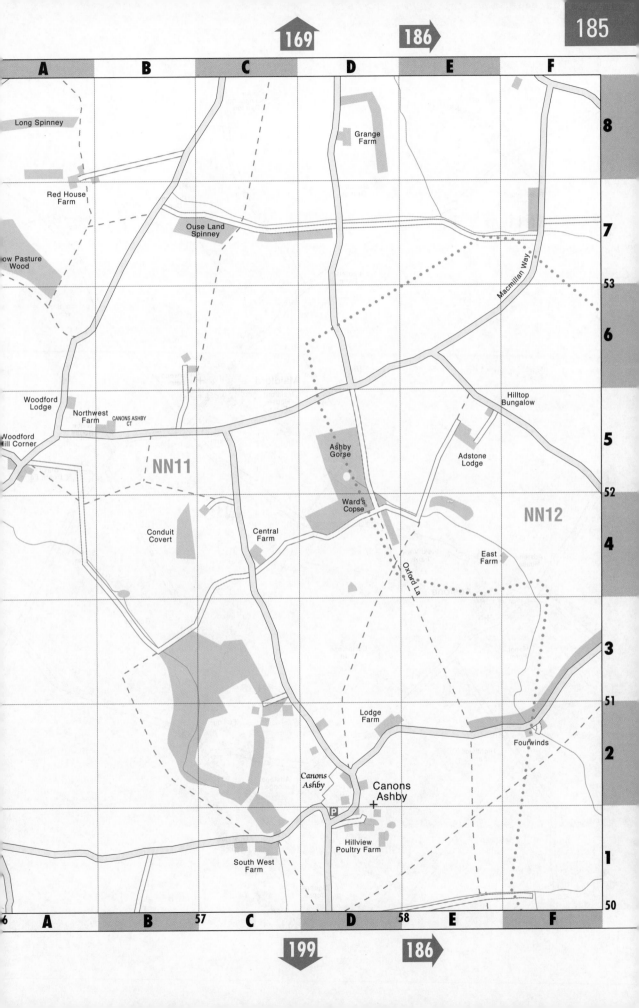

A　B　C　D　E　F

Long Spinney

Red House
Farm

Ouse Land
Spinney

ow Pasture
Wood

Grange
Farm

Macmillan Way

8

7

53

6

Woodford
Lodge

Northwest
Farm

CANONS ASHBY
CT

Woodford
ill Corner

NN11

Hilltop
Bungalow

Ashby
Gorse

Adstone
Lodge

5

52

Ward's
Copse

NN12

Conduit
Covert

Central
Farm

East
Farm

Oxford La

4

Lodge
Farm

3

51

Fourwinds

2

Canons
Ashby

Canons
Ashby

P

Hillview
Poultry Farm

South West
Farm

1

50

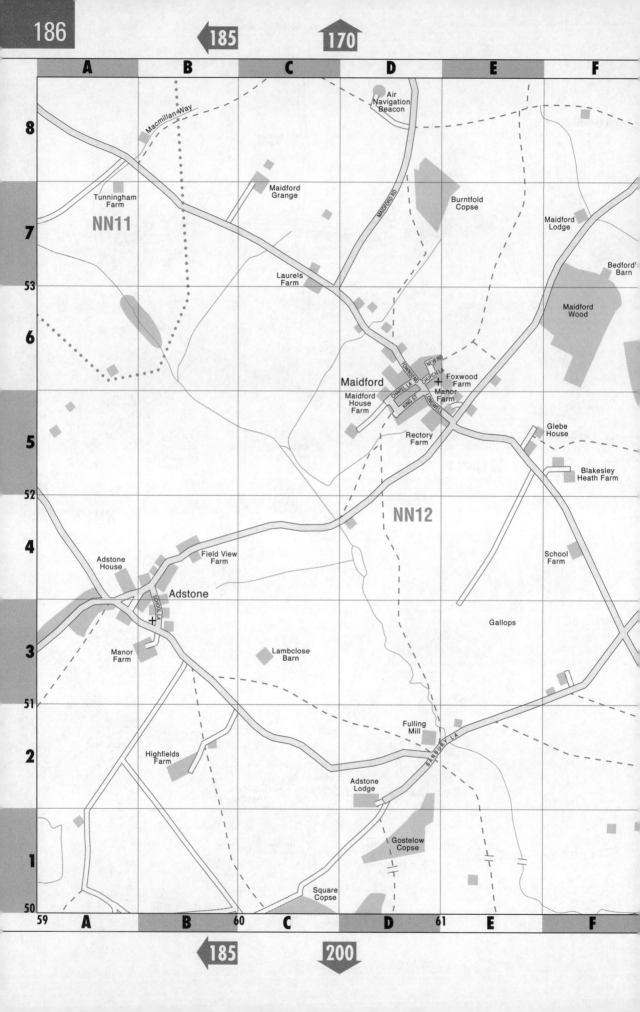

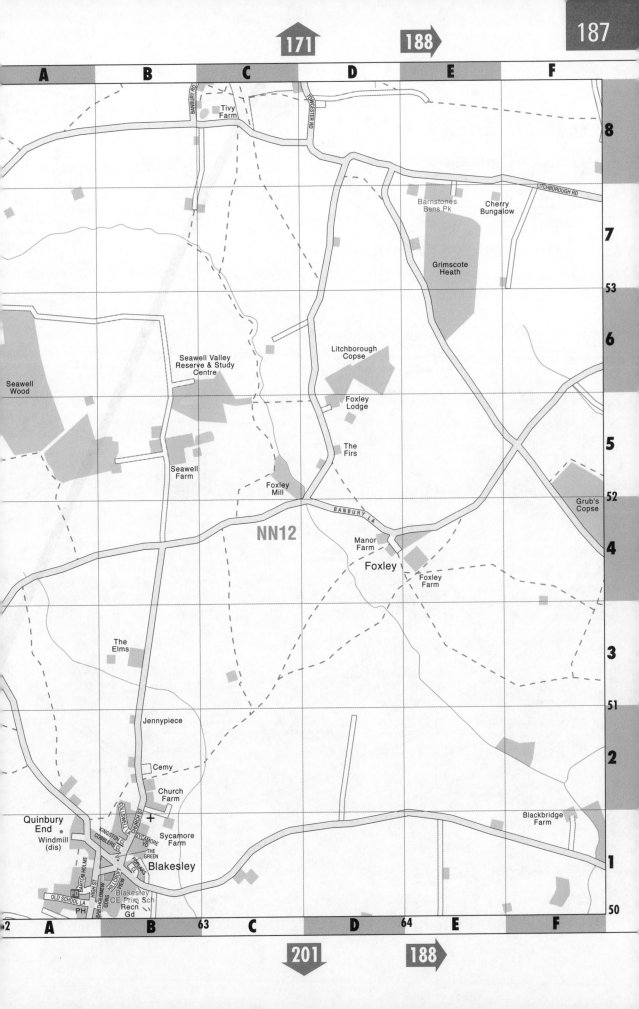

A B C D E F

8
7
53
6
5
52
4
3
51
2
1
50

Banbury Rd
Tivy Farm
Towcester Rd

Litchborough Rd
Barnstones Bsns Pk
Cherry Bungalow

Grimscote Heath

Litchborough Copse

Seawell Valley Reserve & Study Centre

Seawell Wood

Foxley Lodge

The Firs

Seawell Farm

Foxley Mill

Grub's Copse

BANBURY LA

NN12

Manor Farm

Foxley

Foxley Farm

The Elms

Jennypiece

Cemy

Church Farm

Blackbridge Farm

Quinbury End
Windmill (dis)

KINGSTON CL
COBBLERS CL
COLLSWELL CL
CHURCH ST
SYCAMORE YD
THE GREEN

Sycamore Farm

Blakesley

OLD SCHOOL LA
PO
PH
BARTON HOLME
HIGH ST
BARTHOLOMEW GDNS
HILLCROFT
HILLCROFT VIEW
PARK CL

Blakesley CE Prim Sch
Recn Gd

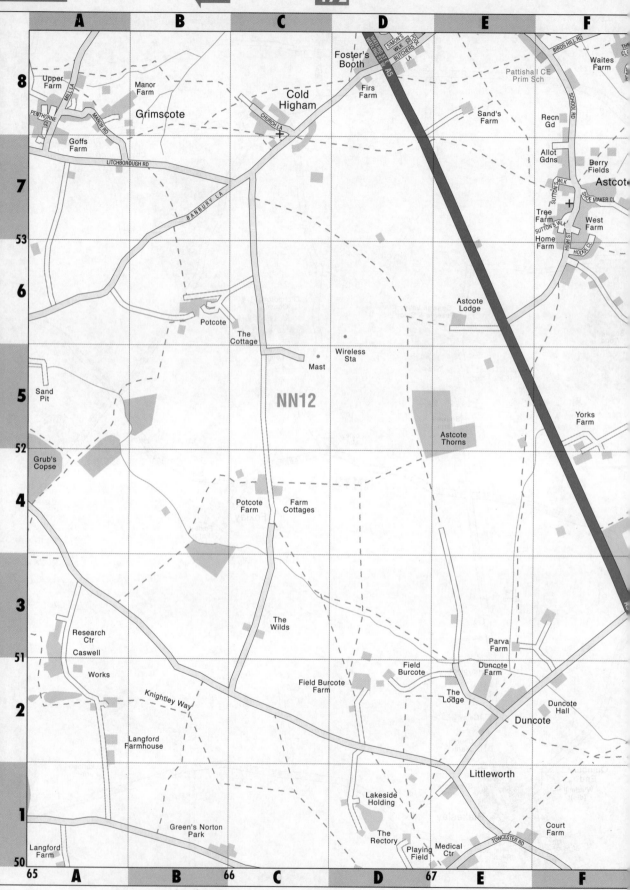

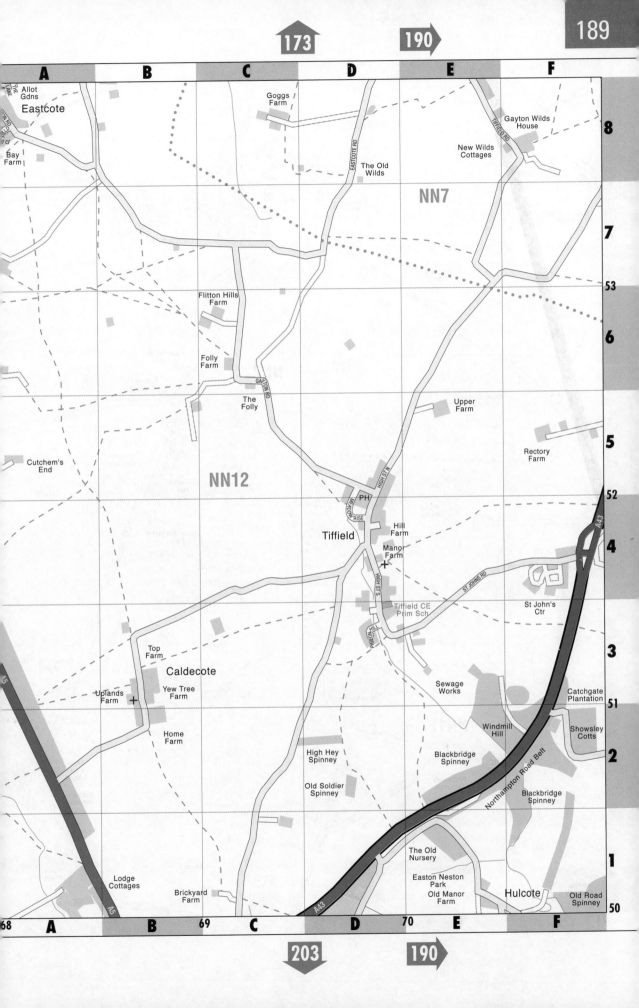

A   B   C   D   E   F

8

BLISWORTH RD

A43

GAYTON RD

Hill
Farm

Highcliffe
Farm

NORTHAMPTON RD

CHAPEL LA

Blisworth
Com Prim
Sch

FORD BANK

WEST BROOK

LITTLE LA

PH

HIGH ST

PO

FASTFIELD

WELSPRING

HOME CL

WINDMILL AVE

Blisworth
Lodge

COURTEENHALL RD

GREENAWAY CL

7

Gayton Wood
Farm

BLISWORTH
MILL

Blisworth Mill

CHURCH LA

ASHLEY CT

BUTTMEAD

CONNEGAR LEYS

Blisworth

GREENSIDE

Grand Union Canal

53

Rectory
Farm

TOWCESTER RD

Stone Works
Farm

6

Glebe
Farm

Tunnel Hill
Farm

NN7

Tunnel Hill
Cottages

Wood Cottage
Farm

70

KNOCK LA

5

A43

Grand Union
Canal Wlk

Windmill
Cottage

Blisworth
Hill

52

Wood
Farm

Blisworth Hill
Farm

STOKE RD

4

Top Farm

Burn
Wood

Blisworth Tunnel

Buttermilk Hall
Farm

3

Midshires Way

Nun Wood

51

NN12

Showsley
Belt

Stoke
Plain
Lodge

2

Showsley
Grounds

Showsley Belt

Station
House

1

SNOWSLEY RD

HIGH ST

Hill
Farm

Stoke
Plain

Nettle
Spinney

MAIN RD

SHUTLANGER RD

50

71   A   B   72   C   D   73   E   F

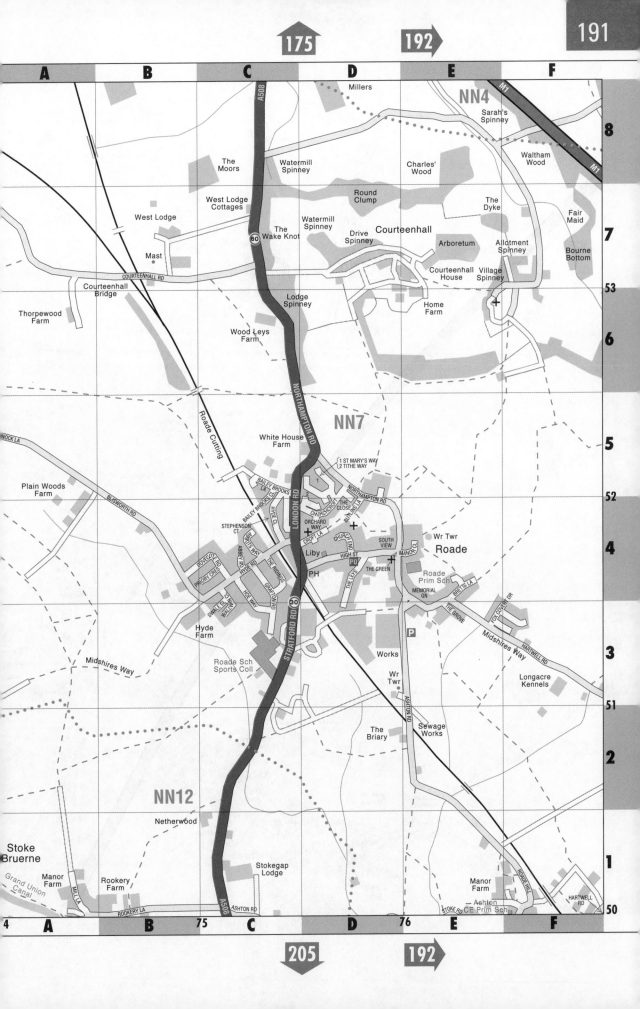

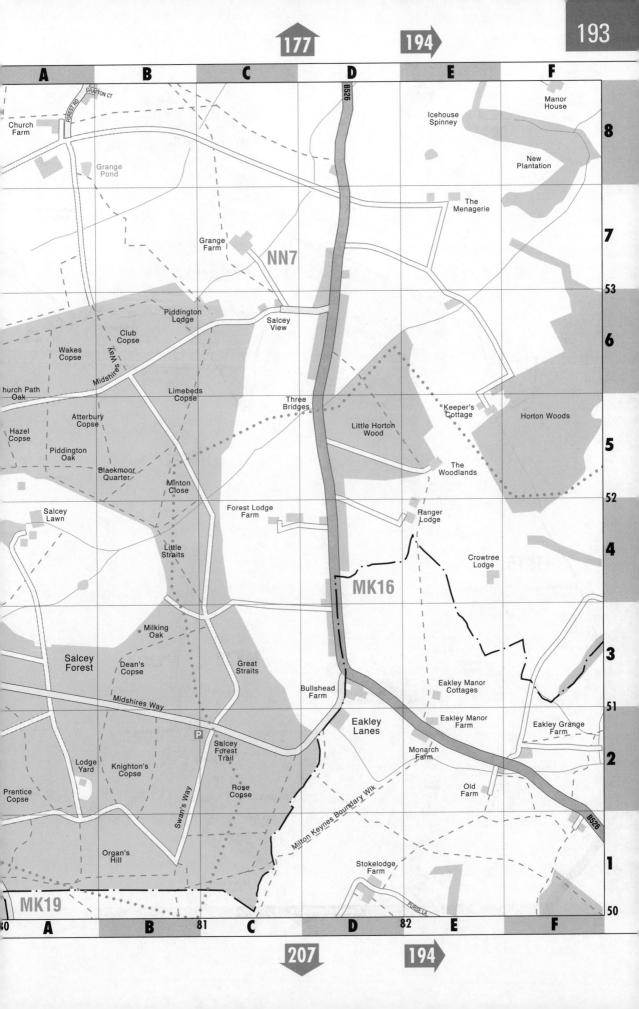

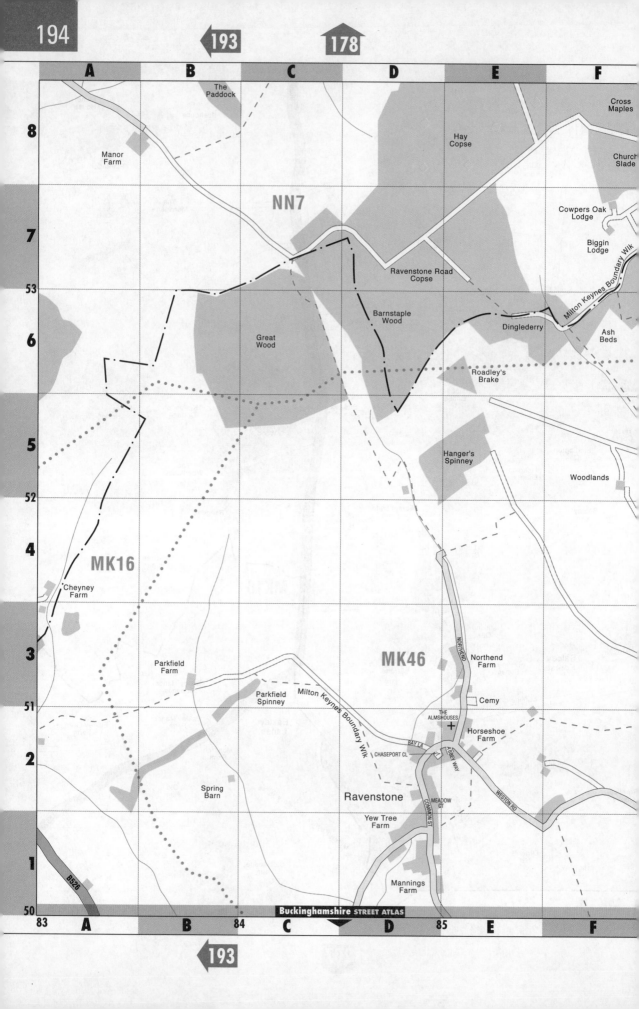

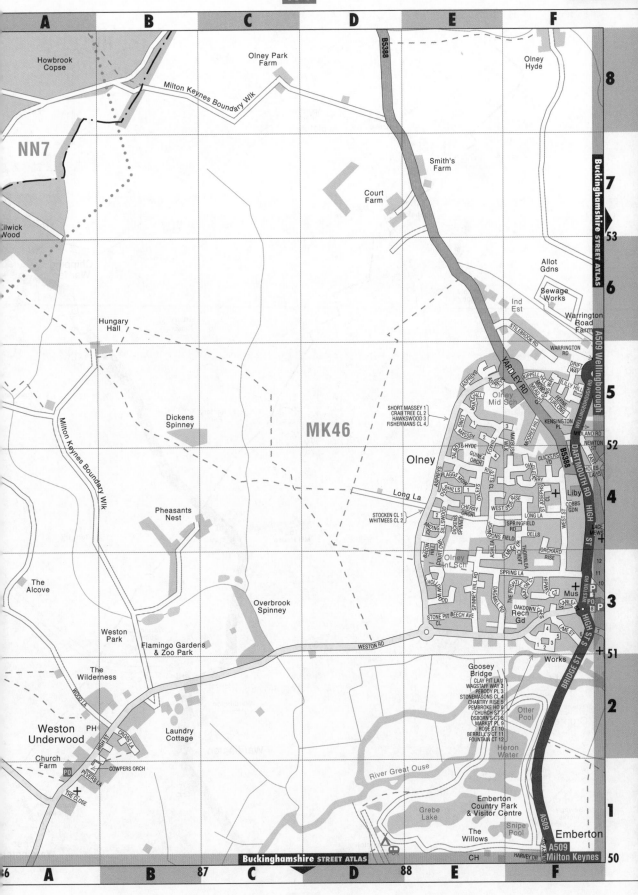

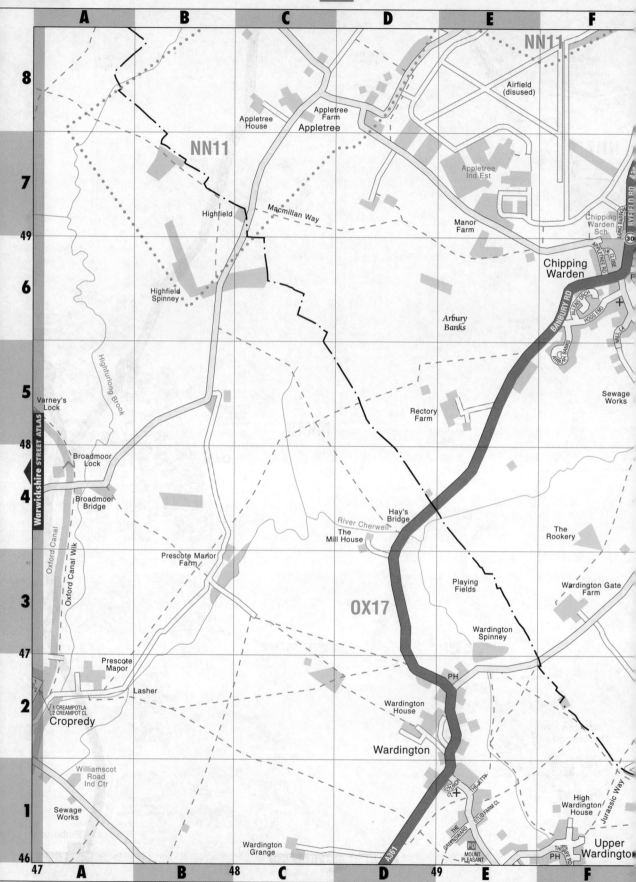

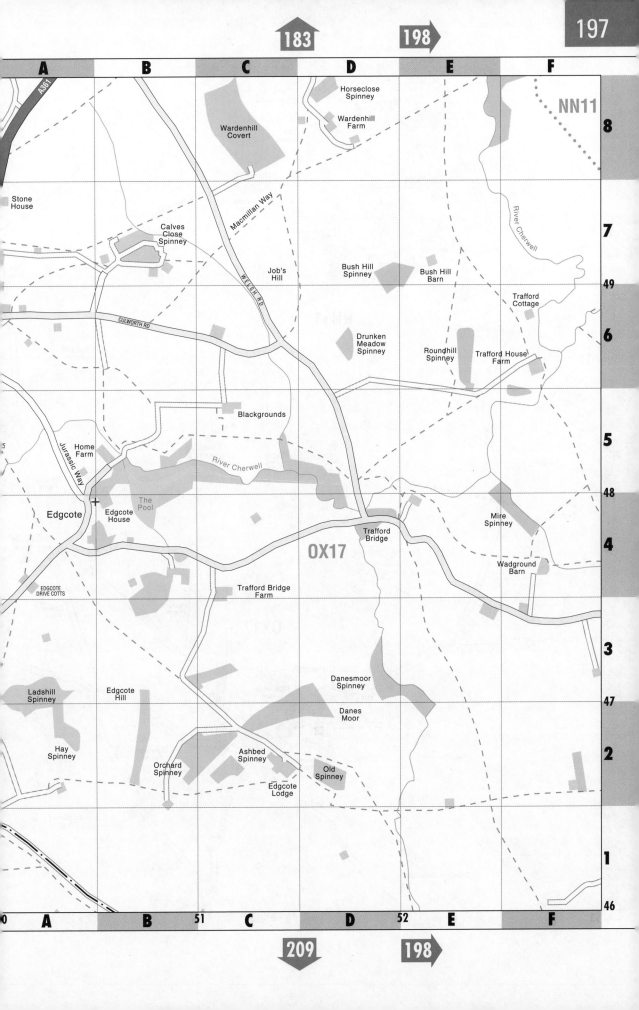

NN11

A B C D E F

8

Stone
House

7

Calves
Close
Spinney

49

Horseclose
Spinney

Wardenhill
Farm

Wardenhill
Covert

Macmillan Way

Job's
Hill

WELSH RD

Bush Hill
Spinney

Bush Hill
Barn

Trafford
Cottage

CULWORTH RD

Drunken
Meadow
Spinney

Roundhill
Spinney

Trafford House
Farm

6

River Cherwell

5

Blackgrounds

Home
Farm

Jurassic Way

River Cherwell

48

Edgcote

The
Pool

Edgcote
House

Trafford
Bridge

Mire
Spinney

OX17

4

EDGCOTE
DRIVE COTTS

Trafford Bridge
Farm

Wadground
Barn

3

Danesmoor
Spinney

Ladshill
Spinney

Edgcote
Hill

47

Danes
Moor

Hay
Spinney

Ashbed
Spinney

2

Orchard
Spinney

Old
Spinney

Edgcote
Lodge

1

46

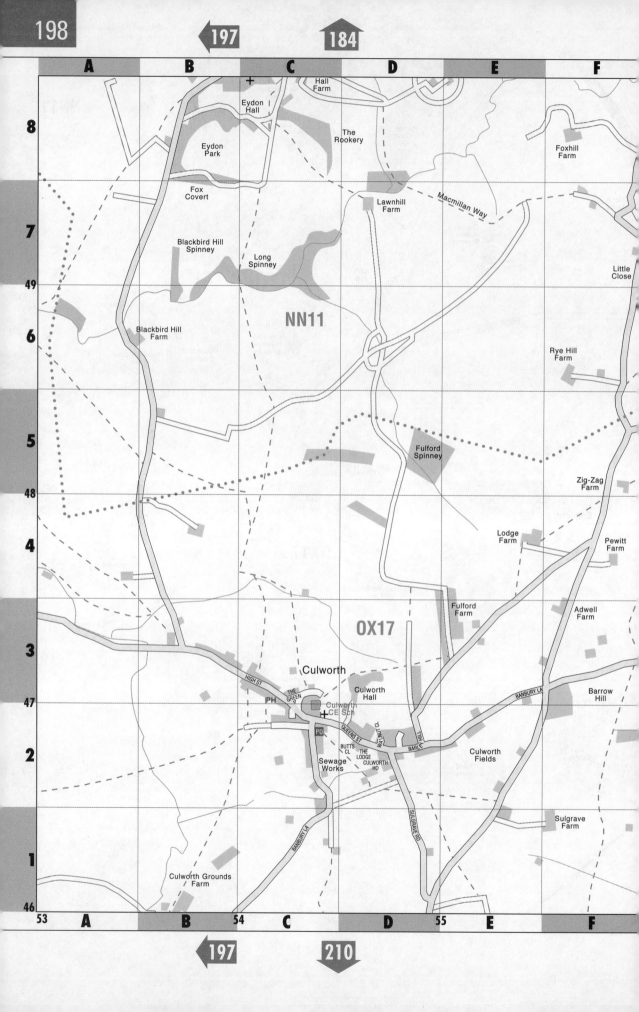

A B C D E F

8

Hall
Farm

Eydon
Hall

Eydon
Park

The
Rookery

Foxhill
Farm

7

Fox
Covert

Lawnhill
Farm

Macmillan Way

Blackbird Hill
Spinney

Little
Close

49

Long
Spinney

NN11

6

Blackbird Hill
Farm

Rye Hill
Farm

5

Fulford
Spinney

Zig-Zag
Farm

48

Lodge
Farm

Pewitt
Farm

4

OX17

Fulford
Farm

Adwell
Farm

3

Culworth

Culworth
Hall

Barrow
Hill

HIGH ST

BANBURY LA

47

PH

THE GREEN

Culworth
CE Sch

2

PO

QUEENS ST

BUTTS
CL

THE
LODGE

CULWORTH
HO

BARL

WALTON

TITHL

Culworth
Fields

Sewage
Works

Sulgrave
Farm

BANBURY LA

SULGRAVE RD

1

46

Culworth Grounds
Farm

53 A B 54 C D 55 E F

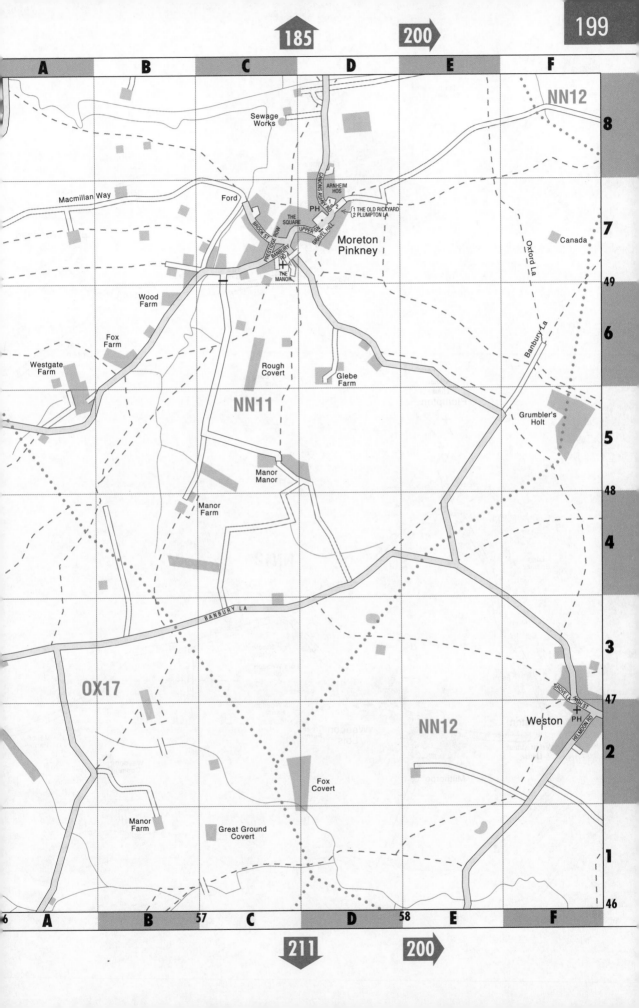

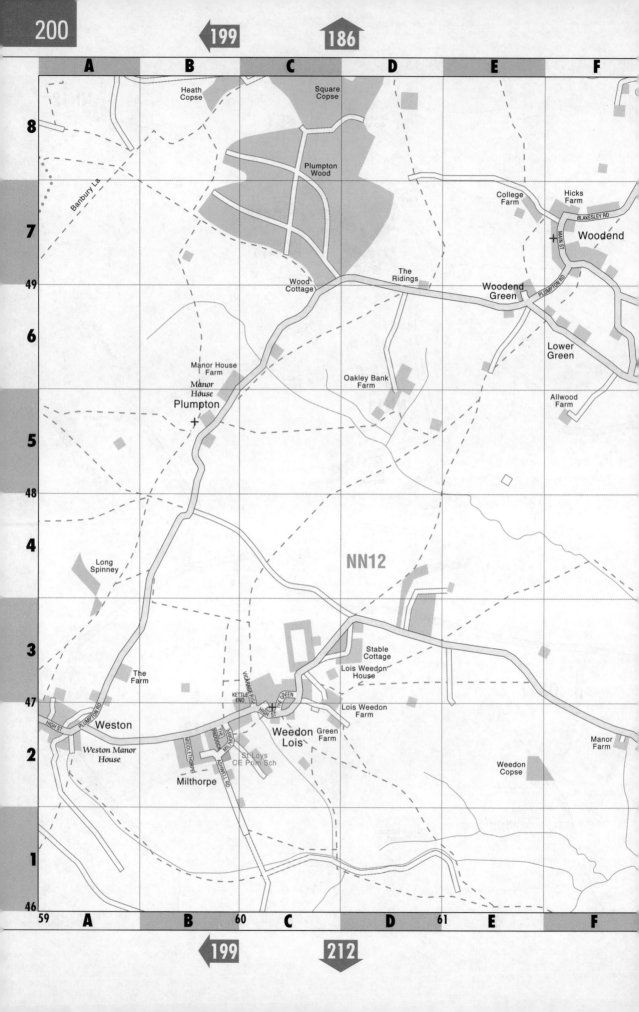

Heath Copse

Square Copse

Plumpton Wood

Banbury La

College Farm

Hicks Farm

BLAKESLEY RD

Woodend

MAIN ST

The Ridings

Wood Cottage

Woodend Green

PLUMPTON RD

Lower Green

Manor House Farm

Manor House

Oakley Bank Farm

Allwood Farm

Plumpton

Long Spinney

NN12

The Farm

Stable Cottage

Lois Weedon House

PLUMPTON RD

VICARAGE RISE

KETTLE END

THE GREEN

HIGH ST

Weston

HIGH ST

Lois Weedon Farm

Manor Farm

Weston Manor House

MIDDLETHORPE

THE PADDOCK

THE MILL

ASHWELL RD

St Loys CE Prim Sch

Weedon Lois

Green Farm

Weedon Copse

Milthorpe

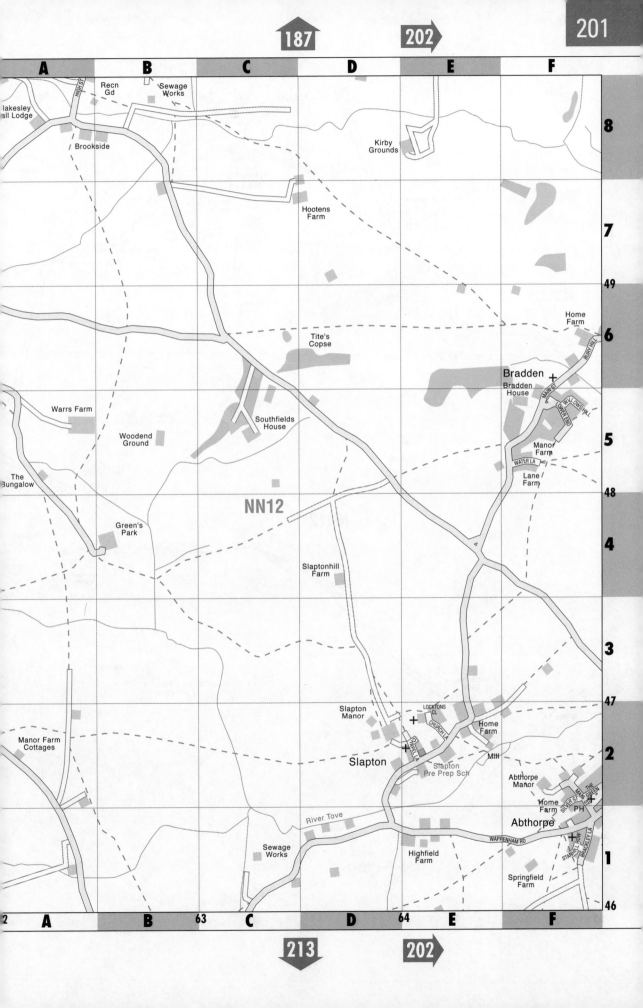

A B C D E F

8

7

49

6

Kirby
Grounds

Hootens
Farm

Tite's
Copse

Home
Farm

Bradden

Bradden
House

BIRT HILL

MAIN ST

LDR WILLOWS HILL

LOWER END

Manor
Farm

WATER LA

Lane
Farm

48

Warrs Farm

Woodend
Ground

Southfields
House

NN12

The
Bungalow

Green's
Park

5

4

Slaptonhill
Farm

3

47

Slapton
Manor

LOCKTONS
CL

CHURCH LA

CHAPEL LA

Home
Farm

Mill

Home
Farm

Abthorpe
Manor

SILVER ST

MAIN ST

THE
GREEN

PH

BRACKLEY LA

STAMHILL ROW

Slapton

Slapton
Pre Prep Sch

River Tove

Abthorpe

WAPPENHAM RD

Manor Farm
Cottages

Sewage
Works

Highfield
Farm

Springfield
Farm

2

46

Blakesley
all Lodge

Recn
Gd

Sewage
Works

HIGH ST

Brookside

201
188

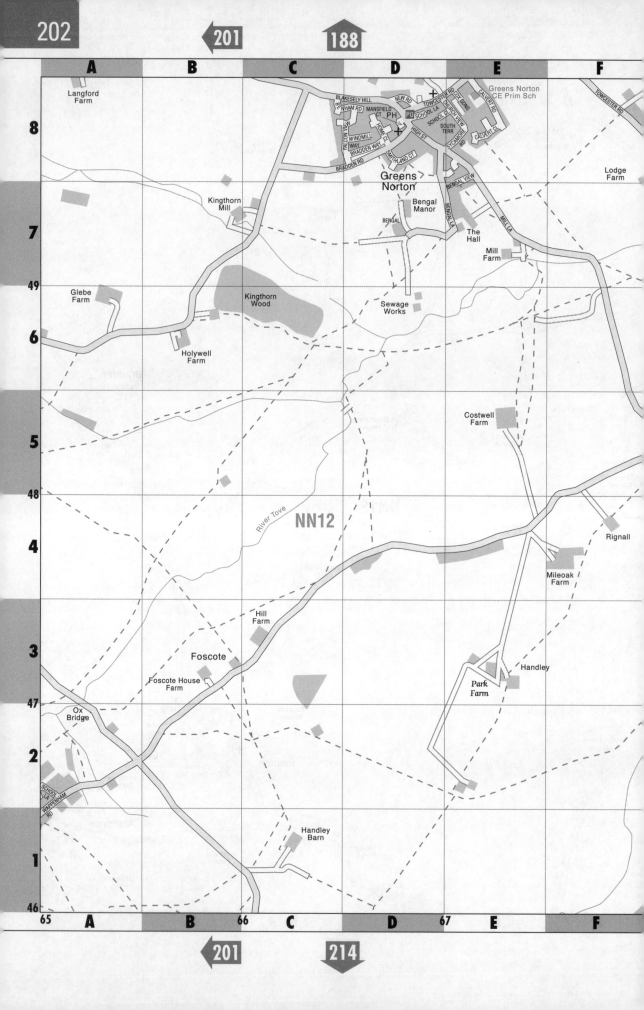

A   B   C   D   E   F

8

Langford
Farm

BLAKESELY HILL
NHAM RD
MANSFIELD
CT   PH
FALCON VIEW
WINDMILL
WAY
BRADDEN WAY
BRADDEN RD
HOME CT
SMITH AND CT
NEW RD
TOWCESTER RD
SCHOOL LA
HIGH ST
CHURCH RD
SCHOOL CL
SOUTH
TERR
CHURCH VIEW
SYCAMORE
RD
COZY GDNS
CALVERT RD
CALVERT CL

Greens Norton
CE Prim Sch

PO

Greens
Norton

Kingthorn
Mill

Bengal Manor

BENGAL VIEW
BENGAL LA

Lodge
Farm

7

BENGAL

The
Hall

MILL LA

Mill
Farm

49

Glebe
Farm

Kingthorn
Wood

Sewage
Works

6

Holywell
Farm

5

Costwell
Farm

48

River Tove

NN12

4

Rignall

Mileoak
Farm

3

Hill
Farm

Foscote

Handley

Park
Farm

Foscote House
Farm

47

Ox
Bridge

2

SCHOOL LA
WAPPENHAM RD

1

Handley
Barn

46

65   A   B   66   C   D   67   E   F

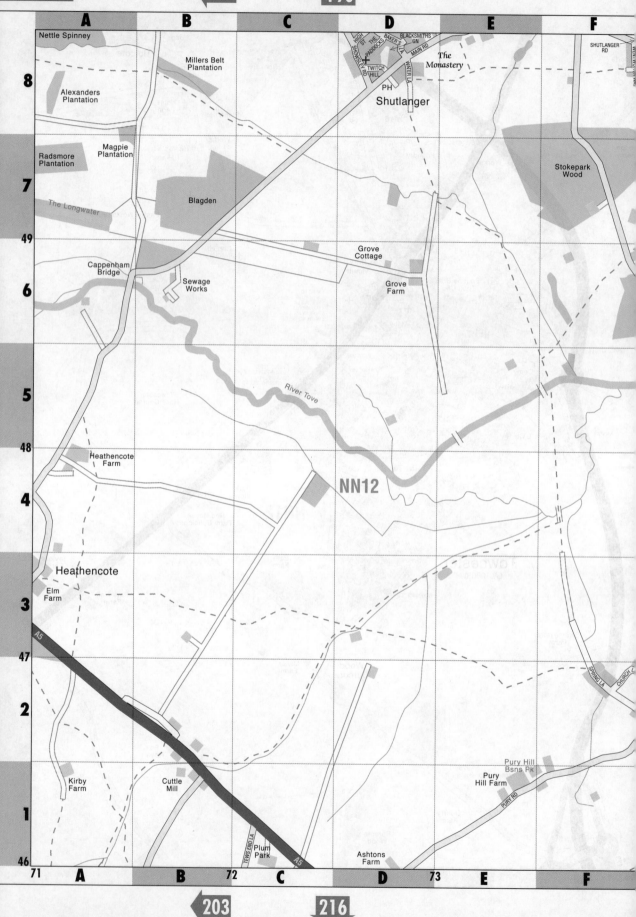

A   B   C   D   E   F

8

Nettle Spinney

Millers Belt
Plantation

Alexanders
Plantation

HIGH ST
SHONSLEY RD
THE PADDOCKS
BAKER'S LA
BLACKSMITHS GN
MAIN RD
WATER LA
TWITCH HILL

SHUTLANGER
RD

The Monastery

PH

Shutlanger

7

Radsmore
Plantation

Magpie
Plantation

Stokepark
Wood

The Longwater

Blagden

49

Grove
Cottage

6

Cappenham
Bridge

Sewage
Works

Grove
Farm

5

River Tove

48

Heathencote
Farm

NN12

4

3

Heathencote

Elm
Farm

A5

47

2

SPRING LA
CHURCH

Pury Hill
Bsns Pk

Kirby
Farm

Cuttle
Mill

Pury
Hill Farm

PURY RD

1

TEWS END LA
Plum
Park

A5

Ashtons
Farm

46

71   A   B   72   C   D   73   E   F

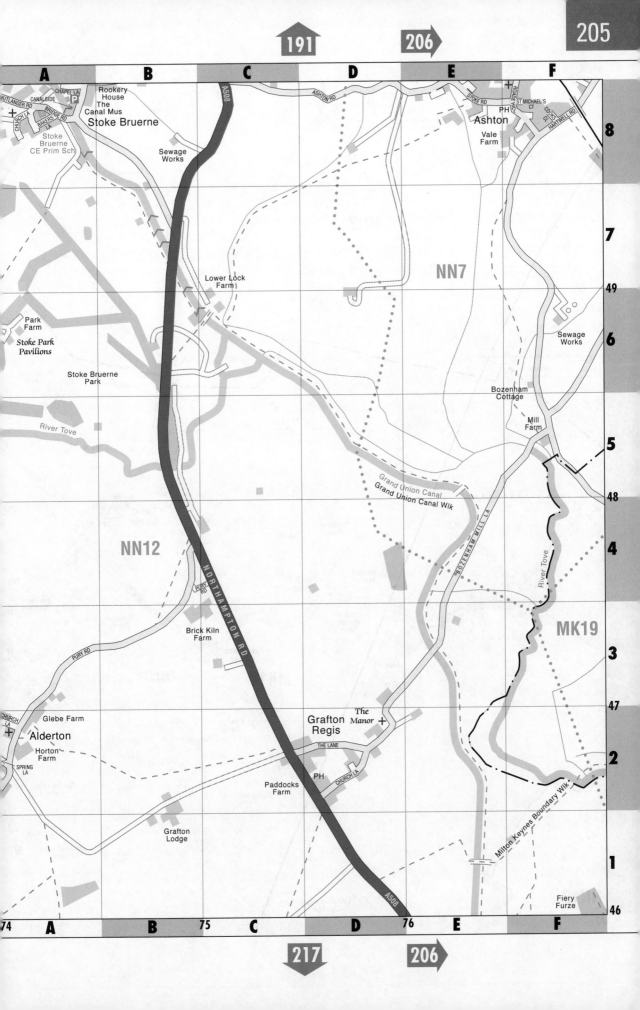

A   B   C   D   E   F

8

7

49

6

5

48

4

3

47

2

1

46

NN7

NN12

MK19

Stoke Bruerne
Rookery House
The Canal Mus
HUTLANGER RD
CANALSIDE
CHURCH LA
BAKERS LA
BRIDGE RD
CHAPEL LA
Stoke Bruerne CE Prim Sch
Sewage Works

Ashton
Ashton Rd
Stoke Rd
ROAD HILL
ST MICHAEL'S CT
PH
COCKS LA
HARTWELL RD
Vale Farm

A508

Lower Lock Farm

Park Farm
Stoke Park Pavilions
Stoke Bruerne Park
River Tove

Bozenham Cottage
Mill Farm
Sewage Works

NORTHAMPTON RD
LAD RD
BURY RD
Brick Kiln Farm

Grand Union Canal
Grand Union Canal Wlk

BOZENHAM MILL LA
River Tove

PURY RD
CHURCH LA
Glebe Farm
Alderton
Horton Farm
SPRING LA

Grafton Regis
The Manor
THE LANE
CHURCH LA
PH
Paddocks Farm
Grafton Lodge

Milton Keynes Boundary Wlk

Fiery Furze

A508

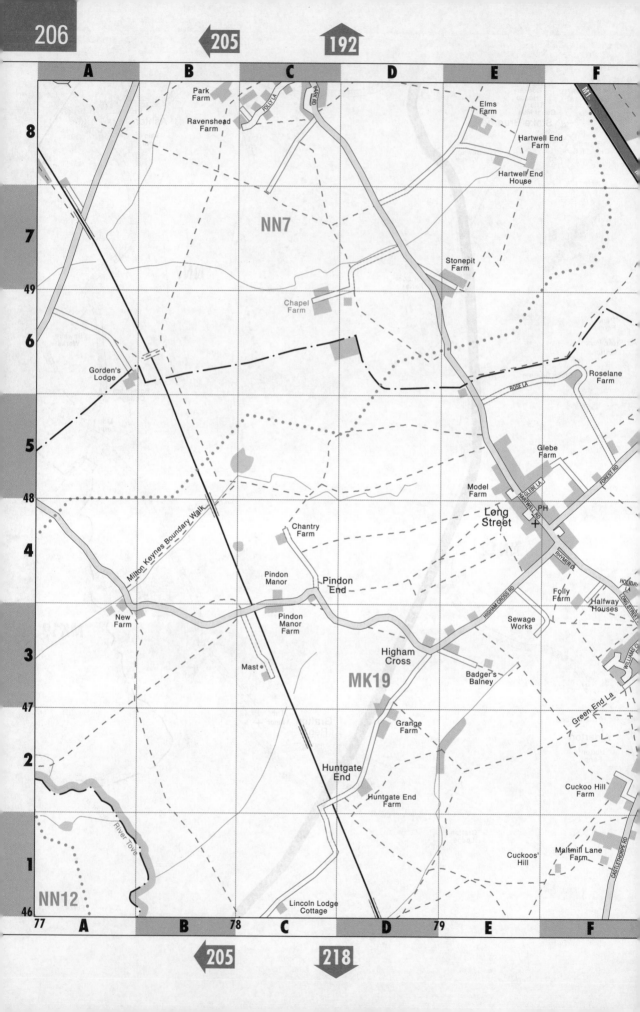

A B C D E F

8

7

49

6

5

48

4

3

47

2

1

46

77 A B 78 C D 79 E F

NN7

NN12

MK19

Park
Farm

Ravenshead
Farm

FOLLY LA

PARK RD

Elms
Farm

Hartwell End
Farm

Hartwell End
House

Stonepit
Farm

Chapel
Farm

Gorden's
Lodge

ROSE LA

Roselane
Farm

Glebe
Farm

GLEBE LA.

FOREST RD

Model
Farm

HARTWELL RD

PH

Long
Street

RHYMER CT

Milton Keynes Boundary Walk

New
Farm

Chantry
Farm

Pindon
Manor

Pindon
End

Pindon
Manor
Farm

HIGHAM CROSS RD

Folly
Farm

Halfway
Houses

HOLIDAY LA

LONG ST RD

Sewage
Works

Mast

Higham
Cross

Badger's
Balney

WILLIAMS RD

Green End La

River Toye

Grange
Farm

Cuckoo Hill
Farm

Huntgate
End

Huntgate End
Farm

Cuckoos'
Hill

Maltmill Lane
Farm

CASTLETHORPE RD

Lincoln Lodge
Cottage

M1

MK16

MK19

Jarvis's Wood

Salcey Green Farm

Forest Farm

Midshire Way

Milton Keynes Boundary Wlk

Milton Keynes Boundary Wlk

Mast

Salcey Green

Lodge Farm

PURSE LA

PURSE LA

Stokepark Wood

FOREST RD

Spinney Lodge

Swan's Way

Littlewood Farm

Midshires Way

Swan's Way

Yew Tree Farm

Hanslope Comb Sch

Stocking Green House

Woad Farm

Tathallend Farm

Hanslope

LONGS END STREET END LA

KITELEE CL

WAYS

STOCKING GREEN

MANDUIT CT

CASTFIELD DR

WRENS MERE CT

WARWICK RD

ALDENE RD

KESWICK RD

STERN DR

LINCOLN CT

GOLD ST

NEVILL CL

NEWPORT RD

Tathall End

CASTLETHORPE RD

HIGH ST

FAITH TERR 1

CARRIERS CL 2

ST JAMES CT

MARKET SQ

THE GREEN

Church End

Manor Farm

MANOR

VICARAGE CT

WEAVERS RD

PARK RD

Three Shires Way

The Grove

Park Farm

Ivy Farm

Buckinghamshire STREET ATLAS

M1 Luton

8

7

49

6

5

48

4

3

47

2

1

46

0   A   B   81   C   D   82   E   F

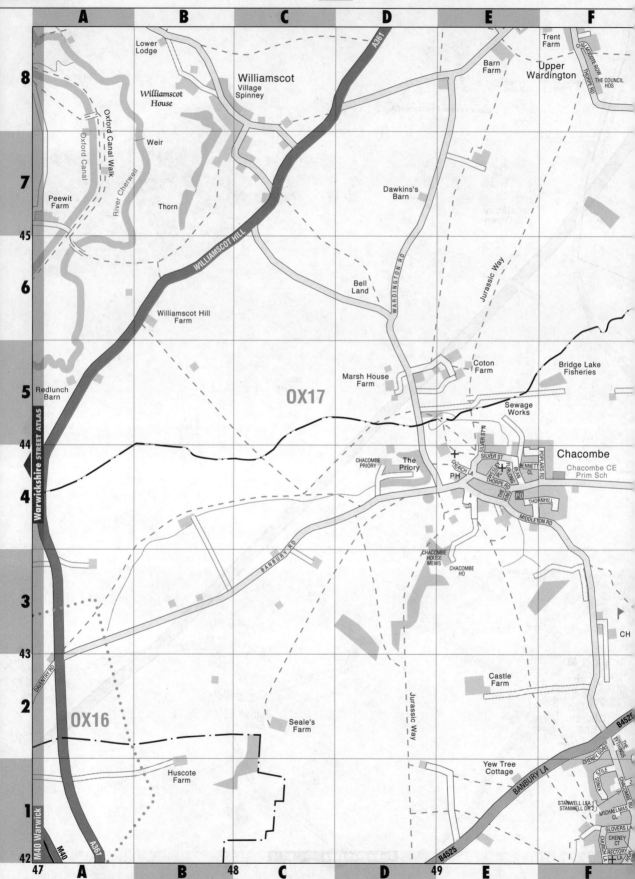

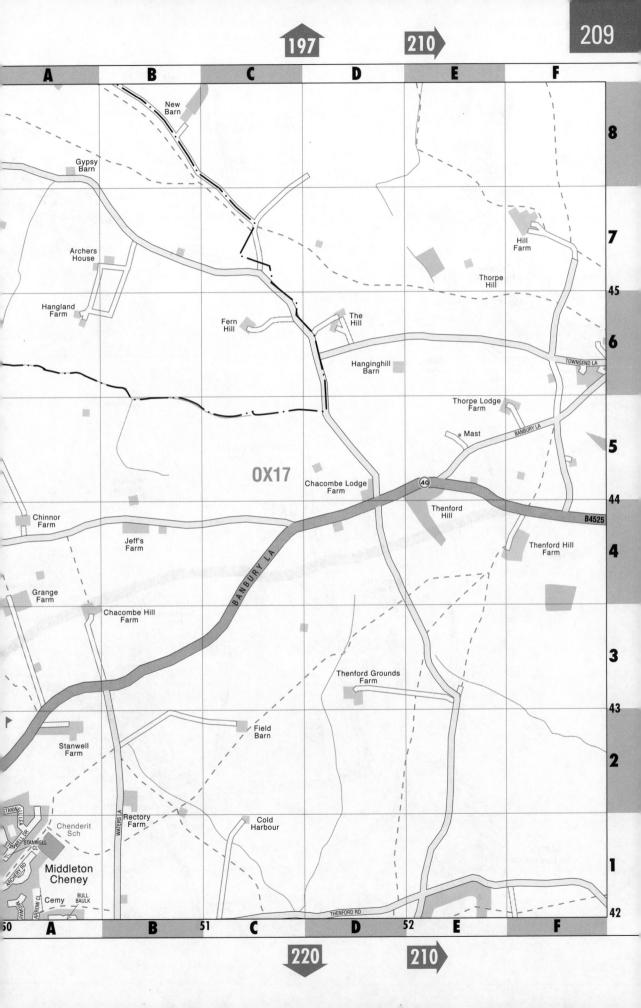

197 210

A B C D E F

8
7
45
6
5
44
4
3
43
2
1
42

New Barn

Gypsy Barn

Archers House

Hangland Farm

Fern Hill

The Hill

Hanginghill Barn

Hill Farm

Thorpe Hill

TOWNSEND LA

Thorpe Lodge Farm

Mast

BANBURY LA

OX17

Chacombe Lodge Farm

40

Thenford Hill

B4525

Chinnor Farm

Jeff's Farm

Grange Farm

Chacombe Hill Farm

BANBURY LA

Thenford Hill Farm

Thenford Grounds Farm

Field Barn

Stanwell Farm

Cold Harbour

THENFORD RD

STANW CALLEY

WATERS LA

Rectory Farm

Chenderit Sch

STANWELL CL

Middleton Cheney

ARCHERY RD

Cemy

BULL BAULK

50 A B 51 C D 52 E F

220 210

← 209
▲ 198

← 209
▼ 221

A B C D E F

8 7 45 6 5 44 4 3 43 2 1 42

53 **A** **B** 54 **C** **D** 55 **E** **F**

Windmill (dis)
Sulgrave Hotel
Happy Lands
Lower Thorpe
Magpie Farm
Spinners Cotts
Castle Hill
Magpie Rd
Thorpe Mandeville
Manor House
Sewage Works
The Warren
Dove Cotts
PH
Costow House
Dean Barn
Painter's Spinney
OX17
B4525
Woods Farm
Marston Hill Farm
Marston Hill
Greatworth Park
Stuchbury Manor Farm
B452
Astral Row
Whittoc Cl
Helmdon Rd
Pever Rd
Dering Cotts
Greatworth Prim Sch
Westthorp
Pargeter
Greatworth
PH
Marston Cl
Hickman Cl
Field View
Kieldsen Cl
Merestone Hos
The Green
PH
South Cl
The Square
Brackley Rd
Church Rd
Floyd's Farm
Marston St Lawrence
Sewage Works
Banbury La
PO
PH
School St
Church St
Manor Rd
Little St
Helmdon Rd
Park La
Stockwell

A B C D E F

8

NN12

Sewage Works

Sulgrave Manor

Rectory Farm

Coolington Farm

Allithorne Wood

7

45

6

Peter's Farm

College Farm

Home Farm

5

Stuchbury Lodge

WRIGHTONS HILL

44

Stuchbury Manor Farm

Stuchbury

OX17

Stuchbury Hall Farm

Helmdon

THE GREEN

BARN CT

4

Washbrook Spinney

Stuchbury Fox Covert

Helmdon Prim Sch

PH

BELL CL

HINTON'S CL

Sewage Works

Grange Farm Barn

3

HELMDON RD

NN13

43

Fatlands Farm

Greatworth Hall

2

Spring Farm

B4525

Bungalow Farm

Redlands House

Glebe Farm

Halse Copse

Ash Vale Farm

Blackpits Barn

1

Greatworth Fields

42

56 A B 57 C D 58 E F

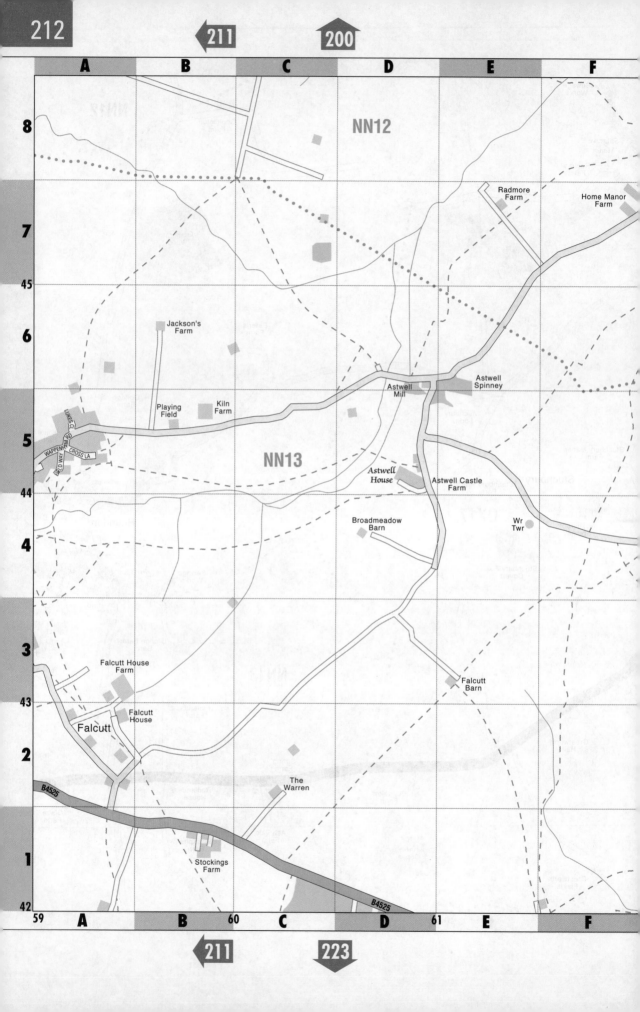

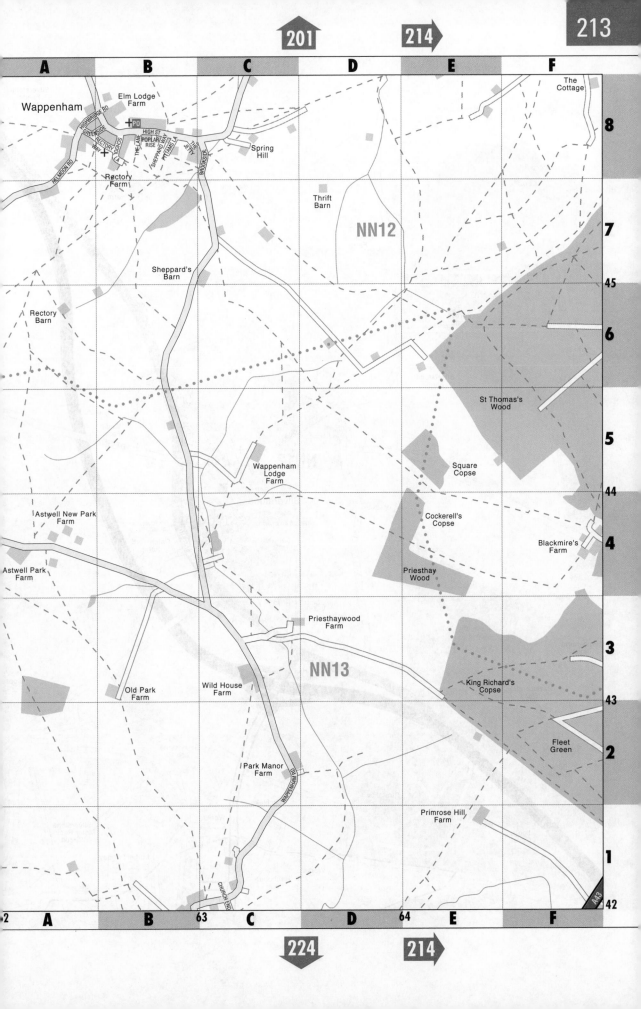

A B C D E F

Wappenham

The Cottage

Elm Lodge
Farm

8

PO
HIGHBRIDGE RD
GREENSIDE
SCHOOLS
RECTORY
WAY
HIGH ST
THE LANE
POPLAR
RISE
SHEPPARD WAY
PITTANS LA
THE
JETTY
HELMDON RD

Spring
Hill

Rectory
Farm

Thrift
Barn

7

NN12

45

Sheppard's
Barn

6

Rectory
Barn

St Thomas's
Wood

5

Square
Copse

Wappenham
Lodge
Farm

44

Astwell New Park
Farm

Cockerell's
Copse

4

Astwell Park
Farm

Blackmire's
Farm

Priesthay
Wood

Priesthaywood
Farm

3

NN13

King Richard's
Copse

Old Park
Farm

Wild House
Farm

43

Fleet
Green

2

Park Manor
Farm

WAPPENHAM RD

Primrose Hill
Farm

1

CHURCH END

A43

42

A B C D E F

8

7

45

6

Silverstone Fields Farm

The Hayes Farm

Sewage Works

Pits Farm

Challock Farm

Bucknell Wood

P ⌂

Forest Walk

The Mill

Silverstone Farm

Windill Farm

WHITMORE CT

KINGSLEY RD

LITTLE LONDON

HILLSIDE AVE

5

THE WILLOWS

Rookery Farm

PIDDLEDOCK

CHURCH ST

BROOK CT

WHITTLEBURY RD

WHITTLEBURY RD

NN12

✛

STOCKS HILL

PH

FROG HALL

ACORN WAY

44

Silverstone Inf Sch

PO

THE SLADE

BLACKMIRES LA

Silverstone

MONKSWOOD

HAZELWOOD

CHAPEL HILL 1
HOME CL 2
THE OLD WOODYARD 3

WALNUT
HIGH ST
CHAPEL DR

OLD ACORN

1 AUSTINS PL
2 BAINES PL

WEST END

GREEN LA

MURSWELL

4

Monk's Wood

Silverstone CE Jun Sch

GRAHAM HILL

BRABHAM CL

MURSWELL

TOWCESTER RD

Catch Yard Farm

THE WOODLANDS

STEWART CL

THE HAWTHORNS

SAYERS CL

CATTLE END

PH

Wild Wood

3

Sandyhurst Copse

Shiplands Copse

BRACKLEY RD

Hazelborough Wood

Bleak Hall Farmhouse

A413

43

Silverstone Tech Pk

2

NN13

Bone Copse

The Straights

Litchlake

DADFORD RD

Works

Silverstone Motor Racing Circuit

1

Lodge Copse

Works

Henhood Farm

Luffield Abbey Farm

A43

42

203
216

A B C D E F

8
7
45
6
5
44
4
43
3
2
1
42

Kirby Farm House

Pury End

Porterswood Farm

Manor Farm

Wr Twr

THE HILL

KINGS LA

CAREY'S RD

Lordsfields Farm

Longhedge Wood

Ladywell Spinney

Dove's Farm

Black Pits

Sholebroke Lodge

Shacks Barn Farm

A413

A413

A413

Washbrook Spinney

TOWCESTER RD

WHITTLEBURY CT

VICARAGE CL

CHURCH WAY

The Home Farm

Sholebroke Farm

NN12

THE CRESCENT

KINGSFIELD PIECE

Whittlebury CE Prim SCh

HIGH ST

PH

PARK CL PK

LODGE PK

LEE'S CL

Deer Park

Buckingham Thick Copse

Whittlebury

Wr Twr

KENNEL RD

West Park Farm

Foxhole Copse

Hotel

CH

The Clumps

Cheese Copse

Coldthorn

Linshire Copse

Chapel Copse

Deer Park

Birch Copse

MK18

MK18

Linshire Farm

A413

68 69 70

A   B   C   D   E   F

8

Tew's End

Paulerspury
CE Prim
Sch

Paulerspury

PH

Plum Park

Grafton
Park

7

Kingstons
Farm

Plumpton
End

45

Plum Park
Farm

6

Park
Farm

The Gullet

Stollage
Farm

Bradlem
Pond

NN12

5

King's
Copse

44

Bear's
Copse

Lady
Copse

4

Say's
Copse

Old Tun Copse

Kennels
Cottages

KENNELS DR

Wakefield
Little Lodge

3

Smalladine
Copse

43

Wakefield Lawn

MK18

2

Wakefield
Lodge

Home
Farm

The
Pheasantry

1

Briary
Wood

Hill
Cops

42

71   A   B   72   C   D   73   E   F

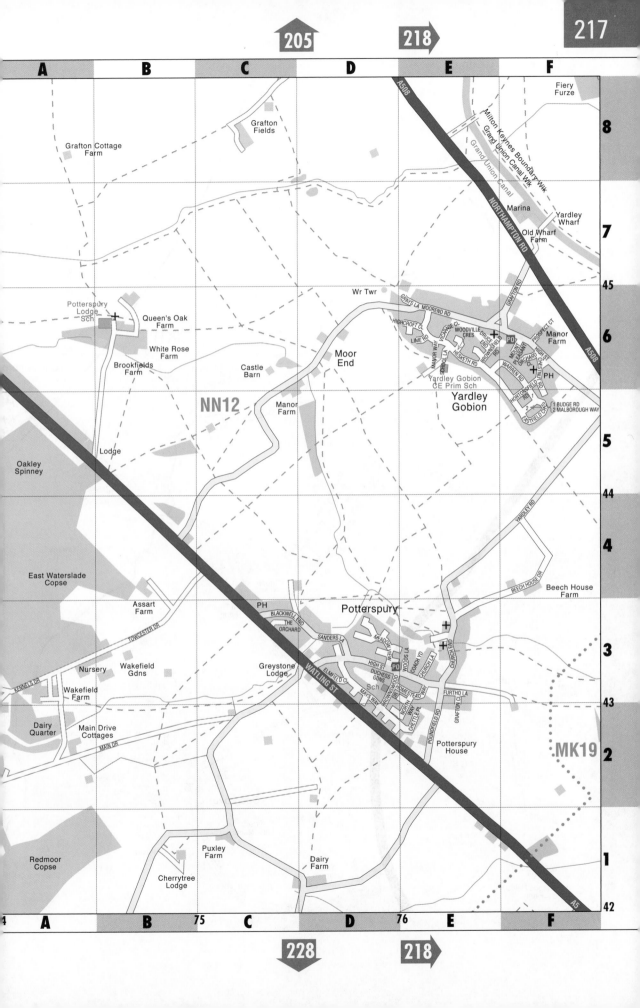

A B C D E F

Fiery Furze

Grafton Fields

Grafton Cottage Farm

Milton Keynes Boundary Wlk
Grand Union Canal Wlk
Grand Union Canal

NORTHAMPTON RD

Marina

Yardley Wharf

Old Wharf Farm

GRAFTON RD

A508

Wr Twr

GRAYS LA
MOOREND RD

Potterspury Lodge Sch

Queen's Oak Farm

White Rose Farm

Brookfields Farm

Castle Barn

Moor End

HIGHCROFT CL
LIME RD

MANOR WAY
SCHOOL LA
VICARAGE CL
WOODVILLE CRES
HESKETH RD
DRUCE END
BROMSFIELD RD

MOUNT PLEASANT
THE ORCHARD
HIGH ST
PROSPECT CT

Manor Farm

WARREN RD

PH

Yardley Gobion CE Prim Sch

HORTONSFIELD RD
EASTFIELD DR
CHESTNUT RD
1
2

1 BUDGE RD
2 MALBOROUGH WAY

NN12

Manor Farm

Yardley Gobion

YARDLEY RD

Lodge

Oakley Spinney

East Waterslade Copse

Beech House Farm

BEECH HOUSE DR

Assart Farm

TOWCESTER DR

PH

BLACKWELL END
THE ORCHARD

Potterspury

SANDERS LA

MEADOW VIEW

HIGH ST
PO
WOODS LA
DUCHESS GDNS
COACH YD
CHURCH LA
CHURCH END

Nursery

Wakefield Gdns

Greystone Lodge

ELMFIELD CL
WATLING ST

Sch
HOMESTEAD

POUNDFIELD RD
GRAFTON CL
FURTHO LA

KENNELS DR

Wakefield Farm

MAYS WAY
NORTH WALK
CHETTLE PL

MK19

Dairy Quarter

Main Drive Cottages

MAIN DR

Potterspury House

Redmoor Copse

Puxley Farm

Cherrytree Lodge

Dairy Farm

A5

217
206

A B C D E F

8

Lincoln Lodge

7

45

NN12

6

MK19

Milford Leys Farm

Lower Balney Grounds

Isworth Farm

Castlethorpe Mill (dis)

Castlethorp

CASTLETHORPE RD

HANSLOPE RD

LODGE FARM CT

Castlethorpe Fst Sch

THE CHESTNUTS

NORTH ST

PH

SOUTH CL

NEW RD

5

Badger's Farm

River Tove

STATION RD

THE CHEQUERS

SCHOOL LA

PROSPECT PL

BENS CL

MALTING

SHEPPERTON CL

44

Milton Keynes Boundary Wlk
Grand Union Canal Wlk
Grand Union Canal

4

Cheley Well

Sewage Works

Thrupp Wharf

PH

NORTHAMPTON RD

Elm Tree Farm

3

Cobb's Bush Farm

The Priory

Furtho

Manor Farm

Mast

43

Dogsmouth Brook

YARDLEY RD

Ivy Cottage

2

Rectory Farm

Cosgrove Village Prim Sch

Elms Farm

MANOR CL

BRIDGE RD

PARK CL

THE GREEN

St Vincent's Well (chalybeate)

MAIN ST

LOCK LA

PO

Cosgrove

THE STOCKS

PH

Hotel

The Little Manor

Cosgrove Hall

STRATFORD RD

Cosgrove Leisure Park

1

Ash Pole Spinney

Broad Water

Knotwood Fields Farm

A508

NORTHAMPTON RD

The Quarries

Cosgrove Leisure Park

42

77 A 78 B C 79 D E F

217
229

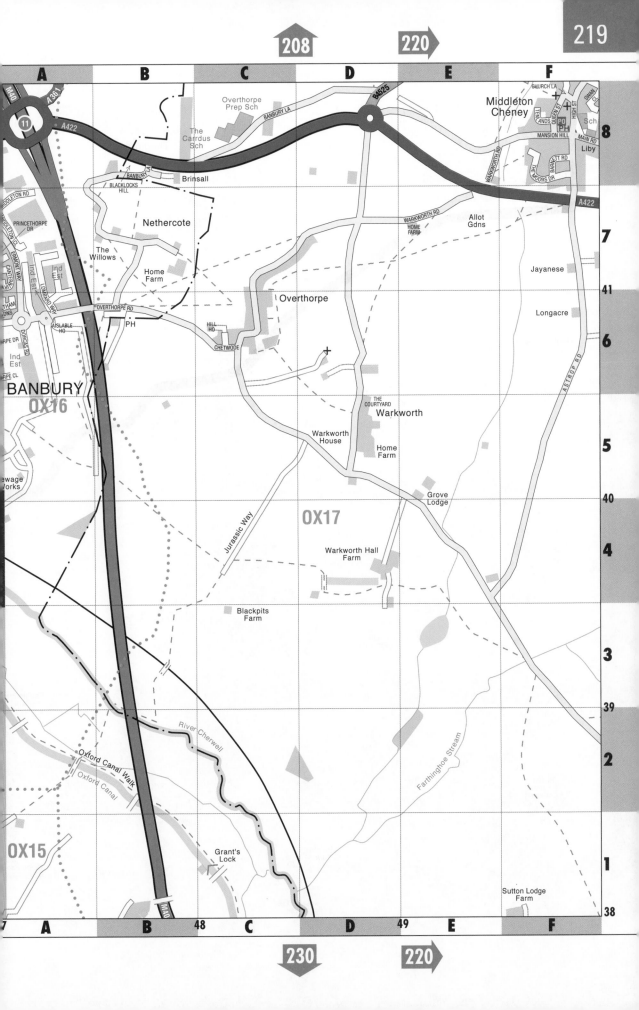

A B C D E F

8

Lower
Middleton
Cheney

BONMAN CL
MIDWAY
BULL BAULK
ARROW CL
PEACOCK'S
YEW TREE CL
DANDS DR
DANDS CL
LEXTON
MAIN RD LA
SLADE LEAS LA
GUNS LA
WATERS LA
ASH TREE CT
THENFORD RD
THE AVENUE
HORTON CRES
RISE HALL LA
POPLARS CL
BRAGGINGTONS
HORTON DR
LONGBRIDGES
HAILSHAM CT
MANOR CL
HORTON RD
HORTON
KINGSTON CL
WASTEL DR
ASHLADE
SALMONS

Thenford
House

Gardener's
Cottage

STABLE
YD

Thenford

+

A422

Thenford
Lodge

7

TULBROOK
STONES

Sewage
Works

Burgess
Farm

41

OX17

Thenford
Grange

6

Middleton Lodge
Farm

Works

Avenue
Bridge

5

Farthinghoe Stream

A422

40

Baldwin's
Spinney

4

Great
Purston

NN13

Little
Purston

Farthinghoe
Park

3

39

Buston
Farm

2

Buston
Farm
Cottages

Sandy La

Astrophill
Farm

1

Coldharbour

38

Rosamond's
Bower

50 A B 51 C D 52 E F

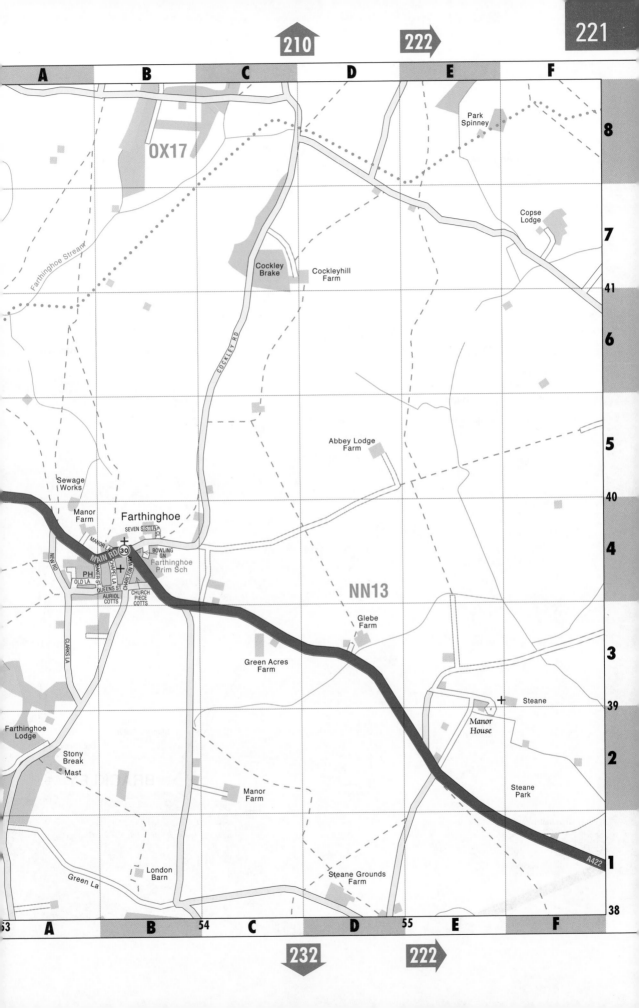

210
222
222

OX17

Park
Spinney

Copse
Lodge

A422

Cockley
Brake

Cockleyhill
Farm

COCKLEY RD

Farthinghoe Stream

Abbey Lodge
Farm

Sewage
Works

Manor
Farm

Farthinghoe

SEVEN SISTERS

MANOR LA

BOWLING
GN

Farthinghoe
Prim Sch

NN13

MAIN RD

30

CHURCH ST

NEW RD

PH

CHAPEL LA

OLD LA

QUEENS ST

AURIOL
COTTS

CHARLTON WY

CHURCH
PIECE
COTTS

Glebe
Farm

Steane

Manor
House

Green Acres
Farm

CLARKS LA

Farthinghoe
Lodge

Stony
Break

Mast

Manor
Farm

Steane
Park

London
Barn

Green La

Steane Grounds
Farm

A422

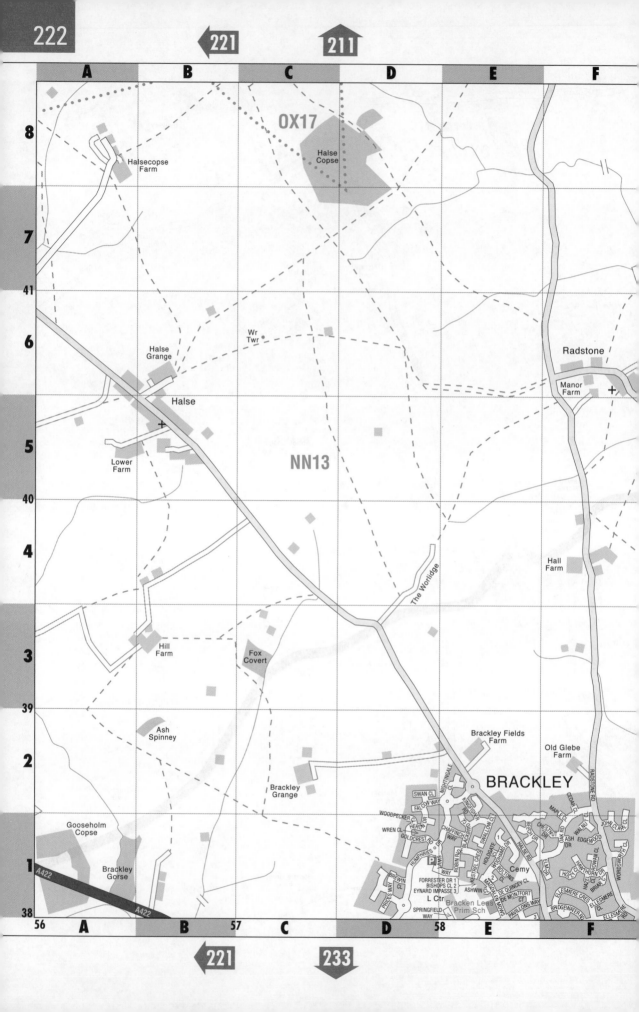

A B C D E F

8

7

41

6

5

40

4

3

39

2

1

38

Falcutt Hall

Crowfield
B4525
Crowfield
Shortgrove Wood
Staplegate Farm
40
Whistley Wood
Pimlico Farm
B4525
Pimlico
Kiln Farm
Hoppersford Farm
Wrighton's Barn
A43
Hoppersford Bridge

NN13

Coldharbour Farm

Fox Covert

Whitfield House Farm
THE AVENUE
CHESTNUT GR
MILL RD
TRENGOTHAL CT
FARRER CL
Inn
CHAPEL LA
Whitfield
Manor Farm
Mill Bridge
Sewage Works
River Great Ouse

Ilett's Farm

Sundale

Foxhill Spinney

Bushey End Wood

NORTHAMPTON RD
Saw Mill

Versions Farm

Airstrip

A43

TURWESTON RD

59 A B 60 C D 61 E F

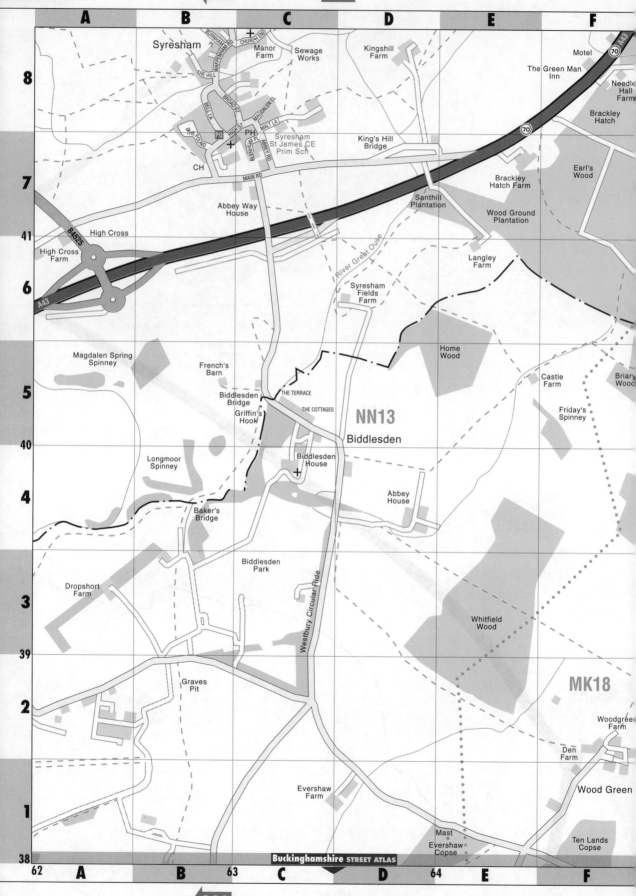

A B C D E F

8

Syresham

Manor Farm

Sewage Works

Kingshill Farm

Motel

The Green Man Inn

Needle Hall Farm

Brackley Hatch

BURNHAM RD
WAPPENHAM PL
CHURCH END
THE HILL
BROAD ST
HIGH ST
MAGDALEN CL
MALT LA
BELL LA
THE POUND
PO
PH
BLENHEIM PL
ABBEY RD
THE CROFT

King's Hill Bridge

Syresham St James CE Prim Sch

CH

MAIN RD

Santhill Plantation

Brackley Hatch Farm

Earl's Wood

7

Abbey Way House

Wood Ground Plantation

41

High Cross

B4525

River Great Ouse

Langley Farm

High Cross Farm

A43

Syresham Fields Farm

6

Home Wood

Castle Farm

Briary Wood

Magdalen Spring Spinney

French's Barn

5

Biddlesden Bridge

THE TERRACE

Griffin's Hook

THE COTTAGES

NN13

Friday's Spinney

Biddlesden

40

Biddlesden House

Longmoor Spinney

Abbey House

4

Baker's Bridge

Dropshort Farm

Biddlesden Park

Westbury Circular Ride

Whitfield Wood

3

39

MK18

Graves Pit

2

Woodgreen Farm

Den Farm

Evershaw Farm

Wood Green

1

Mast

Evershaw Copse

Ten Lands Copse

38

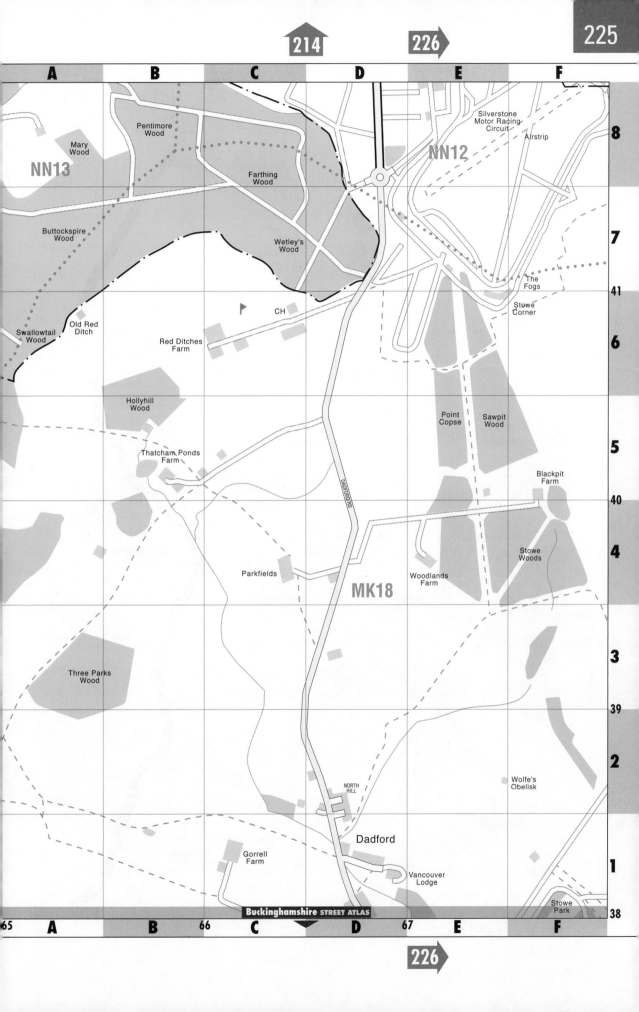

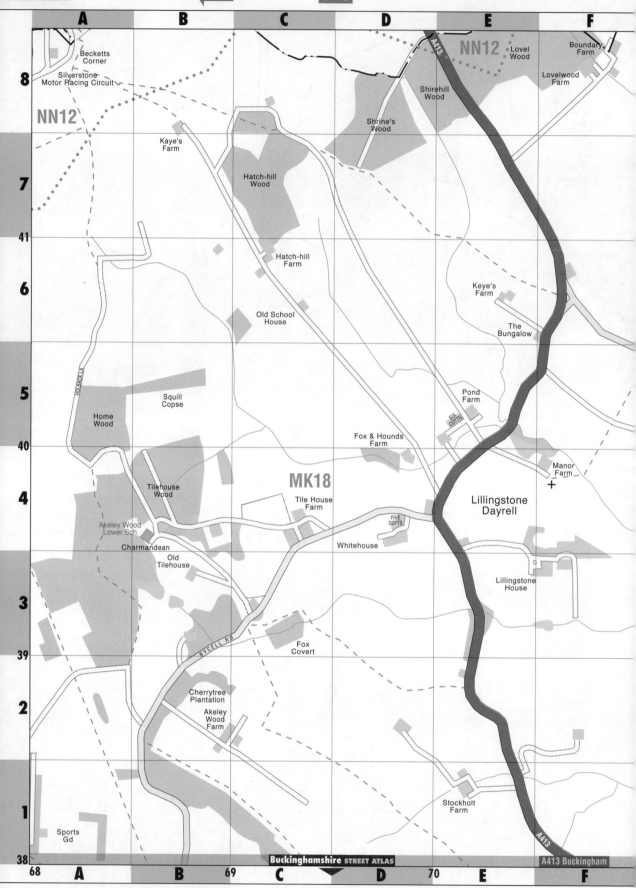

A B C D E F

NN12
Hill
Copse

Manor
Cottages

Manor
House

West Ashalls
Copse

8

Briary
Lodge

Briary Wood
Farm

East Ashalls
Copse

Long
Copse

The
Spinney

DEANSHANGER DR

Manor
Lodge

Forest
Farm

7

41

Valley
Farm

Bradley
Fields Farm

6

Church
Farm

PO

Wicken
Wood

CHURCH LA

BROOKSIDE

Notamore
Copse

WENTWORTH
COTTS

Glebe
Farm

Bridge
Farm

Lillingstone
Lovell

Lilby
Wood

MK19

5

40

Hall
Farm

MK18

Leckhampstead
Wood

4

Hill
Farm

3

39

2

Park
Copse

WICKEN RD

THE SHAW

Lodge
Farm

Wicken
Road
Farm

LONG
ROW

Limes End

1

CHAPEL LA

Pottery
Farm

Leckhampstead
House

38

71 A B 72 C D 73 E F

A B C D E F

8

7

41

MK12

6

5

40

4

MK11

3

39

2

1

38

77 A B 78 C D 79 E F

Knotwood
Fields Farm

Shrob Lodge
Cottages

Shrob Lodge
Farm

Old
Stratford

Old Stratford
Prim Sch

MK19

Chantry
Farm

Manor Farm

Manor
House

Passenham

CH

Mill Farm
Ctyd

Mill Farm

Dogmouth
Bridge

Wheelwrights
Way

Canalside

Stony Stratford
Nature Reserve

Weir

The Mill

PH

St Mary & St Giles
CE Jun Sch

Liby

Stony
Stratford

Cemy

River Great Ouse

Calverton
Cottage

PH

Manor Farm

Calverton

Almshouses

LOWER
WEALD

CHARITY
COTTS

Rectory
Farm

Middle Weald
Farm

MIDDLE
WEALD

Queen Eleanor
Prim Sch

Mast

Grand Union Canal

A5 Milton Keynes (A509)

Buckinghamshire STREET ATLAS

WHITEHORSE YD 1
GEORGE YD 2
COFFERIDGE CL 3
SWINFEN'S YD 4
LONDON HO 5
ANTHONY CT 6
THE RETREAT 7
SWAN TERR 8

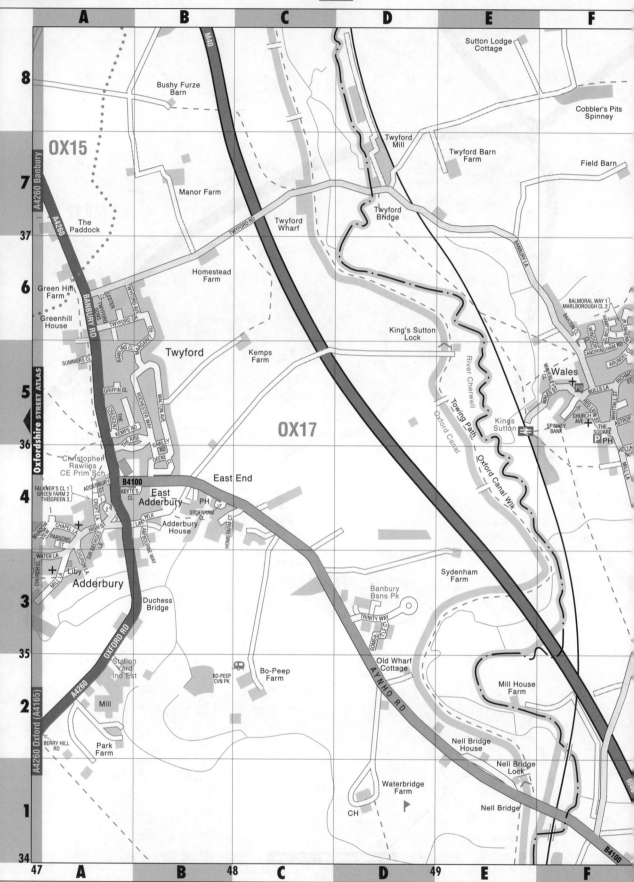

231
221

A B C D E F

8

Colready Farm

Coleready Plantation

Hinton Grounds Farm

7

Forceleap Close

Walltree Farm

THE CHESTNUTS

37

NORRIS ACRE

Airfield

Forceleap Farm

6

FARTHINGHOE RD

Hinton-in-the-Hedges

PH

BADGER'S

DUCKEN

Sports Gd

CARTWRIGHT RD

Washbrook Farm

5

Charlton House Farm

NN13

36

4

Charlton Firs

3

The Cabin

The Dower House

College Barn Spinney

35

Camp Farm

Rowler

OX17

Myers' Copse

2

Rowler's Covert

1

Cross Stones

34

53 A B 54 C D 55 E F

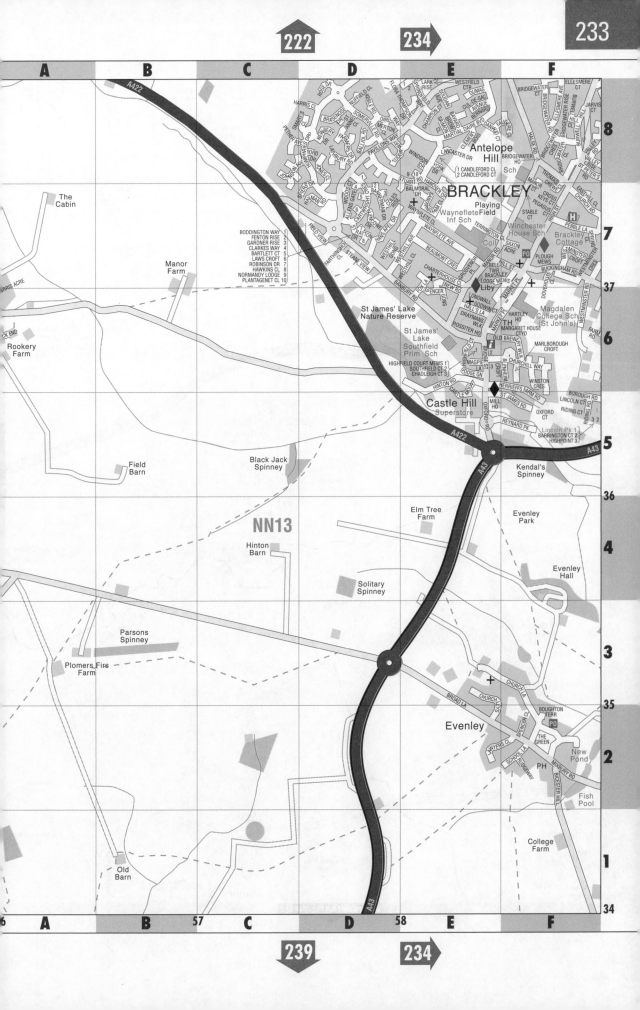

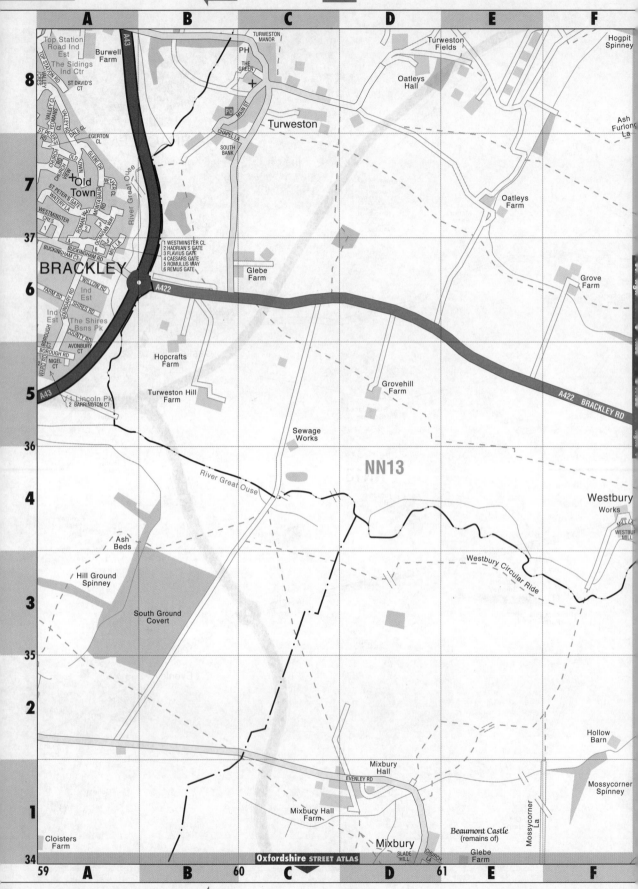

A B C D E F

8

7

37

BRACKLEY

1 WESTMINSTER CL
2 HADRIAN'S GATE
3 FLAVIUS GATE
4 CAESARS GATE
5 ROMULUS WAY
6 REMUS GATE

6

5

Top Station Road Ind Est
The Sidings Ind Ctr
Burwell Farm
St David's Ct

Old Town

St Peter's Gate

Westminster Cres

Ind Est
The Shires Bsns Pk

1 Lincoln Pk
2 Barrington Ct

Hopcrafts Farm

Turweston Hill Farm

TURWESTON MANOR
PH
THE GREEN
PO
CHAPEL LA
SOUTH BANK

Turweston

Glebe Farm

Turweston Fields

Oatleys Hall

Oatleys Farm

Hogpit Spinney

Ash Furlong La

Grove Farm

A422 BRACKLEY RD

36

4

River Great Ouse

Sewage Works

Grovehill Farm

NN13

Westbury Works

Westbury Circular Ride

MILL LA
WESTBURY MILL

Ash Beds

Hill Ground Spinney

South Ground Covert

Westbury

3

35

2

Mixbury Hall

EVENLEY RD

Mossycorner La

Hollow Barn

Mossycorner Spinney

1

Cloisters Farm

Mixbury Hall Farm

Mixbury

SLADE HILL

CHURCH LA

Beaumont Castle (remains of)

Glebe Farm

34

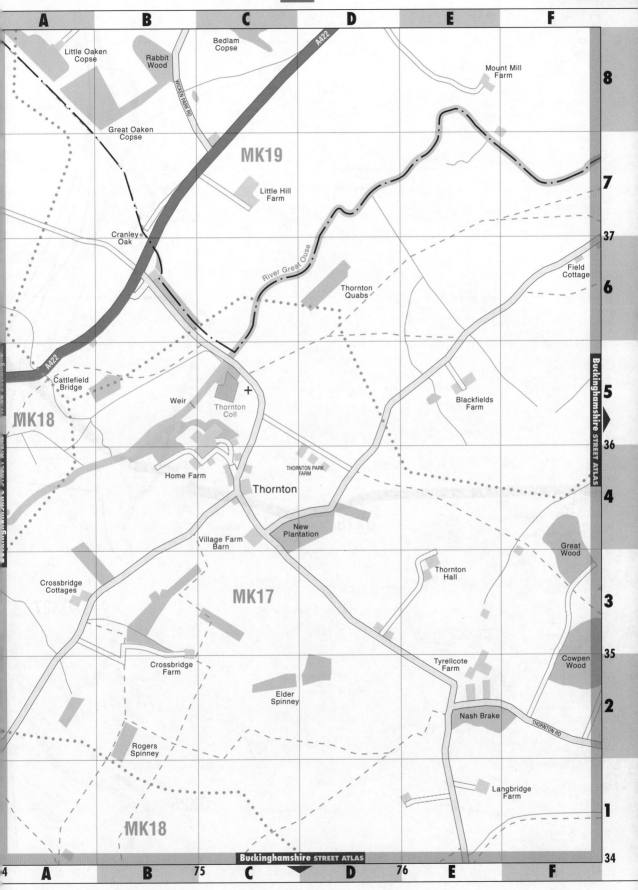

A   B   C   D   E   F

8

Little Oaken
Copse

Rabbit
Wood

Bedlam
Copse

Mount Mill
Farm

Great Oaken
Copse

WICKEN PARK RD

A422

MK19

7

Little Hill
Farm

37

Cranley
Oak

River Great Ouse

Thornton
Quabs

Field
Cottage

6

A422

Cattlefield
Bridge

MK18

Weir

Thornton
Coll

Blackfields
Farm

5

36

Home Farm

THORNTON PARK
FARM

4

Thornton

Village Farm
Barn

New
Plantation

Thornton
Hall

Great
Wood

Crossbridge
Cottages

MK17

3

35

Crossbridge
Farm

Elder
Spinney

Tyrellcote
Farm

Cowpen
Wood

Nash Brake

THORNTON RD

2

Rogers
Spinney

Langbridge
Farm

1

MK18

34

4   A   B   75   C   D   76   E   F

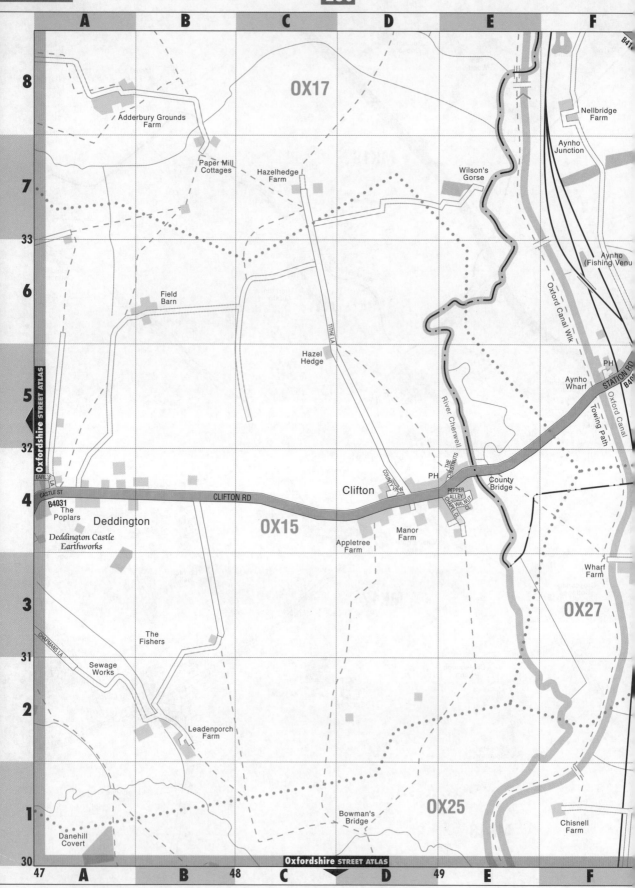

A B C D E F

8

OX17

Adderbury Grounds
Farm

7

Paper Mill
Cottages

Hazelhedge
Farm

Nellbridge
Farm

Aynho
Junction

Wilson's
Gorse

33

Aynho
(Fishing Venu

6

Field
Barn

Oxford Canal Wlk

Hazel
Hedge

TITHE LA

PH

Aynho
Wharf

STATION RO

5

Oxfordshire STREET ATLAS

River Cherwell

B40

Oxford Canal

Towing Path

32

EARL'S LA

CASTLE ST

Clifton

COUNTY FEN

PH

THE CHESTNUTS

County
Bridge

4

B4031

CLIFTON RD

The
Poplars

Deddington

OX15

PEPPER
ALLEY

WALNUT
CL

CHAPEL CL

Deddington Castle
Earthworks

Appletree
Farm

Manor
Farm

Wharf
Farm

3

OX27

CHAPMANS LA

The
Fishers

31

Sewage
Works

2

Leadenporch
Farm

Bowman's
Bridge

OX25

1

Danehill
Covert

Chisnell
Farm

30

A B C D E F

8
BANBURY RD
7
33
6
5
32
4
3
31
2
1
30

Ox House

Pesthouse Wood

NN13

Allot Gdns

Bricklands Farm

Recn Gd

BLACKSMITHS HILL 1
SKITTLE ALLEY 2
THE HILL 3
THE SQUARE 4

B4100 BANBURY RD

B4031

B4100

B4031

B4031

COLLEGE FIELDS

College Farm

CHARLTON RD

RATCLIFFE RD

THE BUTTS

PORTWAY

PORTWAY GDNS

BUTTS CL

BOWLING

LEA

THE GLEBE

CROUGHTON RD

SCHOOL END

LITTLE WAY

ROUNDTOWN

CARTWRIGHT GDNS

AYNHO CT

Friar's Well

AYNHOE PK

Aynho

Aynho Fields

OX17

Ryeland Hill

Northcotehill Covert

Ash Grove

Puckwell

Keeper's Hill

Lower Aynho Grounds

Aynho Park

The Firs

The Mill House

Park Flat

Holloway's Flat

The Oaks

Ockley Brook

Sewage Works

Risley's Corner

Upper Aynho Grounds

Souldern Mill

Old Shaws

WHARF LA

Souldern Manor

FOX LA

PH

BATES LA

HIGH ST

BODWELL

FOXHILL LA

1 CHAPEL ROW
2 THE PADDOCKS
3 COTSWOLD CT

Souldern

OX27

Mast

Ploughley Hill

B4100

Foxhill La

Souldern Grounds

Holtage La

Fox Hill

Inkerman Farm

OX25

Upper Souldern Grounds Farm

Foxhill Barn

M40

M40 Oxford (A34)

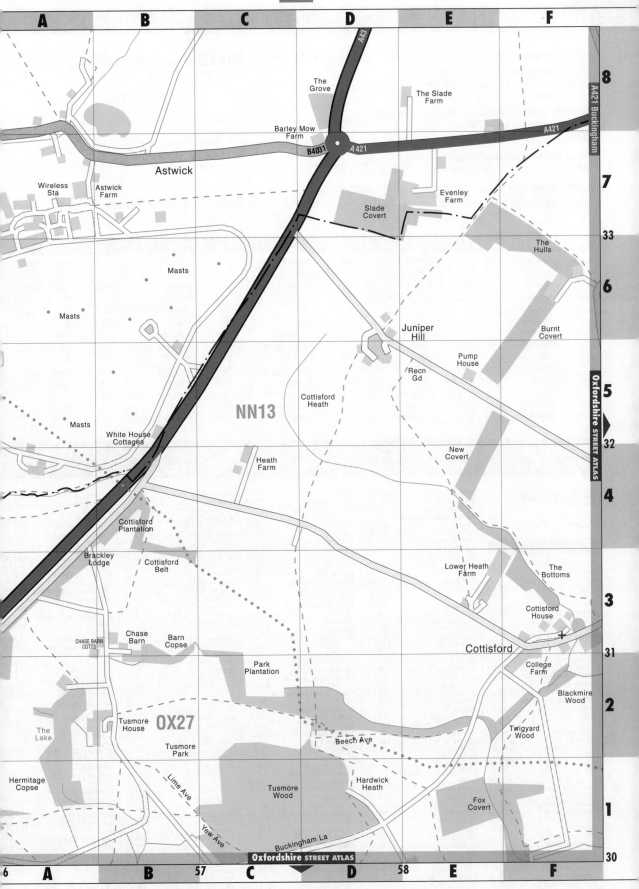

A B C D E F

8

The Grove

The Slade Farm

Barley Mow Farm

A 421

B4031 A 421

Astwick

7

33

Wireless Sta

Astwick Farm

Evenley Farm

Slade Covert

The Hulls

6

Masts

Burnt Covert

Juniper Hill

Masts

Pump House

Recn Gd

Cottisford Heath

5

32

New Covert

Masts

NN13

White House Cottages

Heath Farm

4

Cottisford Plantation

Lower Heath Farm

The Bottoms

Brackley Lodge

Cottisford Belt

3

Cottisford House

CHASE BARN COTTS

Chase Barn

Barn Copse

Cottisford

31

Park Plantation

College Farm

Tusmore House

OX27

Blackmire Wood

2

The Lake

Tusmore Park

Beech Ave

Twigyard Wood

Hermitage Copse

Hardwick Heath

Fox Covert

Tusmore Wood

1

Lime Ave

Yew Ave

Buckingham La

30

Oxfordshire STREET ATLAS

Oxfordshire STREET ATLAS

A421 Buckingham

Index

Place name May be abbreviated on the map

Location number Present when a number indicates the place's position in a crowded area of mapping

Locality, town or village Shown when more than one place has the same name

Postcode district District for the indexed place

Page and grid square Page number and grid reference for the standard mapping

Church Rd 6 Beckenham BR2.........53 C6

Cities, towns and villages are listed in CAPITAL LETTERS

Public and commercial buildings are highlighted in **magenta** Places of interest are highlighted in **blue** with a star★

Abbreviations used in the index

Acad	Academy	Comm	Common	Gd	Ground	L	Leisure	Prom	Promenade
App	Approach	Cott	Cottage	Gdn	Garden	La	Lane	Rd	Road
Arc	Arcade	Cres	Crescent	Gn	Green	Liby	Library	Recn	Recreation
Ave	Avenue	Cswy	Causeway	Gr	Grove	Mdw	Meadow	Ret	Retail
Bglw	Bungalow	Ct	Court	H	Hall	Meml	Memorial	Sh	Shopping
Bldg	Building	Ctr	Centre	Ho	House	Mkt	Market	Sq	Square
Bsns, Bus	Business	Ctry	Country	Hospl	Hospital	Mus	Museum	St	Street
Bvd	Boulevard	Cty	County	HQ	Headquarters	Orch	Orchard	Sta	Station
Cath	Cathedral	Dr	Drive	Hts	Heights	Pal	Palace	Terr	Terrace
Cir	Circus	Dro	Drove	Ind	Industrial	Par	Parade	TH	Town Hall
Cl	Close	Ed	Education	Inst	Institute	Pas	Passage	Univ	University
Cnr	Corner	Emb	Embankment	Int	International	Pk	Park	Wk, Wlk	Walk
Coll	College	Est	Estate	Intc	Interchange	Pl	Place	Wr	Water
Com	Community	Ex	Exhibition	Junc	Junction	Prec	Precinct	Yd	Yard

Index of towns, villages, streets, hospitals, industrial estates, railway stations, schools, shopping centres, universities and places of interest

240 1st–Amb

1st Drift PE9 .... 2 D8
78 Derngate★⃞NN1 .....159 D5

A

A6 Bsns Ctr NN16........ 71 E4
Abbey Cl NN29........164 C2
Abbey Ct
⃞ Daventry NN11....135 C2
Wollaston NN29....146 D3
Abbey Ho ⃞ NN5 ....159 A6
Abbey Lo NN3 ....160 C7
Abbey Prim Sch The
NN4...........................159 C1
Abbey Rd
Northampton NN4.....159 B3
Roade NN7 ....191 C4
Syresham NN13........224 C7
Wellingborough NN8 ...129 F3
Abbey Rise NN29........146 D3
Abbey St
Daventry NN11 ....135 C2
Market Harborough LE16 .. 31 E3
Northampton NN5.....159 A6
Abbey Way
Ravenstone MK46 ....194 E2
Rushden NN10............148 A8
Abbot Cl NN11............153 D8
Abbots Cl NN15..........91 B7
Abbots Way
Kettering NN15 ....91 A6
Northampton NN5 ....158 F6
Roade NN7 ....191 C4
Wellingborough NN8 ....129 F4
Abbotts Cl NN14..........77 D3
Abbotts Way NN10......131 F1
Aberdare Rd NN5........159 A8
Aberdeen Terr NN5.....159 A6
ABINGTON 160 B8
Abington Ave NN3 .....160 A8
Abington Bsns Ctr
NN1..........................160 A7
Abington Cotts NN1....160 A8
Abington Ct NN3........160 B8
Abington Gr NN1........159 F8
Abington Mus★⃞NN1....160 A7
Abington Park Cres
NN3.........................160 C7
Abington Rd NN17 .....36 B7

Abington Sq NN1 .... 159 E6
Abington St NN1........159 D6
ABINGTON VALE 160 C7
Abington Vale Prim Sch
NN3........................160 C6
Ablett Cl NN14.......... 76 D2
ABTHORPE 201 F1
Abthorpe Ave NN2 .....141 D5
Accurate Boot The
NN1.........................159 E7
Ace La NN7..............172 F7
ACHURCH 58 C2
Acorn Cl
Islip NN14 .... 76 B3
Kettering NN15 .... 92 B5
Lubenham LE16 .... 30 E3
Acorn Ind Est NN14 .... 76 B3
Acorn Pk NN15 .... 92 C4
Acorn Way NN12.........214 E4
Acre Cl NN11............135 C6
Acre Ct NN16............ 72 D3
Acre La NN11............141 A6
Acremead PE8........... 28 B3
Acre St NN16............ 72 D3
Adam Bsns Ctr NN16... 71 F5
Adam & Eve St ⃞ LE16 .. 31 E3
Adams Ave NN1 ....159 F7
Adams Cl
Stanwick NN9 ....114 A5
Wellingborough NN8 ...130 B5
Adams Dr NN14 .... 70 B7
Adams Rd NN11 ....184 B6
Adamswood Cl LE16 ...31 C3
ADDERBURY 230 A3
Adderbury Ct OX17 ....230 A4
Addington Park Ind Est
NN14.......................113 C2
Addington Rd
Irthlingborough NN9......113 A5
Woodford NN14.......... 94 D6
Addis Cl NN15 .... 92 C1
Addison Rd
Desborough NN14....... 50 F3
Northampton NN3 ......142 B2
Addlecroft Cl NN2 .....141 B3
Adelaide Ho
Corby NN17 .... 22 F1
⃞ Northampton NN2 ...159 C7
Adelaide Pl ⃞ NN1 ...159 C5
Adelaide St NN2 ....159 C7
Adelaide Terr ⃞ NN2 ...159 C7
Adit View NN9...........131 D8

Admiral Ct
Kettering NN16 ....72 C3
Market Harborough
LE16.........................31 D3
Admirals Way NN11....135 E2
Adnitt Ho LE17.......... 45 E5
Adnitt Rd
Northampton NN1 ....159 F7
Rushden NN10...........132 A2
ADSTONE 186 B4
Afan Cl NN16 .... 72 A5
Affleck Bridge NN9 ....111 F4
Aggate Way NN6........144 D4
Agnes Rd NN2 ....159 C8
Agricultural Hos
CV47.......................166 A5
Ainsdale Cl NN2 ....141 F3
Aintree Dr NN10 ....148 D8
Aintree Rd
Corby NN18 .... 36 E1
Northampton NN3 ....141 F4
Aislable Ho OX16 .....219 A7
Akela Cl NN15 .... 91 C8
Akeley Wood Jun Sch
MK19.......................228 A1
Akeley Wood Lower Sch
MK18.......................226 B4
Alanbrooke Cl NN15....72 E1
Alastor NN8 ....129 B5
Albany Ct LE16 .... 31 F4
Albany Gdns NN18 ..... 36 B2
Albany Rd
Market Harborough
LE16.........................31 F4
Northampton NN1 ....160 A7
Albany The ⃞ NN11....135 C2
Alberta Cl NN18 .... 36 C3
Albert Pl NN1............159 D6
Albert Rd
Finedon NN9 ....111 F5
Market Harborough LE16 .. 31 F3
Rushden NN10...........132 B2
Albert St ⃞ NN16 ..... 72 C2
Albion Ct
Little Harrowden NN9...110 C4
Northampton NN1 ....159 D5
Albion Ho NN1...........159 D5
Albion Pl
Northampton NN1 ....159 D5
Rushden NN10...........132 B1
Albion Rd NN16......... 72 B3
Albisdene Ct NN10......132 C2

Admiral Ct
Alchester Ct NN12 .....203 C5
Alcombe Rd NN1 ....159 E7
Alcombe Terr NN1 .....159 E7
Aldbury Ct ⃞ NN1 .....159 C7
Aldene Rd MK19 ....207 B3
Alder Cl NN14 .... 51 C3
Alder Ct NN3 ....142 F5
Alderley Cl NN5........158 B8
ALDERTON 205 A2
ALDGATE 1 B5
Aldgate Ct PE9 .... 1 A5
Aldsworth Cl NN8......145 E8
Aldwell Cl NN4 ....175 F7
ALDWINCLE 76 F8
Aldwincle Rd NN14 ....76 A6
Aldwinkles Yd ⃞ LE16 ..31 E3
Alexander Ct
Corby NN17 .... 22 A2
Irchester NN29 ....147 B8
Northampton NN3 ......142 E3
Alexander Pl NN9......113 A4
Alexander Rd NN9 .....113 A4
Alexandra Rd
Corby NN17 .... 36 E6
Desborough NN14....... 50 F3
Northampton NN1 ......159 E6
Rushden NN10...........132 D2
Wellingborough NN8 ...130 B5
Alexandra St
Burton Latimer NN15 ... 92 B2
Kettering NN16 .... 72 C2
Alexandra Terr ⃞
NN2.........................141 C3
Alfoxden St NN8 ....129 B3
Alfred St
Irchester NN29 ....147 A8
Kettering NN16 ....72 C2
Northampton NN1 ......159 F6
Rushden NN10...........132 B2
Stanwick NN9 ....113 F4
Alfred Street Jun Sch
NN10.......................132 B2
Alibone Cl NN3 ....126 D1
Alice Ct NN6............100 F6
Alice Dr NN15 .... 92 B1
Alice Gdns NN16 .... 72 D3
Alington Cl NN9 ....112 A5
Aiken Cl NN8............129 F8
Allan Bank NN8.........129 B3
Allans Cl CV23.......... 80 A5
Allans Dr CV23.......... 80 A5
Allard Cl NN3 ....143 D4
Allebone Rd NN6 ......144 E3

Alledge Dr NN14........ 94 D7
Allen Ct NN9 ....112 A5
Allen Rd
Finedon NN9 ....112 A5
Irthlingborough NN9.....112 A5
Northampton NN1 ......160 A7
Rushden NN10...........132 C3
Allens Gate NN13 .....233 D7
Allens Hill NN29 ....164 D3
Allens Orch OX17 .....196 F6
Alliance Ct ⃞ NN8.....130 A5
Alliance Terr NN8......129 F5
Alliston Gdns ⃞ NN2...159 C5
All Saints CE Mid Sch
NN2.........................141 E6
All Saints' CE Prim Sch
NN8.........................130 B4
Alma St
Northampton NN5 ......159 A6
Wellingborough NN8 ...130 A5
Almond Cl
Barby CV23............. 99 C1
Bugbrooke NN7.........173 A4
Almond Gr NN3.........142 C1
Almond Rd NN16....... 72 D4
Almshouses NN6 ....102 B5
Almshouses The
MK46.......................194 E2
Alness Cl NN15 .... 91 E8
Alpine Ct NN15 .... 92 B2
Alpine Way NN5 ....140 A3
Alsace Cl NN5 ....139 F2
Altendiez Way NN15 ... 92 B4
Althorp★⃞NN7 ....139 A7
Althorp Cl
Market Harborough
LE16.........................32 B3
Wellingborough NN8 ...129 C2
Althorpe Pl NN16 ...... 72 D3
Althorp Pl NN18 .... 36 B3
Althorp Rd NN5.........159 A6
Althorp St ⃞ NN1 .....159 C6
Alton St NN4 ....159 B3
Alvington Way LE16 ...31 D5
Alvis Ct NN3 ....143 C4
Alvis Way NN11.........134 F3
Amber Dr NN6..........108 A5
Amberley Rd NN7 .....192 C1
Ambleside Cl
⃞ Northampton NN3 ...142 C4
Wellingborough NN8 ...129 C5
Ambridge Cl NN4 ......174 F8
Ambridge Ct ⃞ NN1 ...159 F6

Ambush St NN5............159 B6
Amen Cnr NN14........113 C8
Amen Pl NN14.........113 C8
Amundsen Cl NN11.....135 B6
Ancell Rd MK11........229 E5
Anchor Dr NN2........141 B6
Anderson Ave CV22....98 A8
Anderson Dr NN15.....72 F1
Anderson Gn NN8......129 C4
Anding Cl MK46.......195 E4
Andrew Cl NN10......132 C7
Andrew Macdonald Cl
LE16................31 F3
Andrews Ave NN13.....238 E6
Andrews Way NN9.....114 B5
Angel Ct 2 LE16......31 E3
Angel La 2 NN8.......130 A4
Angel St
1 Market Harborough
LE16................31 E3
Northampton NN1......159 D5
Angel Yd 19 NN16......72 B2
Anglian Rd NN11......135 B1
Anglia NN3..........141 F6
Angus Ho NN17.......36 F6
Annandale Rd NN17....36 E7
Anna's La NN12.......173 B1
Anne Cl NN10.........132 C7
Anne Rd NN8.........129 E2
Annesley Cl NN3......160 D6
Anne St NN17.........36 E5
Ann Sq NN16..........72 E3
Anscomb Way NN11....184 B6
Ansell Way NN4.......175 C4
Anson Cl
Corby NN17..........36 B7
Daventry NN11........135 C1
ANTELOPE HILL.......233 E8
Anthony Ct MK11......229 D5
Antona Cl NN9.......114 B4
Antona Dr NN9.......114 B4
Antona Gdns NN9.....114 B4
Anvil The NN7........172 F7
APETHORPE...........14 C3
Apethorpe Rd PE8......15 C3
Apollo Cl NN11.......135 B3
Applebarn Cl NN4.....175 C4
Appleby Cl NN9.......110 F1
Appleby Wlk 2 NN3....142 C4
Appledore Cl NN2.....141 C4
Applegarth Cl NN18....36 D3
Applegarth The NN6....121 C4
APPLETREE...........196 C8
Appletree Ct NN9......111 F5
Appletree Ind Est
OX17...............196 E7
Appletree La NN11.....182 F2
Appletree Rd OX17.....196 F6
Approach The NN5.....158 A4
Aquitaine Cl NN5......139 F1
Arbour Ct NN3........142 E4
Arbours Prim Sch The
NN3................142 D3
Arbour View Ct NN3....142 E5
Arbury Banks OX17....196 F5
Archangel Rd 2 NN4....158 F2
Archangel Sq 1 NN4....158 F2
Archer Ave NN11......118 C1
Archers Cl NN2.......141 B5
Archers Spinney CV21..99 B8
Archery Rd OX17......209 A1
Archfield NN8........129 F4
Archfield Terr 2 NN9...112 F2
Arden Cl
3 Daventry NN11.....135 B4
Kettering NN15.......91 F5
Market Harborough
LE16...............32 A4
Ardens Gr NN7........174 A7
Arden Way LE16.......31 F5
Ardington Rd NN1......160 A7
Argyle Pk LE16........48 E8
Argyle St NN5........159 A6
Argyll Ho NN17.......36 E6
Argyll St
Corby NN17..........36 F6
Kettering NN15.......91 B8
Ariel Cl NN5.........140 A1
Arkwright Rd
Corby NN17..........22 C1
Irchester NN29.......147 C7
Arlbury Rd NN3.......143 B4
Armley Cl NN6........121 C4
ARMSTON............59 E8
Armston Rd PE8.......59 B8
Arndale NN2.........140 F5
Arnheim Hos NN11.....199 D7
Arnhill Rd NN17.......10 B1
Arnills Way CV23......100 A2
Arnold Cott MK19......229 B7
Arnold Rd NN2........159 C8
Arnsby Cres NN3......126 B1
Arnsley Rd NN17......23 A1
Arnull Cres NN11......135 B4
Arran Way NN17......36 C8
Arrow Cl OX17........220 A4
Arrow Head Rd NN4....158 F3
ARTHINGWORTH.......68 C4
Arthingworth Rd NN14..50 E4
Arthur St
Northampton NN2.....141 C1
Wellingborough NN8...129 E4
Arthur's Way 1 NN16...72 C2
Artizan Rd NN1.......159 F7
Arum Cl NN10........148 C7
Arundel Cl
Kings Sutton OX17....230 F5

Arundel Cl continued
Thrapston NN14.......76 F2
Arundel Ct
Kettering NN15.......91 F8
Rushden NN10........148 A8
Arundel St 9 NN1......159 C7
Arundel Wlk NN18.....36 B5
Ascot Cl NN18........36 E1
Ascot Rd NN10.......148 D8
Ashbourne Dr NN14....50 E4
Ashbrook Cl NN14.....90 A4
Ashbrow Rd NN4......158 F3
Ashburnham Rd NN1...159 F8
Ashby Cl NN8........129 E7
Ashby Ct
Guilsborough NN6.....103 E7
Kislingbury NN7......157 D3
Moulton NN3.........126 C1
Ashby Dr
Crick NN6...........100 F5
Rushden NN10........148 A8
Ashby Fields Prim Sch
NN11...............135 C5
Ashby Gdns 4 NN3.....126 C1
Ashby Pk NN11.......135 C4
Ashby Rd
Braunston NN11......118 C1
Daventry NN11.......135 B4
Daventry NN11.......135 B7
Daventry NN11.......135 C2
Kilsby CV23.........100 A2
Welton NN11.........119 D1
ASHBY ST LEDGERS...119 D5
Ash Cl
Daventry NN11.......135 C4
Irchester NN29.......147 A7
Ashcroft Cl NN5......140 B1
Ashcroft Gdns NN3....142 A2
Ash Ct NN14.........76 D1
Ashdale Cl NN6.......127 D1
Ashdown Cl NN15.....92 A5
Ashdown Pl NN17......36 E7
Ashdown Rd NN11.....135 C4
Ash Dr
Brackley NN13.......222 F1
Sywell NN6..........143 D7
Ashes The
Bugbrooke NN7.......172 F7
Northampton NN4.....176 B6
Weldon NN17.........38 C8
Ashfield Ave NN9.....114 D6
Ashfield Rd
3 Market Harborough
LE16...............31 E4
Wellingborough NN8...129 E4
Ashfield Rise NN9.....114 C6
Ashford Cl NN13......160 C6
Ashford Lea NN14.....50 E4
Ashgate Ct NN14......70 C7
Ash Gr
Bugbrooke NN7.......172 F7
Desborough NN14.....50 E4
Northampton NN2.....141 B6
Ash La NN4..........175 B4
Ashlade OX17........220 B7
Ashlawn Rd CV22.....98 C7
Ashlawn Sch CV22....98 C7
Ashlea MK46.........195 E3
Ashleigh Cl CV23......99 C2
Ashleigh Ho 6 NN10...132 B2
ASHLEY.............18 E2
Ashley Ave NN17......36 B7
Ashley Ct
Blisworth NN7.......190 D7
Kettering NN16.......72 A3
Ashley La NN3........126 D1
Ashley Rd
Medbourne LE16......18 E6
Middleton LE16......20 B2
Stoke Albany LE16....34 A5
Weston by W LE16....18 C3
Ashley Way
Market Harborough
LE16...............32 B3
Northampton NN3.....142 E2
Ashmead NN3........143 A2
Ashmore NN6........121 C4
Ashpole Spinney NN4...158 C2
Ash Rd NN15.........72 D1
Ashridge Cl NN10.....148 A8
Ash Rise NN2........141 C6
Ash St NN1..........159 C7
Ashton
Oundle.............42 D5
Roade..............205 B8
Ashton CE Prim Sch
NN7...............191 F1
Ashton Cl NN11.......135 A3
Ashton Gr NN8.......129 D8
Ashton Lodge Farm
NN7...............192 A2
Ashton Rd
Hartwell NN7........192 C1
Oundle PE8..........42 B5
Roade NN7..........191 E2
Stoke Bruerne NN7....205 D8
Ash Tree Ct OX17......220 B8
Ashtree Gdns PE9......1 D2
Ashtree Way NN5......158 C7
Ashurst Cres NN18.....36 B4
Ash Way
Braunston NN11......118 B1
Hinton NN11.........184 A6
Ashway The
Brixworth NN6.......106 C1
Brixworth NN6.......125 B8
Ashwell Rd
Rushden NN10........132 D2

Ashwell Rd continued
Weedon Lois NN12....200 B2
Ashwells La NN6......82 B4
Ashwin Cl NN13......222 E1
Ashwood Rd NN5......158 C7
Ashworth St NN11.....135 C1
Askham Ave NN1......129 E1
Aspen Cl
Northampton NN3.....143 C3
Rushden NN10........132 B3
Aspen Ho NN15.......72 A1
Aspreys MK46........195 E4
Astbury Cl NN11......153 C8
ASTCOTE............188 F7
Aster Cl NN3.........160 D6
Aster Rd NN16.......72 D4
Astley Cl LE16........31 D1
Astley Pl NN21.......99 B7
ASTON LE WALLS.....182 F2
Aston Rise NN5.......158 B8
Astral Row OX17......210 E2
ASTROP.............231 B5
Astrop Gdns OX17.....231 A5
Astrop Grange OX17...231 A5
Astrop Rd
Kings Sutton OX17....231 B5
Middleton Cheney
OX17..............219 F6
ASTWICK............239 B7
Athelstan Rd NN16....72 D2
Atterbury Cl NN6......102 D4
Atterbury Way NN4....160 F2
Attlee Cl NN3........142 B4
Attley Cl NN8........129 C5
Attley Way NN9.......113 A3
Auctioneers Ct NN1....159 D4
Auctioneers Way
NN1...............159 D4
Auden Way NN17......36 C8
Audley Cl LE16.......32 B2
Augusta Ave NN4......175 C6
Augustus Rd MK11....229 E4
Auriga St LE16........31 F2
Auriol Cotts NN13.....221 B4
Austin Ho NN14......70 D7
Austins Cl LE16.......31 D3
Austins Pl NN12......214 E4
Austin St NN1........159 D7
Austins Yd NN6......144 E4
Austin Way NN11.....134 F4
Avalon Ct NN14......70 E7
Avebury Rd NN4......175 B8
Avenue Bernard
NN13..............233 E8
Avenue Cl NN11......111 E5
Avenue Inf Sch The
NN8...............130 A5
Avenue Rd
Finedon NN9........111 E5
Rushden NN10........148 F5
Wellingborough NN8...130 A5
Woodford NN14......94 D6
Avenue Terr NN16.....72 C3
Avenue The
Flore NN7...........155 E5
Medbourne LE16......19 C8
Middleton Cheney
OX17..............220 A8
Moulton NN3.........142 E3
Northampton, Dallington
NN5...............158 F7
Northampton, Meadow View
NN2...............140 F6
Northampton NN1.....159 F5
Northampton, Spinney Hill
NN3...............142 A3
Rothwell NN14.......70 D7
Stanwick NN9.......114 A3
Wellingborough NN8...130 A5
Whitfield NN13.......223 D4
Aviemore Gdns NN4...158 E1
Avignon Cl NN5.......140 A2
Avonbury Ct NN13....234 E3
Avon Cl
Daventry NN11.......153 A8
Kettering NN16.......72 A5
Wellingborough NN8...129 C6
Avondale Jun & Inf Schs
NN16..............72 D4
Avondale Mews NN16..72 D3
Avondale Rd NN16....72 D3
Avon Dr NN5.........140 E1
Avon Fields NN6......64 E6
Avon Wks NN16......72 D3
Axe Head Rd NN4.....158 F4
AYNHO.............237 C5
Aynho Cres NN1......141 C5
Aynho Ct OX17.......237 D7
Aynhoe Pk OX17......237 C7
Aynho (Fishing Venue)★
OX17..............236 F6
Aynho Rd OX17.......230 D2
Aynho Wlk NN2.......141 D5
Aynsley Cl NN14......50 F3
Ayr Cl NN18.........36 E1
Azalea Ct NN3........160 D6

B

Back La
Brigstock NN14.......55 F8
Chapel Brampton NN6..124 D1
Collyweston PE8......1 D2
East Farndon LE16....48 B7
Elton PE8...........28 D8
Gayton NN7..........173 E2

Back La continued
Great Brington NN7....138 C6
Holcot NN6..........160 A6
Little Addington NN14..113 B8
Morcott LE15........3 A6
Northampton NN4.....175 F8
Ringstead NN14......95 B3
Scaldwell NN6.......106 F5
South Luffenham LE15..3 D8
Backley Cl NN15......90 E8
Back Rd LE15.........3 E5
Backway NN29........146 D2
Backway The LE16.....31 F2
Bacon Hill MK46......195 E4
Bacon Rd NN8........129 E8
BADBY.............153 A2
Badby Cl NN2........141 E4
Badby Leys CV22.....98 A7
Badby Pk NN11.......135 A5
Badby Rd
Daventry NN11.......153 C1
Newnham NN11.......153 D4
Badby Rd W
Daventry NN11.......153 A7
Daventry NN11.......153 B8
Badby Sch NN11......152 F3
Baden Powell Cres
NN12..............203 C4
Badger La NN4.......175 D3
Badgers Cl NN7.......172 F7
Badgers Hyde NN13...232 F6
Badgers La NN14.....89 C5
Badgers Wlk NN2.....141 B5
Baffin Cl NN14.......70 E7
Bailey Brooks Cl NN7..191 C5
Bailey Brooks La NN7..191 C5
Bailey Ct NN10.......132 B5
Bailiff St NN1........159 D7
Baines Pl NN12.......214 E4
Baines Way NN4......175 E3
Baird Ave NN5........158 A4
Baird Cl NN11.........135 B5
Baird Ct NN8.........129 B6
Baird Rd NN17.......22 D1
Bairstow Rd NN12.....203 C5
Bakehouse Hill
Geddington NN14.....54 A3
Little Addington NN14..113 B8
Bakehouse La
Burton Latimer NN15...92 C3
Mears Ashby NN6.....128 B2
Bakehouse Mews
NN14..............90 B4
Bakehouse Rise NN6...85 B8
Baker Ave NN14......90 A3
Baker Ct NN14.......76 D1
Bakers Cres NN29.....147 A8
Bakers La
Norton NN11.........136 C4
Spratton NN6........105 B4
Stoke Bruerne NN12...205 A8
Walgrave NN6.......108 A4
Woodford NN14......204 D8
Baker's La NN2.......204 D8
Baker St
Farthinghoe NN13....221 B4
Gayton NN7..........173 E2
Irthlingborough NN9..112 F1
Northampton NN2.....159 C8
3 Wellingborough
NN8...............130 A5
Bakewell Cl NN4......174 F8
Balcombe Cl CV22....98 A8
Balcombe Pl NN18....36 A5
Balcombe Rd CV22....98 D8
Balding Cl CV23......99 C1
Baldwin Cl NN3......142 B4
Baler Cl NN11........141 C1
Balfour Cl NN2.......141 C1
Balfour Dr NN14.....70 E7
Balfour Gdns LE16....31 D1
Balfour Rd NN2.......141 D1
Balfour St NN16......72 C4
Balham Cl NN10......147 F8
Balland Way NN4.....175 F7
Ballantyne Rd NN10...132 A1
Balliol Rd
Brackley NN13.......233 D8
Daventry NN11.......153 B8
Balmoral NN18.......36 C3
Balmoral Ave NN10...132 C3
Balmoral Cl
Earls Barton NN6.....144 F3
Market Harborough LE16..32 B2
Towcester NN12......203 B5
Wellingborough NN8...129 E1
Balmoral Ct NN15.....91 C5
Balmoral Dr NN13....233 E7
Balmoral Ho NN2.....141 C1
Balmoral Rd NN2.....141 C1
Balmoral Way OX17...230 F6
Baltic Cl NN18.......36 D3
Bamburg Cl NN18.....36 A1
Bamburgh Cl LE16....32 B3
Bampton Cl NN18.....36 F4
BANBURY...........219 A6
Banbury Bsns Pk
OX17..............230 D3
Banbury Cl
Northampton NN4.....158 D2
Wellingborough NN8...129 C6
Banbury La
Banbury OX17.......219 B8
Banbury OX17.......219 C8
Blakesley NN12......186 D2
Byfield NN11........183 D7
Cold Higham NN12....188 B4
Culworth OX17......198 E3

Banbury La continued
Foxley NN12.........187 D4
Gayton NN7..........173 D4
Great Easton LE16....20 D6
Kings Sutton OX17....230 E6
Middleton Cheney
OX17..............209 C4
Northampton NN4.....158 D1
Rothersthorpe NN7....174 B7
Thorpe Mandeville
OX17..............210 B8
Weston NN12........199 C3
Banbury Rd
Aynho OX17.........237 C7
Brackley NN13.......233 E6
Byfield NN11........183 D7
Chacombe OX17......208 C3
Chipping Warden OX17..196 F6
Litchborough NN11....171 C1
Lower Boddington
NN11..............182 C4
Moreton Pinkney NN11..199 C7
Twyford OX17.......230 A6
Bancroft Cl NN4......176 A6
Bancroft Rd LE16.....20 D1
Bancroft Way NN4....176 A6
Bangrave Rd NN17....37 F8
Bangrave Rd S NN17,
NN18..............37 F6
Bank Cotts LE16......46 C8
Bankfield Dr LE16.....32 A5
Bank Hill View NN9....110 C4
Bankside
Corby NN18..........36 D3
Higham Ferrers NN10..132 B2
Northampton NN2.....141 F3
Woodford Halse NN11..184 C6
Banks The
Broughton NN14......90 B5
Hackleton NN7.......177 B3
Kilsby CV23.........100 A2
Long Buckby NN6.....121 B4
Wellingborough NN9...129 F8
Bank View NN4.......175 B7
Banner Cl NN10......132 A1
Bannerman Dr NN13...233 D7
Bants La NN5........158 E7
Baptists Cl NN7.......172 F7
BARBY.............99 D1
Barby CE Prim Sch
CV23..............118 C8
Barby La
Braunston NN11......118 C2
Rugby CV23.........99 B5
BARBY NORTOFT....99 F6
Barby Rd
Kilsby CV23.........99 F3
Rugby CV23.........98 B7
Bardsley Rd NN17....21 E3
Barford MK11........229 F4
Baring Ho NN5.......159 A7
Baring Rd NN5.......159 A7
Barker Cl NN10......132 C2
Barker Rd NN6.......144 E3
Barksdale Ave NN13...238 E6
Barley Cl
Daventry NN11.......135 C4
Hartwell NN7........192 E2
Rugby CV21.........99 A8
Barley Croft NN6.....100 F6
Barley Ct NN10......148 C8
Barley Dr NN15.......92 C2
Barley Hill OX17......198 D2
Barley Hill Rd NN3....142 F6
Barley La NN2........141 B5
Barlow Cl NN14......70 B7
Barlow Ct NN15......92 B1
Barlow La NN3.......126 C1
Barlows La LE16......34 C5
Barn Acre NN6.......122 D5
Barnard NN18........36 C3
Barnard Cl NN5......158 B8
Barnard Gdns LE16...48 D8
Barnard's Way NN14...56 A6
Barn Cl
Corby NN18..........36 B1
Northampton NN4.....175 F3
Barn Cnr NN4........175 C4
Barn Ct
Helmdon NN13.......211 F4
Little Harrowden NN9..110 C4
Barnes Cl
Daventry NN11.......135 B3
Kettering NN15.......91 B7
Old NN6............107 C7
Barnes Mdw★ NN4....159 F4
Barnes Meadow Intc
NN4...............160 A4
Barneswell Cl NN6....106 B2
Barnet Cl NN4........159 A2
Barnett Cres NN11....184 B6
Barnett Rd OX17......219 F8
Barnfield Cl NN2......141 B4
Barnhill Sq NN3.......143 A6
Barn La NN7.........174 F2
Barn Mews NN4......175 C4
Barn Owl Cl NN4......175 A8
Barnsdale LE16.......20 D6
Barnsdale Cl LE16.....20 D6
Barnsley Sq NN18.....36 C4
Barnstaple Cl NN3.....160 E7
Barns The
Irchester NN29.......131 B1
Mears Ashby NN6.....128 C2

Barnstones Bsns Pk
NN12. . . . . .187 E7
Barn Way NN5 . . . . 140 C2
BARNWELL. 59 B6
Barnwell CE Prim Sch
PE8 . . . . .59 B6
Barnwell Ct NN14 . . . . . . 76 E2
Barnwell Ctry Pk★
PE8. . . . . .41 E3
Barnwell Ctry Pk Visitor
Ctr★▲PE8. . . . . .41 F3
Barnwell Dr NN10 . . . . . 148 A8
Barnwell Gdns NN8 . . . . 129 D7
Barnwell Rd
Northampton NN2 . . . . . . 141 D4
Oundle PE8 . . . . .41 F3
Wellingborough NN8 . . . .129 E7
Barnwell St NN16 . . . . . . 72 D2
Barnwell Workshops
PE8 . . . . .59 B8
Baron Ave
Earls Barton NN6. . . . . . 144 F6
Kettering NN16 . . . . 71 E3
Baron Ct
Corby NN17 . . . . 22 E1
Northampton NN1 . . . . . . 159 F8
Baronson Gdns NN1 . . . . 159 F8
Barons Way NN1. . . . . . . 141 A4
Barrack Rd NN1, NN2 . . . 159 C7
Barracks The NN7 . . . . . 161 D2
Barratt Cl NN10 . . . . 132 B5
Barrett Cl NN8. . . . . 129 C4
Barringers Ct NN29 . . . . 131 B1
Barringers Gdns
NN29 . . . . 131 B1
Barrington Ct NN13 . . . . 233 F5
Barrington Rd NN10 . . . . 148 C8
Barron Cl NN15 . . . . 91 C6
BARROWDEN. 3 E5
Barrowden La LE15 . . . . . .3 E8
Barrowden Rd
Barrowden PE9 . . . . .4 C8
Ketton PE9. . . . . .1 A4
South Luffenham LE15. . . . .3 F7
Barry Prim Sch NN1 . . . . 160 A7
Barry Rd NN1. . . . . 160 A6
Barth Cl NN18 . . . . 36 B2
Bartholomew Gdns
NN12 . . . . 187 A1
Bartlett Ct NN13 . . . . . . 233 D7
Bartley Ho NN16 . . . . . . 71 F4
Barton Cl OX17 . . . . 230 F6
Barton Fields NN6 . . . . . 143 F3
Barton Holme NN12. . . . 187 A1
Barton Rd NN15 . . . . 91 E7
Bartons Cl The **2**
NN5 . . . . 140 F1
BARTON SEAGRAVE 92 A6
Barton Seagrave Prim Sch
NN15 . . . . 92 A6
Barton Sq NN18 . . . . 36 B6
Barwick Ho **10** NN10 . . . 132 B2
Basil Cl NN4 . . . . 175 D6
Bassett Ct NN4 . . . . 175 D2
Bassett Ford Rd PE8 . . . 42 A4
Bassett Lowke Ho
NN1 . . . . 159 D5
Bassett Pl PE8 . . . . 42 A4
Bassett's Ct NN8. . . . . . 129 F4
Bassett Way LE16 . . . . . 67 A8
Bates Ave NN14. . . . . . . 95 B3
Bates Cl
Higham Ferrers NN10 . . . 132 B5
Market Harborough LE16 . . 31 E5
Bates La OX27 . . . . 237 D3
Bath La NN16 . . . . 72 C3
Bath Rd NN16 . . . . 72 C4
Bath St LE16 . . . . 31 E1
Batsmans Dr NN10 . . . . . 132 A4
Battalion Dr NN4 . . . . . . 175 E7
Battle Cl
Cranford St John NN14 . . . 93 A6
Northampton NN4 . . . . . . 175 D7
Baukewell Ct **4** NN3 . . . 142 E3
Baulmsholme Cl NN4 . . . 159 C4
Baunhill Cl NN3. . . . . . . 160 D7
Baxter Cl NN4 . . . . 175 F8
Bayard Brow NN13 . . . . . 233 E8
Bayes St NN16 . . . . 72 A3
Bay La MK46. . . . . 194 D2
Baysdale Ave NN17 . . . . 36 E6
Beacon Cl NN4 . . . . 158 E3
Beaconsfield Pl NN10 . . . 132 B3
Beaconsfield Terr
Northampton NN1 . . . . . . 159 D7
Rushden NN10. . . . . 132 B3
Beanfield Ave NN18. . . . . 36 B5
Beanfield Prim Sch
NN18. . . . . 36 A5
Bean Furlong OX17 . . . . 208 E4
Beardsley Ct NN18. . . . . 36 D5
Beardsley Gdns NN15 . . . 92 A7
Beatrice Rd NN16 . . . . . . 72 B5
Beatty Cl NN11 . . . . 135 E1
Beatty Gdns NN17 . . . . . 36 B7
Beaufort Dr
Kettering NN15 . . . . 92 A6
Northampton NN5 . . . . . . 140 C1
Beauly Ct NN15 . . . . 91 E8
Beaumaris Cl NN10 . . . . 132 C1
Beaumont Cl NN16. . . . . 72 B6
Beaumont Cres NN13 . . . 233 E7
Beaumont Dr NN3 . . . . . 143 C3
Beaune Cl NN5 . . . . 139 F1
Beauvais Ct NN5. . . . . . . 139 F1

Beaver Ctr The NN11. . . . 184 C7
Beck Ct NN8. . . . . 129 D6
Becketts Cl NN11 . . . . . . 183 D7
Beckett's View NN1. . . . 159 E5
Becket Way NN3 . . . . . . 142 B4
Bective Rd NN2 . . . . 141 C4
Bective View NN2. . . . . . 141 D4
Bedale Rd NN8 . . . . 130 A6
Beddoes Cl NN4 . . . . 176 A6
Bede Cl
Corby NN18. . . . . 36 A1
Higham Ferrers NN10 . . . 132 C5
Bede Ho★▲LE15. . . . . .9 D7
Bedford Cl NN15. . . . . . . 91 F5
Bedford Cotts NN7. . . . . 138 D7
Bedford Mans NN1. . . . . 159 D5
Bedford Pl NN1. . . . . 159 D5
Bedford Rd
Denton NN7. . . . . 178 B8
Little Houghton NN7. . . . 160 F3
Northampton NN1 . . . . . . 159 E4
Rushden NN10. . . . . 148 C5
Bedford Rd E NN7 . . . . . 179 D5
Bedford Rd W NN7 . . . . . 179 A6
Beech Ave
Northampton NN3 . . . . . . 142 A1
Olney MK46. . . . . 195 E3
Beech Cl
Bugbrooke NN7 . . . . 172 F7
Corby NN17. . . . . 21 E1
Desborough NN14. . . . . . 51 A3
Hackleton NN7. . . . . 177 B3
Towcester NN12 . . . . . . 203 C4
Beech Cres
Irchester NN29 . . . . 147 A7
Kettering NN15 . . . . 72 D1
Beechcroft Gdns NN3 . . . 142 A2
Beech Ct
Rugby CV22 . . . . 98 F8
Thrapston NN14 . . . . . . 76 D2
Beech Dr
Brackley NN13. . . . . 222 E1
Hinton NN11 . . . . 184 B6
Wellingborough NN8 . . . .129 E5
Beeches Cl LE16 . . . . 46 F2
Beeches The
Deanshanger MK19. . . . . 228 E3
Pattishall NN12 . . . . 172 E1
Beech Gr
Northampton NN3 . . . . . . 142 D5
Rushden NN10. . . . . 131 F3
Beech Hill NN11 . . . . 151 D1
Beech House Dr
NN12 . . . . 217 F4
Beech La NN7 . . . . 157 E4
Beech Rd NN10 . . . . 132 B4
Beechwood Dr NN3 . . . . 142 E1
Beechwood Rd NN5. . . . . 158 C4
Beeston Ave NN3 . . . . . . 160 F8
Beeston Pl NN18. . . . . . . 36 C5
Belfield Ct NN3 . . . . 142 B3
Belfry La NN4. . . . . 175 B5
Belfry Way NN11 . . . . . . 135 E2
Belgrave Cl NN15 . . . . . . 92 A5
Bellamy Rd PE8. . . . . 41 F7
Bell Cl NN13 . . . . 211 F4
Bell Ct
Corby NN18. . . . . 36 D4
5 Wellingborough
NN8. . . . . 130 A5
Belle Baulk NN12 . . . . . . 203 A6
Bell End NN29 . . . . 146 D2
Bellfield LE15. . . . . .3 E8
Bellfields La LE16 . . . . . . 32 A2
Bellfields St LE16 . . . . . . 32 A2
Bellfoundry La **4**
NN16 . . . . 72 B2
Bell Hill
Finedon NN9 . . . . 111 E4
Rothwell NN14. . . . . 70 D7
BELLINGE 143 B1
Bellinge Prim Sch
NN3. . . . . 143 B1
Bell La
Byfield NN11 . . . . 183 C7
Husbands Bosworth
LE17 . . . . 45 E5
Syresham NN13. . . . . . . 224 B8
Bellropes Sq **5** NN3 . . . 143 D2
Bells Cl LE16 . . . . 55 E8
Bell St NN8. . . . . 130 A5
Bell Twr NN18 . . . . 233 F7
Bellway Ct NN3 . . . . 72 A3
Bell View OX17 . . . . 231 F5
Bell Wlk CV21 . . . . 99 A8
Belmont Ct **13** NN1 . . . . 159 C7
Belmont Gdns NN9 . . . . . 114 C6
Belstead Rd NN3. . . . . . . 160 D6
Belton Cl **4** NN4 . . . . . . 175 C8
Belvedere Cl NN5. . . . . . 158 F7
Belvedere Rd NN15 . . . . . 72 D1
Belvoir Cl
Corby NN18. . . . . 36 E2
Northampton NN5 . . . . . . 140 B1
Rushden NN10. . . . . 148 C8
Belvoir Dr NN15 . . . . 92 A6
Bembridge Dr NN2. . . . . 141 B1
Benbow Cl NN11 . . . . 135 E2
Benedict Cl NN10 . . . . . . 147 F8
Benefield Rd
Brigstock NN14 . . . . 39 D2
Deenethorpe NN17 . . . . . 24 C4
Oundle PE8 . . . . 41 C5
Bengal NN12 . . . . 202 D7
Bengal La NN12. . . . . 202 E7
Bengal View NN12. . . . . . 202 E8
Bengeworth Ct **10**
NN8 . . . . 130 A5

Benham Ct NN3 . . . . 142 F3
Benham Rd NN12 . . . . . . 202 D8
Benjamin Sq **6** NN4 . . . 158 F2
Bennett Cl
Chacombe OX17 . . . . . . 208 E4
Daventry NN11 . . . . 135 A4
Stony Stratford MK11 . . . 229 D4
Bennett Rd NN18 . . . . . . 36 D1
Bens Cl MK19. . . . . 218 F5
Bentley Cl NN3 . . . . 143 D4
Bentley Ct NN9 . . . . 111 B1
Bentley Way NN11 . . . . . 134 F3
Bentley Wlk NN18. . . . . . 36 C5
Bergen Wlk NN18 . . . . . . 36 A2
Bergerac Cl NN5. . . . . . . 139 F2
Berkeley Cl NN1. . . . . . . 159 F6
Berkeley Ho **26** NN1. . . . 159 C6
Berkeley St LE16 . . . . . . 46 F2
Berneshaw Cl NN18 . . . . 36 D3
Bern Links NN4. . . . . 159 A3
Bern Side NN4. . . . . 159 A3
Berrell's Ct MK46. . . . . . 195 F3
Berrill St NN29 . . . . 147 A7
Berrister Pl NN9 . . . . 114 E7
Berry Cl
Earls Barton NN6. . . . . . 144 E5
Great Bowden LE16 . . . . 32 A5
Hackleton NN7. . . . . 177 B3
Rothersthorpe NN7 . . . . 174 B3
Berrydale NN3. . . . . 143 D4
Berryfield NN6 . . . . 121 C4
Berry Field Rd LE16 . . . . 20 C1
Berry Green Ct NN9. . . . . 111 B5
Berry Green Pk NN14 . . . 78 E6
Berry Green Rd NN9 . . . . 111 E5
Berry Hill Rd OX17 . . . . . 230 A2
Berry La
Helidon NN11 . . . . 151 C1
Northampton NN3 . . . . . . 175 E5
Berrymoor Ct NN8 . . . . . 129 E2
Berrymoor Rd NN8. . . . . 129 E2
Berry Rd NN10 . . . . 20 C1
Berrywood Dr NN5. . . . . 157 F7
Berrywood Rd NN5 . . . . . 158 A7
Bertha Way NN16 . . . . . . 72 C4
Berwick Ho NN2 . . . . 141 D5
Berwick Rd NN14 . . . . . . 37 E3
Berwick Way NN15 . . . . . 92 A8
Bessemer Gr NN18. . . . . 37 B6
Bestwell Ct **3** NN3. . . . . 161 A8
Bestwood Cl NN14 . . . . . 50 F4
Bestwood Gn NN18 . . . . . 36 C5
Beswick Cl NN14. . . . . . . 52 C3
Bethany Homestead **1**
NN2 . . . . 141 E1
Bethel La NN11 . . . . 170 B7
Betjeman Cl
Daventry NN11 . . . . 135 A3
Higham Ferrers NN10 . . . 132 A5
Betony Wlk NN3 . . . . 148 B8
Bettycroft Cl NN6 . . . . . . 103 E1
Bevan Cl
Warmington PE8 . . . . . . 28 B3
Wellingborough NN8 . . . . 130 C7
Beverley Cl NN14 . . . . . . 70 B7
Beverley Cres NN3. . . . . 142 C1
Beverley Rd NN15. . . . . . 91 D8
Beverley Wlk NN18 . . . . . 36 C5
Bewick Ct NN18 . . . . 36 A4
Bewick Rd NN3 . . . . 160 E8
Bexhill Wlk NN18 . . . . . . 36 B4
Bibury Cl NN8 . . . . 129 D1
Bibury Cres NN3 . . . . . . 142 D6
Bicester Hill NN13 . . . . . 233 F2
Bickerstaffes Rd
NN12 . . . . 203 C5
Bidders Cl NN1. . . . . 159 D4
BIDDLESDEN 224 D5
Bideford Cl NN3 . . . . 160 D7
Bideford Sq NN18. . . . . . 36 F5
Bies Cl NN18 . . . . 36 C2
Big Gn PE8 . . . . 28 C3
Bignal Ct NN15 . . . . 90 E8
Billing Aquadrome★
NN7. . . . . 161 B7
Billing Arbours Ho
NN3 . . . . 142 E4
Billing Brook Rd NN3 . . . 142 F4
Billing Brook Specl Sch
NN3. . . . . 142 F3
Billing La
Moulton NN6 . . . . 126 F1
Northampton NN3,
NN6. . . . . 143 A7
Billing Rd
Brafield-on-t-G NN7. . . . 161 D4
Northampton NN1 . . . . . . 159 F6
Billing Rd E NN3. . . . . . . 160 D7
Billing School Pl NN7. . . . 155 C3
Billington St NN1 . . . . . . 159 F7
Bilsdon Cl NN10 . . . . 147 F8
Bilton Ct NN8. . . . . 129 D5
Binbrook Wlk NN18 . . . . 36 C4
Binder Cl NN10 . . . . 132 A7
Binders Ct NN14 . . . . 37 F2
Bingham Wlk NN18 . . . . . 36 C5
Birchall Rd NN10 . . . . . . 131 F2
Birch Ave NN18 . . . . 36 D4
Birch Barn Way NN2 . . . . 141 B6
Birch Cl
Hinton NN11 . . . . 184 B6
Northampton NN4 . . . . . . 175 E2
Birch Ct NN10 . . . . 132 C2
Birchfield Cres NN3 . . . . 142 C2
Birchfield Rd NN3 . . . . . . 142 B1

Birchfield Rd
Northampton NN1,
NN3. . . . . 142 A1
Wellingborough NN8 . . . . 129 E4
Birchfield Rd E NN3. . . . . 142 C1
Birchington Rd NN17. . . . 22 F2
Birch Rd
Kettering NN16 . . . . 72 D3
Rushden NN10. . . . . 132 C2
Birch Spinney NN3 . . . . . 89 A4
Birch Tree Gdns LE16 . . . 31 F4
Birchvale Ct NN14 . . . . . 50 E4
Birds Hill Rd
Eastcote NN12 . . . . 188 F8
Northampton NN2 . . . . . . 142 F3
Birds Hill Wlk NN3 . . . . . 142 F2
Bird St NN15 . . . . 92 D3
Birkdale Cl
Daventry NN11 . . . . 135 E2
Northampton NN2 . . . . . . 141 B3
Birkdale Dr NN10 . . . . . . 132 D1
Birling Pl NN18 . . . . 36 B5
Birtley Coppice LE16 . . . 31 D4
Bishop Cl LE16. . . . . 48 E8
Bishops Cl NN13 . . . . . . 222 E1
Bishops Ct
4 Daventry NN11 . . . . 135 C2
Higham Ferrers NN10 . . . 132 C7
Bishops Dr NN2 . . . . 141 B3
Bishop's Dr NN15 . . . . . . 91 B6
Bishop Stopford Sch
NN15. . . . . 91 B7
Bishops Way NN18 . . . . . 36 A4
Bitten Cl NN3. . . . . 142 B3
Blackberry Cl NN16 . . . . . 72 B6
Blackberry La NN4 . . . . . 158 F3
Blackbird NN13 . . . . 222 E1
Blackbridge Ct NN14 . . . 76 C2
Blackdown NN11 . . . . . . 151 B3
Blackdown MK11 . . . . . . 229 F4
Blackfriars NN10. . . . . . . 147 F8
Blackfriars Ho **19**
NN1 . . . . 159 C6
Black Lion Hill NN1 . . . . . 159 B5
Blacklocks Hill OX17 . . . 219 B8
Blackmile La NN6 . . . . . . 163 E7
Blackmires La NN12. . . . 214 B5
Blackmoor Ave NN18 . . . 36 F4
Blackpot La PE8 . . . . 42 A5
Blacksmith's Cl NN12 . . . 172 D1
Blacksmiths Gn NN12 . . . 204 D8
Blacksmiths Hill
OX17 . . . . 237 C7
Blacksmiths La
Eydon NN11 . . . . 184 C1
Little Brington NN7 . . . . 138 B4
Blacksmith's La
Aston le W NN11 . . . . . . 182 F2
Pytchley NN14 . . . . 90 F2
Blacksmith's Way
NN7 . . . . 192 C1
Black Swan Spinney
PE8 . . . . 8 A4
BLACKTHORN. 143 B4
Blackthorn Bridge Ct **4**
NN3 . . . . 143 B4
Blackthorn Cl
Kettering NN16 . . . . 72 C6
Spratton NN6 . . . . 105 A1
Blackthorn Prim Sch
NN3. . . . . 143 B4
Blackthorn Rd NN3 . . . . . 143 B4
Blackwall Cl **1** NN4. . . . . 159 A2
Blackwell Cl
Earls Barton NN6. . . . . . 144 E4
Higham Ferrers NN10 . . . 132 B7
Towcester NN12 . . . . . . 203 D4
Blackwell End NN12 . . . . 217 C3
Blackwell Hill NN4. . . . . . 174 F8
Blackwell Rd NN15. . . . . 91 F4
Blackwells Yd NN7. . . . . . 179 B6
BLACKY MORE 175 C2
Blackymore La NN4. . . . . 175 D5
Bladon Cl NN3 . . . . 142 C4
Blake Cl NN11 . . . . 153 E8
Blake Ct NN15 . . . . 92 A8
Blake Rd NN18. . . . . 36 D4
Blakesely Hill NN12 . . . . 202 D8
BLAKESLEY 187 B1
Blakesley CE Prim Sch
NN12. . . . . 187 B1
Blakesley Cl NN2 . . . . . . 141 C5
Blakesley Rd NN12 . . . . . 200 F7
Blake Wlk NN10 . . . . 132 A5
Blanchard Cl **3** NN4 . . . 175 E7
Blandford Ave NN16 . . . . 72 B5
Blandford Ct NN18. . . . . 36 A6
BLATHERWYCKE 12 E4
Blatherwycke Rd PE8 . . . 13 E7
Blaydon Wlk NN8 . . . . . . 129 E6
Bleaklow Cl NN14. . . . . . 50 E3
Bledlow Rise NN4. . . . . . 174 F8
Blencowe Dr NN13 . . . . . 233 D7
Blenheim Cl NN3 . . . . . . 238 B7
Blenheim Ct NN10 . . . . . 148 A8
Blenheim Croft NN13 . . . 233 F6
Blenheim Pl NN13 . . . . . 224 C7
Blenheim Rd
Northampton NN4 . . . . . . 159 B2
Wellingborough NN8 . . . . 129 D7
Blenheim Rise OX17 . . . . 230 F6
Blenheim Way
Kettering NN15 . . . . 91 C5
Market Harborough LE16 . . 31 E5
Blenheim Wlk NN18. . . . . 36 C5
Blinco Rd NN10. . . . . 132 C2
Blind La LE16 . . . . 20 D1

Bliss Charity Sch The
NN7. . . . . 156 C2
Bliss La NN7. . . . . 155 F5
BLISWORTH 190 E7
Blisworth Cl NN4 . . . . . . 159 A2
Blisworth Com Prim Sch
NN7. . . . . 190 D8
Blisworth Mill NN7. . . . . 190 C7
Blisworth Rd
Gayton NN7. . . . . 173 F1
Roade NN7. . . . . 191 B4
Bloomfield Cl NN10 . . . . 132 A2
Blossac Ct NN5 . . . . 139 F1
Blossom Ct **2** NN16. . . . 72 C4
Blossom Way NN3 . . . . . 143 A1
Blotts Barn Bsns Ctr
NN9. . . . . 114 F8
Bluebell Cl
Corby NN18. . . . . 36 C2
Hinton NN11 . . . . 184 B7
Kettering NN16 . . . . 72 C4
Rushden NN10. . . . . 148 C8
Wellingborough NN8 . . . . 130 B6
Bluebell Ct NN3 . . . . 160 C6
Bluebell Pk Cvn Pk **2**
NN3 . . . . 126 C1
Bluebell Rise
Northampton NN4 . . . . . . 175 F1
Rushden NN10. . . . . 148 B8
Blueberry Cl NN6 . . . . . . 87 B6
Blueberry Rise **2**
NN3 . . . . 143 C2
Bluecoat La LE15 . . . . . . .9 D7
Blythe Cl NN14 . . . . 70 E6
Blyton Cl NN18 . . . . 36 C4
Boarden Cl NN3 . . . . 142 A7
Boardman Rd NN15 . . . . 90 F8
Board St NN9. . . . . 112 F2
Boat Horse La NN6. . . . . 101 A3
Boathouse The LE16 . . . . 31 D4
Bobtail Ct NN5. . . . . 140 C1
Boddington CE Sch
NN11. . . . . 182 C7
Boddington Ct NN11 . . . 182 C5
Boddington Mews
NN15 . . . . 91 C8
Boddington Rd
Byfield NN11 . . . . 183 C7
Claydon OX17 . . . . 181 D1
Kettering NN15 . . . . 91 C8
Boddington Way
NN13 . . . . 233 D8
Boden Cl NN18 . . . . 36 A4
Bodiam Cl NN14. . . . . . . 76 E2
Bodiam Pl NN18 . . . . 36 A5
Bodleian Cl NN11 . . . . . . 153 B8
Bognor Rd NN18 . . . . 36 B4
Bolingbroke Pl NN10. . . . 132 C7
Bollinger Cl NN5. . . . . . . 139 F1
Boltons Ct NN13 . . . . . . 222 E1
Bondfield Ave NN2. . . . . 141 D3
Bonham Ct NN16. . . . . . . 72 C3
Bonington Wlk NN18. . . . 36 C5
Bonnington Cl CV21. . . . 80 B1
Bonsor Gdns NN3 . . . . . . 95 A3
Boon Wlk NN17 . . . . 37 B7
Booth Cl NN12 . . . . 172 D1
Booth Dr NN8 . . . . 129 A4
Booth La N NN3 . . . . 142 C4
Booth La S NN3. . . . . 142 D2
Booth Meadow Ct
NN3 . . . . 142 E5
Booth Rise NN3. . . . . 142 D6
Boothville Gn NN3 . . . . . 142 D5
Boothville Prim Sch
NN3. . . . . 142 C4
Bo-Peep Cvn Pk
OX17 . . . . 230 C2
Bordeaux Ave NN5 . . . . . 139 F1
Bordeaux Ct NN5 . . . . . . 139 F1
BOROUGH 135 E2
Borough Ct
Brackley NN13. . . . . 234 A5
Higham Ferrers NN10 . . . 132 B5
Borough Rd NN13. . . . . . 234 A5
Borrowdale Rd NN17. . . . 36 D8
Borrowdale Wlk **3**
NN3 . . . . 142 C4
Bostock Ave NN1 . . . . . . 159 F7
Bostock Mews NN1 . . . . . 159 F7
Boston Cl NN18 . . . . 36 C4
Boswell La MK19. . . . . . . 228 E4
Bosworth Cl
Northampton NN4 . . . . . . 159 A1
Warmington PE8 . . . . . . 28 B3
Bosworth Independent
Coll NN2 . . . . 159 C8
Bosworth Rd
Husbands Bosworth
LE17 . . . . 45 A8
Theddingworth LE17 . . . . 46 C7
Bothy The OX17. . . . . 237 D7
Botmead Rd NN3 . . . . . . 143 D4
Bottom La LE16 . . . . 34 B5
Bougainvillea Dr NN3 . . . 160 C6
BOUGHTON 141 D8
Boughton NN15. . . . . 91 D4
Boughton Cl NN18 . . . . . 36 A4
Boughton Dr NN10 . . . . . 148 A8
Boughton Fair La
NN3 . . . . 126 B4
Boughton Green Rd NN2,
NN3. . . . . 141 D5
Boughton Ho★▲NN14. . . . 73 C8
Boughton La NN3. . . . . . 141 F7
Boughton Prim Sch
NN2. . . . . 141 D8

Boughton Rd
Boughton NN2, NN3 . . . . . 141 F8
Corby NN18 . . . . 36 D2
Moulton NN3 . . . . 126 A1
Boughton Terr NN13 . . . 233 F2
Boundary Ave NN10 . . . 131 E1
Boundary Cres MK11 . . 229 C6
Boundary Rd NN13 . . . . 234 A6
Bourne Cl
Corby NN18 . . . . 36 D2
Wellingborough NN8 . . . 129 C6
Bourne Cres NN5 . . . . . 140 E1
Bourton Cl NN4 . . . . 174 E8
Bourton Way NN11 . . . . 129 E1
Bouverie Rd NN4 . . . . . . 175 E8
Bouverie St **1** NN1 . . . . 159 F6
Bouverie Wlk **5** NN1 . . 159 F6
Bovevell Ct NN4 . . . . . . 158 E2
Bow Ct NN4 . . . . 158 E2
Bowden La
Market Harborough
LE16 . . . . 31 E4
Welham LE16 . . . . 17 E4
Bowden Rd
Northampton NN5 . . . . . 159 A6
Thorpe Langton LE16 . . . 17 A4
Bowden Ridge LE16 . . . 32 A5
Bowen Rd CV22 . . . . 98 D8
Bowen Sq **7** NN11 . . . . 135 C1
Bowhill NN16 . . . . 72 A1
Bowland Dr NN15 . . . . . 92 A5
Bowling Gn NN13 . . . . . 221 B4
Bowling Green Ave
NN15 . . . . 72 B1
Bowling Green La
NN5 . . . . 158 A6
Bowling Green Rd
NN15 . . . . 72 B1
Bowman Cl OX17 . . . . . 220 A8
Bowmans Cl NN4 . . . . . 158 D1
Bowness NN8 . . . . 129 D5
Bowthorpe Cl NN3 . . . . 160 D6
Box Gdns NN8 . . . . 130 A5
Boxwood Dr CV23 . . . . 100 A3
Boyle Rd NN17 . . . . 22 C1
BOZEAT 164 D3
Bozeat Com Prim Sch
NN29 . . . . 164 D3
Bozenham Mill La
NN7 . . . . 205 E4
Brabham Cl NN12 . . . . . 214 D4
Bracadale Wlk NN17 . . 21 C1
Bracken Borough
NN6 . . . . 106 C2
Bracken Cl NN16 . . . . . . 72 B5
Brackendale Dr CV23 . . 99 C1
Bracken Field Sq
NN3 . . . . 142 F7
Brackenhill Cl NN2 . . . 141 E3
BRACKLEY 233 E7
Brackley CE Jun Sch
NN13 . . . . 233 F8
Brackley Cl NN2 . . . . . . 141 D6
Brackley Cottage Hospl
NN13 . . . . 233 F7
Brackley Jun Sch
NN13 . . . . 233 E6
Brackley La NN12 . . . . . 201 F1
Brackley Lodge Mews
NN13 . . . . 233 F7
Brackley Rd
Croughton NN13 . . . . . . 238 D8
Greatworth OX17 . . . . . 210 E1
Silverstone NN12 . . . . . 214 D3
Towcester NN12 . . . . . . 203 B6
Westbury NN13 . . . . . . 234 F5
Brackley Waynflete Inf
Sch NN13 . . . . 233 E7
BRACKMILLS 160 B1
Brackmills Ind Est
NN4 . . . . 160 A2
Bracknell NN8 . . . . 129 C4
Bradbury Rd NN11 . . . . 153 D3
BRADDEN 201 F6
Bradden Cl NN2 . . . . . . 141 D5
Bradden Rd NN12 . . . . . 202 D8
Bradden Way NN12 . . . 202 D8
Bradfield Cl
Rushden NN10 . . . . 132 D3
Wellingborough NN8 . . . 111 A1
Bradfield Rd NN8 . . . . . 111 A1
Bradford Wlk NN18 . . . 36 C5
Bradgate Ho NN1 . . . . . 159 E6
Bradmoor Ct NN3 . . . . . 143 B5
Bradmore Gdns NN18 . . 36 C6
Bradshaw St **29** NN1 . . 159 C6
Bradshaw Way NN29 . . 146 F8
Braemar Cl
NN15 . . . . 91 E8
Braemar Cres NN22 . . . 175 C8
Brafield Leys CV22 . . . 98 A6
BRAFIELD-ON-THE-
GREEN 161 E2
Brafield Rd
Cogenhoe NN7 . . . . 161 E5
Horton NN7 . . . . 177 E3
Braggintons La OX17 . . 220 B8
Braid Ct NN8 . . . . 129 D7
Braithwaite Cl NN15 . . 90 F8
Brakey Rd NN17 . . . . . . 37 F8
Bramber Ct NN18 . . . . . 36 A5
Bramble Cl
Kettering NN16 . . . . 72 B6
Ringstead NN1 . . . . 95 A3
Bramble End NN4 . . . . . 174 F8
Bramble Rd NN12 . . . . . 203 B4

Brambleside
Kettering NN16 . . . . 72 C6
Thrapston NN14 . . . . . . 76 D1
Brambleside Com Prim
Sch NN16 . . . . 72 C6
Brambleside Ct NN16 . . 72 B6
Brambles The NN10 . . . 148 B5
Bramblewood Rd
NN17 . . . . 38 A8
BraMCote Dr NN3 . . . . . 160 F8
Bramhall Rise NN5 . . . 158 B8
Bramley Cl
Cogenhoe NN7 . . . . 161 E5
Market Harborough LE16 . . 31 F5
Rushden NN10 . . . . 131 F3
Bramley Ct NN29 . . . . . 146 D3
Bramley Gr NN3 . . . . . . 143 B2
Bramley Ho **7** NN1 . . . 135 C2
Brammar Ho NN5 . . . . . 158 F7
BRAMPTON ASH 33 E3
Brampton Cl
Kettering NN15 . . . . 92 A5
Wellingborough NN8 . . . 129 D7
Brampton Hill LE16 . . . 33 F4
Brampton La
Boughton NN2, NN6 . . . 141 A7
Chapel Brampton NN6 . . 125 A3
Bramptons Prim Sch The
NN6 . . . . 124 D1
Brampton Valley Way★
NN6 . . . . 124 E4
Brampton Way NN6 . . . 106 B1
Brampton Wlk NN3 . . . 141 F5
Brampton Wood La
NN14 . . . . 50 F7
Bramshill Ave NN16 . . . 72 A6
Bramston Ct PE8 . . . . . 42 A4
Brandenburg Rd NN18 . 35 F2
Brangwyn Wlk NN18 . . 36 E5
Branksome Ave NN2 . . 141 B1
Branksome Ct NN18 . . . 36 A6
Branson Ct NN2 . . . . . . 72 A3
Branson Mews NN17 . . 38 A8
Brasenose Dr NN13 . . . 233 D8
Brashland Dr NN4 . . . . 175 D6
BRAUNSTON 118 C2
Braunston CE Prim Sch
NN11 . . . . 118 C1
Braunston Cl NN4 . . . . 159 A2
Braunston La NN11 . . . 152 C8
Braunston Pl CV22 . . . . 98 D8
Braunston Rd NN11 . . . 135 B2
Braunton Pl NN18 . . . . 36 F4
Brawn Cl NN9 . . . . 131 E8
Brawn Way PE8 . . . . . . 16 D1
BRAYBROOKE 49 F5
Braybrooke Cl NN14 . . 95 C3
Braybrooke Prim Sch
LE16 . . . . 49 E6
Braybrooke Rd
Arthingworth LE16 . . . . 68 D8
Desborough NN14 . . . . 50 F4
Dingley LE16 . . . . 33 A3
Great Oxendon LE16 . . 49 A3
Market Harborough LE16 . . 32 B1
Brayford Ave NN18 . . . 36 F5
Brayford Cl NN3 . . . . . . 160 C7
Breach Cl NN6 . . . . 106 C2
Breakleys Rd NN14 . . . 51 B2
Breck Cl NN18 . . . . 53 B8
Brecon Cl NN16 . . . . . . 72 B6
Brecon St NN5 . . . . 159 A8
Breedon Ct NN18 . . . . . 36 A1
Breezehill NN4 . . . . 175 F6
Brembridge Cl NN6 . . . 127 D2
Brendon Cl NN3 . . . . . . 160 D7
Brent Cl NN15 . . . . 92 A2
Brentford St NN18 . . . . 129 B5
Brer Ct NN4 . . . . 159 F5
Bressingham Gdns
NN4 . . . . 175 C7
Breton Cl NN5 . . . . 140 A1
Bretton Cl NN5 . . . . 140 A1
Bretts La NN7 . . . . 191 E4
Brewery Ct PE8 . . . . . . 41 F4
Brewery Yd NN14 . . . . . 56 E1
Brewin Cl NN13 . . . . . . 222 D1
Briar Cl NN13 . . . . 222 F1
Briar Ct NN9 . . . . 112 F2
BRIAR HILL 158 F3
Briar Hill Prim Sch
NN4 . . . . 158 F3
Briar Hill Rd NN4 . . . . . 159 B2
Briar Hill Wlk NN4 . . . 159 B2
Briar Rd NN16 . . . . 72 E5
Briars The NN4 . . . . 159 A3
Briarwood Way NN29 . . 146 D1
Briary Cl NN12 . . . . 203 B4
Brickett's La NN7 . . . . 155 E5
Brickhill Mews NN8 . . . 129 C4
Brickhill Rd NN8 . . . . . 129 D4
Brick Kiln Cl NN12 . . . 203 D4
Brick Kiln La NN2 . . . . 159 D8
Brick Kiln Rd NN9 . . . . 114 D6
Brickwell Ct NN3 . . . . . 143 A1
Brickyard Spinney Rd
NN3 . . . . 142 B6
Bridewell Ho **21** NN16 . 72 B2
Bridewell La **11** NN16 . 72 B2
Bridge Ct
Corby NN17 . . . . 37 A7
Thrapston NN14 . . . . . . 76 C2
Bridge End PE8 . . . . . . 8 A3
Bridge Ho NN14 . . . . . . 72 B2
Bridge Mdw NN7 . . . . . 178 B8
Bridge Meadow Way
NN4 . . . . 175 F4
Bridgend NN6 . . . . 82 B4

Bridge Rd
Cosgrove MK19 . . . . . . 218 E2
Desgrove NN14 . . . . . . 50 F4
Stoke Bruerne NN12 . . 205 A8
Bridge St
Apethorpe PE8 . . . . 14 D4
Brackley NN13 . . . . 233 E6
Brigstock NN14 . . . . 55 E7
Geddington NN14 . . . . . 54 A2
Kettering NN16 . . . . 72 C3
King's Cliffe NN14 . . . . . 14 A7
Northampton NN1 . . . . 159 C5
Olney MK46 . . . . 195 F2
Raunds NN9 . . . . 114 D7
Rothwell NN14 . . . . 70 D7
Thrapston NN14 . . . . . . 76 C2
Weedon Bec NN7 . . . . . 155 B4
Weldon NN17 . . . . 38 B8
Bridge View PE8 . . . . . 42 A6
Bridgeford St NN13 . . . 233 F8
Bridgewater Cres
NN13 . . . . 233 F8
Bridgewater Ct NN13 . . 233 F8
Bridgewater Dr NN3 . . 160 D7
Bridgewater Ho NN13 . 233 F8
Bridgewater Prim Sch
NN3 . . . . 160 C7
Bridgewater Rd NN13 . 233 F8
Bridgewater Rise
NN13 . . . . 233 F8
Bridge Wlk MK19 . . . . . 228 E4
Bridgford PE8 . . . . 36 C6
Bridgwater Ct NN18 . . . 36 A6
Bridle Cl
Brafield-on-t-G NN7 . . . 161 D2
Wellingborough NN8 . . . 111 A1
Bridle La NN6 . . . . 84 B6
Bridle Path NN7 . . . . . . 161 E2
Bridle Rd
Burton Latimer NN15 . . 92 A2
Hannington NN6 . . . . . . 108 C3
Old NN6 . . . . 107 D7
Bridle Way NN14 . . . . . 90 A6
Briery St NN16 . . . . 36 B1
Brigadier Cl NN4 . . . . . 175 D7
Brigg Ct NN18 . . . . 36 C4
Brighouse Cl NN18 . . . . 36 C4
Brighton Rd NN18 . . . . 36 B4
Bright Trees Rd NN4 . . 54 B3
Brightwell Wlk NN9 . . . 131 D8
BRIGSTOCK 55 E7
Brigstock Latham's CE
Prim Sch NN14 . . . . . 55 F7
Brigstock Rd NN14 . . . 38 A2
Brindlestone Cl NN4 . . 158 C4
Brindley Cl
Daventry NN11 . . . . 135 A5
Rushden NN10 . . . . 131 F4
Brindley Ct NN11 . . . . . 134 B8
Brindley Quay NN11 . . 134 B8
Brindley Rd CV21 . . . . . 80 B1
BRINGHURST 20 C5
Bringhurst Prim Sch
LE16 . . . . 20 C6
Brington Dr NN15 . . . . 91 F5
Brington Prim Sch
NN7 . . . . 138 C5
Brington Rd NN6 . . . . . 121 C3
Brinkhill Wlk NN18 . . . 36 C4
Brinsley Gn NN18 . . . . 36 C6
Brisbane Gdns NN18 . . 36 B2
Briscoe Cl NN2 . . . . . . 141 E6
BRITAIN 173 F1
Britain Cotts NN7 . . . . 173 F1
Britannia Gdns NN8 . . . 130 C4
Britannia Rd NN16 . . . . 72 B5
Britannia Trad Ctr
NN5 . . . . 140 D2
Britannia Wlk LE16 . . . 31 F2
British La **17** NN16 . . . 72 B2
Briton Gdns NN3 . . . . . 142 B1
Briton Rd NN3 . . . . 142 B1
Briton Terr NN3 . . . . . . 142 B1
Britten Cl NN9 . . . . 133 C8
Brittens View NN4 . . . . 126 E8
Brittons Dr NN3 . . . . . . 143 A7
Brixham Wlk NN18 . . . 36 F5
BRIXWORTH 106 A2
Brixworth CE Prim Sch
NN6 . . . . 106 B1
Brixworth Ctry Pk★
NN6 . . . . 125 C8
Brixworth Ctry Pk Visitor
Ctr★ NN6 . . . . 125 C7
Brixworth Hall Pk
NN6 . . . . 106 B2
Brixworth Rd
Creaton NN6 . . . . 104 F4
Holcot NN6 . . . . 126 D8
Spratton NN6 . . . . 105 D1
Broadgate LE16 . . . . . . 20 D7
Broadgate Way PE8 . . . 28 C2
Broadhurst Dr NN3 . . . 161 A8
Broad La NN13 . . . . 233 E3
Broadlands
Brixworth NN6 . . . . 106 A1
Desborough NN14 . . . . 51 C2
Pitsford NN6 . . . . 125 D5
Raunds NN9 . . . . 114 E6
Broad March NN11 . . . 153 D8
Broadmead Ave NN3 . . 142 A1
Broadmead Ct NN3 . . . 142 B2
Broad St
Brixworth NN6 . . . . 106 B1
Earls Barton NN6 . . . . . 144 E4
Northampton NN1 . . . . 159 C6
Syresham NN13 . . . . . . 224 B8

Broadstone Ct NN18 . . 36 A6
Broadwater La NN12 . . 203 A5
Broadway
Kettering NN15 . . . . 91 B8
Northampton NN1,
NN3 . . . . 142 A1
Wellingborough NN8 . . . 130 A3
Broadway E NN3 . . . . . 142 B1
Broadway Terr LE16 . . . 31 F4
Broadway The
Market Harborough
LE16 . . . . 31 F4
Norton NN11 . . . . 136 C4
Brocade Cl **8** NN4 . . . . 158 F2
BROCKHALL 137 D2
Brockhall Cl NN2 . . . . . 141 E4
Brockhall Rd
Flore NN7 . . . . 155 E6
Northampton NN2 . . . . 141 E4
Brockhill Cl NN15 . . . . 72 E1
Brockton St NN2 . . . . . 141 D1
Brockwood Cl NN5 . . . 140 A1
Bromford Cl **8** NN3 . . . 161 A8
Bromley Farm Ct
NN11 . . . . 184 B5
Bromwich Rd **1** CV21 . 80 A1
Bronte Cl NN16 . . . . . . 72 C6
Brontes The NN17 . . . . 36 E6
Brook Ct
Horton NN7 . . . . 177 E2
Silverstone NN12 . . . . . 214 D5
Brooke Cl
Rushden NN10 . . . . 132 B1
Wellingborough NN8 . . . 129 B5
Brooke Gn NN8 . . . . . . 129 B5
Brooke Ho NN17 . . . . . 36 E6
Brooke House Coll
LE16 . . . . 31 E4
Brooke Mews NN8 . . . . 129 B5
Brookend NN4 . . . . 175 E5
Brooke Rd NN18 . . . . . . 53 B8
Brookes Gr NN17 . . . . . 21 E1
Brookes Mews NN6 . . . 144 E5
Brooke Weston City Tech
Coll NN18 . . . . 36 D1
Brook Farm Cl NN10 . . 148 B5
Brookfield Rd
Market Harborough
LE16 . . . . 31 C3
Northampton NN2 . . . . 141 E4
2 Rushden NN10 . . . . . 132 A2
Brookhaven NN14 . . . . 90 B4
Brook La
Great Easton LE16 . . . . 20 D6
Northampton NN5 . . . . 158 F8
Towcester NN12 . . . . . 203 A6
Brookland Cres NN1 . . 142 A1
Brookland Rd NN1,
NN3 . . . . 142 A1
Brooklands Cl NN11 . . 135 C1
Brooklands Gdns LE16 . 31 E4
Brook St E NN8 . . . . . . 130 B4
Brook St W NN8 . . . . . 129 F4
Brooks Cl
Burton Latimer NN15 . . 92 C1
Willoughby CV23 . . . . . 117 D4
Brooksdale Cl NN16 . . 72 B6
Brookside
Bozeat NN29 . . . . 164 D2
Desborough NN14 . . . . 51 B2
Glapthorn PE8 . . . . 26 C1
Hinton NN11 . . . . 184 A6
Lillingstone Lovell
MK18 . . . . 227 A6
Southwick PE8 . . . . . . 26 B5
Stanwick NN9 . . . . 114 A3
Wappenham NN12 . . . . 213 C8
Weedon Bec NN7 . . . . . 155 B3
Brookside Cl
Old Stratford MK19 . . . 229 B6
Yelvertoft NN6 . . . . 82 B4
Brookside La NN11 . . . 153 A2
Brookside Mdws NN14 . 140 E1
Brookside Mews NN6 . . 82 B4
Brookside Pl NN7 . . . . . 156 C2
Brooks Rd NN9 . . . . . . 114 F8
Brook St
9 Daventry NN11 . . . . . 135 C2
Hargrave NN9 . . . . 115 E3
Moreton Pinkney NN11 . 199 C2
Northampton NN1 . . . . 159 B7
Raunds NN9 . . . . 114 D6
Brook Terr
1 Irthlingborough
NN9 . . . . 112 F2
Medbourne LE16 . . . . . 18 C4
Brook Vale NN8 . . . . . . 129 C2
Brooke View NN4 . . . . . 175 C4
Brookway MK19 . . . . . 228 E4
Brook Wlk NN14 . . . . . . 95 A3
Broom Ct **2** NN4 . . . . . 159 A3
Broomhill Cres NN3 . . . 143 A6
Broom Way NN15 . . . . . 90 F8
Brough Cl NN5 . . . . 139 F1
BROUGHTON 90 B4
Broughton Hill NN14 . . 90 A6
Broughton Pl NN3 . . . . 142 B3
Broughton Prim Sch
NN14 . . . . 90 A4
Broughton Rd
Mawsley Village NN14 . . 89 B3
Old NN6 . . . . 107 E8
Pytchley NN6 . . . . 90 E2
Browning Ave NN16 . . 72 C5
Browning Cl
8 Daventry NN11 . . . . . 135 B4
Rushden NN10 . . . . 148 D8

Browning Rd
Rugby CV21 . . . . 99 B8
Wellingborough NN8 . . . 129 C4
Browning Wlk NN17 . . . 36 D8
Brownlow Ct NN3 . . . . 142 E4
Browns Cl
Mawsley Village NN14 . . 89 B4
Moulton NN3 . . . . 126 D2
Brownsfield Rd NN12 . . 217 E6
Brown's La NN14 . . . . . 95 C6
Browns Rd NN11 . . . . . 134 F1
Brown's Way NN1 . . . . 159 E5
Brownswood Dr
NN12 . . . . 217 D3
Browns Yd NN12 . . . . . 203 C6
Bruce St NN5 . . . . 158 F6
Brundall Ct NN3 . . . . . . 160 D7
Brunel Cl
Daventry NN11 . . . . 134 F4
Kettering NN16 . . . . 72 A3
Wellingborough NN8 . . . 129 B6
Brunel Ct NN17 . . . . . . 22 A2
Brunel Dr NN5 . . . . 158 D5
Brunel Rd NN17 . . . . . . 22 A2
Brunswick Gdns NN18 . 35 F2
Brunswick Pl NN1 . . . . 159 E7
Brunswick Wlk NN1 . . . 159 E7
Brunting Rd NN3 . . . . . 142 C8
Bryant Rd NN15 . . . . . . 91 C7
Bryant Way NN10 . . . . 132 B6
Bsns Ctr The NN5 . . . 158 F6
Bsns Exchange The
NN16 . . . . 72 B3
Buccleuch St NN16 . . . 72 B3
Buchanan Cl NN4 . . . . 159 A3
Buckfast Sq NN18 . . . . 36 F4
Buckingham Cl
Northampton NN4 . . . . 175 B7
Wellingborough NN8 . . . 129 E1
Buckingham Ct
Brackley NN13 . . . . 234 A6
Kettering NN15 . . . . 91 F7
Buckingham Rd
Brackley NN13 . . . . 234 A6
Deanshanger MK19 . . . 228 F3
Buckingham Way
NN12 . . . . 203 B5
Buckle Ho NN15 . . . . . . 159 B5
Buckley St MK11 . . . . . 229 F4
Bucknell Wood Forest
Wlk★ NN12 . . . . 214 B6
Bucknill Cres CV21 . . . 99 B7
Bucknills La NN6 . . . . . 100 F5
Buckwell Cl
Desborough NN14 . . . . 51 A3
Wellingborough NN8 . . . 129 E5
Buckwell End NN8 . . . . 129 F4
Buckwell La CV23 . . . . 80 B6
Budge Rd NN12 . . . . . . 217 F5
BUGBROOKE 173 A7
Bugbrooke Com Prim Sch
NN12 . . . . 172 F7
BUGBROOKE DOWNS . 173 C4
Bugbrooke Rd
Gayton NN7 . . . . 173 D2
Kislingbury NN7 . . . . . 157 D3
Nether Heyford NN7 . . . 156 C1
Bugby Dr NN9 . . . . 113 B5
Bugby Way NN9 . . . . . . 114 D7
Bull Baulk OX17 . . . . . 220 A8
Bull Cl NN29 . . . . 164 D3
Bull La PE9 . . . . 1 A6
Bullmatt Bsns Ctr
NN10 . . . . 131 E4
Bullock Rd PE7 . . . . 29 D5
Bulls La OX17 . . . . 230 F5
Bulwell Gn NN18 . . . . . 36 C6
BULWICK 12 C1
Bungalows The
Theddingworth LE17 . . . 46 D8
Walgrave NN6 . . . . 108 A5
Bunkers Hill
Badby NN11 . . . . 152 F2
Foxton LE16 . . . . 30 A5
Bunsty Ct MK11 . . . . . . 229 F5
Bunting Cl NN15 . . . . . 92 A2
Bunting Rd NN2 . . . . . . 141 D1
Bunting's La PE8 . . . . . 28 B3
Burcote Fields NN12 . . 203 D4
Burcote Rd NN12 . . . . . 203 D4
Burcote Wood Bsns Pk
NN12 . . . . 203 B1
Burditt Cl NN11 . . . . . . 70 F6
Burdock Way NN14 . . . 51 A4
Burford Ave NN3 . . . . . 142 D5
Burford Cl LE16 . . . . . . 31 D1
Burford Way NN8 . . . . 129 D1
Burgess Ct NN18 . . . . . 36 A4
Burgess Farm OX17 . . 220 B7
Burgess Row LE16 . . . 21 B8
Burghley Cl
Corby NN18 . . . . 36 F4
Desborough NN14 . . . . 51 A4
Market Harborough
LE16 . . . . 32 A3
Burghley Dr NN18 . . . . 36 F5
Burghley St NN16 . . . . 72 C4
Burham Ct NN4 . . . . . . 175 E5
Burkitt Rd NN17 . . . . . . 21 F3
Burleigh Ho **7** NN10 . . 132 B2
Burleigh Rd NN3 . . . . . 141 C1
Burleigh Terr NN29 . . . 164 D3
Burlington Apartments
NN1 . . . . 160 A7

Burmans Way NN7......161 E6
Burnell Cl NN14......95 B3
Burnham Pl NN13......224 B8
Burnmill Rd LE16......31 E5
Burns Cl NN6......144 F4
Burns Dr NN17......36 D8
Burns Rd
  Daventry NN11......135 B4
  Kettering NN16......72 C5
  Wellingborough NN8......129 C4
Burns St NN1......159 E7
BURROW'S BUSH......130 B6
Burrows Cl NN11......119 E1
Burrows Ct NN3......142 E4
Burrows Farm La
  NN14......113 B8
Burrows Vale NN6......106 C2
Burryport Rd NN4......160 B2
Burton Cl NN11......135 C5
Burtone Cl NN14......90 A4
Burton Ho NN15......92 C2
BURTON LATIMER......92 A1
Burton Rd NN9......111 F6
Burton Terr NN29......164 D3
Burtram Cl NN3......142 E1
Burwell Hill NN13......233 F8
Burwell Hill Cl NN13......233 F8
Burwell Wlk NN18......36 C4
Burwood Rd NN3......142 B2
Bury Cl
  Cottingham LE16......20 C1
  Higham Ferrers NN10......132 C6
Bury Dyke NN6......101 A6
Bury Hill NN12......201 F6
Burystead Pl NN8......130 A4
Burystead Rise NN9......114 E7
Burywell Rd NN8......130 B6
Buscot Park Way 🔟......135 B7
Bushacre Ct NN16......71 F3
Bush Cl NN6......129 E5
Bushey Balk Cl NN18......36 B1
Bush Hill NN3......142 C2
Bushland Rd NN3......142 C2
Buswell Cl NN7......155 B3
Buswell Rise NN14......70 E7
Butcher's La
  Boughton NN2......125 C1
  Pattishall NN12......172 E1
  Pytchley NN14......90 F2
Butchers Paddock
  NN14......93 A7
Bute Cl NN17......36 B8
Butland Rd NN18......36 D2
Butler Gdns LE16......31 C1
Butlers Cl NN11......182 F2
Butlin Cl
  Daventry NN11......135 B3
  Rothwell NN14......70 B7
Butlin Ct NN8......130 C1
Butlins La NN7......191 D4
Buttercup Cl NN18......36 C2
Buttercup Rd NN14......51 A5
Butterfields NN8......129 F2
Buttermead NN7......190 D7
Buttermere NN8......129 C5
Buttermere Cl
  Kettering NN16......71 E3
  Northampton NN3......142 C3
Butterwick Wlk NN18......36 C4
Butt La LE17......45 E5
Buttmead NN7......190 D7
Butts Cl
  Aynho OX17......237 C7
  Culworth OX17......198 D2
Butts Croft Cl NN4......175 C6
Butts Hill Cres NN7......173 A8
Butts Rd
  Northampton NN4......175 C6
  Raunds NN9......114 E6
  Wellingborough NN8......129 F1
Butts The OX17......237 D8
Buxton Dr NN14......50 E4
Bycell Rd MK18......226 B3
BYFIELD......183 D7
Byfield Rd
  Chipping Warden
    OX17......196 F7
  Eydon NN11......184 C2
  Hinton NN11......184 B7
  Northampton NN5......159 A5
  Priors Marston CV47......166 E7
Byfield Sch NN11......183 C7
Bygones Mus★🔟OX17......181 D1
By Pass Way NN7......178 B8
Byron Cl NN12......203 B5
Byron Cres
  Higham Ferrers
    NN10......132 A5
  Rushden NN10......131 E2
Byron Rd
  Corby NN17......36 D8
  Kettering NN16......72 C5
  Wellingborough NN8......129 D4
Byron St NN2......141 F1
Byron Wlk NN11......135 B3
BYTHORN......97 D2

C

Cabot Cl
  Daventry NN11......135 C5
  Rothwell NN14......70 E6
Caernarvon Cl NN12......203 C4
Caesars Gate NN13......234 A6

Caistor Rd NN17......10 C1
Caldbeck Wlk 🗡 NN3......142 C4
CALDECOTE......189 B3
Caldecote Rd LE16......20 E6
CALDECOTT
  Corby......21 C8
  Higham Ferrers......133 C6
Caldecott Rd
  Chelveston NN9......133 B7
  Rockingham LE16......21 B5
Calder Cl NN17......21 D1
Calder Gn NN5......140 E1
Caledonian Ho 🔟
  NN5......159 A6
Calke Ho 🔟 NN11......135 B7
Callcott Dr NN15......92 A8
Calstock Cl NN3......160 D7
Calvert Cl NN12......202 E8
Calvert Ct NN8......129 F8
CALVERTON......229 E3
Calverton Rd MK11......229 D4
Calvert Rd NN12......202 E8
Camberley Cl NN13......143 B2
Cambium Cl NN16......72 C6
Camborne Cl NN4......159 B2
Cambria Cres NN3......142 C1
Cambridge Ave NN17......36 B6
Cambridge St
  Kettering NN16......72 C3
  Northampton NN2......159 C8
  Rothwell NN14......70 D8
  Wellingborough NN8......130 A5
  Wymington NN10......148 A7
Cam Cl NN11......21 C1
Camden Sq NN29......164 D2
Camelot Way NN5......158 A7
Cameron Cl
  Daventry NN11......135 B1
  Northampton NN5......158 E7
Cameron Cres NN5......158 E7
Cameron Ct NN17......36 F5
Cameron Dr NN5......158 E7
Campaign Cl 🖉 NN4......175 E7
Campanula Cl NN3......160 C6
Campbell Cl
  Rushden NN10......148 D8
  Towcester NN12......203 D8
  Weedon Bec NN7......155 A4
Campbell Rd
  Corby NN17......36 F5
  Wellingborough NN8......130 A2
Campbell Sq 🔟 NN1......159 D6
Campbell St NN1......159 C7
Camp Cl NN7......173 A6
CAMP HILL......158 E2
Camp Hill NN7......173 A6
Campion Cl NN10......148 B8
Campion Ct NN3......143 B1
Campion Sch NN7......173 A8
Camp La NN7......157 D3
Camrose Rd NN5......159 A8
Camsdale Wlk LE16......35 C8
Canada Sq NN18......36 C3
Canal La MK19......228 E4
Canal Mus The★
  NN12......205 A8
Canalside
  Market Harborough
    LE16......31 D4
  Old Stratford MK19......229 C7
  Stoke Bruerne NN12......205 A8
Canberra Ho NN17......22 F1
Candace Ct NN5......158 E8
Candleford Cl NN3......143 B4
Candleford Cl NN13......233 E8
Candleford Ct NN13......233 E8
Canford Gn NN18......36 A6
Cannam Cl LE16......20 B1
Cannock Rd NN18......36 F8
Cannon St NN8......130 A5
Canonbury NN8......129 C4
Canon Harnett Ct
  MK12......229 F6
CANONS ASHBY......185 D2
Canons Ashby★......185 D2
Canons Ashby Ct
  NN11......185 B5
Canons Ashby Rd
  NN11......199 D7
Canon St NN16......72 B3
Canons Wlk NN2......141 B4
Canterbury Cl OX16......219 A7
Cantle Cl NN18......36 D3
Capell Gdns NN18......36 E4
Capell Rise NN7......155 E5
Cappenham Ct NN12......203 B6
Captain's Ct NN7......177 E1
Cardigan Cl 🖉 NN5......158 F8
Cardigan Ho NN17......36 E6
Cardigan Pl
  Corby NN17......36 E5
  Kettering NN16......72 D2
Cardigan Rd NN14......37 E2
Cardinal Cl NN4......175 B7
Cares Orch NN7......161 D3
Carey Cl NN3......126 B1
Carey Ct NN3......126 B1
Carey Dr NN7......36 C8
Carey Ho 🖉 NN16......72 B2
Carey Rd
  Hackleton NN7......177 A3
  Towcester NN12......203 C3
Careys Rd LE16......215 F7
Carey St
  Kettering NN16......72 C2
  Northampton NN1......159 E7
Carey Way NN10......132 D3

Carina Rd NN15......91 C5
Carisbrooke Cl NN15......91 F8
Carline Ct NN3......142 E4
Carlisle Cl NN18......36 D1
Carlow Rd NN14......95 A3
Carlow St NN14......95 A3
Carlton Cl NN18......148 A7
Carlton Gdns NN2......141 E2
Carlton Mews NN10......132 C5
Carlton Pl NN18......36 B6
Carlton Rd
  Northampton NN2......141 E2
  Wilbarston LE16......34 D5
Carlton St NN14......72 A3
Carlyle Ave NN5......158 E7
Carmarthen Way
  NN10......148 C8
Carnegie St NN10......132 A2
Carne The MK11......229 E5
Caroline Chisholm Sch
  NN4......175 F5
Carol Trusler Mews
  NN2......159 B7
Carousel Way NN3......160 F7
Carpetbagger & Northants
  Aviation Mus★🔟NN6......68 F3
Carradale Cl NN16......72 A6
Carrdus Sch The
  OX17......219 C8
Carriage Dr NN16......72 C6
Carriers Ct MK19......207 A2
Carrington Gdns 🔟
  NN3......160 F8
Carrington St NN16......72 B2
Carron Cl NN11......21 C1
Carr's Way NN7......157 C6
Carsington Cl NN16......71 E3
Carter Ave NN14......90 A3
Carter Cl NN8......130 B4
Cartmel Pl NN3......142 C3
Cartmel Way NN10......132 D3
Cartill St NN9......114 C6
Cartwright Cres
  NN13......233 D7
Cartwright Gdns
  OX17......237 D7
Cartwright Rd
  Charlton OX17......231 F5
  Northampton NN2......141 C1
Casterbridge Ct NN4......175 E7
Casterton Cl NN9......114 A5
Castilian St NN1......159 D5
Castilian Terr NN1......159 D5
Castillion Ct NN1......159 D5
CASTLE ASHBY......163 A3
Castle Ashby Craft Ctr★
  NN7......162 F3
Castle Ashby Gdns★
  NN7......163 B3
Castle Ashby Rd NN7......179 B7
Castle Ashby Rural
  Shopping Yd★🔟NN7......162 F3
Castle Ave NN5......158 A4
Castle Bush NN5......158 C8
Castle Cl
  Corby NN18......36 A4
  Northampton NN5......158 C8
Castle Ct
  Rushden NN10......148 A8
  Wellingborough NN8......130 B4
Castlefields Cl NN10......132 C6
Castle Gdns NN14......54 B3
CASTLE HILL......233 E5
Castle Hill
  Daventry NN11......135 B1
  Rothwell NN14......70 D7
Castle La NN8......130 B4
Castle Mews NN8......130 B4
Castle Mound CV23......99 C2
Castle Mount NN13......233 E5
Castle Prim Sch NN1......159 D7
Castle Rd
  Lavendon MK46......180 F1
  Wellingborough NN8......130 B4
  Woodford Halse NN11......184 C6
Castle St
  Deddington OX15......236 A4
  Northampton NN1......159 C6
  Wellingborough NN8......130 B4
CASTLETHORPE......218 F6
Castlethorpe Fst Sch
  MK19......218 F5
Castlethorpe Rd
  MK19......206 F1
Castleton Rd NN14......50 E4
Castle View
  Barnwell PE8......59 B7
  Wellingborough NN8......130 B4
Castle Way
  Kettering NN15......91 F6
  Wellingborough NN8......130 A4
Caswell Rd NN4......160 B1
Catchland Cl NN18......36 C2
Catchpole Cl NN18......36 D3
Catesby Cl NN2......141 E4
Catesby End NN11......151 D1
Catesby Rd NN14......70 E7
Catesby St NN16......72 C3
Catlow Cl NN9......114 C8
Catterick Cl NN18......36 E1
Cattle End
  Farthingstone NN12......170 F3
  Silverstone NN12......214 C3
Cattle Hill NN3......143 C2
Cattle Market Rd
  NN1......159 C4
Catton Cl NN6......85 B8
Catton Cres NN2......140 F5

Cauldecott Cl NN4......158 D1
Causeway Cl NN17......21 E2
Causeway The
  Byfield NN11......183 E8
  Northampton NN3......161 C7
Causin Cl NN14......55 F8
Causin Way PE8......40 C6
Cavalry Dr NN11......135 B1
Cavalry Fields NN14......155 A4
Cavalry Hill NN7......155 A4
Cavendish Cl NN15......91 F5
Cavendish Ctyd NN7......22 E1
Cavendish Dr NN3......160 D6
Cawley Ct OX17......230 B5
Caxton Cl NN11......135 A4
Caxton St LE16......31 F1
Caythorpe Sq NN18......36 B6
Cecil Cl NN18......36 E4
Cecil Dr NN18......36 F4
Cecil Rd NN2......141 C2
Cecil St
  Kettering NN16......72 C4
  Rothwell NN14......70 D7
Cedar Cl
  Corby NN17......21 E1
  Northampton NN5......158 E8
Cedar Dr NN14......76 D1
Cedar Gate NN3......142 C7
Cedar Hythe NN6......124 C5
Cedar Rd
  Kettering NN16......72 C4
  Northampton NN1,
    NN3......142 A1
Cedar Rd E NN3......142 A1
Cedar Road Prim Sch
  NN3......142 A1
Cedar Way
  Higham Ferrers NN10......132 B6
  Wellingborough NN8......130 A7
Cedrus Ct NN2......140 F6
Celandine Cl NN10......148 C7
Celeborn Pl NN3......143 B5
Celtic Cl NN10......132 B7
Celtic Way NN6......100 C6
Cemetery La NN10......132 B6
Centaine Rd NN10......132 A1
Centec Ct MK19......229 B7
Central Ave
  Hinton NN11......184 A7
  Kettering NN16......72 D3
  Northampton NN2......141 B6
  Wellingborough NN8......129 E2
Central Mus & Art Gall★
  NN1......159 D5
Centre 2000 NN16......71 F4
Centre Par NN16......72 D4
Centurion Way NN4......175 F5
Chace Rd NN8......130 C4
CHACOMBE......208 F4
Chacombe CE Prim Sch
  OX17......208 F4
Chacombe Ho OX17......208 E3
Chacombe House Mews
  OX17......208 E3
Chacombe Priory
  OX17......208 D4
Chacombe Rd OX17......208 F1
Chadleigh Ct NN13......233 E6
CHADSTONE......162 E2
Chadstone Ave NN2......141 D6
Chadwick Gdns NN5......140 D1
Chaffinch Cl NN4......174 F7
Chaffinch Way NN13......222 E1
Chainbridge Ct NN14......76 C2
Chainbridge La PE28......97 F1
Chalcombe Ave NN2......141 C5
Chalcombe Rd NN2......141 C4
Chalfont Ct 🔟 NN1......159 C7
Chalk La NN1......159 B6
Chalon Ct NN8......129 E1
Chamberlain Ave
  NN8......129 E1
Chamberlain Rd CV21......99 B8
Chamberlain Way
  Higham Ferrers
    NN10......132 C5
  Raunds NN9......114 C5
Chambers Hill NN14......89 B4
Chambers Row NN6......64 E6
Chambers The NN1......159 E6
Champion Ct NN13......233 E8
Chancel Terr PE8......59 B5
Chancery La NN14......76 D2
Chandler Gdns NN14......76 E1
Chandlers Way NN17......36 E5
Channing St 🖉 NN16......72 C2
Chantelle Ct 🔟 NN11......135 B3
Chantry Cl NN3......143 B3
Chantry La NN12......203 C6
Chantry Rise MK46......195 F3
CHAPEL BRAMPTON
  ......124 E2
Chapel Cl
  Clifton OX15......236 E4
  Great Addington NN14......94 B2
  Litchborough NN12......171 C1
  Rushden NN10......132 C3
  Silverstone NN12......214 D4
Chapel Ct PE8......8 B2
CHAPEL END......44 D4

Chapel End
  Croughton NN13......238 C8
  Great Gidding PE28......61 D2
  Piddington NN7......177 A2
Chapel Farm NN7......206 C6
Chapel Fields LE17......62 B3
Chapel Gn NN5......141 A2
Chapel Hill
  Higham Ferrers NN10......132 B7
  Irchester NN29......147 B8
  Islip NN14......76 B2
  Little Addington NN14......113 B7
  Silverstone NN12......214 D4
Chapel Ho NN4......159 B3
Chapel La
  Adderbury OX17......230 A4
  Badby NN11......153 A3
  Barrowden LE15......3 F5
  Blisworth NN7......190 D3
  Brafield-on-t-G NN7......161 C2
  Clipston LE16......66 F8
  Corby NN17......37 B2
  Crick NN6......101 A5
  Daventry NN11......135 C4
  Denford NN14......95 C6
  Elton PE8......28 C8
  Farthinghoe NN13......221 B4
  Flore NN7......155 F5
  Geddington NN14......54 A2
  Great Doddington
    NN29......145 D3
  Hackleton NN7......177 B2
  Ketton PE9......1 C1
  Lilbourne CV23......81 A3
  Lillingstone Lovell
    MK18......227 A1
  Little Harrowden NN9......110 C4
  Maidford NN12......186 A6
  Old NN6......107 C2
  Rushton NN14......52 C2
  Slapton NN12......201 E2
  Stanion NN14......37 E2
  Stanwick NN9......114 A3
  Stoke Albany LE16......34 B4
  Stoke Bruerne NN12......205 A8
  Turweston NN13......234 B7
  Whitfield NN13......223 D8
  Wilbarston LE16......34 C5
Chapel Pl 🔟 NN1......159 E6
Chapel Rd
  Greatworth OX17......210 E1
  Weldon NN17......38 A8
Chapel Row
  Northampton NN3......143 C2
  Souldern OX27......237 E3
Chapel St
  Charwelton NN11......168 A4
  Kilsby CV23......100 A2
  Ringstead NN14......95 A3
  Swinford LE17......62 B3
  Titchmarsh NN14......77 C4
  Warmington PE8......28 B3
Chapel View NN14......90 B5
Chaplins La NN14......51 A3
Chapman Cl NN12......203 C7
Chapman Gr NN17......36 E8
Chapmans Cl
  Irchester NN29......147 B8
  Stoke Albany LE16......34 A4
Chapmans Ct 🔟 NN16......72 C2
Chapmans Dr MK19......229 B7
Chapmans La OX15......236 A3
Chappell Ho 🖉 NN3......126 C1
Chardonnay Cl NN5......140 A2
Chariot Rd NN4......175 F5
Charity Cotts MK19......229 E2
Charlbury Cl NN8......145 E8
Charles Cl
  Higham Ferrers
    NN10......132 C7
  Long Buckby NN6......121 B3
  Old NN6......107 C2
Charlesfield Rd CV22......98 A3
Charles Robinson Ct
  NN8......129 E3
Charles St
  Corby NN17......36 F5
  Kettering NN16......72 B4
  Market Harborough
    LE16......31 D3
  Northampton NN1......159 D7
  Rothwell NN14......70 C6
  Thrapston NN14......76 E2
  Wellingborough NN8......129 E2
Charles Terr 🔟 NN11......135 C1
Charlotte Pl NN16......72 E4
Charlottes Row 🔟
  NN10......132 A2
CHARLTON......231 F4
Charlton Cl NN2......141 C5
Charlton Rd OX17......237 C7
Charlton Way NN13......221 B4
Charnwood 🔟 NN8......130 A5
Charnwood Ave NN3......142 E4
Charnwood Cl 🖉
  NN11......135 B4
Charnwood Ct NN3......142 E2
Charnwood Dr NN15......92 A5
Charnwood Rd NN17......36 F7
Charter Ct NN18......36 D2
Charter Gate NN3......142 B6
Charterhouse Cl
  NN13......233 E7
Charter Rd CV22......98 E8
Chartwell Ave NN3......142 C5
Chartwell Rd 🔟 NN11......135 B7
CHARWELTON......168 B5
Charwelton La NN11......167 D8

harwelton Rd NN11.... **169** C2
hase Barn Cotts
  OX27 .... **239** B3
hase Cl NN14........ **37** E3
hase Farm NN14...... **54** B2
hase Hill NN14....... **54** A3
hase Park Rd NN7 .... **179** A5
haseport Cl MK46..... **194** D2
hase The
  Long Buckby NN6..... **121** B4
  Pitsford NN6 .... **125** D4
hase View Rd NN14.... **54** B3
haston Pl NN16....... **72** E5
hatellerault Ct NN17 .. **36** D8
hater Cl LE16........ **32** A6
hater La PE9 .... **1** A7
hater Mews PE9...... **1** A7
hater St NN3 .... **126** D1
hatsworth Ave
  Kettering NN15 ...... **91** C5
  Northampton NN3 .... **142** F5
hatsworth Dr
  Market Harborough
    LE16 .... **32** B3
  Wellingborough NN8 .. **129** C7
hatsworth Rd NN18... **36** D6
haucer Cl NN2 ...... **141** F1
haucer Ho NN2 ...... **141** F2
haucer Rd
  Rugby CV22 .... **98** A7
  Wellingborough NN8 .. **129** D4
haucer St NN2 ...... **141** F1
haucer Way NN11 .... **135** B2
heaney Dr NN4 ...... **175** E2
heaney Rd NN5 ...... **158** D7
heddar Cl NN5 ...... **158** D7
hedington Cl NN15 ... **92** A5
hedworth Cl NN3 .... **143** D2
heese La **5** NN8..... **130** A4
helfham Cl NN3 ..... **160** D7
helmorton Vale NN14 . **50** E4
helmscote Row
  OX17 .... **208** F8
helmsford Cl NN4 .... **159** A2
heltenham Cl NN15 ... **148** C8
heltenham Rd NN18 .. **36** E1
HELVESTON **133** C8
helveston Cres NN9 ... **133** D5
helveston Dr NN17 ... **36** B7
helveston Rd
  Higham Ferrers NN10 . **132** E7
  Raunds NN9......... **114** C4
  Stanwick NN9 .... **114** B3
henderit Sch OX17 ... **209** A1
heney Ct OX17 ...... **208** F1
heney Gdns OX17.... **208** F2
hepstow Cl
  Kettering NN15 ...... **91** F8
  Northampton NN5 .... **159** A7
hepstow Dr NN8..... **129** C7
hepstow Rd
  Corby NN18 .... **36** D1
  Corby NN18 .... **36** E1
hequers Cl NN18..... **36** E2
hequers La
  Grendon NN7........ **163** E5
  Ravensthorpe NN6.... **103** D1
  Wellingborough NN8 .. **130** A5
hequers The MK19.... **218** F5
heriton Cl NN11...... **135** C6
heriton Rd NN18..... **36** F4
heriton Way NN1..... **160** C6
herradine Ct NN9 .... **114** D6
herry Ave NN4....... **130** A7
herry Blossom Cl
  NN3 .... **143** B2
herry Cl NN3 .... **142** C2
herry Ct NN9 .... **112** E1
herry Hill NN16...... **107** C6
herry Lodge Rd NN3 . **143** B3
herry Orch
  Olney MK46 .... **195** E4
  Rushden NN10....... **132** C1
herry Rd NN16 ...... **72** D4
herry St
  Irthlingborough NN9 .. **112** E1
  Ringstead NN14...... **95** B3
herry Tree Cl
  Desborough NN14..... **51** B2
  Husbands Bosworth
    LE17 .... **45** E5
herry Tree La NN4.... **160** E3
herrytree Wlk NN6 ... **143** D8
herry Wlk NN9 ...... **114** B5
herwell Banks OX17 .. **231** A6
herwell Gn NN5 ..... **140** F1
herwell Terr NN18.... **184** C6
herwell The NN11 .... **134** F1
herwell Wlk NN17 ... **21** C1
hesham Rise NN3 .... **143** B4
hesil Wlk NN18...... **36** A6
hester Ave NN7 ..... **157** B6
hester Cl NN15 ..... **91** B6
hester Ho NN3 ...... **161** B8
hester Rd
  Irchester NN29 ...... **131** A1
  Rushden NN10....... **131** F2
  Wellingborough NN8 .. **130** C4
hestnut Ave
  Corby NN17 .... **21** D1
  Kettering NN15 ...... **72** C1
  Northampton NN4 .... **175** D5
hestnut Cl
  Hinton NN11 .... **184** A6
  Long Buckby NN6..... **121** B3
  Milton Malsor NN7 ... **174** E4
  Rushden NN10....... **131** F3
  Stony Stratford MK11.. **229** D5

Chestnut Cl continued
  Wymington NN10...... **148** B5
Chestnut Ct
  Northampton NN3 .... **142** A2
  Raunds NN9......... **114** D7
Chestnut Dr
  Brackley NN13....... **222** F1
  Desborough NN14..... **51** C2
  Thrapston NN14 ..... **76** D1
Chestnut Gn NN13 ... **223** E4
Chestnut Gr LE16 .... **67** A8
Chestnut Rd
  Northampton NN3 .... **142** A1
  Yardley Gobion NN12.. **217** F6
Chestnuts The
  Castlethorpe MK19 ... **218** F5
  Clifton OX15........ **236** E4
  Hinton-in-t-H NN13 ... **232** F6
Chestnut Terr NN3 ... **142** A2
Chettle Pl NN12...... **217** E2
Chetwode OX17...... **219** C6
Cheviot Cl NN16 ..... **72** B7
Cheviot Ct NN4 ..... **158** E3
Cheviot Ho NN2 ..... **141** C5
Chewton Cl NN5 ..... **158** D7
Cheyne Wlk
  Kettering NN15 ...... **91** E8
  Northampton NN1 .... **159** E5
Chichele Cl NN10 .... **132** B5
Chichele Coll ★ NN10 . **132** B6
Chichele Ct NN10 .... **132** B3
Chichele St NN10 .... **132** C6
Chicheley Cotts NN14 . **76** D2
Chichester Cl
  1 Daventry NN11..... **135** D1
  Rothwell NN14....... **70** E6
Chieftan Bsns Pk
  NN8............... **129** A6
Child's St NN14 ..... **95** C6
Chiltern Ave NN5 .... **158** D8
Chiltern Cl
  Market Harborough
    LE16 .... **31** F5
  Northampton NN5 .... **158** D8
Chiltern Ct **3** NN10 ... **132** A2
Chiltern Prim Sch
  NN5............... **158** E8
Chiltern Rd
  Daventry NN11 ...... **135** B5
  Kettering NN16 ..... **72** B6
Chiltern Way NN5..... **158** E8
Chilwell Ct **3** NN3 ... **160** F8
CHIPPING WARDEN ... **196** F6
Chipping Warden Sch
  OX17.............. **196** F7
Chipsey Ave
  Bugbrooke NN7 ...... **172** F8
  Northampton NN1 .... **160** B6
Chisholm Cl NN4 .... **175** E1
Choakles The NN4 ... **176** B6
Chowns Mill Bsns Pk
  NN9............... **113** B1
Christchurch Dr
  NN11.............. **153** B7
Christchurch Rd NN1 . **160** A7
Christie Way NN15 ... **90** F8
Christine Ct NN9 .... **114** D6
Christopher Ct NN6.. **64** D5
Christopher Rawlins CE
  Prim Sch OX17 ..... **230** A4
Christopher Reeves Lower
  Sch NN29 .... **147** E1
Chulmleigh Wlk NN3.. **160** C7
Church Ave OX17 .... **230** F5
Church Wlk
Church Bank LE16 .... **20** D1
CHURCH BRAMPTON .. **140** C8
CHURCH CHARWELTON
  .... **168** C3
Church Cl
  Adderbury OX17 ..... **230** A3
  Braybrooke LE16 ..... **49** E6
  Caldecott LE16 ...... **21** B8
  Clipston LE16........ **67** A8
  Hartwell NN7........ **192** D2
  Milton Malsor NN7 ... **174** F4
  Wardington OX17 .... **196** E1
  West Haddon NN6.... **102** C5
  Wicken MK19........ **228** B3
  Wymington NN10..... **148** B5
Churchcroft NN7 .... **191** D4
Church Dr NN18 ..... **53** C8
CHURCH END **183** D7
Church End NN13 .... **238** D8
CHURCH END **207** A2
Church End
  Piddington NN7 ...... **177** A2
  Potterspury NN12 .... **217** E3
  Roade NN7 .... **191** D4
  Syresham NN13...... **224** C8
Church Farm Cl
  NN29.............. **164** D3
Church Farm Way
  LE16.............. **68** C7
Churchfield Cl NN2 ... **141** E4
Church Fields NN11... **152** C7
Church Gdns NN6.... **103** E1
Church Gn
  Badby NN11 .... **153** A2
  Barnwell PE8........ **59** B6
  Northampton NN5 .... **140** F2
  Woodford NN14...... **94** D6
Church Hall Rd NN10.. **131** F1
Church Hill
  Badby NN11 .... **152** F2
  Barnwell PE8........ **59** B6
  Finedon NN9 .... **111** E4
  Geddington NN14 .... **54** A3

Church Hill continued
  Hollowell NN6 .... **104** B4
  Moulton NN3 .... **126** C1
  Northampton NN4 .... **175** E6
  Ravensthorpe NN6 ... **103** D1
Churchill Ave
  Irthlingborough NN9 .. **113** B5
  Northampton NN3 .... **142** B4
  Wellingborough NN8 .. **129** E7
Churchill Cl NN14 .... **70** E7
Churchill Rd
  Earls Barton NN6..... **144** F4
  Welton NN11 .... **135** E8
Churchill Way
  Brackley NN13....... **233** F6
  Burton Latimer NN15 . **92** B2
  Daventry NN11 ...... **153** E7
  Kettering NN15 ..... **72** F1
Church La
  Adderbury OX17 ..... **230** A3
  Alderton NN12....... **204** F2
  Barnwell PE8........ **59** B6
  Barrowden LE15 ..... **3** F4
  Blisworth NN7....... **190** D7
  Bozeat NN29 .... **164** D3
  Brafield-on-t-G NN7... **161** E2
  Broughton NN14 ..... **89** F6
  Bugbrooke NN7 ...... **172** E7
  Burton Latimer NN15 . **92** C2
  Bythorn PE28........ **97** D4
  Caldecott LE16 ...... **21** B8
  Chacombe OX17 ..... **208** E4
  Church Brampton NN6.. **140** B8
  Claydon OX17 .... **181** D1
  Clipston LE16........ **67** A8
  Cold Ashby NN6...... **84** A5
  Cold Higham NN12 ... **188** C8
  Covington PE18 ..... **116** C2
  Cranford St John NN14 . **93** B7
  Croughton NN13 ..... **238** D5
  Deanshanger MK19... **228** E4
  Denford NN14 .... **95** C6
  Dingley LE16 .... **33** A4
  Duddington PE9...... **5** B6
  East Carlton LE16 .... **34** F7
  East Carlton LE16 .... **35** A7
  East Haddon NN6 .... **122** D4
  Evenley NN13 .... **233** F3
  Grafton Regis NN12 .. **205** D2
  Great Doddington
    NN29............. **145** D6
  Harlestone NN7 ..... **139** E6
  Harrington NN6...... **69** B6
  Hellidon NN11 .... **151** C1
  Husbands Bosworth
    LE17 .... **45** E5
  Kislingbury NN7...... **157** D3
  Lillingstone Lovell
    MK18 .... **227** A6
  Lyddington LE15 ..... **9** D6
  Maidford NN12 ...... **186** D7
  Middleton Cheney
    OX17............. **208** F1
  Morcott LE15........ **3** A6
  Nether Heyford NN7 .. **156** B2
  Newton Bromswold
    NN10............. **149** D8
  Northampton, Bellinge
    NN3.............. **161** A8
  Northampton NN1 .... **159** D5
  Pitsford NN6 .... **125** D5
  Potterspury NN12 .... **217** E3
  Slapton NN12........ **201** E2
  Slipton NN14 .... **75** A3
  South Kilworth LE17 .. **63** C8
  South Luffenham LE15. **3** E8
  Spratton NN6........ **105** B1
  Stanford on A NN6 ... **62** F2
  Stibbington PE8...... **8** D2
  Stoke Bruerne NN12 .. **205** A8
  Stoke Doyle PE8 ..... **41** D1
  Sywell NN6 .... **127** E3
  Thornby NN6 .... **84** D4
  Thorpe Langton LE16.. **17** A5
  Walgrave NN6 .... **108** A4
  Warmington PE8 ..... **28** B3
  Welford NN6 .... **64** E5
  Wicken MK19........ **228** B3
  Wilby NN8 .... **129** B1
  Wollaston NN29...... **146** D3
  Wymington NN10..... **148** B5
  Yardley Hastings NN7. **179** B7
  Yelden NN44 .... **133** F3
Church Leys NN13 ... **233** E3
Church Mount NN6 .. **103** F6
Church Piece Cotts
  NN13.............. **221** B4
Church Pk PE8 ...... **7** D8
Church Rd
  Brackley NN13....... **233** F7
  Braunston NN11 ..... **118** B1
  Greatworth OX17 .... **210** E1
  Hargrave NN9 .... **115** F1
  Ketton PE9 .... **1** A5
  Piddington NN7 ...... **177** A2
  Pytchley NN14 ...... **91** A1
  Spratton NN6........ **124** B8
  Upper Boddington
    NN11............. **182** C7
Church Row PE8...... **42** F3
Church Sq **6** LE16 ... **31** E3
Church St
  Blakesley NN12 ...... **187** B1
  Boughton NN2....... **141** C8
  Brigstock NN14...... **55** F7
  Brixworth NN6....... **106** B3
  Broughton NN14 ..... **90** B4
  Burton Latimer NN15 . **92** C3

Church St continued
  Byfield NN11 .... **183** D7
  Charwelton NN11 .... **168** B4
  Clifton u D CV23 .... **80** A5
  Cogenhoe NN7....... **162** A6
  Cottingham LE16 .... **20** D1
  Crick NN6 .... **100** F6
  Easton o t H PE9 .... **2** A6
  Finedon NN9 .... **111** E4
  Hargrave NN9 .... **115** E2
  Helmdon NN13 ...... **211** F3
  Husbands Bosworth
    LE17 .... **45** E5
  Irthlingborough NN9 .. **112** F2
  Isham NN14......... **91** F1
  Long Buckby NN6..... **121** B4
  Market Harborough LE16 . **31** E3
  Mears Ashby NN6 .... **128** B2
  Moulton NN3 .... **126** C1
  Naseby NN6......... **85** B8
  Nassington PE8 ..... **15** F5
  Nether Heyford NN7 .. **156** B2
  Newnham NN11 ..... **153** E4
  Olney MK46 .... **195** F3
  Oundle PE8 .... **42** A5
  Pattishall NN12 ..... **172** E1
  Polebrook PE8 ...... **42** F3
  Raunds NN9......... **114** E7
  Ringstead NN14...... **95** B3
  Rothersthorpe NN7 .. **174** A6
  Rushden NN10....... **132** B2
  Sibbertoft LE16 ..... **47** A2
  Silverstone NN12 .... **214** D5
  Stanwick NN9 .... **114** A3
  Staverton NN11 ..... **152** C7
  Stony Stratford MK11.. **229** D5
  Sulgrave OX17 ...... **210** F7
  Titchmarsh NN14.... **77** C4
  Wadenhoe PE8 ...... **58** A3
  Warmington PE8 ..... **28** B2
  Watford NN6 .... **120** C6
  Weedon Bec NN7..... **155** C3
  Weldon NN17........ **38** B7
  Wellingborough NN8 .. **130** A4
  Wilbarston LE16 ..... **34** C5
  Woodford Halse NN11.. **184** C6
  Woodford NN14...... **94** D6
CHURCH STOWE **171** D8
Church View
  Brackley NN13....... **234** A7
  Broughton NN14 ..... **90** A4
  Burton Latimer NN15 . **92** C3
  Ecton NN6 .... **143** F4
  Greens Norton NN12.. **202** E8
  Keyston PE28........ **97** A3
  Moulton NN3 .... **126** C2
  Northampton NN4 .... **175** E5
  Raunds NN9......... **114** D7
  Walgrave NN6 .... **108** A5
  Weldon NN17........ **38** B7
Church View Rd NN14.. **51** B2
Churchway NN3 ..... **160** D8
Church Way
  Denton NN7......... **178** B8
  Ecton NN6 .... **143** F4
  Grendon NN7........ **163** D5
  Northampton NN3 .... **160** E7
  Preston Capes NN11.. **169** D2
  Thorpe Malsor NN14.. **71** A3
  1 Wellingborough
    NN8.............. **130** A4
  Whittlebury NN12 ... **215** C5
Church Way Ct NN3.. **160** D8
Church Wlk
  Barby CV23 .... **99** C1
  Bozeat NN29 .... **164** D3
  Corby NN17 .... **37** B6
  Daventry NN11 ...... **135** C2
  Denford NN14 .... **95** C6
  5 Irthlingborough
    NN9.............. **112** F2
  Kettering NN16 ..... **72** B2
  Kilsby CV23 .... **100** A3
  King's Cliffe PE8 .... **13** E7
  Little Addington NN14.. **113** B8
  Lubenham LE16...... **30** F3
  Market Harborough
    LE16 .... **32** A2
  Newton Bromswold
    NN10............. **149** D8
  Northampton NN3 .... **143** D8
  Ringstead NN14...... **95** B3
  Weldon NN17........ **38** B7
Cider Cl LE15........ **3** F5
Cinnamon Cl **5** NN4 . **175** D6
Circus End NN5...... **140** C1
Circus Gr PE8 .... **42** F2
Cirrus Pk NN3 ...... **142** A7
Cissbury Rd NN4..... **158** F4
Clailey Ct MK11...... **229** F5
Clannell Rd NN4..... **175** A8
Clare Ave NN11 ..... **135** C2
Clare Cl NN6 .... **144** F4
Clare Cres NN12 .... **203** B5
Clare Dr NN14 ...... **76** E3
Claregate NN4....... **175** B8
Claremont Ave MK11.. **229** E4
Claremont Ct **13** NN1.. **159** C6
Claremont Dr LE16... **32** A3
Clarence Ave NN2 ... **141** C2
Clarence Ct NN10 ... **148** A8
Clarence Rd
  Kettering NN16 ..... **72** C1
  Stony Stratford MK11.. **229** E5
Clarence St LE16..... **31** F3
Clare St
  Northampton NN1 .... **159** E7

Cha–Cob **245**

Clare St continued
  Raunds NN9......... **114** D6
Clare Wlk NN10 ..... **132** B5
Clark Cres NN12 .... **203** C8
Clarke Cl
  Kettering NN16 ..... **72** A4
  Little Addington NN9 . **113** B4
Clarke Ct NN6 ...... **144** F4
Clarke Ho NN1....... **160** A8
Clarke Rd
  Corby NN17 .... **36** D8
  Northampton NN1 .... **160** A8
Clarkes Dale LE16 ... **20** D6
Clarke St LE16 ...... **31** D3
Clarkes Way
  Brackley NN13....... **233** D7
  Welton NN11 .... **135** D8
Clarks La NN13 ..... **221** A3
Claudius Way NN8 ... **130** E2
Claughton Rd NN4 ... **159** D3
CLAY COTON **82** A6
CLAYDON **181** D1
Claydon Cl NN8...... **129** E5
Clayfield Cl NN3 .... **142** B6
Clay La NN17 .... **10** B1
Clayland Cl NN29 ... **164** C2
Claylands The NN7 .. **161** E6
Clay Pit La MK46 .... **195** F3
Claystones NN4...... **158** D2
Clearway House Ind Est
  OX16.............. **219** A7
Cleaver Ct NN15 .... **72** A1
Cleavers La NN6 .... **107** D7
Cleburne Cl NN9..... **114** A4
Clee Rise NN5 ...... **158** D8
Cleeve Way NN8 .... **129** D1
Clement Bois NN13 .. **233** E8
Clevedon Ct **1** NN11 . **135** B7
Cleveland Ave NN16 . **72** C6
Cleveland Pl NN4 ... **159** A2
Clickers Dr NN5 .... **158** D4
Clickers Pl NN5...... **158** C4
Clickers Yd NN46 ... **195** F4
Clifden Terr NN6 .... **122** D4
Cliffe Rd PE9 .... **2** A3
CLIFTON **236** D4
Clifton Cl
  Kettering NN15 ..... **72** C1
  Long Buckby NN6..... **121** C4
Clifton Dr PE8 ...... **41** E5
Clifton Gr NN15 ..... **72** C1
Clifton Rd OX15..... **236** B4
Clifton Sq NN17..... **36** E8
CLIFTON UPON
  DUNSMORE **80** A6
Cliftonville NN1 ..... **159** E5
Cliftonville Ct **11** NN1 . **159** F6
Cliftonville Rd NN1 .. **159** F5
Clinton Rd NN4 ..... **159** B3
CLIPSTON **66** F8
Clipstone Cl NN14 .. **70** C8
Clipston Endowed Prim
  Sch LE16 .... **67** A8
Clipston Field Pl **7**
  NN3.............. **143** C2
Clipston La LE16 .... **48** E3
Clipston Rd
  East Farndon LE16.... **48** B4
  Great Oxendon LE16 . **48** D2
Clipston St LE16 .... **31** F1
Clipston Way NN5 ... **140** D1
Clive Cl NN15....... **72** E1
Clock Mdw NN1 .... **183** C7
Clock Tower Ct NN3 . **142** E6
Cloisters The
  Daventry NN11 ...... **135** D2
  Priors Hardwick CV47. **166** A5
  Rushden NN10....... **132** B2
  Wellingborough NN8 . **130** B3
CLOPTON **78** E5
Close Rd NN7........ **156** B1
Close The
  Chipping Warden
    OX17............. **196** F6
  Eastcote NN12....... **188** F8
  Easton o t H PE9 .... **1** F4
  Greatworth OX17 .... **210** E1
  Irthlingborough NN9 .. **112** F1
  Kettering NN15 ..... **91** B8
  Northampton NN2 .... **141** C4
  Roade NN7 .... **191** D4
  Swinford LE17 ...... **62** B4
  Weston Underwood
    MK46 .... **195** A4
Cloutsham St NN1 ... **159** E7
Clovelly Ct NN18..... **36** F4
Clover Dr
  Rushden NN10....... **148** C8
  Thrapston NN14 ..... **76** D2
Clover Field NN4 .... **175** F2
Clover Gdns NN16 ... **72** B4
Clover La NN4 ...... **141** B5
Club La NN14........ **94** D6
Club St NN16 .... **72** C3
Clumber Ct NN18 ... **36** B6
Clumber Dr NN3 .... **160** E7
Clun Wlk NN17 ..... **21** C1
Clwyd Wlk NN17 ... **21** C1
Clydesdale Rd NN17 . **36** D7
Coach Ho The NN3... **160** B7
Coaching Wlk NN3... **142** D2
Coach Yd NN12...... **217** B3
Coales Gdns LE16.... **31** D5
Coalport Cl NN14 ... **50** F4
Cobblers Cl NN12 ... **187** B1

Cobbler's Pl NN29 . . . . . . 164 D2
Cobblestone Ct NN4 . . . . . 158 D2
Cobbs Gdn MK46 . . . . 195 F4
Cobb's La NN29 . . . . 146 D3
Cobden St NN16 . . . . 72 A3
Cob Dr NN4 . . . . 158 B1
Cobbrook La PE28 . . . . 79 C2
Cobley Cl NN11 . . . . 184 D6
Cockbrook La PE28 . . . . . . 79 C2
Cockerell Rd NN17 . . . . 37 B8
Cockerill's Mdw CV21 . . . . . 99 A8
Cockley Rd NN13 . . . . 221 C6
Codlin Cl NN3 . . . . 143 B1
Coffee Tavern La 9
   NN10 . . . . 132 B2
Cofferidge Cl MK11 . . . . . . 229 D5
Cogan Cres NN14 . . . . 70 B6
COGENHOE 161 E5
Cogenhoe Mill Cvn Cite
   NN7 . . . . 162 A7
Cogenhoe Prim Sch
   NN7 . . . . 161 F5
Coggins Cl NN9 . . . . 114 C6
COLD ASHBY 84 B5
Cold Ashby Rd
   Guilsborough NN6 . . . . . . 103 E7
   Thornby NN6 . . . . 84 D4
Coldermeadow Ave
   NN18 . . . . 36 A3
COLD HIGHAM 188 C8
Coldstream Cl NN11 . . . . . 135 B1
Coldstream La NN4 . . . . . . 175 E8
Cole Ct
   Kettering NN16 . . . . 72 B4
   Rauns NN9 . . . . 114 C5
Coleman Cl NN6 . . . . 101 A6
Coleman St NN14 . . . . 114 D6
Coleraine Cl NN2 . . . . 141 A5
Coleridge Way NN17 . . . . . . 36 C8
Coleridge Wlk NN11 . . . . . 135 B4
Coles Cl NN15 . . . . 92 B2
Coles Rise NN13 . . . . 233 D7
Cole St NN10 . . . . 131 E4
College Field Cl NN3 . . . . . 143 C3
College Fields OX17 . . . . . 237 C3
College Grounds The
   NN3 . . . . 126 B1
College Rd CV23 . . . . 117 E3
College St Mews 28
   NN1 . . . . 159 C6
College St
   Higham Ferrers
     NN10 . . . . 132 C6
   Irthlingborough NN9 . . . . 112 F2
   Northampton NN1 . . . . . . 159 C6
   Rushden NN10 . . . . 132 B2
   Wellingborough NN8 . . . . 129 E4
   Wollaston NN29 . . . . 146 D2
Colley Rise LE15 . . . . 9 C7
Collingcroft Cl NN4 . . . . . 175 A7
Collingdale Rd NN3 . . . . . . 142 D2
Collingham Cl NN9 . . . . . . 114 A5
COLLINGTREE 175 B4
Collingtree CE Prim Sch
   NN4 . . . . 175 C4
Collingtree Ct NN4 . . . . . . 175 B3
COLLINGTREE PARK 175 C5
Collingtree Rd NN4,
   NN7 . . . . 175 A4
Collingwood Ave NN17 . . 36 A7
Collingwood Bsns Ctr
   NN1 . . . . 159 C6
Collingwood Rd NN1 . . . . 141 F1
Collingwood Way
   NN11 . . . . 135 E3
Collins Cl NN12 . . . . 203 C7
Collins Hill NN7 . . . . 155 E6
Collins St NN1 . . . . 159 F7
Collmead Ct NN3 . . . . 143 B4
Collswell La NN12 . . . . 187 B1
Collyns Way PE9 . . . . 1 D2
COLLYWESTON 1 D2
Collyweston Cross Rds
   PE8 . . . . 6 A6
Collyweston Rd NN3 . . . . . 143 C4
Colmar Cl NN11 . . . . 135 A4
Colne Cl NN17 . . . . 21 C1
Colne Way NN5 . . . . 140 E1
Colonial Dr NN4 . . . . 175 C5
Colseed Rd NN14 . . . . 89 B4
Colsons Way MK46 . . . . . . 195 F5
Coltsfoot Rd NN10 . . . . . . 148 C7
Columbus Cres NN14 . . . . . 70 E6
Columbus Cl NN11 . . . . . . 135 B5
Colwell Rd NN8 . . . . 130 C4
Colwyn Rd NN1 . . . . 159 E8
Colyers Ave NN18 . . . . 36 B3
Comfrey Cl NN10 . . . . 148 B7
Commercial Rd
   Corby NN17 . . . . 37 B6
   Kettering NN16 . . . . 72 B2
Commercial St
   Higham Ferrers NN10 . . . 132 B5
   Northampton NN1 . . . . . . 159 C5
Commercial Way
   NN8 . . . . 130 A4
Common St MK46 . . . . 194 D1
Compton Gn NN18 . . . . 36 A6
Compton Ho NN1 . . . . 159 B6
Compton Pl NN16 . . . . 72 E2
Compton St NN8 . . . . 130 C5
Compton St
   Desborough NN14 . . . . . . 51 A3
   Northampton NN1 . . . . . . 159 B6
Compton Way NN6 . . . . . . 144 E3
Coneygree NN4 . . . . 175 F8

Coneygree Ct NN3 . . . . . . 143 B1
Coneywell Ct NN3 . . . . . . 142 F1
Conifer Rise NN3 . . . . 142 E1
Coniston Ave NN3 . . . . . . 142 B3
Coniston Cl
   Daventry NN11 . . . . 135 B2
   Higham Ferrers NN10 . . . 132 B8
   Wellingborough NN8 . . . . 129 C5
Coniston Rd NN16 . . . . 71 F2
Connaught Rd LE16 . . . . . . 31 F4
Connaught St
   Kettering NN16 . . . . 72 D3
   Northampton NN1 . . . . . . 159 D7
Connegar Leys NN7 . . . . . . 190 E7
Connell Cl LE16 . . . . 30 F3
Connell St NN17 . . . . 36 F5
Connolly Cl NN14 . . . . 70 F7
Connolly Dr NN14 . . . . 70 F7
Connolly Rd NN5 . . . . 157 F8
Constable Dr
   Kettering NN15 . . . . 92 A7
   Wellingborough NN8 . . . . 129 F7
Constable Rd
   Corby NN18 . . . . 36 E5
   Rugby CV21 . . . . 80 B1
Constable Wlk NN14 . . . . . 94 D7
Conway Cl
   Northampton NN5 . . . . . . 140 E2
   Rushden NN10 . . . . 148 A8
   Wellingborough NN8 . . . . 129 C6
Conway Dr
   Burton Latimer NN15 . . . . 92 B2
   Thrapston NN14 . . . . 76 F2
Conway Wlk NN17 . . . . 21 D1
Conyngham Rd NN3 . . . . . 142 F2
Cony Wlk NN4 . . . . 175 F3
Cook Cl
   Daventry NN11 . . . . 135 C5
   Rothwell NN14 . . . . 70 E6
Cooks Cl NN7 . . . . 205 F6
Cooks Rd NN17 . . . . 37 F8
Cook's Terr NN6 . . . . 121 A3
Cook's Way NN6 . . . . 121 A3
Coomb Rd NN18 . . . . 36 D1
Co-operative Row
   NN10 . . . . 132 B1
Cooper Cl NN12 . . . . 203 C8
Cooper Ct NN14 . . . . 76 D1
Cooper Dr NN8 . . . . 129 F8
Copelands Rd NN14 . . . . . . 51 C3
Copenhagen Rd NN18 . . . . 36 A1
Copperfield Cl NN16 . . . . . 72 C6
Copper Leaf Cl NN3 . . . . . 142 C6
Coppertree Wlk NN14 . . . . 76 D1
Coppice Cl
   Burton Latimer NN15 . . . . 92 C4
   Daventry NN11 . . . . 153 C8
Coppice Dr NN3 . . . . 142 A5
Coppice The NN14 . . . . 76 D1
Copse Cl
   Burton Latimer NN15 . . . . 92 C3
   Northampton NN2 . . . . . . 140 F5
Copymoor Cl NN4 . . . . 176 A6
Cora Rd NN16 . . . . 72 E4
Corbieres Cl NN5 . . . . 140 A2
CORBY 36 E3
Corby Com Coll NN17 . . . . 36 F6
Corby Com Hospl
   NN17 . . . . 36 D6
Corby Gate Bsns Pk
   NN17 . . . . 22 F1
Corby Rd
   Cottingham LE16 . . . . 35 E8
   Gretton NN17 . . . . 22 B6
   Stanion NN14 . . . . 37 E3
   Weldon NN17 . . . . 38 A7
Cordon Cl NN3 . . . . 143 B3
Cordon Cres NN14 . . . . . . 144 F4
Cordwainer Gr NN14 . . . . . 76 D1
Cordwainer Ho NN5 . . . . . 159 A5
Cordwainers NN10 . . . . . . 132 C1
Corfe Cl NN18 . . . . 36 E2
Corner Cl NN29 . . . . 147 E1
Cornfield Cl NN2 . . . . 141 B5
Cornfield Way NN15 . . . . . . 92 C1
Cornflower Cl NN4 . . . . . . 175 F2
Cornhill Cl NN5 . . . . 140 C3
Corn Kiln Cl NN14 . . . . . . 161 F6
Corn La 7 NN8 . . . . 130 A4
Cornwall Cl NN17 . . . . 36 C6
Cornwall Rd NN16 . . . . 72 D3
Cornwell Bsns Pk
   NN4 . . . . 160 B2
Coronation Ave
   Rothwell NN14 . . . . 70 D7
   Rushden NN10 . . . . 131 E1
Coronation Cres PE8 . . . . . 39 E7
Coronation Rd
   Newnham NN11 . . . . 153 D4
   Stony Stratford MK11 . . . . 229 E5
Corporation St NN17 . . . . . 36 E6
Corran Cl NN5 . . . . 158 E8
Cory Gdns NN7 . . . . 157 C7
COSGROVE 218 D2
Cosgrove L Pk ✶
   MK19 . . . . 218 F1
Cosgrove Rd
   Northampton NN2 . . . . . . 141 C5
   Old Stratford MK19 . . . . . 229 C7
Cosgrove Village Prim Sch
   MK19 . . . . 218 E2
Cosgrove Way NN2 . . . . . . 141 C5
Cosy Nook NN14 . . . . 76 C2
COTON 103 E4
Coton Manor Gdns ✶
   NN6 . . . . 103 E4

Coton Rd
   Guilsborough NN6 . . . . . . 103 F5
   Ravensthorpe NN6 . . . . . 103 E4
   Rugby CV21 . . . . 80 A1
Cotswold Ave
   Kettering NN16 . . . . 72 B5
   Northampton NN5 . . . . . . 158 D8
Cotswold Cl NN11 . . . . . . 135 B5
Cotswold Ct OX27 . . . . . . 237 E3
Cotswold Dr NN8 . . . . 129 D1
Cottage Cl NN2 . . . . 141 A4
Cottage Gdns
   Northampton NN3 . . . . . . 143 B3
   Rushden NN10 . . . . 148 C2
Cottages The NN13 . . . . . . 224 C5
Cottagewell Ct NN3 . . . . . 142 F1
COTTARVILLE 142 D1
Cottarville NN3 . . . . 142 D1
COTTERSTOCK 27 A2
Cotterstock Rd PE8 . . . . . . 41 F7
COTTESBROOKE 104 F8
Cottesbrooke Gdns
   NN4 . . . . 175 D7
Cottesbrooke Grange
   NN6 . . . . 105 A8
Cottesbrooke Hall ✶
   NN6 . . . . 105 A8
Cottesbrooke Hall Gdns ✶
   NN6 . . . . 105 A8
Cottesbrooke Pk
   NN11 . . . . 135 A5
Cottesbrooke Rd NN17 . . . . 36 B7
Cottesloe Ct MK11 . . . . . . 229 F5
Cottesmore Ave NN15 . . . . 92 A5
Cottesmore Cl NN15 . . . . . 140 B1
Cottesmore Way NN8 . . . . 129 D4
COTTINGHAM 20 D1
Cottingham CE Prim Sch
   LE16 . . . . 20 C1
Cottingham Dr NN3 . . . . . 142 B7
Cottingham Rd
   Corby NN17 . . . . 36 E6
   Corby NN18 . . . . 36 B7
   Rockingham LE16 . . . . . . 21 A4
Cottingham Way NN14 . . . . 76 C2
COTTISFORD 239 E3
COTTON END 159 C4
Cotton End
   Long Buckby NN6 . . . . . . 121 D4
   Northampton NN4 . . . . . . 159 C4
Cotton Mdw NN5 . . . . 158 E7
Cottons The
   Rockingham LE16 . . . . . . 21 B4
   Wellingborough NN8 . . . . 129 D7
Coulon Cl NN29 . . . . 147 A7
Coulthard Cl NN12 . . . . . . 203 D8
Council Hos
   Farthingstone NN12 . . . . . 170 E3
   Guilsborough NN6 . . . . . . 103 F7
   Hannington NN6 . . . . 108 C3
   Podington NN29 . . . . 147 E1
Council Ho's LE16 . . . . 48 B8
Council Hos The
   Long Buckby Wharf
     NN6 . . . . 136 E7
   Upper Wardington
     OX17 . . . . 208 F8
Council Houses NN6 . . . . . 106 F6
Council St
   Bozeat NN29 . . . . 164 D4
   Wollaston NN29 . . . . 146 D2
Countess Ct NN5 . . . . 159 A7
Countess Rd NN5 . . . . 159 A7
Countryman Mews
   LE16 . . . . 32 A5
Countryside NN11 . . . . . . 118 B1
Counts Farm Rd NN18 . . . . 36 F4
County Rd NN13 . . . . 234 A6
County View OX15 . . . . . . 236 D4
Courier Rd NN17 . . . . 37 B8
Court Cnr MK46 . . . . 195 E4
Court Dr NN16 . . . . 72 B6
COURTEENHALL 191 E7
Courteenhall Cl NN2 . . . . . 141 D5
Courteenhall Rd NN7 . . . . 191 A7
Court House Cl NN6 . . . . . 104 F4
Court La NN6 . . . . 64 D3
Courtman Rd NN9 . . . . . . 114 A4
Court Mews NN8 . . . . 130 B4
Courtney Rd NN10 . . . . . . 132 A1
Court Rd 11 NN1 . . . . 159 C5
Courtwood NN9 . . . . 114 A3
Courtyard La NN11 . . . . . . 153 A3
Courtyard The
   Ecton NN6 . . . . 143 F4
   Islip NN14 . . . . 76 B3
   4 Kettering NN16 . . . . . . 72 C3
   Middleton Cheney
     OX17 . . . . 219 D5
   Northampton NN5 . . . . . . 142 C1
Courtyard Workshops
   LE16 . . . . 31 E1
Coventry Rd LE16 . . . . 31 D3
Coverack Cl NN4 . . . . 159 B1
Coverdale NN2 . . . . 140 F5
Covert Cl NN2 . . . . 141 A4
COVINGTON 116 D2
Covington Gr NN8 . . . . . . 130 A6
Covington St NN1 . . . . 160 A7
Cowbeck Cl NN4 . . . . 175 E5
Cowgill Cl NN3 . . . . 143 B3
Cowley Cl NN4 . . . . 175 D6
Cowley Rd NN11 . . . . 135 B3
Cowley Way CV23 . . . . 99 F2
Cowper Cl
   Earls Barton NN6 . . . . . . 145 A4
   Irthlingborough NN9 . . . . 112 F1
Cowper Factory NN1 . . . . . 159 E7

Cowper & Newton Mus
   The ✶ MK46 . . . . 195 F3
Cowper Rd
   Daventry NN11 . . . . 135 B2
   Wellingborough NN8 . . . . 129 C4
Cowpers Orch MK46 . . . . . 195 A1
Cowper St
   Kettering NN16 . . . . 72 B4
   Northampton NN1 . . . . . . 159 E7
Cowper Terr NN2 . . . . 141 F1
Cowslip Cl
   Corby NN18 . . . . 36 D2
   Rushden NN10 . . . . 148 C8
Cowslip Hill NN14 . . . . 89 B5
Cow Yd NN2 . . . . 141 B3
Cox Gdns NN12 . . . . 202 E8
Cox's Cl NN6 . . . . 121 B3
Cox's La NN4 . . . . 90 A5
Cox's La NN11 . . . . 151 C1
Crab Apple Way NN14 . . . . 76 E1
Crabb St NN10 . . . . 132 B1
Crabb Tree Dr NN3 . . . . . . 143 A7
Crabtree Cl
   Hartwell NN7 . . . . 192 E2
   Wellingborough NN8 . . . . 129 F2
Crab Tree Cl MK46 . . . . . . 195 E5
Crabtree Ho 8 NN11 . . . . 135 C2
Crabtree La NN6 . . . . 84 B5
Cracknuts La NN4 . . . . . . 160 C2
Craddock Ct NN29 . . . . . . 147 B8
Cragside NN8 . . . . 129 C6
Craigie NN4 . . . . 129 C4
Cranbrooke Rd NN2 . . . . . 141 C1
Crane Cl
   Broughton NN14 . . . . 90 A5
   Rushden NN10 . . . . 132 B4
   Wellingborough NN8 . . . . 130 A2
Cranesbill Cl NN14 . . . . . . 51 A4
Crane Wlk NN3 . . . . 142 E6
Cranford CE Prim Sch
   NN14 . . . . 93 B7
Cranford Ho 1 NN2 . . . . . 141 C3
Cranford Rd
   Burton Latimer NN15 . . . . 92 D2
   Great Addington NN14 . . . 94 A4
   Kettering NN15 . . . . 92 C6
   Northampton NN2 . . . . . . 141 C3
CRANFORD ST ANDREW
   . . . . 93 A8
CRANFORD ST JOHN 93 A7
Cranford Terr 6 NN2 . . . . 141 C3
Cranleigh Rd NN15 . . . . . . 91 B7
Cranmere Ave NN1 . . . . . . 160 B6
Cransley Ct NN14 . . . . 89 B3
Cransley Gdns NN17 . . . . . 36 B7
Cransley Hill NN14 . . . . . . 90 A4
Cransley Rd NN14 . . . . 70 E1
Cransley Rise NN14 . . . . . . 89 B4
Cranstoun St NN1 . . . . 159 D7
Craven St NN1 . . . . 159 D7
Crawford Ave NN5 . . . . . . 158 E7
Crawford Gr NN17 . . . . 36 E8
Crawley Ave NN8 . . . . 129 D7
Craxford Rd NN17 . . . . 10 B1
Creampot Cl OX17 . . . . . . 196 A2
Creampot La OX17 . . . . . . 196 A2
CREATON 104 E4
Creaton Rd NN6 . . . . 104 D5
Crediton Cl NN3 . . . . 160 D7
Creed Rd PE8 . . . . 41 E7
Creighton Cres NN15 . . . . . 91 F6
Crescent Cl LE16 . . . . 31 F4
Crescent The
   Burton Latimer NN15 . . . . 92 C4
   Easton o t H PE9 . . . . 1 F5
   Flore NN7 . . . . 155 F6
   Hackleton NN7 . . . . 177 A3
   Kettering NN15 . . . . 91 B8
   Ketton PE9 . . . . 1 A7
   Market Harborough LE16 . . 31 F4
   Moulton NN3 . . . . 126 D1
   Northampton NN1 . . . . . . 159 F8
   Pattishall NN12 . . . . 172 E1
   Rothwell NN14 . . . . 70 C6
   Rushden NN10 . . . . 131 E2
   Twyford OX17 . . . . 230 A5
   Wellingborough NN8 . . . . 129 D7
   Whittlebury NN12 . . . . . . 215 C5
Creslow Ct MK11 . . . . 229 F5
Cresswell Rd NN10 . . . . . . 131 F2
Crestline Ct NN3 . . . . 143 A5
Crestwood Gdns NN3 . . . . 142 F5
Crestwood Rd NN3 . . . . . . 142 F5
Creswell Wlk NN17 . . . . . . 21 C1
CRICK 101 A5
Crick Cl NN17 . . . . 22 A1
Cricketers Gn NN17 . . . . . . 38 C8
Cricklade Cl NN3 . . . . 160 D6
Crickley Cres NN4 . . . . . . 158 E3
Crick Prim Sch NN6 . . . . . 100 F4
Crick Rd
   Rugby CV21, CV23 . . . . . . 99 D7
   West Haddon NN6 . . . . . . 102 A5
   Yelvertoft NN6 . . . . 82 A2
Crimea Cl 2 NN4 . . . . 175 E7
Crispian Cl NN10 . . . . 132 A2
Crispian Ho NN1 . . . . 159 D7
Crispin Cotts NN6 . . . . . . 108 A4
Crispin Ho NN1 . . . . 159 B6
Crispin Pl 14 NN16 . . . . . . 72 B2
Crispin St
   14 Northampton NN1 . . . . 159 C6
   Rothwell NN14 . . . . 70 E7
Crispin Way St NN9 . . . . . 114 C8
Crocket Cl NN14 . . . . 141 E2
Crockwell Hill NN11 . . . . . 119 F1
Crocus Way NN10 . . . . . . 148 B7
Croft Cl NN8 . . . . 129 C5

Crofters Cl NN4 . . . . 175 B7
Croft La
   Adderbury OX17 . . . . . . 230 A4
   Roade NN7 . . . . 191 D4
   Staverton NN11 . . . . 152 B7
Croftmeadow Ct NN3 . . . . 143 B4
Croft The
   Daventry NN11 . . . . 153 C8
   Hanging Houghton NN6 . . 106 C8
   1 Northampton NN5 . . . . 140 F1
   Rugby CV21 . . . . 99 A8
Croft Way
   Rushden NN10 . . . . 132 D3
   Weedon Bec NN7 . . . . . . 155 A3
Cromarty Ct NN17 . . . . 36 F5
Cromarty Ho NN17 . . . . . . 36 F5
Crome Cl NN8 . . . . 129 F8
Cromer Rd NN9 . . . . 111 F4
Cromwell Cl NN14 . . . . 51 A3
Cromwell Cres LE16 . . . . . 31 C5
Cromwell Ct NN8 . . . . 130 B5
Cromwell Ho NN8 . . . . . . 130 B4
Cromwell Rd
   Kettering NN16 . . . . 72 A2
   Rushden NN10 . . . . 132 C2
Cromwell St 15 NN1 . . . . . 159 C7
Cronin Ctyd NN18 . . . . 37 F2
Cronin Rd NN18 . . . . 37 E2
CROPREDY 196 A2
Crosby Rd LE16 . . . . 31 F1
Cross Bank LE16 . . . . 20 C5
Cross Brooks NN4 . . . . . . 175 F6
Cross Ct NN10 . . . . 72 A3
Crosse Cl NN7 . . . . 155 C4
Cross Hill NN6 . . . . 106 B3
Crosshills MK11 . . . . 229 D4
Cross Keys Ct NN13 . . . . . 233 F7
Cross Keys Dr NN13 . . . . . . 76 C2
Cross La
   Aldwincle NN14 . . . . 57 L1
   Braunston NN11 . . . . 118 C1
   Helmdon NN13 . . . . 212 A5
   Weston Underwood
     MK46 . . . . 195 B2
Cross Rd NN8 . . . . 130 B6
Cross St
   Covington PE18 . . . . 116 C2
   Daventry NN11 . . . . 135 D2
   Kettering NN16 . . . . 72 A3
   Market Harborough LE16 . . 31 F2
   Moulton NN3 . . . . 126 C1
   Rothwell NN14 . . . . 70 E7
Cross The
   Great Houghton NN4 . . . . 160 D4
   Gretton NN17 . . . . 10 C1
Cross Tree Rd MK19 . . . . . 228 B3
Cross Waters Cl NN4 . . . . . 175 F6
Cross Way NN9 . . . . 131 D8
Crouch Rd NN9 . . . . 112 F1
CROUGHTON 238 D4
Croughton All Saints CE
   Prim Sch NN13 . . . . 238 C8
Croughton Cl NN2 . . . . . . 141 C5
Croughton Rd OX17 . . . . . 237 D7
Crowberry Ave NN3 . . . . . 142 C6
CROWFIELD 223 F8
Crow La NN3 . . . . 161 C7
Crown Apartments 13
   NN16 . . . . 72 A4
Crown Ct
   Corby NN18 . . . . 36 E5
   Oundle PE8 . . . . 42 A5
Crown Ct NN10 . . . . 131 E4
Crown La
   Barrowden LE15 . . . . 3 C5
   Rothwell NN14 . . . . 70 C7
   West Haddon NN6 . . . . . 102 C4
Crownsmead NN4 . . . . . . 158 D1
Crown St NN16 . . . . 72 B3
Crown Way NN10 . . . . 131 E4
Crowthorp Rd NN3 . . . . . . 143 C5
Croxdale Cl NN2 . . . . 140 F5
Croxen Cl NN15 . . . . 92 C2
Croyde Ave NN18 . . . . 36 F4
Croyland Hall Her Ctr
   Mus ✶ NN8 . . . . 130 A4
Croyland Prim Sch
   NN8 . . . . 129 E3
Croyland Rd NN8 . . . . 129 E3
Crucible Rd NN17 . . . . 37 B7
Crystal Ct NN16 . . . . 72 D3
Cubleigh Cl NN3 . . . . 142 C6
Cuckoo Cl LE15 . . . . 3 E5
Cukow Ct NN14 . . . . 89 B4
Cullahill Ct NN14 . . . . 158 E2
Culloden Ct NN17 . . . . 36 F5
Culloden Dr NN15 . . . . 91 F6
Culme Cl PE8 . . . . 41 E7
Culross Wlk NN18 . . . . 36 C3
CULWORTH 198 C3
Culworth CE Sch
   OX17 . . . . 198 C2
Culworth Cres NN2 . . . . . 141 C5
Culworth Ho OX17 . . . . . . 198 D2
Culworth Rd OX17 . . . . . . 197 B6
Cumberland Ave NN9 . . . . 114 A4
Cumberland Cl NN3 . . . . . 142 A3
Cumbrae Dr NN3 . . . . 143 C2
Cunliffe Dr NN16 . . . . 72 A4
Cunliffe Rd Ind Est
   NN16 . . . . 72 A4
Cunningham Cl
   Daventry NN11 . . . . 135 E2
   Higham Ferrers NN10 . . . 132 B5
Cupar Cres NN17 . . . . 36 F5
Curgenven Cl NN11 . . . . . 183 E7
Curlbrook Cl NN4 . . . . 176 A6
Curlew Way NN11 . . . . . . 135 C3

Currie Rd NN2 . . . . 141 C1
Curtis Mews NN8 . . . . . . 129 C7
Curtlee Hill NN4 . . . . 175 F5
Curver Way NN17 . . . . . . 22 D1
Cyclamen Cl NN14 . . . . . 50 F3
Cyclamen Cl NN3 . . . . . . 160 C6
Cypress Cl NN14 . . . . 50 F3
Cypress Ct NN3 . . . . 142 E3
Cyril St NN1 . . . . 159 E6
Cytringen Cl NN15 . . . . . 91 A7

D

DADFORD 225 D1
Dadford Rd NN12,
MK18 . . . . 225 D5
Daffodil Dr NN10 . . . . . . 148 B7
Dag La NN29 . . . . 164 D2
Dagnall Rd MK46 . . . . . . 195 E3
Dahlia Rd NN16 . . . . 72 D4
Daimler Cl
  Daventry NN11 . . . . 135 A3
  Northampton NN3 . . . . . 143 D4
Dainty Gr NN4 . . . . 175 E3
Dairy Cl
  Brixworth NN6 . . . . 106 A1
  West Haddon NN6 . . . . . 102 D4
Dairy Cotts LE17 . . . . . . 45 A4
Dairy Field NN6 . . . . 103 D1
Dairy Ground OX17 . . . . 231 A6
Dairymeadow Ct NN3 . . . 142 F6
Dairy Way NN9 . . . . 131 E8
Daisy Bank Ave NN14 . . . 70 C7
Daisy Cl NN18 . . . . 36 C2
Daisy Croft NN10 . . . . . . 148 C8
Dakin Cl PE8 . . . . 13 F8
D'albini Cl LE16 . . . . 34 B4
Dalby Cl NN16 . . . . 72 A6
Dale Ave NN8 . . . . 129 C5
Dale Cl
  Brackley NN13 . . . . 234 A7
  Daventry NN11 . . . . 135 B5
  Mears Ashby NN6 . . . . . 128 C2
  Wellingborough NN8 . . . 129 C5
Dale Farm Cotts NN6 . . . 128 C2
Dale Ho 1 NN8 . . . . 129 F4
Dale St
  Corby NN17 . . . . 36 D7
  Wellingborough NN8 . . . 129 F4
Dalestones NN4 . . . . 158 D2
Daleswood Rise PE8 . . . . 13 F8
Dale The NN8 . . . . 129 C5
Dalkeith Ave 20 NN16 . . . 72 B2
Dalkeith Pl NN16 . . . . . . 72 B2
Dalkeith Rd NN8 . . . . 129 F1
Dallacre Cl LE16 . . . . 34 C4
Dallacre Farm LE16 . . . . 34 D4
DALLINGTON 158 F8
Dallington Cl NN14 . . . . . 54 A2
Dallington Ct NN5 . . . . . . 158 F8
Dallington Gn 2 NN5 . . . . 158 F8
Dallington Haven 5
  NN5 . . . . 158 F8
Dallington Park Rd
  NN5 . . . . 158 F8
Dallington Rd NN5 . . . . . 159 A7
Dallison Cl LE16 . . . . 48 E8
DALSCOTE 173 B1
Dalston Wlk 6 NN3 . . . . . 142 C4
Dalton Rd NN17 . . . . 21 E2
Damherst Piece NN6 . . . . 106 C2
Damson Cl NN14 . . . . 76 E1
Damson Dell NN3 . . . . . . 161 A8
Dance Way NN8 . . . . 129 F8
Dando Cl NN29 . . . . 146 D1
Dands Cl OX17 . . . . 220 A8
Dands Dr OX17 . . . . 220 A8
Dane Ct NN11 . . . . 118 C1
Danefield Rd NN3 . . . . . . 142 B1
Daneholme Ave NN11 . . . 135 C4
Dane Ridge NN5 . . . . 158 C6
Danes Backside NN7 . . . . 141 B3
Danes Camp Way
  NN4 . . . . 158 A3
Danesholme Jun & Inf Sch
  NN18 . . . . 36 A2
Danesholme Rd NN18 . . . 36 A2
Danes Way NN6 . . . . 100 C7
Danetre Dr NN11 . . . . . . 135 D2
Danetree Gdns NN3 . . . . 142 B2
Danetre Hospl NN11 . . . . 153 C8
Danetre Sch NN11 . . . . . 135 E1
Danewood Gdns NN3 . . . 142 B2
Danford Cl PE8 . . . . 41 F4
Danfords PE8 . . . . 41 F5
Daniaud Ct NN13 . . . . . . 233 E8
Daniell Wlk NN18 . . . . . . 36 D5
Daniels Rd NN8 . . . . 130 C1
Dapplestone Cl NN4 . . . . 158 D2
Darby Cl NN8 . . . . 129 A5
Dardis Cl 2 NN2 . . . . 141 E1
Darenth Ct 16 NN1 . . . . . 159 C7
Darescroft LE16 . . . . 20 B1
Dark La
  Braunston NN11 . . . . . . 118 C3
  Great Harrowden NN9 . . 110 D3
Darley Cl NN16 . . . . 72 C6
Darley Dale Rd NN17 . . . 36 D8
Dart Cl NN17 . . . . 21 D2
Dartford 2 NN4 . . . . 159 A2
Dartmouth Rd MK46 . . . 195 F4
Dartmouth Row 3
  NN11 . . . . 135 D1
Darwin Ct NN17 . . . . 37 C4
Darwin Ho NN17 . . . . . . 22 F1
Darwin Rd NN17 . . . . . . 37 C8
Darwin Wlk NN5 . . . . . . 140 C1
Dash Farm Cl NN17 . . . . 38 A8

DAVENTRY 135 D3
Daventry Abbey Jun Sch
  The NN11 . . . . 135 D1
Daventry Cty Pk★
  NN11 . . . . 135 D5
Daventry Cty Pk Visitor Ctr
  NN11 . . . . 135 D5
Daventry Rd
  Banbury OX16 . . . . 208 A2
  Barby CV23 . . . . 118 C8
  Kilsby CV23 . . . . 100 A1
  Newnham NN11 . . . . . . 153 D4
  Norton NN11 . . . . 136 C5
  Staverton NN11 . . . . . . 152 B1
  Staverton NN11 . . . . . . 152 C7
  Willoughby CV23 . . . . . 117 C7
Daventry Tert Coll
  NN11 . . . . 153 B8
Daventry William Parker
  Sch NN11 . . . . 135 C3
Davey Rd NN17 . . . . 37 C8
Davies Cl
  Kettering NN16 . . . . . . 90 F8
  Market Harborough
  LE16 . . . . 31 D5
Da Vinci Cl NN5 . . . . 158 A5
Davis Cl NN14 . . . . 70 E6
Davis Ct NN17 . . . . 37 A6
Davy Cl NN8 . . . . 129 A6
Dawkins Ct NN14 . . . . . . 90 A4
Dayrell Rd NN4 . . . . 158 F2
Dayrell Sq 5 NN4 . . . . . . 158 F2
Dayton St NN10 . . . . 132 A2
Deacon Cl
  Market Harborough
  LE16 . . . . 31 D5
  Rushden NN10 . . . . 132 D3
Deacons Ct NN3 . . . . 143 C4
Deal Cl NN1 . . . . 159 D7
Deal St NN1 . . . . 159 C7
Dean Cl
  Rands NN9 . . . . 114 D7
  Rushden NN10 . . . . 148 A8
Deancourt Dr NN5 . . . . . 140 A1
Deane Par CV21 . . . . 99 A8
Deane Rd CV21 . . . . 99 B8
DEANSHANGER 228 D4
Deanshanger Dr
  NN12 . . . . 216 F1
Deanshanger Prim Sch
  MK19 . . . . 228 E3
Deanshanger Rd
  Old Stratford MK19 . . . . 229 B6
  Wicken MK19 . . . . 228 B3
Deans Row NN7 . . . . 173 E2
Deansway NN3 . . . . 143 C4
Dean Wlk 6 NN11 . . . . . . 135 B4
Debbs Cl MK11 . . . . 229 E5
Debdale Rd
  Northampton NN3 . . . . . 142 D2
  Wellingborough NN8 . . . 129 F5
Deben Rd NN17 . . . . 21 D1
De Capel Cl NN14 . . . . . . 94 D6
DEDDINGTON 236 A4
Deddington Castle
  Earthworks★ OX15 . . . 236 A4
Deeble Rd NN15 . . . . 72 F1
DEENE 23 F6
Deene Cl
  Adderbury OX17 . . . . . . 230 B4
  Corby NN17 . . . . 36 E7
  Market Harborough
  LE16 . . . . 32 A3
Deene End NN17 . . . . . . 38 C8
Deene Pk★ NN17 . . . . . . 23 E5
Deene Rd
  Deene NN17 . . . . 11 D3
  Harringworth NN17 . . . . 10 F7
Deeneside NN17 . . . . 38 B8
DEENETHORPE 24 B4
Deenethorpe La NN17 . . . 24 B5
Deepdale LE16 . . . . 20 D7
Deep Side PE9 . . . . 1 F4
Deer Cl NN14 . . . . 175 F2
Deerings Rd CV21 . . . . . . 99 A8
Deer Park Rd NN3 . . . . . . 142 A6
Dee Wlk NN11 . . . . 135 A1
De Ferneus Dr NN7 . . . . . 114 D7
Delamere Dr NN15 . . . . . 92 A5
Delamere Rd NN4 . . . . . . 159 C2
Delapre Abbey★ NN4 . . . 159 D3
Delapre Cres NN4 . . . . . . 159 C2
Delapre Crescent Rd
  NN4 . . . . 159 C3
Delapre Ct NN4 . . . . 159 C2
Delapre Pl NN18 . . . . 36 A3
Delapre Prim Sch
  NN4 . . . . 159 B3
Delapre St NN4 . . . . 159 B3
De Lisle Cl LE16 . . . . 31 D2
Dell Cres NN3 . . . . 143 B5
Dell Pl NN10 . . . . 132 C2
Dells MK46 . . . . 195 F4
Dells Cl PE28 . . . . 61 D2
Dell The NN6 . . . . 144 E4
Delta Way NN2 . . . . 141 A5
Delves The NN9 . . . . 114 C6
De Montfort Dr NN13 . . . 222 E1
Dempsey Dr NN14 . . . . . 70 F6
Demswell NN6 . . . . 106 C2
Denbeigh Ho 5
  NN10 . . . . 132 B2
Denbigh Rd NN3 . . . . 160 D6
Denby Dale NN8 . . . . 129 D7
Dencora Bsns Pk
  NN8 . . . . 129 A4
Dene Cl
  Kettering NN16 . . . . . . 72 A5

Dene Cl continued
  Wellingborough NN8 . . . 129 C6
Denfield Park Jun Sch
  NN10 . . . . 132 C3
DENFORD 95 C5
Denford Dr NN15 . . . . . . 91 F5
Denford Rd
  Corby NN17 . . . . 36 B8
  Ringstead NN14 . . . . . . 95 C4
  Thrapston NN14 . . . . . . 95 D8
Denford Way NN8 . . . . . . 129 D7
Denington Ct NN8 . . . . . . 130 A2
Denington Ind Est
  NN8 . . . . 130 B2
Denington Rd NN8 . . . . . 130 A2
Denman Cl LE16 . . . . 34 A4
Denmark Cl NN18 . . . . . . 35 C7
Denmark Ct NN10 . . . . . . 132 C1
Denmark Rd
  Northampton NN1 . . . . . 159 E6
  Rushden NN10 . . . . 132 C1
Denne Cl NN18 . . . . 36 C1
Denney Cres NN11 . . . . . 135 B2
Denston Cl NN4 . . . . 159 B1
Dent Cl NN5 . . . . 157 F7
DENTON 178 A4
Denton Cl
  Irchester NN29 . . . . 147 B8
  Rushden NN10 . . . . 132 C3
Denton Ct NN15 . . . . 92 B2
Denton Prim Sch
  NN7 . . . . 178 C8
Denton Rd NN7 . . . . 178 B6
De Quincey Cl NN13 . . . . 222 E1
Derby Mews NN1 . . . . . . 159 F8
Derby Rd NN1 . . . . 159 F8
Dering Cotts OX17 . . . . . 210 E2
Derling Dr NN9 . . . . 114 E6
Derngate NN1 . . . . 159 D5
De Roos Way LE16 . . . . . 34 B4
Derry The NN6 . . . . 100 F5
Derwent Cl
  Daventry NN11 . . . . 135 A1
  Northampton NN8 . . . . . 140 F1
  Wellingborough NN8 . . . 129 E5
Derwent Cres NN16 . . . . 71 F2
Derwent Ct NN5 . . . . 140 F2
Derwent Ho PE8 . . . . 42 A6
Derwent Wlk NN17 . . . . . 21 D2
DESBOROUGH 51 C2
Desborough Rd
  Arthingworth LE16 . . . . 49 F1
  Braybrooke LE16 . . . . . . 49 F5
  Rothwell NN14 . . . . 70 C7
  Rushton NN14 . . . . 52 B2
  Stoke Albany LE16 . . . . 34 B3
De Vere Rd NN14 . . . . . . 76 D2
Deveron Wlk NN17 . . . . . 21 D1
Devon Dr NN15 . . . . 91 D6
Devon Ox Rd CV23 . . . . . 99 F2
Devonshire Cl
  Boughton NN2 . . . . 141 C8
  Wellingborough NN8 . . . 129 E6
Devonshire Ho 6
  NN5 . . . . 159 A6
Devon Way NN3 . . . . 142 A5
Devon Wlk NN10 . . . . . . 132 C1
Dewar Dr NN11 . . . . 135 A4
Dexter Way PE8 . . . . 28 B3
Diamond Ct NN3 . . . . 131 E8
Diamonds Bsns Ctr
  NN9 . . . . 113 A3
Diamond Way NN9 . . . . . 113 A2
Diana Ho NN8 . . . . 129 D5
Diana Way NN15 . . . . 92 B1
Dibbin Cl NN17 . . . . 38 B8
Dickens Dr
  Kettering NN16 . . . . . . 72 B6
  Old Stratford MK19 . . . . 229 B6
Dickens Spinney
  MK46 . . . . 195 E4
Dick's Hill LE16 . . . . 47 C5
Dickson Cl 4 NN4 . . . . . . 158 F3
Digby St NN16 . . . . 72 C3
Dimock Sq NN4 . . . . 158 F2
Dingledery MK46 . . . . . . 195 F4
Dingle Rd NN10 . . . . 131 E2
Dingle The
  Daventry NN11 . . . . 153 C8
  Rugby CV21 . . . . 99 B8
DINGLEY 33 A4
Dingley La LE16 . . . . 32 F6
Dingley Rd LE16 . . . . 32 B6
Dingley Terr LE16 . . . . . . 31 F3
Disbrowe St NN9 . . . . . . 133 C7
Diswell Brook Way
  MK19 . . . . 228 E5
Ditchford Cl NN4 . . . . . . 175 F4
Ditchford Rd NN8 . . . . . . 131 C5
Dixon Rd NN2 . . . . 141 E6
Dixon Wlk NN17 . . . . 37 A6
Dobbins Cl OX17 . . . . 231 A6
Dobson Cl NN4 . . . . 160 F2
Dobson Wlk NN18 . . . . . 36 D5
Dockham Way NN16 . . . . 100 E6
Docklewell Cl NN12 . . . . 203 A4
Doctors La
  Eydon NN11 . . . . 184 C1
  Great Doddington
  NN29 . . . . 145 E6
Doddington Ct NN8 . . . . 129 F2
Doddington Rd
  Earls Barton NN6 . . . . . 145 A4
  Great Doddington NN9 . 145 F8
  Wellingborough NN8 . . . 129 F2
  Wilby NN8 . . . . 145 B8
Doddridge 1 NN1 . . . . . . 159 C5

Doddridge Ho 21
  NN1 . . . . 159 C6
Doddridge Rd 1 LE16 . . . 31 E4
Doddridge St 24 NN1 . . . 159 C6
DODFORD 154 F6
Dog La
  Napton on t H CV47 . . . 150 A7
  South Kilworth LE17 . . . 63 C8
Dolben Ave NN9 . . . . 113 F4
Dolben Cl NN9 . . . . 111 E4
Dolben Sq NN9 . . . . 111 F4
Dolver Cl NN18 . . . . 36 C2
Donald Greaves Ho
  NN17 . . . . 21 D1
Donaldson Ave NN14 . . . 90 A3
Don Cl NN17 . . . . 21 D1
Donellan Gn NN3 . . . . . . 142 F6
Donne Cl
  Higham Ferrers
  NN10 . . . . 132 A5
  Kettering NN16 . . . . . . 72 C6
Donovan Ct NN3 . . . . 160 E8
Dorcas Rd OX16 . . . . 219 A6
Dorchester Ct NN5 . . . . . 140 B2
Dore Cl NN3 . . . . 143 B5
Doris Rd NN16 . . . . 72 E4
Dorking Wlk NN18 . . . . . 36 C3
Dorman Cl NN3 . . . . 142 B4
Dorothy Rd NN16 . . . . . . 72 C2
Dorset Gdns NN2 . . . . . . 141 D3
Dorset Rd
  Corby NN17 . . . . 36 C6
  Northampton NN2 . . . . . 141 D3
Doubles The NN11 . . . . . 135 B1
Douglas Cl NN15 . . . . 91 E8
Douglas Rd NN5 . . . . 157 F8
Douglass Dr LE16 . . . . . . 31 F4
Doulton Cl NN14 . . . . 50 F3
Dove Cl NN3 . . . . 143 B5
Dovecote
  Barrowden LE15 . . . . . . 3 F5
  Kettering NN15 . . . . . . 91 F7
  Rands NN9 . . . . 114 E7
  Weston by W LE16 . . . . 18 B3
  Yarwell PE8 . . . . 16 A8
Dovecote Dr
  Denton NN7 . . . . 162 B1
  Little Addington NN14 . . 113 B7
Dovecote Rd NN7 . . . . . . 191 C4
Dovecote The
  King's Cliffe PE8 . . . . . . 13 F7
  Pitsford NN6 . . . . 125 D5
Dovecote Yd NN14 . . . . . 110 A5
Dove Cotts OX17 . . . . . . 210 A6
Dovedale Gr NN14 . . . . . 50 E4
Dovedale Rd NN17 . . . . . 36 E7
Dovehouse Cl
  Brackley NN13 . . . . 233 F7
  Stanwick NN9 . . . . 113 F3
  Welford NN6 . . . . 64 E6
Dovehouse Ct MK19 . . . . 228 E4
Dover Cl NN10 . . . . 132 C1
Dovercourt NN5 . . . . 159 B5
Dove's La NN3 . . . . 126 D1
Downing Way NN11 . . . . 153 C7
Downs The NN9 . . . . 110 E1
Downsway NN1 . . . . 175 B6
Downwood Cl NN3 . . . . . 143 C3
Dowthorpe End NN6 . . . . 144 F4
Dowthorpe Hill NN6 . . . . 144 F3
Drake Cl
  Corby NN17 . . . . 36 B8
  Daventry NN11 . . . . 135 C1
  Rothwell NN14 . . . . 70 E7
Drake Lee Mews NN16 . . 72 B1
Draper's Cl PE8 . . . . 28 C3
Drapery NN1 . . . . 159 C6
DRAUGHTON 87 E6
Draughton Rd NN6 . . . . . 87 B7
Draycott Cl NN3 . . . . 160 D7
Draymans Wlk NN13 . . . 233 E6
Drayson La NN6 . . . . 100 F6
DRAYTON
  Corby 20 A5
  Daventry 135 A2
Drayton Cl
  Corby NN18 . . . . 36 B4
  Islip NN14 . . . . 76 B3
  Rushden NN10 . . . . 148 A8
Drayton Fields Ind Est
  NN11 . . . . 135 A5
Drayton Leys CV22 . . . . . 98 A7
Drayton Pk NN11 . . . . . . 135 B5
Drayton Pl NN9 . . . . 112 F3
Drayton Rd
  Bringhurst LE16 . . . . . . 20 B5
  Drayton LE16 . . . . 19 D7
  Irthlingborough NN9 . . . 112 F3
  Lowick NN14 . . . . 75 E6
  Medbourne LE16 . . . . . 19 A5
Drayton Way NN11 . . . . . 135 A5
Drayton Wlk NN12 . . . . . 141 D4
Dresden Cl NN18 . . . . . . 35 F2
Driffield Gr NN17 . . . . . . 36 F7
Drift The
  Collyweston PE9 . . . . . . 1 D2
  Sutton PE5 . . . . 8 F3
Drift Way MK46 . . . . 195 F5
Drill Hall Ct NN15 . . . . . . 72 A1
Drive The
  Horton NN7 . . . . 177 E1
  Kettering NN15 . . . . . . 72 B1
  Northampton, Duston
  NN5 . . . . 158 A7
  Northampton, Phippsville
  NN1 . . . . 141 F1
  Rushden NN10 . . . . 132 C1
  Wellingborough NN8 . . . 130 A3

Cur–Eag   247

Droue Ct NN14 . . . . 70 C7
Drovers Wlk NN2 . . . . . . 141 A5
Drove The
  Collyweston PE9 . . . . . . 1 D1
  Nassington PE8 . . . . . . 15 E5
Druce End PE8 . . . . 217 E6
Druids Way NN3 . . . . 141 F5
Drum La 30 NN1 . . . . 159 C6
Drummond Cl NN6 . . . . . 125 D4
Drydale Ave NN3 . . . . . . 142 B3
Dryden Ave NN11 . . . . . . 135 B2
Dryden Cl NN11 . . . . 184 A7
Dryden Rd
  Northampton NN5 . . . . . 158 F7
  Towcester NN12 . . . . . . 203 C5
  Wellingborough NN8 . . . 130 C5
Dryden's Cl NN14 . . . . . . 77 C4
Dryden St
  Kettering NN16 . . . . . . 72 B3
  Rands NN9 . . . . 114 C6
Dryden Way
  Corby NN17 . . . . 36 C8
  Higham Ferrers NN10 . . 132 B5
Dryland Rd NN3 . . . . 142 C2
Dryland St NN16 . . . . . . 72 B2
Dryleys Ct NN3 . . . . 143 B5
Drywell Ct NN3 . . . . 143 A1
Duchess Cl NN16 . . . . . . 72 B4
Duchess End NN6 . . . . . . 128 C2
Duchess Gdns NN12 . . . . 217 D3
Duchy Cl
  Chelveston NN9 . . . . . . 133 B8
  Higham Ferrers NN10 . . 132 C5
Duck End
  Cranford St John NN14 . 93 B7
  Denford NN14 . . . . 95 D6
  Hinton-in-t-H NN13 . . . 232 F6
  Wollaston NN29 . . . . . . 146 D3
Duck La
  Harpole NN7 . . . . 157 C6
  Oundle PE8 . . . . 42 A5
Duck St
  Elton PE8 . . . . 16 D1
  Rushden NN10 . . . . 132 B2
Duckworth Dell NN3 . . . 142 F6
Duckworth Rd NN17 . . . . 36 B7
DUDDINGTON 5 B6
Duffy Pl CV21 . . . . 99 A8
Dugdale Cl NN14 . . . . . . 76 D2
Dukelands NN7 . . . . 155 A3
Dukes Ct NN15 . . . . 92 C2
Dukes Green Rd NN7 . . . 157 D3
Duke St
  Burton Latimer NN15 . . 92 B2
  Kettering NN16 . . . . . . 72 B3
  Northampton NN1 . . . . . 159 D7
  Polebrook PE8 . . . . 42 F3
  Wellingborough NN8 . . . 129 E1
Dulce Rd NN5 . . . . 158 C8
Dulley Ave NN15 . . . . . . 91 F1
Dulverton Rd NN3 . . . . . 160 D7
Dumas Cul-De-Sac
  NN13 . . . . 233 E8
Dumble Cl NN18 . . . . 36 D2
Dunbar Ct NN15 . . . . 91 E8
Duncan Cl NN3 . . . . 141 F7
Duncan Ct NN8 . . . . 129 D3
Duncan Rd NN17 . . . . . . 36 B7
DUNCOTE 188 E2
Dundee St NN5 . . . . 158 F4
Dunedin Rd NN18 . . . . . . 36 C2
Dungee Rd MK43 . . . . . . 165 E2
Dunkirk Ave NN14 . . . . . 51 B3
Dunmore Rd LE16 . . . . . . 32 A1
Dunn Cl NN6 . . . . 101 A6
Dunnock La NN4 . . . . 175 F3
Dunnock Rd NN18 . . . . . 36 E3
Dunslade Cl LE16 . . . . . . 32 B2
Dunslade Gr LE16 . . . . . . 32 B2
Dunslade Rd LE16 . . . . . . 32 A2
DUNSMORE 80 C6
Dunsmore Ave CV22 . . . . 98 C8
Dunster St NN1 . . . . 159 D6
Durban Rd NN16 . . . . . . 72 D2
Durham Cl NN17 . . . . 36 B6
Durness Cl NN15 . . . . . . 91 E8
Dusthill Rd NN14 . . . . . . 55 D8
DUSTON 158 C7
Duston Eldean Prim Sch
  NN5 . . . . 140 B1
Duston Mill La NN5 . . . . 158 D4
Duston Rd NN5 . . . . 158 E6
Duston Sch The NN5 . . . . 158 A8
Duston Wildes NN5 . . . . 140 A2
Dybdale Cres NN8 . . . . . 129 E5
Dychurch La
  Bozeat NN29 . . . . 164 E3
  Northampton NN1 . . . . . 159 D6
Dyson Cl CV21 . . . . 80 A1
Dyson Dr NN16 . . . . 72 A4

E

Eady Cl NN3 . . . . 126 E1
Eady Rd NN15 . . . . 92 B1
Eady's Row NN14 . . . . . . 94 D7
Eagle Dr NN4 . . . . 159 F2
Eaglehurst NN6 . . . . 106 C2
Eagle La NN14 . . . . 71 B1
Eaglesfield NN11 . . . . . . 136 C4
Eaglethorpe PE8 . . . . 28 B4

EAKLEY LANES 193 D2
Ealing Terr NN10 ...... 132 A3
EARLS BARTON 144 F3
Earls Barton Inf Sch
NN6 .... 144 E4
Earls Barton Jun Sch
NN6 .... 144 E4
Earls Barton Mus★
NN6 .... 144 E4
Earls Barton Rd
 Great Doddington
 NN29 .... 145 C5
 Mears Ashby NN6 ...... 128 B2
Earlsfield Cl NN4 ...... 176 A6
Earl's La OX15 .... 236 A4
Earl Spencer Prim Sch
NN5 .... 159 A8
Earl St NN1 .... 159 D7
Earlstrees Ct NN17 ..... 21 F2
Earlstrees Ind Est
NN17 .... 21 F2
Earlstrees Rd NN17 ..... 21 F2
EAST ADDERBURY 230 B4
East Ave
 Burton Latimer NN15 ... 92 B3
 Corby NN17 .... 36 F5
 Kettering NN15 .... 72 C2
East Bank NN3 .... 142 E6
Eastbourne Ave NN18 .... 36 B5
Eastbrook NN18 .... 36 B4
Eastbrook Hill NN14 .... 51 C3
East Butterfield Ct
NN3 .... 142 F5
EAST CARLTON 35 A7
East Carlton Countryside
Pk★ LE16 .... 35 B8
East Carlton Pk LE16 ... 35 B7
East Cl NN15 .... 72 C2
EASTCOTE 189 A8
Eastcote Rd NN7 .... 189 D8
East Cres
 Rushden NN10 .... 131 F2
 Weldon NN17 .... 38 C8
East Dr NN15 .... 72 C2
EAST END 230 B4
East End NN6 .... 106 F5
Eastern Ave N NN2 ..... 141 D4
Eastern Ave S NN2 ..... 141 D3
Eastern Cl NN2 .... 141 D5
Eastern Way NN11 ...... 135 C2
EAST FARNDON 48 B7
Eastfield NN7 .... 190 D7
Eastfield Cl NN5 ...... 140 C1
Eastfield Cres
 Finedon NN9 .... 112 A5
 Yardley Gobion NN12 ... 217 D3
Eastfield Dr MK19 ..... 207 A3
Eastfield Prim Sch
NN3 .... 142 B3
Eastfield Rd
 Brixworth NN6 .... 106 B1
 [3] Irthlingborough
 NN9 .... 112 F2
 Northampton, Duston
 NN5 .... 158 B8
 Northampton, Far Cotton
 NN4 .... 159 C3
 Wellingborough NN8 .... 130 C6
 Wollaston NN29 .... 146 E2
Eastfields NN11 .... 118 C1
Eastfields Cres PE8 .... 15 E6
East Gr NN10 .... 132 B3
EAST HADDON 122 D5
East Haddon CE Prim Sch
NN6 .... 122 D5
East Haddon Rd NN6 ..... 122 D8
Easthill NN13 .... 233 F7
East Hunsbury Prim Sch
NN4 .... 175 B6
Eastlands Rd NN9 ...... 112 A5
East Langham Rd
NN9 .... 114 D7
Eastleigh Rd NN15 ..... 91 D7
East Leys Ct NN3 ...... 142 C7
Eastmead Ct NN3 ...... 143 A1
Easton Garford CE Sch
PE9 .... 2 A5
Easton La NN29 .... 164 C3
EASTON MAUDIT 163 F2
EASTON ON THE HILL 2 A4
Easton Way NN7 .... 163 E4
Easton Wlk NN17 ...... 37 B6
East Oval NN5 .... 140 F2
East Paddock Ct NN3 ... 143 A4
East Park Par NN1 ..... 159 F8
East Priors Ct NN3 .... 143 A4
East Rd PE8 .... 42 A5
East Rising NN4 .... 175 D7
East St
 Irchester NN29 .... 147 B8
 Long Buckby NN6 ...... 121 D4
 Market Harborough
 LE16 .... 31 D3
 Northampton NN1 ...... 159 F6
 Olney MK46 .... 195 F4
 Stanwick NN9 .... 114 A3
East View OX17 .... 210 E2
East Wlk NN15 .... 72 C2
Eastwood Gr CV21 ...... 99 C8
Eastwood Rd PE8 ...... 42 A5
Eaton Rd NN5 .... 159 B4
Eaton Wlk NN10 .... 132 B2
Ebbw Vale Rd NN5 ..... 131 E8
Ebenezer Pl [16] NN16 ... 72 B2
Ebony Ct NN11 .... 184 D5

Eccles Rd PE8 .... 7 D8
Eckland Lodge Bsns Pk
NN14 .... 50 D6
ECTON 143 F4
ECTON BROOK 143 D2
Ecton Brook Prim Sch
NN3 .... 143 D2
Ecton Brook Rd NN3 .... 143 D2
Ecton Hall NN6 .... 143 F4
Ecton La NN6 .... 127 D2
Ecton Leys CV22 .... 98 A7
Ecton Park Rd NN3 ..... 143 C3
Ecton St [11] NN1 ...... 159 E6
Ecton Village Prim Sch
NN6 .... 143 F4
Edale Gn NN14 .... 50 E4
Eden Cl
 Daventry NN11 .... 135 A1
 Northampton NN3 ..... 142 B4
Eden Ct NN6 .... 120 C6
Eden St NN15 .... 72 C2
Edgar Mobbs Way
NN5 .... 158 E5
Edgar Rd NN16 .... 72 D3
EDGCOTE 197 A4
Edgcote Drive Cotts
OX17 .... 197 A4
Edgehill Dr NN11 ..... 135 D6
Edgehill Rd NN5 ...... 140 D1
Edgell St NN16 .... 72 C2
Edgemead Cl NN3 ..... 142 E7
Edgemont Rd NN3 ..... 142 E1
Edges Ct NN3 .... 142 C7
Edgewood NN13 .... 222 F1
Edinburgh Cl
 Market Harborough
 LE16 .... 31 F4
 Rothwell NN14 .... 70 C6
Edinburgh Ho NN5 ..... 158 C8
Edinburgh Mews
NN2 .... 141 C2
Edinburgh Rd
 Kettering NN16 .... 72 D3
 Northampton NN2 ..... 141 C2
 Wellingborough NN8 ... 129 E1
Edinburgh Sq [3]
NN11 .... 135 B3
Edison Cl NN8 .... 129 A6
Edison Ct NN8 .... 129 A6
Edison Ctyd NN17 ..... 21 F3
Edison Dr NN5 .... 158 D4
Edith Rd NN16 .... 72 E4
Edith St NN1 .... 159 E6
Edmonds Cl NN8 .... 130 A4
Edmonds Dr PE9 .... 1 A5
Edmund St NN16 .... 72 D2
Edward Cl
 Higham Ferrers
 NN10 .... 132 C7
 Kettering NN15 .... 91 C7
Edwardian Cl NN4 ..... 175 E7
Edward Rd
 Irchester NN29 .... 147 B7
 Kettering NN15 .... 91 C7
 Market Harborough
 LE16 .... 31 D5
Edwards Cl NN11 ...... 183 D7
Edwards Dr NN8 .... 129 D5
Edward Watson Cl
NN2 .... 141 B5
Edwinstowe Cl NN3 .... 160 E7
Egerton Cl NN13 ...... 234 A7
Egmont Ave MK11 ...... 229 E4
Eider Cl
 Burton Latimer NN15 .. 92 A2
 Daventry NN11 .... 135 C3
Eismann Way NN17 ..... 37 C7
Ekins Cl NN3 .... 142 D2
Elan Ct NN10 .... 131 E3
Eldean Rd NN5 .... 140 B1
Elderberry Ct NN3 .... 143 C3
Elder Dr NN14 .... 135 C4
Eldon Cl NN6 .... 100 E6
Eldon Way NN6 .... 100 E6
Eleanor Ct NN6 .... 102 C5
Eleonore Ho NN3 ...... 142 C3
Elgin St NN5 .... 158 F6
Eliot Cl NN16 .... 72 C6
Elizabeth Cl
 Earls Barton NN6 ..... 144 E5
 Wellingborough NN8 ... 129 C2
Elizabeth Ct NN10 .... 132 C7
Elizabeth Rd
 Daventry NN11 .... 135 B3
 Kettering NN16 ...... 72 D3
 Rothwell NN14 .... 70 C6
 West Haddon NN6 ..... 102 C5
Elizabeth St
 Corby NN17 .... 36 E6
 Northampton NN1 ..... 159 F6
Elizabeth Way
 Earls Barton NN6 ..... 144 E5
 Higham Ferrers NN10 .. 132 C5
 Irthlingborough NN9 .. 131 E8
Elizabeth Wlk [6] NN1 .. 159 F6
ELKINGTON 83 A5
Elkington La CV23 ..... 99 B1
Elkington Rd NN6 ..... 82 B4
Elkins Cl NN6 .... 82 B4
Ellen Cl NN6 .... 100 F6
Ellesmere Ave
 Brackley NN13 .... 233 F8
 Northampton NN5 ..... 158 E7
Ellesmere Cl NN13 .... 222 F1
Ellesmere Cres NN13 .. 222 F1
Ellesmere Ct NN13 .... 233 F8
Ellesmere Rd NN13 .... 222 F1
Ellfield Ct NN3 ...... 142 F3

Elliot Ho [1] NN10 .... 132 A2
Elliot Way NN10 ...... 132 A5
Ellis La NN14 .... 89 B4
Ellison Cl NN9 .... 114 C7
Elm Cl
 Brafield-on-t-G NN7 .. 161 D2
 Hargrave NN9 .... 115 F2
Elm Ct NN14 .... 76 D1
Elm Dr
 Brackley NN13 .... 222 F1
 Deanshanger MK19 .... 228 D5
 Hinton NN11 .... 184 A6
 Market Harborough
 LE16 .... 31 C2
Elmfield Cl NN12 ..... 217 D3
Elm Gr NN4 .... 176 A6
Elmhurst Ave NN3 ..... 142 A2
Elmhurst Ct NN3 ...... 142 A2
Elmington Cotts PE8 .. 42 C8
Elmington Rd NN3 ..... 143 C5
Elmlea Dr MK46 .... 195 F4
Elm Rd
 Burton Latimer NN15 .. 92 C4
 Kettering NN15 .... 72 D1
Elms Dr CV22 .... 98 F8
Elms Dyke NN15 ...... 135 E8
Elm St
 [19] Northampton NN1 .. 159 C7
 Wellingborough NN8 ... 129 F5
Elm Way NN7 .... 177 C3
Elm Wlk
 Corby NN17 .... 21 D1
 Higham Ferrers NN10 .. 132 B6
Elmwood Wlk NN5 ..... 140 A1
Elsden Rd NN8 .... 130 C5
ELTON 28 E8
Elton CE Prim Sch PE8 . 28 D8
Elton Cl
 Desborough NN14 ..... 50 E3
 Northampton NN3 ..... 143 B5
Elton Hall★ PE8 ...... 28 D6
Elton Rd PE8 .... 16 C7
Elwes Way NN3 .... 143 B2
Elysium Terr NN2 ..... 159 C8
Embankment NN8 ...... 130 C2
EMBERTON 195 F1
Emberton Ctry Pk &
Visitor Ctr★ MK46 .... 195 E1
Emerald Way NN1 ...... 159 B5
Emerton Gdns MK11 .... 229 D5
Emery Cl NN11 .... 135 E8
Emley Cl NN3 .... 142 F1
Emmanuel Cl NN11 .... 153 C8
Encon Ct NN3 .... 141 F7
Enfield Cl NN5 .... 157 F8
English Martyrs RC Prim
Sch CV21 .... 99 A7
Ennerdale Cl
 Daventry NN11 .... 135 A2
 Kettering NN16 ...... 72 A2
 Northampton NN3 .... 142 A3
Ennerdale Rd
 Corby NN17 .... 21 E1
 Northampton NN3 .... 142 A4
 Rushden NN10 .... 132 D3
Ensleigh Cl NN15 .... 92 C1
Enstone Ct NN8 ...... 129 E1
Enterprise Ct NN16 .. 71 F4
Enterprise Ct NN8 ... 129 B6
Enterprise Ind Pk
NN17 .... 22 F1
Enterprise Rd NN9 ... 114 D7
Entwood Dr NN3 ...... 143 B6
Epping Cl NN15 ...... 92 A5
Epping Wlk [4] NN11 .. 135 B4
Epsom Cl NN10 .... 148 D8
Epsom Wlk NN18 ...... 36 C3
Equestrian Way NN7 .. 155 B4
Ericsson Cl NN11 .... 135 C5
Ermine Rd NN3 .... 143 C5
Ermont Way OX16 ..... 219 A7
Erskin Wood NN6 ..... 105 B1
Esher Ct NN3 .... 142 D4
Eskdaill Pl NN16 .... 72 B3
Eskdaill St NN16 .... 72 B3
Eskdale Ave
 Corby NN17 .... 36 E7
 Northampton NN3 .... 142 B3
Eskdale Cl NN8 ...... 129 C6
Essenden Ct MK11 .... 229 F5
Essen La CV23 .... 100 A3
Essex Cl NN17 .... 36 B6
Essex Gdns LE16 ..... 31 D1
Essex Pl NN15 .... 91 D5
Essex Rd NN10 .... 132 C1
Essex St NN2 .... 159 C8
Essex Terr NN2 ...... 159 C8
Ethel St NN1 .... 159 E6
Eton Cl NN7 .... 155 C4
Eton Ct [3] NN2 ..... 141 C3
Ettrick Cl NN16 ..... 72 A6
Euro Bsns Pk LE16 ... 32 B4
Euro Hub NN18 .... 37 A4
Euston Rd NN4 .... 159 C3
Evans Cl NN11 .... 135 E1
Eva Rd NN16 .... 72 E3
Evelyn Way NN29 ..... 147 C7
Evelyn Wlk NN9 ...... 114 D6
EVENLEY 233 E2
Evenley Rd
 Mixbury NN13 .... 234 D1
 Northampton NN2 .... 141 C5
Evensford Wlk NN9 ... 131 D8
Everard Cl CV23 ..... 80 A5
EVERDON 170 B8
Everdon Cl
 Northampton NN2 .... 141 E4
 Rugby CV22 .... 98 E8

Everdon Pk NN11 ...... 135 A5
Everdon Rd NN12 ..... 170 E3
Everdon Stubbs Nature
Trail★ NN11 .... 170 C6
Everdon Stubbs Woodland
Trust Wood★ NN11 .... 170 D6
Everest Ho NN16 ..... 36 E6
Everest La NN17 ..... 36 E6
Evergreen Dr NN14 ... 113 B7
Everitt Cl NN8 ...... 130 B2
Evesham Cl NN8 ...... 129 E1
Evesham Ct NN3 ...... 143 A7
Evison Ct NN14 ...... 70 C6
Evison Rd NN14 ...... 70 C6
Ewenfield Rd NN9 .... 111 F4
Excalibur Cl NN5 .... 158 A7
Excelsior Cl NN8 .... 129 B4
Excelsior Ct NN9 .... 112 C2
Excelsior Gdns NN5 .. 157 F8
Exeter Cl NN11 ...... 153 C8
Exeter Inf Sch NN18 . 36 F5
Exeter Pl NN1 .... 159 E7
Exeter St NN16 ...... 72 C5
Exmoor Cl NN3 .... 160 D7
Exmouth Ave NN18 .... 36 F4
Express Cl NN9 ...... 131 E8
Express Pk
 Kettering NN16 ...... 71 F3
 Rushden NN10 .... 131 D3
Eyam Cl NN14 .... 50 E3
EYDON 184 C1
Eyeletter Ho [7] NN5 . 159 A6
Eynard Impasse NN13 . 222 E1
Eynon Cl NN3 .... 126 B1

F

Factory La [9] LE16 .. 31 E3
Fairfax Rd LE16 ..... 31 E1
Fairfax Rise NN6 .... 85 B8
Fairfield NN7 .... 174 B2
Fairfield Rd
 Isham NN14 .... 91 E1
 Market Harborough
 LE16 .... 31 D4
 Northampton NN2 .... 141 E2
 Paulerspury NN12 ... 216 B7
Fairfields Sch NN2 .. 141 E1
Fairground Way NN3 .. 160 E2
Fairhurst Way NN6 ... 144 F4
Fair La NN14 .... 76 E3
Fairlight Ct [3] NN18 . 36 B5
Fairmead Cres NN10 .. 147 F8
Fairmead Rise NN2 ... 140 F6
Fair Mile NN7 .... 141 A6
Fairoaks Dr NN9 ..... 114 C7
Fairoaks The NN3 .... 160 F8
Fairway
 Market Harborough
 LE16 .... 31 D4
 Northampton NN2 .... 141 E2
Fairway The
 Daventry NN11 .... 135 F2
 Kettering NN15 ...... 91 A8
 Wellingborough NN9 .. 110 A1
Faith Terr MK19 ..... 207 A2
Falcon Dr MK19 ...... 229 B7
Falconers Cl NN11 ... 135 C3
Falconer's Hill Com Jun &
 Inf Schs NN11 ...... 135 C3
Falconers Rise NN4 .. 175 A8
Falcon View NN12 .... 202 F8
Falcon Way NN13 ..... 222 D2
FALCUTT 212 A2
Falcutt Way NN2 ..... 141 D5
Falkner's Cl OX17 ... 230 A4
Fallowfield NN9 ..... 129 E8
Fallowfields NN6 .... 101 A6
Fallow Wlk NN2 ...... 141 A6
Falmer Wlk NN18 ..... 36 B4
Falster Cl NN18 ..... 36 A2
Faracre Ct NN3 ...... 143 B1
Faraday Cl
 Daventry NN11 .... 135 A4
 Northampton NN5 .... 158 D5
 Wellingborough NN8 .. 129 A6
Faraday Ct
 Thrapston NN14 ...... 76 E2
 Wellingborough NN8 .. 129 A6
Faramir Pl NN3 ...... 143 B6
Far Brook NN6 .... 125 B8
Farebrother Cl NN11 . 183 D7
Fareham Ave CV22 ... 98 E8
Far End NN5 .... 158 F6
Faringdon Cl NN3 ... 143 A7
Farm Cl
 Brigstock NN14 ..... 55 F7
 Holcot NN6 .... 126 A5
 Northampton NN2 .... 141 B4
Farmclose Rd NN4 ... 175 E6
Far Meadow Ct NN3 .. 142 E5
Farm Rd
 Brackley NN13 ...... 234 A4
 Wellingborough NN8 . 129 E6
Farmstead Rd NN6 ... 143 B7
Farm Stile NN11 .... 182 C8
Farmyard The NN7 ... 163 A3
Farnborough Cl
 Corby NN18 .... 36 E1

Farnborough Cl continued
 Northampton NN15 .... 91 D
Farnborough Dr [8]
 NN11 .... 135 B
Farndale Ave NN17 ... 36 E
Farndale View LE16 .. 31 C
FARNDISH .... 147 B
Farndish Cl NN10 ... 131 F
Farndish Rd NN29 ... 147 B
Farndon Ct NN3 ..... 142 F
Farndon Fields Prim Sch
 LE16 .... 48 E8
Farndon Rd
 Great Oxendon LE16 . 48 D
 Hinton NN11 .... 184 A
 Lubenham LE16 ...... 30 F
 Market Harborough
 LE16 .... 31 D
 Marston Trussell LE16 . 47 D
Farnham Dr NN10 .... 147 F8
Farnworth Cl NN5 ... 140 C
Farraxton Sq NN4 ... 158 E2
Farrer Cl NN13 ..... 223 D
Farthing Ct CV21 ... 99 B8
FARTHINGHOE 221 B4
Farthinghoe Cl NN13 . 233 D
Farthinghoe Prim Sch
 NN13 .... 221 B4
Farthinghoe Rd OX17 . 231 F5
FARTHINGSTONE 170 F2
Farthingstone Rd
 Litchborough NN12 .. 171 B3
 Weedon Bec NN7 .... 155 B1
Faugere Cl NN13 .... 233 F8
Favell Way NN3 ..... 160 D8
Fawsley Leys CV23 .. 98 A7
Fawsley Rd
 Everdon NN11 ...... 170 A8
 Northampton NN4 ... 159 C2
 .... 88 C3
Faxton Cl NN3 ...... 141 D4
Faxton End NN6 ..... 107 D7
Fay Cl NN11 .... 184 A7
Feast Field Cl NN29 . 146 D1
Featherbed La
 Geddington NN18 ... 37 B1
 Rugby CV21 .... 80 A1
Federation Ave NN14 . 50 F2
Fegans Ct MK11 ..... 229 D6
Fellmead Rd NN3 .... 143 C5
Fellows Ct NN29 .... 146 C3
Fellows Way CV21 ... 98 F8
Fell Wlk NN18 ...... 36 D6
Fengate Cl NN3 ..... 143 C5
Fenn Cl PE8 .... 15 E5
Fennel Ct NN4 ...... 175 D5
Fenners Cl NN10 .... 132 C7
Fenny Compton Rd
 OX17 .... 181 D1
Fenton Rise NN13 .. 233 D7
Fenwick Dr CV21 ... 99 A8
Ferguson's Cl PE8 .. 43 A3
Fermoy Ct NN7 ..... 138 B4
Fermyn Cl NN14 .... 55 F8
Fermyn Pl NN18 .... 36 A3
Fermyn Woods Ctry Pk★
 NN14 .... 56 A7
Fern Dale Cl NN14 .. 54 B3
Ferndale Rd NN3 ... 142 D2
Ferne Furlong MK46 . 195 F5
Fernfield Ct LE16 .. 32 B4
Fernie Chase LE16 .. 17 A6
Fernie Ct NN15 .... 92 A5
Fernie Ct LE17 .... 45 E6
Fernie Field NN3 .. 142 C6
Fernie Rd LE16 .... 31 F3
Fernie Way NN8 .... 129 D4
Fern Ley Cl LE16 .. 32 B2
Fernmoor Dr NN9 ... 112 F2
Fern Rd NN10 ...... 131 E3
Ferrers Ct NN10 ... 132 C7
Ferrers Specialist Arts
 Coll The NN10 .... 132 C5
Ferrestone Rd NN8 . 130 A6
Ferris Row NN3 .... 160 F7
Ferro Fields NN6 .. 106 C3
Fessey Rd NN11 .... 183 D8
Festival Cl NN9 ... 113 B5
Festival Rd NN12 .. 172 C1
Fetter St NN1 ..... 159 D5
Fettledine Rd NN9 . 113 B5
Field Cl NN6 ...... 102 C4
Field Cotts NN18 .. 53 B8
Fieldgate Ct NN4 . 175 F6
Fieldhead Cl LE16 . 31 C3
Fieldmill Rd NN3 . 143 B1
Field Rose Sq [4] NN3 . 143 C2
Field St NN16 .... 72 B3
Field Street Ave NN16 . 72 B3
Fields View NN8 .. 130 B4
Field View
 Brackley NN13 .... 233 D7
 Braunston NN11 ... 118 C1
 Marston St Lawrence
 OX17 .... 210 B2
Fieldway NN3 ..... 142 B1
Field Way NN13 ... 212 A5
Fiennes Ct NN11 .. 135 B6
Fiensgate NN4 .... 158 D1
Fife St NN5 ...... 158 F7
Fifth Ave NN13 ... 238 E2
Fifth St E NN13 .. 238 E7
Fifth St NN13 .... 238 E7
Filey Ct NN18 .... 36 B4
Filleigh Way NN13 . 160 C7
Finch Dr NN15 .... 92 A6
Finch-Hatton Dr NN17 . 10 C1

FINEDON 111 E4
Finedon Hall NN9 . . . . 111 E4
Finedon Inf Sch NN9 . . . . 111 F5
Finedon Mulso CE Jun Sch
NN9 . . . . 112 A5
Finedon Rd
Burton Latimer NN15 . . . . . 92 B1
Irthlingborough NN9 . . . . . . 112 E3
Wellingborough NN8 . . . . . 130 B6
Finedon Road Ind Est
NN8 . . . . 130 B8
Finedon St NN15 . . . . 92 B1
Finedon Station Rd
NN9 . . . . 111 A6
Fineshade Cl
Kettering NN15 . . . . 92 A5
King's Cliffe PE8 . . . . 13 E7
Fineshade Gr NN17 . . . . . . 36 E7
Finland Way NN18 . . . . 36 A2
Finney Dr NN4 . . . . 175 E3
Firbank Cl NN3 . . . . 160 F8
Firdale Ave NN10 . . . . 132 B4
Fire Quarters The
NN7 . . . . 155 C4
Fir Rd NN16 . . . . 72 D2
Firs Ct NN4 . . . . 175 F8
First Ave NN8 . . . . 129 D3
Firs The
Daventry NN11 . . . . 135 C3
Market Harborough
LE16 . . . . 31 C3
First La NN5 . . . . 158 F6
First St NN13 . . . . 238 F6
Firsview Dr NN5 . . . . 140 C1
Fir Tree Gr NN29 . . . . 164 D2
Firtree La LE17 . . . . 62 C3
Fir Tree Wlk
Market Harborough
LE16 . . . . 31 E4
Northampton NN3 . . . . 142 E2
Fisher Ave CV22 . . . . 98 E8
Fisher Cl NN14 . . . . 76 E1
Fishermans Cl MK46 . . . . 195 E4
Fishers Cl
Kilsby CV23 . . . . 99 F2
Northampton NN3 . . . . 143 B1
Fishpond Cl NN7 . . . . 162 B1
Fishponds Rd NN3 . . . . 143 B1
Fish St NN1 . . . . 159 D6
Fishton Cl NN15 . . . . 91 C7
Fitzroy Ct NN6 . . . . 102 B4
Fitzroy Pl NN1 . . . . 159 B6
Fitzwilliam Ct
4 Rushden NN10 . . . . 132 A2
Wymington NN10 . . . . 148 A7
Fitzwilliam Dr NN15 . . . . . . 92 A5
Fitzwilliam Leys
NN10 . . . . 132 B7
Fitzwilliam Rd NN9 . . . . . 112 F3
Fitzwilliam St NN10 . . . . . 132 A2
Five Acres Fold NN4 . . . . 158 F3
Five Cotts MK18 . . . . 226 D4
Fiveways NN6 . . . . 104 C1
Fjord Wlk NN18 . . . . 36 A2
Flaggs Mdw MK46 . . . . 195 E4
Flamingo Gardens & Zoo
Pk★ MK46 . . . . 195 B3
Flatford Cl NN18 . . . . 36 D1
Flatlets The NN9 . . . . 112 F2
Flavius Gate NN13 . . . . . . 234 A7
Flaxland Cl LE16 . . . . 32 B3
Flaxlands Ct NN3 . . . . 142 F3
Flaxwell Ct NN3 . . . . 160 F8
Fleet St NN16 . . . . 72 A2
Fleetwind Dr NN4 . . . . 175 D7
Fleetwood Cl LE16 . . . . 31 D1
Fleetwood Gdns LE16 . . . . 31 D1
Fleming Cl NN8 . . . . 129 B7
Fleming Rd NN17 . . . . 22 A2
Flensburg Cl NN18 . . . . 36 B2
Fletcher Gdns NN14 . . . . . . 76 D1
Fletcher Rd NN10 . . . . 132 A3
Fletton Way PE8 . . . . 41 F6
Fleur Cl NN11 . . . . 184 C6
Flintcomb Rise NN3 . . . . . 143 B3
Flinters Cl NN4 . . . . 175 F7
Flitton Ct MK11 . . . . 229 F5
Flora Thompson Dr
NN13 . . . . 233 E8
FLORE 155 F4
Flore CE Prim Sch
NN7 . . . . 155 E5
Flore Hill NN7 . . . . 155 D5
Florence Rd NN1 . . . . 159 F7
Floribunda Dr NN4 . . . . . . 158 F2
Florin Pl CV21 . . . . 99 A8
Flowerhill Dr NN8 . . . . 130 B6
Flying Dutchman Way 2
NN11 . . . . 135 A3
Fog Cotts NN6 . . . . 120 B5
Folly La
Hartwell NN7 . . . . 206 C8
Little Brington NN7 . . . . . . 138 B4
Folly Rd MK19 . . . . 228 D4
Fontwell Cres NN18 . . . . . . 36 E1
Foot La NN9 . . . . 133 C8
Ford Bank LE16 . . . . 20 D6
Ford Dr NN13 . . . . 233 D8
Ford St NN16 . . . . 72 C2
Forest App PE8 . . . . 13 F7
Forest Cl NN15 . . . . 92 D3
Forest Ct NN10 . . . . 132 D3
Foresters Pl CV21 . . . . 99 B7
Forest Gate Rd NN17 . . . . . 36 E7
Forest Glade
Hartwell NN7 . . . . 192 D2
Kettering NN16 . . . . 72 C6
Forest Rd
Hanslope MK19 . . . . 207 A6
Hartwell NN7 . . . . 192 D2
Northampton NN4 . . . . . . 159 C3
Piddington NN7 . . . . 177 A1
Forest View NN7 . . . . 192 D2
Forfar St NN5 . . . . 158 F7
Forge Ho NN14 . . . . 70 D7
Forge The NN10 . . . . 132 B1
Forrester Dr NN13 . . . . . . 222 E1
Forrester Gr NN14 . . . . 76 E1
Forresters The NN9 . . . . . . 114 D5
Forstal Cl NN18 . . . . 36 D3
Fort Pl NN1 . . . . 159 B6
Forty Foot La MK44 . . . . . . 149 A1
Fosberry Cl NN4 . . . . 175 F6
FOSCOTE 202 B3
Foskett Cl NN10 . . . . 132 A3
Foskitt Ct NN3 . . . . 143 B1
Fosse Cl NN8 . . . . 129 D1
Fosse Gn NN10 . . . . 132 C3
Foster Cl NN15 . . . . 90 F8
Foster Ct NN18 . . . . 36 E5
FOSTER'S BOOTH 188 D8
Foster's Booth Rd
NN12 . . . . 172 D1
Fothergill Cl LE16 . . . . 32 B3
FOTHERINGHAY 27 D7
Fotheringhay Castle★
PE8 . . . . 27 E6
Fotheringhay Ct NN14 . . . . 76 E2
Fotheringhay Mews
PE8 . . . . 42 A5
Fotheringhay Rd
Corby NN17 . . . . 36 B8
Nassington PE8 . . . . 15 F4
Foundry Ct 5 NN11 . . . . . 135 C1
Foundry Pl NN11 . . . . 135 C1
Foundry St 13 NN1 . . . . . . 159 C5
Foundry Wlk
4 Daventry NN11 . . . . . . 135 C1
Thrapston NN14 . . . . 76 C1
Fountain Ct MK46 . . . . 195 F3
Four Crosses Ho
CV23 . . . . 117 E3
Fourth Ave
Croughton NN13 . . . . 238 E6
Wellingborough NN8 . . . . . 129 D3
Fourth St NN13 . . . . 238 E6
Fowey Cl NN8 . . . . 129 C6
Fox Cl CV21 . . . . 80 B1
Fox Covert Dr NN7 . . . . . . 191 E3
Foxcovert Rd NN3 . . . . 143 B6
Fox Coverts NN14 . . . . 89 A4
Foxendale Sq NN3 . . . . . . 143 D2
Foxfield Way NN4 . . . . 175 F2
Foxford Cl NN4 . . . . 174 F8
Foxglove Ave NN11 . . . . . 184 B6
Foxglove Cl
Corby NN18 . . . . 36 E2
Northampton NN4 . . . . . . 175 F2
Rushden NN10 . . . . 148 C8
Foxglove Rd NN14 . . . . 51 A5
Foxgoles Cl MK19 . . . . 228 F5
Foxgrove Ave NN2 . . . . . . 141 B4
Foxhill MK46 . . . . 195 E5
Foxhill La OX27 . . . . 237 E3
Foxhill Rd NN6 . . . . 102 B3
Fox Hill Rd NN3 . . . . 143 D2
Fox La
Brackley NN13 . . . . 233 E7
Souldern OX27 . . . . 237 E3
Foxlands NN14 . . . . 51 B2
FOXLEY 187 D4
Fox St NN14 . . . . 70 C7
FOXTON 30 E8
Foxton Canal Mus★
LE16 . . . . 30 C8
Foxton Ct NN15 . . . . 72 A1
Foxton Locks Ctry Pk★
LE16 . . . . 30 C8
Foxton Prim Sch LE16 . . . . 30 D8
Foxton Rd
Foxton LE16 . . . . 30 B7
Lubenham LE16 . . . . 30 D5
Foxwell Sq NN3 . . . . 142 F7
Foxwood Cl NN10 . . . . 131 E2
Fox Yd 7 LE16 . . . . 31 E3
Franciscan Cl NN10 . . . . . 147 F8
Francis Ct NN10 . . . . 131 E3
Francis Dickins Cl
NN29 . . . . 146 E3
Francis Row NN7 . . . . 171 E6
Francis St
8 Northampton NN1 . . . . 159 C7
Raunds NN9 . . . . 114 B4
Francis Terr NN9 . . . . 114 B4
Frank Large Wlk NN5 . . . . 158 A7
Franklin Cres NN5 . . . . 158 D7
Franklin Ct NN5 . . . . 159 A6
Franklin Fields NN17 . . . . . 37 A8
Franklin's Cl NN6 . . . . 143 F4
Franklin St NN5 . . . . 158 F6
Franklin Way NN11 . . . . . . 135 B5
Frankston Ave MK11 . . . . . 229 E5
Fraser Cl NN11 . . . . 135 D2
Fraser Rd NN3 . . . . 142 D6
Freehold St NN2 . . . . 159 C8
Freeman's Endowed CE
Jun Sch NN8 . . . . 129 E4
Freeman's La NN14 . . . . . . 95 C6
Freeman Way NN9 . . . . . . 112 B5
Freeschool St 9 NN1 . . . . 159 C5
Fremeaux Terr NN2 . . . . . . 141 B2
French Dr NN15 . . . . 72 F1
Frensham Cl 2 NN4 . . . . . 158 F3
Friar's Ave NN4 . . . . 159 C1
Friars Cl NN8 . . . . 130 A3
Friar's Cl NN4 . . . . 159 B1
Friar's Cres NN4 . . . . 159 C1
Friars Sch NN8 . . . . 130 A3
Friary Cl NN11 . . . . 135 D2
Friary The NN1 . . . . 159 D6
Frinton Cl NN10 . . . . 147 F8
Frisby La LE15 . . . . 3 D8
Friston Cl NN15 . . . . 92 A5
Frobisher Cl NN11 . . . . 135 E2
Frog Hall
Brixworth NN6 . . . . 106 A2
Silverstone NN12 . . . . 214 D5
Frog La NN11 . . . . 182 C7
Front St NN14 . . . . 95 C6
Frost Cl NN14 . . . . 51 B4
Frost Ct NN29 . . . . 145 D6
Frosts Ct NN4 . . . . 175 E5
Frosty Hollow NN4 . . . . . . 175 C6
Froxhill Cres NN6 . . . . 106 A1
Froxhill Wlk NN6 . . . . 106 A1
Fuchsia Cl NN3 . . . . 160 C6
Fuchsia Way NN10 . . . . . . 148 B7
Fulford Dr NN2 . . . . 141 E3
Fullen La NN17 . . . . 22 D8
Fullerburn Ct 2 NN3 . . . . 142 E3
Fuller Rd NN3 . . . . 142 C8
Fullers Cl NN14 . . . . 76 F8
Fuller St NN16 . . . . 72 C2
Fullingdale Rd NN3 . . . . . 142 B2
Fullwell Rd NN29 . . . . 164 D4
Fulmar La NN8 . . . . 130 A8
Fulwell Ave NN17 . . . . 10 C1
Furber Ct NN3 . . . . 142 D4
Furlong Rd NN14 . . . . 51 C3
Furlongs The LE16 . . . . 32 B3
Furnace Cotts NN9 . . . . . . 111 A5
Furnace Dr
Daventry NN11 . . . . 135 A4
Thrapston NN14 . . . . 76 D1
Furnace La
Finedon NN9 . . . . 111 A5
Kettering NN16 . . . . 72 A5
Nether Heyford NN7 . . . . . 172 A8
Furnace Lane Ind Est
NN9 . . . . 111 B5
Furnells Cl NN9 . . . . 114 D7
FURTHO 218 A3
Furtho Ct MK19 . . . . 229 B7
Furtho La NN12 . . . . 217 E3
Furze Ct 5 NN4 . . . . 159 A3
Furze Rd NN7 . . . . 161 D2
Furze Wlk NN2 . . . . 141 E2
Fusilier Rd NN11 . . . . 135 B1
Fusilier Way NN7 . . . . 155 A4
Fydell Row LE15 . . . . 3 A6
Fyfe Rd NN17 . . . . 36 B8
Fylingdale NN2 . . . . 140 F5

G

Gable Cl NN11 . . . . 135 B1
Gable Court Mews
NN3 . . . . 142 D1
Gables The NN15 . . . . 72 B1
Gadesby Ct NN3 . . . . 142 E3
Gainage Cl NN18 . . . . 36 C1
Gainsborough Ave
NN15 . . . . 92 A7
Gainsborough Cres
CV21 . . . . 80 B1
Gainsborough Ct NN18 . . . . 36 D5
Gainsborough Dr
NN8 . . . . 129 F7
Gainsborough Rd
NN18 . . . . 36 C4
Gainsborough Way
NN11 . . . . 135 C6
Gains La PE28 . . . . 61 D2
Galahad Ct NN5 . . . . 158 A8
Galane Cl NN4 . . . . 158 D1
Gallery Cl NN3 . . . . 143 A6
Gallery La PE8 . . . . 42 A5
Gallery The★ PE8 . . . . 42 A5
Galley Hill MK11 . . . . 229 F5
Gallfield Ct NN3 . . . . 161 C8
Galliard Ct NN1 . . . . 159 F7
Gallow Field Rd LE16 . . . . . 30 E7
Gallowhill Rd NN4 . . . . . . 160 B1
Gambrel Rd NN5 . . . . 158 D6
Gamston Wlk NN18 . . . . . . 36 B6
Gander Cl NN17 . . . . 38 A7
Gannet La NN8 . . . . 130 A8
Ganton Cl NN11 . . . . 135 F3
Gapstile Cl NN14 . . . . 51 A4
Gap The NN29 . . . . 146 E2
Gardenfield NN10 . . . . 132 B5
Gardenfields Cl NN9 . . . . . 113 B5
Garden Fields Ct
NN29 . . . . 147 C8
Gardens The
East Carlton LE16 . . . . 35 A7
Kettering NN16 . . . . 72 A4
Whilton NN11 . . . . 137 D6
Gardiner St LE16 . . . . 31 C3
Gardner Cl NN9 . . . . 114 C7
Gardner Rise NN13 . . . . . . 233 D7
Garfield Cl NN2 . . . . 141 C3
Garfield Ho NN2 . . . . 141 B3
Garfield St
Kettering NN15 . . . . 91 B8
Northampton NN2 . . . . . . 141 B3
Garford La PE9 . . . . 2 A5
Garners Way NN7 . . . . 157 C7
Garrard Way NN16 . . . . 71 F3
Garrick Rd NN1 . . . . 160 B7
Garrow Cl NN9 . . . . 112 E3
Garsdale NN2 . . . . 140 F5
Garston Rd NN18 . . . . 36 C1
Gas St 14 NN1 . . . . 159 C5
Gatcombe Ho 3
NN10 . . . . 132 B2
Gateford Ct NN18 . . . . 36 B6
Gatehouse Cl CV21 . . . . 99 A8
Gatehouse La LE16 . . . . 20 F6
Gate La NN14 . . . . 90 B5
Gatelodge Cl NN3 . . . . 142 E6
Gates Cl NN9 . . . . 112 E3
Gateway Cl NN4 . . . . 175 F6
Gaultney The NN14 . . . . 51 A3
Gawaine Ct NN5 . . . . 158 A7
Gaydon Ho NN17 . . . . 22 C1
Gayhurst Cl NN3 . . . . 142 B7
GAYTON 173 F2
Gayton CE Prim Sch
NN7 . . . . 173 E2
Gayton Rd
Blisworth NN7 . . . . 190 C8
Eastcote NN12 . . . . 172 F1
Tiffield NN12 . . . . 189 C6
GEDDINGTON 54 B3
Geddington CE Prim Sch
NN14 . . . . 54 B2
Geddington Rd NN18 . . . . . . 37 D5
Gedling Cl NN3 . . . . 160 F8
Gees Farm Cl NN7 . . . . . . 179 A5
GEESTON 1 B4
Geeston Rd PE9 . . . . 1 B5
Geldock Rd NN3 . . . . 143 A1
Genner Rd NN17 . . . . 22 B1
Gentian Cl NN10 . . . . 148 C8
George Blackall Ct
NN17 . . . . 36 C8
George Nutt Ct NN4 . . . . . 159 C2
George Row NN1 . . . . 159 C5
Georges Ave NN7 . . . . 173 A7
Georges Cl NN7 . . . . 173 A7
Georges Dr NN4 . . . . 175 E3
George St
Burton Latimer NN15 . . . . . 92 D3
Corby NN17 . . . . 36 E6
Higham Ferrers NN10 . . . . 132 C7
Irthlingborough NN9 . . . . . 112 E1
Kettering NN16 . . . . 72 B1
Rushden NN10 . . . . 132 B2
Wellingborough NN8 . . . . . 130 A5
George Yd MK11 . . . . 229 D5
Gerandria Ct CV22 . . . . 98 E8
Gerrard Gdns LE16 . . . . 48 D8
Gervase Sq NN3 . . . . 143 C1
Gharana Nivas NN8 . . . . . . 130 B5
Gibbons Dr NN14 . . . . 70 E7
Gibbsacre Ct NN3 . . . . 143 C1
Gibraltar Ct 23 NN1 . . . . . 159 C7
Gibson Dr
Rugby CV21 . . . . 80 A1
Upper Benefield PE8 . . . . . . 39 F7
Gibson La NN5 . . . . 158 F8
Giffard Ct
Market Harborough
LE16 . . . . 31 D3
Northampton NN5 . . . . . . 159 A5
Gifford Ct NN5 . . . . 158 C8
Gilbert Cl LE16 . . . . 32 B2
Gilbert Scott Ct NN12 . . . . 203 B6
Gilbey Cl NN9 . . . . 110 E1
Gilchrist Ave NN17 . . . . 37 A8
Gillingham Rd NN15 . . . . . . 90 F8
Gillitts Rd NN8 . . . . 129 E3
Gillsway NN2 . . . . 141 A4
Gilson's Cl LE15 . . . . 3 A6
Gingles Ct CV21 . . . . 99 A8
Gipsy La
Irchester NN29 . . . . 146 E8
Kettering NN16 . . . . 71 E2
Gipsy Lane Turn
NN29 . . . . 146 F7
Gisburne Rd NN8 . . . . 130 A6
Glade Cl
Burton Latimer NN15 . . . . . 92 C3
Northampton NN3 . . . . . . 143 B1
Glades The NN4 . . . . 175 F2
Glade The NN9 . . . . 110 E1
Gladiator Cl NN4 . . . . 175 F5
Gladstone Cl NN5 . . . . 141 A1
Gladstone Ct 7 NN16 . . . . . 72 C2
Gladstone Rd NN5 . . . . 159 A8
Gladstone St
Desborough NN14 . . . . 51 A4
Kettering NN16 . . . . 72 C2
Market Harborough LE16 . . 31 F2
Raunds NN9 . . . . 114 D6
Ringstead NN14 . . . . 95 C3
Rothwell NN14 . . . . 70 D7
Glaisdale Cl NN2 . . . . 140 F5
Glaister Pl NN16 . . . . 72 D2
Glamis Cl NN10 . . . . 132 D1
Glan y Mor Terr NN2 . . . . . 141 C5
GLAPTHORN 26 C2
Glapthorn CE Lower Sch
PE8 . . . . 26 B2
Glapthorn Rd PE8 . . . . 41 F6
Glasgow St NN5 . . . . 158 F6
Glassbrook Rd NN10 . . . . . 132 A2
Glassthorpe La NN7 . . . . . 157 A6
Glastonbury Cl NN15 . . . . . 91 F8
Glastonbury Rd
Corby NN18 . . . . 36 A6
Northampton NN4 . . . . . . 159 C1
Glaston Rd LE15 . . . . 3 A5
Glebe Ave
Broughton NN14 . . . . 90 B4
Kettering NN15 . . . . 91 B8
Northampton NN4 . . . . . . 175 E8
Glebe Cl
Holcot NN6 . . . . 126 E8
Glebe Cl continued
Northampton NN4 . . . . . . 175 E8
Glebe Ct PE8 . . . . 58 A4
Glebe Dr NN13 . . . . 234 A7
Glebe Farm Cl NN4 . . . . . 175 C4
Glebe Farm Ct NN29 . . . . 145 E6
Glebe La
Great Houghton NN4 . . . . 160 E2
Hanslope MK19 . . . . 206 E5
Harlestone NN7 . . . . 139 E7
Pitsford NN6 . . . . 125 D5
Staverton NN11 . . . . 152 C7
Glebeland Cres NN5 . . . . . 159 A8
Glebeland Gdns NN5 . . . . 140 F1
Glebeland Rd NN5 . . . . . . 158 F8
Glebelands NN6 . . . . 105 B1
Glebeland Wlk 1
NN5 . . . . 158 F8
Glebe Rd
Burton Latimer NN15 . . . . . 92 A2
Cogenhoe NN7 . . . . 161 E6
Deanshanger MK19 . . . . . . 228 E5
Market Harborough
LE16 . . . . 32 A2
Mears Ashby NN6 . . . . 128 B2
Glebe Rise OX17 . . . . 231 A5
Glebe The
Aynho OX17 . . . . 237 D7
Badby NN11 . . . . 153 A2
Daventry NN11 . . . . 153 C8
Glebe Way
Cogenhoe NN7 . . . . 161 E6
Northampton NN4 . . . . . . 175 E8
Glen Ave NN7 . . . . 174 B2
Glen Bank NN8 . . . . 130 A4
Glen Baulk Rd NN14,
NN16 . . . . 71 C4
Glencoe Dr NN15 . . . . 91 E8
Glendale Ct NN3 . . . . 143 C1
Glendon Rd NN14 . . . . 70 E7
Glendower Cl NN11 . . . . . 135 A4
Gleneagles Cl
Daventry NN11 . . . . 135 E3
Kettering NN15 . . . . 91 F8
Gleneagles Dr NN8 . . . . . . 129 D7
Glenfield Cl NN10 . . . . 131 F2
Glenfield Dr NN29 . . . . . . 145 D5
Glengary NN3 . . . . 142 D7
Glenshee Cl NN15 . . . . 91 E8
Glenville NN3 . . . . 142 B4
Gloucester Ave NN4 . . . . . 159 B1
Gloucester Cl
2 Kettering NN16 . . . . 72 C2
Northampton NN4 . . . . . . 159 B2
Weedon Bec NN7 . . . . 155 B4
Gloucester Cres
Northampton NN4 . . . . . . 159 B2
Rushden NN10 . . . . 132 C3
Gloucester Ct NN14 . . . . . . 70 C6
Gloucester Ho NN4 . . . . . . 159 C2
Gloucester Pl NN8 . . . . . . 130 A4
Glover Ct LE16 . . . . 20 C1
Glovers Cl NN9 . . . . 131 E8
Glovers La
Middleton Cheney
OX17 . . . . 208 F1
Raunds NN9 . . . . 114 C5
Glyndebourne Gdns
NN18 . . . . 36 A4
Goadby's Yd 9 NN16 . . . . . 72 B2
Gocker Wood Cl NN18 . . . . 36 B1
Goddard Ct 5 LE16 . . . . . . 31 E4
Godwin Ct NN13 . . . . 233 E6
Godwin Rd NN17 . . . . 21 F3
Godwin Wlk NN5 . . . . 140 D2
Goffs Yd NN29 . . . . 164 D2
Goldcrest Ct NN3 . . . . 143 A5
Goldcrest Rd NN13 . . . . . . 222 D1
Goldenash Ct NN3 . . . . 142 F5
Golding Cl NN11 . . . . 135 C2
GOLDINGS 143 A5
Goldings Rd NN3 . . . . 143 A5
Goldsmith Dr NN17 . . . . 36 D8
Goldsmith Rd NN8 . . . . . . 129 C4
Gold St
Clipston LE16 . . . . 66 F8
Desborough NN14 . . . . 51 A3
Hanslope MK19 . . . . 207 A2
Kettering NN16 . . . . 72 B2
Northampton NN1 . . . . . . 159 C5
Podington NN29 . . . . 147 E2
Walgrave NN6 . . . . 108 A5
Wellingborough NN8 . . . . . 130 A6
Gold Street Mews 6
NN1 . . . . 159 C5
Golf La NN6 . . . . 140 C8
Goodacre Cl CV23 . . . . 80 A5
Goodens La NN29 . . . . 145 F6
Goodhew Cl NN15 . . . . 90 F8
Good Shepherd RC Prim
Sch The NN2 . . . . 141 C3
Goodwin Cl NN8 . . . . 130 A8
Goodwood Ave NN3 . . . . . 141 F5
Goodwood Cl
Corby NN18 . . . . 36 E1
Market Harborough LE16 . . 32 B3
Goodwood Rd NN10 . . . . . 148 D8
Goose Gn NN13 . . . . 233 E6
Goosemere MK19 . . . . 228 E4
Goran Ave MK11 . . . . 229 E4
Gordon Rd
Oundle PE8 . . . . 42 A6
Wellingborough NN8 . . . . . 130 B5
Gordon St
Kettering NN16 . . . . 72 C2

Gordon St continued
Northampton NN2 . . . . **159** C8
Rothwell NN14 . . . . **70** D6
Rushden NN10 . . . . **131** F2
Gordon Terr NN14 . . . . **74** F2
Gores La LE16 . . . . **32** A3
Gorricks MK11 . . . . **229** D4
Gorse Cl NN2 . . . . **141** B6
Gorseholm Ct 10 NN9 . . **112** F2
Gorse Rd
Hinton NN11 . . . . **184** B7
Kettering NN16 . . . . **72** E4
Spratton NN6 . . . . **124** B8
Gosforth NN8 . . . . **129** C4
Goslar The NN8 . . . . . . **129** B3
Gotch Cl NN15 . . . . **91** F4
Gotch Rd NN15 . . . . **91** F5
Gough Cl NN15 . . . . **72** E1
Goughs Cotts NN5 . . . . **158** C7
Gould Cl NN11 . . . . **118** B1
Goulsbra Rd NN10 . . . . **148** D8
Goward St LE16 . . . . **31** E3
Gower Cl NN15 . . . . **91** C6
Gowerton Rd NN4 . . . . **176** C8
Grace Ct NN15 . . . . **92** B1
Gracelands LE16 . . . . . . **31** C2
Graeme Rd PE5 . . . . **8** F2
Grafton Cl
Hartwell NN7 . . . . **192** D2
Potterspury NN12 . . . . . **217** E3
Wellingborough NN8 . . . **129** D7
Grafton Ct NN7 . . . . . . **193** A8
Grafton Dr NN17 . . . . . . **36** B8
Grafton Ho NN1 . . . . . . **159** B6
Grafton Pl 10 NN1 . . . . **159** C7
Grafton Rd
Brigstock NN14 . . . . **55** E4
Cranford St John NN14 . . . **93** A4
Geddington NN14 . . . . . . **54** B2
Roade NN7 . . . . **191** C4
Rushden NN10 . . . . **132** D2
Yardley Gobion NN12 . . . **217** F6
GRAFTON REGIS **205** D2
Grafton St Ind Est
NN1 . . . . **159** B7
Grafton St
Kettering NN16 . . . . **72** A4
Northampton NN1 . . . . . **159** C7
Grafton View NN4 . . . . **175** E6
Grafton Way
Northampton NN5 . . . . . **140** B2
Rothersthorpe NN7 . . . . **174** A4
Graham Hill NN12 . . . . **214** D4
Graham Hill Rd NN12 . . **203** C7
Granary Cl LE16 . . . . **31** F6
Granary Ct NN4 . . . . . . **175** C7
Granary Rd NN4 . . . . . . **175** C7
Granby Cl NN18 . . . . **36** B6
Grandborough Cl
NN6 . . . . **106** C1
Grange Ave NN5 . . . . . . **140** B1
Grange Cl
Denton NN7 . . . . **162** B1
Earls Barton NN6 . . . . . . **144** E5
Irchester NN29 . . . . **147** B7
Grange Com Sch NN16 . . **72** E3
Grange Ct
Brixworth NN6 . . . . **106** B2
Horton NN7 . . . . **177** D1
Stony Stratford MK12 . . . **229** F6
Grange La
Pitsford NN6 . . . . **125** E6
Thorpe Langton LE16 . . . **17** A5
GRANGE PARK **175** E3
Grange Pl NN16 . . . . **72** E4
Grange Rd
Broughton NN14 . . . . **90** B4
Geddington NN14 . . . . . . **53** F4
Islip NN14 . . . . **76** B1
Kettering NN16 . . . . **72** A3
Northampton NN3 . . . . . **142** C3
Stanion NN14 . . . . **37** E2
Stanwick NN9 . . . . **114** A3
Wellingborough NN9 . . . **110** E1
Grange Road Workshops
NN14 . . . . **53** F2
Grange Sch The
NN11 . . . . **135** A1
Grangeway NN10 . . . . . **148** A8
Grange Way NN29 . . . . **147** B7
Grangewood NN4 . . . . . **175** A7
Grant Cl NN15 . . . . **90** F7
Grantham Wlk NN18 . . . **36** B4
Grantown Cl NN15 . . . . **91** E8
Grant Rd NN8 . . . . **130** B5
Granville St
Kettering NN16 . . . . **72** C2
Market Harborough LE16 . . **31** F2
Grasmere Gn NN8 . . . . **129** B4
Grasmere Rd NN8 . . . . . **71** F2
Grasmere Way NN10 . . **132** B8
Graspin La NN3 . . . . . . **160** D8
Grass Cl NN12 . . . . **203** B3
Grasscroft NN2 . . . . . . **141** A4
Grass Croft NN6 . . . . . **121** A3
Grassmere Ave NN3 . . **142** E2
Grass Slade NN6 . . . . . **106** C2
Gravel Hill NN11 . . . . . **199** D7
Gravely St NN10 . . . . . **131** F2
Gray Cl NN6 . . . . **145** A4
Grays Cl NN12 . . . . **216** D8
Gray's Cl NN17 . . . . **36** E5
Grays Dr NN14 . . . . **37** E3
Grays La
Paulerspury NN12 . . . . . **216** D8

Grays La continued
Yardley Gobion NN12 . . . . **217** E6
Gray St
Irchester NN29 . . . . **147** A7
Northampton NN1 . . . . . **159** F2
Greasley Wlk NN18 . . . . **36** B6
GREAT ADDINGTON **94** B2
Great Addington CE Prim
Sch NN14 . . . . **94** B3
GREAT BILLING **143** C3
Great Billing Way
NN3 . . . . **143** C4
GREAT BOWDEN **32** A6
Great Bowden CE Prim
Sch LE16 . . . . **32** A6
Great Bowden Hall
LE16 . . . . **31** E7
Great Bowden Rd LE16 . . **32** A4
GREAT BRINGTON **138** D7
Great Central Walk Nature
Trail ★ CV22 . . . . **98** D6
Great Central Way
NN11 . . . . **184** C7
Great Cl NN6 . . . . **124** D1
GREAT CRANSLEY **89** F6
Great Creaton Prim Sch
NN6 . . . . **104** F4
GREAT DODDINGTON
. . . . **145** D5
Great Doddington Prim
Sch NN29 . . . . **145** E6
GREAT EASTON **20** E7
Great Easton Rd
Bringhurst LE16 . . . . **20** C6
Caldecott LE16 . . . . **21** A7
Drayton LE16 . . . . **20** A5
Great Easton LE16 . . . . . **20** F6
Great Field Ct NN3 . . . . **142** E5
Great Folds Rd NN18 . . . **35** F1
GREAT GIDDING **61** D3
Great Gidding CE Prim
Sch PE28 . . . . **61** D3
Great Ground Wlk
NN4 . . . . **175** F2
Great Gull Cres NN3 . . **142** F6
GREAT HARROWDEN
. . . . **110** D2
Great Holme Ct NN3 . . **142** E5
GREAT HOUGHTON **160** F2
Great La
Bugbrooke NN7 . . . . **172** F7
Hackleton NN7 . . . . **177** B3
Greatmeadow NN3 . . . . **143** C4
Greatmeadow Rd
NN3 . . . . **143** B4
Great North Rd
Stibbington PE8 . . . . **8** C2
Wothorpe PE9 . . . . **2** B8
GREAT OAKLEY **53** B8
GREAT OXENDON **48** E3
Great Park St NN8 . . . . **130** A5
Great Russell St NN1 . . **159** D7
GREATWORTH **210** E2
Greatworth Prim Sch
OX17 . . . . **210** E2
Grebe Cl
Hinton NN11 . . . . **184** B6
Thrapston NN14 . . . . **76** E3
Greenacre Dr
Rushden NN10 . . . . **148** B8
Stanion NN14 . . . . **37** E2
Green Acres Cvn Pk
LE16 . . . . **31** C6
Greenaway Cl NN7 . . . . **190** E7
Greenbank Ave NN15 . . **72** E3
Greenbank Terr NN14 . . **95** B3
Green Cl
Irthlingborough NN9 . . . **131** D8
Wellingborough NN8 . . . **129** C7
Green Dale Sq 8
NN3 . . . . **143** C2
Green End NN2 . . . . . . **141** B2
Green End La MK19 . . . **207** A3
Green Farm OX17 . . . . . **230** A4
Green Farm Cl CV23 . . . **81** A6
Greenfield Ave
Kettering NN15 . . . . **71** F1
Northampton NN3 . . . . . **142** B3
Greenfield Rd NN3 . . . . **142** A2
Greenfields Sch NN2 . . **141** B5
Greenfield Way NN10 . . **132** A1
Greenhill Rd
Elton PE7 . . . . **29** B6
Elton PE8 . . . . **28** F8
Kettering NN15 . . . . **91** A8
Long Buckby NN6 . . . . . **121** A3
Greenhill Rise NN18 . . . **36** B5
Greenhills Cl NN2 . . . . **141** B6
Greenhills Rd NN2 . . . . **141** B6
Greening Rd NN14 . . . . **70** C7
Green La
Ashley LE16 . . . . **18** F2
Braybrooke LE16 . . . . . . **49** F5
Charlton OX17 . . . . **231** E5
Desborough NN14 . . . . . **50** D3
Duddington PE9 . . . . **5** B6
Husbands Bosworth
LE17 . . . . **45** E5
Kettering NN16 . . . . **72** B2
Market Harborough LE16 . . **31** E1
Northampton NN4 . . . . . **175** E5
Silverstone NN12 . . . . . **214** D4
Stanwick NN9 . . . . **113** F3
Stoke Albany LE16 . . . . . **34** B4

Green La continued
Thrapston NN14 . . . . **76** D2
Towcester NN12 . . . . . . **203** A5
Weston by W LE16 . . . . . **18** C6
Greenland Wlk NN18 . . . **36** A2
Greenlaw NN8 . . . . **129** B4
Green Oaks Prim Sch
NN2 . . . . **141** D4
Green Rd NN7 . . . . **161** E2
Greenside
Blisworth NN7 . . . . **190** D7
Northampton NN3 . . . . . **142** B3
Wappenham NN12 . . . . **213** B8
Greenslade Cl NN15 . . . **91** A8
GREENS NORTON **202** D8
Greens Norton CE Prim
Sch NN12 . . . . **202** E8
Green St
Milton Malsor NN7 . . . . **174** E4
Northampton NN1 . . . . . **159** B5
Wollaston NN29 . . . . . . **146** E2
Greensward The
OX17 . . . . **196** E1
Green The
Abthorpe NN12 . . . . **201** F2
Adderbury OX17 . . . . . . **230** A4
Barby CV23 . . . . **99** C1
Blakesley NN12 . . . . **187** B1
Brafield-on-t-G NN7 . . . **161** E2
Braunston NN11 . . . . . . **118** C1
Byfield NN11 . . . . **183** D7
Caldecott LE16 . . . . **21** B8
Chelveston NN9 . . . . . . **133** C8
Church Stowe NN7 . . . . **171** D7
Clipston LE16 . . . . **67** A8
Cosgrove MK19 . . . . . . **218** F2
Cranford St John NN14 . . **93** A6
Culworth OX17 . . . . **198** C3
Deanshanger MK19 . . . **228** E4
Dodford NN7 . . . . **154** E6
Evenley NN13 . . . . **233** C7
Everdon NN11 . . . . **170** A8
Flore NN7 . . . . **155** F5
Great Bowden LE16 . . . . **32** B6
Great Brington NN7 . . . **138** D7
Great Houghton NN4 . . **160** E2
Guilsborough NN6 . . . . . **103** E7
Hanslope MK19 . . . . . . **207** A3
Harlestone NN7 . . . . **139** D4
Hellidon NN11 . . . . **151** C1
Helmdon NN13 . . . . **211** F4
Hollowell NN6 . . . . **104** B4
Husbands Bosworth
LE17 . . . . **45** E5
Kislingbury NN7 . . . . . . **157** D3
Lilbourne CV23 . . . . **81** A6
Little Addington NN14 . . **113** B8
Lower Boddington
NN11 . . . . **182** B5
Lubenham LE16 . . . . **30** E3
Lyddington LE15 . . . . **9** D7
Marston St Lawrence
OX17 . . . . **210** B1
Mawsley Village NN14 . . **89** B4
Nether Heyford NN7 . . . **156** B1
Newnham NN11 . . . . . . **153** D4
Northampton, Grange Park
NN4 . . . . **175** F3
Northampton, Hardingstone
NN4 . . . . **175** F8
Northampton, Kingsthorpe
NN2 . . . . **141** B3
10 Northampton NN1 . . **159** C5
Orlingbury NN14 . . . . . . **110** A5
Paulerspury NN12 . . . . **216** B7
Priors Marston CV47 . . . **166** D7
Roade NN7 . . . . **191** D4
Staverton NN11 . . . . . . **152** B7
Titchmarsh NN14 . . . . . . **77** C4
Turweston NN13 . . . . . **234** C8
Twywell NN14 . . . . **75** A1
Wadenhoe PE8 . . . . **58** A4
Weedon Lois NN12 . . . . **200** D3
West Haddon NN6 . . . . **102** B4
Weston by W LE16 . . . . . **18** B3
Whilton NN11 . . . . **137** D6
Woodford NN14 . . . . **94** D6
Greenview Dr
Northampton NN2 . . . . . **141** E3
Towcester NN12 . . . . . . **203** B6
Greenway
Braunston NN11 . . . . . . **118** B1
Eastcote NN12 . . . . **173** A1
Northampton NN3 . . . . . **160** C8
Greenway Ave NN3 . . . **142** D4
Greenway The NN11 . . **153** C8
Greenwood Cl
Byfield NN11 . . . . **183** C7
Moulton NN3 . . . . **142** C8
Greenwood Rd NN15 . . **159** A6
Greenyard The NN7 . . **179** B7
Greeve Cl NN18 . . . . **36** C1
Greeves Cl NN5 . . . . . . **139** F1
Gregory St 8 NN1 . . . . **159** C5
Gregory Wlk NN18 . . . . **36** C4
Grenadier Rd NN11 . . . **135** B1
GRENDON **163** E5
Grendon Ave NN17 . . . . **36** B7
Grendon CE Prim Sch
NN7 . . . . **163** D6
Grendon Lakes
Watersports Ctr ★
NN7 . . . . **145** C1
Grendon Rd NN6 . . . . . **144** E1
Grendon Wlk NN3 . . . . **141** F5
Grenville Cl
Corby NN17 . . . . **36** A8
Daventry NN11 . . . . **135** E1

Grenville Cl continued
Rothwell NN14 . . . . **70** E6
Grenville Gdns LE16 . . . **31** D1
Gresham Dr NN4 . . . . . **158** E2
Gresley Cl NN11 . . . . . . **135** A4
GRETTON **10** C1
Gretton Brook Rd
Corby NN17 . . . . **21** E3
Corby NN17 . . . . **22** C4
Gretton Ct NN8 . . . . . . **129** D7
Gretton Prim Sch
NN17 . . . . **22** C8
Gretton Rd
Corby NN17 . . . . **22** F3
Harringworth NN17 . . . . **10** E7
Lyddington LE15 . . . . **9** D5
Rockingham NN17 . . . . . **21** B5
Weldon NN17 . . . . **38** A8
Gretton Road Ind Est
NN17 . . . . **38** A8
Greville Ave NN3 . . . . . **142** A4
Greville Cl NN12 . . . . . **141** C8
Greyfriars NN1 . . . . **159** C6
Greyfriars Rd NN15 . . . **153** B8
Greys The NN7 . . . . **155** B4
Grieg Wlk NN18 . . . . **36** A2
Griffin Cl OX17 . . . . **230** A5
Griffin Rd LE16 . . . . **49** E4
Griffiths Cl NN5 . . . . . . **157** F8
Griffith St NN10 . . . . . . **132** B1
Grimmer Wlk NN9 . . . . **131** D8
Grimsby Cl NN18 . . . . . . **36** C4
GRIMSCOTE **188** B8
Grindleford Cl NN14 . . . **50** E3
Grizedale Cl
Corby NN17 . . . . **36** D8
Kettering NN16 . . . . **72** A6
Grombold Ave NN9 . . . **114** C6
Grooms La NN6 . . . . . . **105** A4
Grosvenor Cl NN15 . . . . **92** A5
Grosvenor Ctr NN1 . . . **159** D6
Grosvenor Gdns NN2 . . **141** D4
Grosvenor Ho NN2 . . . . **141** D4
Grosvenor Pl NN13 . . . **233** E7
Grosvenor Rd NN15 . . . . **92** A5
Grosvenor Way NN15 . . **91** F5
Groundwell Ct 1
NN3 . . . . **142** F1
Grovebury Dell NN2 . . . **141** A4
Grove Farm Cl NN6 . . . **121** D4
Grove Farm La NN3 . . . **126** D2
Grove La NN12 . . . . **199** F3
Grovelands NN11 . . . . . **153** A8
Grove Pl NN9 . . . . **114** C5
Grove Rd
Brafield-on-t-G NN7 . . . **161** D3
Northampton NN1 . . . . . **159** E7
Rushden NN10 . . . . **132** C2
Thrapston NN14 . . . . **76** D1
Grove St
Higham Ferrers
NN10 . . . . **132** C6
Raunds NN9 . . . . **114** D5
Wellingborough NN8 . . . **129** E4
Grove The
Corby NN18 . . . . **37** C6
Kettering NN15 . . . . **72** B1
Moulton NN3 . . . . **126** C2
Ringstead NN14 . . . . **95** A3
Roade NN7 . . . . **191** E3
Wollaston NN29 . . . . . . **146** D1
Grove Way NN9 . . . . . . **111** E3
Grove Works NN15 . . . . **159** E7
Grundy Ct NN15 . . . . . . **91** B8
Guildhall Rd NN1 . . . . . **159** D5
Guillemot La NN8 . . . . . **130** A4
GUILSBOROUGH **103** E6
Guilsborough CE Prim Sch
NN6 . . . . **103** E7
Guilsborough Hill
NN6 . . . . **104** B5
Guilsborough Rd
Ravensthorpe NN6 . . . . **103** D1
West Haddon NN6 . . . . **102** C5
Guilsborough Sch
NN6 . . . . **103** D8
Guinea Orch MK46 . . . . **195** E4
Gullet La LE16 . . . . **18** F2
Gumley Rd LE16 . . . . . . **30** C7
Gunnell Cl NN15 . . . . . . **90** F8
Gunnsbrook Cl LE16 . . . **32** A6
Gunthorpe Pl NN18 . . . . **36** B6
Gurston Rise NN3 . . . . **143** C4
Gynwell NN6 . . . . **85** B8

H

Hachenburg Pl NN10 . . **132** C5
HACKLETON **177** C3
Hackleton Prim Sch
NN7 . . . . **177** A3
Hackwood Rd NN11 . . . **153** E8
Haddon Cl
Rushden NN10 . . . . **132** A1
Wellingborough NN8 . . . **129** D8
Haddon Ct NN6 . . . . . . **122** C5
Haddonian Rd LE16 . . . . **31** F1
Haddonstone Show Gdn ★
NN6 . . . . **122** D4
Hadfield Cl CV23 . . . . . . **80** A5
Hadleigh Ho 4 NN10 . . **132** B2
Hadrian's Gate NN13 . . **234** A2
Hafod Cl NN18 . . . . **36** C2
Hagley Cl LE16 . . . . **32** B3
Haigh Dr NN15 . . . . **72** C1
Hailsham Ct OX17 . . . . . **220** B8
Haines Rd NN4 . . . . **159** C3

Hale Ave MK11 . . . . **229** E6
Halfmoon Mews PE8 . . . **42** A4
Halford St NN14 . . . . **76** C1
Halford Way NN11 . . . . **135** E4
Halfway Thorn NN6 . . . **124** C1
Halifax Sq NN18 . . . . **36** B4
Hallam Cl NN3 . . . . **142** B4
Hallaton Rd LE16 . . . . . . **18** F4
Hall Ave NN10 . . . . **132** A4
Hall Cl
Arthingworth LE16 . . . . . **68** C1
Harpole NN7 . . . . **157** B6
Kettering NN15 . . . . **90** F8
Kilsby CV23 . . . . **100** A4
Kislingbury NN7 . . . . . . **157** D1
Naseby NN6 . . . . **66** B4
Northampton NN5 . . . . . **158** C6
Old Stratford MK19 . . . . **229** B6
Weston by W LE16 . . . . . **18** B4
Hall Dr
Finedon NN9 . . . . **111** E4
Long Buckby NN6 . . . . . **121** C4
Hall Farm Cl NN6 . . . . . **106** B3
Hall Gdns
East Haddon NN6 . . . . . **122** D5
Loddington NN14 . . . . . . **70** C1
Polebrook PE8 . . . . **43** A3
Hall Hill NN14 . . . . **55** F7
Hall La
Ashley LE16 . . . . **18** E2
Drayton LE16 . . . . **20** A8
Kettering NN15 . . . . **90** F8
South Luffenham LE15 . . . **3** A8
Welford NN6 . . . . **64** D6
Wittering PE8 . . . . **7** C8
Hall Mead Ct NN7 . . . . **172** E6
Hall Meadow Prim Sch
NN15 . . . . **90** F7
Hall Piece Cl NN3 . . . . **143** C3
Hall's Cl
Geddington NN14 . . . . . . **54** B3
Weldon NN17 . . . . **38** A8
Hall's La NN13 . . . . **233** E6
Hallwood Rd NN16 . . . . . **72** C5
Hall Yd
Collyweston PE9 . . . . **1** C2
King's Cliffe PE8 . . . . **13** F7
HALSE **222** B5
Halse Rd NN13 . . . . **222** F7
Halswell NN3 . . . . **142** D4
Hambledon Rise NN4 . . **158** E5
Hamblin Ct NN10 . . . . . **132** B2
Hamilton Ct NN6 . . . . . **124** D1
Hamilton Ho
Corby NN17 . . . . **36** E5
Northampton NN2 . . . . . **141** C5
Hamilton La NN7 . . . . . **138** D6
Ham La NN15 . . . . **95** A4
Hamlet Gn NN15 . . . . . **158** F8
Hammas Leys NN6 . . . . **121** C4
Ham Meadow Dr NN3 . . **143** C2
Hammerstone La
NN4 . . . . **158** F3
Hammond Way LE16 . . . **31** E4
Hampden Cres NN16 . . . **72** D3
Hampton Court Cl
NN12 . . . . **203** B5
Hampton Ct LE16 . . . . . **31** F3
Hampton Dr OX17 . . . . . **230** F6
Hampton Ho 1 NN10 . . **132** B2
Hampton St NN1 . . . . . **159** B7
Hamsterly Pk NN3 . . . . **143** A6
Hanbury Ct NN11 . . . . . **135** B6
Handcross Ct NN18 . . . . **36** B4
Handcross Way NN10 . . **132** C5
Handley Cl NN5 . . . . . . **140** A1
Hanemill Ct NN3 . . . . . **143** C1
Hangerfield Ct NN3 . . . **142** F4
HANGING HOUGHTON
. . . . **106** C8
HANNINGTON **108** C3
Hanover Cl NN15 . . . . . . **92** A7
Hanover Ct NN3 . . . . . . **143** B4
Hanover Dr NN13 . . . . . **233** E7
Hans Apel Dr NN13 . . . **233** D7
HANSLOPE **207** B3
Hanslope Comb Sch
MK19 . . . . **207** A3
Hanslope Rd MK19 . . . . **218** F7
Harbidges La NN6 . . . . **121** A4
Harborough Rd
Braybrooke LE16 . . . . . . **49** F3
Brixworth NN6 . . . . **106** C3
Clipston LE16 . . . . **48** A2
Desborough LE16, NN14 . . **50** D7
Dingley LE16 . . . . **32** D5
Dingley LE16 . . . . **32** E1
Dingley LE16 . . . . **33** A3
East Farndon LE16 . . . . . **48** C8
Great Oxendon LE16 . . . **48** F4
Kelmarsh NN6 . . . . **67** F5
Lubenham LE16 . . . . **31** A3
Maidwell NN6 . . . . **87** B4
Market Harborough
LE16 . . . . **31** C7
Marston Trussell LE17 . . . **30** A1
Northampton NN2 . . . . . **141** C4
Rushden NN10 . . . . **132** C1
Stoke Albany LE16 . . . . . **34** B4
Theddingworth LE17 . . . . **46** D8
Harborough Rd N
NN2 . . . . **141** B6
Harborough Way
NN10 . . . . **132** C1
Harcourt Sq NN16 . . . . **144** E4
Harcourt St
9 Kettering NN16 . . . . . **72** C2

Harcourt St *continued*
Market Harborough LE16 31 D3
Raunds NN9 114 D6
Harcourt Way NN4 158 E3
Hardays La NN6 102 B4
Harden Cl NN18 53 A8
Harding Cl NN15 72 F1
HARDINGSTONE 175 E8
Hardingstone La NN4 175 D8
Hardingstone Prim Sch NN4 175 E7
Harding Terr NN1 159 C7
Hardlands Rd NN5 158 C8
Hardwater Rd NN29 145 D4
HARDWICK 128 D8
Hardwick Cl NN8 129 E5
Hard wick Hall Way 10 NN11 135 B7
Hardwick Jun & Inf Sch NN8 129 C5
Hardwick Rd
Gretton NN17 10 B1
Little Harrowden NN9 110 B3
Northampton NN4 175 C8
Priors Marston CV47 166 D7
Wellingborough, Hatton Park NN8 129 D6
Wellingborough, Hatton Park NN8 129 E5
Wellingborough NN8 129 A7
Hardy Dr NN4 175 F7
Harebell Sq 1 NN3 143 D2
Harefield Rd NN3 143 B5
Harefoot Cl NN5 158 B8
Haresmoor Dr NN12 203 C4
Hares Run NN14 89 C5
HARGRAVE 115 E2
Hargrave Ct NN9 112 E1
Harksome Hill NN4 158 E2
Harlech NN18 36 C3
Harlech Ct NN14 76 F2
HARLESTONE 139 D5
Harlestone Ct NN5 158 F7
Harlestone Ho NN5 159 A7
Harlestone Prim Sch NN7 139 E5
Harlestone Rd
Church Brampton NN6 124 D1
Harlestone NN7 139 F6
Northampton NN5 140 B2
Harley Way
Brigstock NN14 56 C8
Lower Benefield PE8 40 D3
Harmans Way NN7 155 B4
Harnett Dr MK12 229 F6
Harold St 10 NN1 159 E6
Harpers Cl NN18 53 B8
Harper's Ct NN14 55 F7
HARPOLE 157 D6
Harpole Prim Sch NN7 157 D6
Harrier Pk NN4 175 B8
HARRINGTON 69 B4
Harrington Rd
Desborough NN14 50 F3
Kelmarsh NN6 67 F3
Loddington NN14 70 D1
Old NN6 107 D7
Rothwell NN14 70 C6
HARRINGWORTH 10 F7
Harringworth Rd NN17 10 C2
Harris Cl
Brackley NN13 233 D8
Northampton NN4 175 F7
Raunds NN9 114 D7
Harrison Cl
Market Harborough LE16 48 D8
Rugby CV21 99 B8
Wellingborough NN8 129 D5
Harrison Ct NN7 172 F7
Harris Rd NN17 21 C1
Harrod Dr LE16 32 A4
Harrogate Ct NN18 36 B4
Harrold Rd NN29 164 D3
Harrowden Rd
Finedon NN9 111 D3
Northampton NN4 160 B2
Orlingbury NN14 110 A5
Wellingborough NN8 129 F6
Harrowick La NN6 144 E4
Harrow La NN11 135 D6
Harrow Way NN2 140 F6
Harry Cl NN6 121 B3
Harry Potter Ho NN15 72 B1
Hartburn Cl NN3 161 C8
Hartland Dr LE16 32 B3
Hartley Dr NN15 92 A7
Hartley Ho NN13 233 F6
HARTWELL 192 D1
Hartwell CE Prim Sch NN7 192 D1
Hartwell Cl NN2 141 D5
Hartwell Rd
Ashton NN7 205 F8
Hanslope MK19 206 E4
Roade NN7 192 A2
Hartwood Croft NN16 72 C6
Harvest Cl
Burton Latimer NN15 92 C2
Daventry NN11 135 D6
Harvest Way NN2 140 F5
Harvey Cl NN9 114 B5
Harvey Dr MK46 195 F1
Harvey La NN3 142 B8
Harvey Rd
Rushden NN10 148 B7
Wellingborough NN8 129 E3
Harvey Reeves Rd NN5 159 A5
Harwood Dr NN16 72 A6
HASELBECH 86 A8
Haselrig Sq 4 NN4 158 F2
Hassocks Hedge NN4 158 C2
Hastings MK11 229 E5
Hastings Rd NN2 141 D3
Hastings Wlk 4 NN18 36 B5
Hatchdoyle La PE8 41 D1
Hatfield Cl
Corby NN18 36 E3
6 Northampton NN4 175 C8
Wellingborough NN8 129 C7
Hatherley Cl NN6 101 A6
Hathersage Cl NN14 50 E4
Hatton Ave NN8 129 F5
Hatton Cl NN3 142 A6
Hatton Hall 5 NN8 129 F5
Hatton La NN17 10 B1
HATTON PARK 129 E6
Hatton Park Rd NN8 129 F5
Hatton St NN8 129 F5
Hautboy La PE8 28 B3
Havelock Cotts PE8 42 A5
Havelock Ho 4 NN16 72 C4
Havelock Jun & Inf Schs NN14 51 A3
Havelock Mews NN16 72 B3
Havelock St
Desborough NN14 51 A3
Kettering NN16 72 C3
Wellingborough NN8 130 A5
Haven Cl NN5 159 A7
Haweswater Rd NN16 71 E3
Hawfinch Gn NN14 51 B4
Hawke Rd NN11 135 E1
Hawkesbeard Pl 3 NN3 143 C2
Hawkins Cl
Brackley NN13 233 D7
Corby NN17 21 B1
Daventry NN11 135 E2
Rothwell NN14 70 E7
Stony Stratford MK11 229 D5
Hawk Ridge NN4 158 F1
Hawkshead NN8 129 B3
Hawksmoor Way NN5 140 D1
Hawksnest NN4 175 A8
Hawkstone Cl NN5 158 D7
Hawkswood MK46 195 F5
Hawkwell Est MK19 229 B7
Hawson Cl NN15 91 C7
Hawthorn Ave NN14 89 C5
Hawthorn Cl NN15 92 B1
Hawthorn Com Prim Sch NN15 91 B8
Hawthorn Dr
Brackley NN13 222 F1
Daventry NN11 135 C3
Thrapston NN14 76 D1
Towcester NN12 203 C8
Hawthorne Cl NN11 184 E6
Hawthorne Rd NN9 112 A4
Hawthorne Wlk NN17 21 E1
Hawthorn Rd
Burton Latimer NN15 92 B1
Kettering NN15 91 B8
Northampton NN3 142 A1
Hawthorns The
Desborough NN14 51 C2
Higham Ferrers NN10 132 B6
Silverstone NN12 214 D3
Hawthorn Way NN8 129 E5
Hay Cl
Corby NN18 53 B8
Rushden NN10 148 B8
Haycroft Wlk NN2 141 A5
Hayden Ave NN9 112 A5
Hayden Rd NN10 132 C2
Hayden Wlk NN10 132 C2
Haydock Cl NN18 53 E8
Haydown Gn NN5 158 D8
Hayes Rd MK19 228 F5
Hayes Wlk PE8 16 D1
Hayeswood Rd NN3 142 F4
Hay La NN9 112 E1
Hayman Rd NN13 233 D7
Haynes La NN6 105 B1
Haynes Rd NN16 72 D2
Hayride The NN4 175 A7
Haystack The NN11 135 D6
Hayway
Irthlingborough NN9 112 E1
Rushden NN10 132 A4
Hayway Inf Sch NN10 132 B3
Hazeland Ho NN14 51 A3
Hazel Cl
Brackley NN13 222 F1
Hartwell NN7 192 E2
Hazel Copse NN4 175 F1
Hazel Cres NN12 203 B5
Hazel Croft NN11 118 C1
Hazelden Cl NN29 146 D1
Hazeldene Rd NN2 141 F3
Hazel Leys Prim Sch NN18 36 D4
Hazel Rd NN15 72 C1
Hazelwood NN12 214 C4
Hazelwood Ct 1 NN16 72 B1
Hazelwood La NN16 72 B1
Hazelwood Rd
Corby NN17 36 E7
Northampton NN1 159 D5
Headingley Rd NN10 132 D2
Headlands
Desborough NN14 51 C3
Kettering NN15 91 B8
Headlands Prim Sch NN3 142 C2
Headlands The
Market Harborough LE16 31 F4
Northampton NN3 142 C2
Wellingborough NN8 129 F6
Headway NN18 53 A8
Healey Cl NN3 143 D4
Hearndon Ct NN8 129 E3
Hearth St LE16 31 D3
Heart Of The Shires Sh Village NN7 136 F2
Heathcote Gr NN14 50 E4
HEATHENCOTE 204 A3
Heatherbreea Gdns NN10 131 F3
Heather Ct
Northampton NN4 159 A2
Rushden NN10 132 A2
Heatherdale Way NN2 141 E3
Heather La NN3 142 E4
Heather Rd NN16 72 D4
Heathers The NN29 146 E2
Heathfield Way NN5 141 A1
Heathfield Wlk NN18 36 B4
Heath Gn NN5 140 F1
Heath Rise NN8 129 D6
Heath Terr NN12 203 C6
Heathville NN5 140 F1
Heath Way
Burton Latimer NN15 92 C3
Rugby CV22 98 D8
H E Bates Way NN10 132 A2
Hecham Way NN10 132 B7
Hedge End NN4 175 C6
Hedgely Ct NN4 159 A2
Hedgerow Dr NN2 141 A5
Hedgerow La NN14 89 C5
Hedgerow Way NN11 135 C6
Hedges The NN10 132 C4
Hedgeway NN4 175 C6
HELLIDON 151 D1
Hellidon Cl NN2 141 E4
Hellidon Rd CV47 166 D7
HELMDON 211 F4
Helmdon Cres NN2 141 C4
Helmdon Prim Sch NN13 211 F4
Helmdon Rd
Greatworth OX17 210 E2
Northampton NN2 141 C5
Sulgrave OX17 210 F7
Wappenham NN12 213 A8
Weston NN12 199 F2
Helmsley Way NN18 36 B5
Hemans Rd NN11 135 B3
Hembury Pl NN4 158 F3
Hemery Way NN15 90 F8
HEMINGTON 60 E7
Hemington Rd PE8 42 F2
Hemmingwell Rd NN8 130 A7
Hempland Cl NN18 53 B8
Hemplow Dr NN6 64 B2
Henders MK11 229 E5
Henley Cl
Kettering NN15 91 F5
Wellingborough NN8 129 C6
Henley Ct NN6 120 C6
Henley Ho NN17 36 E6
Henry Bird Ct NN4 159 D4
Henry Bird Way NN4 159 D4
Henry Chichele Prim Sch NN10 132 B7
Henry Gotch Prim Sch NN15 72 D1
Henry Smith Ho 2 NN11 135 B3
Henry St NN1 159 E7
Henshaw Rd NN8 129 E3
Hensmans La NN29 164 D3
Henson Cl NN16 71 F5
Henson Pk NN16 71 F5
Henson Way NN16 71 E4
Herbert Gdns NN12 203 D8
Herbert St NN1 159 C6
Hereford Cl NN14 51 C4
Hereward Rd NN4 159 B2
Herford Cl NN18 36 A2
Heritage Ct NN16 72 B1
Heritage Way
Corby NN17 22 B2
Raunds NN9 114 E7
Hermitage Rd LE16 33 E3
Hermitage Way NN4 175 D7
Herne Hill Ct NN4 158 E2
Herne Rd PE8 42 B4
Heron Ave NN14 76 E3
Heron Cl
Burton Latimer NN15 92 A2
Hinton NN11 184 B6
Towcester NN12 203 C3
Wellingborough NN8 130 A7
Heron Ct NN11 135 C3
Heron Dr NN13 222 D1
Heronsford NN4 174 E8
Herons Wood Cl PE8 41 E5
Herrieffs Farm Rd NN13 233 F6
Herriotts Ct 11 NN8 130 A5
Herriotts La NN8 130 A5
Hertford Ct
Daventry NN11 153 C7
Northampton NN3 143 A1
Hertford Rd NN15 91 C6
Hervey Cl NN3 142 D2
Hervey St NN1 159 E7
Hesketh Cres NN12 203 C4
Hesketh Rd NN12 217 E6
Hesperus NN8 129 B4
Hester St NN2 159 C8
Hever Cl
Rushden NN10 148 C8
Thrapston NN14 76 E2
Hewlett's Cl NN29 164 D2
Hexham Ct NN4 159 A2
Heyford Rd NN5 157 F7
Heygate St LE16 31 E4
Hiawatha NN8 129 B4
Hibiscus Cl NN3 160 C6
Hickman Cl OX17 210 D2
Hickmire NN29 146 D3
Hicks Ct NN12 203 D4
Hicks Rd NN12 203 C4
Hidcote Cl
Corby NN18 36 E2
Northampton NN4 175 C7
Wellingborough NN8 129 D2
Hidcote Way 3 NN11 135 B7
Hield Cl NN18 36 C1
Higgins Sq NN4 158 F2
HIGHAM CROSS 206 D3
Higham Cross Rd MK19 206 E4
HIGHAM FERRERS 132 D6
Higham Ferrers Jun & Inf Schs NN10 132 B6
Higham Park Rd NN10 149 A5
Higham Rd
Burton Latimer NN15 92 C1
Chelveston NN9 133 B7
Little Irchester NN8, NN29 130 D1
Rushden NN10 132 B4
Stanwick NN9 113 F3
High Barns Cl NN4 175 E2
Highbridge Rd NN12 213 A8
Highbrook NN18 36 B4
Highcroft LE17 45 E6
Highcroft Cl NN12 217 E6
Highcross St LE16 31 C3
Highdown Cl NN4 158 E3
Highfield
Duddington PE9 5 B7
Woodford NN14 94 C7
Highfield Cotts LE15 3 E8
Highfield Court Mews NN13 233 E6
Highfield Cres NN15 91 C6
Highfield Ct NN13 233 E6
Highfield Gr NN17 36 F7
Highfield Pk NN6 104 D4
Highfield Rd
Daventry NN11 135 B3
Irthlingborough NN9 112 F2
Kettering NN15 91 B7
Mears Ashby NN6 128 C4
Northampton NN1 142 A1
Rushden NN10 131 F1
Thrapston NN14 76 E2
Wellingborough NN8 130 B5
Highfields
Polebrook PE8 42 F3
Towcester NN12 203 C3
Highfields Com Prim Sch NN15 91 B7
Highfield St
Finedon NN9 112 B5
Market Harborough LE16 31 D3
Highfield Way NN7 179 B6
HIGHGATE 28 D8
Highgate Gn PE8 28 D8
High Gn NN2 141 B3
High Greeve NN4 176 A6
Highgrove Ct 2 NN10 132 B2
High Hill Ave NN14 70 C7
Highlands Ave NN3 142 A4
Highlands Dr NN11 135 B5
High Leys The NN6 100 F4
High March NN11 153 E8
High March Cl NN11 153 E8
Highpoint NN13 233 F5
High St Mews 4 NN8 129 F4
High St N NN12 189 D5
High St Pl NN8 129 F4
High St S
Olney MK46 195 F3
Rushden NN10 132 B1
Tiffield NN12 189 D4
High St The NN6 103 D1
High Slade NN6 125 C8
High St
Adderbury OX17 230 A4
Astcote NN12 188 F7
Blakesley NN12 187 A1
Blisworth NN7 190 D7
Bozeat NN29 164 D2
Brackley NN13 233 F7
Braunston NN11 118 B1
Brigstock NN14 55 F8
Brixworth NN6 106 B3
Broughton NN14 90 A4
Bugbrooke NN7 172 F7
Burton Latimer NN15 92 C2
Byfield NN11 183 D7
Charwelton NN11 168 A4
High St *continued*
Chelveston NN9 133 C8
Clipston LE16 67 A8
Collyweston PE9 1 D2
Corby NN17 37 A6
Cottingham LE16 20 C1
Cranford St John NN14 93 A6
Creaton NN6 104 F4
Crick NN6 100 F5
Croughton NN13 238 C8
Culworth OX17 198 C3
Daventry NN11 135 C2
Deanshanger MK19 228 E4
Denford NN14 95 C6
Desborough NN14 51 A3
Duddington PE9 5 B6
Earls Barton NN6 144 E4
Easton o t H PE9 2 A5
Ecton NN6 143 F3
Everdon NN11 170 A8
Eydon NN11 184 C1
Finedon NN9 111 F5
Flore NN7 155 E5
Gayton NN7 173 E2
Great Doddington NN7 145 E6
Great Easton LE16 20 D7
Great Houghton NN4 160 E2
Greens Norton NN12 202 D8
Gretton NN17 10 C1
Guilsborough NN6 103 F6
Hanslope MK19 207 A2
Harpole NN7 157 C6
Harrington NN6 69 A5
Higham Ferrers NN10 132 B5
Husbands Bosworth LE17 45 E5
Irchester NN29 147 B8
Irthlingborough NN9 112 E2
Islip NN14 76 B2
Kettering NN16 72 B2
Ketton PE9 1 A6
Kislingbury NN7 157 D4
Lamport NN6 87 D2
Little Addington NN14 113 B8
Long Buckby NN6 121 C4
Market Harborough LE16 31 E3
Middleton Cheney OX17 219 F8
Milton Malsor NN7 174 E4
Morcott LE15 3 A6
Moulton NN3 126 C1
Naseby NN6 85 B8
Northampton, Collingtree NN4 175 C4
Northampton, Great Billing NN3 143 C2
Northampton, Hardingstone NN4 175 F8
Northampton, Kingsthorpe NN2 141 B3
Northampton, Weston Favell NN3 142 D1
Northampton, Wootton NN4 175 E6
Olney MK46 195 F4
Paulerspury NN12 216 C8
Pitsford NN6 125 C4
Podington NN29 147 E2
Potterspury NN12 217 D3
Preston Capes NN11 169 D2
Pytchley NN14 90 F2
Raunds NN9 114 D7
Ringstead NN14 95 B3
Roade NN7 191 D4
Rothwell NN14 70 C7
Rugby CV21 99 A8
Rushden NN10 132 B2
Rushton NN14 52 C2
Scaldwell NN6 106 F5
Shutlanger NN12 190 D1
Silverstone NN12 214 D4
Souldern OX27 237 E3
Spratton NN6 105 B1
Stanion NN14 37 E2
Stanwick NN9 113 F3
Stony Stratford MK11 229 D6
Swinford LE17 62 B3
Syresham NN13 224 B8
Thrapston NN14 76 D2
Titchmarsh NN14 77 D4
Twywell NN14 74 F1
Walgrave NN6 108 A5
Wappenham NN12 213 B8
Weedon Bec NN7 155 B4
Weedon Lois NN12 200 C2
Weldon NN17 38 B8
Welford NN6 64 E6
Wellingborough NN8 129 F5
Welton NN11 119 E1
West Haddon NN6 102 C4
Weston NN12 199 F2
Weston Underwood MK46 195 B2
Whittlebury NN12 215 C4
Wollaston NN29 146 D2
Woodford Halse NN11 184 C6
Woodford NN14 94 D7
Wymington NN10 148 B5
Yardley Gobion NN12 217 F6
Yardley Hastings NN7 179 B6
Yelvertoft NN6 82 B3
High Stack NN6 121 C3
High View
Deanshanger MK19 228 E5
Northampton NN4 175 E6

High Woods NN6 . . . . . .143 D8
Hilda Pl NN16 . . . . 72 E4
Hillary Cl NN11 . . . . .135 B5
Hillary Rd NN10 . . . . .131 F1
Hillberry Rise NN3 . . . . .143 D4
Hill Cl
 Northampton NN5 . . . . .140 C2
 Walgrave NN6 . . . . . . .107 F5
Hill Crest NN7 . . . . .174 C1
Hillcrest Ave
 Burton Latimer NN15 . . . 92 B5
 Kettering NN15 . . . . 72 D1
 Market Harborough
 LE16 . . . . 31 D4
 Northampton NN3 . . . . .142 A3
Hillcrest Cl NN14 . . . . 76 E3
Hillcrest La LE17 . . . . 45 E5
Hillcrest Rd NN7 . . . . . . .173 E1
Hillcroft View NN12 . . . . .187 B1
Hilldrop Rd NN8 . . . . . . .175 B7
Hill Farm Est NN14 . . . . .113 C7
Hill Farm Rise NN4 . . . . .175 A8
Hillfield Rd PE8 . . . . 41 E6
Hill Gdns LE16 . . . . 31 C3
Hill Ho OX17 . . . . .219 C6
Hill House Ct NN12 . . . . .172 D1
Hill House Gdns NN9 . . . .113 F3
Hillmorton La
 Clifton u D CV23 . . . . . . 80 A4
 Lilbourne CV23 . . . . 80 F5
 Yelvertoft NN6 . . . . 82 A4
Hillmorton Prim Sch
 CV21 . . . . 99 B8
Hill Rd NN11 . . . . .182 C5
Hill Row NN11 . . . . .134 C8
Hillside
 Chelveston NN9 . . . . . .133 B8
 Daventry NN11 . . . . . . .135 E2
 Great Harrowden NN9 . .110 E4
 Hartwell NN7 . . . . .192 D2
 West Haddon NN6 . . . . .102 B4
Hillside Ave
 Kettering NN15 . . . . 91 C8
 Silverstone NN12 . . . . .214 E5
Hillside Cl NN29 . . . . . . .164 D2
Hillside Cotts PE28 . . . . . 97 A4
Hillside Cres
 Nether Heyford NN7 . . .156 C1
 Weldon NN17 . . . . 38 A7
Hillside Rd
 Flore NN7 . . . . .155 D6
 Market Harborough LE16 . 31 F4
 Nether Heyford NN7 . . .156 C1
 Piddington NN7 . . . . . . .177 B1
 Wellingborough NN8 . . .130 C7
Hillside Terr NN16 . . . . . . 72 A2
Hillside Way NN3 . . . . . . .160 C8
Hill St
 Brackley NN13 . . . . .233 F7
 Kettering NN16 . . . . 72 A3
 Raunds NN9 . . . . .114 D6
 Wellingborough NN8 . . .129 F4
Hillstone Ct NN9 . . . . . . .113 F3
Hill The
 Aynho OX17 . . . . .237 C7
 Great Houghton NN4 . . .160 E2
 Middleton LE16 . . . . 35 B8
 Pury End NN12 . . . . . . .215 F7
 Syresham NN13 . . . . . . .224 B8
Hilltop
 Blisworth NN7 . . . . .174 C1
 Dodford NN7 . . . . .154 F5
 Great Harrowden NN9 . .110 E5
HILL TOP 141 D4
Hill Top NN2 . . . . .141 D4
Hilltop Ave
 Desborough NN14 . . . . . 50 F4
 Kettering NN15 . . . . 91 F5
Hilltop Rd
 Brixworth NN6 . . . . . . .106 B1
 Desborough NN14 . . . . . 50 F4
Hill Top Rd NN9 . . . . . . .110 D4
Hill View NN11 . . . . .184 C1
Hilmorton Rd CV22 . . . . . 98 F8
Hind Stile NN10 . . . . .132 B5
HINTON 184 A6
Hinton Ave NN18 . . . . 36 A4
Hinton Cl
 Hinton NN11 . . . . .184 B6
 Northampton NN2 . . . . .141 C5
HINTON-IN-THE-HEDGES
 . . . . .232 F6
Hinton Manor Ct
 NN11 . . . . .184 B6
Hinton Rd
 Brackley NN13 . . . . .233 E6
 Hinton NN11 . . . . .184 B5
 Northampton NN2 . . . . .141 C5
Hinton's Cl NN13 . . . . . . .211 F3
HINWICK 165 D7
Hinwick Cl NN15 . . . . 91 F5
Hinwick Hall Coll of F Ed
 NN29 . . . . .147 C1
Hinwick Rd
 Podington NN29 . . . . . .147 D1
 Wollaston NN29 . . . . . .146 E1
Hipwell Ct NN4 . . . . .175 E7
Hirondelle Cl NN5 . . . . . .139 F1
Hobbs Hill NN14 . . . . 70 C6
Hobby Cl NN4 . . . . .175 B8
Hocknell Cl NN14 . . . . . .175 F6
Hockney Ave NN15 . . . . . 92 A7
Hodge Cl NN12 . . . . .188 F6
Hodges La NN7 . . . . .157 D4
Hodge Way NN16 . . . . 72 D2

Hodnet Cl NN4 . . . . .175 C7
Hoe Way NN7 . . . . .191 C4
Hogarth Cl NN8 . . . . .129 F7
Hogarth Dr NN15 . . . . 92 A7
Hogarth Wlk NN18 . . . . . . 36 E5
Hogg End OX17 . . . . .196 F6
Hogg La OX17 . . . . .231 F5
Holback La MK18 . . . . . . .226 A5
Holbein Gdns NN4 . . . . . .174 E8
Holbein Wlk NN18 . . . . . . 36 D5
Holbush Way NN9 . . . . . .112 E3
HOLCOT 126 E8
Holcot Cl NN8 . . . . .129 E8
Holcot La
 Scaldwell NN6 . . . . . . .107 A5
 Sywell NN6 . . . . .127 E4
Holcot Leys CV22 . . . . . . 98 A7
Holcot Rd
 Brixworth NN6 . . . . . . .106 D2
 Moulton NN3 . . . . .126 C5
 Walgrave NN6 . . . . . . .107 F4
Holcutt Cl NN4 . . . . .175 F7
HOLDENBY 123 D3
Holdenby
 Holdenby NN6 . . . . . . .123 D4
 Kettering NN15 . . . . 91 D5
Holdenby Cl LE16 . . . . . . 32 B3
Holdenby House Gdns &
 Falconry Ctr ★ ⁴ NN6 . .123 C4
Holdenby Rd
 East Haddon NN6 . . . . .122 E5
 Northampton NN2 . . . . .141 E4
 Spratton NN6 . . . . .124 B8
Holdgate Ct NN13 . . . . . .222 E1
Holes La MK46 . . . . .195 F4
Holiday La MK19 . . . . . . .206 F4
Holkham Cl NN18 . . . . . . 36 D2
Holland Rise OX17 . . . . . .230 F4
Hollands Dr NN15 . . . . . . 92 C2
Hollies The
 Higham Ferrers NN10 . . .132 B5
 Moulton NN3 . . . . .126 B2
 Wellingborough NN8 . . .129 E5
Hollingside Dr NN2 . . . . .141 F3
Hollington Rd NN9 . . . . . .114 D6
Holloway The CV47 . . . . .166 D7
Hollow Bank NN3 . . . . . .142 C6
HOLLOWELL 104 B5
Hollowell Cl NN10 . . . . . .148 D8
Hollowell Ct ³ NN8 . . . . .129 F4
Hollowell Rd NN14 . . . . . .104 E4
Hollow The
 Ravensthorpe NN6 . . . . .103 E1
 Stanwick NN9 . . . . .114 A3
Hollow Way
 Aynho OX17 . . . . .237 C7
 Eydon NN11 . . . . .184 B1
Hollow Wood MK46 . . . . .195 E3
Holly Bush La CV47 . . . . .166 D7
Holly Cl
 Brackley NN13 . . . . .222 F1
 Market Harborough LE16 . 31 E4
Hollyhill NN12 . . . . .203 B4
Holly La NN14 . . . . 90 A6
Holly Lodge Dr NN2 . . . . .141 D6
Holly Rd
 Kettering NN16 . . . . 72 C4
 Northampton NN1 . . . . .159 F8
 Rushden NN10 . . . . . . .131 E3
Holly Wlk NN9 . . . . .111 D4
Holman Cl NN3 . . . . .142 D2
Holm Cl NN7 . . . . .155 A2
Holme Cl
 Wellingborough NN9 . . .110 E1
 Wilbarston LE16 . . . . 34 D5
Holmecross Rd NN3 . . . . .142 E5
Holmes Ave NN9 . . . . . . .114 E5
Holmes Dr PE9 . . . . 1 B5
Holme Way CV23 . . . . 99 D1
Holmfield Dr NN9 . . . . . .114 E6
Holmfield Terr NN16 . . . . .121 A4
Holmfield Way NN3 . . . . .160 C8
Holmfirth Wlk NN18 . . . . . 36 C4
Holmleigh Ct NN15 . . . . .158 C7
Holmwood Cl NN5 . . . . . .140 A1
Holt Rd LE16 . . . . 19 C8
Holt View LE16 . . . . 20 D7
Holyoake Rd NN29 . . . . . .146 D2
Holyoake Terr NN6 . . . . . .121 C4
Holyrood Ct NN5 . . . . . . .158 F7
Holyrood Rd NN5 . . . . . . .158 F7
Holyrood Wlk NN18 . . . . . 36 C3
Home Acre NN7 . . . . .161 B4
Home Cl
 Blisworth NN7 . . . . .190 D7
 Corby NN18 . . . . 36 B1
 Dingley NN16 . . . . 33 A3
 Eastcote NN12 . . . . . . .188 F8
 Greens Norton NN12 . . .202 D8
 Irthlingborough NN9 . . .131 E8
 Middleton Cheney
 OX17 . . . . .220 B8
 Northampton NN4 . . . . .175 C2
 Silverstone NN12 . . . . .214 D4
 Staverton NN11 . . . . . . .152 C8
 Towcester NN12 . . . . . .203 C5
Home Ct NN14 . . . . 76 D2
Home Farm OX17 . . . . . . .219 E7
Home Farm Cl
 Corby NN18 . . . . 53 B8
 Creaton NN6 . . . . .104 F5
 East Farndon LE16 . . . . . 48 B7
 Northampton NN3 . . . . .161 B8
 Weedon Bec NN7 . . . . .154 F2
Home Farm Ct
 Adderbury OX17 . . . . . .230 B4
 Norton NN11 . . . . .136 C4

Home Farm Gr LE16 . . . . . 68 C7
Home Farm La NN5 . . . . .125 C4
Home Farm Rd NN14 . . . . . 37 E2
Home Farm Yd NN6 . . . . .104 B5
Homefield NN11 . . . . .153 C8
Homestead Cl NN3 . . . . . .126 D1
Homestead Ct NN2 . . . . . .141 E1
Homestead Dr NN7 . . . . . .173 A7
Homestead Rise NN14 . . . . 74 E6
Homestead The NN14 . . . . 74 F1
Homestead Way
 Northampton NN2 . . . . .141 E1
 Potterspury NN12 . . . . .217 E3
Homewelland Ho LE16 . . . . 31 D4
Honey Hill Dr MK19 . . . . .228 E5
Honey Holme NN6 . . . . . .106 A1
Honeypot La LE17 . . . . 45 E5
Honeystones NN3 . . . . . . .126 C1
Honeysuckle Rd NN14 . . . . 51 A5
Honeysuckle Way
 NN3 . . . . .160 C6
Honiton Gdns NN18 . . . . . 36 E4
Hood Cl NN17 . . . . 36 B8
Hood Rd NN11 . . . . .135 C1
Hood St NN1 . . . . .159 E7
Hood Wlk NN15 . . . . 91 D8
Hookhams Path NN29 . . . .146 E2
Hopes Pl NN2 . . . . .141 B3
Hope St NN29 . . . . .164 D4
Hopmeadow Ct ²
 NN3 . . . . .143 B4
Hoppet Cl NN18 . . . . 53 A8
HOPPING HILL 140 C1
Hopping Hill Gdns
 NN5 . . . . .140 D1
Hopping Hill Prim Sch
 NN5 . . . . .158 C8
Hopton Cl NN11 . . . . .135 D6
Hopton Fields LE16 . . . . . 48 D8
Hornbeam Cl
 Podington NN29 . . . . . .147 E2
 Wellingborough NN8 . . .129 E5
Hornbeam Ct
 Desborough NN14 . . . . . 51 D3
 Northampton NN3 . . . . .142 D3
Hornby Rd NN6 . . . . .144 E5
Horncastle Cl NN11 . . . . .135 C6
Horne Cl CV21 . . . . 99 B8
Horn La MK11 . . . . .229 D5
Horrell Ct NN10 . . . . .132 A2
Horrock's Way NN15 . . . . . 72 F1
Horsefair Ct LE16 . . . . 31 D4
Horsefair Gn MK11 . . . . . .229 D5
Horse La NN11 . . . . 11 F5
Horselease Cl NN18 . . . . . 53 A8
Horse Market
 Kettering NN16 . . . . 72 B2
 Northampton NN1 . . . . .159 C6
Horsemoor Sq ⁶
 NN3 . . . . .143 C2
Horsepool The CV23 . . . . . 81 A7
Horseshoe Cl
 Brixworth NN6 . . . . . . .106 C2
 Creaton NN6 . . . . .104 F4
Horse Shoe La LE16 . . . . . 32 B6
Horseshoe St NN1 . . . . . .159 C5
Horse Well Ct NN3 . . . . . .142 C7
Horsham Wlk NN18 . . . . . 36 B5
Horsley Rd NN2 . . . . .141 C1
HORTON 177 D1
Horton Cl OX17 . . . . .220 A8
Horton Cres OX17 . . . . . . .220 A8
Horton Dr OX17 . . . . .220 A8
Horton Pk NN7 . . . . .177 E2
Horton Rd
 Brafield-on-t-G NN7 . . . .177 D7
 Hackleton NN7 . . . . . . .177 C2
 Middleton Cheney
 OX17 . . . . .220 A7
Hortonsfield Rd NN12 . . . .217 F5
Hortons' La NN14 . . . . 76 D2
Hoskyn Cl OX17 . . . . 98 F8
Hospital Bungalow
 NN6 . . . . .126 D7
Hospital Hill NN14 . . . . . . 70 D7
Hothorpe Rd LE17 . . . . . . 46 D8
Houghton Hill NN4 . . . . . .160 A1
Hove Rd NN10 . . . . .132 C2
Hove St NN18 . . . . 36 B4
Howard Ave NN17 . . . . . . 36 B7
Howard Biley Gdns
 NN3 . . . . .142 C3
Howard Cl NN11 . . . . .135 D1
Howard Ct ³ NN8 . . . . . . .130 B5
Howard La NN2 . . . . .141 C8
Howard Rd NN29 . . . . . . .146 D2
Howard's Ct NN29 . . . . . .146 D2
Howards Mdw PE8 . . . . . . 13 F7
Howard St NN16 . . . . 72 A2
Howard Way LE16 . . . . 31 D1
Howcut La NN7 . . . . .178 E3
Howden Gn NN14 . . . . 50 E4
Howe Cres
 Corby NN17 . . . . 36 A7
 Daventry NN11 . . . . . . .135 E1
Hoxton Cl NN3 . . . . .142 E6
Hoylake NN8 . . . . .129 C7
Hoylake Dr NN2 . . . . .141 F3
Hoy Wlk NN17 . . . . 21 C1
Hubble Rd NN17 . . . . 21 F1
Hudson Cl
 Corby NN18 . . . . 36 C3
 Daventry NN11 . . . . . . .135 C5
Hudson Dr NN4 . . . . .158 E1
HULCOTE 189 F1
Hulcote NN12 . . . . .203 F8
Hulme Way NN8 . . . . .129 C6

Humber Cl
 Daventry NN11 . . . . . . .134 F4
 Northampton NN5 . . . . .140 F2
Humber Gdns NN8 . . . . . .129 C6
Humber Wlk NN17 . . . . . . 21 D2
Humfrey La NN2 . . . . .141 C8
Humphries Dr NN13 . . . . .233 D8
Hunsbarrow Rd NN4 . . . . .158 E4
Hunsbury Cl NN11 . . . . . .158 F1
Hunsbury Gn NN4 . . . . . .158 D2
HUNSBURY HILL 158 F1*
Hunsbury Hill Ave
 NN4 . . . . .158 E3
Hunsbury Hill Ctry Pk★
 NN4 . . . . .158 F1
Hunsbury Hill Rd
 NN4 . . . . .158 D1
Hunsbury Ironstone
 Railway Mus★ ⁴ NN4 . . .158 E2
Hunsbury Park Prim Sch
 NN4 . . . . .158 F2
Hunslet La NN4 . . . . .158 E2
Hunt Cl
 Brixworth NN6 . . . . . . .106 B2
 Towcester NN12 . . . . . .203 C7
 Wellingborough NN8 . . .129 F8
Hunters Cl
 Husbands Bosworth
 LE17 . . . . 45 E6
 Northampton NN2 . . . . .141 D6
Hunters Rd NN17 . . . . 22 F1
Hunter St NN1 . . . . .159 D7
Hunters' Way NN6 . . . . . .106 B2
HUNTGATE END 206 D2
Huntingdon Cl NN18 . . . . . 36 E1
Huntingdon Gdns LE16 . . . 31 E1
Huntingdon Rd NN14 . . . . . 76 E2
Hunting Way PE8 . . . . 14 C4
Huntsham Cl NN3 . . . . . .160 D7
Huntsmead NN3 . . . . . . .143 D4
Hunt St NN16 . . . . 36 D5
Hurst Cl NN15 . . . . 92 C4
HUSBANDS BOSWORTH
 . . . . 45 D5
Husbands Bosworth CE
 Prim Sch LE17 . . . . 45 E5
Hussar Cl NN11 . . . . .135 B1
Hutchinson Ave NN14 . . . . 90 B3
Hutts Cl NN11 . . . . .183 D7
Huxley Cl NN8 . . . . .129 A4
Huxloe Rise NN3 . . . . . . .142 E6
Huxlow Science Coll
 NN9 . . . . .112 E3
Hyacinth Way NN10 . . . . .148 B7
Hyde Dr NN7 . . . . .191 C4
Hyde Dr NN9 . . . . .112 A5
Hyde Rd NN7 . . . . .191 C4

I

Ibsen Wlk NN18 . . . . 36 A2
Ibstock Cl NN3 . . . . .143 A6
Icknield Dr NN4 . . . . .158 E1
Ickworth Cl ¹² NN11 . . . . .135 B7
Ideal Bldgs ¹⁷ NN1 . . . . . .159 C7
Ilex Cl NN4 . . . . .159 F1
Ilmor Ave NN6 . . . . .106 C3
Imperial Ct NN10 . . . . . . .132 A2
Independent St CV23 . . . .100 A3
Indmere Cl NN4 . . . . .158 C1
Ingleborough Way
 NN5 . . . . .158 D8
Inglewood Ct NN3 . . . . . .143 C1
Inham Cl NN18 . . . . 36 C2
Inkerman Way PE8 . . . . . . 41 F5
Inlands Cl NN11 . . . . .135 D1
Inlands Rise NN11 . . . . . .135 D1
Inlands The NN11 . . . . . . .135 D1
Inn Yard Ct LE16 . . . . 68 C3
Insignia Cl ⁷ NN4 . . . . . . .175 E7
Inwood Cl NN18 . . . . 36 C2
io Centre The NN5 . . . . . .140 C2
Iona Rd NN17 . . . . 36 C8
IRCHESTER 147 B7
Irchester Com Prim Sch
 NN29 . . . . .147 A8
Irchester Country Pk
 Trail ★ NN29 . . . . .130 D1
Irchester Country Pk
 Visitor Ctr★ NN29 . . . .130 D1
Irchester Cry Pk★
 NN29 . . . . .130 F1
Irchester Narrow Gauge
 Rly Mus★ ⁴ NN8 . . . . . .130 D1
Irchester Rd
 Podington NN10 . . . . . .147 B4
 Rushden NN10 . . . . . . .131 F2
 Wollaston NN29 . . . . . .146 F3
Irchester Turn NN29 . . . . .131 A2
Ireton Rd LE16 . . . . 31 E1
Iron Cross NN11 . . . . .167 B2
Irondale Cl NN4 . . . . .158 E3
Iron Duke Cl NN11 . . . . . .135 B4
Iron Pikes NN6 . . . . .106 C1
Ironstone Ct NN9 . . . . . . .111 F4
Ironstone La NN4 . . . . . . .158 E3
Ironstone Way NN6 . . . . . .106 C3
Ironwood Ave NN14 . . . . . 51 A4
IRTHLINGBOROUGH 112 D2
Irthlingborough Inf Sch
 NN9 . . . . .112 D2
Irthlingborough Jun Sch
 NN9 . . . . .112 D2
Irthlingborough Rd
 Finedon NN9 . . . . .112 B4
 Little Addington NN14 . . .113 B7
 Wellingborough NN8 . . .130 E4

Irvine Dr NN12 . . . . .203 D8
Irving St NN17 . . . . 36 E8
Isebrook Ct NN15 . . . . 92 A2
Isebrook Hospl NN8 . . . . .130 B3
Isebrook Sch NN15 . . . . . . 91 E7
Ise Com Coll NN15 . . . . . . 72 D1
Ise Rd NN15 . . . . 72 C1
Ise Vale Ave NN14 . . . . . . 51 B3
Ise View Rd NN14 . . . . 51 B3
ISHAM 91 E1
Isham CE Prim Sch
 NN14 . . . . 91 F1
Isham Cl NN2 . . . . .141 D5
Isham Rd
 Orlingbury NN14 . . . . . .110 A5
 Pytchley NN14 . . . . 91 B3
Islay Wlk NN17 . . . . 36 C1
Isley Valley Ind Est
 NN8 . . . . .130 D7
Islington NN14 . . . . 77 B4
Islington Ct NN12 . . . . . . .203 D5
Islington Rd NN12 . . . . . .203 D5
ISLIP 76 B3
Ivens La NN12 . . . . .171 C1
Ivy Ct NN11 . . . . .135 B1
Ivydene Terr NN14 . . . . . . 90 A4
Ivy La NN9 . . . . .111 F4
Ivy Rd
 Kettering NN16 . . . . 72 D4
 Northampton NN1 . . . . .159 F8
Ixworth Cl NN3 . . . . .142 F5

J

Jackdaw NN3 . . . . .161 C8
Jacklin Ct NN8 . . . . .129 C7
Jack Parnell Cl NN5 . . . . .158 B6
Jackson Cl
 Market Harborough
 LE16 . . . . 48 E8
 Northampton NN2 . . . . .141 E6
Jackson Rd CV21 . . . . 80 A1
Jackson's La NN8 . . . . . . .129 F5
Jackson's Lane Flats ¹
 NN8 . . . . .129 F5
Jackson Way NN15 . . . . . . 90 F8
Jacorrin Cl NN2 . . . . .141 E6
Jacques Rd NN15 . . . . 92 C1
Jamb The NN17 . . . . 37 A6
James Lewis Ct NN3 . . . . .142 C2
James Rd NN8 . . . . .130 A2
James St NN29 . . . . .147 B7
James Watt Ave NN17 . . . . 37 A8
James Watt Cl NN11 . . . . .135 A4
Jardine Cl NN3 . . . . .142 D1
Jarretts Yd NN4 . . . . .175 D4
Jarvis Ct NN13 . . . . .233 F8
Jasmine Ct NN16 . . . . 72 D5
Jasmine Gdns NN10 . . . . .148 B7
Jasmine Ho NN4 . . . . .159 A2
Jasmine Rd
 Kettering NN16 . . . . 72 D4
 Northampton NN3 . . . . .143 C5
Jasper Wlk NN3 . . . . .142 D6
Javelin Cl NN5 . . . . .158 C8
Jay Rd NN18 . . . . 36 E3
JBJ Bsns Pk NN7 . . . . . . .174 D2
Jean Rd NN16 . . . . 72 E3
Jellicoe Cl NN11 . . . . .135 E1
Jenkinson Rd NN12 . . . . . .203 D4
Jenkins Rd CV21 . . . . 80 A1
Jenner Cres NN2 . . . . .141 B5
Jennings Cl
 ⁴ Daventry NN11 . . . . . .135 D1
 Higham Ferrers NN10 . . .132 B5
Jersey Cl NN8 . . . . .130 B6
Jersey Ct NN3 . . . . .142 F1
Jervis Cl NN11 . . . . .135 E1
Jerwood Way LE16 . . . . . . 31 F2
Jesus Hospl NN14 . . . . 70 D7
Jetty The
 Creaton NN6 . . . . .104 F4
 Hackleton NN7 . . . . . . .177 B3
 Wappenham NN12 . . . . .213 B8
 Wardington OX17 . . . . .196 E1
Jeyes Cl NN3 . . . . .126 B1
Jibwood NN14 . . . . 89 B5
Jitty The NN14 . . . . 89 B4
Joan Pyel Cl NN9 . . . . . . .131 E8
Job's Yd NN15 . . . . 72 B2
John Beverly Mews
 NN14 . . . . 70 C6
John Clare Cl NN13 . . . . .222 F1
John Clare Ct NN16 . . . . . 72 C6
John Clare Way NN17 . . . . 36 D8
John Clark Way NN10 . . . .132 C3
John Eagle Cl NN9 . . . . . .113 F4
John Gray Rd NN29 . . . . .145 D6
John Hellins Prim Sch
 NN12 . . . . .217 D3
John Lea Way NN8 . . . . . .130 A1
John Pyel Rd NN9 . . . . . .112 E1
John Smith Ave NN14 . . . . 70 E7
Johnson Ave
 Brackley NN13 . . . . .233 C8
 Wellingborough NN8 . . .130 A1
Johnson Cl NN11 . . . . . . .135 B3
Johnson Ct NN4 . . . . .159 D4
Johnsons Field MK46 . . . .195 E4
Johns Rd NN7 . . . . .157 A1
John St
 Rushden NN10 . . . . . . .132 B2
 Thrapston NN14 . . . . . . 76 C2
John White Cl The
 NN10 . . . . .132 C6
Jones Cl NN13 . . . . .233 D8
Jordan Cl LE16 . . . . 32 A3

Joseph Priestle y Ct **6**
NN15 . . . . 135 C1
Joshua Sq NN4 . . . . 158 F2
Jowett Cl NN15 . . . . 92 A8
Jubilee Ave NN18 . . . . . . 36 D5
Jubilee Cl
  Byfield NN11 . . . . 183 D7
  Islip NN14 . . . . 76 B3
  Long Buckby NN6 . . . . . 121 A4
  Northampton NN4 . . . . . 158 F3
Jubilee Cres NN8 . . . . . 129 F2
Jubilee Ct PE8 . . . . 39 E7
Jubilee Dr NN6 . . . . 108 B5
Jubilee Gdns
  Market Harborough
  LE16 . . . . 31 F4
  Rushden NN10 . . . . 148 C8
Jubilee Rd NN11 . . . . . . 135 B2
Jubilee St
  Irthlingborough NN9 . . . 112 E1
  Rothwell NN14 . . . . 70 D6
Jubilee Terr
  Isham NN14 . . . . 110 F8
  Stony Stratford MK11 . . 229 E5
Judes Ct NN15 . . . . 72 A1
Judges Ct NN6 . . . . 104 F4
Judith Rd NN16 . . . . 72 E4
Julian Way NN2 . . . . 141 A3
Junction Rd NN2 . . . . . . 141 E1
Juniper Cl NN12 . . . . . . 203 B4
Juniper Ct NN3 . . . . 143 D3
JUNIPER HILL 239 E6
Juniper Thorn NN6 . . . . 106 C1
Jura Cl NN17 . . . . 36 B8
Justin Park Cvn Site
  LE16 . . . . 48 F7
Jutland Way NN16 . . . . . 72 A2

K

K2 Ho NN5 . . . . 141 A1
Kane Wlk NN17 . . . . 36 E8
Kangaroo Spinney
  NN8 . . . . 130 E3
Karlstad Cl NN18 . . . . . . 36 A2
Kathleen Dr NN16 . . . . . 72 E4
Katrine Cl NN17 . . . . 21 B1
Kealdale Rd NN3 . . . . . . 142 A4
Keating Cl NN15 . . . . . . 92 A8
Keats Cl
  Earls Barton NN6 . . . . . 144 F4
  Great Houghton NN4 . . . 160 F1
Keats Dr
  Kettering NN16 . . . . 72 C6
  Towcester NN12 . . . . . . 203 B5
Keats Rd
  Daventry NN11 . . . . 135 B3
  Wellingborough NN8 . . . 129 D4
Keats Way
  Corby NN17 . . . . 36 C8
  Higham Ferrers NN10 . . 132 C3
  Rushden NN10 . . . . 131 E3
Keble Cl NN11 . . . . 153 B8
Keble Ct NN8 . . . . 129 F4
Keble Rd NN13 . . . . 233 D8
Kedleston Cl **3** NN4 . . . 175 C8
Keebles Cl NN14 . . . . . . 37 E2
Keepers Cl NN4 . . . . 175 F3
Kelburn Rd NN4 . . . . 175 B7
Keld Cl NN18 . . . . 36 D2
KELMARSH 67 F3
Kelmarsh Hall ★ NN6 . . . 67 F4
Kelmarsh Rd
  Arthingworth LE16 . . . . . 68 C7
  Clipston LE16 . . . . 67 A7
  Corby NN17 . . . . 36 C7
Kelmscott Cl NN3 . . . . . 143 A5
Kelsall Cl NN5 . . . . 158 B8
Kelthorpe Cl PE9 . . . . . . 1 A4
Kelvin Gr NN17 . . . . 37 A7
Kemp Ho NN17 . . . . 21 F3
Kemps Cl NN14 . . . . 89 B4
Kemps Rd OX17 . . . . 230 A5
Kempton Cl NN18 . . . . . 53 E8
Kendal Cl
  Northampton NN3 . . . . . 142 D4
  Rushden NN10 . . . . 132 D1
  Wellingborough NN8 . . . 129 D6
Kendalls Cl LE16 . . . . . . 34 C5
Kenilworth NN18 . . . . . . 36 C3
Kenilworth Cl
  Daventry NN11 . . . . 135 B1
  Northampton NN5 . . . . . 158 B8
  Rushden NN10 . . . . 132 C1
Kenilworth Dr NN15 . . . . 91 F8
Kenilworth Gdns NN14 . . 76 F2
Kenmore Dr NN14 . . . . . 51 B2
Kenmuir Ave NN2 . . . . . 141 F2
Kenmuir Cres NN2 . . . . . 141 F2
Kenmuir Gdns NN2 . . . . 141 F2
Kenmuir Rd NN9 . . . . . . 111 F4
Kennedy Cl NN11 . . . . . . 135 E1
Kennel Hill NN14 . . . . . . 55 F7
Kennel Rd NN12 . . . . 215 C3
Kennels Dr NN12 . . . . . . 216 E3
Kennet Terr NN6 . . . . . . 106 B2
Kennet Cl NN8 . . . . 129 C6
Kennet Gn NN5 . . . . 140 F2
Kensington Cl
  Kings Sutton OX17 . . . . 230 F6
  Rushden NN10 . . . . 131 E3
  Towcester NN12 . . . . . . 203 B4
Kensington Gdns NN15 . . 91 B8
Kensington Pl MK46 . . . . 195 F5
Kensington Wlk NN18 . . . 36 C3
Kent Cl
  Corby NN17 . . . . 36 C7

Kent Cl *continued*
  Northampton NN5 . . . . . 158 C6
Kentford Cl NN14 . . . . . . 175 D4
Kenton Ct NN15 . . . . 92 A8
Kent Pl NN15 . . . . 91 D6
Kent Rd
  Northampton, Duston
  NN5 . . . . 158 B6
  Rushden NN10 . . . . 132 C3
  Wellingborough NN8 . . . 129 F1
Kentstone Cl NN2 . . . . . 140 F4
Kent The CV21 . . . . 80 A2
Kerley Cl NN14 . . . . 90 A3
Kerrfield Est NN5 . . . . . . 158 C7
Kestian Cl LE16 . . . . 31 D5
Keston Way NN9 . . . . . . 114 B5
Kestrel Cl NN3 . . . . 142 D1
Kestrel Cres NN13 . . . . . 222 E1
Kestrel La NN8 . . . . 130 A7
Keswick NN8 . . . . 129 B5
Keswick Dr
  Northampton NN3 . . . . . 142 C4
  Rushden NN10 . . . . 132 D3
Keswick Rd MK19 . . . . . 207 B2
Ketco Ave PE9 . . . . 1 B7
KETTERING 72 E3
Kettering Gdns **2**
  NN1 . . . . 159 E6
Kettering General Hospl
  NN16 . . . . 71 F2
Kettering Parkway
  NN15 . . . . 91 D5
Kettering Rd
  Broughton NN14 . . . . . . 90 B5
  Burton Latimer NN15 . . . 92 B3
  Geddington NN14 . . . . . 54 A1
  Great Harrowden NN9 . . 110 E4
  Isham NN14 . . . . 91 E1
  Islip NN14 . . . . 75 E1
  Market Harborough LE16 . 32 B2
  Moulton NN3 . . . . 126 F2
  Northampton NN1 . . . . . 159 E8
  Northampton, Spinney Hill
  NN3 . . . . 142 A3
  Pytchley NN14 . . . . 90 F2
  Rothwell NN14, NN16 . . 70 E5
  Stanion NN14 . . . . 37 E2
  Walgrave NN6 . . . . 108 C6
  Weldon NN17 . . . . 38 B7
  Woodford NN14 . . . . . . 94 B8
  Wothorpe PE9 . . . . 2 C8
Kettering Rd N NN3 . . . . 142 C5
Kettering Sta NN15 . . . . 72 A1
Kettering Town FC
  NN16 . . . . 72 B5
Kettle End NN12 . . . . . . 200 C3
KETTON 1 A6
Ketton CE Prim Sch
  PE9 . . . . 1 A5
Ketton Rd PE9 . . . . 1 C3
Keyham Ct NN3 . . . . 143 A5
Keys Cl NN11 . . . . 135 D1
Keys La CV47 . . . . 166 E1
KEYSTON 97 A4
Keystone NN4 . . . . 158 C3
Keyston Rd PE18 . . . . . . 116 D2
Keyte's Cl OX17 . . . . 230 A4
KG House Bsns Ctr **4**
  NN5 . . . . 140 F1
Kielder Ct NN15 . . . . 92 A4
Kieldsen Cl OX17 . . . . . . 210 B1
Kiel Wlk NN3 . . . . 36 A2
Kilborn Cl NN8 . . . . 129 E7
Kilburn Rd NN8 . . . . 129 E6
Kilburn Pl NN10 . . . . 132 B4
Kilby Cl NN8 . . . . 129 E3
Kiln La
  Litchborough NN12 . . . . 171 C1
  Welton NN11 . . . . 135 B3
Kiln Way NN8 . . . . 129 D4
KILSBY 100 A3
Kilsby CE Prim Sch
  CV23 . . . . 100 A3
Kilsby La CV21 . . . . 99 C7
Kilsby Rd
  Barby CV23 . . . . 99 C1
  Crick NN6 . . . . 100 F2
  Watford NN11 . . . . 120 B7
Kilvey Rd NN4 . . . . 160 B2
Kilworth Rd
  Husbands Bosworth
  LE17 . . . . 45 D4
  Rugby CV21 . . . . 99 B7
  Swinford LE17 . . . . 62 C4
Kimble Cl NN14 . . . . 175 B8
Kimbolton Ct NN14 . . . . 76 E2
Kimbolton Rd
  Chelveston NN9 . . . . . . 133 D8
  Higham Ferrers NN10 . . 132 C6
Kinewell Cl NN14 . . . . . . 95 A3
Kinewell Lake Nature
  Trail ★ NN14 . . . . 95 A3
King Cup Cl NN10 . . . . . 148 C7
King Edward Rd NN1 . . . 160 A7
Kingfisher Cl
  Hinton NN11 . . . . 184 B6
  Northampton NN4 . . . . . 175 A7
  Ringstead NN14 . . . . . . 95 A3
Kingfisher Dr NN16 . . . . 143 D8
Kingfisher Rd NN13 . . . . 222 E2
Kingfisher Way NN15 . . . 92 A2
King George Cres
  MK11 . . . . 229 E6
King John Sch The
  NN14 . . . . 76 D1
Kingmaker Way NN4 . . . 159 A2
King Richard Ct NN4 . . . 175 C6

Kings Arms La PE8 . . . . . 42 F3
Kings Ave NN10 . . . . 132 C2
Kingsbrook NN18 . . . . . . 36 B3
Kingsbrook Sch MK19 . . 228 F4
Kings Cl NN11 . . . . 175 F3
KING'S CLIFFE 13 E8
King's Cliffe Endowed
  Prim Sch PE8 . . . . 13 F7
Kings Cliffe Rd PE8 . . . . 14 C4
Kings Corner Cl
  NN11 . . . . 184 C6
Kingscroft Cl NN3 . . . . . 143 C1
Kings Ct NN14 . . . . 51 B3
King's Ct **2** LE16 . . . . . . 31 E4
Kingsfield Bsns Pk
  NN5 . . . . 141 A1
Kingsfield Cl NN5 . . . . . . 141 A1
Kingsfield Piece
  NN2 . . . . 215 C4
Kingsfield Way NN5 . . . . 141 A1
King's Forest PE8 . . . . . . 13 F7
Kings Gn NN11 . . . . 153 C7
King's Head Pl LE16 . . . . 31 E3
KING'S HEATH 140 E2
King's Heath Prim Sch
  NN5 . . . . 140 F2
Kingshill Dr MK19 . . . . . 228 E5
Kings La
  Barrowden LE15 . . . . 3 F5
  Pury End NN12 . . . . 215 F7
  Yelvertoft NN6 . . . . 82 B4
Kingsland Ave NN2 . . . . 141 D3
Kingsland Cl NN2 . . . . . . 141 D3
Kingsland Gdns NN2 . . . 141 D3
Kingsley Ave
  Daventry NN11 . . . . 135 B1
  Kettering NN16 . . . . 72 B5
  Rugby CV21 . . . . 98 F8
Kingsley Dr NN17 . . . . . . 36 D8
Kingsley Gdns **3**
  NN2 . . . . 141 E1
KINGSLEY PARK 141 F2
Kingsley Park Mid Sch
  NN2 . . . . 141 D1
Kingsley Park Terr
  NN2 . . . . 141 F1
Kingsley Prim Sch
  NN2 . . . . 141 F2
Kingsley Rd
  Northampton NN2 . . . . . 141 E1
  Rothwell NN14 . . . . 70 C7
  Silverstone NN12 . . . . . 214 E5
Kingsley Sch NN15 . . . . . 72 F1
Kingsmead
  King's Cliffe PE8 . . . . . . 13 F8
  Northampton NN2 . . . . . 141 A5
Kings Meadow La
  NN10 . . . . 132 B7
Kings Meadow Sch
  NN3 . . . . 142 C7
Kingsmead Pk NN10 . . . 148 C7
Kingsmith Dr NN9 . . . . . 114 E6
Kings Park Rd NN3 . . . . . 141 F6
Kings Pk NN7 . . . . 155 A3
Kings Pl NN10 . . . . 132 C2
Kings Rd
  Oundle PE8 . . . . 42 A6
  Rushden NN10 . . . . 132 C2
  Weldon NN17 . . . . 38 B7
King's Rd LE16 . . . . 31 E3
Kings St NN8 . . . . 130 A5
Kings Stile OX17 . . . . 208 F1
KINGS SUTTON 231 A4
Kings Sutton Prim Sch
  OX17 . . . . 231 A5
Kings Sutton Sta
  OX17 . . . . 230 E5
King St
  Desborough NN14 . . . . . 51 B3
  Earls Barton NN6 . . . . . 144 E5
  Kettering NN16 . . . . 72 C3
  Long Buckby NN6 . . . . . 121 B4
  Maidford NN12 . . . . 186 D5
  Northampton NN1 . . . . . 159 C6
  Stony Stratford MK11 . . 229 E6
Kingsthorne Distribution
  Pk NN6 . . . . 71 E4
KINGSTHORPE 141 C3
Kingsthorpe Ave NN6 . . . 36 B7
Kingsthorpe Bsns Ctr
  NN2 . . . . 141 B4
Kingsthorpe Com Coll
  NN2 . . . . 141 E5
Kingsthorpe Gr NN2 . . . . 141 C2
Kingsthorpe Grove Prim
  Sch NN2 . . . . 141 C2
Kingsthorpe Ho NN2 . . . 141 C5
KINGSTHORPE HOLLOW
  . . . . 141 D1
Kingsthorpe Mid Com Sch
  NN2 . . . . 141 B4
Kingsthorpe Rd NN2 . . . 141 C1
Kingsthorpe Sh Ctr **2**
  NN2 . . . . 141 C3
Kingsthorpe Village Prim
  Sch NN2 . . . . 141 B3
Kingston Ave MK11 . . . . 229 E5
Kingston Cl
  Blakesley NN12 . . . . . . 187 B1
  Daventry NN11 . . . . 135 B3
  Long Buckby NN6 . . . . . 121 B4
Middleton Cheney
  OX17 . . . . 220 A7
Kingston Way LE16 . . . . 31 E6
King Style Cl NN6 . . . . . . 100 F6

Kingsway
  Northampton NN2 . . . . . 141 B4
  Wellingborough NN8 . . . 129 E2
Kingswell Rd NN2 . . . . . . 141 B4
Kingswell St NN1 . . . . . . 159 C5
Kingswood Pl NN18 . . . . 36 A3
Kingswood Prim Sch
  NN18 . . . . 36 C3
Kingswood Sch The
  NN18 . . . . 36 A3
Kinross Cl NN3 . . . . 142 A4
Kipling Dr NN12 . . . . 203 B5
Kipling Rd
  Corby NN17 . . . . 36 D8
  Kettering NN16 . . . . 72 C5
Kippell Hill MK46 . . . . . . 195 F5
Kipton Cl NN14 . . . . 70 E7
Kipton Field NN14 . . . . . 70 E7
Kirby Cl
  Corby NN18 . . . . 36 A3
  Northampton NN4 . . . . . 175 F7
Kirby Ct NN15 . . . . 91 C5
Kirby Hall ★ NN17 . . . . . 23 B6
Kirby Ho LE16 . . . . 31 F3
Kirby La NN17 . . . . 23 C5
Kirby Rd NN17 . . . . 10 C1
Kirkby Rd CV21 . . . . 98 F8
Kirkhams Cl NN6 . . . . . . 82 C3
Kirkstone Wlk **7**
  NN3 . . . . 142 C4
Kirkwall NN17 . . . . 21 C1
Kirton Cl NN3 . . . . 143 B5
Kirton End NN14 . . . . . . 143 B4
KISLINGBURY 157 E4
Kislingbury Prim Sch
  NN7 . . . . 157 D4
Kislingbury Rd
  Bugbrooke NN7 . . . . . . 173 A8
  Rothersthorpe NN7 . . . . 174 A7
Kitchener Cl NN11 . . . . . 135 B4
Kitchen Gdns NN14 . . . . 89 F6
Kitelee Cl MK19 . . . . 207 A3
Kites Cl NN4 . . . . 175 A8
Kits Cl NN17 . . . . 192 D2
Knaphill Cres NN4 . . . . . 158 F4
Knibb Pl NN15 . . . . 91 F6
Knibb St NN16 . . . . 72 C2
Knightlands Rd NN9 . . . . 112 F3
Knightley Cl NN11 . . . . . 183 D7
Knightley Rd NN2 . . . . . . 141 C1
Knighton Cl NN5 . . . . . . 140 A3
Knightons Way NN6 . . . . 106 C1
Knights Cl
  Bozeat NN29 . . . . 164 D2
  Corby NN18 . . . . 36 A5
  Earls Barton NN6 . . . . . 144 E4
Knightscliffe Way
  NN5 . . . . 140 D1
Knights Ct
  Northampton, Little Billing
  NN3 . . . . 143 B1
  Northampton NN1 . . . . . 159 F8
  Wellingborough NN8 . . . 129 F5
Knight's End Rd LE16 . . . 32 B6
Knights Hill NN6 . . . . . . 85 B8
Knight's La NN2 . . . . 141 B3
Knights Mews NN10 . . . . 132 C1
Knob The OX17 . . . . 231 A5
Knock La NN7 . . . . 190 F5
Knoll Cl NN16 . . . . 72 B4
Knoll St LE16 . . . . 31 C3
Knoll The
  Brixworth NN6 . . . . 106 C2
  Grendon NN7 . . . . 163 D5
KNOTTING 149 E3
KNOTTING GREEN 149 F1
Knowle Cl NN3 . . . . 160 C6
Knowles Cl NN10 . . . . . . 132 C3
Knowle Way **2** NN11 . . . 135 B7
Knox Cl NN8 . . . . 130 B4
Knox Rd NN8 . . . . 130 B5
KNUSTON 131 D1
Knuston Dr NN10 . . . . . . 131 F2
Knuston Spinney
  NN10 . . . . 131 E1
Knutsford La NN6 . . . . . . 121 C4
Kylesku Cres NN15 . . . . . 91 E8
Kynnesworth Gdns
  NN10 . . . . 132 C6
Kyoto Cl NN3 . . . . 142 A6

L

Laburnum Cl
  Hinton NN11 . . . . 184 B6
  Wellingborough NN8 . . . 129 E5
Laburnum Cres
  Kettering NN16 . . . . 72 D4
  Northampton NN3 . . . . . 142 A3
Laceby Wlk NN3 . . . . . . 142 F5
Lacemakers Ct NN10 . . . 148 C8
Lace Mews MK46 . . . . . . 195 F4
Lacock Ho **7** NN11 . . . . 135 B7
Laddermakers Yd
  NN7 . . . . 172 E7
Ladybower Cl NN16 . . . . 71 E3
Ladybridge Dr NN4 . . . . 174 E8
Lady Cl NN11 . . . . 153 D3
Lady Croft NN11 . . . . . . 135 B1
Lady Hollows Dr NN4 . . . 176 A6
Ladymead Cl NN4 . . . . . . 158 D1
Lady's La
  Mears Ashby NN6 . . . . . 128 B2
  Northampton NN1 . . . . . 159 C6
Lady Smock Cl NN4 . . . . 175 F2
Ladywell Cl NN8 . . . . 130 A7
Ladywell Mews NN14 . . . 70 D7

Jos–Lar **253**

Lady Winefride's Wlk
  NN3 . . . . 143 B2
Lahnstein Ct **12** NN16 . . 72 B2
Lake Ave NN15 . . . . 90 F8
Lake Cres NN11 . . . . 135 A2
Lakeside
  Irthlingborough NN9 . . . 131 D7
  Northampton NN3 . . . . . 143 A7
Lakeside Bglws NN15 . . . 91 E6
Lakeside Cl NN14 . . . . . . 76 D3
Lakeside Dr NN3 . . . . . . 143 D3
Lakeside Lodges 143 A7
Lakeview Gn NN3 . . . . . . 142 C4
Lake Wlk
  Adderbury OX17 . . . . . . 230 B4
  Northampton NN4 . . . . . 175 C4
Lalgates Ct NN5 . . . . 158 F8
Lambert's Cl LE15 . . . . . 3 A6
Lambourne Way
  OX17 . . . . 230 B4
Lambrook Dr NN4 . . . . . 175 C7
Lammas Cl
  Husbands Bosworth
  LE17 . . . . 45 E5
  Orlingbury NN14 . . . . . . 110 A5
Lammas Ctyd NN17 . . . . 23 A1
Lammas Rd NN17 . . . . . 23 A1
LAMPORT 87 D2
Lamport Cl NN15 . . . . . . 91 D5
Lamport Ct NN11 . . . . . . 135 A5
Lamport Dr NN11 . . . . . . 135 A5
Lamport Hall ★ NN6 . . . 87 D1
Lamport Rd
  Draughton NN6 . . . . 87 E6
  Old NN6 . . . . 107 F7
Lamva Ct MK11 . . . . 229 F5
Lancaster Dr
  Brackley NN13 . . . . 233 E8
  Thrapston NN14 . . . . . . 76 F2
Lancaster Rd
  Kettering NN16 . . . . 72 C3
  Rothwell NN14 . . . . 70 E7
Lancaster St NN10 . . . . . 132 C7
Lancaster Way
  Northampton NN4 . . . . . 159 A1
  Rushden NN10 . . . . 132 C3
Lancers Way NN7 . . . . . . 155 B4
Lanchester Way NN11 . . . 134 F3
Lancum Ho NN8 . . . . . . 129 E5
Landcross Dr NN3 . . . . . 160 C7
Landimore Rd NN4 . . . . . 176 A7
Landor NN8 . . . . 129 C4
Landor Cl NN17 . . . . 21 D1
Landsdown Dr NN3 . . . . 142 E2
Landseer
  Rugby CV21 . . . . 80 B1
  Wellingborough NN8 . . . 129 F8
Landseer Ct NN18 . . . . . 36 D5
Lanercost Wlk
  Northampton NN3 . . . . . 142 C4
  8 Northampton NN3 . . . 142 C4
Laneside Hollow NN4 . . . 175 C6
Lane The
  Ashby St L CV23 . . . . . . 119 B5
  Denton NN7 . . . . 178 B8
  Eastcote NN12 . . . . 173 A1
  Easton o t H PE9 . . . . . 2 A5
  Grafton Regis NN12 . . . 205 D2
  Rothersthorpe NN7 . . . . 174 B6
  Wappenham NN12 . . . . 213 B8
  Weston by W LE16 . . . . 18 B4
Langdale NN14 . . . . 50 F3
Langdale Ct NN8 . . . . . . 129 D5
Langdale Gr NN17 . . . . . 36 D8
Langdale Rd NN2 . . . . . . 141 D3
Langdale Wlk LE16 . . . . . 31 E1
Langdon Cl NN11 . . . . . . 135 B5
Langford Dr NN4 . . . . . . 175 D5
Langham Cl NN6 . . . . . . 104 F5
Langham Pl
  Northampton NN2 . . . . . 159 C8
  Walgrave NN6 . . . . 108 A5
Langham Rd NN9 . . . . . . 114 D7
Langley Cl NN4 . . . . 158 E3
Langley Cres NN9 . . . . . 113 B5
Langley Ct NN15 . . . . . . 92 B2
Langley Way NN15 . . . . . 91 C6
Langley Wlk NN18 . . . . . 36 D5
Langport Gn NN18 . . . . . 36 B6
Langsett Cl
  Kettering NN16 . . . . 71 E3
  Northampton NN3 . . . . . 142 F1
Langton Ct
  Corby NN18 . . . . 36 B6
  Market Harborough LE16 . 31 E3
Langton Pl NN14 . . . . . . 91 E1
Langton Rd LE16 . . . . . . 32 A7
Langton Rise NN11 . . . . 137 C6
Lansdown Cl NN11 . . . . . 135 D5
Lansom Cl NN15 . . . . . . 92 C3
Lapford Rd NN18 . . . . . . 36 E4
Lapland Wlk NN18 . . . . . 36 B2
Lapstone Ho NN5 . . . . . . 159 A5
Lapwing Cl NN4 . . . . 175 A7
Larch Cl
  Hinton NN11 . . . . 184 A6
  Irchester NN29 . . . . 147 A7
Larch Dr NN11 . . . . 135 C5
Larch La NN5 . . . . 140 B2
Larch Rd
  Corby NN17 . . . . 21 D1
  Kettering NN15 . . . . 72 C1
Larchwood Cl NN8 . . . . . 129 E5
Larkhall La NN7 . . . . 157 D6

Larkhall Way NN7....157 C7
Larkhill NN10....132 A4
Larkin Gdns NN10....132 A5
Lark La NN4....175 F4
Lark Rise
  Brackley NN13....233 E8
  Northampton NN3....143 B4
Larkwood Cl NN16....72 C6
Larratt Rd NN17....38 A8
Larwood Cl NN2....141 A5
Lasham Ct NN3....143 C1
Latham Rd PE8....41 F7
Latham's Hospl PE8....59 B6
Latham St NN14....55 F7
Lathbury Rd NN13....233 D8
Lathkill St LE16....31 F1
Latimer MK11....229 E4
Latimer Cl
  Burton Latimer NN15....92 C2
  Gretton NN17....10 C1
Latimer Com Arts Coll
  NN15....92 A6
Latimer Cres LE16....31 F2
Latimer Rd NN17....36 E8
Lattimore Cl NN6....102 C5
Latymer Cl LE16....49 E5
Latymer Ct **4** NN1....159 C6
Lauda Way NN12....203 C8
Lauderdale Ave NN4....159 A2
Laud's Rd NN6....101 A5
Laughton Rd LE16....30 C4
Launcelot Ct NN5....158 A7
Launde Pk LE16....32 C4
Laundry Rd PE8....14 C4
Laurel Ct
  Northampton NN3....142 E3
  4 Wellingborough
  NN8....130 B5
Laurel Pl NN12....203 D5
Laurel Rd NN16....72 C4
Laurels The
  Ecton NN6....143 F3
  Moulton NN3....126 B2
Laurel Valley NN4....175 D4
Lavant Wlk NN3....141 F5
Lavender Cl
  Corby NN18....36 D2
  Thrapston NN14....76 D2
Lavender La NN7....177 D1
Lavender Way NN10....148 C8
Lavendon Ct NN15....92 A5
Lavenham Cl NN3....142 F5
Lavery Ct NN18....36 D5
Lawns The
  Corby NN18....36 A4
  Kettering NN16....72 A1
  Kilsby CV23....100 A2
  Northampton NN5....158 E8
Lawrence Cl
  Kettering NN15....92 A8
  Raunds NN9....114 B5
Lawrence Ct
  Corby NN18....36 D5
  Long Buckby NN6....121 B4
  22 Northampton NN1....159 C7
Laws Croft NN13....233 D7
Laws La NN9....111 F4
Law's La PE5....13 F7
Lawson Cres NN3....143 C1
Lawson St
  Kettering NN16....72 C3
  Raunds NN9....114 D6
Lawton Rd NN10....132 C3
Lawyers Cl NN13....233 E2
LAXTON....11 F5
Laxton Cl NN17....36 B8
Laxton Ct NN15....92 A5
Laxton Dr PE8....42 B7
Laxton Jun Sch PE8....42 A5
Laywood Cl NN9....114 C7
Laywood Way NN9....131 E8
Leafields NN3....160 F8
Leah Bank NN4....159 A2
Leah Cl NN18....53 A8
Lealand The LE16....48 B8
Leamington Way
  NN11....135 A2
Leam The NN11....134 F1
Lea Rd NN1....159 F8
Leatherland Ct **18**
  NN16....72 B2
Lea Way NN8....129 D3
Leben Sq NN3....143 C5
Leckhampstead Rd
  MK19....228 A3
Ledaig Way NN3....142 A4
Ledbury Rd NN15....91 F5
Leeds Cl NN18....36 F2
Lees Cl NN12....215 C4
Leeson Cres NN15....91 F6
Leeson Ct NN12....203 D4
Leeson Rd NN12....203 C4
Lees St NN9....112 E1
Lee's Way NN14....54 A3
Lee Way NN9....114 D7
Legg Rd PE8....7 D8
Legion Cres NN16....71 F3
Leicester Cl NN16....72 A3
Leicester La LE16....31 D7
Leicester Par NN2....159 C8
Leicester Rd
  Husbands Bosworth
    LE17....45 D7
  Market Harborough
    LE16....31 D5

Leicester St
  Kettering NN16....72 A3
  Northampton NN1....159 C7
Leicester Terr **2**
  NN2....159 C7
Leighton Cl NN8....129 F8
Leighton Pl NN8....129 F4
Leighton Rd NN18....36 D5
Leith Ct NN4....158 E3
Lely Ct NN18....36 D5
Lennon Cl CV21....99 C8
Lennox Wlk NN5....140 D2
Lensway NN14....89 B5
Lenthall Sq LE16....31 E1
Lenton Ct NN14....90 A3
Leonard La **1** NN3....126 C1
Leonardo Ct NN18....36 D5
Lerwick Way NN17....36 C8
Leslie Rd NN2....159 B7
Lesson Rd NN6....106 B1
Lester Ct OX17....230 A6
Letts Rd NN3....159 B3
Leven Way NN17....21 B1
Lever Rd CV21....80 A1
Levitts Rd NN3....173 A8
Lewin Cl NN14....70 B7
Lewin Rd NN18....36 B1
Lewis Ho NN14....91 E1
Lewis Rd
  Kettering NN15....91 C7
  Northampton NN5....159 A4
Lexden Cl NN4....175 F7
Lexton Gdns OX17....220 B8
Leyland Dr NN2....141 A5
Leyland Trad Est NN8....130 D4
Leyland View NN8....130 D4
Leys Ave
  Desborough NN14....51 C3
  Rothwell NN14....70 C7
Leys Cl
  Denton NN7....162 B1
  Long Buckby NN6....121 C4
Leys Gdns NN18....130 B6
Leyside Ct NN3....143 B5
Leys La NN4....160 F1
Leys Rd
  Earls Barton NN6....144 D4
  Pattishall NN12....172 D1
  Rugby CV21....99 C7
  Wellingborough NN8....130 B6
Leys The
  Bugbrooke NN7....172 E6
  Denton NN7....162 B1
  Long Buckby NN6....121 C4
  Northampton NN2....141 B2
  Orlingbury NN14....110 A5
  Roade NN7....191 D4
  Upper Boddington
    NN11....182 C8
  Welford NN6....64 E5
  Woodford NN14....94 D7
  Yardley Hastings NN7....179 A4
Leyswell Ct **4** NN3....161 A8
Liberty Dr NN5....140 C1
Lichfield Cl NN7....157 D3
Lichfield Dr NN4....175 B7
Liddington Way NN2....141 B5
Lightfoot La LE16....20 B1
Lilac Cl NN14....76 D3
Lilac Ct NN8....129 C5
Lilac Gr NN10....148 B7
Lilac Pl NN15....72 D1
LILBOURNE....81 A6
Lilbourne Rd CV23....80 C5
LILFORD....58 E4
Lilford Pl NN16....72 D3
Lilford Rd NN14....77 C8
Liliput Rd NN4....160 C3
Lilley Homes The
  NN8....129 F2
Lilley Terr NN9....112 F2
LILLINGSTONE DAYRELL....226 E4
LILLINGSTONE LOVELL....227 A5
Lillington Ct NN18....36 B6
Lillycourt Ho NN16....72 A2
Lilly Hill MK46....195 F5
Lime Ave
  Eydon NN11....184 C1
  Long Buckby NN3....121 C4
  Northampton NN3....142 A1
  Oundle PE8....41 F7
Lime Cl
  Broughton NN14....90 A5
  Hartwell NN7....192 E2
Lime Ct NN9....112 F2
Lime Farm Way NN4....160 F2
Limefields Way NN4....175 D6
Lime Gr
  Bugbrooke NN7....173 A7
  Rushden NN10....132 B4
  Wellingborough NN8....130 A7
Limehurst Cl NN5....140 C1
Limehurst Rd NN5....158 C8
Limehurst Sq NN5....158 C8
Lime Rd
  Kettering NN16....72 D4
  Yardley Gobion NN12....217 E6
Lime St
  Irthlingborough NN9....112 F2
  Olney MK46....195 F3
  Rushden NN10....132 B4
Limes The
  9 Daventry NN11....135 C1
  11 Irthlingborough
    NN9....112 F2
  Stony Stratford MK11....229 E5

Limes The continued
  Thorpe Langton LE16....17 A5
  Thrapston NN14....76 B2
Lime Terr NN9....112 F2
Lime Tree Mews NN15....72 B1
Lime Trees Gr NN17....37 A6
Limlow Cl NN4....158 E3
Limoges Ct NN5....140 A2
Linacre Cl NN3....142 F6
Lincoln Ct
  Brackley NN13....233 F5
  Hanslope MK19....207 A2
  Market Harborough LE16....31 F5
Lincoln Ho NN5....159 A5
Lincoln Pk NN13....233 F5
Lincoln Rd NN5....159 A5
Lincoln St NN2....141 C3
Lincoln Way
  Corby NN18....36 C4
  Daventry NN11....153 C8
Lindale Cl NN3....142 B3
Linden Ave
  Higham Ferrers NN10....132 B7
  Kettering NN16, NN16....72 D1
Linden Cl NN15....72 D1
Linden Gr PE28....97 A2
Linden Rd NN3....142 A1
Lindens The
  Northampton NN1....159 E5
  Towcester NN12....203 C6
Lindisfarne Dr NN15....91 F8
Lindisfarne Rd NN17....21 C1
Lindisfarne Way
  Northampton NN4....175 C8
  Thrapston NN14....76 F2
Lindrick Cl NN11....135 C4
Lindsay Ave NN3....142 B2
Lindsay St NN16....72 B3
Lindsay Terr NN3....142 A2
Lindsey Cl PE8....14 F1
Lindsey Gdns LE16....48 D8
Lingfield Terr NN2....141 F2
Lingfield Wlk NN18....36 C2
Lings Prim Sch NN3....142 F4
Lings Way NN3....143 A4
Lingswood Pk NN3....143 A3
Link La NN14....89 B4
Link Rd
  Northampton NN2....141 B6
  Rushden NN10....148 B7
Links Rd NN8....130 C8
Links The NN15....91 B8
Link Way
  Bugbrooke NN7....173 A7
  Towcester NN12....203 C5
Linley Dr NN14....50 F4
Linley Gn NN5....158 D8
Linnell Way NN16....71 F4
Linnet Cl NN8....130 A7
Linnet Dr NN15....92 A6
Linnet Rd NN12....203 C3
Linnetts La NN10....132 B5
Lion Ct NN4....159 D4
Lismore Cl NN3....143 C2
Lismore Wlk NN17....21 C1
Lister Cl NN17....22 A1
Lister Dr NN4....158 E1
Lister Rd NN8....130 A5
LITCHBOROUGH....171 D1
Litchborough Rd
  Farthingstone NN12....170 F3
  Grimscote NN12....188 A7
Litchfield Cl
  Brixworth NN6....106 B2
  Kettering NN16....72 C6
Litchfield La NN6....104 F4
LITTLE ADDINGTON....113 B7
Little Back La NN11....151 D1
LITTLE BILLING....143 B1
Little Billing Way
  NN3....143 A1
Little Bowden Manor
  LE16....31 F3
Little Bowden Sch
  LE16....31 F2
LITTLE BRAUNSTON....118 D1
LITTLE BRINGTON....138 C4
Little Cl
  Bozeat NN29....164 C2
  Chapel Brampton NN6....124 D1
LITTLE CRANSLEY....90 A5
LITTLE CREATON....105 A3
Little Cross St NN1....159 B6
Littledale NN8....129 D6
LITTLE EVERDON....154 A1
Little Field NN4....175 F4
Little Field Cl NN12....189 A8
Little Gn PE8....28 B3
Little Greeve Way
  NN4....176 A6
Little Gull Cl NN3....142 F6
LITTLE HARROWDEN....110 B4
Little Harrowden Com
  Prim Sch NN9....110 C4
Little Horton Ho NN7....177 E2
Little Horton House Dr
  NN7....177 E2
LITTLE HOUGHTON....161 A3
LITTLE IRCHESTER....130 C1
Little La
  Aynho OX17....237 C7
  Blisworth NN7....190 D8
  Great Harrowden NN4....160 E2
  Ravensthorpe NN6....103 D1
  Stanion NN14....37 E3
  Wollaston NN29....146 D3

Little La continued
  Yardley Hastings NN7....179 A7
Little London
  Deanshanger MK19....228 E4
  Silverstone NN12....214 D5
Little Mdw NN18....36 B1
LITTLE OAKLEY....54 A8
Little Park St **6** NN8....130 A5
Little Priel Rd NN7....155 B4
Little St
  Rushden NN10....132 C1
  Sulgrave OX17....211 A8
  Yardley Hastings NN7....179 B6
Littlewood Cl NN5....159 A8
Littlewood St NN1....70 E7
LITTLEWORTH....188 E1
LITTLE WYMINGTON....148 A7
Livingstone Cl NN14....70 F7
Livingstone Rd NN11....135 C4
Llewellyn Wlk NN18....36 D5
Lloyd Cl NN8....130 B8
Lloyd's Rd NN17....37 B7
Loach Ct NN3....142 A6
Loatlands Prim Sch
  NN14....50 F3
Loatland St NN14....50 F3
Lobelia Rd NN16....72 C4
Lockcroft Sq **6** NN3....143 D2
Lock La MK19....218 A2
Locks Gn PE8....16 A8
Locks The CV21....80 B1
Locktons Cl NN12....201 E2
Lockwood Cl NN2....141 C4
LODDINGTON....70 C2
Loddington CE Prim Sch
  NN14....70 D1
Loddington Rd NN14....89 F7
Loddington Way NN14....89 B4
Lodge Ave NN4....175 C4
Lodge Cl
  Little Houghton NN7....161 B3
  Northampton, Hopping Hill
    NN5....140 B1
  Northampton NN4....175 F3
Lodge Ct **1** NN8....130 B5
Lodge Farm Ct MK19....218 F6
Lodge Farm Ind Est
  NN5....140 C2
Lodge Flats NN6....122 D5
Lodge Green Rd NN17....36 E8
Lodge La NN6....121 F3
Lodge Park Tech Coll
  NN17....21 B1
Lodge Pk NN12....215 C4
Lodge Rd
  Daventry NN11....135 C2
  Little Houghton NN7....161 A3
  Rushden NN10....148 A8
Lodge The OX17....198 D2
Lodge Way
  Irthlingborough NN9....131 E8
  Northampton NN5....140 C3
Lodore Gdns NN3....142 C3
Logan Cres LE16....31 C4
Logan Ct LE16....31 D4
Logan St LE16....31 D3
Logwell Ct NN3....142 F1
Loire Cl NN5....140 A2
Lombard Way OX16....219 A6
Lombardy Rd NN3....142 D3
Lomond Ct NN17....21 C1
Lomond Dr NN15....91 F8
London End
  Earls Barton NN6....144 D4
  Irchester NN29....147 B8
  Titchmarsh NN14....77 D3
  Upper Boddington
    NN11....182 C8
London Ho MK11....229 D5
London Rd
  Bozeat NN29....164 C3
  Braunston NN11....118 A1
  Daventry NN11....153 D8
  Kettering NN15....91 C8
  Little Irchester NN8....130 C1
  Northampton, Far Cotton
    NN4....159 C2
  Northampton, Wootton
    NN4....175 D5
  Old Stratford MK19....229 C6
  Raunds NN9....114 C6
  Roade NN7....191 C4
  Stony Stratford MK11....229 E5
  Towcester NN12....203 D5
  Wansford PE8....8 B3
  Wellingborough NN8....130 B3
  Willoughby CV23....117 E3
  Wollaston NN29....146 D1
  Wothorpe PE9....2 F7
Lone Pine Ct NN6....106 B2
Long Acre NN7....161 D3
Long Acres **4** NN4....175 B8
Long Acres Dr NN9....112 E3
Long Barrow OX17....196 F7
Long Breech NN6....89 B5
Long Brimley Cl LE16....32 B3
LONG BUCKBY....121 B4
Long Buckby Inf Sch
  NN6....121 B4
Long Buckby Jun Sch
  NN6....121 B3
Long Buckby Pocket Pk★
  NN6....121 A4
Long Buckby Rd NN6....120 E5
Long Buckby Sta NN6....121 A2
LONG BUCKBY WHARF....136 E7

Longburges OX17....220 B8
Long Cl NN18....36 B1
Longcroft La NN12....216 C8
Long Croft Rd NN14,
  NN18....37 C3
Longdown La CV23....118 B7
Longfellow Dr NN16....72 C6
Longfellow Rd NN8....129 B4
Long Furlong CV22....98 A8
Long La
  Olney MK46....195 F4
  Warmington PE8....28 B2
Longland Ct NN3....142 B2
Longland Rd NN3....142 C2
Longlands The LE16....32 B3
Longleat Cl LE16....32 B3
Longleat Ct **5** NN4....175 C8
Longleat Gr NN15....91 C5
Long Mallows Rise **9**
  NN3....143 C2
Long March NN11....153 E8
Long March Ind Est
  NN11....153 E8
Long Marsh NN8....130 B3
Long Marsh Sq NN3....143 A6
Long Massey MK46....195 E5
Long Mdw NN4....176 B6
Longmead Ct NN3....143 B4
Longmynd Dr NN5....158 D8
Long Row
  Leckhampstead MK18....227 E5
  Woodford NN14....94 D7
Long Row Cl NN11....170 A8
LONG STREET....206 E4
Long Street Rd MK19....207 A3
Longueville Ct NN3....142 E4
Long Wall NN13....233 E6
Longwell NN12....186 B5
Lonsborough Dr NN15....90 E8
Lonsdale Rd NN15....91 B7
Loop Rd PE28....97 A3
Lordswood Cl NN4....176 A6
Lorne Ct NN17....36 F6
Lorne Rd NN1....159 C7
Lorraine Cres NN3....142 B5
Lorraine Dr NN3....142 C5
Loseby Cl NN10....148 A8
Lotus Ct NN15....72 B1
Louisa Dr NN16....72 C4
Louisa Lilley Homes The
  7 NN9....112 F2
Louisburg Cl **4** NN4....175 C4
Louise Rd NN1....159 D7
Lounts Cres LE16....20 D7
Lovap Way NN18....36 B1
Lovat Dr NN5....158 E7
Lovell Cl NN9....114 A4
Lovell Ct **12** NN9....112 F2
Lovers La PE5....8 F3
Lovett Rd NN1....183 D8
Lowbury Ct NN4....158 E3
Lower Adelaide St
  NN2....159 C7
Lower Bath St NN1....159 B6
LOWER BENEFIELD....40 C6
LOWER BODDINGTON....182 D5
LOWER CATESBY....151 D4
Lower Cross St NN1....159 B6
Lower Ecton La NN3....143 D3
Lower End NN12....201 F5
LOWER END
  Brafield-on-the-
    Green....161 E3
  Grendon....163 E7
  Hartwell....192 C1
Lower End
  Hartwell NN7....192 C1
  Pytchley NN14....91 A1
Lower Farm Rd NN3....141 F7
LOWER GREEN
  Blakesley....200 F6
  Willoughby....117 A5
Lower Harding St **11**
  NN1....159 C6
LOWER HARLESTONE....139 E5
Lower Hester St NN2....159 C8
Lower Hilmorton Rd **5**
  CV21....80 A1
Lower King St NN14....51 B3
Lower Lea Pl CV21....99 B8
Lower Meadow Ct
  NN3....142 E5
LOWER MIDDLETON
  CHENEY....220 B8
Lower Mounts NN1....159 D6
Lower Pastures NN18....53 A8
Lower Priory St NN1....159 B7
Lower Rd
  Milton Malsor NN7....174 E4
  Stoke Albany LE16....34 B5
Lower St
  Desborough NN14....51 A3
  Great Addington NN14....94 B2
  Great Doddington
    NN29....145 E6
  Kettering NN16....72 A2
  Pury End NN12....216 A7
  Rugby CV21....99 C8
  Twywell NN14....75 A1
  Willoughby CV23....117 C4
Lower Stable Yd
  NN12....203 D8
Lower Steeping NN14....51 B2
Lower Thrift St NN1....159 F6
Lower Weald MK19....229 E2

LOWER WEEDON 155 A3
Low Farm Pl NN3 ..... 141 F7
Low Greeve NN4 .... 176 A6
LOWICK 75 F6
Lowick Cl NN8 .... 129 D7
Lowick Ct NN3 .... 142 C7
Lowick La NN14 .... 76 F7
Lowick Rd
  Aldwincle NN14 ...... 76 E7
  Islip NN14 .... 76 B3
Lowlands Cl NN3 ...... 143 C5
Low March NN11 ...... 153 D7
Lowood NN1 .... 159 F5
Lowry Cl
  Corby NN18 .... 36 D4
  Northampton NN3 .... 142 B4
  Wellingborough NN8 .. 129 C7
Loxton Cl NN5 .... 140 C1
Loyd Rd NN1 .... 160 A6
LUBENHAM 30 E3
Lubenham All Saints CE
  Prim Sch LE16 .... 30 F3
Lubenham Hill LE16 ... 31 C2
Lubenham Rd
  East Farndon LE16 ... 31 B1
  Marston Trussell LE16 . 30 D1
Lucas Cl NN3 .... 131 E8
Lucas La NN7 .... 177 B3
Lucas Rd NN6 .... 121 A3
LUDDINGTON IN THE
  BROOK 61 B4
Luddington Rd PE8,
  PE28 .... 61 C3
Ludlow Cl NN3 .... 143 A7
Ludlow Wlk NN18 .... 36 E1
Luffenham Rd LE15 ... 3 F6
Lukes Cl NN13 .... 212 A5
Lulworth Wlk NN18 ... 36 A4
Lumber La NN12 ..... 216 B7
Lumbertubs La NN3 .. 142 D5
Lumbertubs Prim Sch
  NN3 .... 142 F3
Lumbertubs Rise
  NN3 .... 142 D5
Lumbertubs Way NN3 . 142 E3
Lunchfield Ct NN3 .... 126 C1
Lunchfield Gdns NN3 . 126 C1
Lunchfield La NN3 .... 126 C1
Lunchfield Wlk 7
  NN3 .... 126 C1
Lundie Cl NN9 .... 114 D7
Lundy Ave NN18 ..... 36 E4
Lupin Cl NN16 .... 72 D4
Lutterworth Rd
  Northampton NN1 .... 160 A6
  Swinford LE17 ...... 62 B6
LUTTON 44 C4
Lutton Rd PE8 .... 43 C3
LYDDINGTON 9 C7
Lyddington Rd
  Caldecott LE15, L16 .. 9 D2
  Gretton NN17 .... 10 A1
Lydia Ct NN10 .... 132 A2
Lyle Ct NN8 .... 129 C7
Lyncrest Ave NN5 .... 158 E7
Lyncroft Prim Sch
  NN5 .... 158 E7
Lyncroft Way NN4 ... 141 B1
Lyndhurst Rd CV21 ... 98 F8
Lyneford Way NN10 .. 147 F8
Lyne Wlk NN7 .... 177 B3
Lynmore Cl NN4 ..... 158 C1
Lynmouth Ave NN3 .. 160 C7
Lynmouth Pl NN18 ... 36 E4
Lynton Ave NN2 ..... 141 C6
Lynton Gr NN18 ..... 36 F4
Lynwood Cl NN5 ..... 72 B5
Lytham Cl NN2 ...... 141 E3
Lytham Ct NN8 ...... 129 C7
Lyttleton Rd NN5 .... 159 A7
Lyveden New Bield★
  PE8 .... 57 A7
Lyveden Pl NN16 .... 72 D3
Lyveden Rd
  Brigstock NN14 ..... 55 F7
  Northampton NN4 ... 160 A1
Lyveden Way NN18 ... 36 E2

M

Macadam Cl NN11 ... 134 F5
Macadam Rd NN17 ... 22 A1
McGibbon Wlk NN9 .. 131 D8
McInnes Way NN9 ... 114 D7
Mackenzie Rd NN9 ... 114 C5
Mackintosh La NN15 . 92 B1
Mackworth Dr NN9 .. 111 E4
Mackworth Gn NN9 .. 111 F4
Maclean Cl NN3 ..... 160 C7
Macmillan Way NN3 . 142 B4
Macon Cl NN5 .... 139 F2
Madams Gdns NN14.. 70 D7
Madams Hill NN14 ... 70 D7
Madeline Cl NN14 ... 32 A5
Madison Apartments
  NN16 .... 72 A3
Magdalen Cl
  Daventry NN11 ..... 153 B8
  Stony Stratford MK11 . 229 D6
  Syresham NN13 ..... 224 C8
Magdalen College Sch (St
  John's) NN13 ...... 233 F6
Magdalen College Sch
  (Waynflete) NN13 ... 233 E7
Magdalene Cl NN14 .. 54 B3
Magdalen Ho MK11 .. 229 D6

Magdalen Mdws
  NN13 .... 222 E1
Magdalen Rd CV23 ... 117 E3
Magee St NN1 .... 159 F7
Magellan Cl
  Daventry NN11 ..... 135 C5
  Rothwell NN14 ..... 70 E6
Magnolia Cl NN3 .... 160 D6
Magnolia Dr
  Daventry NN11 ..... 135 C4
  Rushden NN10 ..... 148 B7
Magpie La NN13 .... 233 E6
Magpie Rd
  Sulgrave OX17 ..... 210 E7
  Towcester NN12 .... 203 C3
Maida Cl NN4 .... 175 E7
Maidencastle NN3 ... 143 B3
MAIDFORD 186 D6
Maidford Rd
  Corby NN17 .... 36 C7
  Farthingstone NN12 . 170 D1
MAIDWELL 87 B7
Maidwell Hall (Prep Sch
  for Boys) NN6 ..... 87 B6
Maidwell Prim Sch
  NN6 .... 87 B6
Maidwell Rd
  Haselbech NN6 ..... 86 B8
  Maidwell NN6 ...... 87 D7
Main Dr NN12 ...... 217 B2
Main Rd
  Collyweston PE9 .... 1 D2
  Crick NN6 .... 100 F5
  Dingley LE16 ...... 32 F3
  Earls Barton NN6... 144 D6
  Farthinghoe NN13 .. 221 B4
  Grendon NN7 ...... 163 D6
  Hackleton NN7 ..... 177 B3
  Kelmarsh NN6 ..... 67 F3
  Kilsby CV23 .... 99 F3
  Middleton Cheney
    OX17 .... 220 A8
  Northampton, Duston
    NN5 .... 158 B7
  Northampton, Far Cotton
    NN4 .... 159 B3
  Shutlanger NN12 ... 204 D8
  Syresham NN13 .... 224 C7
  Upper Heyford NN7 . 156 D4
  Wilby NN8 .... 129 B1
Main St
  Abthorpe NN12 .... 201 F2
  Aldwincle NN14 .... 76 F8
  Apethorpe PE8 ..... 14 C4
  Ashby St L CV23 ... 119 C5
  Ashley LE16 .... 18 F2
  Aston le W NN11 ... 182 F2
  Badby NN11 .... 152 F2
  Barnwell PE8 ...... 59 B5
  Bradden NN12 ..... 201 F5
  Caldecott LE16 ..... 21 B8
  Charlton OX17 .... 231 F4
  Church Stowe NN7 . 171 E8
  Claydon OX17 ..... 181 D1
  Clifton u D CV23 ... 80 A5
  Cold Ashby NN6 ... 84 B5
  Cosgrove MK19 .... 218 E2
  Cottesbrooke NN6 . 105 A8
  Denton NN7 .... 162 B1
  Drayton LE16 ..... 20 A5
  East Farndon LE16 . 48 B7
  East Haddon NN6 . 122 D5
  Farthingstone NN12 170 E3
  Foxton LE16 .... 30 A8
  Great Addington NN14 94 B2
  Great Bowden LE16 . 32 A6
  Great Brington NN7 . 138 D7
  Great Gidding PE28 . 61 D3
  Great Oxendon LE16 48 E3
  Hannington NN6 ... 108 C3
  Helidon NN11 ..... 151 D1
  Holcot NN6 .... 126 E8
  Little Brington NN7 . 138 C4
  Little Harrowden NN9 110 C4
  Loddington NN14 ... 70 C1
  Lowick NN14 ...... 75 F6
  Lubenham LE16 .... 30 F3
  Lyddington LE15 ... 9 C7
  Mawsley Village NN14 89 B4
  Medbourne LE16 ... 19 A7
  Middleton LE16 .... 35 C8
  Orton NN14 .... 70 A3
  Polebrook PE8 ..... 43 A3
  Rockingham LE16.... 21 B4
  Slipton NN14 ...... 75 A3
  Southwick PE8 ..... 26 B5
  Stoke Dry LE15 .... 9 A7
  Sudborough NN14 .. 56 D1
  Sutton Bassett LE16 . 18 A1
  Tansor PE8 .... 27 D2
  Theddingworth LE17 46 D8
  Thorpe by Water LE15 10 A5
  Thurning PE8 ...... 60 D3
  Turweston NN13 ... 234 C8
  Upper Stowe NN7 .. 171 F6
  Wadenhoe PE8 .... 58 A4
  Wakerley LE15..... 4 A4
  Watford NN6 ...... 120 C6
  Wilbarston LE16 ... 34 C5
  Willoughby CV23 ... 117 E3
  Woodend NN12 .... 200 F7
  Woodnewton PE8 .. 14 E1
Makepeace Ho NN11 . 118 C1
Malabar Fields NN11 . 153 B8
Malaslea NN14 ...... 89 B4

Malborough Way
  NN12 .... 217 F5
Malcolm Ct NN17 .... 36 F6
Malcolm Dr NN5 .... 158 E7
Malcolm Rd NN2 .... 141 F2
Malcolm Terr NN2 ... 141 F2
Malham Ct NN8..... 129 D6
Malham Dr NN16 ... 72 A5
Mallard Cl
  Earls Barton NN6... 144 F5
  Higham Ferrers NN10 132 C8
  Northampton NN4 .. 158 F2
  Thrapston NN14 ... 76 D3
Mallard Dr
  Burton Latimer NN15 92 A2
  Hinton NN11 ...... 184 B6
Mallery Cl NN10 .... 132 D3
Mallets Cl MK11 .... 229 E5
Mallory Way NN11 .. 135 C5
Mallows Dr NN9 .... 114 C7
Mallows Yd NN29 .. 164 D3
Mall The NN16 ..... 72 B2
Malmo Cl NN18 .... 36 A2
Malpas Dr NN5 ..... 158 B8
Malthouse Cl
  Irthlingborough NN9 112 F2
  Northampton NN4 .. 159 D4
Malthouse Ct NN12 . 203 C6
Malting La NN14 .... 54 A3
Maltings Cl NN17 ... 10 B1
Maltings Field MK19 218 F5
Maltings Rd NN17.... 10 B1
Maltings The
  Ashley LE16 .... 18 F3
  10 Market Harborough
    LE16 .... 31 E3
  Rothwell NN14 ..... 70 C7
  Wollaston NN29.... 146 D3
  Wothorpe PE9 ..... 2 E8
Malting Way NN7 ... 192 D1
Malt La NN13 ...... 224 C8
Malt Mill Cl CV23 .. 100 A2
Malt Mill Mews CV23 100 A2
Malton Wlk NN18 ... 36 B5
Malvern Cl
  Kettering NN16 .... 72 B7
  Wellingborough NN8 129 D1
Malvern Dr MK11 ... 229 F4
Malvern Gr NN5 .... 158 D8
Malzor La NN7 ..... 174 E4
Manchester Rd NN29 146 C3
Mander Cl NN5 ..... 157 F8
Mandeville Cl NN3 .. 142 B4
Manfield Rd NN1 ... 160 A7
Manfield Way NN3 .. 142 B4
Manitoba Cl NN18 .. 36 B3
Manitoba Pl NN11 .. 184 C1
Manitoba Way NN11 184 C1
Manna Ho NN1 ..... 159 D6
Manning Ct NN3 .... 142 C7
Manningham Rd NN9 114 A4
Manning Rd NN3 ... 142 C7
Mannings Rise NN10 132 C5
Manning St NN10 ... 132 C1
Mannington Gdns
  NN4 .... 175 C7
Mannock Rd NN8 ... 129 E3
Manor Cl
  Bozeat NN29 ...... 164 D3
  Charwelton NN11 .. 168 A4
  Cosgrove MK19 .... 218 E2
  Great Addington NN14 94 B2
  Great Harrowden NN9 110 D2
  Hanslope MK19 .... 207 A2
  Harpole NN7 ...... 157 C6
  Hinton NN11 ...... 184 B7
  Irchester NN29 .... 147 B8
  Isham NN14....... 110 F8
  Middleton Cheney
    OX17 .... 220 A8
  Roade NN7 .... 191 E4
  Sulgrave OX17 .... 210 F8
  Thrapston NN14 ... 76 D2
Manor Ct
  Brackley NN13 .... 233 F8
  Cottingham LE16 .. 20 C1
  Grendon NN7 ..... 163 D5
  Little Harrowden NN9 110 C4
  Northampton NN2 . 141 B3
  Rushden NN10 .... 148 C8
  2 Wellingborough
    NN8 .... 130 B5
Manor Dr
  Corby NN18 .... 36 A4
  Irthlingborough NN9 113 A2
Manor Farm
  Apethorpe PE8..... 14 C4
  Hannington NN6 .. 108 C3
Manor Farm Cl
  Barby CV23 .... 99 C2
  Broughton NN14 .. 90 B4
  Walgrave NN6 .... 108 A5
Manor Farm Cotts
  NN13 .... 238 C8
Manor Farm Ct
  Cogenhoe NN7 .... 162 A6
  Titchmarsh NN14.. 77 C4
Manor Farm Rd
  Northampton NN3 . 143 B2
  Raunds NN9....... 114 A6
Manorfield Cl NN3 . 161 B8
Manorfield Rd NN3 . 161 B8
Manorfields Rd MK19 229 B6
Manor Gdns
  Farthingstone NN12 170 F3
  Norton NN11 ...... 136 C4
  Pytchley NN14..... 90 F2

Manor Gdns continued
  Stanwick NN9 ..... 114 A3
Manor Ho The NN14 . 76 D2
Manor House Cl NN6 144 E5
Manor House Gdns
  NN9 .... 114 D6
Manor House Mus★
  NN16 .... 72 B1
Manor La
  Clifton u D CV23 ... 80 A5
  Farthinghoe NN13 . 221 B4
  Newnham NN11 .... 153 E4
  Whilton NN11 ..... 137 D5
  Wymington NN10... 148 A5
Manor Pk
  Claydon OX17 ..... 181 D1
  Nether Heyford NN7 156 C2
Manor Pl NN15 ..... 91 B8
Manor Rd
  Brackley NN13 .... 233 E7
  Daventry NN11 .... 135 D1
  Earls Barton NN6.. 144 E5
  Great Bowden LE16 . 32 A6
  Grendon NN7 ..... 163 D5
  Grimscote NN12 .. 188 A8
  Hanging Houghton NN6 106 C8
  Hinton NN11 ...... 184 B6
  Kilsby CV23 .... 100 A3
  Mears Ashby NN6 . 128 B2
  Medbourne LE16 .. 19 A7
  Moulton NN3 ..... 142 C8
  Northampton NN2 . 141 B3
  Pitsford NN6 ...... 125 D5
  Rothwell NN14 .... 70 B7
  Rushden NN10 .... 148 B8
  Rushton NN14 .... 52 C2
  Spratton NN6 ..... 105 B1
  Stanion NN14..... 37 E2
  Staverton NN11 ... 152 B7
  Sulgrave OX17 .... 210 F8
  Sutton PE5 .... 8 F2
  Weedon Bec NN7 .. 155 B3
Manor Sch & Sports Coll
  NN9 .... 114 E6
Manor St NN9 ...... 114 D6
Manor The NN11 ... 199 C7
Manor View PE9 ... 1 A6
Manor Way
  Higham Ferrers
    NN10.............. 132 C5
  Yardley Gobion NN12 217 E6
Manor Wlk
  Hanging Houghton
    NN6 .... 106 C8
  Market Harborough LE16 31 E3
  Nether Heyford NN7 156 C2
Mansard Cl NN5 .... 158 E6
Manse Cl
  Rushden NN10 .... 132 C3
  Stony Stratford MK11 229 D6
Mansefield Cl NN14 . 51 A3
Mansel Cl MK19 .... 218 D2
Mansell Cl NN12 ... 203 C8
Mansfield Ct NN12 . 202 D8
Mansfield Ct NN9 .. 113 F4
Mansfield Way NN7 147 A8
Manshead Ct MK11 . 229 F5
Mansion Cl NN3 .... 142 A6
Mansion Hill OX17 . 219 F8
Mantlefield Rd NN18 36 B6
Manton Ct NN10 ... 132 C2
Manton Rd
  Corby NN17 .... 22 C7
  Irthlingborough NN9 112 C2
  Rushden NN10 .... 132 C1
Manton Spinney
  NN10 .... 131 E2
Maple Cl
  Brackley NN13 .... 222 F1
  Braunston NN11 .. 118 D1
  Bugbrooke NN7 ... 172 F7
  Hinton NN11 ..... 184 A6
  Towcester NN12 .. 203 B4
Maple Ct NN17 .... 21 E1
Maple Dr NN8 ..... 129 E5
Maplefelds Sch NN18 36 D5
Maple Rd
  Kettering NN16 ... 72 D4
  Rushden NN10 .... 132 C2
Maples The NN11 .. 135 D1
Mapletoft St NN9 .. 114 C5
Maple Wood NN10 . 148 B7
Mapperley Dr NN3 . 160 F8
Marchwood Cl NN3 . 142 F6
Marconi Ctyd NN17 . 22 B1
Marecroft LE16 .... 66 F7
Mare Fair NN1 ..... 159 C5
Margaret Ave NN8 . 129 E2
Margaret House Ctyd
  NN13 .... 233 F6
Margaret Rd
  Kettering NN16 ... 72 E3
  Twyford OX17 .... 230 B5
Margaret St NN1 ... 159 D7
Marion Sq NN16 ... 72 E3
Maritime Way NN11 135 C4
Marjoram Cl 6 NN4 175 D6
Market Cross NN9 . 112 F2
MARKET HARBOROUGH
  .... 31 C2
Market Harborough CE
  Prim Sch LE16..... 31 D3
Market Harborough
  District Hospl LE16 31 D3
Market Harborough Mus★
  LE16 .... 31 E3
Market Harborough Sta
  LE16 .... 32 A3

Market Hill NN14 ... 70 D7
Market Pl
  Brackley NN13..... 233 E6
  Kettering NN16 ... 72 B1
  Long Buckby NN6 . 121 B4
  Olney MK46 ...... 195 F3
  Oundle PE8 .... 42 A5
Market Rd NN14 ... 76 D2
Market Sq
  3 Daventry NN11.. 135 C2
  Hanslope MK19 ... 207 A2
  Higham Ferrers NN10 132 C6
  Northampton NN1 . 159 C6
  Stony Stratford MK11 229 D5
  3 Wellingborough
    NN8 .... 130 A4
Market St
  Kettering NN16 ... 72 B2
  Northampton NN1 . 159 E7
  Wellingborough NN8 130 A4
Market Street Mews 10
  NN16 .... 72 B2
Market Wlk NN1 ... 159 E7
Markham Cl NN5 .. 140 C1
Markham Wlk NN18 36 B5
Marks Cl NN9...... 114 A3
Marlborough Ave
  NN8 .... 129 D7
Marlborough Cl
  Kettering NN15 ... 72 F1
  Kings Sutton OX17 230 F6
Marlborough Croft
  NN13 .... 233 F6
Marlborough Rd NN5 159 A6
Marlborough Way
  LE16. .... 31 E5
Marlow Cl
  Daventry NN11 ... 135 B1
  Rothwell NN14 .... 70 C6
Marlow Ct
  Corby NN18 .... 36 B5
  Medbourne LE16 .. 19 A8
Marlowe Cl NN4 ... 175 B7
Marlow Rd NN12 .. 203 D5
Marlstones NN4 ... 158 D2
Marnock Sq 3 NN4 158 F2
Marquee Dr NN3 .. 160 F7
Marriots Rd NN6 .. 121 C3
Marriott Cl NN9.... 131 E8
Marriott St NN2 ... 159 C8
Marseilles Cl NN5 . 139 F1
Marshall Ct 2 LE16 31 F2
Marshalls Ct NN9 .. 114 D6
Marshall's Rd NN9 . 114 C6
Marsh Cl NN6 ..... 101 A5
Marsh La NN9 ..... 113 B3
Marshleys Ct NN3.. 143 B5
Marsh The NN6 ... 101 A5
Marshwell Ct 5 NN3 161 A8
Marsons Dr NN6 .. 100 F5
Marston Hill
  Marston St Lawrence
    OX17 .... 210 B3
  Priors Marston CV47 166 E7
Marston La LE16 ... 48 A7
Marston Rd
  Greatworth OX17 . 210 E2
  Lubenham LE16 ... 30 D2
MARSTON ST LAWRENCE
  .... 210 A1
MARSTON TRUSSELL .. 47 C8
Marston Trussell Rd
  LE16. .... 47 F7
Marston Way NN11 135 D6
Martel Cl NN5 ..... 157 F8
Martha Wallis Ct 1
  NN16 .... 72 B2
Martial Daire Bvd
  NN13 .... 233 E8
Martin Cl NN10 ... 132 B4
Martindale NN2.... 140 F5
Martin Rd NN15.... 91 C7
Martins La NN4 ... 175 E8
Martins Rd NN7... 177 A1
Martins Yd NN5 .. 159 B7
Martlet Cl NN4 ... 175 E5
Martonia 1 NN1 .. 159 F7
Marvills Mill Rd NN4 159 C4
Marwood Cl NN3 . 160 C7
Masefield Cl NN8 . 129 C4
Masefield Dr NN10 131 E3
Masefield Rd NN16 72 C5
Masefield Way
  Corby NN17 ...... 36 D8
  Northampton NN2 141 E4
Mason Cl
  Oundle PE8 ...... 42 A5
  Thrapston NN14 . 76 D1
Massey Cl NN4 ... 175 E8
Matchless Cl NN5 . 140 A1
Matlock Way NN14 50 E4
Matson Cl NN14 .. 70 B6
Matson Ct NN9 ... 114 E7
Matthew Clarke Ho 4
  LE16. .... 31 E4
Matthews Cl NN14 52 C3
Mauduit Cl NN3 ... 207 A3
Maunsell Rise NN14 70 B6
Mauntley Ave NN14 55 F7
Maurice Rd LE16 .. 48 D8
Mawsley Chase NN14 89 C5
Mawsley Cres NN16 71 F2
Mawsley La NN14 . 89 C8
Mawsley Lo NN14 . 89 B3

Mawsley Prim Sch
NN14................................89 B5
MAWSLEY VILLAGE.......89 A4
Maxwell Wlk NN18.......36 E5
May Bank NN11.........153 B8
Maybush Wlk MK46....195 E5
May Cl NN10...........148 C7
Maye Dicks Rd NN10....148 C8
Mayfield Rd
Daventry NN11.........135 C3
Desborough NN14........51 C3
Northampton NN3.......142 B3
Maylan Rd NN17.........21 F3
Mays Way NN12........217 D3
Mazewood Gate PE8....13 E7
Meacham Cl NN14........90 A3
Meadow Cl
Daventry NN11.........135 D6
Higham Ferrers NN10...132 B6
Market Harborough LE16..31 F4
Northampton NN5.......140 B2
Ringstead NN14..........95 A3
Wellingborough NN8....130 D8
Meadow Ct
[6] Kettering NN16......72 B2
Ravenstone MK46.......194 D2
Towcester NN12........203 C5
Meadowdale Prim Sch
LE16...................32 B4
Meadow Dr NN10......132 B6
Meadow Farm Cl NN7..155 F5
Meadow Gate PE8.......14 E2
Meadow La
Denford NN14...........95 C6
Little Houghton NN7....161 A4
Raunds NN9............114 A6
Thornhaugh PE8..........7 F5
Thrapston NN14.........76 D2
Meadowlands NN9.....110 B3
Meadow Rd
Kettering NN16.........72 A2
Rothwell NN14...........70 C6
Meadow Rise NN12....189 D8
Meadowside Inf Sch
NN15...................92 B2
Meadowside Jun Sch
NN15...................92 B2
Meadow St LE16.........31 E4
Meadows The
Northampton NN4......175 F1
Northampton NN4......175 F2
Old Stratford MK19.....229 B6
Wellingborough NN9...110 E1
Meadow Sweet Rd
NN10..................148 C7
Meadowsweet Wlk
NN4..................175 F2
Meadow The NN3......142 C1
Meadowvale NN9.....112 F1
MEADOW VIEW........140 F6
Meadow View
Adderbury OX17.......230 A4
Great Addington NN14...94 C3
Higham Ferrers NN10...132 A6
Potterspury NN12......217 D3
Meadow Way NN9.....112 F1
Meadow Wlk
Higham Ferrers NN10...132 B6
[9] Irthlingborough
NN9..................112 F2
Mead Rd NN15..........90 F8
Meads Ct NN15..........92 B1
Meadslade NN7.......192 D2
Meadway
Bugbrooke NN7........172 F7
Northampton NN3......160 D8
Meadway Cl NN15......91 D8
MEARS ASHBY........128 C2
Mears Ashby Prim Sch
NN6..................128 B2
Mears Ashby Rd
Earls Barton NN6.....144 C6
Wilby NN8.............129 A1
MEDBOURNE............18 F6
Medbourne Cl NN3....142 B7
Medbourne Rd
Ashley LE16............18 E4
Drayton LE16...........19 E4
Medbourne LE16.........18 C8
Medellin Hill NN3.....142 F6
Medinah Cl NN4......175 D5
Medina Rd NN17........21 C1
Medlicott Cl NN18......53 A8
Medway Cl
Market Harborough
LE16...................32 A3
Northampton NN5......140 E2
Medway Dr
Northampton NN5......140 F2
Wellingborough NN8...129 C6
Medway Ho PE8.........42 A6
Medway The NN11.....135 A1
Medwin NN3............129 B4
Meeting La
Burton Latimer NN15...92 C2
Corby NN17.............37 B7
Irthlingborough NN9...112 F2
[15] Kettering NN16....72 B2
Northampton NN5......158 C7
Rothwell NN14..........70 C6
Towcester NN12.......203 C6
Meissen Ave NN14......50 F3
Melbourne Ho
Corby NN17.............22 F1
[4] Northampton NN5..159 A6

Melbourne La NN5.....158 C6
Melbourne Rd NN5.....158 F6
Melbourne St [3] NN1..159 F6
Melbourne Wlk [4]
NN1...................159 F6
Melbury La NN3.......143 B3
Melbury Pl NN3.......143 B3
Melchbourne Rd
MK44..................149 F4
Melchester Cl NN4....175 E7
Meldon Cl NN4........175 C8
Melford Cl NN18........36 D2
Mellor Rd CV21..........99 B8
Melloway Rd NN10....131 E2
Melrose Ave NN5......158 E7
Melrose Cl NN15........91 F8
Meltham Cl NN3.......142 F1
Melton Rd NN8........130 C5
Melton Rd N NN8......130 B5
Melton St NN16.........72 B3
Melville St NN1........159 F7
Membris Way NN11...184 A6
Memorial Gn NN7.....191 E4
Mendip Cl NN16........72 B5
Mendip Ct NN11.......135 B5
Mendip Rd NN5.......158 D7
Meon Cl NN17...........21 C1
Meon Way NN5........158 D8
Mercer Ct CV22.........98 F8
Mercer's Row [3] NN1..159 C5
Mercia Gdns NN3.....142 C1
Mercury Cl NN11......135 A4
Mercury Dr NN4.......160 A2
Mere Cl
Brafield-on-the-G NN7..161 D2
[1] Northampton NN4..175 B8
Mere Farm Bsns Units
NN6...................108 D4
MEREFIELD............175 B7
Merefields NN9.......112 E3
Merestone Hos OX17..210 B1
Merestone Rd NN18....36 D3
Mere Way NN4........175 C8
Mereway Com Coll
NN4...................159 B1
Merlin Gr [5] NN4.....175 B8
Merrivale Cl NN15......90 F7
Merrycot La NN6........82 B4
Merrydale Sq NN3.....143 A6
Merryhill NN4.........158 E2
Merry Tom La NN6....124 D4
Mersey Cl NN4.........159 A2
Mershe Cl NN4........175 F7
Merthyr Rd NN5......159 A8
Merton Cl NN13.......233 D8
Merton Rd NN11......153 B7
Mescalero Cres NN3..160 B7
Methodist Homestead [4]
NN2...................141 E1
Mews Cotts LE16........48 E3
Mews The
Brixworth NN6........106 B2
Brockhall NN11.......137 C2
Great Bowden LE16......31 E7
Long Buckby NN6.....121 B4
Northampton NN3....160 D8
[4] Rugby CV21........80 A1
Michaelmas Cl OX17..208 F1
Michael's Wlk LE16.....21 B4
Mickleborough Cl
LE16....................18 B3
Mickle Hill PE18......116 D7
Micklewell La NN3....142 F6
Middlebrook Gn LE16..32 A4
Middledale Rd LE16.....32 A3
Middlefield Cl NN14....95 B3
Middle Grass NN9....112 E3
Middle Greeve NN4...176 A6
Middle La LE16..........34 B4
Middlemarch [5] NN3..143 B4
Middlemead Ct NN3...143 A1
Middlemore NN3.....142 F6
Middle St
Elton PE8...............28 D8
Foxton LE16............30 E8
Isham NN14............110 F8
Kilsby CV23............100 A3
Nether Heyford NN7..156 C2
Middlethorpe NN12...200 B2
MIDDLETON.............35 B8
MIDDLETON CHENEY...209 A1
Middleton Cheney Com
Prim Sch OX17........219 F8
Middleton Cl
Banbury OX16.........219 A7
Northampton NN2....141 C5
Middleton Rd
Ashley LE16............19 B3
Banbury OX16.........219 A7
Bringhurst LE16........20 C4
Chacombe OX17......208 E4
Middle Weald MK19..229 E1
Middlewell Ct [2] NN3..142 F1
Middlewich Cl NN11..135 C6
Midfield Ct NN3......142 E5
Midland Bsns Ctr
NN10..................132 C6
Midland Bsns Units
NN8...................130 D6
Midland Cotts NN14...52 C3
Midland Rd
Higham Ferrers
NN10..................132 C6
Olney MK46...........195 F5

Midland Rd continued
Raunds NN9...........114 E7
Rushden NN10.........132 A3
Thrapston NN14........76 C1
Wellingborough NN8..130 B4
Midland Works Bsns Ctr
NN8...................130 D6
Midway
Blisworth NN7........174 B2
Middleton Cheney
OX17..................209 A1
Milbury Rd NN4......144 F3
Milby La NN14..........54 A2
Mildmay Cl PE8.........41 E5
Miles Cl NN9...........114 B5
Miles La NN6..........121 C4
Mile St NN29..........164 D3
Milford Ave MK11....229 E4
Military Rd NN1......159 D7
Militia Cl NN4.........175 E7
Milking Slade La PE28..61 F3
Millais Rd NN18.........36 E5
Millbank NN3.........143 D2
Millbrook Cl NN15....159 A4
Millbrook Inf Sch
NN15...................91 F8
Millbrook Jun Sch
NN15...................91 F8
Millburn Dr NN5......158 A6
Mill Cl
Braunston NN11......118 B1
Corby NN18.............36 B1
Raunds NN9...........114 C6
Milldale Gdns NN15....91 D8
Mill Dale Rd NN15......91 D8
Millenium Cl NN15.....91 A7
Millennium Way
NN11..................135 C2
Miller Cl
Kettering NN15.........91 C6
Thrapston NN14........76 E1
Miller Hill NN4.......158 E2
Miller Rd NN15.........92 B1
Millers Cl
Lower Boddington
NN11..................182 C5
Rushden NN10........131 F2
Miller's Cl
Finedon NN9..........112 A5
Kislingbury NN7......157 D2
Millers Gdns LE16......31 B2
Millers La NN8........145 F8
Millers Pk NN6.......130 A1
Miller St NN9..........114 D7
Millers Way NN4.....175 F3
Miller's Yd [5] LE16....31 E3
Mill Est NN10.........148 B7
Mill Farm Ctyd MK19..229 B1
Millfield Ave LE16......20 D1
Millfields PE8...........41 F6
Mill Fields NN10......132 B7
Millfields Ave CV21....98 F8
Millglade The NN14....91 F1
Mill Greene Ct [3]
NN16....................72 C4
Mill Hill
Corby NN18.............53 B7
Lubenham LE16.........30 E3
Mill Hill Rd LE16......31 F3
Mill Ho
Brackley NN13........233 E5
[6] Northampton NN2..141 B2
Millholm Rd NN14.....51 B2
Millhouse Ct NN5....159 B5
Millies La NN17........12 C1
Mill La
Adderbury OX17......230 A3
Barrowden LE15.........4 A5
Brackley NN13........234 A6
Brigstock NN14.........55 F7
Caldecott LE16..........21 B8
Chipping Warden OX17..196 F6
Cogenhoe NN7........162 A7
Croughton NN13.....238 C2
Earls Barton NN6.....145 A3
Greens Norton NN12..202 E7
Grimscote NN12......172 B1
Isham NN14............91 F1
Islip NN14..............76 C3
Ketton PE9..............1 A5
Kings Sutton OX17...230 F4
Kislingbury NN7......157 D3
Lowick NN14...........75 F6
Northampton, Kingsthorpe
NN2, NN5.............141 B2
Northampton NN2....159 B7
Old NN6.................88 E3
Oundle PE8.............27 B1
Stoke Bruerne NN12..191 A1
Stony Stratford MK11..229 D6
Wadenhoe PE8.........58 A3
Westbury NN13.......234 F4
Mill Marina Cvn Pk
NN14....................76 C1
Mill Mdw NN2........141 D5
Mill Rd
Bozeat NN29..........164 C2
Cottingham LE16.......20 C2
Great Gidding PE28....61 E3
Gretton LE15, NN17.....9 F2
Irthlingborough NN8..131 B7
Islip NN14..............76 B3
Kettering NN16.......141 F5
Kislingbury NN7......157 D3
Northampton NN2....159 C7
Oundle PE8.............41 F4

Mill Rd continued
Wellingborough NN8..130 B5
Whitfield NN13.......223 E4
Woodford NN14.........94 C7
Yarwell PE8.............16 A7
Mill Rd Ind Est NN8...130 C6
Mill Road Pas [5] NN16..72 C2
Mills Cl NN6..........144 F4
Millside Cl NN2......141 D5
Mill St PE9..............5 B6
Millstone Cl NN4....158 D2
Millway NN5..........158 C6
Millway Prim Sch
NN5...................158 D6
Millwood Way PE8.....13 E7
Milner Rd NN9........111 F4
MILTHORPE............200 B2
Milthorpe NN12......200 B2
Milton Ave NN8.......129 C3
Milton Bridge NN4...176 A6
Milton Ct
Kettering NN16.........72 C5
Milton Malsor NN7...174 E3
MILTON MALSOR.....174 E4
Milton Parochial Prim Sch
NN7...................174 E4
Milton Rd
Corby NN17.............36 C8
Daventry NN11.......135 B2
Gayton NN7...........173 F2
Little Irchester NN8..130 C1
Oundle PE8.............41 F5
Milton St N NN2......141 E1
Milton St
Higham Ferrers NN10..132 B5
Northampton NN2....141 F1
Milton Terr PE8.........44 C4
Milverton Cres NN3..160 D7
Mimosa Cl NN3......160 C6
Minden Cl NN18........35 F2
Minehead Cl NN18.....36 A6
Minerva Way NN8....129 D5
Minster Ho [2] NN1..159 D6
Minton Cl NN14.........50 F3
Mirfield Cl NN18........36 C5
Mistletoe Pl NN3.....142 C1
Mitchell Cl NN5......140 D2
Mitchell Rd NN17......22 B2
Mitchell St NN16.......72 C5
Mitchison Cl CV23....118 C8
MIXBURY..............234 D1
Mixbury Rd NN13....233 F2
Moat Farm Dr CV21....99 A7
Moat La NN12.........203 C6
Moat Pl NN1..........159 B6
Moat Yd NN12........203 C6
Mobbs Miller Ho NN1..160 A7
Moffatt Terr NN8.....130 A5
Molesworth Bglws PE9..1 A6
Monarch Ctyd NN4...160 A2
Monarch Rd NN2....141 C1
Monarch Terr NN2...159 C8
Monfield Coll NN14.....50 E2
Monk's Hall Rd NN1..159 F7
Monks Park Rd NN1..159 F7
Monks Pond St NN1..159 B6
Monks Rd NN29......146 D3
Monks Way
Corby NN18.............36 A4
Crick NN6.............101 A6
Wellingborough NN8..130 A3
Monkswood NN12...214 C4
Monmouth Cl NN14....76 F2
Monmouth Rd NN5..159 A7
Monroe Cl LE16.........31 D5
Monson Way PE8.......41 E7
Montabaur Rd NN13..234 A7
Montagu Cl NN15......91 D5
Montague Cres NN5..140 D2
Montague Ct NN14.....76 D2
Montague Dr CV23....100 A3
Montague St NN10...132 A2
Montagu Sch NN16....72 D5
Montagu St NN16......72 C2
Montagu Terr PE8.....59 B6
Montcalm Cl NN15.....72 F1
Monterly Gate NN14...55 F7
Montfort Cl NN5.....158 E6
Montgomery Cl NN15..72 E1
Montgomery Way
NN4...................175 D7
Montrose Cl LE16......31 D1
Montrose St NN17......36 F6
Montsaye Com Coll
NN14...................70 B7
Moonshine Gap NN6..128 D6
Moore Cl
Corby NN17.............36 D8
Kettering NN15.........92 A7
Moor End PE8...........60 D3
MOOR END............217 D6
Moorend Rd NN12...217 E6
Moores Cl NN17......172 F7
Moores Hill MK46.....195 F5
Moore St NN2........141 F1
Moor Field NN12.....203 B5
Moorfield Gn NN14....70 B6
Moorfield Rd NN14....70 B6
Moorfield Sq NN3....143 A6
Moorhouse Way NN15..90 E8
Moorings The NN14....94 E6
Moor La CV23.........117 D3
Moorland Cl NN13...142 E2
Moorlands NN8.......129 D7
Moorlands The NN10..132 A6
Moor Rd NN10........132 A2
Moors Cl MK19.......228 E4
Moors Dr The OX17..219 F8

Moors La CV21, CV23...99 D8
Morby Ct NN15.........92 B1
MORCOTT..............3 A5
Morcott Rd LE15........3 D5
Mordaunt Cl NN14.....75 E6
Mordaunt La NN5....140 D1
Morehay La
King's Cliffe PE8........13 E6
King's Cliffe PE8........13 F7
More Rd NN11.........135 B4
Moreton Ave NN8...129 D2
MORETON PINKNEY..199 D7
Moreton Rd NN11....184 C1
Moreton Way NN2...141 C5
Morgan Cl NN3.......143 C4
Morgan Dr NN6......106 C3
Morgans Cl PE8........43 A3
Moriston Cl NN17......21 C1
Morland Rd NN18.....36 E5
Morley St
Kettering NN16.......72 B2
Market Harborough
LE16....................31 E3
Morley Wlk NN17.....36 C8
Morning Star Rd [1]
NN11..................135 A3
Morris Ave NN10.....131 F1
Morris Cl NN8........129 A6
Morrison Park Rd
NN6...................102 C5
Morris Rd
Daventry NN11.......134 F3
Northampton NN2....141 D3
Morse Way NN14.......51 B4
Mortar Pit Rd NN3...143 C5
Mortimer Cl NN4.....159 A2
Morton Ct CV22........98 F8
Mortons Bush NN4...176 A6
Moss Cl NN12.........203 C8
Moss Ct NN16..........72 B3
Moss Wlk NN18........36 A2
Motala Cl NN18........36 A2
Motherwell Ho NN17...37 A8
Motspur Dr NN2......141 B1
Motts The NN7.......157 B6
Moulds La LE16........20 D7
MOULTON..............126 C2
Moulton Coll NN3....126 C1
Moulton Crossing
NN3...................142 A8
Moulton La NN2, NN3..141 D8
MOULTON PARK.....142 A6
Moulton Park Bsns Ctr
NN3...................142 A6
Moulton Prim Sch
NN3...................126 C1
Moulton Rd
Holcot NN6...........126 B6
Pitsford NN6.........125 D3
**Moulton Sch & Science
Coll** NN3.............126 B1
Moulton Way NN3...142 C6
Moulton Way N NN3..142 C6
Moulton Way S NN3..142 C6
Mountbatten Dr NN14..95 C3
Mountbatten Ho
NN11..................153 B8
Mountbatten Way
NN9...................114 C4
Mountclair Ct NN3...160 B6
Mountfield Rd
Irthlingborough NN9..112 F3
Northampton NN3....142 A3
Mount Hill Ave MK19..229 B7
Mount Pleasant
Earls Barton NN6.....144 F4
Harpole NN7.........157 C7
Morcott LE15............3 A6
Wardington OX17....196 E5
Woodford Halse NN11..184 D6
Yardley Gobion NN12..217 F6
Mount Pleasant Rd
LE15....................3 A6
Mounts Bsns Ctr NN1..159 D7
Mounts Ct [1] NN3...142 E3
Mounts La NN11......153 E4
Mounts The NN6.....121 B3
Mow Mead MK46.....195 F5
Mowsley Ct LE17.......45 E6
Mowsley Rd
Husbands Bosworth
LE17....................45 E6
Theddingworth LE16..46 C8
Moyeady Ave CV22....98 E8
Muirfield Dr NN11....135 E2
Muirfield Rd NN8....129 C7
Mulberry Cl
Desborough NN14.....51 A5
Northampton NN5...158 F7
Wellingborough NN8..129 E5
Mulberry Ct LE16.......20 A5
Mull Dr NN17...........36 C8
Mullions The NN4....175 E5
Mulso Rd NN9........112 A4
Mumford Dr NN7....174 A2
Muncaster Gdns NN4..175 D7
Muncaster Way NN6..102 C5
Murcott Info..........121 A4
Murcott Cl NN6......121 A4
Murray Ave NN2......141 D1
Murray Ho NN1......160 A8
Murray Wlk NN18.....36 E5
Mursley Ct MK11....229 F5
Murswell Cl NN12...214 D4
Murswell La NN12...214 D4
MUSCOTT.............137 B3
Muscott La NN5.....158 C6
Muscott St NN5.....159 A6

Museum Way NN3 160 F7
Musgrave Cl NN4 175 F7
Mushroom Field Rd NN3 143 D2
Musk Cl LE16 20 D7
Musott Cl NN7 155 E6
Musson Cl NN9 112 E2
Myers Cl OX17 231 F5
Myers Rd CV21 99 C8
Myers Way OX17 231 F5
Myrtle Rd NN16 72 D4

N

Nags Head La NN9 115 F2
Nansen Cl
Daventry NN11 135 C5
Rothwell NN14 70 E6
Nansen Wlk NN18 36 B2
Nantwich Dr NN11 135 D6
Naomi Cl NN3 142 F1
Napier Cl
Daventry NN11 153 D8
Wellingborough NN8 129 A4
NAPTON ON THE HILL 150 A7
Narvik Rd NN18 36 A2
NASEBY 66 B1
Naseby Battle & Farm Mus★ NN6 85 B7
Naseby CE Prim Sch NN6 66 B1
Naseby Cl
Market Harborough LE16 31 E2
Wellingborough NN8 129 D7
Naseby Dr NN11 135 C6
Naseby Ho NN16 71 F3
Naseby Rd
Clipston LE16 66 F8
Corby NN17 36 C7
Haselbech NN6 85 F8
Kettering NN16 72 E3
Sibbertoft LE16 46 F2
Thornby NN6 84 E4
Welford NN6 65 C5
Naseby Sq LE16 31 E2
Naseby St NN2 159 C8
Nash Ct NN15 92 A8
Nasmith Ave NN17 37 A8
Nasmyth Rd NN11 134 F5
NASSINGTON 15 E5
Nassington Prim Sch PE8 15 F5
Nassington Rd
Woodnewton PE8 14 F1
Yarwell PE8 15 F7
Navigation Row NN1 159 C4
Navisford Cl NN14 76 E3
NBC Depot NN2 141 E3
Neale Ave NN16 72 B5
Neale Cl
Northampton NN3 160 E8
Wollaston NN29 146 C3
Near Side NN5 158 F6
Near The Church LE16 17 A5
Needham Rd NN9 113 F4
Neene Ct 13 NN9 112 F2
Nelson Ave NN11 184 B6
Nelson Cl NN11 135 E2
Nelson Dr NN14 70 E7
Nelson Rd NN17 36 B8
Nelson St
Kettering NN16 72 C3
Market Harborough LE16 31 D3
24 Northampton NN1 159 C7
Nelson's Yd NN12 203 C6
Nene Cl
Kettering NN15 92 A5
Raunds NN9 114 D7
Wansford PE8 8 A3
Wellingborough NN8 129 C6
Nene Cres NN17 21 C1
Nene Ct
Thrapston NN14 76 D2
Wellingborough NN8 130 C3
Nene Dr NN5 140 F2
Nene Ent Ctr NN2 159 C8
Nene La NN12 203 A6
Nene Park (Rushden & Diamonds FC) NN9 113 A2
Nene Pl NN5 141 A2
Nene Rd
Burton Latimer NN15 92 A2
Higham Ferrers NN10 132 B5
Nene Rise NN7 161 F6
Neneside Cl NN7 155 B3
Nene Side Cl NN11 152 F3
Nene Univ Coll Northampton NN2 141 E5
Nene Valley Bsns Pk PE8 42 B5
Nene Valley Ret Pk NN1 159 B4
Nene Valley Way NN3 160 D5
Nene View
Irthlingborough NN14 112 F2
Islip NN14 76 B3
Oundle PE8 41 F6
Nene Way
Kislingbury NN7 157 C3
Northampton NN5 141 A2
Oundle PE8 41 F7
Sutton PE5 8 F2
Nene Whitewater Ctr★ NN4 160 B3
Nene Wlk
Daventry NN11 135 A1
Northampton NN5 140 F2
Nepcote Cl NN15 91 D8
Nesbitt Cl NN3 160 E8
Nest Farm Cres NN8 130 A8
Nest Farm Rd NN8 130 A7
Nest La NN8 130 B7
Nether Cl NN13 234 A7
NETHERCOTE 219 B7
Netherfield Gr NN17 36 F8
Netherfield Rd NN15 91 C7
Nether Gn LE16 67 A8
NETHER HEYFORD 156 B1
Nether Jackson Ct 3 NN3 143 B4
Nether La NN7 155 F4
Nethermead Ct NN3 142 F4
Nethertown Way NN14 89 B4
Nettle Gap Cl NN4 175 F6
Neuville Way NN14 50 F3
Nevill Cl MK19 207 B2
Neville Day Cl PE9 1 F5
Neville Ho NN17 36 E6
NEVILL HOLT 19 D8
Nevill Holt Rd LE16 19 F6
Nevis Cl NN17 21 C1
Newark Dr NN18 36 C6
NEW BARTON 144 F5
Newbery Dr NN13 233 D8
New Bldgs 7 NN16 72 B2
Newbold Cl PE8 41 E6
Newbolt Cl NN12 216 B8
NEWBOTTLE 231 E7
Newbottle & Charlton CE Prim Sch OX17 231 F5
Newbridge NN6 136 D8
Newbridge La NN9 114 A3
Newbury Cl
Corby NN18 36 D1
Rushden NN10 132 D3
Newbury Dr NN11 135 C6
Newby Ct NN3 142 C3
New College Farm NN6 127 A6
Newcombe Rd NN5 159 A7
Newcombe St LE16 31 E2
Newcomen Rd NN8 130 B5
New Croft NN7 155 B3
NEW DUSTON 140 B2
Newell Rd NN14 95 B3
New Forest Way NN11 135 B4
NEW HACKLETON 177 A3
New Hall NN11 153 B7
Newham Cl NN14 70 C7
Newington Rd NN2 141 C4
New La PE8 8 C1
Newland NN1 159 C6
Newland Rd NN6 108 A5
Newlands
Brixworth NN6 106 B2
3 Daventry NN11 135 C1
Kings Sutton OX17 231 A6
Naseby NN6 66 C1
Newlands Ctr NN16 72 B2
Newland Sq NN2 141 C4
Newlands Rd NN6 64 E5
Newland St
Braybrooke LE16 49 E5
Kettering NN16 72 B2
Newland Wlk 5 NN1 159 D6
Newlife Apartments 15 NN1 159 C6
Newman St
Burton Latimer NN15 92 B2
Higham Ferrers NN10 132 C7
6 Kettering NN16 72 C2
Newmarket Cl NN18 36 D1
NEWNHAM 153 E4
Newnham Dr NN11 135 A5
Newnham Prim Sch NN11 153 D4
Newnham Rd NN2 141 D3
Newnham Windmill★ NN11 153 D7
Newport Pagnell Rd
Horton NN7 177 D1
Northampton NN4, NN7 176 A7
Newport Pagnell Rd W NN4 175 D8
Newport Rd
Hanslope MK19 207 B2
Northampton NN5 159 A7
New Post Office Sq NN17 36 E6
New Rd
Brackley NN13 233 E6
Castlethorpe MK19 218 F5
Collyweston PE9 1 C2
Easton o t H PE9 2 A5
Farthinghoe NN13 221 A4
Geddington NN14 54 A2
Greens Norton NN12 202 D8
Maidford NN12 186 D6
Northampton NN4 175 E6
Oundle PE8 42 A6
New South Bridge Rd NN4 159 C4
New St
Brixworth NN6 106 A2
Daventry NN11 135 C1
Desborough NN14 51 A3
Earls Barton NN6 144 F4
Irchester NN29 147 B8
New St *continued*
Irthlingborough NN9 112 F2
Oundle PE8 42 A5
Rothwell NN14 70 D7
Stony Stratford MK11 229 D5
Weedon Bec NN7 155 C3
Wellingborough NN8 130 A5
Newstead Cl NN3 143 D3
Newstead Ct NN15 91 C5
Newstone Cres NN4 158 E4
New Street Ct NN29 147 B8
New Terr NN11 183 D7
NEWTON 53 E3
NEWTON BROMSWOLD 149 D8
Newton Cl
Daventry NN11 135 A4
Rushden NN10 132 D1
Wellingborough NN8 129 B6
Newton Ct CV23 80 A8
Newton Gr NN17 22 A1
Newton Manor La CV23 80 A8
Newton Rd
Clifton u D CV23 80 A7
Geddington NN14 54 A3
Higham Ferrers NN10 132 E5
Kettering NN15 91 F5
Northampton NN5 158 D8
Rushden NN10 132 E1
Wollaston NN29 146 D2
Newton Road Com Prim Sch NN10 132 C2
Newton St MK46 195 F4
Newton Way LE16 49 F6
Newtown
Brigstock NN14 55 E8
Woodford NN14 94 D7
New Town PE9 2 A5
Newtown Rd
Little Irchester NN8 130 C1
Raunds NN9 114 E5
New Town Rd 2 NN1 159 F6
Newtown St NN14 94 D7
Nibbits La NN11 118 C1
Nicholas Hawksmoor Prim Sch NN12 203 B5
Nicholas La NN9 112 E1
Nicholas Rd NN9 112 E1
Nicholas Way NN10 131 F3
Nicholls Ct NN3 142 E5
Nicholls Ho 1 NN4 159 A3
Nichols St NN14 51 A4
Nichols Way NN9 114 C7
Nielson Rd NN8 130 C8
Nigel Ct NN13 234 A5
Nightingale Cl
Brackley NN13 222 E2
Daventry NN11 135 D6
Nightingale Ct NN2 141 D1
Nightingale Dr
Desborough NN14 51 B4
Towcester NN12 203 C3
Nightingale La NN8 130 B7
Nine Arches Way NN14 76 C2
Niort Way NN8 129 C8
Nippendale NN10 132 C2
Nithsdale Ave LE16 31 F2
Nithsdale Cres LE16 31 F2
Nithsdale Rd NN17 36 D7
Noble Ave NN9 113 A5
Nobold Ct LE16 66 F8
NOBOTTLE 138 E2
Noel Mews NN3 142 B4
Nook The
Corby NN17 37 B6
Cottingham LE16 20 D1
Easton o t H PE9 2 A5
Norbury Cl LE16 31 D3
Norfolk Cl NN17 36 C7
Norfolk St NN2 159 C8
Norfolk Terr NN2 159 C8
Norman-D-Gate NN1 159 E5
Norman-D-Gate Ind Est NN1 159 E5
Normandy Lo NN13 233 E8
Norman Rd NN3 142 B1
Norman Way
Irchester NN29 147 C8
Wellingborough NN8 129 D2
Normead Sq 4 NN3 143 D2
Norris Acre NN13 232 F6
Norris Cl NN15 92 A8
Norris Way NN10 131 E3
Norris Way Ind Est NN10 131 E3
Norse Wlk NN18 36 A2
Northall NN6 108 A5
Northall Mews NN16 72 A2
Northall St NN16 72 B3
Northam Ct NN16 72 B4
NORTHAMPTON 159 E4
Northampton Acad NN3 142 F2
Northampton Christian Sch NN1 160 A8
Northampton Coll
Northampton NN1 159 D6
Northampton, The Arbours NN3 142 D3
Northampton General Hospl NN1 159 E5
Northampton High Sch NN4 175 E8
Northampton Ho 7 NN1 159 D6
Northampton La N NN3 142 C8
Northampton La S NN3 142 C7
Northampton Prep Sch NN4 160 E3
Northampton Rd
Blisworth NN7 174 D1
Brackley NN13 223 A1
Brixworth NN6 106 B1
Broughton NN14 90 A3
Chapel Brampton NN6 124 E1
Cosgrove MK19 217 F7
Denton NN7 178 B8
Earls Barton NN6 144 D5
Ecton NN6 143 F4
Harpole NN7 157 C5
Kettering NN15 71 F1
Litchborough NN12 171 E2
Market Harborough LE16 31 F3
Orlingbury NN14 109 F5
Roade NN7 191 D5
Rushden NN10 131 E4
Towcester NN12 203 C7
Welford NN6 64 E4
Wellingborough NN8 129 D3
West Haddon NN6 102 C4
Yardley Hastings NN7 179 A6
Northampton Sch for Boys NN1 160 A6
Northampton Sch for Girls
Northampton NN3 142 A4
Northampton NN3 142 A5
Northampton Science Pk NN3 141 F6
Northamptonshire Fire & Rescue HQ NN3 142 C6
Northamptonshire Gram Sch NN6 125 D4
Northampton Sta NN1 159 B5
Northampton (Sywell) Airport NN6 127 E5
Northampton Town FC NN5 158 E5
Northampton & Lamport Rly★ NN6 124 F1
Northants County Cricket Club★ NN1 160 A8
Northants Ent Pk NN2 141 E6
North Ave NN15 92 B3
Northbank LE16 31 E3
Northbrook NN18 36 B4
North Cape Wlk NN18 36 A2
North Cl NN11 118 D1
Northcote St NN2 159 C7
Northend MK46 194 E3
North End NN10 132 B7
Northen Way NN8 129 F8
Northern Cl NN17 22 B8
Northern Way NN11 135 D4
Northfield Ave
Kettering NN16 72 A3
Ringstead NN14 95 B3
North Field Cl NN16 72 A4
Northfield Gn NN6 122 D5
Northfield La PE8 15 E5
Northfield Point NN16 72 A4
Northfield Rd
Broughton NN14 71 C1
Northampton NN5 140 B1
Northfield Way NN2 141 B4
North Folds Rd NN18 35 F1
Northgate NN12 203 C7
Northgate Sch NN2 141 C2
North Hayes Ct NN3 142 F5
North Hill MK18 225 D2
North Holme Ct NN3 142 D5
NORTH KILWORTH 45 A3
North La LE16 30 D8
North Lea LE16 18 B3
Northleigh Gr LE16 31 D4
North Leys Ct NN3 142 C7
North Luffenham Rd LE15 3 B8
North Meadow View NN5 157 F7
North Oval NN5 140 F2
North Paddock Ct NN3 142 F4
North Park Dr NN16 72 C5
North Portway Cl NN3 142 F7
North Priors Ct NN3 143 A4
North Rd
Clifton u D CV23 80 A6
Earls Barton NN6 144 E5
Northampton NN3 141 F6
South Kilworth LE17 63 D8
North St
Castlethorpe MK19 218 F5
Daventry NN11 135 C2
Kilsby CV23 99 F3
Mears Ashby NN6 128 B2
Oundle PE8 42 A5
Raunds NN9 114 E7
Rothersthorpe NN7 174 B6
Rushden NN10 132 B3
Swinford LE17 62 B4
Titchmarsh NN14 77 C4
Wellingborough NN8 129 F5
Northumberland Cl NN15 91 D6
Northumberland Rd NN15 91 D6
Northumbria Gdns NN3 142 B1
North Way
Deanshanger MK19 228 E5
Potterspury NN12 217 E2
North Western Ave NN2 141 A4
Northwood Rd NN3 142 B2
Nortoft NN6 103 F7
NORTON 136 C4
Norton Cl NN11 135 D2
Norton Cres NN12 203 B6
Norton Leys CV22 98 A6
Norton Rd
Corby NN17 36 C7
Daventry NN11 135 D2
Northampton NN2 141 C3
Norton St NN14 70 E7
Norway Cl NN18 36 A3
Norwood Rd NN5 157 F8
Notre Dame Mews 3 NN1 159 D6
Nuffield Cl NN13 233 D8
Nunneley Way LE16 31 F5
Nunnery Ave NN14 70 C7
Nunn Mills Rd NN1 159 E4
Nuns La NN6 121 B4
Nurseries The
Horton NN7 177 D1
3 Moulton NN3 126 C1
Northampton NN1 159 F5
Nursery Cl
Little Houghton NN7 161 A4
Maidwell NN6 87 B7
Nursery Ct NN6 128 B2
Nursery Dr NN8 130 B7
Nursery End LE16 31 C2
Nursery Gdns NN9 112 E2
Nursery La NN2 141 C3
Nutcote NN6 85 B8
Nuthall Cl NN3 160 F8

O

Oak Ave NN7 174 B1
Oak Cl
Broughton NN14 90 B4
Hartwell NN7 192 E2
Irchester NN29 147 A7
Market Harborough LE16 31 F4
Towcester NN12 203 C4
Oakdown Cres MK46 195 F3
Oak Dr NN11 184 B6
Oakfield NN10 132 A4
Oak Gr NN11 135 C5
Oakgrove Pl NN4 175 D6
Oakham Cl
Desborough NN14 50 F4
Northampton NN3 142 B7
Rushden NN10 148 A8
Oakham La NN11 152 B7
Oak La NN6 100 F6
Oaklands
Bugbrooke NN7 173 A7
Weedon Bec NN7 155 A2
Oaklands Dr NN3 142 E1
Oaklands Pk 4 LE16 31 F2
Oakleas Rise NN14 76 D1
Oaklee Cl PE8 58 A3
Oakleigh Cl NN9 114 C7
Oakleigh Dr NN5 140 C1
Oakley Ct NN18 36 A1
Oakley Dr
Moulton NN3 126 D1
Wellingborough NN8 129 D3
Oakley Hay Ind Est NN18 36 A1
Oakley Mews LE16 31 D3
Oakley Pond NN18 53 B8
Oakley Rd
Corby NN17 37 A6
Corby NN18 36 C3
Pipewell NN14 52 D8
Rushden NN10 131 F3
Rushton NN14 52 E5
Oakley St
Kettering NN16 72 B4
Northampton NN1 159 D7
Oakmont Cl NN4 175 C5
Oakpark Cl NN3 143 A6
Oakpits Way NN10 132 C1
Oak Rd
Brackley NN13 222 F1
Kettering NN15 72 D1
Oaks Dr NN10 132 B6
Oak St
20 Northampton NN1 159 C7
Rushden NN10 132 B4
Weedon Bec NN7 155 A2
Oaks The NN4 175 F3
Oak Terr 6 NN9 112 F2
Oak Tree Cl NN14 50 F3
Oaktree Ct 2 NN16 72 B1
Oak Tree Ct NN14 76 F8
Oak View NN9 110 F1
Oakway NN8 129 F7
Oak Way NN9 112 F2
Oakway Jun & Inf Sch NN8 130 A7
Oakwood Cl PE8 27 D2
Oakwood Rd NN1 142 A1
Oathill Cl NN6 106 B1
Oat Hill Dr NN3 143 D2
Oat Hill Rd NN12 203 C4
Oathill Rise NN15 92 C2
Oban Cl NN15 91 E8

Obelisk Cl NN2 . . . . **141** C8
Obelisk Rd NN9 . . . . **112** A5
Obelisk Rise NN2 . . . . . . **141** C6
Occupation Rd
  Corby NN17 . . . . **36** F7
  Middleton LE16 . . . . **20** B2
  Oundle PE8 . . . . **42** A7
Octagon The NN17 . . . . . . **37** A8
Octagon Way NN3 . . . . . **142** F2
Octavian Way NN13 . . . . **234** A7
Odeon Bldgs NN17 . . . . . . **37** A7
OLD **107** D7
Old Barn Ct NN3 . . . . . . **142** F3
Old Brewery Wlk
  NN13 . . . . **233** F6
Old Brickyard The
  NN6 . . . . **102** C4
Old Carpenters Cl
  NN3 . . . . **143** C2
Old Cl NN4 . . . . **175** E2
Old Coach Ho The
  LE16 . . . . **35** A7
Old Coffee Mills The **6**
  LE16 . . . . **31** F2
Old Dairy Farm★
  NN7 . . . . **171** E6
Old Depot The NN7 . . . . **155** B4
Old Dry La NN14 . . . . **55** F8
Olde Forde Cl NN6 . . . . . **106** B1
Olde Hall Cl NN6 . . . . . . **105** B1
Oldenburg Rd NN18 . . . . . **35** F3
Old End NN7 . . . . **177** A1
Oldenmead Ct NN3 . . . . **142** F3
Olden Rd NN3 . . . . **143** C5
Old Farm PE8 . . . . **41** C1
Old Farm La NN14 . . . . . . **76** B3
Old Forge Dr NN6 . . . . . **102** C4
Old Forge La NN11 . . . . **169** C2
Old Gn LE16 . . . . **18** F6
Old Gorse Way NN14 . . . . **89** A4
Old Gram School The
  NN6 . . . . **103** F6
Old Great North Rd PE8 . . **8** C2
Old Greens Norton Rd
  NN12 . . . . **203** B7
Old Hall La NN7 . . . . **30** F3
Old Holt Rd LE16 . . . . **19** A7
Oldland Rd NN18 . . . . **36** D3
Old Leicester Rd PE8 . . . . **8** A3
Old Manor Ct NN11 . . . . **135** E8
Old North Rd PE8 . . . . **8** A4
Old Oak Dr NN12 . . . . . . **214** D4
Old Oundle Rd PE8 . . . . . . **7** A6
Old Quarry Ct NN3 . . . . **142** E4
Old Rd
  Braunston NN11 . . . . . **134** C8
  Scaldwell NN6 . . . . . . **107** A7
  Stanion NN14 . . . . **37** E2
  Walgrave NN6 . . . . **107** F5
Old Rectory Dr PE8 . . . . . . **8** A6
Old Rickyard The
  NN11 . . . . **199** D7
Old School Cotts
  NN6 . . . . **105** A8
Old School La NN12 . . . . **187** A1
Old School Mews LE16 . . **31** E3
Old Stable Yd MK19 . . . **229** C7
OLD STRATFORD **229** B7
Old Stratford Prim Sch
  MK19 . . . . **229** B6
Old Sulehay Rd PE8 . . . . **15** C8
Old Tiffield Rd NN12 . . . **203** C8
Old Towcester Rd
  NN4 . . . . **159** C4
OLD TOWN **234** A7
Old Town NN13 . . . . . . **234** A7
Old Vineyard The
  NN10 . . . . **132** B6
Old Woodyard The
  NN12 . . . . **214** D4
Old Yew Ct NN2 . . . . . . **141** B3
Oleander Cres NN3 . . . . **143** C4
Oliver Cl NN10 . . . . **132** C2
Oliver St NN2 . . . . **141** E1
Ollerton Wlk NN18 . . . . . **36** E8
Ollis Cl NN17 . . . . **36** E8
OLNEY **195** E4
Olney Inf Sch MK46 . . . . **195** E3
Olney Mid Sch MK46 . . . **195** F5
Olney Rd MK46 . . . . **195** F1
Olympia Cl NN4 . . . . **175** B8
Olympic Way
  Kettering NN15 . . . . **91** A7
  Wellingborough NN8 . . . **129** C5
ONLEY **98** D2
Onley La CV22 . . . . **98** D6
Onley Pk CV23 . . . . **117** C8
Oransay Cl NN3 . . . . **143** C2
Orchard Cl
  Badby NN11 . . . . **152** F3
  Desborough NN14 . . . . . **50** B3
  East Haddon NN6 . . . . **122** D5
  Finedon NN9 . . . . **111** F5
  Hannington NN6 . . . . . **108** C3
  Hollowell NN6 . . . . . . **104** B5
  Milton Malsor NN7 . . . . **174** E4
  Northampton NN4 . . . . **175** E6
  Orlingbury NN14 . . . . . **110** A5
  Oundle PE8 . . . . **41** F6
  Ringstead NN14 . . . . . . **95** C3
  Rushden NN10 . . . . . . **131** F3
  Spratton NN6 . . . . **124** B8
  Towcester NN12 . . . . . **203** C4
  Walgrave NN6 . . . . **107** F5

Orchard Cl *continued*
  Warmington PE8 . . . . . . **28** B3
  Weedon Bec NN7 . . . . . **155** C3
  Weldon NN17 . . . . **38** B8
  Wilbarston LE16 . . . . . . **34** C5
  Wollaston NN29 . . . . . . **146** D3
  Yardley Gobion NN12 . . **217** F6
  Yelvertoft NN6 . . . . **82** B4
Orchard Cotts NN6 . . . . **125** C5
Orchard Cres
  Kettering NN16 . . . . **72** C4
  Woodnewton PE8 . . . . . **14** E2
Orchard Ct
  Pattishall NN12 . . . . . . **172** D1
  Woodford NN14 . . . . . . **94** C7
Orchard Est NN14 . . . . . . **90** F2
Orchard Field NN14 . . . . . **93** A6
Orchard Gn NN3 . . . . . . **142** C2
Orchard Hill NN3 . . . . . **143** A1
Orchard Ho NN17 . . . . . . **38** B8
Orchard La
  Denton NN7 . . . . **162** B1
  Gretton NN17 . . . . **10** C1
  King's Cliffe PE8 . . . . . . **13** E7
  Woodnewton PE8 . . . . . **14** E2
Orchard Pl NN29 . . . . . . **147** A8
Orchard Rd
  Finedon NN9 . . . . **111** F5
  Raunds NN9 . . . . **114** B5
Orchard Rise
  Long Buckby NN6 . . . . . **121** D4
  Olney MK46 . . . . **195** F3
Orchard Sch The NN16 . . **72** B5
Orchard St
  Daventry NN11 . . . . . . **135** B2
  Market Harborough LE16 . **31** E4
   8 Northampton NN5 . . **159** A6
Orchards The NN6 . . . . . **103** D1
Orchard Terr
  Finedon NN9 . . . . **111** F5
  Welford NN6 . . . . **64** E6
  Wellingborough NN8 . . . **129** F5
Orchard The
  Apethorpe PE8 . . . . **14** C4
  Bozeat NN29 . . . . **164** D3
  Flore NN7 . . . . **155** F5
  Kislingbury NN7 . . . . . . **157** D3
  Potterspury NN12 . . . . **217** C3
  Sibbertoft LE16 . . . . **47** A2
  Staverton NN11 . . . . . . **152** B7
  Upper Boddington
  NN11 . . . . **182** C7
Orchard Way
  Cogenhoe NN7 . . . . . . **161** F6
  Easton o t H PE9 . . . . **1** F6
  Harpole NN7 . . . . **157** C6
  Kings Sutton OX17 . . . . **231** A5
  Northampton NN5 . . . . **158** C6
  Roade NN7 . . . . **191** D4
  Thrapston NN14 . . . . . . **76** E1
Orchid Cl NN14 . . . . **51** A4
Ordnance Ho NN7 . . . . . **155** A4
Ordnance Rd NN7 . . . . . **154** F3
Oriel Rd NN11 . . . . **153** C7
Oriel Way NN13 . . . . . . **233** D8
Orient Ho NN1 . . . . **159** E6
Orient Way NN8 . . . . . . **130** A4
Orion Way NN15 . . . . **91** C5
ORLINGBURY **110** A5
Orlingbury Rd
  Great Harrowden
  NN9 . . . . **110** D2
  Isham NN14 . . . . **110** C7
  Little Harrowden NN9 . . **110** B4
  Pytchley NN14 . . . . **90** F1
Ormond Pl NN14 . . . . . . **110** E8
Orson Leys CV22 . . . . **98** A7
ORTON **70** A3
Orton Pl NN8 . . . . **129** D7
Orton Rd
  Kettering NN15 . . . . **91** F5
  Loddington NN14 . . . . . . **70** D2
Orwell Cl
  Clifton u D CV23 . . . . . . **80** A5
  Raunds NN9 . . . . **114** D7
  Wellingborough NN8 . . . **129** C6
Osborn Cl NN8 . . . . **129** E3
Osborne Cl NN10 . . . . . . **132** D4
Osborne Rd NN2 . . . . . . **141** C2
Osborn's Ct MK46 . . . . . **195** F3
Osbourne Cl NN18 . . . . . . **36** E2
Osier Bed La NN17 . . . . . **24** B5
Osiers The NN14 . . . . **51** D2
Osier Way NN14 . . . . **76** C1
Osler Cl NN2 . . . . **141** B5
Oslo Gdns NN18 . . . . **36** A3
Osmond Dr NN3 . . . . . . **143** A5
Osprey Dr NN11 . . . . . . **135** C3
Osprey La NN8 . . . . **130** B7
Osprey Rise NN4 . . . . . . **175** B8
Osprey View **6** NN4 . . . **175** B8
Ostlers La MK11 . . . . . . **229** D6
Ostlers Way NN15 . . . . . . **91** B7
Oswald Rd NN10 . . . . . . **132** C2
Osyth Cl NN4 . . . . **160** B2
Oulton Rise NN3 . . . . . . **141** F4
OUNDLE **42** A6
Oundle CE Prim Sch
  PE8 . . . . **41** F5
Oundle Dr NN3 . . . . **142** B7
Oundle & Kings Cliffe Mid
  Sch PE8 . . . . **41** E7
Oundle Mus★✿ PE8 . . . . **41** F5
Oundle Rd
  Elton PE8 . . . . **16** F1
  Thrapston NN14 . . . . . . **76** E2
  Weldon NN17 . . . . **38** E7

Oundle Rd *continued*
  Woodnewton PE8 . . . . . **14** F1
Oundle Sch PE8 . . . . **42** A5
Our Lady of Walsingham
  RC Prim Sch NN17 . . . . . **36** F7
Our Lady & Pope John RC
  Sch NN18 . . . . **36** A4
Our Lady's Convent Prep
  Sch NN15 . . . . **71** F1
Our Lady's RC Jun & Inf
  Sch NN8 . . . . **129** D3
Ousebank Way MK11 . . . **229** D5
Ouse Cl NN8 . . . . **129** C6
Ouse La NN12 . . . . **203** A6
Outlaw La NN8 . . . . **129** F5
Oval Cres NN10 . . . . **132** D2
Oval Rd
  Rugby CV22 . . . . **98** D8
  Rushden NN10 . . . . . . **132** D2
Oval The
  Kettering NN15 . . . . **91** B8
  Market Harborough LE16 . **31** E4
Overdale Cl LE16 . . . . **32** A3
OVER END **28** E7
Overfield Ave LE16 . . . . . **31** F5
Overhills MK46 . . . . **195** E4
Overleys Ct NN3 . . . . . . **143** B5
Overmead Rd NN3 . . . . . **143** D2
Overslade Cl NN4 . . . . . . **175** A8
Overslade Ho NN4 . . . . . **175** A8
OVERSTONE **127** B1
Overstone Cl NN3 . . . . . **126** E1
Overstone Cres NN6 . . . . **127** B1
Overstone Hts NN6 . . . . **127** D3
Overstone La NN6 . . . . . **126** F1
Overstone Lakes Cvn Pk
  NN6 . . . . **143** D8
OVERSTONE LODGE . . . **143** B5
Overstone Park Sch
  NN6 . . . . **143** B8
Overstone Prim Sch
  NN6 . . . . **127** A1
Overstone Rd
  Moulton NN3 . . . . **126** D1
  Northampton NN1 . . . . **159** D7
  Sywell NN6 . . . . **127** D3
OVERTHORPE **219** D6
Overthorpe Ind Est
  OX16 . . . . **219** A7
Overthorpe Prep Sch
  OX17 . . . . **219** C8
Overthorpe Rd OX16 . . . **219** B6
Ovett Cl NN15 . . . . **90** F4
Owen Cl NN8 . . . . **129** B5
Owen Mews NN8 . . . . . . **129** B5
Owen Way NN10 . . . . . . **132** A5
Owl Cl NN3 . . . . **141** F7
Owl End La NN11 . . . . . . **182** C5
Owl End Way NN11 . . . . **182** C5
Oxburgh Ct **7** NN4 . . . . **175** C4
Oxendon Hall LE16 . . . . . **48** E3
Oxendon Rd
  Arthingworth LE16 . . . . . **49** A1
  Braybrooke LE16 . . . . . . **49** D5
  Clipston LE16 . . . . **48** B1
  East Farndon LE16 . . . . . **48** B5
Oxfield Park Dr MK19 . . **229** C7
Oxford Cl
  Daventry NN11 . . . . . . **135** C1
  Earls Barton NN6 . . . . **144** F3
Oxford Ct NN13 . . . . . . **233** F5
Oxford Rd
  Adderbury OX17 . . . . . **230** A3
  Corby NN17 . . . . **36** C6
  Evenley NN13 . . . . **233** E5
Oxford St
  Daventry NN11 . . . . . . **135** C1
  Finedon NN9 . . . . **112** B5
  Kettering NN16 . . . . **72** A3
  Northampton NN4 . . . . **159** B3
  Rothwell NN14 . . . . **70** D8
  Stony Stratford MK11 . . **229** D5
  Wellingborough NN8 . . . **129** F4
  Wymington NN10 . . . . **148** A7
Oxleys MK46 . . . . **195** E4
Oxwich Cl NN4 . . . . **160** A1

P

Packer Rd NN15 . . . . **90** B8
Packwood Ave CV21 . . . . . **99** C8
Packwood Cl **9** NN11 . . **135** B7
Paddock Cl NN6 . . . . **103** D1
Paddock Ct LE16 . . . . **31** E3
Paddock End NN14 . . . . . **89** B4
Paddock La
  Desborough NN14 . . . . . **51** A3
  Mears Ashby NN6 . . . . **128** B2
  Medbourne LE16 . . . . . . **19** D8
Paddock Mews NN6 . . . . . **51** A3
Paddock Mill Ct **1**
  NN3 . . . . **143** B4
Paddocks Cl NN6 . . . . . . **108** A5
Paddocks Rd NN10 . . . . . **131** F3
Paddocks The
  Brixworth NN6 . . . . . . **106** B3
  Bugbrooke NN7 . . . . . **172** F7
  Moulton NN3 . . . . **126** C4
  Orlingbury NN14 . . . . . **109** F5
  Shutlanger NN12 . . . . . **204** D8
  Souldern OX27 . . . . . . **237** E3
  Stanion NN14 . . . . **37** F3
  Yelvertoft NN6 . . . . **82** A5
Paddocks Way NN3 . . . . **143** A1
Paddock The
  Crick NN6 . . . . **100** F5

Paddock The *continued*
  Lower Boddington
  NN11 . . . . **182** C5
  Raunds NN9 . . . . **114** C4
  Weedon Lois NN12 . . . . **200** B2
  Welton NN11 . . . . **135** E8
  Woodnewton PE8 . . . . . **14** E2
Paddox Cl CV22 . . . . **98** F8
Paddox Ct CV23 . . . . . . **100** A3
Paddox Prim Sch
  Rugby CV22 . . . . **98** D8
  Rugby CV22 . . . . **98** E8
Padmans Cl NN14 . . . . . . **89** B4
Padwell Ct **2** NN3 . . . . . **161** A8
Pagent Ct NN14 . . . . **95** A7
Paget Cl NN4 . . . . **160** E2
Paget Ho NN5 . . . . **140** E1
Paget Rd LE16 . . . . **30** E3
Pagnell Ct NN4 . . . . **176** A7
Palace Ct **8** NN10 . . . . . **132** B2
Palk Rd NN8 . . . . **130** B4
Palmer Ave NN9 . . . . . . **113** B4
Palmer Cl NN8 . . . . **129** D7
Palmer Ct NN8 . . . . **129** F5
Palmer's Cl CV21 . . . . **99** B8
Palmer Sq NN3 . . . . **143** C1
Palmerston Ct **5**
  NN1 . . . . **159** E6
Palmerston Ho **4**
  NN1 . . . . **159** E6
Palmerston Rd NN1 . . . . **159** E6
Palm Rd NN10 . . . . **131** E3
Pantell Way NN10 . . . . . **132** A7
Panters La NN14 . . . . **75** A1
Parade Bank NN3 . . . . . . **126** C1
Parade The NN1 . . . . . . **159** C6
Paradise Ave NN15 . . . . . . **91** D6
Paradise Ho **2** NN8 . . . **129** F5
Paradise La NN15 . . . . . . **91** D6
Pargeter Cl OX17 . . . . . . **210** E2
Park Ave
  Kettering NN16 . . . . **72** B4
  Northampton, Abington
  NN1 . . . . **160** A8
  Northampton NN5 . . . . **140** B1
  Raunds NN9 . . . . **114** C5
  Rushden NN10 . . . . . . **132** A2
Park Ave N NN3 . . . . **142** A1
Park Ave S NN3 . . . . **160** B7
Park Cl
  Badby NN11 . . . . **153** A3
  Brafield-on-t-G NN7 . . . **161** E2
  Cosgrove MK19 . . . . . . **218** F2
  Earls Barton NN6 . . . . **144** D4
  Isham NN14 . . . . **110** F8
  King's Cliffe PE8 . . . . . . **14** A8
  Northampton NN5 . . . . **140** A1
  Sywell NN6 . . . . **127** D2
  Watford NN6 . . . . **120** C6
  Whittlebury NN12 . . . . **215** C4
Park Cnr NN5 . . . . **158** F6
Park Cres **8** NN3 . . . . . **130** A5
Park Cres E NN5 . . . . . . **140** F2
Park Cres W NN5 . . . . . . **140** F1
Park Dr
  Market Harborough
  LE16 . . . . **31** E4
  Northampton NN5 . . . . **140** F1
Park End NN13 . . . . **238** D8
Park End Works
  NN13 . . . . **238** D7
Parker Rd PE8 . . . . **7** D8
Parkers Terr NN9 . . . . . . **111** F4
Parker Way NN10 . . . . . **132** B7
Park Farm Barns NN7 . . **139** E6
Park Farm Ct NN14 . . . . . **77** C4
Park Farm Ind Est
  NN8 . . . . **129** A5
Park Farm Way NN8 . . . **129** A3
Parkfield Ave NN4 . . . . . **159** C1
Parkfield Cres NN4 . . . . **159** C2
Parkfield Rd
  Brixworth NN6 . . . . . . **106** A1
  Long Buckby NN6 . . . . . **121** A4
Parkham Ind Est
  NN10 . . . . **131** D3
Park Hill Rd NN3 . . . . . . **142** D3
Park Ho LE16 . . . . **31** E4
Park Jun Sch
  Kettering NN16 . . . . **72** C4
  Wellingborough NN8 . . . **130** A5
Park La
  Earls Barton NN6 . . . . **144** D4
  Gayton NN7 . . . . **173** E2
  Harpole NN7 . . . . **157** C6
  Hartwell NN7 . . . . **192** C1
  Northampton NN5 . . . . **140** A2
  Paulerspury NN12 . . . . **216** B7
  Sulgrave OX17 . . . . . . **210** F7
  Watford NN6 . . . . **120** C6
Parklands
  Crick NN6 . . . . **100** C7
  Stanwick NN9 . . . . **113** F3
  Sywell NN6 . . . . **127** D1
Parklands Ave NN3 . . . . **142** A5
Parklands Cl NN14 . . . . . **70** D1
Parklands Cres NN3 . . . . **142** A5
Parklands Mid Sch
  NN3 . . . . **142** A5
Parklands Prim Sch
  NN3 . . . . **142** A4
Park Leys NN11 . . . . **135** C1
Park Lo NN17 . . . . **36** E6
Park Mews
  Market Harborough
  LE16 . . . . **31** E4
  Towcester NN12 . . . . . **203** C6

Park Mews *continued*
  Wellingborough NN8 . . . **130** A5
Park Pl NN10 . . . . **132** B2
Park Rd
  Burton Latimer NN15 . . . **92** B2
  Hanslope MK19 . . . . . . **207** B1
  Hartwell NN7 . . . . **192** C1
  Irthlingborough NN9 . . . **112** F1
  Kettering NN16 . . . . **72** C4
  Raunds NN9 . . . . **114** C6
  Rushden NN10 . . . . . . **132** C1
  Stony Stratford MK11 . . **229** D5
  Titchmarsh NN14 . . . . . **77** C4
  Wellingborough NN8 . . . **130** A5
Parkside NN3 . . . . **143** D2
Park Spinney Cl NN6 . . . . **84** A5
Park Sq NN5 . . . . **140** F2
Park St
  Earls Barton NN6 . . . . **144** D4
  King's Cliffe PE8 . . . . . . **13** F7
  Raunds NN9 . . . . **114** C6
  Towcester NN12 . . . . . **203** C6
  Wollaston NN29 . . . . . . **146** A5
Park The PE28 . . . . **97** A3
Park View
  Kettering NN16 . . . . **72** B4
  Moulton NN3 . . . . **142** E8
  Northampton NN5 . . . . **158** B8
  Thrapston NN14 . . . . . . **76** D2
  Wellingborough NN8 . . . **130** B4
Park View Cl NN3 . . . . . **126** E1
Park View Ho NN10 . . . . **132** A3
Park View Rd NN12 . . . . **203** D5
Parkway
  Nassington PE8 . . . . **15** F5
  Northampton NN3 . . . . **142** E8
Parkway Cl PE8 . . . . **15** F5
Park Wlk
  Brigstock NN14 . . . . . . **55** E7
  Easton o t H PE9 . . . . **2** A6
  Northampton NN5 . . . . **140** F2
Parkwood St NN5 . . . . . . **159** B5
Parnell Cl NN6 . . . . **102** C5
Parracombe Way
  NN3 . . . . **160** C7
Parsons Cl
  Ecton NN6 . . . . **143** F4
  Nether Heyford NN7 . . . **156** C2
Parsons' Cl NN7 . . . . . . **163** D5
Parsons Gr NN17 . . . . **22** A1
Parsons Meade NN4 . . . . **158** E2
Parsons Rd
  Daventry NN11 . . . . . . **134** F5
  Irchester NN29 . . . . . . **147** B8
Parsons St
  Adderbury OX17 . . . . . **230** A4
  Woodford Halse NN11 . . **184** C6
Partridge Cl
  Charwelton NN11 . . . . . **168** A5
  Northampton NN2 . . . . **141** B6
Partridge La NN11 . . . . . **184** C1
Parva Ct NN3 . . . . **142** E3
Pascoe Cres **1** NN11 . . . **135** A4
Pashler Gdns NN14 . . . . . **76** D2
PASSENHAM **229** C5
Pasteur Cl NN2 . . . . **141** B5
Pasteur Ctyd NN17 . . . . . **37** B8
Pasture End NN14 . . . . . . **89** C5
Pasture Mobile Home Pk
  NN14 . . . . **51** C8
Pastures The
  Market Harborough
  LE16 . . . . **31** C3
  Northampton NN2 . . . . **141** A5
  Wellingborough NN9 . . . **110** E1
Pasture The NN11 . . . . . **135** C1
Paterson Rd NN8 . . . . . . **130** B8
Patrick Cl NN15 . . . . **91** C6
Patrick Rd
  Corby NN17 . . . . **36** D4
  Kettering NN15 . . . . **91** C6
Patricks La MK19 . . . . . **228** E4
Patrick St LE16 . . . . **31** F2
Patterdale Wlk **1**
  NN3 . . . . **142** E4
Patterson Cl NN3 . . . . . . **142** E1
PATTISHALL **172** E1
Pattishall CE Prim Sch
  NN12 . . . . **188** F8
PAULERSPURY **216** C8
Paulerspury CE Prim Sch
  NN12 . . . . **216** B8
Pavilion Dr
  Northampton NN4 . . . . **159** F1
  Oundle PE8 . . . . **41** E6
Pavillons Way NN13 . . . . **233** E8
Paxford Cl NN8 . . . . **129** E1
Paxton Cl MK46 . . . . **195** F3
Paxton Rd NN3 . . . . **142** D4
Payne's La LE16 . . . . **18** F7
Peace Cl NN4 . . . . **158** F3
Peace Hill NN7 . . . . **172** E7
Peacock Dr NN14 . . . . . . **95** B3
Peacock Pl **6** NN1 . . . . . **159** D6
Peacock's Cl OX17 . . . . . **220** A8
Peake Cl LE16 . . . . **35** B8
Peak The NN7 . . . . **156** C1
Pearmain Ave NN8 . . . . **129** F7
Pearmain Ct NN3 . . . . . . **143** A2
Pearson Mews NN29 . . . **146** D2
Peartree Cl NN11 . . . . . . **135** C4
Pear Tree Cl
  Bozeat NN29 . . . . **164** D3
  Northampton NN3 . . . . **143** A2
Pear Tree Gdns LE16 . . . . **31** D2
Peaselands NN14 . . . . . . **50** F4
Pebble Cotts LE17 . . . . . . **46** D8
Pebbleford Rd NN15 . . . . **91** D8

Pebble La
  Brackley NN13..........233 F7
  4 Wellingborough
  NN8..................130 A4
Pebody Pl MK46........195 F3
Peck Way NN10.........132 B4
Pegasus Ct NN13.......233 F7
Pegasus Way NN10......131 E4
Peg's La
  Clipston LE16..........66 F8
  Denford NN14..........95 C6
Pelham Ct NN3.........142 D4
Pell Ct NN3............142 E3
Pells Cl NN6..........103 E7
Pemberton St NN10.....132 A3
Pembroke Cl
  Rushden NN10.........132 C1
  Thrapston NN14........76 C2
Pembroke Cres NN5.....159 B8
Pembroke Gdns NN5.....159 A8
Pembroke Ho MK46......195 F3
Pembroke Rd NN5.......159 B8
Pembroke Way NN11.....153 B7
Penarth Rd NN5.......159 A8
Pen Ct NN1............159 D4
Pendered Rd NN8.......130 A1
Pendle Ave NN16........72 A6
Pendle Rd NN5........158 C8
Penfold Cl NN2........141 B4
Penfold Dr NN3........143 B3
Penfold Gdns NN3......143 C3
Penfold La NN3........143 C3
Pen Gn La NN17.........37 A8
Peninsular Cl **12** NN4...175 D7
Penistone Rd NN3......142 E3
Penistone Wlk **3**
  NN3..................142 E3
Pennard Cl NN4........160 B2
Penn Gdns NN4........175 B7
Pennine Ct NN11.......135 B5
Pennine Way
  Kettering NN16.........72 B6
  Northampton NN5......158 D7
Pennycress Pl NN3.....143 D1
Penny La NN9..........114 D7
Penrhyn Cl NN18........36 F3
Penrhyn Ct NN14........76 E2
Penrhyn Rd NN4.......159 C3
Penrith Dr NN8........129 D6
Pentelowes The PE18...116 D2
Penthorne Cl NN12.....188 A8
Pentlands MK11........229 F4
Penvale Rd NN4........175 B7
Pepper Alley OX15.....236 E4
Peppercorn Way NN4...175 D6
Perceval Cl NN5.......140 D1
Perch Cl NN11.........135 B6
Percival Rd CV22........98 D8
Percy Rd
  Northampton NN1......159 F7
  Woodford Halse NN11...184 C6
Peregrine Pl NN4......175 A8
Perkins Cl LE16........31 F4
Perkins Ct **4** NN8....130 A5
Perkins Rd NN9........131 E8
Perkins Way NN11......153 E4
Perry Cl NN15..........91 A7
Perry St NN1..........159 F7
Pershore Cl NN8.......145 C4
Perth Ho NN17..........22 F1
Peterborough Rd
  Morcott LE15............3 C4
  Wansford PE8............8 A3
  Warmington PE8........28 C4
Peters La NN6.........106 F5
Pether Ave NN13.......233 C8
Petherton Ct NN16......72 B3
Pettiver Cres **2** CV21...80 A1
Petworth Dr LE16.......32 B2
Petworth Gdns NN18....36 B5
Pevensey Cl NN10......132 C1
Pevensey Wlk **2** NN18...36 B5
Peverel Cl NN10.......132 C6
Peverel's Way NN5.....158 E6
Peveril Rd
  Greatworth OX17......210 E2
  Northampton NN5......158 C7
Pevers La MK46.........195 A1
Pevrel Pl NN14.........50 E4
Pexley Ct PE8..........41 E5
Pheasant Way NN2.....141 A5
Pheonix Parkway
  NN17..................37 B8
Philip Way NN10.......132 C7
Phillips Way NN6......121 C4
Phipps Rd NN11.......184 B6
PHIPPSVILLE............141 F1
Phoenix Ct NN8........130 B3
Phoenix Parkway
  NN17..................22 B2
Phoenix St **23** NN1...159 C6
Piccadilly Bldgs **3**
  NN16..................72 B1
Piccadilly Cl NN4.....158 F2
Pickering Ct NN18......36 B4
Pickerings The NN6....106 C1
Picks Cl LE16..........32 B3
PIDDINGTON...........177 B2
Piddington La NN7.....177 A2
Piddington Roman Villa
  Mus★ NN7............177 B2
Piece The
  Cogenhoe NN7........161 F6
  Spratton NN6.........105 B1
Pie Cnr NN7...........127 D3
Pied Bull Cl PE9.........1 A6
Pierce Cres PE8........28 C3
Pigeon Hill NN12......189 D3

Pightles Terr NN10....132 C1
Pightles Wlk NN10....132 C1
Pigott's La NN15.......92 C2
Pike La NN1...........159 C6
Pikemead Ct NN3......143 B4
Pike Rd NN18...........36 A1
Pilgrims La NN7.......173 A7
Pilgrims Pl NN14......159 C2
Pilgrim Way NN8......129 F3
Pilot Rd NN17..........37 C8
PILTON................58 C5
Pilton Cl NN3.........143 C5
Pilton Rd PE8..........58 A4
PIMLICO...............223 F6
Pincet La LE17.........45 A6
Pindar Rd NN8........129 E2
Pindar Rise NN3......142 E6
PINDON END...........206 C4
Pine Ave NN6.........127 D1
Pine Cl
  Desborough NN14......51 C2
  Irchester NN29.......147 A7
  Northampton NN4......175 F3
  Wellingborough NN8...148 A8
Pine Copse Cl NN5....140 A2
Pine Cres NN6........127 D1
Pine Ct NN7..........138 C4
Pine Gr CV21..........80 A1
Pineham Ave NN2......141 D6
Pine Rd NN15..........72 C1
Pine Ridge NN3.......142 F7
Pines The LE16........32 A6
Pine Tree Ct NN14.....76 B3
Pine Trees NN3.......142 C1
Pinetrees Cl NN7......177 B3
Pine Wlk NN17.........21 E1
Pinewood Cl NN16......72 B6
Pinewood Rd NN3.....142 B3
Pinfold Cl LE15.........3 E8
Pinfold Gn NN11......152 F3
Pinfold La LE15.........3 E8
Pingle La LE15..........3 B6
Pioneer Ave
  Burton Latimer NN15...92 B2
  Desborough NN14......50 F2
Pioneer Cl **10** NN4...175 E7
Piper Cl NN8.........129 F8
Pipers Cl
  Irthlingborough NN9...112 F2
  Kettering NN15.........72 C1
Piper's Hill Rd NN15...91 C8
Pippin Cl
  Cogenhoe NN7........161 E5
  Rushden NN10.........131 E3
  Wellingborough NN8...129 F4
Pippin La NN3.........143 A2
Pitchers La LE16........20 D7
Pit La PE9..............1 A7
PITSFORD.............125 D5
Pitsford & Brampton Sta★
  NN6..................124 E2
Pitsford Prim Sch
  NN6..................125 D5
Pitsford
  Chapel Brampton
  NN6..................124 E1
  Moulton NN3.........126 B2
Pitstone Rd NN4......158 E3
Pittams Cl NN6.......121 B3
Pittams La NN12......213 B8
Pittoms La CV23.......99 C1
Pitt St NN8..........129 E4
Plank Hos NN12.......203 C5
Plantagenet Cl NN13...233 E8
Plantagenet Sq **7**
  NN4..................158 F2
Playford Cl NN14......70 F7
Plaza 2&4 The **1**
  NN1..................159 E7
Pleasant Row NN14....94 D7
Plessey Cl NN12......203 D5
Pleydell Gdns NN4....159 C2
Pleydell Rd NN4......159 C2
Plough Cl
  Daventry NN11.......135 D6
  Rothwell NN14........70 D2
Plough La NN2........141 A6
Ploughmans Way
  NN4..................175 F3
Ploughmans Wlk
  NN2..................141 B5
Ploughmans Yd **11**
  LE16..................31 E3
Plough Mews NN13....233 F7
Plover Cl NN12.......203 C3
Plowden Cl NN11......182 F2
Plum Park La NN12....216 D8
PLUMPTON............200 B5
Plumpton Ct NN18.....36 B5
PLUMPTON END........216 D7
Plumpton La NN11....199 D7
Plumpton Rd
  Weston NN12.........200 A2
  Woodend NN12.......200 F6
Plumtree Ave NN8....130 A7
Poachers Cl NN4......175 F3
Poachers Way NN2....141 B5
Pochin Dr LE16.........31 F5
PODINGTON...........147 E2
Podington Rd NN10....148 A4
Podmore Way NN14....90 A3
Poets Way NN11......153 E5
Poitiers Ct NN5.......139 F1
Pokas Cotts NN9......133 C8

Polar Star Cl NN11....135 A4
POLEBROOK.............43 A3
Polebrook Airfield Nature
  Reserve★ PE8.........43 F3
Polebrook CE Prim Sch
  PE8...................43 A3
Polebrook Ct PE8......42 F3
Polegate Ct NN18......36 B5
Police Flats NN17......36 E6
Pollards Ct LE15........3 F5
Pollard St NN16........72 B4
Polopit NN14..........77 D3
Polwell La NN15........92 A4
Pomfret Arms Cl NN4..159 C4
Pomfret Rd NN12.....203 C6
Pond Bank NN7.......190 D8
Ponder St NN14........70 D7
Pond Farm Cl NN5....158 C7
Ponds Cl NN9.........114 C6
Pond Wood Cl NN3....142 B6
Pool Cl NN12.........188 D8
Poole St NN1.........159 D4
Pool Farm Ct NN11....184 A5
Pool St NN11.........184 B5
Pope Rd NN8.........129 C3
Popham Ct NN9.......114 C7
Poplar Cl
  Daventry NN11.......135 C5
  Irchester NN29.......147 A7
  Rushden NN10........148 A8
  Towcester NN12.......203 C4
Poplar Ct NN3........142 D5
Poplar Pl
  Wellingborough NN8...129 F4
  Wollaston NN29.......146 E2
Poplars Cl
  Blakesley NN12.......187 B1
  Middleton Cheney
  OX17..................220 A8
  Raunds NN9..........114 C6
Poplars Ct
  Market Harborough
  LE16..................31 D4
  Scaldwell NN6.........106 F6
Poplar's Farm Rd
  NN15..................92 B8
Poplars La NN6.......126 E8
Poplars Rd OX17......208 F4
Poplar St NN8........130 A5
Poplars The
  Guilsborough NN6....103 E7
  Long Buckby NN6.....121 B3
  Northampton NN1.....159 C7
Poppy Cl NN10.......148 C8
Poppyfield Ct
  Northampton NN3.....142 F4
  Thrapston NN14.......76 D3
Poppy Fields NN16.....71 F3
Poppy Leys NN6......125 B8
Porlock Cl NN5.......158 E8
Portchester Gdns **4**
  NN3..................160 F8
Porter's Cl MK19.....228 E4
Porter's La PE9........2 A5
Portland Ct NN11.....135 D1
Portland Pl NN1......159 E6
Portland Rd
  Irthlingborough NN9...112 F2
  Rushden NN10........132 B2
Portlow La NN6.......100 F6
Port Rd NN5..........140 A2
Portree Wlk NN17......36 C8
Portstone Cl NN5.....140 A2
Portway
  Aynho OX17.........237 D7
  Croughton NN13......238 E7
Portway Cres NN13....238 E7
Portway Dr NN13......238 D7
Portway Gdns OX17...237 D7
Portwey Cl NN6.......106 C1
Postle Cl CV23.........99 F2
Post Office Ln NN17....37 B6
Potter Ct NN9........114 A4
Potters End NN14.....183 D7
POTTERSPURY..........217 D3
Potterspury Lodge Sch
  NN12..................217 A6
Pound Cl
  Corby NN18...........36 B2
  Ringstead NN14........95 B3
  Wicken MK19.........228 A4
Pound Ct NN3........126 B1
Poundfield Rd NN12...217 E2
Pound La
  Badby NN11..........152 F3
  Bugbrooke NN7.......173 A7
  Eastcote NN12........172 F1
  Moulton NN3.........126 C1
  Northampton NN3.....143 C2
Pound Pl NN9........111 F4
Pound The
  Great Brington NN7...138 C6
  Horton NN7..........177 E1
  Nether Heyford NN7...156 B1
  Syresham NN13.......224 B7
Powys NN18...........36 E2
Poyntz Gdns NN5.....158 E8
Poyntz La NN5........158 E8
Pratt Rd NN10........132 C2
Prebendal Gn PE8.....15 F8
Premier Ct NN3......142 A7
Premier Way NN8.....131 E4

Prentice Ct NN3......143 A5
Prentice Wlk NN17.....37 A6
Prescott Cl NN3......143 C4
Presland Way NN9....112 F7
Pressland Dr NN10....132 C6
Prestbury Rd NN5.....140 A1
Prestidge Row NN11...199 C7
PRESTON CAPES.......169 D2
Preston Ct
  Burton Latimer NN15..92 C3
  Northampton NN3.....142 E3
PRESTON DEANERY....176 E4
Preston Deanery Rd
  NN7..................176 B1
Preston Dr NN11......135 C6
Preston Hedges Prim Sch
  NN4..................175 F6
Preston Rd NN11......184 C2
Prestwold Way NN3...143 B5
Pretoria Cotts NN9....114 C1
Prices Way NN13......222 D1
Pride Pl LE16..........31 D2
Pridmore Cl PE8.......14 E2
Priestley Ct NN17......22 D1
Priestwell Ct NN6....122 D5
Primrose Cl
  Corby NN18...........36 C2
  Kettering NN16........72 D4
Primrose Gdns NN9...114 C5
Primrose Hill
  Daventry NN11.......135 C2
  Northampton NN2.....159 C8
  Raunds NN9..........114 D6
Primrose Pl NN8......130 C5
Primrose Wlk
  Hinton NN11.........184 B6
  Northampton NN4.....175 F2
Primula Cl NN3.......160 C6
Primula Ct NN2.......159 C8
Prince Cl NN11.......135 B3
Prince Of Wales Row
  NN3..................126 D1
Prince Rupert Ave
  NN14..................50 F3
Princes Ave NN14......51 B3
Princes Cl NN7.......155 A3
Princes Ct NN16.......72 B3
Princess Anne Bldg
  NN2..................141 C4
Princess Cl NN3......160 B6
Princess Marina Hospl
  NN5..................158 B6
Princess St NN16......72 C3
Princess Way NN8....129 E2
Prince St NN6........144 E5
Princes Wlk **4** NN1...159 D6
Princethorpe Dr
  OX16..................219 A7
Prince William Rd PE8..41 E5
Prince William Sch
  PE8...................42 B4
Princewood Rd NN17...21 E3
Printers Yd NN16......72 B2
Priors Cl NN10.......147 F8
Priors Ct
  Corby NN17............23 A1
  Priors Marston CV47..166 D7
PRIORS HARDWICK....166 A5
Priors Hardwick Rd
  NN11..................182 B8
Priors Haw Rd NN17....23 A1
PRIORS MARSTON......166 E8
Priors Marston Rd
  Byfield NN11.........167 B8
  Hellidon NN11........151 C1
Priors Sch The CV47...166 D8
Priory Cl
  Daventry NN11.......135 D1
  Northampton NN3.....160 B6
Priory Cres NN7......191 C4
Priory Ct
  Geddington NN14......54 A2
  Weedon Bec NN7.....155 A2
Priory Ho NN1........159 B6
Priory Rd
  Wellingborough NN8...129 F3
  Wollaston NN29......146 D3
Pritchard Cl NN3......143 C6
Probyn Cl NN3.......143 A6
Promenade The NN8...129 E6
Prospect Ave
  Irchester NN29.......147 A7
  Rushden NN10........132 B4
Prospect Cl NN29.....146 D3
Prospect Ct NN12.....217 F6
Prospect Pl MK19.....218 F5
Prospect Rd MK11....229 C5
Prospect Way NN11...134 F3
Provence Cl NN5......139 F1
Pudding Bag La
  NN29..................164 D3
Puddledock NN12.....214 D5
Pumping Station Cott
  LE16..................21 A7
Pump Pl MK19........229 B7
Purbeck Rd NN10.....131 D2
Purse La NN16........207 F8
Purser Rd NN1.......159 F8
Purvis Rd NN10.......132 A2
PURY END.............215 F8
Pury Hill Bsns Pk
  NN12..................204 E1
Pury Rd NN12........203 A3
PUXLEY...............228 D5
Pye Ct CV23..........117 D3
Pyghtles The
  Daventry NN11.......135 B1

Pyghtles The continued
  Wollaston NN29......146 D1
Pyghtle The
  Earls Barton NN6....144 E5
  Olney MK46..........195 F3
  Wellingborough NN8...129 F6
Pyghtle Way NN4.....175 A7
Pyket Way NN3.......160 E8
Pyke Way NN6........101 A6
Pym Cl NN8..........130 B6
Pyramid Cl NN3......142 E2
PYTCHLEY..............90 F2
Pytchley Cl NN6......106 B2
Pytchley Ct
  Corby NN17...........36 B8
  West Haddon NN6....102 C4
Pytchley Dr NN6......121 B4
Pytchley Endowed CE
  Prim Sch NN14.......90 F2
Pytchley La NN15......91 C5
Pytchley Lodge Ind Est
  NN15..................91 C6
Pytchley Lodge Rd
  NN15..................91 C5
Pytchley Rd
  Kettering NN15........91 C6
  Orlingbury NN14.....109 F5
  Rugby CV22...........98 C8
  Rushden NN10.......131 F3
Pytchley Rise NN8....129 D3
Pytchley St NN1......159 E6
Pytchley View NN3....126 D1
Pytchley Way
  Brixworth NN6.......106 B2
  Northampton NN5....140 B2
Pywell Ct NN17........22 E2
Pywell Rd NN17........22 E2

Q

Quakers Cl NN7.......172 F7
Quantock Cl
  Daventry NN11.......135 B5
  Kettering NN15........92 A5
Quantock Cres NN5...158 D8
Quarry Green Cl
  MK19..................228 B3
Quarry Park Cl NN3...142 B6
Quarry Rd
  Brixworth NN6.......106 C3
  Northampton NN5....140 D4
Quartercroft NN3.....142 E2
Quarterstone NN4....158 D1
Quebec Cl
  Corby NN18...........36 C1
  5 Northampton NN4..175 E7
Queen Eleanor Prim Sch
  Northampton NN4....159 B2
  Stony Stratford MK11..229 F4
Queen Eleanor Rd
  Geddington NN14......54 A3
  Northampton NN4....159 C2
Queen Eleanor St
  MK11..................229 E6
Queen Eleanor Terr
  NN4..................159 C2
Queensberry Rd NN15..72 B1
Queensbury Ct NN15...72 B1
Queens Cl LE16........34 C5
Queens Cres NN2.....141 D2
Queensland Gdns
  NN2..................141 C1
QUEEN'S PARK........141 C1
Queens Park Ind Est
  NN2..................141 B1
Queen's Park Par
  NN2..................141 C2
Queen's Pk NN7.......155 A3
Queens Rd
  Daventry NN11.......135 B3
  Wilbarston LE16.......34 D5
  Wollaston NN29......146 D2
Queen's Rd
  Northampton NN1....159 E7
  Towcester NN12......203 C6
Queen's Sq NN17......36 E5
Queens St
  Culworth OX17.......198 D2
  Farthinghoe NN13....221 B4
  Wellingborough NN8..130 A5
Queen St
  Bozeat NN29.........164 C2
  Desborough NN14.....51 B3
  Earls Barton NN6....144 F5
  Geddington NN14......54 A2
  Irthlingborough NN9...112 E2
  Kettering NN16........72 B2
  Market Harborough
  LE16..................32 A2
  Middleton Cheney
  OX17..................219 F8
  Rushden NN10........132 B2
  Stony Stratford MK11..229 E6
  Thrapston NN14.......76 E2
  Weedon Bec NN7.....155 A2
Queensway
  Burton Latimer NN15..92 B1
  Higham Ferrers NN10..132 C5
  Wellingborough NN8..129 D3
Queenswood Ave
  NN3..................142 D5
Quernstone La NN4...158 E3
QUINBURY END........187 A1

QUINTON 176 B1
Quinton Green Cotts
　NN7 . . . . 192 C7
Quinton House Sch
　NN5 . . . . 158 B5
Quinton La NN11 . . . . 184 C6
Quinton Rd NN4 . . . . 175 F5
Quintonside NN4 . . . . . . 175 F3
Quorn Cl
　Kettering NN15 . . . . 92 A5
　Wellingborough NN8 . . . . 129 D4
Quorn Rd NN10 . . . . 132 A3
Quorn Way NN1 . . . . 159 B7

R

Racecourse Rd PE9 . . . . 2 D5
Racedown NN8 . . . . 129 B3
Radleigh Cl NN4 . . . . 159 A2
Radleigh St NN4 . . . . 141 E1
Radnor Way NN15 . . . . . . 92 A5
RADSTONE 222 F6
Radstone Rd NN13 . . . . . 222 F6
Radstone Rd NN13 . . . . . 222 F2
Radstone Way NN2 . . . . . 141 C5
Raeburn Rd NN2 . . . . 141 F2
Raeburn Sch NN2 . . . . 141 F2
Raglan Cl NN10 . . . . 132 D1
Raglan St NN1 . . . . 159 E6
Ragsdale Ct NN14 . . . . 70 E7
Ragsdale St NN14 . . . . 70 E7
Ragsdale Wlk NN3 . . . . . . 142 C6
Railport App NN6 . . . . . . 100 B6
Railside La NN17 . . . . 37 A6
Railway Cotts
　Church Brampton
　　NN6 . . . . 140 A7
　Kilsby CV23 . . . . 100 A6
　Nether Heyford NN7 . . . . 172 A8
Railway View NN16 . . . . . . 72 A2
Raincliffe Cl OX17 . . . . . . 237 C7
Rainsborough Cres
　NN4 . . . . 158 F4
Rainsborough Gdns
　LE16 . . . . 48 D8
Rainsbrook Ave CV22 . . . . 98 E8
Rainsbrook Valley Rly★
　CV22 . . . . 98 C6
Raisins Field Cl NN3 . . . 143 C3
Rakestone Cl 4 NN4 . . . . 175 D6
Raleigh Cl
　Corby NN17 . . . . 36 A8
　Rothwell NN14 . . . . 70 E7
Raleigh Ct NN11 . . . . 135 B5
Ramsay Cl NN9 . . . . 114 C7
Randall Cl NN9 . . . . 131 E8
Randall Ho NN1 . . . . 159 F7
Randall Rd NN2 . . . . 141 E1
Rands Way NN9 . . . . 114 E5
Ranelagh Rd NN8 . . . . . . 130 B4
Rankine Ho NN17 . . . . 36 D8
Rannoch Cl NN15 . . . . 91 E8
Rannoch Way NN17 . . . . . 21 C1
Ransome Rd NN4 . . . . . . 159 D3
Rate's La PE8 . . . . 13 F7
Rathbone Cl CV21 . . . . 99 A8
Rathlin NN17 . . . . 36 C8
RAUNDS 114 C6
Raunds Park Inf Sch
　NN9 . . . . 114 E6
Raunds Rd
　Chelveston NN9 . . . . 133 C8
　Stanwick NN9 . . . . 114 A4
Raven Dr NN15 . . . . 92 A6
Ravensbank NN10 . . . . . . 132 B4
Ravenscourt NN17 . . . . . . 36 F8
Ravens Croft NN4 . . . . . . 175 A7
RAVENSTHORPE 103 E1
Ravensthorpe Rd
　NN6 . . . . 122 D5
RAVENSTONE 194 D2
Ravens Way NN3 . . . . 161 C8
Rawley Cres NN5 . . . . . . 140 A1
Rawlings 2 NN11 . . . . 135 D1
Rawlins OX17 . . . . 230 A5
Ray Cl PE8 . . . . 41 F7
Raymond Cl NN29 . . . . . . 146 E1
Raymond Rd NN5 . . . . . . 159 A7
Raynsford Rd NN5 . . . . . 158 F8
Rea Cl NN4 . . . . 175 C7
Rectory Cl
　Barby CV23 . . . . 99 C1
　Crick NN6 . . . . 100 F5
　Stanwick NN9 . . . . 113 F4
　Swinford LE17 . . . . 62 C4
Rectory Ct LE16 . . . . 48 B6
RECTORY FARM 143 C4
Rectory Farm Ct PE8 . . . . 28 D8
Rectory Farm Mews
　PE8 . . . . 28 D8
Rectory Farm Prim Sch
　NN3 . . . . 143 C5
Rectory Farm Rd
　NN3 . . . . 143 D4
Rectory Gdns NN9 . . . . . 112 E2
Rectory Hill NN14 . . . . 93 A7
Rectory La
　Barby CV23 . . . . 99 C1
　Holcot NN6 . . . . 126 E8
　Market Harborough
　　LE16 . . . . 32 C4
　Medbourne LE16 . . . . 19 A7
　Middleton Cheney
　　OX17 . . . . 208 F1

Rectory La continued
　Milton Malsor NN7 . . . . . . 174 E3
　Orlingbury NN14 . . . . 110 A5
　Walgrave NN6 . . . . 108 A4
　Woodford NN14 . . . . 94 D6
　Yardley Hastings NN7 . . . 179 A7
Rectory Rd NN10 . . . . 132 B2
Rectory Road Bsns Ctr
　NN10 . . . . 132 B3
Rectory Way NN12 . . . . . 213 B8
Rectory Wlk NN15 . . . . . . 91 F7
Redbourne Ct MK11 . . . . 229 F5
Redbourn Pk NN4 . . . . 160 B3
Redding Cl NN10 . . . . 148 A7
Redgrave Cl NN15 . . . . . . 90 F7
Redgrave Ct NN8 . . . . . . 129 F8
Red Hill Cres NN29 . . . . . 146 D3
Redhill Way NN9 . . . . 110 E1
Red House La NN6 . . . . . 108 E4
Redhouse Rd NN14 . . . . . 109 C4
Red House Rd NN3 . . . . . 142 B7
Red House Wharf
　NN7 . . . . 155 C4
Redland Cl LE15 . . . . 3 F5
Redland Dr NN2 . . . . 141 A4
Redliech Cl LE16 . . . . 32 B3
Red Lion St OX17 . . . . . . 230 F5
Red Lodge Rd NN17 . . . . . 12 A1
Redmile's La PE9 . . . . 1 A5
Redmoor NN12 . . . . 203 B4
Red Row NN9 . . . . 114 D6
Redruth Cl NN4 . . . . 159 B1
Redwell St NN8 . . . . 129 F6
Redwell Jun & Inf Sch
　NN8 . . . . 129 E7
Redwell L Ctr NN8 . . . . . . 129 E7
Redwell Rd NN8 . . . . 129 F6
Redwing Ave NN3 . . . . . . 142 C6
Redwood Cl NN29 . . . . . . 147 A7
Red Wood Cl NN14 . . . . . . 51 C2
Reedham Cl NN5 . . . . 140 C1
Reedhill NN4 . . . . 158 E1
Reedway NN3 . . . . 142 A4
Reffield Cl NN12 . . . . 203 D5
Regal Cl NN15 . . . . 141 F6
Regal Ct NN10 . . . . 132 C1
Regal Dr NN16 . . . . 72 C6
Regency Cl NN7 . . . . 155 B4
Regency Ct
　5 Daventry NN11 . . . . 135 C2
　Finedon NN9 . . . . 112 A5
　Rushden NN10 . . . . 132 B3
Regent Cl NN15 . . . . 92 A2
Regent Rd NN15 . . . . 92 A2
Regents Hall MK11 . . . . . . 229 D6
Regent St
　Desborough NN14 . . . . 51 B3
　Finedon NN9 . . . . 111 F4
　Kettering NN16 . . . . 72 C3
　Northampton NN1 . . . . . . 159 C6
　Wellingborough NN8 . . . . 130 A5
Regent Way NN7 . . . . 177 D1
Regiment Cl NN4 . . . . 175 E7
Reigate Wlk NN18 . . . . 36 B3
Reims Ct NN5 . . . . 140 A4
Remus Gate NN13 . . . . . . 234 A6
Rendelsham Cl NN16 . . . . 72 A6
Rennishaw Way NN2 . . . 141 F3
Repton Ct NN3 . . . . 142 D4
Reservoir Cl
　Irthlingborough NN9 . . . . 131 E8
　Stanion NN14 . . . . 37 F3
Reservoir Hos NN6 . . . . . . 125 D5
Reservoir Rd NN14 . . . . . . 72 B4
Resthaven Rd NN4 . . . . . 175 D6
Restormel Cl NN10 . . . . . 132 D1
Retford Ct NN3 . . . . 142 F4
Retreat The
　Easton o t H PE9 . . . . 1 F5
　Stony Stratford MK11 . . . 229 D5
Reynard Pk NN13 . . . . . . 233 F5
Reynard Way NN2 . . . . . . 141 D6
Reynolds Cl
　Kettering NN15 . . . . 92 A8
　Rugby CV21 . . . . 80 B1
　Wellingborough NN8 . . . . 129 F7
Reynolds Rd NN18 . . . . . . 36 E5
Reynoldston Cl NN4 . . . . 160 C1
Rhodes Cl
　Daventry NN11 . . . . 135 C5
　Market Harborough
　　LE16 . . . . 31 C2
Rhosili Rd NN4 . . . . 160 A2
Rhymer Cl MK19 . . . . 206 F4
Rhymer Ho NN2 . . . . 141 D5
Ribble Cl
　Northampton NN5 . . . . . . 140 F2
　Wellingborough NN8 . . . . 129 D6
Ribblesdale Ave NN17 . . . 36 E7
Richard Cl NN15 . . . . 91 C6
Richardsons La NN14 . . . . 70 D2
Richardson Way NN9 . . . 114 E7
Richmond Ave NN15 . . . . 91 F8
Richmond Cl NN10 . . . . . 132 C1
Richmond Ct NN12 . . . . . 203 C5
Richmond Rd
　Corby NN17 . . . . 36 E6
　Towcester NN12 . . . . 203 C6
Richmond St OX17 . . . . . 231 A5
Richmond Terr NN5 . . . . 159 B6
Rickyard Rd NN3 . . . . 142 E3
Rickyard Wlk NN4 . . . . . . 175 F2
Ridding Cl NN18 . . . . 36 D3
Rides Ct NN3 . . . . 142 C7
Ridge Rd NN14 . . . . 76 C4
Ridge The NN29 . . . . 145 E7
Ridge View LE16 . . . . 31 E5

Ridgeway
　Northampton NN3 . . . . . . 160 D8
　Stony Stratford MK11 . . . 229 F4
　Wellingborough NN8 . . . . 129 F7
Ridgeway Prim Sch
　LE16 . . . . 31 F5
Ridgeway The
　Barby CV23 . . . . 118 E8
　Kilsby CV23 . . . . 100 A1
　Market Harborough LE16 . 31 F5
　Welton NN11 . . . . 119 E1
Ridgeway W LE16 . . . . 31 E5
Ridgmont NN2 . . . . 228 E5
Ridgmont Cl MK19 . . . . . 228 E5
Ridgway Rd NN3 . . . . 92 B8
Riding Ct NN13 . . . . 233 F5
Riding The MK19 . . . . 228 D5
Ridings The
　Brixworth NN6 . . . . 106 C2
　Desborough NN14 . . . . 50 E4
　Northampton, Grange Park
　　NN4 . . . . 175 E2
　Northampton NN1 . . . . . . 159 D6
　Roade NN7 . . . . 191 C4
Riding The MK19 . . . . 228 D5
Ridley Cl 1 NN11 . . . . 135 C2
Ridley St NN16 . . . . 72 A4
Riggall Cl NN14 . . . . 90 A3
Riley Cl
　Daventry NN11 . . . . 134 F4
　Market Harborough LE16 . 31 B2
　Northampton NN3 . . . . . . 143 C5
Riley Rd NN16 . . . . 71 E4
Rillwood Ct NN3 . . . . 142 E4
RINGSTEAD 95 B3
Ringstead CE Prim Sch
　NN14 . . . . 95 B3
Ringstead Cl
　Corby NN17 . . . . 36 B8
　Kettering NN15 . . . . 91 F5
Ringstead Rd
　Denford NN14 . . . . 95 C5
　Great Addington NN14 . . . 94 C2
Ringtail Cl NN9 . . . . 131 E8
Ring The OX17 . . . . 208 E4
Ring Way NN4 . . . . 159 A3
Ringwell Cl NN9 . . . . 112 E3
Ringwood NN2 . . . . 141 A5
Ripley Cl LE16 . . . . 32 B3
Ripley Rd LE16 . . . . 20 D1
Ripley Wlk NN18 . . . . 36 C3
Ripon Cl NN4 . . . . 159 A2
Risdene Ct 11 NN10 . . . . . 132 B2
Rise The
　Northampton NN2 . . . . . . 141 B3
　Twyford OX17 . . . . 230 A5
Ritchie Pk LE16 . . . . 48 E8
Rivercrest Rd MK19 . . . . 229 B6
River La PE8 . . . . 28 C8
Riverside LE16 . . . . 32 A4
Riverside Bsns Pk
　NN3 . . . . 160 E7
Riverside Cl PE8 . . . . 42 A4
Riverside Ct
　Kislingbury NN7 . . . . 157 D4
　Market Harborough
　　LE16 . . . . 31 D2
　Weedon Bec NN7 . . . . . . 155 B3
Riverside Dr NN7 . . . . 155 B3
Riverside Ind Est LE16 . . 32 A4
Riverside Maltings
　PE8 . . . . 42 A6
Riverside Spinney PE8 . . . 8 A3
Riverside Way
　Islip NN14 . . . . 76 B2
　Northampton NN1 . . . . . . 159 F5
Riverside Way Ind Est
　NN1 . . . . 159 F5
Riverstone Way NN4 . . . 158 D2
Riverview NN15 . . . . 111 B8
Riverview Gdns NN14 . . . 95 C6
Riverwell NN3 . . . . 143 D2
Rivetts Cl MK46 . . . . 195 E4
Rixon Cl NN3 . . . . 142 E1
Rixon Rd NN18 . . . . 130 C7
RNIB Rushton Hall Sch
　NN14 . . . . 52 B2
ROADE 191 E4
Roade Hill NN7 . . . . 191 F1
Roade Prim Sch NN7 . . . 191 E4
Roade Sch Sports Coll
　NN7 . . . . 191 C3
Roadins Cl NN15 . . . . 91 A7
ROAD WEEDON 155 C4
Robbins Ct CV22 . . . . 98 F8
Robb's La NN14 . . . . 75 F6
Roberson Cl NN12 . . . . . . 203 C4
Robert Hill Cl CV21 . . . . . 80 A1
Roberts Cl MK19 . . . . 228 E4
Roberts Field NN7 . . . . . . 156 B1
Robert's La PE8 . . . . 42 F2
Robert Smyth Sch The
　LE16 . . . . 31 E5
Robertson Cl CV23 . . . . . . 80 A5
Roberts St
　Bozeat NN29 . . . . 164 C2
　Rushden NN10 . . . . 132 C2
　Wellingborough NN8 . . . . 129 E4
Robert St NN1 . . . . 159 D7
Robin Cl
　Kettering NN15 . . . . 92 A6
　Towcester NN12 . . . . 203 C3
Robinia Cl NN4 . . . . 158 E3
Robin La NN8 . . . . 130 A7
Robin Ride NN13 . . . . 222 E1
Robins Cl NN7 . . . . 192 C1
Robins Field PE8 . . . . 8 A4
Robinson Cl NN16 . . . . . . 71 F4

Robinson Dr NN13 . . . . . 233 D7
Robinson Ho NN3 . . . . . . 142 E4
Robinson Rd NN10 . . . . . 132 C2
Robinson Way
　Kettering NN16 . . . . 71 F4
　Northampton NN4 . . . . . . 176 A6
Robinswood PE8 . . . . 8 A4
Roche Cl NN11 . . . . 153 C8
Rochelle Way NN5 . . . . . 140 A2
Rochester Cl NN15 . . . . . . 91 F7
Rochester Gdns LE16 . . . 31 D1
Rochester Rd NN18 . . . . . 36 E2
Rochester Way OX17 . . . 230 B5
Roche Way NN8 . . . . 129 F6
Rockcroft 3 NN4 . . . . 175 D6
Rock Hill NN14 . . . . 70 D7
Rockhill Rd NN6 . . . . 121 A3
ROCKINGHAM 21 B4
Rockingham Castle &
　Gdns★ LE16 . . . . 21 B3
Rockingham Cl
　1 Daventry NN11 . . . . 135 B4
　Thrapston NN14 . . . . 76 E2
Rockingham Ct NN10 . . . 148 A8
Rockingham Hills PE8 . . . 41 E7
Rockingham Ind Est
　LE16 . . . . 32 B3
Rockingham Mews
　NN17 . . . . 37 A7
Rockingham Motor
　Speedway★ NN17 . . . . 22 E4
Rockingham Paddocks
　NN16 . . . . 72 B6
Rockingham Prim Sch
　NN17 . . . . 37 A8
Rockingham Rd
　Caldecott LE16 . . . . 21 B6
　Corby, Great Oakley
　　NN14 . . . . 53 A3
　Corby NN17 . . . . 21 E2
　Cottingham LE16 . . . . 20 E2
　Gretton LE16, NN17 . . . . . 21 E7
　Kettering NN16 . . . . 72 A5
　Market Harborough LE16 . 32 B4
　Northampton NN4 . . . . . . 159 C2
Rockleigh Cl NN9 . . . . . . 112 A5
Rock Rd
　Finedon NN9 . . . . 112 A5
　Oundle PE8 . . . . 41 F6
Rock St NN8 . . . . 129 F5
Roderick Ct 9 NN11 . . . . 135 B4
Roderick Way 7
　NN11 . . . . 135 B4
Rodewell Ho NN14 . . . . . . 70 D7
Rodney Cl NN11 . . . . 135 E1
Rodney Dr NN17 . . . . 36 B8
Roe Rd NN1 . . . . 160 A8
Rogers Cl NN14 . . . . 90 A3
Rokeby Inf Sch CV22 . . . . 98 A8
Rokeby Jun Sch CV22 . . . 98 A8
Rokeby Wlk NN5 . . . . 140 D1
Roland Way NN10 . . . . . . 132 B6
Rolfe Cres NN7 . . . . 156 B1
Rolleston Cl LE16 . . . . 32 A4
Roman Cl
　Northampton NN4 . . . . . . 175 F5
　Weldon NN17 . . . . 38 B8
Roman Dr PE8 . . . . 8 D2
Roman Way
　Brackley NN13 . . . . 234 A7
　Daventry NN11 . . . . 135 C5
　Desborough NN14 . . . . 51 B2
　Higham Ferrers NN10 . . . 132 B7
　Irchester NN29 . . . . 147 B7
　Market Harborough LE16 . 31 E4
　Northampton NN4 . . . . . . 175 E4
　Raunds NN9 . . . . 114 E6
　Thrapston NN14 . . . . 76 E3
Romany Rd NN2 . . . . 141 E2
Romney Rd NN18 . . . . 36 E5
Romulus Cl NN4 . . . . 175 F5
Romulus Way NN13 . . . . 234 A6
Rookery Farm★
　NN12 . . . . 191 B1
Rookery La
　Northampton NN2 . . . . . . 141 A5
　Stoke Bruerne NN12 . . . . 191 B1
Rookery The NN4 . . . . . . 175 E3
Rookwell Dr LE16 . . . . 31 F1
Roper Cl CV21 . . . . 99 A8
Rose Ave
　Rushden NN10 . . . . 131 F1
　Weldon NN17 . . . . 38 B8
Rosebay Rd NN14 . . . . 51 A5
Rosebery Ave NN5 . . . . . 158 F6
Rosebery St
　Burton Latimer NN15 . . . . 92 B1
　Kettering NN16 . . . . 72 C2
　Ringstead NN14 . . . . 95 B3
Rose Cl
　Broughton NN14 . . . . 90 B5
　Corby NN18 . . . . 36 E2
　Hartwell NN7 . . . . 192 E2
　Rothwell NN14 . . . . 70 E6
Rose Cotts NN14 . . . . 113 B7
Rose Ct
　Irchester NN29 . . . . 147 B8
　Olney MK46 . . . . 195 F3
　Weldon NN17 . . . . 38 B8
Rose Dale LE17 . . . . 45 A4
Rosedale Ave NN17 . . . . . 36 E6
Rosedale Rd NN2 . . . . . . 141 D3
Rose Dr NN13 . . . . 233 D8
Rose Hall La OX17 . . . . . 220 A8
Rose Hill NN4 . . . . 112 A5
Rose Hill Way NN14 . . . . . 89 C5
Roseholme Rd NN1 . . . . 160 A8
Rose La MK19 . . . . 206 E6
Rosemoor Cl LE16 . . . . . . 32 B3

Rosemoor Dr NN4 . . . . . 175 C7
Rosemount Dr NN15 . . . . 91 C7
Rosenella 3 NN4 . . . . 158 F3
Rose Paddock NN14 . . . . . 94 D7
Roses Cl NN29 . . . . 146 C3
Rose Terr NN14 . . . . 94 D7
Rosette Cl NN5 . . . . 158 C8
Rosewood Ave CV22 . . . . 98 A8
Rosewood Cl NN11 . . . . . 135 C5
Rosewood Ct NN8 . . . . . . 130 C3
Rosewood Pl NN16 . . . . . . 72 C4
Rosgill Pl NN3 . . . . 142 B2
Rossendale Dr NN15 . . . . 92 A5
Rossetti Rd NN18 . . . . 36 E5
Rossiter Ho NN13 . . . . . . 233 E4
Ross Rd NN5 . . . . 158 C4
Rotherhithe Cl 9
　NN4 . . . . 158 F2
ROTHERSTHORPE 174 A7
Rothersthorpe Ave
　NN4 . . . . 159 A3
Rothersthorpe CE Prim
　Sch NN7 . . . . 174 A6
Rothersthorpe Cres
　NN4 . . . . 159 A3
Rothersthorpe Rd
　Kislingbury NN7 . . . . 157 E2
　Northampton NN7 . . . . . . 159 A3
Rothesay Rd NN2 . . . . . . 141 F2
Rothesay Terr NN2 . . . . . 141 F2
ROTHWELL 70 D8
Rothwell Grange Cotts
　NN16 . . . . 71 B5
Rothwell Grange Ct
　NN16 . . . . 71 B5
Rothwell Jun Sch
　NN14 . . . . 70 D7
Rothwell Rd
　Desborough NN14 . . . . 51 A2
　Harrington NN6 . . . . 69 B5
　Kettering NN16 . . . . 71 D4
　Kettering NN16 . . . . 71 F3
Rothwell Victoria Inf Sch
　NN14 . . . . 70 D7
Rotten Row NN29 . . . . . . 146 D2
Rotton Row NN9 . . . . 114 D7
Roughton Cl NN15 . . . . . . 91 B6
Round Cl NN11 . . . . 119 E1
Roundel The NN6 . . . . . . 143 B6
Roundhill Cl LE16 . . . . 32 B2
Roundhill Rd NN15 . . . . . . 91 C7
ROUND SPINNEY 142 E7
Round The NN14 . . . . 89 B4
Roundtown OX17 . . . . 237 C7
Roundway The NN11 . . . . 135 D6
Roundwood Way NN5 . . 157 F8
Roveley Ct MK11 . . . . 229 F5
Rowallen Way 2
　NN11 . . . . 135 A4
Rowan Ave
　Market Harborough
　　LE16 . . . . 31 E1
　Mawsley Village NN14 . . . 89 B4
　Northampton NN3 . . . . . . 142 C5
Rowan Cl
　Brackley NN13 . . . . 222 F1
　Northampton NN4 . . . . . . 175 C5
　Towcester NN12 . . . . 203 B4
　Wellingborough NN8 . . . . 129 C5
Rowan Ct NN17 . . . . 21 E1
Rowan Gate Prim Sch
　NN8 . . . . 130 B6
Rowans The NN11 . . . . . . 135 C4
Rowan Way NN11 . . . . . . 184 B6
Rowe Cl CV21 . . . . 99 C8
Rowell Way PE8 . . . . 42 B4
Rowlandson Cl NN3 . . . . 142 E1
Rowlett Cl NN10 . . . . 132 C5
Rowlett Com Prim Sch
　NN17 . . . . 37 B6
Rowlett Rd NN17 . . . . 36 D8
Rowley Way NN17 . . . . . . 141 E6
Rowtree Rd NN4 . . . . 175 B6
Roxton Cl NN15 . . . . 92 A5
Royal Cl NN11 . . . . 135 B3
Royal Gdns NN14 . . . . 50 E7
Royal Oak Ind Est
　NN11 . . . . 134 F3
Royal Oak La OX17 . . . . . 220 A8
Royal Oak Way N
　NN11 . . . . 134 F3
Royal Oak Way S
　NN11 . . . . 134 F2
Royal Star Dr NN11 . . . . . 135 A4
Royal Terr NN1 . . . . 159 C7
Royce Cl NN17 . . . . 21 F1
Rubens Wlk NN18 . . . . 36 E5
Rubicon Ho NN1 . . . . 159 C7
Ruddington Cl NN3 . . . . . 160 E7
Rudge Mews NN5 . . . . . . 157 F2
Rudgeway NN13 . . . . 233 F2
Rufford Ave NN3 . . . . 160 E7
Rufford Cl NN15 . . . . 92 A5
Rufford Wlk NN18 . . . . 36 E5
RUGBY 99 A7
Rugby Cl LE16 . . . . 31 D2
Rugby Rd
　Barby CV23 . . . . 99 C1
　Kilsby CV21, CV23 . . . . . . 99 E5
　Lilbourne CV23 . . . . 80 F6
　South Kilworth LE17 . . . . . 62 C6
　Swinford LE17 . . . . 62 B3
Ruins The NN12 . . . . 203 C6
Runnell La PE8 . . . . 15 F5
Runnymede Gdns 5
　NN3 . . . . 142 F1
Rupert Rd LE16 . . . . 31 E1
Rush Cl NN7 . . . . 192 E2

RUSHDEN 132 E2
Rushden Com Coll The NN10 132 A4
Rushden Hospl NN10 148 B8
Rushden Rd
Newton Bromswold NN10 149 C7
Wymington NN10 148 A6
Rushden Station Transport Mus★ NN10 132 B3
Rushes La LE16 30 F3
Rushes The NN15 111 B8
Rushmere Ave NN1 160 B6
Rushmere Cl
Islip NN14 76 B3
Raunds NN9 114 C5
Rushmere Cres NN1 160 B6
Rushmere Rd NN1 160 B5
Rushmere Way
Northampton NN1 160 B6
Rushden NN10 132 B4
Rushmills NN4 160 B3
RUSHTON 52 C2
Rushton Prim Sch NN14 52 C2
Rushton Rd
Desborough NN14 51 C3
Rothwell NN14 70 E8
Wilbarston LE16 34 C4
Rushton Triangular Lo★ NN14 52 A2
Rushwell Cl NN14 94 B3
Rushy End NN4 175 B6
Ruskin Ave NN8 129 C4
Ruskin Jun & Inf Sch NN8 129 C3
Ruskin Rd
Daventry NN11 153 C8
Northampton NN2 141 C4
Russell Ct NN10 132 B2
Russell Hill PE8 8 A6
Russell Rise NN7 155 E5
Russell Sq NN3 142 C6
Russell St
Kettering NN16 72 C2
Stony Stratford MK11 229 D5
Russell Street Sch MK11 229 D5
Russell Way NN10 132 B6
Russet Dr NN3 143 A2
Russett Cl LE16 31 F5
Rutherford Ct NN17 22 B1
Rutherford Dr NN8 129 A5
Rutherford Way NN11 134 F4
Rutherglen Rd NN17 36 F7
Ruth Gdns NN16 72 E3
Rutland Cl NN17 36 B7
Rutland Ct NN14 50 F4
Rutland St NN16 72 C3
Rutland Wlk
Market Harborough LE16 31 F5
Northampton NN3 142 B7
Rycroft Cl NN8 129 D5
Rydal NN8 129 B3
Rydal Mount NN3 142 C3
Rydalside
Kettering NN15 72 D1
Northampton NN4 158 F3
Ryder Ct NN18 52 F8
Ryder View NN8 129 C7
Ryeburn Way NN8 129 E5
Ryebury Hill NN8 111 E2
Rye Cl
Burton Latimer NN15 92 C2
Rushden NN10 148 C8
Ryefields NN6 124 B8
Ryehill Cl
Irthlingborough NN9 131 E8
Isham NN14 91 E1
Long Buckby NN6 121 A3
Northampton NN5 140 C2
Ryehill Ct NN5 140 C2
Ryehill Rd NN3 142 F3
Ryeland MK11 229 E6
Ryeland Rd NN5 158 A8
Ryeland Way NN5 140 A1
Ryland Rd
Moulton NN3 142 C8
Northampton NN2 141 E2
Rylands Cl LE16 32 B3
Ryle Dr NN8 129 A4
Rylstone The NN8 129 B4
Ryngwell Cl NN6 106 B1

S

Sackville St
Kettering NN16 72 A4
Raunds NN9 114 D6
Thrapston NN14 76 D2
Sacrewell Farm & Ctry Ctr★ PE8 8 B5
Saddleback Rd NN5 158 D6
Saddlers Sq NN3 142 F6
Saddlers The NN4 175 F3
Saddlers Way NN9 114 B5
Saffron Cl NN4 175 D5
Saffron Rd NN10 132 B6
Sage Cl NN3 142 E4
Saimon Cl NN13 233 E8
St Alban's Cl
Kettering NN15 73 A1
Northampton NN3 142 B3
St Albans Pl NN29 146 D2
St Alban's Rd NN3 142 B3
St Amandas Cl NN15 72 F2
St Andrews CE Prim Sch NN3 143 C2
St Andrew's CE Prim Sch NN16 72 A4
St Andrews Cl
Broughton NN14 90 B4
Great Easton LE16 20 D7
St Andrew's Cl NN14 77 D3
St Andrews Cres
Rugby CV22 98 A8
Wellingborough NN8 129 E2
St Andrews Ct NN1 159 C6
St Andrew's Ct NN14 90 B4
St Andrews Dr NN11 135 E3
St Andrew's Ho 9 NN1 159 F6
St Andrew's Hospl NN1 159 F6
St Andrews La NN14 77 D4
St Andrew's La NN14 93 A7
St Andrew's Rd
East Haddon NN6 122 D5
Northampton NN2 159 B7
St Andrew's St
Kettering NN16 72 B3
Northampton NN1 159 C6
St Andrews Way NN14 90 B4
St Andrew's Wlk NN17 37 B6
St Annes Cl
Brackley NN13 233 D8
Daventry NN11 153 C8
St Anne's Rd NN15 73 A1
St Ann's Ct PE8 41 F5
St Anthonys Cl NN11 153 B8
St Anthony's Hill NN14 51 A2
St Anthony's Rd NN15 72 F1
St Augustine's Cl NN15 73 A1
St Augustin Way NN11 135 D1
St Barnabas CE Sch NN8 129 F4
St Barnabas' Cl NN15 73 A1
St Barnabas Ho 10 NN1 159 C6
St Barnabas St NN8 129 F4
St Bartholemews Ho 5 NN1 159 C6
St Bartholomew's Cl NN15 73 A1
St Benedicts Mount NN4 158 E2
St Bernards Ct NN15 72 F1
St Botolphs Gn PE8 28 E7
St Botolph's Rd NN15 91 F7
St Brendan's RC Inf Sch NN18 36 B6
St Catharine's Rd NN15 73 A1
St Catherines Cl NN11 153 B8
St Cecilia's Cl NN15 72 F1
St Chad's Cl NN15 73 A1
St Christopher's Cl NN15 73 A1
St Christopher's Dr PE8 42 B4
St Christopher's Wlk NN3 160 B7
St Clements Ct NN15 91 B7
St Crispin Ave NN8 129 F2
St Crispin Cl NN15 92 C3
St Crispin Cres NN5 157 F8
St Crispin Dr NN5 158 A7
St Crispin Rd NN6 144 F4
St Davids Cl NN6 106 B1
St David's Cl NN15 72 F1
St David's Ct NN13 234 A8
St Davids RC Mid Sch NN2 141 C3
St David's Rd
Brixworth NN6 106 A1
Northampton NN2 141 C2
Rushden NN10 131 D3
St Dunstan's Cl NN15 91 F8
St Dunstans Rise NN4 158 E1
St Edmunds Cl NN11 153 C7
St Edmund's Hospl NN1 159 E7
St Edmund's Rd NN1 159 E6
St Edmund's St NN1 159 E6
St Edward's RC Prim Sch NN15 91 E7
St Emilion Cl NN5 139 F1
St Francis Ave NN5 159 A8
St Francis' Cl NN15 73 A1
St Georges Ave CV22 98 A8
St George's Ave NN2 159 D8
St Georges Cl NN12 203 C5
St Georges Ho 2 NN1 159 C6
St George's Pl NN2 159 C8
St George's St NN1 159 C7
St George's Way NN10 131 F3
St Giles' Cl NN15 73 A1
St Giles Mews MK11 229 D6
St Giles's Cl NN14 51 A3
St Giles' Sq NN1 159 D5
St Giles' St NN1 159 D6
St Giles' Terr NN1 159 D6
St Gregory's RC Prim Sch NN3 142 D3
St Gregory's Rd NN3 142 D3
St Helens Cl NN6 84 D4
St Hilda's Cl NN11 153 C8
St Hughes Cl NN11 153 C8
St James' CE Prim Sch NN5 159 A7
St James Cl
2 Daventry NN11 135 C1
Hanslope MK19 207 A2
St James' Cl
Kettering NN15 92 A8
Rushden NN10 132 C4
St James' Cres NN14 76 E2
ST JAMES' END 159 A5
St James Inf Sch NN11 135 C1
St James' Lake Nature Reserve★ NN13 233 E6
St James' Mill Rd NN5 159 A4
St James Mill Rd E NN1 159 B4
St James' Park Rd NN5 159 A6
St James Rd
Brackley NN13 233 F5
Corby NN18 37 A6
St James' Rd NN5 159 A5
St James Ret Pk NN1 159 B5
St James St NN11 135 C1
St Johns Ave CV22 98 E8
St John's Ave NN2 141 C6
St Johns Cl
Daventry NN11 153 B8
Rothersthorpe NN7 174 A6
St Johns Ct NN1 159 D5
St John's Ho
8 Northampton NN1 159 C6
3 Wellingborough NN8 129 F5
St John's La MK19 228 B4
St John's Pl NN17 37 B6
St Johns Rd NN12 189 E4
St John's Rd NN15 91 F8
St John's Sq NN11 135 C2
St John's St
Northampton NN1 159 D5
Wellingborough NN8 129 F5
St John's Terr NN1 159 D5
St John's Way NN7 177 A2
St John's Wlk NN3 142 D1
St Josephs Cl MK46 195 F4
St Joseph's Cl NN15 73 A1
St Joseph's RC Prim Sch LE16 31 E3
St Julien Cl NN5 140 A2
St Katharine's Way NN29 131 B1
St Katherine's Ct 25 NN1 159 C6
St Katherine's Sq 27 NN1 159 C6
St Katherine's St 2 NN1 159 C5
St Laurence Way NN9 113 F4
St Lawrence CE Jun Sch NN12 203 C5
St Lawrence CE Lower Sch NN10 148 A5
St Lawrence Ct 12 NN1 159 E6
St Lawrence Ho 3 NN1 159 C6
St Lawrence Rd NN12 203 C5
St Lawrence Rd S NN12 203 C4
St Lawrence Wlk NN10 148 B5
St Leonards Cl CV47 166 D8
St Leonard's Cl NN15 72 F1
St Leonards Ct NN4 159 C3
St Leonard's Rd NN4 159 C3
St Loys CE Prim Sch NN12 200 B2
St Luke's CE Prim Sch NN5 158 C6
St Lukes Cl
Northampton NN5 157 F8
Spratton NN6 105 B1
St Luke's Cl NN15 92 A8
St Luke's Ho 12 NN1 159 C6
St Luke's Hospl LE16 31 D5
St Luke's Rd NN18 37 A5
St Magdalenes Rd NN15 72 F2
St Margarets Ave NN10 132 A1
St Margaret's Gdns 3 NN5 140 F1
St Mark's Cl
Kettering NN15 73 A1
Rushden NN10 131 E2
St Mark's Cres NN2 141 B6
St Marks Ho 7 NN1 159 C6
St Mark's Rd NN18 37 A5
St Martins Cl NN2 141 C4
St Martins Ho 1 NN1 159 C6
St Martins Yd 3 LE16 31 E3
St Martyn's Way NN7 155 B3
St Mary & St Giles CE Jun Sch MK11 229 E6
St Mary's Ave
Finedon NN9 111 F5
Rushden NN10 132 B1
Stony Stratford MK11 229 E6
St Mary's CE Prim Sch
Burton Latimer NN15 92 C2
Kettering NN16 72 C2
St Marys Cl
Thrapston NN14 76 F3
Woodnewton PE8 14 E2
St Mary's Cl
Nassington PE8 15 E5
Priors Hardwick CV47 166 A5
St Marys Ct NN7 173 F2
St Mary's Ct
Finedon NN9 111 E5
Market Harborough LE16 32 A4
22 Northampton NN1 159 C6
St Marys Hill PE8 14 E2
St Mary's Hospl NN15 72 C1
St Mary's Paddock NN8 130 C4
St Mary's Pl LE16 31 F3
St Mary's RC Prim Sch
Aston le W NN11 182 F2
Northampton NN5 140 F1
St Marys Rd NN29 146 E2
St Mary's Rd
Bozeat NN29 164 D2
Kettering NN15 72 C1
Market Harborough LE16 31 F3
St Mary's St NN1 159 C6
St Mary's Way
Nassington PE8 15 E5
Roade NN7 191 D5
Weedon Bec NN7 155 B3
St Matthew's Par NN2 141 F1
St Matthew's Rd NN15 73 A1
St Matthew's Sch NN3 142 A1
St Michael's Ave NN1 159 E7
St Michael's Ct NN7 205 F8
St Michaels Gdns NN15 91 C8
St Michael's La NN29 146 D2
St Michael's Mount NN1 159 E7
St Michael's Rd
Kettering NN15 91 C8
Northampton NN1 159 D6
St Nicholas Cl
Kettering NN15 72 F2
Market Harborough LE16 31 F2
St Nicholas Ct NN29 145 E6
St Nicholas Rd NN29 145 D6
St Nicholas Way
Islip NN14 76 B3
Market Harborough LE16 31 F2
St Oswald's Cl NN15 91 F8
St Osyths La PE8 42 A5
St Patrick's RC Prim Sch NN18 36 D4
St Patrick St 11 NN1 159 C7
St Paul's Ct
Kettering NN15 72 B1
Stony Stratford MK11 229 D6
St Pauls Gdns NN14 76 D2
St Paul's Rd NN2 159 C8
St Paul's Terr NN2 159 C8
St Peter's Ave
Kettering NN16 72 C1
Kettering NN16 72 C2
Rushden NN10 131 F3
St Peter's CE Jun Sch NN9 114 E6
St Peters Cl NN11 153 B8
St Peter's Cl NN14 37 F2
St Peters Ct NN9 114 D6
St Peter's Gate NN13 234 A7
St Peter's Gdns NN3 142 D1
St Peter's Ho 20 NN1 159 C6
St Peter's Ind Sch NN3 143 A3
St Peter's Mews 12 NN16 72 C2
St Peters Rd PE8 41 F7
St Peter's Rd NN13 233 F8
St Peter's Sch NN15 91 B8
St Peters Sq 12 NN1 159 C5
St Peter's St NN1 159 B5
St Peters's Way NN9 112 F2
St Peters Way NN7 161 F6
St Peter's Way
Corby NN17 37 A6
Northampton NN1 159 C5
Weedon Bec NN7 155 B3
St Peters Wlk 5 NN1 159 C5
St Philip's Cl NN15 73 A1
St Rochus Dr NN8 130 A1
St Rumbolds Dr OX17 231 A5
St Saviour's Rd NN15 73 A1
St Simon's Cl NN15 73 A1
St Stephens Ho 9 NN1 159 C6
St Stephen's Rd NN15 73 A1
St Swithins Cl NN15 72 F2
St Theresa's Cl NN15 72 F2
St Thomas Ho NN1 159 D6
St Thomas More RC Prim Sch NN16 71 F1
St Thomas Rd NN7 161 D3
St Valentine's Cl NN15 72 F1
St Vincents Ave NN15 72 F2
St Wilfrids Rd PE8 41 F7
Salcey Ave NN7 192 D2
Salcey Cl
2 Daventry NN11 135 B4
Hartwell NN7 192 E2
Kettering NN15 92 A5
Salcey Forest Trail★ NN7 192 F4
Salcey Forest Trail (Rose Copse)★ NN7 193 B2
SALCEY GREEN 207 B7
Salcey Rise NN7 177 B1
Salcey St NN4 159 C2
Salcombe Rd NN18 36 E4
Salem Cl NN6 121 A3
Salem La 9 NN8 130 A5
Salen Cl NN15 92 B5
Salford Cl NN6 64 E6
Salisbury Rd NN8 130 C5
Salisbury St
Kettering NN16 72 C4
Northampton NN2 159 C8
Salisbury Wlk NN18 36 E1
Sallow Ave NN3 143 C3
Sallow Rd NN17 22 E1
Salmons La OX17 220 B8
Salthouse Rd NN4 160 C2
Salt Pikes NN6 125 B8
Saltwell Sq 5 NN3 143 C2
Samuel Pl NN17 37 A8
Samuels Cl NN9 113 F3
Samwell Way NN4 158 C1
Sandby Rd NN18 36 E4
Sanders Cl
Braunston NN11 118 B1
Wellingborough NN8 111 B1
Sanders La NN12 217 D3
Sanders Lodge Ind Est NN10 131 D3
Sanderson Cl NN15 91 A8
Sanders Rd NN8 111 B1
Sanders Terr NN6 121 B4
Sandfield Cl NN3 142 B6
Sandhill Rd 2 NN5 159 A6
Sandhills NN6 105 A1
Sandhills Cl NN2 141 B6
Sandhills Rd NN2 141 B6
Sandhurst Cl NN4 175 B8
Sandiland Rd NN3 142 B2
Sandlands Ave NN14 55 F7
Sandlands Cl NN14 55 F7
Sandover NN4 175 D6
Sandown Cl NN18 36 E1
Sandpiper Cl NN15 92 A2
Sandpiper La NN8 130 A7
Sandringham Cl
Brackley NN13 233 E7
Northampton NN1 160 B7
Rushden NN10 132 A1
Towcester NN12 203 C4
Wellingborough NN8 129 E2
Sandringham Ct NN15 91 D5
Sandringham Rd
Kings Sutton OX17 230 F5
Northampton NN1 160 A7
Sandringham Way LE16 32 B3
Sandringham Wlk NN18 36 E2
Sands Cl NN12 172 D1
Sandy Cl NN8 129 F6
Sandy Hill La NN3 126 E2
Sandyhome Rd NN12 203 C5
Sandy La
Church Brampton NN6 140 D8
Harpole NN7 157 E7
Northampton NN5 139 F2
Saneco La NN6 106 B3
Sansom Ct NN3 142 D4
Sansome Cl NN7 177 B3
Saplings The NN16 72 C6
Sapphire Cl NN15 72 C1
Sarek Pk NN4 174 F7
Sargeants La NN4 175 C4
Sargent Rd NN18 36 E4
Sarjeant Ct NN14 70 D7
Sarrington Rd NN17 36 F8
Sartoris Rd NN10 131 F2
Saruman La NN3 143 B6
Sassoon Cl NN8 129 C6
Sassoon Mews NN8 129 B6
Saunders Cl NN16 72 B1
Savill Cl NN4 175 C7
Sawyers Cres NN9 133 B8
Saxby Cres NN8 130 C4
Saxilby Cl NN18 36 C4
Saxon Acre NN13 233 F7
Saxon Ave NN4 175 E3
Saxon Cl
Desborough NN14 51 A3
Higham Ferrers NN10 132 B7
Market Harborough LE16 31 F4
Saxon Dale NN16 72 C6
Saxon Ho NN6 106 B2
Saxon Hts NN6 125 B8
Saxonlea Cl NN10 131 E3
Saxon Rise
Earls Barton NN6 144 E3
Irchester NN29 147 C8
Northampton NN5 158 B7
Saxon St NN3 142 B1
Saxon Way NN9 114 E6
Saxon Way E NN18 53 A8
Saxon Way W NN18 52 F8
Sayers Cl NN12 214 D3
SCALDWELL 106 F6
Scaldwell Rd
Brixworth NN6 106 D4
Old NN6 107 C7
Scapa Rd NN17 36 C8
Scarborough St NN9 112 E2
Scarborough Wlk NN18 36 B4
Scarletwell St NN1 159 B6
Scarplands The NN5 158 C6
Scharpwell NN9 112 E3
Scholars Ct NN1 159 D5
Scholars Row NN14 89 B4

School Cl
Braunston NN11 . . . . .118 D1
Greens Norton NN12. . . . .202 D8
Yelvertoft NN6. . . . . .82 A4
School End OX17 . . . . .237 C7
School Farm Yd LE16 . . . . . .18 B3
School Gdns CV21 . . . . .80 A1
School Hill
Irchester NN29 . . . . .147 B8
Middleton LE16 . . . . .35 C8
Newnham NN11. . . . . .153 D4
School La
Abthorpe NN12 . . . . .202 A2
Adstone NN12 . . . . .186 B3
Badby NN11. . . . . .152 F3
Barrowden LE15 . . . . .3 F5
Braybrooke LE16 . . . . .49 F5
Bythorn PE28. . . . . .97 D4
Castlethorpe MK19 . . . . . . .218 F5
Cottingham LE16 . . . . .20 C1
Denford NN14. . . . . .95 C6
Elton PE8. . . . . .28 D8
Evenley NN13 . . . . .233 F2
Everdon NN11. . . . . .170 A8
Eydon NN11. . . . . .184 C1
Greens Norton NN12. . . . .202 D8
Hannington NN6 . . . . .108 C2
Harpole NN7 . . . . .157 B6
Hartwell NN7. . . . . .192 D2
Higham Ferrers NN10 . . . . .132 B7
Husbands Bosworth
LE17 . . . . .45 E5
Irchester NN29 . . . . .147 A8
Islip NN14 . . . . .76 B2
Kettering NN16 . . . . .72 B2
Kislingbury NN7. . . . . .157 D4
Little Harrowden NN9 . . . . .110 C4
Lubenham LE16 . . . . .30 F3
Market Harborough LE16 . . .31 E3
Morcott LE15. . . . . .3 A6
Moulton NN3 . . . . .126 C1
Naseby NN6. . . . . .85 B8
Northampton NN4 . . . . .175 E3
Priors Marston CV47. . . . . .166 D8
Quinton NN7. . . . . .176 B1
Rothwell NN14. . . . . .70 D7
Scaldwell NN6. . . . . .106 F6
Swinford LE17 . . . . .62 B4
Titchmarsh NN14. . . . . .77 C4
Wappenham NN12. . . . . . . .213 B8
Warmington PE8 . . . . .28 B3
Weldon NN17. . . . . .38 B8
Wilbarston LE16 . . . . .34 C5
Yardley Gobion NN12. . . . . .217 E6
Yelvertoft NN6. . . . . .82 B4
School Pl NN18 . . . . .36 D5
School Rd
Gretton NN17 . . . . .10 B1
Irchester NN29 . . . . .147 A8
Mawsley Village NN14. . . . . .89 B4
Pattishall NN12 . . . . .188 F8
Spratton NN6. . . . . .105 B1
School St
Daventry NN11 . . . . .135 A2
Rugby CV21 . . . . .80 A1
Sulgrave OX17 . . . . .210 F7
Woodford Halse NN11. . . . .184 C6
School Wlk NN8 . . . . .130 A1
Scirocco Cl NN3 . . . . .141 E6
Scoborough Rd LE16,
LE17. . . . . .30 A1
Scotgate NN17 . . . . .10 F7
Scotia Cl NN4 . . . . .160 C2
Scotland End LE16 . . . . . . .31 F1
Scotland Rd LE16 . . . . .32 A2
Scotland St NN16 . . . . .72 C5
Scotney Cl 1 NN14 . . . . .175 C8
Scotney Way NN14. . . . . . .76 E2
Scots Mere NN9 . . . . .112 D3
Scott Ave NN14 . . . . .70 E7
Scott Cl
Daventry NN11 . . . . .135 C4
Market Harborough LE16 . . .31 E5
Ravensthorpe NN6 . . . . . . .103 D1
Scotter Wlk NN18 . . . . .36 C4
Scott Rd
Corby NN17 . . . . .37 A6
Kettering NN16 . . . . .72 C5
Wellingborough NN8 . . . . . .129 C3
Scotts La LE16 . . . . .34 C5
Scriveners La NN12 . . . . .216 A8
Scrivens Hill NN11 . . . . . . .184 D6
Scully Cl 8 NN4 . . . . .175 E7
Scythe Cl NN11 . . . . .135 C6
Seaford Wlk NN18 . . . . . . .36 B5
Seagrave Ct NN3 . . . . .143 B5
Seagrave St NN15. . . . . . . .91 C8
Sears Cl NN7 . . . . .155 E6
Sears Ho NN1 . . . . .159 F7
Seaton Cres NN18 . . . . . . .36 E4
Seaton Dr NN3 . . . . .142 F1
Seaton Rd
Barrowden LE15 . . . . .3 C4
Harringworth NN17. . . . . .10 E8
Second Ave NN8. . . . . .129 D3
Second Drift PE9 . . . . .2 D8
Second La NN5 . . . . .158 F6
Second St NN13 . . . . .238 E6
Sedbergh Rd NN18. . . . . . . .36 C4
Sedge Cl NN14. . . . . .76 C1
Sedgemoor Ct NN11 . . . . .135 C6
Sedgemoor Way
NN11. . . . . .135 C6
Sedgwick Cl NN3 . . . . .142 F3
Sedlescombe Pk CV22 . . .98 A8

Seedfield Cl NN3 . . . . .142 E1
Selby Cl LE16 . . . . .48 E8
Selby Ct NN15 . . . . .91 F8
Selby Gdns NN29 . . . . .164 C2
Selby Wlk NN18. . . . . .36 C4
Selsey Rd NN18. . . . . .36 B5
Selston Wlk NN3. . . . . .160 D7
Selwyn Cl NN11. . . . . .153 C7
SEMILONG 159 D8
Semilong Ho 4 NN2 . . . . .159 C7
Semilong Rd NN2 . . . . .159 C8
Senna Dr NN12 . . . . .203 C8
Sentinel Rd NN4 . . . . .158 E1
Sentry Cl 6 NN4. . . . . .175 E7
Senwick Dr NN8 . . . . .130 C4
Senwick Rd NN8. . . . . .130 C4
Setchells Yd PE8 . . . . .41 F5
Settlers Fields NN15 . . . . .91 A7
Seven Sisters Cl
NN13. . . . . .221 B4
Severn Cl NN8. . . . . .129 C6
Severn Ct NN15. . . . . .92 B2
Severn Dr NN5 . . . . .140 F2
Severn Ho PE8. . . . . .42 A6
Severn The NN11 . . . . .135 A1
Severn Way NN16 . . . . .72 A5
Severn Wlk NN17 . . . . .21 C1
Sewter Gdns PE8 . . . . .15 E6
Sexton Cl NN11 . . . . .135 B3
Seymour Pl PE8 . . . . .41 E7
Seymour St NN5 . . . . .159 A6
Shackleton Cl NN14. . . . . . .70 E7
Shackleton Dr NN11 . . . . .135 C5
Shadowfax Dr NN3. . . . . . .143 C5
Shaftesbury Ho NN18 . . . .130 A3
Shaftesbury Rd NN18 . . . . . .36 B6
Shaftesbury St NN16 . . . . . .72 C2
Shakespeare Ave
NN11. . . . . .135 B2
Shakespeare Dr NN15. . . . . .92 A2
Shakespeare Ho 2
NN1 . . . . .159 E7
Shakespeare Rd
Kettering NN16 . . . . .72 B5
Northampton NN1 . . . . .159 E7
Rushden NN10. . . . . .131 E2
Wellingborough NN8 . . . . . .129 C4
Shakespeare Way
NN17 . . . . .36 D8
Shale End NN5 . . . . .140 A3
Shannon Cl NN10 . . . . .132 D3
Shannon Ct NN18 . . . . .36 E4
Shannon Way NN15. . . . . . .92 B2
Shap Gn NN3 . . . . .142 C4
Shard Cl NN4 . . . . .175 D6
Sharman Cl NN11 . . . . .135 C5
Sharman Rd
Northampton NN5 . . . . .159 A5
Wellingborough NN8 . . . . . .129 F4
Sharmans Cl NN7. . . . . . . .162 A6
Sharman Way NN14. . . . . . .70 F7
Sharpes La NN6 . . . . .121 B4
Sharplands NN7 . . . . .163 D5
Sharrow Pl 7 NN3 . . . . . .143 D2
Shatterstone 2 NN4 . . . . .175 D6
Shaw Cl NN8 . . . . .129 B5
Shawell Rd LE17 . . . . .62 A4
Shaw The MK18 . . . . .227 F1
Sheaf Cl NN5 . . . . .140 B2
Sheaf St NN11 . . . . .135 C1
Shearwater La NN8 . . . . . .130 A7
Shedfield Way NN4 . . . . . .175 C6
Sheep St
Kettering NN16 . . . . .72 B1
Northampton NN1 . . . . .159 C6
Wellingborough NN8 . . . . . .130 A4
Sheerwater Dr NN3. . . . . . .143 D3
Sheffield Cl NN9. . . . . .114 C5
Sheffield Way NN6. . . . . . . .144 E3
Sheffield Wlk NN18 . . . . . . .36 B4
Sheila Pl NN16 . . . . .72 E4
Sheldons La NN6 . . . . .108 A5
SHELFLEYS 174 E8
Shelford Cl NN3 . . . . .143 B5
Shelland Cl LE16. . . . . .32 C2
Shelley Cl
Daventry NN11 . . . . .135 B2
Towcester NN12 . . . . .203 B5
Shelleycotes Rd NN6. . . . .106 A1
Shelley Dr
Corby NN17 . . . . .21 D1
Higham Ferrers NN10 . . . . .132 B5
Shelley Rd
Kettering NN16 . . . . .72 C5
Wellingborough NN8 . . . . . .129 B4
Shelley St NN2 . . . . .141 F1
Shelmerdine Rise
NN9 . . . . .114 D6
Shelsley Dr NN3 . . . . .141 F4
Shelton Ct
Corby NN17 . . . . .22 E7
Wollaston NN29. . . . . .146 D2
Shelton Rd
Corby NN17 . . . . .22 E2
Raunds NN9. . . . . .114 E4
Shepherd Dr NN2 . . . . .141 A5
Shepherds Hill NN29 . . . . .146 F1
Shepherds Wlk
Bugbrooke NN7 . . . . .173 A8
Harpole NN7 . . . . .157 C6
Sheppard Way NN12 . . . . .213 B8
Shepperton Ct
Castlethorpe MK19 . . . . . . .218 F5
Northampton NN3 . . . . .143 C2
Sheppey La NN7. . . . . .177 B3
Shepton Ct NN18 . . . . .36 A6
Sheraton Dr NN14 . . . . . . .142 C2

Sheraton Mews NN3 . . . . .142 C2
Sherborne Way NN14. . . . . .76 E2
Sherborne Wlk NN18. . . . . .36 A6
Sheriff Ho NN9 . . . . .112 E1
Sheriff Rd NN1 . . . . .159 F7
Sherrard Rd LE16 . . . . .31 E5
Sherwood Ave NN2 . . . . . .140 F6
Sherwood Cl NN17. . . . . . . .36 E8
Sherwood Dr
Daventry NN11 . . . . .135 B4
Kettering NN15 . . . . .91 F5
Shetland Way NN17. . . . . . .21 C1
Shieling Ct NN18 . . . . .36 A1
Ship La PE8 . . . . .41 F4
Shipton Way NN10. . . . . . . .131 C3
Shire Pl NN3 . . . . .143 C5
Shire Rd NN17 . . . . .21 C1
Shires Bsns Pk The
NN13. . . . . .234 A6
Shires Rd NN13. . . . . .234 A6
Shirley Rd NN10 . . . . .132 B3
Shoal Creek NN4 . . . . .175 C5
Shoe Maker Cl NN12 . . . . .188 F7
Shoemakers Ct NN10 . . . .132 B2
Shop La NN7 . . . . .179 B6
Shoreham Ct NN18. . . . . . . .36 B5
Short Cl PE8. . . . . .28 B3
Short La
Cogenhoe NN7. . . . . .162 A6
Thorpe Malsor NN14 . . . . . .71 B3
Wellingborough NN8 . . . . . .129 F5
Shortlands Cl NN13 . . . . . .211 F3
Shortlands The NN9 . . . . .113 B5
Short Massey MK46 . . . . . .195 E5
Short Stocks NN10 . . . . . . .132 D2
Shortwoods Cl NN9 . . . . . .114 C5
SHOTLEY 11 B7
Shotwell Mill La NN14. . . . .70 D8
Showsley Rd NN12. . . . . . .204 D8
Shrewsbury Ave LE16 . . . . .32 B2
Shropshire Cl LE16. . . . . . . .31 E4
Shropshire Pl LE16. . . . . . . .31 E4
Shrubberies The NN14 . . . .94 D7
Shrubfield Gr NN17 . . . . . . .36 F8
Shuckburgh Cres CV22. . . .98 D8
Shuckburgh Rd CV47. . . . .166 D8
Shurville Cl NN6. . . . . .144 F3
SHUTLANGER 204 D8
Shutlanger Rd NN12 . . . . .190 F1
SIBBERTOFT 46 F2
Sibbertoft Rd
Clipston LE16. . . . . .47 E1
Husbands Bosworth
LE17 . . . . .45 F2
Marston Trussell LE16 . . . . .47 B6
Sibley Rd NN9 . . . . .112 B4
SIBSON 16 F8
Siddeley Way NN11 . . . . . .134 F3
Siddons Cl PE8 . . . . .41 E7
Siddons Way NN3. . . . . . . .126 D1
Sidebrook Ct NN18 . . . . . . .36 A6
Sidegate La NN8. . . . . .130 F5
Sidings Ind Ctr The
NN13. . . . . .234 A8
Sidings The NN9 . . . . .131 D8
Sidlaw Ct MK11 . . . . .229 F4
Sidmouth Wlk NN18 . . . . . .36 F4
Sidney Rd
Rugby CV22 . . . . .98 D8
Woodford Halse NN11. . . . .184 C6
Silkweavers Mews
NN14 . . . . .70 D7
Sillswood MK46 . . . . .195 E4
Silverdale Gr NN10. . . . . . . .131 E2
Silverdale Rd NN3 . . . . . . .142 D2
Silver St N OX17 . . . . .208 E4
Silver St
Abthorpe NN12 . . . . .201 F2
Brixworth NN6. . . . . .106 B3
Broughton NN14 . . . . .90 A5
Chacombe OX17 . . . . .208 E4
Kettering NN16 . . . . .72 B2
Northampton NN1 . . . . .159 C6
Stony Stratford MK11 . . . . .229 D5
Walgrave NN6. . . . . .108 A5
Wellingborough NN8 . . . . . .130 A4
SILVERSTONE 214 D4
Silverstone CE Jun Sch
NN12. . . . . .214 D4
Silverstone Cl NN2. . . . . . .141 D5
Silverstone Inf Sch
NN12. . . . . .214 D5
Silverstone Motor Racing
Circuit * NN12. . . . . .225 E8
Silverstone Tech Pk
NN12. . . . . .214 E2
Silverwood Ct NN15. . . . . . .91 C8
Silverwood Rd NN15 . . . . . .91 C8
Simborough Way LE16 . . . . .32 B3
Simon de Senlis Ct
NN1 . . . . .159 D7
Simon de Senlis Prim Sch
NN4. . . . . .175 B8
Simon's Wlk
17 Northampton NN1 . . . . .159 C6
Pattishall NN12 . . . . .172 D1
Simpson Ave NN10. . . . . . .132 C7
Simpson Barracks
NN4 . . . . .175 D6
Sinclair Dr NN8. . . . . .129 B6
Sir Christopher Hatton
Sch NN8 . . . . .130 A6
Sir Georges La OX17 . . . . .230 A4
Sir John Brown Ct
NN16 . . . . .72 A2
Sir John Pascoe Way
NN5 . . . . .158 C8
Sissinghurst Dr NN14 . . . . .76 F2

Siward View NN5 . . . . .140 D2
Six Cotts MK18 . . . . .226 E5
Sixth St NN13. . . . . .238 E7
Six Willows NN9 . . . . .110 B3
Skagerrak Cl NN18. . . . . . . .36 A2
Skawle Ct NN3 . . . . .142 F3
Skeffington Cl NN14 . . . . . .54 A2
Skegness Wlk NN18. . . . . . .36 C4
Skelton Wlk 4 NN3 . . . . . .142 C4
Sketty Cl NN4 . . . . .160 C1
Skiddaw Wlk NN3. . . . . . . .142 C4
Skinner Ave NN5 . . . . .158 D5
Skinner's Hill NN10 . . . . . .132 B2
Skin Yard La NN6. . . . . . . .121 B4
Skippon Cl LE16 . . . . .31 D2
Skippons Ct NN6. . . . . .85 B8
Skipton Cl
Corby NN18. . . . . .36 B4
Northampton NN4 . . . . .175 B7
Skittle Alley OX17 . . . . . . .237 C7
Skye Rd NN17 . . . . .36 B8
Slade Cl NN14 . . . . .54 B3
Slade Cres NN15. . . . . .91 B7
Slade Hill NN13. . . . . .234 D1
Slade Ho NN11 . . . . .153 C8
Slade Leas OX17 . . . . .220 B8
Sladeswell Dr 1 NN3 . . . .161 A8
Slade The
Daventry NN11 . . . . .153 C8
Silverstone NN12. . . . . .214 E5
Slade Valley Ave NN14 . . . .70 F7
SLAPTON 201 D2
Slapton Pre Prep Sch
NN12. . . . . .201 E2
Slate Drift PE9. . . . . .1 E3
Slaters Cl NN12 . . . . .132 D2
Slawston Rd
Medbourne LE16 . . . . .18 E7
Welham LE16 . . . . .17 F6
Slim Cl NN15 . . . . .72 F1
Slips The NN9 . . . . .110 E2
Slip The NN6 . . . . .106 C2
SLIPTON 75 A3
Slipton La
Slipton NN14 . . . . .75 A3
Sudborough NN14 . . . . .56 C1
Sloe La NN14 . . . . .89 C5
Smart's Cl NN13 . . . . .233 D8
Smarts Est CV23 . . . . .100 A3
Smith Cl NN7 . . . . .177 A1
Smith Ct NN9 . . . . .114 D5
Smitherway NN17 . . . . .173 A8
Smithfield Pl NN9 . . . . .114 D6
Smithland Ct NN12. . . . . . .202 D8
Smiths Ct NN4. . . . . .159 D4
Smith St NN6. . . . . .105 A1
Smiths Yd NN9 . . . . .110 B3
Smithy The
Deanshanger MK19 . . . . . .228 E4
Northampton NN3 . . . . .142 D1
Rushden NN10. . . . . .132 B1
Smyth Cl LE16 . . . . .31 E5
Smyth Ct NN3 . . . . .142 E3
Snetterton Cl NN3 . . . . . . .141 F4
Snowbell Sq 1 NN3 . . . . .143 C2
Snowshill Cl 4 NN11. . . . .135 B7
Soane Cl NN8. . . . . .129 F8
Soar Gn NN17 . . . . .21 C1
Solly's Way NN12. . . . . . . .203 C5
Somerford Rd NN8. . . . . . .129 E6
Somerset St NN1 . . . . .159 E7
Somerton Ct NN18. . . . . . . .36 A6
Somerville Ct OX17 . . . . . .230 D3
Somerville Rd
Brackley NN13. . . . . .233 D8
Daventry NN11 . . . . .153 B8
Sondes Cl PE8 . . . . .41 E7
Sondes Rd NN17. . . . . .22 E2
Sopwith Way NN11 . . . . . . .135 B5
Sorrel Cl
Isham NN14. . . . . .91 F1
Northampton NN4 . . . . .175 E5
Sorrels The NN14 . . . . .91 F1
Sotheby Rise NN3. . . . . . . .143 D3
Soudan Ave NN13. . . . . . . .233 E8
SOULDERN 237 E3
Sourton Pl NN11. . . . . .135 D6
Southall Rd NN17 . . . . .37 B6
Southampton Rd
NN4 . . . . .159 C3
Southam Rd CV47. . . . . . . .166 D7
South Ave NN15 . . . . .92 B3
South Bank NN13 . . . . .234 B7
South Bridge Ct PE8 . . . . . .41 F4
Southbrook NN18. . . . . .36 B3
Southbrook Jun & Inf
Schs NN11 . . . . .135 E1
South Cl
Braunston NN11 . . . . .118 D1
Greatworth OX17 . . . . .210 D1
Long Buckby NN6. . . . . .121 B3
Rushden NN10. . . . . .132 C1
South Copse NN4 . . . . .175 B7
Southcourt NN3 . . . . .142 C7
Southcrest NN4. . . . . .158 F1
South End Jun & Inf Schs
NN10. . . . . .148 B8
Southfield Ave NN4 . . . . . .159 D3
Southfield Ct NN13 . . . . . . .233 E6
Southfield Dr NN15 . . . . . . .91 F4
Southfield Prim Sch
NN13. . . . . .233 E6
Southfield Rd
Gretton NN17 . . . . .10 C1
Northampton NN5 . . . . .158 B6
SOUTHFIELDS 143 A7
Southfields NN10 . . . . .132 C1

Southfield Sch for Girls
NN15. . . . . .91 C7
South Fields Dr NN6 . . . . .101 A5
South Folds Rd NN18 . . . . .35 F1
Southgate Dr
Kettering NN15 . . . . .72 C6
Towcester NN12 . . . . .203 D5
South Gr NN10. . . . . .148 B5
South Holme Ct NN3 . . . . .142 B6
SOUTH KILWORTH 63 D8
South Kilworth CE Prim
Sch LE17 . . . . .63 C8
South Kilworth Rd
NN6 . . . . .64 B5
Southlands NN15 . . . . .72 B1
Southleigh Gr LE16 . . . . . . .31 E5
SOUTH LUFFENHAM 3 D8
South March NN11. . . . . . . .153 C8
South Meadow View
NN5 . . . . .158 A5
South Oval NN5. . . . . .140 F1
South Paddock Ct
NN3 . . . . .142 F4
South Pk NN10 . . . . .132 B1
South Pl NN11 . . . . .135 B1
South Portway Cl
NN3 . . . . .142 F6
South Priors Ct NN3 . . . . .143 A3
South Rd
Clifton u D CV23 . . . . .80 A5
Corby NN17 . . . . .37 B6
Oundle PE8 . . . . .42 A4
South St
Castlethorpe MK19 . . . . . . .218 F5
Isham NN14. . . . . .110 F8
Northampton NN1 . . . . .159 C6
Weedon Bec NN7. . . . . .155 C3
Wollaston NN29. . . . . .146 D2
Woodford Halse NN11. . . . .184 C6
South Terr
Greens Norton NN12. . . . . .202 E8
Northampton NN1 . . . . .159 F6
South Vale NN7. . . . . .179 A5
South View
Brixworth NN6. . . . . .106 B4
Harpole NN7 . . . . .157 C6
Nether Heyford NN7 . . . . . .156 B1
Roade NN7 . . . . .191 A4
Whilton NN11 . . . . .137 C6
South Way NN11 . . . . .135 D1
SOUTHWICK 26 B5
Southwick Hall * PE8 . . . .26 C5
Southwood Hill NN4 . . . . .159 A3
Southwood Ho NN3 . . . . . .130 A3
Sovereign Ct
Northampton NN3 . . . . .142 F6
Rushden NN10. . . . . .132 B3
Sovereign Pk LE16 . . . . . . .31 F1
Sovereigns Ct NN16. . . . . . .72 C6
Sower Leys Rd NN18 . . . . . .36 C4
Spalding Rd NN18 . . . . .36 C4
Spanslade Rd NN3 . . . . . . .143 A1
Sparke Cl NN8. . . . . .129 D7
Spartan Cl NN7 . . . . .175 F5
Spectacle La NN3. . . . . . . .125 F1
Speedwell Rd NN14 . . . . . . .51 A4
Speke Dr NN11 . . . . .135 C5
Spelhoe St NN3. . . . . .142 F6
Spencelayh Cl NN8 . . . . . .129 F7
Spencer Bridge Rd
NN5 . . . . .159 A7
Spencer Cl
Bugbrooke NN7 . . . . .173 D3
Chapel Brampton NN6. . . . .124 D1
Earls Barton NN6. . . . . .144 F4
Evenley NN13 . . . . .233 F2
Spencer Ct
Corby NN17 . . . . .36 E5
Rushden NN10. . . . . .132 A3
West Haddon NN6 . . . . .102 C4
Spencer Gdns
Bozeat NN29 . . . . .164 D2
Brackley NN13. . . . . .233 E6
Spencer Haven NN5. . . . . .159 A7
Spencer Par
Northampton NN1 . . . . .159 D6
Stanwick NN9 . . . . .113 F3
Spencer Rd
Irthlingborough NN9 . . . . . .112 E1
Long Buckby NN6. . . . . .121 B3
Northampton NN1 . . . . .159 E7
Rushden NN10. . . . . .132 A3
Stanion NN14. . . . . .37 E3
Wellingborough NN8 . . . . . .130 A1
Spencer St
Burton Latimer NN15 . . . . . .92 B2
Kettering NN16 . . . . .72 B4
Market Harborough
LE16 . . . . .31 D3
Northampton NN5 . . . . .159 A5
Raunds NN9 . . . . .114 E6
Ringstead NN14. . . . . .95 B3
Rothwell NN14. . . . . .70 D8
Spencer Wlk NN18 . . . . . . .36 E5
Spendlove Ct NN17 . . . . . . .10 C1
Spenfield Ct NN3 . . . . .142 F3
Spenser Cres NN11 . . . . . .135 A3
Spens Ho NN2 . . . . .141 D5
Spey Cl NN8 . . . . .129 C6
Spiers Dr NN13 . . . . .233 D7
Spilsby Cl NN18. . . . . .36 C4
Spinners Cotts NN15 . . . . .210 F7
Spinney Bank OX17 . . . . . .230 F5
Spinney Cl
Boughton NN2. . . . . .141 C7
Market Harborough
LE16 . . . . .31 C3
Rushden NN10. . . . . .131 F2

Spinney Cl *continued*
Thrapston NN14 . . . . **76** D1
Towcester NN12 . . . . **203** C3
Warmington PE8 . . . . **28** B2
Spinney Dr
Kettering NN15 . . . . **91** D7
Northampton NN4 . . . . . . **175** C4
Spinney Gr NN17 . . . . **36** F2
SPINNEY HILL **142** A3
Spinney Hill NN11 . . . . . . **118** D1
Spinney Hill Cres
NN3 . . . . **142** A4
Spinney Hill Rd
Northampton NN3 . . . . . . **142** A4
Olney MK46 . . . . **195** E3
Spinney La
Kettering NN15 . . . . **91** D7
Wellingborough NN8 . . . . **129** C2
Spinney Rd
Burton Latimer NN15 . . . . . **92** C3
Irthlingborough NN15 . . . . **112** F2
Rushden NN10 . . . . **131** F1
Weldon NN17 . . . . **38** C7
Spinney Rise
Daventry NN11 . . . . **135** C1
Denford NN14 . . . . **95** C6
Spinney St NN9 . . . . **114** D6
Spinney Terr [8] NN9 . . . . **112** F2
Spinney The NN4 . . . . **175** E2
Spinney Way NN3 . . . . . . **142** A5
Sponne House Sh Ctr
NN12 . . . . **203** C6
Sponne Sch Tech Coll
NN12 . . . . **203** B6
Sponnes Rd NN12 . . . . . . **203** C5
Spotted Cow La
NN11 . . . . **136** D5
SPRATTON **105** C1
Spratton CE Prim Sch
NN6 . . . . **105** B1
Spratton Hall Sch
NN6 . . . . **105** B1
Spratton Rd NN6 . . . . **106** A2
Spring Bank LE16 . . . . **18** F7
Springbanks Way [2]
NN4 . . . . **175** B8
Spring Cl
Boughton NN2 . . . . **125** C1
Brackley NN13 . . . . **233** F7
Daventry NN11 . . . . **153** C8
Hollowell NN6 . . . . **104** B4
Irthlingborough NN9 . . . . . **112** F2
Kilsby CV23 . . . . **100** A2
Springer Straight [1]
NN4 . . . . **158** F3
Springfield
Flore NN7 . . . . **155** E5
Northampton NN4 . . . . . . **175** E7
Springfield Ave NN15 . . . . **76** D3
Springfield Cl NN15 . . . . . **91** C7
Springfield Ct
[1] Market Harborough
LE16 . . . . **31** F2
Northampton NN3 . . . . . . **142** F3
Springfield Gdns
MK19 . . . . **228** E4
Springfield Gr NN17 . . . . . **36** F8
Springfield Rd
Kettering NN15 . . . . **91** C7
Olney MK46 . . . . **195** F4
Oundle PE8 . . . . **41** F7
Rushden NN10 . . . . **148** D8
Walgrave NN6 . . . . **107** F5
Wilbarston LE16 . . . . **34** C4
Springfields NN12 . . . . . . **203** B5
Springfield St LE16 . . . . . **31** F2
Springfield Way
NN13 . . . . **233** E8
Spring Gdns
Burton Latimer NN15 . . . . . **92** C3
Earls Barton NN6 . . . . **144** F4
Higham Ferrers NN10 . . . . **132** B6
Northampton NN1 . . . . . . **159** D5
Rothwell NN14 . . . . **70** D7
Towcester NN12 . . . . **203** D5
Wellingborough NN8 . . . . **129** F4
Springhill Gdns LE16 . . . . **31** C2
Springhill Hos CV22 . . . . . **98** C8
Spring Ho [2] NN8 . . . . . . **129** F4
Spring La
Alderton NN12 . . . . **204** F2
Flore NN7 . . . . **155** E5
Northampton NN1 . . . . . . **159** B6
Olney MK46 . . . . **195** F3
[8] Wellingborough
NN8 . . . . **130** A4
Spring Lane Prim Sch
NN1 . . . . **159** B6
SPRING PARK **141** A5
Spring Rise NN15 . . . . **91** C7
Spring St [4] NN9 . . . . . . **112** F2
Springs The
Northampton NN4 . . . . . . **159** A3
Swinford LE17 . . . . **62** C4
Spring Terr
Irthlingborough NN9 . . . . . **112** F2
Medbourne LE16 . . . . **19** A6
Springwell Cl NN4 . . . . . . **175** F3
Springwood Ct NN3 . . . . . **142** F5
Spruce Ct
Kettering NN16 . . . . **72** C2
Northampton NN3 . . . . . . **142** E3
Spurlings PE8 . . . . **41** F5
Spyglass Hill NN4 . . . . . . **175** B6
Square The
Aynho OX17 . . . . **237** C7
Earls Barton NN6 . . . . **144** E4
Greatworth OX17 . . . . **210** E1

Square The *continued*
Holdenby NN6 . . . . **123** D4
Kings Sutton OX17 . . . . . . **230** F5
Market Harborough LE16 . . **31** E3
Moreton Pinkney NN11 . . . **199** C7
Northampton NN4 . . . . . . **175** F3
Pitsford NN6 . . . . **125** C4
Raunds NN9 . . . . **114** D6
South Luffenham LE15. . . . . . . **3** D8
Thorpe Malsor NN14 . . . . . **71** B3
Welford NN6 . . . . **64** E6
Yardley Hastings NN7 . . . **179** A6
Squire Cl NN18 . . . . **36** A4
Squires Wlk NN3 . . . . **142** B3
Squirrel Cl NN4. . . . . **175** F2
Squirrel La NN5 . . . . **158** C7
Stable Ct
Brackley NN13. . . . . **233** F7
[4] Northampton NN2 . . . **141** C3
Pitsford NN6 . . . . **125** D4
Stablegate Way LE16. . . . . **32** A3
Stable Hill NN14 . . . . **55** F7
Stable Mews NN29. . . . . . **147** D1
Stables La NN6 . . . . **140** B8
Stables The PE8 . . . . **8** A3
Stable Yd
Loddington NN14. . . . . **70** C1
Thenford NN13 . . . . **220** E8
Stadtpeine Cl NN17 . . . . . . **36** C7
Staffa Wlk NN17 . . . . **36** B8
Stafford Cl NN11. . . . . **135** D5
Stafford Pl NN3. . . . . **141** F7
Stafford Rd NN17 . . . . **22** C8
Staffords La NN6 . . . . **102** B4
Stagshaw Dr [2] NN4. . . . **175** C8
Staines Cl NN5 . . . . **158** E6
Stalbridge Wlk NN18. . . . . **36** A4
Stamford Cl LE16 . . . . **31** E2
Stamford La PE8. . . . . **28** B3
Stamford Rd
Corby NN14, NN18,
NN17. . . . . **37** E4
Deenethorpe NN17 . . . . . . **23** E2
Duddington PE9 . . . . **5** C7
Easton o t H PE9 . . . . **2** B5
Geddington, Little Oakley
NN14. . . . . **54** B5
Geddington NN14 . . . . **54** A1
Kettering NN16 . . . . **72** E5
Ketton PE9. . . . . **1** C8
South Luffenham LE15. . . . . **3** D7
Weldon NN17. . . . . **38** A4
Stamford Wlk NN18. . . . . . **36** C4
Stanbridge St NN11. . . . . **229** F5
Standens Barn Prim Sch
NN3. . . . . **160** F8
Standens Barn Rd
NN3. . . . . **142** F1
Standing Stones NN3 . . . **143** B3
Standside NN5 . . . . **158** F6
Stanfield Rd NN5 . . . . . . **158** C6
Stanford Hall [2] LE17 . . . **62** F3
STANFORD ON AVON **62** F2
Stanford Rd
Cold Ashby NN6. . . . . **84** A5
Swinford LE17 . . . . **62** D3
Stanford Way NN4 . . . . . **175** C8
Stanhill Row NN12. . . . . . **201** F1
Stanhope Rd NN2. . . . . . . **141** D1
Stanier Cl NN16. . . . . **72** A3
Stanier Rd NN17 . . . . **21** F1
STANION **37** F2
Stanion CE Prim Sch
NN14. . . . . **37** E3
Stanion La
Corby NN18 . . . . **37** B6
Corby NN18 . . . . **37** D5
Stanion Rd NN14. . . . . **38** C1
Stanley Boddington Ct
NN15. . . . . **91** C8
Stanley Cl MK46 . . . . **195** F3
Stanley Mews [5] NN8 . . . **130** B5
Stanley Rd
Northampton NN5 . . . . . . **159** A6
Wellingborough NN8 . . . . **130** B5
Stanley St
Northampton NN2 . . . . . . **159** C8
Rothwell NN14. . . . . **70** E7
Stanley Way NN11 . . . . . . **135** C5
Stannard Way NN6. . . . . . **106** B2
Stanton Ave NN3 . . . . **142** A4
Stanton Cl
Desborough NN14. . . . . . . **51** B4
Wellingborough NN8. . . . . **111** B1
Stanway Cl LE16 . . . . **32** A3
Stanwell Cl OX17 . . . . **209** A1
Stanwell Dr OX17 . . . . . . **209** A1
Stanwell Lea OX17. . . . . . **209** A2
Stanwell Way NN8 . . . . . . **129** C3
STANWICK **113** E4
Stanwick Prim Sch
NN9. . . . . **114** A3
Stanwick Rd
Higham Ferrers
NN10. . . . . **132** C8
Raunds NN9 . . . . **114** B4
Star Cnr CV23 . . . . **99** C1
Starmers La NN7. . . . . . . **157** D4
Starmer's Yd NN5. . . . . . . **158** C7
Starvold Ct NN6 . . . . **105** A1
Station Cl
Daventry NN11 . . . . **135** D2
Ecton NN3 . . . . **143** C1
Long Buckby NN6. . . . . . . **121** B3
Station Cotts NN18. . . . . . **53** D7
Station Ct NN11 . . . . **184** C6
Station Gdns NN11 . . . . . **184** C6

Station Mews NN3 . . . . . **143** C2
Station Rd
Aynho OX15, OX17 . . . . . **237** A6
Blisworth NN7 . . . . **174** B2
Brixworth NN6. . . . . **106** A4
Burton Latimer NN15 . . . . . **92** A2
Castlethorpe MK19 . . . . . **218** F5
Clifton OX17. . . . . **236** F5
Cogenhoe NN7. . . . . **161** E6
Corby NN17 . . . . **37** A6
Cottesbrooke NN6 . . . . . . **105** A7
Desborough NN14. . . . . . . **51** A4
Earls Barton NN6. . . . . . . **144** E3
Earls Barton NN6. . . . . . . **144** F1
Finedon NN9 . . . . **111** D6
Great Bowden LE16. . . . . . **32** A6
Gretton NN17 . . . . **10** B1
Helmdon NN13 . . . . **211** F4
Husbands Bosworth
LE17. . . . . **45** D3
Irchester NN44 . . . . **147** C8
Irthlingborough NN9 . . . . **113** A2
Kettering NN15 . . . . **72** B1
Ketton PE9. . . . . **1** A5
King's Cliffe PE8 . . . . **13** F7
Lilbourne CV23 . . . . **81** A7
Little Houghton NN7 . . . . **161** C5
Long Buckby NN6. . . . . . . **121** A2
Morcott LE15. . . . . **3** B6
Nassington PE8 . . . . **15** F5
Northampton NN3 . . . . . . **143** C1
North Kilworth LE17 . . . . . . **45** A4
Oundle PE8 . . . . **42** A6
Raunds NN9. . . . . **115** B7
Ringstead NN14 . . . . **94** F2
Rushden NN10. . . . . **132** A3
Rushton NN14 . . . . **52** C2
Theddingworth LE17 . . . . . **46** D8
Watford NN6 . . . . **120** C5
Welton NN11 . . . . **119** E1
West Haddon NN6. . . . . . . **102** B4
Woodford Halse NN11. . . . **184** C6
Station Yard Ind Est
OX17. . . . . **230** A2
Stavanger Cl NN18. . . . . . . **36** A2
Staveley Way NN6 . . . . . . **106** C3
STAVERTON **152** C7
Staverton CE Prim Sch
NN11. . . . . **152** C7
Staverton Leys CV22 . . . . . **98** A7
Staverton Rd NN11. . . . . . **135** B1
Steadfold La PE9 . . . . **1** C8
Steane View NN13 . . . . . . **233** D7
Steel Cl MK11. . . . . **76** D1
Steele Rd NN8 . . . . **129** D4
Steel Rd NN17 . . . . **22** E2
Steene St NN5 . . . . **159** A6
Stefen Way NN11 . . . . **153** B7
Stenhouse Cl NN6 . . . . . . **121** D4
Stenson St NN5 . . . . **159** A6
Stent Mews NN4 . . . . **175** F8
Stephen Bennett Cl
NN5 . . . . **158** C8
Stephenson Cl NN11 . . . . **134** F4
Stephenson Ct
Kilsby CV23 . . . . **99** F2
Roade NN7 . . . . **191** C4
Stephenson Way NN17 . . . . **37** A8
Sterling Bsns Pk NN4 . . . **160** C2
Sterling Cl NN14. . . . . **70** C1
Sterndale Cl NN14 . . . . **50** E4
Stevens Cl NN6 . . . . **144** F5
Stevenson St NN4. . . . . . . **159** C2
Stevens St LE16. . . . . **31** D3
Stewart Cl NN3 . . . . **126** B2
Stewart Dr NN12. . . . . **214** D4
Stewarts Rd NN8 . . . . **130** B8
Steyning Cl NN18. . . . . **36** A5
STIBBINGTON **8** D2
Stilebrook Rd MK46 . . . . . **195** F6
Stile Cl NN11 . . . . **135** A2
Stimpson Ave NN1. . . . . . **159** F7
Stimpson Avenue Prim
Sch NN1 . . . . **159** F7
Stinford Leys LE16. . . . . . . **32** B3
Stirling Cl NN18 . . . . **36** E2
Stirling St NN5 . . . . **158** F6
Stirrup Ho NN5 . . . . **159** B5
Stitchman Ho [8] NN5 . . . **159** A6
Stockbridge Rd NN17 . . . . . **22** A1
Stocken Cl MK46. . . . . **195** E4
Stockholme Cl NN18 . . . . . **36** A2
Stocking Cl NN7 . . . . **192** D1
Stocking Green Cl
MK19 . . . . **207** A3
Stockley St [6] NN1. . . . . **159** E6
Stockmead Rd NN3 . . . . . **161** A8
Stocks Gn PE8. . . . . **28** C8
Stocks Hill
Finedon NN9 . . . . **111** E4
[8] Moulton NN3 . . . . **126** C1
Silverstone NN12. . . . . . . **214** D5
Stock's Hill PE9 . . . . **1** A5
Stock's Hill NN17 . . . . **37** B6
Stocks The MK19 . . . . **218** E2
Stockwell Ave NN4. . . . . . **175** D5
Stockwell Cl LE16. . . . . **32** B3
Stockwell La
Hellidon NN11 . . . . **151** D1
Sulgrave OX17. . . . . **210** F8
Stockwell Rd NN7 . . . . . . **174** F4
Stockwell Way NN7 . . . . . **174** F4
Stockwood Dr NN17 . . . . . . **21** F1
STOKE ALBANY **34** A4
Stoke Albany Rd LE16 . . . . **18** E1
STOKE BRUERNE **205** B8

Stoke Bruerne CE Prim
Sch NN12 . . . . **205** A8
STOKE DOYLE **41** C1
Stoke Doyle Rd PE8. . . . . . **41** D4
Stoke Firs Cl NN4. . . . . . . **175** F6
Stoke Hill
Oundle PE8 . . . . **41** F5
Stoke Albany LE16 . . . . . . **34** A4
Stoke Rd
Ashton NN7 . . . . **205** D4
Blisworth NN7. . . . . **190** E4
Desborough NN14 . . . . **51** A7
Lyddington LE15 . . . . **9** C7
Stokes Rd NN18 . . . . **36** D4
Stonebridge Ct NN3 . . . . . **142** F3
Stone Circle Rd NN3 . . . . . **142** E7
Stone Cl
Wellingborough NN8 . . . . **129** F8
Wollaston NN29. . . . . **146** D2
Stone Hill Ct NN3 . . . . **142** E4
Stonehill Way NN6 . . . . . . **125** B8
Stonehouse Ct CV23 . . . . . **81** A6
Stone House Mews
NN6 . . . . **84** E4
Stonehurst Cl NN7. . . . . . **192** C1
Stonelea Rd NN9 . . . . **127** D3
Stoneleigh Chase
NN5 . . . . **140** D1
Stonemasons Cl
MK46 . . . . **195** F3
Stone Pit Cl MK46. . . . . . . **195** E3
Stonepit Dr LE16. . . . . **20** D1
Stoneway
Badby NN11. . . . . **152** F2
Hartwell NN7 . . . . **192** E2
Stone Way NN5. . . . . **158** B7
Stonewold Cl NN2. . . . . . . **141** A4
Stoney Fields NN14 . . . . . . **89** B4
Stoneyhurst NN4 . . . . **158** F3
Stoney Piece Cl NN29. . . . **164** C2
Stony Hill NN12. . . . . **216** C8
STONY STRATFORD **229** E5
Stony Stratford Nature
Reserve ★ [1] MK11 . . . . . **229** D7
Stook The NN11 . . . . **135** C6
Storefield Cotts NN14. . . . . **53** A4
Stornoway Rd NN17. . . . . . **21** C1
Stotfold Ct MK11. . . . . **229** E4
Stourhead Dr NN4 . . . . . . **175** C7
Stour Rd
Corby NN17 . . . . **21** D1
Northampton NN5 . . . . . . **158** F6
Stour The NN11 . . . . **153** A8
Stourton Cl NN8 . . . . **129** D1
Stow Cl NN8. . . . . **129** D1
Stowe Wlk NN3 . . . . **141** F5
Stradlers Cl NN4. . . . . **175** E5
Stratfield Cl NN15 . . . . **91** D5
Stratford Arc MK11 . . . . . **229** E5
Stratford Dr NN4 . . . . **175** D5
Stratford Rd
Cosgrove MK19 . . . . **218** D1
Deanshanger MK19 . . . . . **228** F4
Roade NN7 . . . . **191** D3
Stony Stratford MK12 . . . . **229** F6
Strathay Wlk NN11 . . . . . . **21** C1
Strath Cl CV21 . . . . **99** A7
Stratton Cl
Market Harborough
LE16 . . . . **31** D7
Northampton NN3 . . . . . . **160** D7
Stratton Dr NN13 . . . . . . **233** D7
Strawberry Hill NN3 . . . . . **143** C3
Strawberry Hill Cotts
MK44 . . . . **149** F2
Straws Cl NN9 . . . . **112** E1
Stream Bank Cl NN8 . . . . **129** D4
Streambank Rd NN3 . . . . . **142** E6
Streatfield Rd NN5. . . . . . **159** A8
Streather Ct NN9 . . . . **114** C5
Streather Dr NN17 . . . . **36** E7
Streeton Way NN6 . . . . . . **144** E5
Street The LE15. . . . . **3** E8
Strelley Ave NN3. . . . . **160** F8
Stringer's Hill NN14. . . . . . **90** F2
STRIXTON **164** C8
Strixton Manor Bsns Ctr
NN29. . . . . **164** C8
Strode Rd NN8 . . . . **130** B5
Stronglands Ct PE8. . . . . . **41** F6
Stuart Cl
Kettering NN16 . . . . **72** C2
Northampton NN4 . . . . . . **174** F7
Stuart Cres LE16 . . . . **30** F7
Stuart Rd
Brackley NN13. . . . . **233** E8
Corby NN17 . . . . **36** F6
Market Harborough LE16 . . **31** E2
Stubbing End NN18 . . . . . . **53** B8
Stubble Cl NN2. . . . . **141** A6
Stubbs Cl NN8 . . . . **129** F7
Stubbs La NN15. . . . . **92** A8
Stubbs Rd NN11 . . . . **170** B7
STUCHBURY **211** A5
Studfall Ave NN17 . . . . **36** E8
Studfall Cl NN17. . . . . **36** E7
Studfall Inf Sch NN17 . . . . **36** E8
Studfall Jun Sch NN17 . . . . **36** E8
Stud Farm Cl OX17 . . . . . **196** E1
Studland Rd NN2 . . . . **141** B1
Sturdee Cl NN11 . . . . **135** D1
Sturgess Ct NN15 . . . . **92** C2
Sturminster Way NN18. . . . **36** A6
Sturton Wlk NN18. . . . . **36** C4
Styles Pl NN6. . . . . **82** B3
SUDBOROUGH **56** C1
Sudborough Rd
Brigstock NN14 . . . . **56** A4

Spi–Swe 263

Sudborough Rd *continued*
Slipton NN14 . . . . **75** A6
Suffolk Pl NN15 . . . . **91** D6
SULBY **65** B8
Sulby Hall Old Dr NN6. . . . **46** B1
Sulby Rd
Northampton NN3 . . . . . . **142** E6
Welford NN6 . . . . **65** A8
Sulehay Rd PE8. . . . . **7** C1
SULGRAVE **210** F8
Sulgrave Dr NN17. . . . . **36** C7
Sulgrave Manor ★
OX17 . . . . **211** A8
Sulgrave Rd
Culworth OX17 . . . . **198** D1
Northampton NN5 . . . . . . **158** F7
Summerfield Rd NN15 . . . . **91** C8
Summerfields NN15 . . . . . **158** E2
Summerhouse Rd
NN3 . . . . **142** A6
Summerlee Mews
NN9 . . . . **111** F4
Summerlee Rd NN9. . . . . . **111** F4
Summer Leys Nature
Res ★ [1] NN29. . . . . **145** F4
Summers Cl OX17 . . . . **230** A5
Summers Way LE16 . . . . . . **31** D2
Summit Rise NN4 . . . . **175** D7
Sunderland St NN5 . . . . . . **159** A6
Sundew Ct NN4. . . . . **158** D1
Sun Hill NN14. . . . . **70** C7
Sunley Ct NN15 . . . . **91** C8
Sunningdale Cl NN2 . . . . . **141** E2
Sunningdale Dr
Daventry NN11 . . . . **135** E3
Rushden NN10. . . . . **148** D8
Sunny Bank
Arthingworth LE16 . . . . **68** C7
Holcot NN6 . . . . **126** E8
SUNNYSIDE **141** D5
Sunnyside
Ecton NN6 . . . . **143** F4
Northampton NN4 . . . . . . **175** E6
Woodford NN14. . . . . **94** D7
Sunny Side NN6 . . . . **144** D4
Sunnyside Prim Sch
NN2. . . . . **141** D6
Sunny View NN7 . . . . **179** B6
Sunset Ct NN3 . . . . **143** A2
Sun Yd NN12 . . . . **203** D5
Surfleet Cl NN18. . . . . **36** C4
Surrey Cl NN17 . . . . **36** C6
Surrey Rd NN15. . . . . **91** D6
Surtees Way NN12. . . . . . **203** C7
Sussex Cl NN5 . . . . **158** C6
Sussex Dr [6] NN1. . . . . . **159** C6
Sussex Pl NN10 . . . . **132** B4
Sussex Rd NN15 . . . . **91** C6
Sutcliffe Rd PE8. . . . . **7** D8
Sutherland Rd NN18 . . . . . **36** D4
SUTTON **8** F2
Sutton Acre NN7. . . . . **155** E5
SUTTON BASSETT **18** A1
Sutton Cl
Aston le W NN11 . . . . **182** F3
Northampton NN2 . . . . . . **141** D6
Sutton Ct LE16 . . . . **31** E1
Sutton Heath Rd PE5, PE8,
PE9 . . . . **8** D6
Sutton Rd
Great Bowden LE16. . . . . . **32** B6
Oundle PE8 . . . . **42** B4
Sutton Bassett LE16 . . . . . **32** E7
Weston by W LE16. . . . . . . **18** B3
Sutton St NN7 . . . . **155** F5
Sutton's Wlk NN12. . . . . . **188** F7
Swain Cl NN3. . . . . **142** E3
Swale Cl
Corby NN17 . . . . **21** D1
Roade NN7 . . . . **191** C3
Swale Dr
Northampton NN5 . . . . . . **140** F3
Wellingborough NN8 . . . . **129** C6
Swallow Cl
Brackley NN13. . . . . **222** E1
Kettering NN15 . . . . **92** B6
Northampton NN4 . . . . . . **175** A7
Swallow Dr NN10 . . . . **132** B5
Swanage Ct NN18. . . . . **36** A6
Swan Ave NN14. . . . . **55** E8
Swan Cl
Brackley NN13. . . . . **222** D2
Burton Latimer NN15 . . . . . **92** A2
Hinton NN11 . . . . **184** B6
Middleton Cheney
OX17. . . . . **219** F8
Thrapston NN14 . . . . **76** D3
Swan Ct NN6 . . . . **87** D1
Swanhill PE8 . . . . **8** A4
Swann Dale NN11 . . . . **135** D1
Swann Dale Cl NN11 . . . . . **135** D1
Swansea Cres NN5. . . . . . **159** A7
Swansea Rd NN5 . . . . **159** A8
Swansgate Ctr The [9]
NN8. . . . . **130** A4
Swans La [6] NN8 . . . . . . **130** A4
Swanspool Ct NN8 . . . . . . **130** A4
Swanspool Par NN8. . . . . . **130** A3
Swan St NN1 . . . . **159** D5
Swan Terr MK11 . . . . **229** D1
Swan Valley Way
NN4 . . . . **174** C8
Swedish Hos NN7. . . . . . . **139** D4
Sweetacre Cl NN7 . . . . . . **163** D4

Swift Cl NN4 175 F3
Swift Way NN13 222 E1
Swinburne Cl NN16 72 C6
Swinburne Rd NN8 129 B4
Swinfen's Yd MK11 229 D5
SWINFORD 62 C3
Swinford CE Prim Sch LE17 62 B4
Swinford Cnr LE17 62 A8
Swinford Hollow NN3 161 A8
Swinford Rd LE17 62 A8
Swingbridge St LE16 30 E8
Swinnertons La NN6 82 B4
Swinneyford Rd NN12 203 C5
Swyncombe Gn NN7 192 C1
Sycamore Ave NN11 184 B6
Sycamore Cl
Corby NN17 21 E1
Daventry NN11 135 C5
Kettering NN16 72 D4
Rushden NN10 132 C2
Towcester NN12 203 C4
Sycamore Dr
Desborough NN14 51 D2
Sywell NN6 143 D8
Sycamore Rd
Greens Norton NN12 202 E8
Northampton NN5 158 C7
Sycamores The LE17 63 D8
Sycamore Yd NN12 187 B1
Sydenham Cl OX17 230 B4
Sydney St NN16 72 D2
Syers Green Cl NN6 121 A4
Syers Green La NN6 121 A4
Sykes Ct NN17 37 A8
Syke The NN14 55 F7
Syles Cl NN6 102 B5
Sylmond Gdns NN10 148 A7
Sylvanus Ho NN8 129 D5
Symington St NN5 159 A7
Symington Way LE16 31 E3
SYRESHAM 224 B8
Syresham St James CE Prim Sch NN13 224 C7
Syresham Way NN2 141 C5
SYWELL 127 D3
Sywell Airport Bsns Pk NN6 127 F4
Sywell Ave NN8 129 D6
Sywell CE Prim Sch NN6 127 D3
Sywell Ctry Pk★ NN6 144 A7
Sywell Rd
Holcot NN6 126 F8
Mears Ashby NN6 128 A1
Overstone NN6 127 B1
Wellingborough NN8 129 C6
Sywell Way NN8 129 D6

T

Taborley Cl NN3 142 E1
Tadcaster Cl NN11 135 C6
Taggies Yd NN14 109 F5
Tailby Ave NN16 72 A5
Tainty Cl NN9 111 E5
Talan Rise NN3 143 C5
Talavera Cl NN11 135 B1
Talavera Way NN3 142 D6
Talbot Rd
Northampton NN1 159 E7
Rushden NN10 131 F1
Wellingborough NN8 130 C5
Talbot Rd N NN8 130 C5
Talbots Hyde MK46 195 E4
Talbot Yd LE16 31 E3
Tall Trees Cl NN4 174 F8
Tallyfield End NN4 158 E3
Tally-Ho Cotts PE8 60 E7
Tamar Cl NN5 140 E2
Tamar Gn NN17 21 D1
Tamarisk Dr NN3 142 C6
Tamar Sq NN11 135 A1
Tancred Cl 1 NN4 175 E7
Taney Ct PE8 42 A5
Tanfield La NN1 160 C5
Tanfields Gr NN17 36 E8
Tanglewood NN4 175 D4
Tanner's La NN16 72 B2
Tanner St NN1 159 C5
Tannery The LE15 4 A5
Tann Rd NN9 111 F5
Tanser Cott LE17 63 C8
TANSOR 27 D2
Tansor Cl NN17 36 B8
Tansy Cl NN4 158 D1
Tantree Way NN6 106 C2
Tapeley Gdns NN4 175 D7
Taper Way NN11 135 B3
Tarn Croft NN3 142 B3
Tarragon Way NN4 175 D6
Tarrant Cl NN3 126 D1
Tarrant Way NN3 126 D1
Tarrys End NN6 82 B4
Tasman Way NN14 70 E6
Tate Gr NN4 175 F7
TATHALL END 207 D2
Tattersall Cl NN3 142 A5
Taunton Ave
Corby NN18 36 B6
Northampton NN3 160 C7
Tavern La 1 NN11 135 C1
Tavern Wlk NN18 36 A4
Tavistock Cl 3 NN3 143 D2
Tavistock Rd NN15 92 A5
Tavistock Sq NN18 36 F4
Tay Cl NN17 21 D1
Taylor Ave NN3 142 C1
Taylor Cl NN8 129 C7
Taylors Gn PE8 28 B2
Teal Cl
Burton Latimer NN15 91 F2
Daventry NN11 135 C4
Higham Ferrers NN10 132 C8
Northampton NN4 174 E8
Teal La NN8 130 B7
Teasel Cl NN10 148 C7
Teasel Dr NN14 51 A4
Tebbitt Cl NN6 121 B4
Tebbutt Cl NN14 70 F7
Tebbutt's Yd NN6 144 E4
Tees Cl NN8 129 C6
Teesdale NN3 142 F6
Teesdale Rd NN17 36 D7
TEETON 104 D1
Teeton La NN6 104 E3
Teeton Rd
Guilsborough NN6 103 F5
Ravensthorpe NN6 103 E1
Telfords La NN17 37 A8
Telford Way
Kettering NN16 71 F4
Northampton NN5 158 D4
Temperance Terr MK11 229 C6
Templar Dr NN2 141 A4
Templar Rd NN15 72 F1
Temple Bar 21 NN1 159 C7
Temple Ct NN10 132 B7
Tenbury Way NN14 70 F7
Tenby Rd NN5 159 A8
Ten Cotts
Church Brampton NN6 140 B8
Wormleighton CV47 181 B8
Tenlands OX17 219 F8
Tennyson Cl
3 Northampton NN5 158 F8
Towcester NN12 203 B5
Tennyson Dr NN17 36 D8
Tennyson Rd
Daventry NN11 135 B3
Kettering NN16 72 B2
Rothwell NN14 70 C7
Rushden NN10 131 F2
Wellingborough NN8 129 D3
Tennyson Road Inf Sch NN10 131 F2
Ten Pines NN3 142 F7
Tenter Cl NN10 132 B5
Tenter La NN9 111 F5
Tenter Rd NN3 141 F7
Tentsmuir Cl NN16 72 A6
Terrace The NN13 224 C5
Terrington Cl NN13 233 E7
Test Gn NN17 21 D1
Tettenhall Cl NN18 36 A1
Teviot Cl
Corby NN17 21 D1
Northampton NN5 140 E2
Tewkesbury Cl
Northampton NN4 159 A1
Wellingborough NN8 129 D6
Tewkesbury Dr NN10 148 D8
TEW'S END 216 C8
Tews End La NN12 216 C8
Thackers Cl PE8 8 A4
Thames Ct NN15 92 B2
Thames Rd
Daventry NN11 135 A1
Northampton NN4 175 C7
Wellingborough NN8 129 C6
Thames Rise NN16 72 A4
Thames Wlk NN17 21 D1
Thatch Meadow Dr LE16 32 B3
Thatchwell Ct NN3 160 F8
THE ARBOURS 142 C3
Theatre Ct NN1 159 D5
Thebwell Rd 3 NN3 142 F1
THEDDINGWORTH 46 C8
Theddingworth Rd
Husbands Bosworth LE17 46 A6
Lubenham LE16 30 C2
Marston Trussell LE16 47 B8
THENFORD 220 E8
Thenford Rd OX17 209 D1
Thenford St NN1 159 E6
Thetford Cl NN18 36 B1
Third Ave NN8 129 D3
Third St NN13 238 E6
Thirlestane Cres NN4 159 B3
Thirlestane Rd NN4 159 B3
Thirlmere NN8 129 C5
Thirlmere Ave NN3 142 C3
Thirlmere Cl
Daventry NN11 135 A2
Kettering NN16 71 E3
Thirlmere Flats NN16 71 E3
Thirsk Rd NN18 36 C5
Thistle Ct 3 NN4 159 A3
Thistle Dr NN14 51 A5
Thistleholme Cl NN2 141 E3
Thoday Cl NN14 90 A3
Thomas Becket RC Sch NN3 142 B5
Thomas Chapman Gr NN4 159 C4
Thomas Cl
Byfield NN11 183 D6
Thomas Cl *continued*
Corby NN18 36 D4
Crick NN6 101 A6
Thomas Crewe Cl NN13 233 F7
Thomas Flawn Rd NN9 131 D8
Thomas Rd NN15 91 C7
Thomas Rippin Cl NN14 54 A2
Thomas St
Northampton NN1 159 D7
Wellingborough NN8 130 B5
Thomas Webb Cl 10 NN11 135 C2
Thompson Cl NN5 158 A6
Thompson Way NN15 90 F8
Thorburn Rd NN3 160 E8
Thoresby Ct NN18 36 C5
Thornapple Cl NN3 143 C4
Thornborough Cl LE16 32 A2
Thornbridge Cl NN10 132 A1
THORNBY 84 E4
Thornby Dr NN2 141 B3
Thornby Rd
Cold Ashby NN6 84 B5
Naseby NN6 85 B8
Thorn Cl NN16 72 B6
Thorne Ct NN18 36 C5
Thornfield NN3 143 C4
Thorngate St NN16 72 C2
THORNHAUGH 7 F5
Thornhill OX17 208 F4
Thorn Hill NN4 159 A3
Thornlea Croft MK46 195 F3
THORNTON 235 C4
Thornton Cl
Crick NN6 101 A6
Flore NN7 155 F5
Newnham NN11 153 D3
Thornton Coll MK17 235 C5
Thornton Park Farm MK17 235 D4
Thornton Rd
Northampton NN2 141 B1
Thornton MK17 235 F2
Thoroughsale Rd NN17 36 E7
THORPE BY WATER 10 A6
Thorpe Cl
Banbury OX16 219 A6
Wellingborough NN8 129 C5
Thorpe Ct NN14 77 C7
Thorpe Dr OX16 219 A6
THORPE LANGTON 17 A5
Thorpe Langton Rd LE16 17 D6
THORPE MALSOR 71 B3
THORPE MANDEVILLE 210 B7
Thorpe Rd
Chacombe OX17 208 E4
Earls Barton NN6 144 E2
Lyddington LE15 9 D6
Northampton NN4 159 C3
Thorpe Waterville NN14 77 A8
Upper Wardington OX17 208 F8
Thorpe St NN9 114 D5
THORPE UNDERWOOD 69 C7
Thorpeville NN3 142 D7
THORPE WATERVILLE 77 C8
Thorplands Prim Sch NN3 142 E5
Thor Wlk NN18 36 A2
THRAPSTON 76 E1
Thrapston Prim Sch NN14 76 D1
Thrapston Rd
Finedon NN9, NN14 93 C2
Woodford NN14 94 D8
Three Shires Hospl NN1 159 F5
Thrift Mews 13 NN1 159 F6
Thrift St
Higham Ferrers NN10 132 B5
Irchester NN29 147 A7
Wollaston NN29 146 D2
Thrupp Bridge NN4 176 A6
Thrush La NN8 130 B6
Thruxton Dr NN3 141 F4
Thurburn Cl NN14 90 B5
THURNING 60 D2
Thurning Rd PE8, PE28 79 F7
Thursby Rd NN1 160 B7
Thurso Wlk NN17 21 D1
Thurspit Pl 8 NN3 143 D2
Thurston Dr NN15 91 A8
Thyme Ct NN3 142 E3
Tibbs Way NN7 173 A6
Tideswell Cl
Desborough NN14 50 E4
Northampton NN4 174 F8
Tiffany Gdns NN4 175 C6
TIFFIELD 184 D4
Tiffield CE Prim Sch NN12 189 D3
Tiffield Rd NN7 189 E8
Tilbury Rd NN6 122 C5
Tilbury Rise NN6 122 C5
Tilley Hill Cl PE8 41 E7
Timken Ho 3 NN11 135 A4
Timken Lo NN11 135 A4
Timken Way NN11 135 A4
Timor Ct MK11 229 D6
Timpson Cl NN16 72 C5
Timson Cl LE16 31 D5
Tingdene Rd NN9 111 F5
Tinkers Cres NN6 128 B2
Tinsley Cl NN3 143 B3
Tintagel Cl NN10 132 D1
Tintern Ave NN5 159 A7
Tintern Ct NN15 91 F8
Tippings La LE15 3 F5
Tiptoe Cl NN3 143 C3
TITCHMARSH 77 D4
Titchmarsh CE Prim Sch NN14 77 C4
Tithe Barn Cl NN9 114 E7
Tithe Barn Rd NN8 130 A4
Tithe Barn Way NN4 174 B8
Tithe Cl
Holcot NN6 126 E8
Ringstead NN14 95 A3
Tithe La OX15, OX17 236 C6
Tithe Rd NN7 155 A2
Tithe Way NN7 191 D5
Titley Bawk Ave NN6 144 F6
Titty Ho NN9 114 C5
Tiverton Ave NN2 141 C7
TIXOVER 4 E5
Tixover Grange PE9 4 F8
Todd's Hill PE9 5 B6
Todmorden Cl NN18 36 C5
Tofts Cl NN14 77 D4
Tollbar NN10 132 B5
Toll Bar La PE28 97 B4
Toll Bar Rd NN14 76 B2
Toller Pl NN15 91 F6
Toller St NN16 72 C3
Tollgate Cl NN2 141 B2
Tollgate Pl NN18 37 B6
Tollgate Way NN5 158 D6
Tompson Cl NN11 118 C1
Toms Cl
Northampton NN4 175 C3
Theddingworth LE17 46 D8
Tonmead Rd NN3 142 E3
Top Cl NN14 76 F3
Top Dysons NN14 92 F7
Top End
Little Addington NN14 113 B7
Pytchley NN14 90 F2
Top Farm Ct NN11 184 B6
Top Farm La NN29 145 E7
Top Lo NN17 5 A1
Top Station Rd NN13 234 A8
Top Station Road Ind Est NN13 234 A8
Topwell Ct NN3 143 A1
Top Yard Farm LE16 31 F6
Torch Way LE16 48 F8
Tordoff Pl NN16 72 B2
Torksey Cl NN18 36 A1
Torridge Cl NN16 71 F4
Torridon Cl NN17 21 C1
Torrington Cres NN8 129 D6
Torrington Gn NN8 129 E6
Torrington Rd NN8 129 E6
Torville Cres NN15 91 A8
Totnes Cl NN18 36 F4
Toulouse Cl 11 NN4 175 E7
Touraine Cl NN5 139 F2
Tove La NN12 203 A6
Tovey Dr NN11 135 D1
TOWCESTER 203 B3
Towcester Cl NN18 36 E1
Towcester Dr NN12 217 B3
Towcester Inf Sch NN12 203 C5
Towcester Rd
Blisworth NN7 190 B6
Greens Norton NN12 188 E1
Litchborough NN12 171 C1
Milton Malsor NN7 174 E5
Northampton NN4 159 B2
Old Stratford MK19 229 B7
Silverstone NN12 214 E4
Towcester NN12 203 A8
Whittlebury NN12 215 C5
Tower Cl NN9 112 A4
Tower Ct
Lubenham LE16 30 F3
Northampton NN6 143 B7
Wollaston NN29 146 F3
Tower Field Sq NN3 143 A6
Tower Hill Cl NN4 158 E3
Tower Hill Rd NN18 36 A4
Tower Sq NN5 158 F6
Tower St NN1 159 C6
Town Cl NN9 110 C3
Town Cnr NN5 158 F6
Townley Way NN6 144 E5
Townsend
Hinton NN11 184 B6
Maidford NN12 186 D6
Towns End NN6 121 C4
Townsend Cl
Hanging Houghton NN6 106 C8
Wellingborough NN8 129 F4
Townsend Ct PE8 39 E7
Townsend La
Thorpe Mandeville OX17 209 F6
Upper Boddington NN11 182 B8
Townsend Leys NN10 132 B8
Townsend Rd NN6 107 F5
Townson Cl NN6 107 D7
Townwell La NN29 147 B8
Towrise OX17 210 F8
Towton Ct NN4 159 A1
Trafalgar Rd NN16 72 A2
Trafalgar Rd Ind Est NN16 72 A2
Trafalgar Way NN11 135 D1
Trafford Rd NN10 132 D2
Trailli La NN14 94 D6
Treen Cl NN14 76 F2
Treetops NN3 143 A5
Trefoil Cl NN10 148 C7
Trelawney NN8 129 B5
Trenery Way NN4 159 D4
Trengothal Ct NN13 223 D4
Trent Cl
Northampton NN5 140 F2
Wellingborough NN8 129 C6
Trent Cres NN15 92 B1
Trentham Cl NN4 175 C7
Trent Ho PE8 42 A6
Trent Rd
Corby NN17 21 D1
Kettering NN16 72 A5
Wittering PE8 7 D8
Trent Wlk NN11 135 A1
Tresham Gn NN5 140 D1
Tresham Inst
Corby NN17 36 E6
Kettering NN15 72 C1
Kettering NN15 91 D8
Tresham Inst (Wellingborough Campus) NN8 130 A5
Tresham St
Kettering NN16 72 C3
Rothwell NN14 70 D7
Trevithick Rd NN17 37 C8
Trevor Cl NN5 158 E7
Trevor Cres NN5 158 E7
Trimley Cl NN3 160 D6
Trinity Ave NN2 141 D1
Trinity CE Lower Sch NN14 76 F8
Trinity Cl
Daventry NN11 153 B8
Old Stratford MK19 229 B7
Trinity Ct NN14 70 C6
Trinity Ctr NN8 129 A7
Trinity Rd NN14 70 C6
Trinity Way OX17 230 D3
Trinity Wlk NN18 36 E4
Triumph Gdns NN5 139 F1
Trojan Ctr NN8 130 B8
Tromso Cl NN18 36 A2
Troon Cres NN8 129 C7
Troutbeck Wlk NN3 142 C4
Trussell Rd NN3 143 C1
Tudely Cl NN4 175 F7
Tudor Ct 4 NN16 72 C2
Tudor Gdns MK11 229 E4
Tudor Rd NN1, NN2 142 A2
Tudor Way
Brackley NN13 233 E8
Wellingborough NN8 129 E7
Tudor Wlk NN10 132 C3
Tulbrook Stones OX17 220 B7
Tulip Dr NN10 148 B7
Tungstone Way LE16 31 E1
Tunnel Hill Cotts NN4 159 A2
Tunwell La NN17 37 B7
Turnberry Ct NN8 129 C7
Turnberry La NN4 175 C5
Turnbrook Cl NN9 112 E3
Turnells Mill La NN8 130 A1
Turner Cl
Kettering NN15 92 A8
Rugby CV21 99 B8
Turner Rd
Corby NN18 36 E5
Wellingborough NN8 129 F7
Turners Ct NN4 175 D7
Turners Farm Cl NN6 108 C2
Turner St NN1 159 F7
Turners Yd PE8 41 F5
Turn Furlong NN2 141 A5
Turnpike Cl LE16 31 D5
Turvins Mdw CV47 166 D8
TURWESTON 234 C8
Turweston Manor NN13 234 C8
Turweston Rd NN13 223 A1
Tweed Cl
Burton Latimer NN15 92 B2
Daventry NN11 153 A8
Tweed Rd NN5 158 E6
Twickenham Ct 5 NN18 36 B5
Twigden Rd NN7 157 D3
Twistle The NN11 183 C7
Twitch Hill NN12 204 D8
TWYFORD 230 B5
Twyford Ave
Raunds NN9 114 C7
Twyford OX17 230 A6
Twyford Cl 7 NN3 161 A8
Twyford Gdns OX17 230 A6
Twyford Gr OX17 230 A6
Twyford Rd OX17 230 C7
TWYWELL 75 A1
Twywell Hills & Dales Nature Res★ NN14 93 F8
Tyebeck Ct NN2 141 B3
Tyes Ct NN3 142 F3
Tyler Way NN14 76 E1
Tymecrosse Gdns LE16 31 D5
Tynan Cl NN15 92 A8
Tyne Cl NN8 129 C6

Tyne Rd
  Corby NN17 . . . . 21 D1
  Daventry NN11 . . . . 153 A8
  Northampton NN5 . . . . . . 158 A8
Tyringham Cl NN3 . . . . . . 142 D1
Tyrrell Way NN12 . . . . . . 203 C8
Tyson Ctyd NN18 . . . . 37 E7
Tythings The OX17 . . . . . 208 F2

U
Uist Wlk NN17 . . . . 21 C1
Ullswater Cl
  Higham Ferrers NN10 . . . . 132 B8
  Wellingborough NN8 . . . . 129 C5
Ullswater Rd NN16 . . . . . . 71 E2
Underbank La NN3 . . . . . 142 C6
Underwood Rd NN14 . . . . . 70 C7
Union St
  Desborough NN14 . . . . 51 B3
  Finedon NN9 . . . . 112 A5
  Kettering NN16 . . . . 72 A3
Unity Cl NN29 . . . . 146 C3
Unity Coll NN2 . . . . 141 D1
Unity St NN14 . . . . 51 A2
Univ Coll Northampton NN2 . . . . 141 D1
Univ of Leicester (Northampton Ctr) NN2 . . . . 159 C8
Upland Rd NN3 . . . . 142 C2
UPPER ASTROP 231 C7
Upper Astrop Rd OX17 . . . . 231 A5
Upper Bath St NN1 . . . . . 159 C6
UPPER BENEFIELD 39 F7
UPPER BODDINGTON
  . . . . 182 D8
UPPER CATESBY 151 F4
Upper Cross St 18 NN1 . . . . 159 C6
Upper Dane NN14 . . . . 50 E3
Upperfield Gr NN17 . . . . . 36 E8
Upper George St NN10 . . . . 132 C7
Upper Glen Ave NN7 . . . . 174 B2
Upper Gn NN11 . . . . 199 D7
Upper Green Pl LE16 . . . . 32 A6
UPPER HARLESTONE
  . . . . 139 D4
Upper Havelock St 7 NN8 . . . . 130 A5
UPPER HEYFORD 156 D3
Upper Higham La NN10 . . . . 133 C3
Upper High St NN7 . . . . . 157 C7
Upper Kings Ave NN10 . . . . 132 C7
Upper Mounts NN1 . . . . . 159 D6
Upper Park Ave NN10 . . . 131 F1
Upper Priory St 7 NN1 . . . . 159 C7
Upper Queen St NN10 . . . . 132 C3
Upper St NN16 . . . . 72 A2
Upper Steeping NN14 . . . . 51 B2
UPPER STOWE 171 E6
Upper Thrift St NN1 . . . . 159 F6
UPPER WARDINGTON
  . . . . 196 F1
UPPER WEEDON 155 A2
Uppingham Rd
  Caldecott LE16 . . . . 9 B2
  Corby NN17 . . . . 36 A7
  Medbourne LE16 . . . . 19 A8
Uppingham St NN1 . . . . . 159 B7
UPTON 158 C5
Upton Cl NN2 . . . . 141 D6
Upton Way NN4, NN5 . . . 158 D3
Usher Ho NN2 . . . . 141 C5

V
Vale Cl CV21 . . . . 99 A8
Valentine Way NN3 . . . . . 143 C3
Vale St NN16 . . . . 72 A3
Vale The NN11 . . . . 141 F1
Valley Cl NN13 . . . . 234 A4
Valley Cres
  Brackley NN13 . . . . 234 A8
  Northampton NN3 . . . . . . 143 B1
Valley End NN12 . . . . 172 D1
Valley Rd
  Brackley NN13 . . . . 234 A8
  Northampton NN3 . . . . . . 143 B1
  Wellingborough NN8 . . . . 129 F1
  Weston by W LE16 . . . . . . 18 B3
Valley Rise
  Brackley NN13 . . . . 233 F8
  Desborough NN14 . . . . 51 B2
Valley Way LE16 . . . . 32 B4
Valley Wlk NN16 . . . . 72 E2
Vancouver Cl NN18 . . . . . . 36 B2
Vantage Mdw NN3 . . . . . . 143 D3
Vara Cl NN18 . . . . 36 B2
Vardon Cl NN8 . . . . 129 C7
Varley Cl NN8 . . . . 129 E8
Vaughan Cl LE16 . . . . 48 E8
Vaux Rd NN8 . . . . 111 A1
Velbert Ho NN11 . . . . 21 E1
Velocette Way NN5 . . . . . 140 A1
Venture Cl NN17 . . . . 22 F1
Verdant Vale 1 NN4 . . . . 175 D6
Vermont Standing 3 NN16 . . . . 72 C3
Vernier Cl NN11 . . . . 135 A3

Vernon Ave CV22 . . . . 98 E8
Vernon Cl NN11 . . . . 153 E8
Vernon Ct NN11 . . . . 71 F5
Vernon Ct 10 NN1 . . . . . 159 F6
Vernon Rd NN12 . . . . 203 D5
Vernon St NN1 . . . . 159 F6
Vernon Terr NN1 . . . . 159 F6
Vernon Terrace Prim Sch
  NN1 . . . . 159 F6
Vernon Wlk 7 NN1 . . . . 159 F6
Verwood Cl NN3 . . . . 142 F5
Veteran Cl NN4 . . . . 175 E7
Vian Way NN17 . . . . 36 B8
Vicarage Cl
  Hackleton NN7 . . . . 177 A3
  Northampton NN2 . . . . . . 141 A3
  Wellingborough NN8 . . . . 129 D6
  Whittlebury NN12 . . . . . . 215 C5
  Yardley Gobion NN12 . . . . 217 E6
Vicarage Ct MK19 . . . . . . 207 B2
Vicarage Farm Rd
  NN8 . . . . 129 D6
Vicarage Hill NN11 . . . . . 153 A2
Vicarage La
  Denton NN7 . . . . 178 B8
  East Haddon NN6 . . . . . . 122 D5
  Mears Ashby NN6 . . . . . . 128 B2
  Northampton NN3 . . . . . . 141 B3
  Podington NN29 . . . . 147 E2
  Priors Marston CV47 . . . . 166 E8
Vicarage Rd
  Northampton NN5 . . . . . . 159 A7
  Rushden NN10 . . . . 132 C3
  Stony Stratford MK11 . . . 229 D6
Vicarage Rise NN12 . . . . . 200 C3
Vicarage Wlk MK11 . . . . . 229 D6
Vicar La NN11 . . . . 135 D2
Viceroy Cl NN14 . . . . 114 E6
Vickers Cl NN14 . . . . 70 F7
Victoria Ave LE16 . . . . 31 D5
Victoria Cl
  Earls Barton NN6 . . . . . . 144 E5
  Rushden NN10 . . . . 132 B3
  West Haddon NN6 . . . . . . 102 C5
Victoria Ct
  10 Kettering NN16 . . . . . . 72 C2
  Rothwell NN14 . . . . 70 D7
  Rushden NN10 . . . . 132 B3
  Woodford NN14 . . . . 94 C7
Victoria Gdns NN1 . . . . . 159 D5
Victoria Ho NN1 . . . . 159 E6
Victoria Pk NN8 . . . . 130 B2
Victoria Prim Sch
  NN8 . . . . 130 B6
Victoria Prom NN8 . . . . . 159 D5
Victoria Rd
  Cogenhoe NN7 . . . . 161 E5
  Finedon NN9 . . . . 111 F5
  Northampton NN1 . . . . . . 159 E6
  Oundle PE8 . . . . 42 A6
  Rushden NN10 . . . . 132 B3
  Wellingborough NN8 . . . . 130 B4
Victoria St
  Burton Latimer NN15 . . . . 92 B2
  Desborough NN14 . . . . 51 A3
  Earls Barton NN6 . . . . . . 144 F5
  Irthlingborough NN9 . . . . 112 E1
  Kettering NN16 . . . . 72 B2
  Northampton NN1 . . . . . . 159 D6
Vienne Cl NN5 . . . . 157 F8
Viking Cl NN16 . . . . 72 C6
Viking Way NN18 . . . . 36 B1
Villagers Cl NN4 . . . . 175 E5
Villa La NN9 . . . . 113 F3
Villa Rise NN10 . . . . 132 B7
Villa Way NN4 . . . . 175 E5
Vincent Cl NN5 . . . . 157 F8
Vinco Terr PE8 . . . . 28 D8
Vine Cl PE8 . . . . 42 A5
Vine Hill Cl NN10 . . . . . . 132 A6
Vine Hill Dr NN10 . . . . . . 132 B6
Violet Cl NN18 . . . . 36 D2
Violet La
  Creaton NN6 . . . . 104 F4
  Rothwell NN14, NN6 . . . . . 71 C6
Viscount Rd NN3 . . . . 143 C6
Vislok Cl LE16 . . . . 31 E1
Vivian Rd NN8 . . . . 130 B5
Vokes Cl NN3 . . . . 143 A1
Volunteer Cl NN4 . . . . . . 175 E6
Vulcan Cl NN11 . . . . 135 A3
Vyse Rd NN2 . . . . 141 C8

W
Wadcroft 3 NN16 . . . . . . 72 B2
Wadd Close La NN11 . . . . 137 D6
Wade Meadow Ct
  NN3 . . . . 142 F4
WADENHOE 58 A4
Wadenhoe La PE8 . . . . 57 F4
Wadenhoe Rd NN14 . . . . . 57 E1
Wades Cl PE8 . . . . 14 F1
Wadham Ct NN11 . . . . . . 153 C7
Waggoners Way NN7 . . . . 173 A4
Wagstaff Way MK46 . . . . 195 F3
Wagtail Cl NN3 . . . . 142 C7
Waingrove NN3 . . . . 143 B4
Wainwright Ave NN14 . . . . 76 D1
Wake Cl NN3 . . . . 130 A1
Wakefield NN8 . . . . 129 C4
Wakefield Dr NN16 . . . . . . 64 D5
Wakefield Rd NN2 . . . . . . 141 D4
Wakefield Way NN7 . . . . . 156 C1
Wakehurst Dr NN4 . . . . . 175 C7

WAKERLEY 4 A3
Wakerley Cl PE8 . . . . 41 D5
Wakerley Great Wood Forest Trail ★⬛ LE15 . . . 4 C2
Wakerley Great Wood Orienteering Course★
  LE15 . . . . 4 B2
Wakerley Rd
  Barrowden LE15 . . . . 4 A4
  Harringworth NN17 . . . . . 10 F7
Wake Way NN4 . . . . 175 F3
Walcot Cl NN15 . . . . 41 E7
Walcote Rd LE17 . . . . 63 C8
Walcot Rd LE16 . . . . 31 E2
WALES 230 F5
Wales St
  Kings Sutton OX17 . . . . . . 230 F5
  Rothwell NN14 . . . . 70 C7
Walford Pl CV22 . . . . 98 F8
WALGRAVE 108 B5
Walgrave Cl NN3 . . . . 161 B8
Walgrave Prim Sch
  NN6 . . . . 108 A5
Walgrave Rd
  Holcot NN6 . . . . 107 E1
  Old NN6 . . . . 107 E6
  Walgrave NN6 . . . . 108 B4
Walker Dr NN12 . . . . 203 C8
Walkers Acre NN6 . . . . . . 108 A5
Walkers Field PE8 . . . . 13 F8
Walkers La NN6 . . . . 140 B8
Walker's La 5 NN16 . . . . 72 B2
Walker Sq NN16 . . . . 72 B2
Walkers Way NN4 . . . . . . 175 E5
Walker's Way NN9 . . . . . . 111 F4
Walks The PE9 . . . . 1 D2
Walk The NN6 . . . . 124 B8
Wallace Gdns NN2 . . . . . . 141 F2
Wallace Rd NN2 . . . . 141 F2
Wallace Terr NN2 . . . . 141 F2
Wallbeck Cl NN2 . . . . 141 C4
Walledwell Ct 4 NN3 . . . 142 F1
Wallingford End 6
  NN3 . . . . 161 A8
Wallis Cl NN15 . . . . 91 C8
Wallis Cres NN15 . . . . 91 C8
Wallis Rd NN15 . . . . 91 C8
Wallwin Cl NN7 . . . . 191 C4
Walmer Rd NN10 . . . . 132 D1
Walnut Cl
  Brackley NN13 . . . . 222 F1
  Braunston NN11 . . . . 118 D2
  Clifton OX15 . . . . 236 E4
  Culworth OX17 . . . . 198 D2
  Silverstone NN12 . . . . . . 214 D4
  Weldon NN17 . . . . 38 B8
Walnut Cres NN16 . . . . 72 D4
Walnut Gdns OX17 . . . . . 181 D1
Walnut Gr NN3 . . . . 142 C1
Walnut Tree Cl NN14 . . . . 94 D6
Walnut Tree Ct NN10 . . . 132 B7
Walsingham Ave NN15 . . . 91 F8
Waltham NN17 . . . . 36 D8
Waltham Gdns OX16 . . . . 219 A6
Walton Ave OX17 . . . . 230 B5
Walton Heath Way
  NN2 . . . . 141 E3
Walton Pl NN18 . . . . 36 B6
Wansell Rd NN17 . . . . 37 F8
WANSFORD 8 B4
Wansford Pl NN17 . . . . 36 B8
Wansford Rd
  Elton PE8 . . . . 16 E3
  Yarwell PE8 . . . . 7 F2
Wansford Sta ★ PE8 . . . . 16 E8
Wansford Wlk NN3 . . . . . 142 E6
Wantage Cl
  Hackleton NN7 . . . . 177 B3
  Moulton NN3 . . . . 126 E1
Wantage Pl NN29 . . . . . . 147 B8
Wantage Rd
  Irchester NN29 . . . . 147 B8
  Northampton NN1 . . . . . . 160 A8
WAPPENHAM 213 A8
Wappenham Rd
  Abthorpe NN12 . . . . 201 F1
  Helmdon NN13 . . . . 212 A5
  Syresham NN13 . . . . 213 C2
Wardens Lo 2 NN11 . . . 135 C2
WARDINGTON 196 D2
Wardington Rd OX17 . . . 208 D6
Wardle Ct NN16 . . . . 72 B3
Wardle's Cl NN7 . . . . 138 C7
Wardlow Cl NN4 . . . . 174 F8
Ward Rd NN13 . . . . 234 A5
Wards La NN6 . . . . 82 C3
Wareham Gn NN18 . . . . . . 36 B6
Warehouse The LE16 . . . . 31 D4
Wareing La NN7 . . . . 178 B8
Ware Orch CV23 . . . . 99 C2
Ware Rd CV23 . . . . 99 C2
WARKTON 73 A4
Warkton La NN15, NN16 . . . 73 B2
Warkton Way NN17 . . . . . . 36 B8
WARKWORTH 219 D5
Warkworth Rd OX17 . . . . 219 E7
WARMINGTON 28 C2
Warmington Sch NN8 . . . . 28 B3
WARMONDS HILL 132 A6
Warmonds Hill NN10 . . . . 132 B5
Warners Hill NN29 . . . . . 164 D2
Warnham NN8 . . . . 129 B5
Warren Bridge PE8 . . . . . . 41 B1
Warren Cl NN29 . . . . 147 C7
Warren End
  Desborough NN14 . . . . 51 B4
  Mawsley Village NN14 . . . . 89 A4

Warren Hill NN16 . . . . 71 E3
Warren La
  Bythorn PE28 . . . . 97 D4
  Clopton PE14 . . . . 78 F1
Warren Rd
  Northampton NN5 . . . . . . 158 F7
  Stanion NN14 . . . . 37 E3
  Wothorpe PE9 . . . . 2 E7
  Yardley Gobion NN12 . . . . 217 F6
Warrens Cl NN9 . . . . 112 F2
Warren The
  Northampton NN4 . . . . . . 175 F8
  Thorpe Mandeville OX17 . . . . 210 A6
Warren Yd MK12 . . . . 229 F6
WARRINGTON 180 B1
Warrington Rd MK46 . . . . 195 F5
Warth Park Way NN9 . . . 114 B7
Wartnaby St LE16 . . . . 31 D3
Warwick Ave NN14 . . . . . . 37 E3
Warwick Cl
  Market Harborough LE16 . . . . 31 F5
  Northampton NN5 . . . . . . 158 B8
  Raunds NN9 . . . . 114 D5
Warwick Ct
  Daventry NN11 . . . . 135 B1
  Kettering NN15 . . . . 91 F8
Warwick Gdns NN14 . . . . . 76 F2
Warwick Ho NN5 . . . . 158 F7
Warwick Prim Sch
  NN8 . . . . 129 F1
Warwick St NN11 . . . . . . 135 B1
Warwick Way NN17 . . . . . . 36 C6
Warwick Rd
  Hanslope MK19 . . . . 207 A3
  Upper Boddington
    NN11 . . . . 182 C7
  Wellingborough NN8 . . . . 130 A2
Washbrook Cl NN3 . . . . . . 143 B1
Washbrook La NN6 . . . . . 143 F5
Washbrook Rd NN10 . . . . 132 A3
Washingley La PE7 . . . . . . 44 F6
Washington Ct NN14 . . . . . 76 E3
Washington Sq NN16 . . . . . 72 D3
Washington St NN2 . . . . . 141 C3
Washle Dr OX17 . . . . 220 B7
Water Cl MK19 . . . . 229 B7
Waterfall Way LE16 . . . . . 18 F6
Waterfield Pl LE16 . . . . . . 31 E5
Waterhouse Gdns
  NN15 . . . . 92 A7
Watering La NN4 . . . . 175 C3
Water La
  Adderbury OX17 . . . . 230 A3
  Bradden NN12 . . . . 201 F5
  Chelveston NN9 . . . . 133 C4
  Cottingham LE16 . . . . 35 D8
  Northampton NN4 . . . . . . 175 E6
  Shutlanger NN12 . . . . . . 204 D8
  Towcester NN12 . . . . 203 C5
  Weldon NN17 . . . . 38 A8
Waterlee Furlong
  NN6 . . . . 106 C1
Waterloo NN11 . . . . 135 C1
Waterloo Way NN9 . . . . . 131 D8
Waterlow Bridge NN9 . . . 111 F5
Water Meadow Cl
  NN18 . . . . 36 B1
Watermeadow Dr
  NN3 . . . . 142 F6
Watermill Cl NN14 . . . . . . 51 D3
Waterpike NN18 . . . . 36 C2
Waterpump Ct NN3 . . . . . 142 F5
Waters Edge PE8 . . . . 16 B8
Waterside Way NN4 . . . . . 160 B4
Waters La OX17 . . . . 209 B1
Watersmeet NN1 . . . . 160 C6
Water St NN16 . . . . 72 C2
Watervill Way NN14 . . . . 113 B8
Waterworks Way LE17 . . . 45 F5
Watery La
  Brackley NN13 . . . . 234 A7
  Nether Heyford NN7 . . . . 156 C2
WATFORD 120 C6
Watford Rd
  Crick NN6 . . . . 101 A2
  West Haddon NN6 . . . . . . 102 B3
Watkin Cl NN1 . . . . 159 D7
Watkin Terr NN1 . . . . 159 D7
Watling St E
  Pattishall NN12 . . . . 188 D8
  Towcester NN12 . . . . 203 C6
Watling St W
  Pattishall NN12 . . . . 188 D8
  Towcester NN12 . . . . 203 C6
Watling St
  Kilsby CV23 . . . . 100 A3
  Potterspury NN12 . . . . . . 217 D2
  Weedon Bec NN7 . . . . . . 155 C4
Watson Ave LE16 . . . . 48 D8
Watson Cl
  Corby NN17 . . . . 21 E2
  Oundle PE8 . . . . 41 E7
  Wellingborough NN8 . . . . 129 C7
Watson Rd NN6 . . . . 121 B2
Watts Cl MK19 . . . . 207 A3
Watts La CV21 . . . . 99 B8
Watts Way NN16 . . . . 121 C9
Wavell Cl NN15 . . . . 72 E1
Waveney Cl NN11 . . . . . . 153 C8
Waveney Way NN5 . . . . . . 140 F1
Waver Cl NN18 . . . . 36 B3
Waverley Ave NN17 . . . . . . 37 C6
Waverley Cl OX17 . . . . . . 230 F5
Waverley Rd
  Kettering NN15 . . . . 91 D8
  Northampton NN2 . . . . . . 141 E1

Waverley Rd *continued*
  Rugby CV21 . . . . 80 A1
Waynflete Ave NN13 . . . . 233 E7
Waynflete Cl NN13 . . . . . 233 E7
Waypost Ct NN3 . . . . 142 F3
Wayside Acres 3
  NN4 . . . . 175 B8
Weares Cl LE15 . . . . 3 B5
Weaver Cl NN16 . . . . 72 B6
Weavers End MK19 . . . . . 207 B2
Weavers Rd NN8 . . . . 129 D4
Weavers Sch NN8 . . . . . . 129 D4
Weavers The NN4 . . . . . . 175 C6
Webb Cl PE8 . . . . 42 B5
Webb Rd NN14 . . . . 114 C7
Webbs Factory NN2 . . . . 141 D1
Webbs La NN6 . . . . 127 D3
Webster Cl NN14 . . . . 114 D7
Weddell Way NN4 . . . . . . 160 C2
Wedgwood Cl NN14 . . . . . 50 F3
Wedmore Cl NN15 . . . . . . 158 D7
Wedmore Ct NN18 . . . . . . 36 B6
WEEDON BEC 155 A3
Weedon Bec Prim Sch
  NN7 . . . . 155 B3
Weedon La NN11 . . . . 136 C4
WEEDON LOIS 200 C2
Weedon Rd
  Farthingstone NN12 . . . . 170 F3
  Kislingbury NN7 . . . . 157 C5
  Nether Heyford NN7 . . . . 156 B2
  Newnham NN11 . . . . 153 E4
  Northampton NN5 . . . . . . 158 D5
WEEKLEY 72 F6
Weekley Glebe Rd
  NN16 . . . . 72 D5
Weekley Wood La
  NN16 . . . . 72 E6
Weekly Cl NN14 . . . . 113 B8
Weggs Farm Rd NN5 . . . 139 F1
Weighbridge Way
  NN9 . . . . 114 C5
Weinahr Cl LE16 . . . . 34 C5
Weir Cl NN8 . . . . 129 F7
Weir The 14 NN11 . . . . . 135 B7
Welbeck Ct
  Corby NN18 . . . . 36 C5
  Kettering NN15 . . . . 91 F8
Welbourne Cl NN9 . . . . . 114 C6
WELDON 38 C8
Weldon CE Prim Sch
  NN17 . . . . 38 A8
Weldon Cl NN8 . . . . 129 D7
Weldon North Ind Est
  NN17 . . . . 22 F1
Weldon Rd NN17 . . . . 37 C7
Weldon St 2 NN16 . . . . . 72 C3
WELFORD 64 E5
Welford Ave NN9 . . . . . . 113 B5
Welford Cl NN3 . . . . 113 B5
Welford Gr NN17 . . . . 36 C7
Welford Rd
  Husbands Bosworth
    LE17 . . . . 45 E3
  Northampton NN2 . . . . . . 141 B4
  Sibbertoft LE16 . . . . 46 D2
  South Kilworth LE17 . . . . 63 D7
  Spratton NN6 . . . . 124 A8
  Thornby NN6 . . . . 84 D4
  Welford NN6 . . . . 64 E7
Welford Sibbertoft & Sulby Endowed Sch
  NN6 . . . . 64 E5
WELHAM 17 E5
Welham La
  Great Bowden LE16 . . . . . 32 C8
  Welham LE16 . . . . 17 E8
Welham Rd
  Great Bowden LE16 . . . . . 32 B8
  Thorpe Langton LE16 . . . . 17 B5
  Welham LE16 . . . . 18 A8
  Weston by W LE16 . . . . . . 18 A4
Welland Ave LE16 . . . . . . 30 E7
Welland Bsns Pk LE16 . . . 32 B4
Welland Cl
  Caldecott LE16 . . . . 21 C8
  Daventry NN11 . . . . 152 F8
  Gretton NN17 . . . . 22 B8
  Raunds NN9 . . . . 114 C7
Welland Ct
  Burton Latimer NN15 . . . . 92 B2
  Desborough NN14 . . . . . . 51 A3
  3 Market Harborough
    LE16 . . . . 31 F2
  Market Harborough
    LE16 . . . . 32 A4
Welland Gn NN5 . . . . 140 F2
Welland Mdws PE9 . . . . . . 4 F8
Welland Park Com Coll
  LE16 . . . . 31 E2
Welland Park Rd LE16 . . . 31 E2
Welland Rd NN16 . . . . 72 A5
Welland Rise LE16 . . . . . . 46 F2
Welland Vale Rd NN17 . . . 21 E1
Welland Way LE16 . . . . . . 20 D1
Welland Way NN5 . . . . . . 141 A2
Welland Wlk NN5 . . . . . . 140 F2
Well Hill Cl NN6 . . . . 100 F5
WELLINGBOROUGH 130 D6
Wellingborough Jun Sch
  NN8 . . . . 130 B3
Wellingborough Rd
  Broughton NN14 . . . . 90 B3
  Earls Barton NN6 . . . . . . 144 F6
  Finedon NN9 . . . . 111 F4

Wellingborough Rd
continued
Great Harrowden NN9 . . . . .**110** E1
Irthlingborough NN9 . . . . .**131** C8
Isham NN6 . . . .**110** F8
Little Harrowden NN9 . . . . .**110** B3
Mears Ashby NN6 . . . .**128** C2
Northampton, Cottarville
NN3 . . . .**142** E1
Northampton NN1 . . . .**159** F6
Olney MK46 . . . .**195** F5
Rushden NN10 . . . .**131** F3
Sywell NN6 . . . .**127** F4
Wellingborough NN8 . . . . .**111** E1
Wellingborough Sch
Wellingborough NN8 . . . . .**130** B3
Wellingborough NN8 . . . . .**130** B4
Wellingborough Sta
NN8 . . . .**130** C5
Wellington Pl 18 NN1 . . . .**159** C7
Wellington Rd NN9 . . . . . .**114** C5
Wellington St
Kettering NN16 . . . .**72** C3
Northampton NN1 . . . .**159** D6
Wellington Terr NN14 . . . . .**76** B2
Wellington Wks 1
NN16. . . . .**72** C3
Well La
Barnwell PE8 . . . .**59** B7
Everdon NN11 . . . .**170** A8
Guilsborough NN6 . . . .**103** F6
Rothwell NN14 . . . .**70** D7
Staverton NN11 . . . .**152** B7
Welton NN11 . . . .**119** E1
Wells Cl
Husbands Bosworth
LE17 . . . .**45** E5
Kettering NN15 . . . .**90** F8
Wells Ct NN3 . . . .**142** C8
Wells Gn NN8 . . . .**36** B6
Wellspring NN7 . . . .**190** D7
Well St NN9 . . . .**111** F5
Wells The NN9 . . . .**111** F5
Well Yd NN2 . . . .**141** B3
Welsh Rd
Aston le W NN11 . . . .**182** C8
Chipping Warden OX17 . . .**197** C6
WELTON **119** E1
Welton CE Prim Sch
NN11 . . . .**119** E1
Welton La NN11 . . . .**135** D6
Welton Pk NN11 . . . .**119** E1
Welton Pl CV22 . . . .**98** D8
Welton Rd
Braunston NN11 . . . .**118** D1
Daventry NN11 . . . .**135** C3
Wenlock Way NN5 . . . .**140** D1
Wensleydale NN2 . . . .**140** F5
Wensleydale Pk NN17 . . . . .**36** D8
Wentin Cl NN18 . . . .**36** C1
Wentworth Ave NN8 . . . . .**129** C7
Wentworth Cl NN11 . . . . . .**135** E3
Wentworth Cotts
MK18 . . . .**227** A5
Wentworth Dr PE8 . . . .**41** E7
Wentworth Rd
Finedon NN9 . . . .**112** A5
Rushden NN10 . . . .**132** A2
Wentworth Way
Northampton NN2 . . . .**141** E3
Stoke Bruerne NN12 . . . . .**204** F8
Weskers Cl LE16 . . . .**67** A7
Wesley Ct NN9 . . . .**114** D6
Wesley Pl OX17 . . . .**208** E4
Wesley Rd CV21 . . . .**99** A8
Wessex Cl NN16 . . . .**72** B6
Wessex Way NN3 . . . .**142** B1
West Ave NN15 . . . .**92** B3
West Bank NN3 . . . .**142** E6
Westbrook NN8 . . . .**129** B4
West Brook
Blisworth NN7 . . . .**190** D8
Newnham NN11 . . . .**153** D4
WESTBURY **234** F4
Westbury Cl NN5 . . . .**158** D7
Westbury Mill NN11 . . . . . .**234** F4
Westbury Wlk NN18 . . . .**36** B6
West Cotton Cl NN4 . . . . .**159** C4
Westcott Way
Corby NN18 . . . .**36** D5
Northampton NN3 . . . .**160** E7
West Cres NN10 . . . .**131** E2
West Ct NN11 . . . .**135** C1
West End
Bugbrooke NN7 . . . .**172** E7
Scaldwell NN6 . . . .**106** F5
Silverstone NN12 . . . .**214** C4
Welford NN6 . . . .**64** D4
West Haddon NN6 . . . .**102** B4
Westerburgh Sq
NN11 . . . .**153** C8
Westerdale NN2 . . . .**140** F5
Western Ave
Daventry NN11 . . . .**153** B8
Easton le H PE9 . . . .**1** F5
Market Harborough
LE16 . . . .**31** D1
Nether Heyford NN7 . . . . .**156** B1
Western La NN11 . . . .**135** B2
Western Dr MK19 . . . .**207** A3
Western View NN1 . . . .**159** B5
Western Way NN8 . . . .**129** D3
West Farm Cl NN6 . . . .**108** C3
West Farm Dr LE15 . . . .**3** E5
WEST FARNDON **183** F3

Westfield Ave
Deanshanger MK19 . . . . . .**228** D5
Rauns NN9 . . . .**114** B4
Rushden NN10 . . . .**131** F2
Westfield Barns CV47 . . . .**166** D7
Westfield Cl LE16 . . . .**31** C3
Westfield Cres NN6 . . . .**64** E6
Westfield Ctr NN13 . . . . . .**233** E8
Westfield Dr NN9 . . . .**114** B4
Westfield Ho 8 NN16 . . . . . .**72** B2
Westfield Pl NN10 . . . .**131** F2
Westfield Rd
Northampton, Duston
NN5. . . . .**158** B8
Northampton NN5 . . . .**158** F6
Wellingborough NN8 . . . . .**129** E4
Westfields
Little Harrowden NN9 . . . . .**110** B3
Wellingborough NN8 . . . . .**130** D3
West Fields PE9 . . . .**1** F5
Westfields Ave NN10 . . . . .**132** B5
Westfields Rd NN17 . . . .**36** E8
Westfields St NN10 . . . . . .**132** B5
Westfields Terr NN10 . . . . .**132** B5
West Furlong NN15 . . . .**71** F1
Westgate La LE16 . . . .**30** E3
Westgate Rd NN5 . . . .**158** D6
West Glebe Rd NN17 . . . . . .**36** F7
WEST HADDON **102** C4
West Haddon Endowed CE
Prim Sch NN6 . . . .**102** B4
West Haddon Rd
Cold Ashby NN6 . . . .**84** A5
Crick NN6 . . . .**101** B6
Guilsborough NN6 . . . .**103** D7
Ravensthorpe NN6 . . . . . .**103** C1
Watford NN6 . . . .**120** D7
Westhaven PE9 . . . .**2** A5
Westhill Ave NN13 . . . .**233** E7
Westhill Cl
Brackley NN13 . . . .**233** E7
Kettering NN15 . . . .**71** F1
Westhill Dr NN15 . . . .**71** F1
Westhill Gdns NN13 . . . . . .**233** D7
WESTHORP **183** C7
Westhorp OX17 . . . .**210** E2
Westhorpe
Ashley LE16 . . . .**18** E2
Sibbertoft LE16 . . . .**46** F2
Westhorpe La NN11 . . . . . .**183** C7
Westhorpe Mews
NN11 . . . .**183** C6
Westland Cl LE16 . . . .**30** E3
Westlea Rd NN6 . . . .**127** D3
Westleigh Cl NN1 . . . .**159** F8
Westleigh Pk NN3 . . . .**141** E6
Westleigh Rd NN15 . . . .**92** B8
Westley Cl NN15 . . . .**92** B1
West Leys Ct NN3 . . . .**142** C7
West Lodge Rural Ctr ★
NN14. . . . .**51** C6
West March NN11 . . . .**153** D7
Westmead Ct NN3 . . . .**142** F1
West Mill PE9 . . . .**1** F4
Westminster Cl NN13 . . . . .**234** A7
Westminster Cres
NN13 . . . .**234** A7
Westminster Croft
NN13 . . . .**233** F7
Westminster Dr NN15 . . . . . .**91** F7
Westminster Rd
Brackley NN13 . . . .**233** F6
Wellingborough NN8 . . . . .**129** E7
Westminster Wlk
NN18 . . . .**36** C4
Westmoreland Cl PE8 . . . . .**15** E5
Westmorland Dr NN14 . . . . .**51** C4
WESTON **200** A2
WESTON BY WELLAND
. . . .**18** A3
Westone Ave NN3 . . . .**142** E1
WESTON FAVELL **160** E8
Weston Favell CE Prim
Sch NN3 . . . .**142** D1
Weston Favell Ctr
NN3. . . . .**142** F2
Weston Favell Sch
NN3. . . . .**142** D3
Weston Mill La NN3 . . . . . .**160** E6
Weston Rd
Ashley LE16 . . . .**18** D3
Olney MK46 . . . .**195** D3
Ravenstone MK46 . . . .**194** E2
Sulgrave OX17 . . . .**211** A8
Sutton Bassett LE16 . . . . . .**18** A2
Welham LE16 . . . .**17** F5
WESTON UNDERWOOD
. . . .**195** A2
Westonville PE9 . . . .**1** D2
Weston Way NN3 . . . .**160** C8
Weston Wlk NN18 . . . .**36** C6
West Oval NN5 . . . .**140** F1
Westover Rd NN15 . . . .**71** F1
West Paddock Ct
NN3 . . . .**142** F4
West Priors Ct NN3 . . . . . .**143** A4
West Ridge NN2 . . . .**141** D3
West Rising NN4 . . . .**175** D7
West Side Side Rise MK46 .**195** F4
West St
Broughton NN14 . . . .**90** A5
Earls Barton NN6 . . . .**144** E4
Easton o t H PE9 . . . .**2** A5
Ecton NN6 . . . .**143** F4
Geddington NN14 . . . .**54** A3
Kettering NN16 . . . .**72** B1
King's Cliffe PE8 . . . .**13** E7

West St *continued*
Long Buckby NN6. . . . .**121** A4
Moulton NN3 . . . .**126** C1
Northampton NN1 . . . .**159** F6
Olney MK46 . . . .**195** F4
Oundle PE8 . . . .**41** F5
Rauns NN9 . . . .**114** D6
Rushden NN10 . . . .**132** B2
Stanwick NN9 . . . .**113** E3
Weedon Bec NN7. . . . .**155** B3
Welford NN6 . . . .**64** E6
Wellingborough NN8 . . . . .**129** F4
Woodford NN14 . . . .**94** C7
West View
Corby NN17 . . . .**37** B7
Daventry NN11 . . . .**135** B1
Westvilla Cotts NN8 . . . . .**129** F4
West Villa Rd NN8 . . . .**129** F4
Westway NN15 . . . .**71** F1
West Way
Earls Barton NN6 . . . .**144** D5
Weedon Bec NN7. . . . .**155** B3
Westway The NN11 . . . . . .**153** D8
Westwood Rd CV22 . . . .**98** F7
Westwood Way NN3 . . . . .**142** D1
Westwood Wlk NN18. . . . . . .**36** C5
Wetenhall Rd NN9 . . . .**114** A4
Wetheral Cl NN3 . . . .**142** C4
Weymouth Cl NN18 . . . .**36** B6
Whaddon Cl NN4 . . . .**158** E1
Whaddon Field NN6 . . . . .**106** C1
Whalley Gr NN7 . . . .**161** F6
Wharf Cl MK19. . . . .**229** B7
Wharfedale Rd NN17 . . . . . .**21** E1
Wharfe Gn NN5 . . . .**140** F2
Wharf La
Old Stratford MK19 . . . . . .**229** C7
Souldern OX27. . . . .**237** B4
Wharf Rd NN10 . . . .**132** B6
Wharton Cl NN8 . . . .**129** F5
Wheat Cl NN11 . . . .**135** C6
Wheatcroft Gdns
NN10 . . . .**132** C2
Wheatens Cl NN6 . . . .**125** C8
Wheatfield Dr NN15. . . . . . .**92** C2
Wheatfield Gdns NN3 . . . .**142** B1
Wheatfield Rd NN3 . . . . . .**142** B1
Wheatfield Rd N NN3. . . . .**142** B2
Wheatfield Rd S NN3. . . . .**142** B1
Wheatfield Terr NN3 . . . . .**142** B1
Wheatley Ave NN17 . . . .**36** F6
Wheeler's Rise NN13 . . . . .**238** C8
Wheel La LE15 . . . .**3** C1
Wheelwright Cl NN9 . . . . .**114** E7
Wheelwright Ho NN14 . . . . .**70** D7
Wheelwrights Way
MK19 . . . .**229** C7
Wheelwrights Yd
NN29 . . . .**164** D2
Whernside NN8 . . . .**129** B4
Whernside Way NN5 . . . . .**158** C8
WHILTON **137** D6
Whilton Lo NN11 . . . .**136** D8
WHILTON LOCKS **136** F6
Whilton Mill ★ NN11 . . . . .**137** C6
Whilton Rd
Great Brington NN7 . . . . . .**138** C7
Northampton NN2 . . . .**141** D4
Whistlefield Cotts
NN6 . . . .**143** C7
Whistlets Cl NN4. . . . .**158** D1
WHISTON **162** D6
Whiston Rd
Cogenhoe NN7. . . . .**162** C6
Denton NN7. . . . .**162** B2
Northampton NN2 . . . .**141** D4
Whitby Cl NN15 . . . .**91** F8
Whitecroft Gdns
NN11 . . . .**184** B7
White Delves NN8 . . . .**129** E7
White Doe Dr NN3 . . . .**142** C7
Whitefield Rd NN5 . . . .**140** C1
Whitefield Way NN4 . . . . .**114** C7
Whiteford Dr NN15 . . . .**91** C7
Whitefriars NN10 . . . .**131** F1
Whitefriars Jun & Inf Schs
NN10 . . . .**147** F8
Whitegates NN4 . . . .**158** D1
Whiteheart Cl NN3. . . . . . .**143** B2
Whitehill MK46 . . . .**195** D5
Whitehill Rd NN14 . . . .**50** E3
WHITE HILLS **141** B6
White Hills Cres NN2. . . . .**141** A6
Whitehills Prim Sch
NN2. . . . .**141** A6
White Hills Way NN2 . . . . .**141** B6
White Horse Yd
Stony Stratford MK11 . . . . .**229** D5
Towcester NN12 . . . .**203** C6
White House Ct NN10 . . . . .**132** C1
White House Ind Est
NN6. . . . .**144** D6
Whiteland Rd NN3 . . . .**142** C2
Whiteman La NN14 . . . .**70** C7
White Post Ct NN17 . . . .**21** E2
Whitesands Way NN4 . . . .**158** C2
Whitethorns Cl LE17 . . . . . .**62** B3
White Way NN6 . . . .**144** E5
WHITFIELD **223** B3
Whitfield Way NN2. . . . . . .**141** D5
Whiting Ct NN3 . . . .**142** C8
Whitmees Ct MK46. . . . . . .**195** E4
Whitmore Ct NN12. . . . . . .**214** D5
Whitney Cl NN9 . . . .**114** C5
Whitney Rd NN15 . . . .**92** B1
Whitsundale Cl NN9 . . . . .**111** F4
Whittall St OX17 . . . .**230** F5

Whittam Cl NN9 . . . .**114** C7
Whittemore Rd NN10 . . . . .**132** D3
WHITTLEBURY **215** C4
Whittlebury CE Prim Sch
NN12. . . . .**215** C4
Whittlebury Cl NN2 . . . . . .**141** D5
Whittlebury Ct NN12. . . . . .**215** C5
Whittlebury Rd NN12 . . . . .**214** E5
Whittle Cl
Daventry NN11 . . . .**135** A5
Wellingborough NN8 . . . . .**129** B6
Whittle Rd NN17 . . . .**37** B8
Whittles Cross NN4 . . . . . .**176** A6
Whittlesea Terr NN14. . . . . .**94** D6
Whitton Cl OX17 . . . .**210** E2
Whittons La NN12. . . . .**203** C6
Whitwell Cl PE8 . . . .**41** E5
Whitworth Ave NN17 . . . . . .**37** A8
Whitworth Cres NN6 . . . . .**144** E5
Whitworth Rd
Northampton NN1 . . . .**159** F7
Wellingborough NN8 . . . . .**130** C5
Whitworth Way
Irthlingborough NN9 . . . . .**131** E8
Wellingborough NN8 . . . . .**130** B2
Whytewell Rd NN8 . . . .**129** F6
Wick Cl NN18 . . . .**36** D3
WICKEN **228** A3
Wicken Park Rd
MK19. . . . .**228** B1
Wicken Rd MK18. . . . .**227** E1
Wickery Dene NN4. . . . . . .**176** A6
Wicksteed Cl NN15 . . . .**91** C6
Wicksteed L Pk ★
NN15. . . . .**91** D6
Wiggins Cl CV21 . . . .**99** B8
WIGSTHORPE **59** B2
Wigston Rd 3 CV21. . . . . . .**80** A1
WILBARSTON **34** D5
Wilbarston CE Prim Sch
LE16 . . . .**34** C5
Wilbarston Rd LE16 . . . .**34** B4
Wilberforce St 3
NN1 . . . .**159** E6
WILBY **129** A1
Wilby CE Prim Sch
NN8. . . . .**129** B1
Wilby Cl NN17 . . . .**36** B8
Wilbye Grange NN8. . . . . .**129** D2
Wilby La NN29. . . . .**145** D6
Wilby Park Mobile Home
Pk NN8 . . . .**129** C2
Wilby Rd NN6 . . . .**128** D2
Wilby St NN1 . . . .**159** F6
Wilby Way NN8 . . . .**129** D1
Wilce Ave NN8. . . . .**130** A1
Wildacre Rd NN10 . . . .**131** E2
Wild Cherry Cl NN11 . . . . .**184** B6
Wildern La NN4. . . . .**175** C5
Wilford Ave NN3. . . . .**160** F8
Wilkie Cl NN15 . . . .**90** F8
Wilkie Rd NN8 . . . .**129** F8
Wilks Wlk NN4 . . . .**175** E3
Willetts Cl NN17 . . . .**36** E8
Willey Cl MK11 . . . .**229** F4
William Rd NN6. . . . .**121** B3
Williams Cl MK19 . . . .**206** F3
WILLIAMSCOT **208** C8
Williamscot Hill OX17 . . . .**208** B6
Williamscot Road Ind Ctr
OX17. . . . .**196** A1
William St
Burton Latimer NN15 . . . . .**92** B2
Finedon NN9 . . . .**112** A4
Kettering NN16 . . . .**72** B4
Northampton NN1 . . . .**159** D7
William Steele Way
NN10 . . . .**132** C5
Williams Terr NN11 . . . . . .**135** B2
Williams Way
Higham Ferrers NN10 . . . .**132** B5
Northampton NN4 . . . .**175** E3
William's Way NN29. . . . . .**146** E1
William Trigg Cl NN9 . . . . .**131** E8
Willis Way NN12 . . . .**203** C5
Williton Cl NN3 . . . .**160** D7
Willmott Rd NN10. . . . .**148** C8
WILLOUGHBY **117** C3
Willoughby Cl NN11 . . . . . .**135** B3
Willoughby Pl CV22 . . . .**98** D7
Willoughby Rd LE15. . . . .**3** A6
Willoughby Way NN7 . . . . .**177** A1
Willowbrook Appartments
The NN8 . . . .**130** B4
Willowbrook East Ind Est
NN17. . . . .**22** C2
Willow Brook Rd NN17 . . . .**36** C8
Willow Brook Sq
NN3 . . . .**143** D2
Willow Cl
Desborough NN14 . . . .**51** C3
Hinton NN11 . . . .**184** A6
Spratton NN6 . . . .**124** A8
Towcester NN12 . . . .**203** C5
Willow Cres
Great Houghton NN4 . . . . .**160** F2
Market Harborough
LE16 . . . .**31** C2
Willow Ct NN1 . . . .**160** A7
Willow Gr NN3 . . . .**229** B6
Willow Herb Cl NN10. . . . .**148** C2
Willow Herb Wlk NN14. . . . .**51** A4
Willow La
Great Houghton NN4. . . . . .**160** E2
King's Cliffe PE8 . . . .**13** F7
Stanion NN14. . . . .**37** F2
Stony Stratford MK11 . . . . .**229** C5

Willow Rd
Brackley NN13. . . . .**234** A6
Kettering NN15 . . . .**72** C1
Willow Rise NN3 . . . .**161** B8
Willows Hill NN12. . . . .**201** F5
Willows The
Daventry NN11 . . . .**135** C4
Kings Sutton OX17. . . . . . .**231** A6
Little Harrowden NN9 . . . . .**110** B3
Silverstone NN12. . . . .**214** C5
Thrapston NN14 . . . .**76** C1
Willow Tree Gdns
CV21 . . . .**99** A8
Willow View NN7 . . . .**157** C3
Wills Cl NN6 . . . .**103** E7
Willson Cl LE16 . . . .**32** A3
Wilmington Wlk 1
NN18 . . . .**36** B5
Wilson Cl NN11 . . . .**135** A4
Wilson Cres NN9. . . . .**112** E1
Wilson Rd 5 NN10 . . . .**132** A2
Wilson Terr NN16 . . . .**72** B4
Wilson Way NN6 . . . .**144** E3
Wilton Cl NN14 . . . .**51** A2
Wilton Rd NN15. . . . .**91** F8
Wimbledon St NN5 . . . . . .**159** A6
Wimborne Cl NN3 . . . .**143** D3
Wimborne Pl NN11 . . . .**135** C5
Wimborne Wlk NN18. . . . . . .**36** A7
Wimpole NN8 . . . .**129** C4
Wimpole Ho 5 NN11. . . . . .**135** B7
Wincanton Cl NN18 . . . .**36** B6
Wincely Cl NN11 . . . .**135** C6
Winchester Cl NN4. . . . . . .**159** C1
Winchester House Sch
NN13. . . . .**233** F7
Winchester Rd
Northampton NN4 . . . .**159** C1
Rushden NN10 . . . .**132** C1
Winchilsea Dr NN17 . . . .**10** B1
Windermere Cl NN11. . . . . .**135** B2
Windermere Dr
Higham Ferrers NN10 . . . .**132** B8
Wellingborough NN8 . . . . .**129** C6
Windermere Rd NN16 . . . . .**71** F2
Windermere Way
NN3 . . . .**142** C4
Windflower Pl 2
NN3 . . . .**143** D2
Windgate Way PE8. . . . .**8** A2
Windingbrook La
NN4 . . . .**175** C5
Winding Way NN14 . . . .**76** E2
Windmill Ave
Blisworth NN7 . . . .**190** F8
Kettering NN15, NN16. . . . .**72** C2
Rauns NN9 . . . .**114** D6
Windmill Banks NN10. . . . .**132** C2
Windmill Bsns Ctr 7
NN10. . . . .**132** A2
Windmill Cl
Cottingham LE16 . . . .**20** C1
Wellingborough NN8 . . . . .**129** E2
Wollaston NN29. . . . .**146** E2
Windmill Cotts NN15. . . . . .**92** B4
Windmill Ct NN16. . . . .**72** D3
Windmill Gdns NN11 . . . . .**152** C7
Windmill Glade NN6 . . . . .**106** A1
Windmill Gr NN9 . . . .**114** D6
Windmill La
Denton NN7. . . . .**178** B8
Rauns NN9 . . . .**114** C6
Staverton NN11 . . . .**152** C7
Windmill Prim Sch
NN9. . . . .**114** C7
Windmill Rd
Irthlingborough NN9 . . . . .**112** E1
Rushden NN10 . . . .**132** A2
Windmill Rise LE16 . . . .**20** D1
Windmill Terr NN7. . . . . . .**141** D4
Windmill Way
Greens Norton NN12. . . . .**202** D8
Lyddington LE15 . . . .**9** C3
Windmill Wlk NN15 . . . .**72** C1
Windrush Rd NN4. . . . .**175** F8
Windrush Way NN5 . . . . . .**141** A2
Windsor Ave NN14 . . . .**50** F2
Windsor Cl
Daventry NN11 . . . .**135** B1
Kings Sutton OX17. . . . . . .**230** F6
Long Buckby NN6. . . . .**121** B3
Towcester NN12 . . . .**203** B4
Weedon Bec NN7. . . . .**155** B4
Wilbarston LE16 . . . .**34** C4
Windsor Cres NN5 . . . .**158** E6
Windsor Ct
Market Harborough
LE16 . . . .**31** D4
Northampton NN3 . . . .**143** C2
Windsor Dr
Brackley NN13. . . . .**233** E8
Thrapston NN14 . . . .**76** E2
Windsor Gdns NN16. . . . . . .**72** A2
Windsor Ho NN5 . . . .**158** C8
Windsor Pl NN17 . . . .**36** E5
Windsor Rd
Rushden NN10. . . . .**132** C3
Wellingborough NN8 . . . . .**129** F1
Windyridge NN2 . . . .**141** D3
Winemar Cl MK19 . . . .**207** A3
Wingate Cl NN15 . . . .**72** E1
Wing Rd LE15. . . . .**3** A6
Winnington Cl NN3 . . . . . .**143** C5
Winsford Way NN3 . . . . . .**160** D7
Winsland Ct NN6 . . . .**126** E8
Winstanley Rd NN8. . . . . . .**130** B5
Winston Cl
Nether Heyford NN7 . . . . .**156** B1

Winston Cl continued
Northampton NN3 . . . . **142** C5
Woodford Halse NN11 . . . . **184** D5
Winston Cres NN13 . . . . **233** F6
Winston Dr NN14 . . . . **91** D1
Winter Bourne Ct
NN18 . . . . **36** B6
Winterburn Ct NN16 . . . . **71** E3
Winthorpe Way NN18 . . . **36** C6
WINWICK **102** B8
Winwick Rd PE28 . . . . **61** D1
Winwood Cl MK19 . . . . . **228** E5
Wire La LE16 . . . . **19** D2
Wisley Cl NN4 . . . . **175** C7
Wisteria Cl NN10 . . . . . . **148** B7
Wisteria Way NN3 . . . . . **160** C6
Witham Gn NN5 . . . . **140** E2
Witham Ho NN2 . . . . **141** E1
Witham The NN11 . . . . . . **134** F1
Witham Way NN5 . . . . . . **140** F1
Witham Wlk NN5 . . . . . . **140** F2
Witheys The NN4 . . . . . . **175** F2
WITTERING **7** D8
Wittlich Rd NN8 . . . . **130** B6
Witton Rd NN5 . . . . **158** C8
Woburn Cl LE16 . . . . **32** A3
Woburn Ct NN10 . . . . . . **148** A8
Woburn Gate NN3 . . . . . **143** D3
Wodhams Dr NN13 . . . . . **222** E1
Wold Farm Ind Pk
NN6 . . . . **107** D7
Wold Rd NN15 . . . . **92** E2
Wolfe Cl NN15 . . . . **72** F1
WOLLASTON **146** F2
Wollaston Com Prim Sch
NN29 . . . . **146** D2
Wollaston Mus★
NN29 . . . . **146** D2
Wollaston Rd
Bozeat NN29 . . . . **164** C5
Irchester NN29 . . . . **146** F6
Wollaston Sch NN29 . . . . **146** E2
Wollaton Gdns 🔢
NN3 . . . . **160** F8
Wollongong Ho NN17 . . . . **36** F8
Wolsey Cl NN6 . . . . **101** A6
Wolverton Rd MK11 . . . . **229** E6
Wood Avens Cl NN4 . . . . **158** C1
Woodbine Cotts NN6 . . . **108** A5
Woodborough Gdns 🔢
NN3 . . . . **160** F8
Woodbreach Dr LE16 . . . . **32** B3
WOOD BURCOTE **203** C2
Woodcock St NN15 . . . . . **92** D3
Woodcote Ave NN3 . . . . . **142** A5
Woodcroft Cl NN12 . . . . **203** C3
Woodcroft Way NN15 . . . **91** C8
WOODEND **200** F7
WOODEND GREEN **200** E6
Woodfield PE9 . . . . **1** D1
Woodfield Gr NN17 . . . . . **36** E7
WOODFORD **94** C6
Woodford CE Prim Sch
NN14 . . . . **94** D6
Woodford Chase NN6 . . . **127** C2
Woodford Cl NN15 . . . . . . **91** F5
Woodford Glebe NN6 . . . . **64** E5
WOODFORD HALSE **184** C6
Woodford Halse CE Sch
NN11 . . . . **184** D6
Woodford La NN14 . . . . . . **75** E6

Woodford Rd
Byfield NN11 . . . . **183** D7
Eydon NN11 . . . . **184** B2
Great Addington NN14 . . . . **94** C1
Little Addington NN14 . . . . **94** C3
Woodford St 🔢 NN1 . . . . **159** E6
Woodford Wlk 🔢
NN1 . . . . **159** E6
Woodgate LE16 . . . . **30** E8
Woodgate Cl LE16 . . . . . . **32** B2
Woodgate Rd NN4 . . . . . **175** F6
WOOD GREEN **224** F1
Woodhall Cl NN4 . . . . . . **158** D1
Wood Hill NN1 . . . . **159** D5
Woodhill Rd NN5 . . . . . . **140** C1
Wood La
Hartwell NN7 . . . . **192** E2
King's Cliffe PE8 . . . . **13** E7
Oundle PE8 . . . . **41** D4
Weston Underwood
MK46 . . . . **195** A2
Woodland Ave
Kettering NN15 . . . . **92** A5
Northampton NN3 . . . . . . **142** A1
Overstone NN6 . . . . **127** B1
Woodland Dr NN5 . . . . . . **140** B1
Woodland Dr NN15 . . . . . **92** C4
Woodland Hospl The
NN16 . . . . **71** B5
Woodland Rd NN10 . . . . **132** A3
Woodlands NN4 . . . . **175** E1
Woodlands Ave NN17 . . . . **21** F1
Woodlands Cl NN14 . . . . . **55** F7
Woodlands Ct
🔢 Kettering NN16 . . . . **72** C4
Watford NN6 . . . . **120** C6
Woodlands Grange
NN6 . . . . **145** A4
Woodlands La NN18 . . . . . **53** C8
Woodlands Mews
NN14 . . . . **55** F7
Woodlands Rd
Irchester NN29 . . . . **147** A7
Weldon NN17 . . . . **38** C7
Woodlands The
Geddington NN14 . . . . **54** B3
Market Harborough
LE16 . . . . **31** C4
Silverstone NN12 . . . . . . **214** D4
Stanwick NN9 . . . . **114** A3
Staverton NN11 . . . . **152** B7
Woodland View Prim Sch
NN4 . . . . **175** E3
Woodland Wlk NN3 . . . . **143** B6
Woodleigh Pl NN17 . . . . . **36** E6
Woodley Chase NN5 . . . . **140** B1
Woodmans Cl MK19 . . . . **228** E4
WOODNEWTON **14** F2
Woodnewton Inf Sch
NN17 . . . . **36** C8
Woodnewton Rd PE8 . . . . **15** D4
Woodnewton Way
NN17 . . . . **36** C7
Woodpecker Cl NN13 . . . **222** D1
Woodpecker Way NN4 . . **174** F7
Wood Rd PE8 . . . . **13** F7
Woodrush Way NN3 . . . . **142** C7
Woods Ct
Brackley NN13 . . . . **233** D7
Rushden NN10 . . . . **132** B3

Woodsfield NN6 . . . . **106** A2
Woodside
Stony Stratford MK11 . . . . **229** E6
Sywell NN6 . . . . **127** D1
Woodside Ave NN3 . . . . . **142** D4
Woodside Cres NN3 . . . . **142** D4
Woodside Gn NN5 . . . . . **140** F1
Woodside Pk NN17 . . . . . . **38** C7
Woodside Way NN5 . . . . **140** F1
Woodside Wlk NN5 . . . . **140** E1
Woods La NN12 . . . . **217** E3
Wood St
Corby NN17 . . . . **36** E6
Geddington NN14 . . . . **54** B3
Higham Ferrers NN10 . . . . **132** C5
Kettering NN16 . . . . **72** C4
Northampton NN1 . . . . . . **159** D6
Wellingborough NN8 . . . . **129** F4
Woodstock 🔢 NN1 . . . . . **159** F6
Woodstock Cl NN8 . . . . . **129** E7
Woodvale Prim Sch
NN3 . . . . **143** A5
Woodville Cres NN12 . . . **217** E6
Woodward Cl NN11 . . . . **135** E1
WOODWELL **94** A8
Woodwell Cotts NN4 . . . . **94** A8
Woodwell Hill NN14 . . . . . **50** F2
Woodyard Cl NN14 . . . . . **55** F8
Woodyard The NN7 . . . . **163** A3
Wooldale Rd NN4 . . . . . . **175** E4
Woolmans MK11 . . . . **229** F4
Woolmonger St 🔢
NN1 . . . . **159** C5
Woolrich Gdns MK11 . . . **229** E5
Woolscott Rd CV23 . . . . **117** C4
Woolston Ct NN17 . . . . . . **10** C1
WOOTTON **175** F5
Wootton Brook Cl
NN4 . . . . **175** C6
Wootton Ct NN12 . . . . . **203** D5
WOOTTON HALL **175** C8
Wootton Hall Pk NN7 . . **175** D8
Wootton Hill Farm
NN4 . . . . **174** F8
Wootton Hope Dr
NN4 . . . . **175** F6
Wootton Prim Sch
NN4 . . . . **175** E4
Wootton Rd NN7 . . . . . . **176** A2
Wootton Trad Est
NN4 . . . . **175** F6
Worcester Cl
Corby NN18 . . . . **36** E1
Northampton NN3 . . . . . . **143** B2
West Haddon NN6 . . . . . . **102** C5
Worcester Dr LE16 . . . . . . **31** E5
Worcester Way NN11 . . . **153** C7
Wordsworth Ave NN17 . . . **21** D1
Wordsworth Cl
Brackley NN13 . . . . **222** F1
Towcester NN12 . . . . **203** B5
Wordsworth Rd
Daventry NN11 . . . . **135** B3
Kettering NN16 . . . . **72** C5
Wellingborough NN8 . . . . **129** B3
Worksop Gdns NN18 . . . . **36** B6
Works The 🔢 NN1 . . . . . **159** E6
WORMLEIGHTON **181** B8
Wormleighton Way
NN14 . . . . **54** A3
Worthing Rd NN18 . . . . . . **36** B5

WOTHORPE **2** D8
Wothorpe Hill PE9 . . . . . . **2** C7
Wothorpe Villas PE9 . . . . . **2** D8
Wrekin Cl NN4 . . . . **158** E3
Wrenbury Rd NN5 . . . . . **140** A1
Wren Cl
Brackley NN13 . . . . **222** D1
Corby NN18 . . . . **36** E3
Kettering NN15 . . . . **92** A6
Northampton NN4 . . . . . . **175** F3
Towcester NN12 . . . . **203** C3
Wrendyke Cl LE15 . . . . **3** A6
Wrenn Sch
Wellingborough NN8 . . . . **130** A3
Wellingborough NN8 . . . . **130** B3
*Wren Spinney Com Specl
Sch* NN15 . . . . **71** F1
Wrightons Hill NN13 . . . . **211** F4
Wright Rd NN6 . . . . **121** B3
Wroe Cl NN18 . . . . **36** C1
Wroe The NN10 . . . . **132** B7
Wyatt St NN16 . . . . **72** C2
Wyatt Way PE8 . . . . **41** E6
Wychwood Cl NN5 . . . . . **140** A1
Wyckley Cl NN9 . . . . **112** E3
Wycliffe Rd NN1 . . . . . . **160** A6
Wye Cl NN8 . . . . **129** C6
Wye The NN11 . . . . **153** A8
Wykeham Rd NN10 . . . . **132** C7
Wyman Cl NN29 . . . . **164** D2
Wymersley Cl NN4 . . . . . **160** F2
WYMINGTON **148** B5
Wymington Pk NN10 . . . **132** B1
Wymington Rd
Podington NN29 . . . . **147** E3
Rushden NN10 . . . . **148** B8
Wyndham Way NN16 . . . . **71** E4
Wysall Rd NN3 . . . . **143** B5

Y

Yaffle Cres NN14 . . . . **51** B4
Yardley Cl NN17 . . . . **21** D1
Yardley Dr NN2 . . . . **141** D6
YARDLEY GOBION **217** E5
*Yardley Gobion CE Prim
Sch* NN12 . . . . **217** E6
YARDLEY HASTINGS **179** B6
Yardley Hastings Prim Sch
NN7 . . . . **179** A7
Yardley Rd
Cosgrove MK19 . . . . **218** D2
Grendon NN7 . . . . **163** D4
Olney MK46 . . . . **195** F5
Yardley Gobion NN12 . . . . **217** F4
Yarrow NN8 . . . . **129** B3
Yarrow Cl NN10 . . . . **148** C7
Yarrow Ho NN2 . . . . **141** C5
YARWELL **16** A8
Yarwell Ct NN15 . . . . **91** C6
Yarwell Junc★ PE8 . . . . **16** B7
Yarwell Rd PE8 . . . . **8** A3
Yarwell Sq NN4 . . . . **158** F2
Yateley Dr NN15 . . . . **92** A5
YELDEN **133** F3
Yelden Cl NN10 . . . . **131** F2
Yeldon Ct NN8 . . . . **111** B1
YELVERTOFT **82** C4

Yelvertoft Prim Sch
NN6 . . . . **82** B4
Yelvertoft Rd
Crick NN6 . . . . **101** A8
Lilbourne CV23 . . . . **81** D6
Northampton NN2 . . . . . . **141** C3
West Haddon NN6 . . . . . . **102** B5
Yeoman Cl NN14 . . . . **95** A3
Yeoman Dr NN2 . . . . **141** B5
Yeoman Mdw NN4 . . . . . **174** F8
Yeomanry Cl NN11 . . . . . **135** B1
Yeomanry Ct LE16 . . . . . . **31** E3
Yeomanry Way NN11 . . . **135** B1
Yeomans Cl NN13 . . . . . . **234** A8
Yeomans Ct NN15 . . . . . . **92** C2
Yew Cl NN17 . . . . **21** E1
Yew Tree Cl
Middleton Cheney
OX17 . . . . **220** A8
Yewtree Ct NN3 . . . . **142** D5
Yew Tree Gdns NN7 . . . . **155** F5
Yew Tree Gr NN11 . . . . . **153** B8
Yew Tree La NN6 . . . . . . **124** B8
Yew Tree Rise NN13 . . . . **238** D8
York Ave NN7 . . . . **161** F6
York Cl
Higham Ferrers
NN10 . . . . **132** C7
Towcester NN12 . . . . **203** C4
York Ct NN12 . . . . **203** C5
York Dr NN13 . . . . **233** E8
Yorke Cl NN9 . . . . **111** E5
York Ho NN1 . . . . **159** F6
York Rd
Corby NN18 . . . . **36** C5
Higham Ferrers NN10 . . . . **132** C2
Kettering NN16 . . . . **72** B2
Northampton NN1 . . . . . . **159** E6
Rushden NN10 . . . . **132** C1
Stony Stratford MK11 . . . . **229** D5
Wellingborough NN8 . . . . **130** B5
Wollaston NN29 . . . . **146** D3
York Ride NN7 . . . . **155** B4
York St LE16 . . . . **31** F3
York Way NN9 . . . . **114** C7

Z

Zion Hill NN6 . . . . **108** A5

Addresses

Name and Address	Telephone	Page	Grid reference

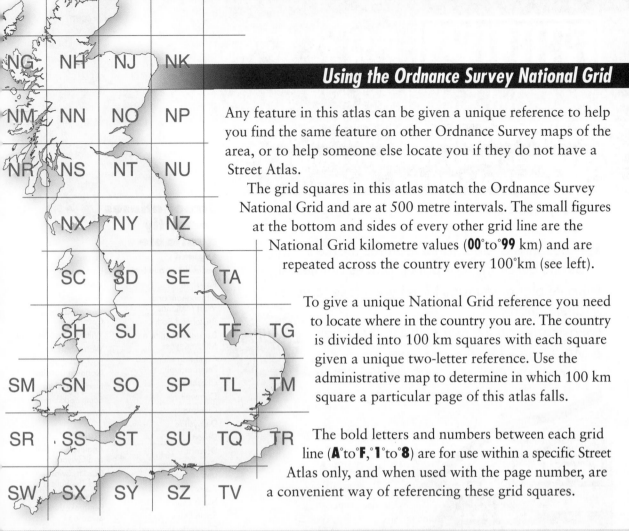

Any feature in this atlas can be given a unique reference to help you find the same feature on other Ordnance Survey maps of the area, or to help someone else locate you if they do not have a Street Atlas.

The grid squares in this atlas match the Ordnance Survey National Grid and are at 500 metre intervals. The small figures at the bottom and sides of every other grid line are the National Grid kilometre values (**00**° to °**99** km) and are repeated across the country every 100°km (see left).

To give a unique National Grid reference you need to locate where in the country you are. The country is divided into 100 km squares with each square given a unique two-letter reference. Use the administrative map to determine in which 100 km square a particular page of this atlas falls.

The bold letters and numbers between each grid line (**A**° to °**F**, °**1** to °**8**) are for use within a specific Street Atlas only, and when used with the page number, are a convenient way of referencing these grid squares.

Example   The railway bridge over DARLEY GREEN RD in grid square B1

Step 1: Identify the two-letter reference, in this example the page is in **SP**

Step 2: Identify the 1 km square in which the railway bridge falls. Use the figures in the southwest corner of this square: Eastings **17**, Northings **74**. This gives a unique reference: **SP 17 74**, accurate to 1°km.

Step 3: To give a more precise reference accurate to 100 m you need to estimate how many tenths along and how many tenths up this 1 km square the feature is (to help with this the 1 km square is divided into four 500 m squares). This makes the bridge about **8** tenths along and about **1** tenth up from the southwest corner.

This gives a unique reference: **SP 178 741**, accurate to 100°m.

Eastings (read from left to right along the bottom) come before Northings (read from bottom to top). If you have trouble remembering say to yourself Along the hall, THEN up the stairs !

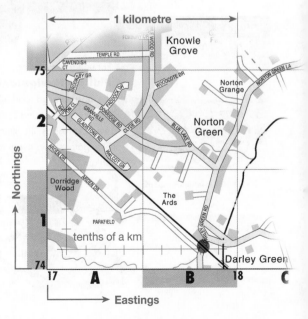

PHILIP'S MAPS

the Gold Standard for drivers

◆ **Philip's street atlases cover all of England, Wales, Northern Ireland and much of Scotland**

◆ Every named street is shown, including alleys, lanes and walkways

◆ Thousands of additional features marked: stations, public buildings, car parks, places of interest

◆ Route-planning maps to get you close to your destination

◆ Postcodes on the maps and in the index

◆ Widely used by the emergency services, transport companies and local authorities

PHILIP'S STREET ATLAS London
More streets
More lanes and alleys
More named buildings
More house numbers
More clear routes
'Absolutely fabulous'
www.london-taxi.co.uk
'Must buy' Evening Standard

PHILIP'S STREET ATLAS Fife & Tayside
Dundee, Dunfermline, Kirkcaldy, Perth, Stirling
30 New speed camera locations with speed limits

PHILIP'S STREET ATLAS Dorset
Bournemouth and Poole
Christchurch, Dorchester, Weymouth
30 New speed camera locations with speed limits

PHILIP'S STREET ATLAS Co Armagh Co Down
Armagh, Banger, Craigavon, Downpatrick, Newry, Newtownards
Includes route-planning map

PHILIP'S NAVIGATOR Britain
'The reigning champion of road atlases'
The Sunday Times
● With speed cameras from PocketGPSWorld.com
● Britain's best-selling UK road atlas

For national mapping, choose **Philip's Navigator Britain** the most detailed road atlas available of England, Wales and Scotland. Hailed by Auto Express as 'the ultimate road atlas', Navigator shows every road and lane in Britain.

Street atlases currently available

England

Bedfordshire and Luton	Surrey
Berkshire	East Sussex
Birmingham and West Midlands	West Sussex
Bristol and Bath	Tyne and Wear
Buckinghamshire and Milton Keynes	Warwickshire and Coventry
Cambridgeshire and Peterborough	Wiltshire and Swindon
Cheshire	Worcestershire
Cornwall	East Yorkshire Northern Lincolnshire
Cumbria	North Yorkshire
Derbyshire	South Yorkshire
Devon	West Yorkshire

Surrey
East Sussex
West Sussex
Tyne and Wear
Warwickshire and Coventry
Wiltshire and Swindon
Worcestershire
East Yorkshire Northern Lincolnshire
North Yorkshire
South Yorkshire
West Yorkshire

Dorset

County Durham and Teesside

Essex

North Essex

South Essex

Gloucestershire and Bristol

Hampshire

North Hampshire

South Hampshire

Herefordshire Monmouthshire

Hertfordshire

Isle of Wight

Kent

East Kent

West Kent

Lancashire

Leicestershire and Rutland

Lincolnshire

Liverpool and Merseyside

London

Greater Manchester

Norfolk

Northamptonshire

Northumberland

Nottinghamshire

Oxfordshire

Shropshire

Somerset

Staffordshire

Suffolk

Wales

Anglesey, Conwy and Gwynedd

Cardiff, Swansea and The Valleys

Carmarthenshire, Pembrokeshire and Swansea

Ceredigion and South Gwynedd

Denbighshire, Flintshire, Wrexham

Herefordshire Monmouthshire

Powys

Scotland

Aberdeenshire

Ayrshire

Dumfries and Galloway

Edinburgh and East Central Scotland

Fife and Tayside

Glasgow and West Central Scotland

Inverness and Moray

Lanarkshire

Scottish Borders

Northern Ireland

County Antrim and County Londonderry

County Armagh and County Down

Belfast

County Tyrone and County Fermanagh

Philip's maps and atlases are available from bookshops, motorway services and petrol stations

For further details visit
www.philips-maps.co.uk